NOMINATED FOR EISNER, IGNATZ, AND LIBRIS AWARDS.
WINNER OF TWO HARVEY AWARDS: BEST WRITER AND BEST GRAPHIC ALBUM OF PREVIOUSLY PUBLISHED WORK.

FEATURED ON THE GLOBE AND MAIL'S LIST OF THE 100 BEST BOOKS OF THE YEAR AND QUILL AND QUIRE'S LIST OF THE FIVE BEST CANADIAN NON-FICTION BOOKS OF THE YEAR.

"Chester Brown is a comic-book artist who has turned his inimitable style to a compelling moment in Canadian history. Not a graphic novel so much as a graphic history book, and one that transforms history into legend."
—CBC CANADA READS TOP 10

"If you love to read a gripping story, if you are awed by the talent of an artist, then look no further: Chester Brown's LOUIS RIEL is comix history in the making, and with it, history never looked so good." —THE GLOBE AND MAIL

"Complete with exhaustive footnotes and an index, it has the thoroughness of a history book yet reads with the personalized vision of a novel. LOUIS RIEL coalesces many of the themes Brown had explored in his earlier works: the relative 'truth' of nonfiction, the relationship between madness and religious experience, the dubious intentions of authority." —TIME

"[LOUIS RIEL] is extraordinary. Brown makes no bones about whose side he's on (the dispossessed Métis'), but he leaves the eternal questions about Riel himself—madman or visionary, traitor or patriot—to readers' judgment.... [T]he words work flawlessly with the muted atmospherics and minimalist settings." —MACLEAN'S

"Brown has invented a biographical form unique to his medium. LOUIS RIEL has too vivid a personal spin to pass as documentary, but it's not quite historical fiction, either—Brown's not interested in making things up."
—THE VILLAGE VOICE

"Chester Brown's graphic novel LOUIS RIEL: A COMIC-STRIP BIOGRAPHY is an overwhelming, eye-boggling achievement, my favourite book of the year. What you have here is Brown at the height of his abilities as an artist, his handling of line and composition is absolutely beautiful, and he's made a fascinating and intelligent portrait of one of Canada's most controversial historical figures. To me, this isn't just one of the best books of the year, it's one of the most important graphic novels ever published."
—Lee Henderson, NATIONAL POST

"LOUIS RIEL is gripping reading, filled with drama and poetry, in which plain words and stunning images carry equal weight in telling the story. It sounds like a cliche, but it's probably true that LOUIS RIEL is destined to become a Canadian classic."
—CALGARY HERALD

"LOUIS RIEL turns out to be a tour de force, a groundbreaking work of graphic storytelling." —EDMONTON JOURNAL

"Even the most uneventful drawings have a curious kind of power, due to Brown's ability to express character in a few brief, economical lines. When the panels do get busy, as in the latter stages of the rebellion, the effect is that much more powerful."
—VANCOUVER SUN

"An impressive work of art that delivers the narrative goods with a cinematic punch." —THE GAZETTE (Montreal)

"The brilliance of Chester Brown's 'comic strip biography' of Louis Riel is that it is fascinating and compelling without compromising the basic facts."
—WINNIPEG FREE PRESS

"Brown invokes with a minimalist style the world of early Canada in the making. The speed and ease of the format allowed me to become readily immersed in a mood, a time, a place, and an historical tale. It is an original form of literate storytelling which Brown vividly proves is often underrated for its power and possibility. Every school in the land that worries about literacy and an appreciation of history among its charges should have it on the curriculum as required reading."
—THE HALIFAX HERALD

"Métis leader Louis Riel has been the subject of biographies, sculptures, museum exhibitions and, more than anything else, strong opinions. But, oddly enough, the most compelling re-telling of the Riel story comes in the form of acclaimed comic artist Chester Brown's minimalist graphic biography. This book is a gift to Canada, a story told with compassion and reserve that captures the essence of one of the North American West's great rebels."
—Hal Niedzviecki, OTTAWA CITIZEN

"...généreuse, puissante et inspirée, peut-être même incontournable en matière de bande dessinée et de document historique....Et on goûtera fort l'élégance du dessin de Brown...[...generous, powerful and inspired, perhaps even essential both as a graphic novel and as a work of history.... And readers will be deeply affected by the elegance of Brown's drawings.]" —LE DEVOIR (Montreal)

"Despite its extensive annotation and bibliography, LOUIS RIEL is a refreshingly unacademic look at Canadian history, a subject too often dismissed as dull."
—REGINA LEADER-POST

"Brown dresse un portrait saisissant, profondément humain et parfois lyrique à souhait d'une figure qui, après son exécution, est entrée dans la légende d'un pays encore divisé à son propos. Pour ce faire, il a eu à démontrer son extraordinaire maîtrise de la narration graphique et a eu recours à une ligne claire pure, agréable à contempler....LOUIS RIEL est sans contredit un sommet de la BD canadienne, peu importe nos allégeances et nos opinions politiques. [Brown creates a portrait that is striking, profoundly human and at times lyrical of a figure who, after his execution, became a legend in a country that is still divided over him. In order to do this, (Brown) demonstrates an extraordinary mastery of graphic narration and a beautiful clear-line drawing style.... LOUIS RIEL is without a doubt a summit for the Canadian comic-strip, regardless of our allegiances and political opinions.]"
—LE SOLEIL (Quebec)

"The hero, martyr and madman that was Louis Riel all get examined in this tale that may be too familiar to high school history students, yet is strangely new and exciting with Brown's telling."
—THE COAST (Halifax)

"Brown's comic-strip biography of the controversial Métis leader is a crisp page-turner." —FAST FORWARD (Calgary)

"Brown's storytelling and exquisite drawing make LOUIS RIEL a jam-packed action adventure story that both teens and adults will enjoy."
—CANADIAN BOOK REVIEW ANNUAL

"As a comic which challenges the presumptuousness of its own narrative, delighting in conflicting scholarly references, LOUIS RIEL is a sophisticated polemic, unabashed and humane."
—MONTREAL REVIEW OF BOOKS

"This is more than 272 pages of stunning Chester Brown drawings portraying one of the most fascinating stories of revolution North American history has to offer. It's a groundbreaking piece of art, seriously. This book is as thorough and obsessive as Henry Darger, but without the mental illness. It's as consistent as Hergé but a lot more honest and heartfelt. It's perfect, really, and if you have never read a comic novel before, this is definitely the place to start."
—VICE

"His epic is a serious work of history, an attempt to boil down the events, accurately and intelligently, which impinged on Louis Riel's life.... Did Riel really have a forehead that looks like a ski slope? Did Schultz, one of the villains, possess a nose that would give Pinocchio pause? It doesn't matter, really. Somehow these caricatures fit the personalities beautifully."
—Maggie Siggins, PRAIRIE DOG (Regina)

"Chester Brown's LOUIS RIEL has certainly become one of the handful of must-have graphic novels released in the last ten years. More than any of his peers, Brown employs narrative and storytelling strategies that seem to come straight from some unknown place." —THE COMICS REPORTER

"A ripping historical yarn that offers an idiosyncratic take on the still-controversial Métis rebel leader." —HOUR (Montreal)

"...the story...is told with compression and masterful pacing. Canada's history unfolds here with an orderly inevitability, engrossing and—thanks to Brown's simple line (he credits Harold Gray's LITTLE ORPHAN ANNIE) and his meticulous composition in every panel—enriching." —THE GEORGIA STRAIGHT (Vancouver)

"It's a credit to Brown's plainspoken artistry and flair for narrative that it's a page-turner till the end." —THE BOSTON PHOENIX

"The compelling, sparsely elegant, heavily researched book, which contains endnotes, a bibliography and an index, creates in Brown's fluid combining of pictures and words an intensely vivid narrative of a complex hero."
—CANADIAN ART

"LOUIS RIEL: A COMIC-STRIP BIOGRAPHY is yet another landmark work by Chester Brown, an artist considered to be one of the greatest cartoonists living today.... Not overly intellectualized yet dense with detail, the book is a wonderful combination of factual resources and powerful art and storytelling."
—QUILL AND QUIRE

"For history buffs, art lovers or anyone with an interest in the life Louis Riel, Chester Brown's book is a must-have addition to the collection."
—THE BRANDON SUN

"LOUIS RIEL is an educational, moving, challenging graphic novel that shows a talented cartoonist at the peak of his storytelling."
—THE OKLAHOMAN

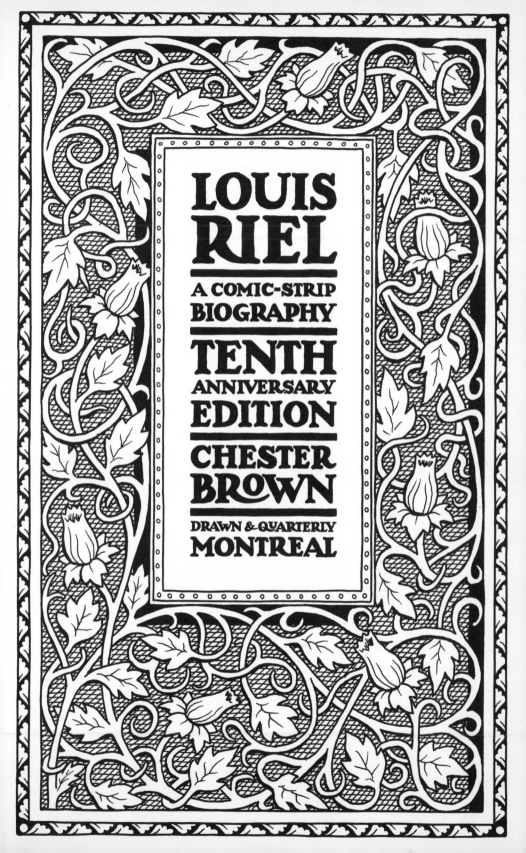

LOUIS RIEL

A COMIC-STRIP
BIOGRAPHY

TENTH
ANNIVERSARY
EDITION

CHESTER
BROWN

DRAWN & QUARTERLY
MONTREAL

Also by Chester Brown:
ED THE HAPPY CLOWN (1989)
THE PLAYBOY (1992)
I NEVER LIKED YOU (1994)
THE LITTLE MAN (1998)
PAYING FOR IT (2011)

www.drawnandquarterly.com

First edition: September 2013.
Printed in Canada.
10 9 8 7 6 5 4 3 2 1
A version of this graphic novel was first published in book form in September 2003.

Library and Archives Canada Cataloguing in Publication
Brown, Chester, 1960–, author, artist
    Louis Riel : a comic-strip biography / Chester Brown. -- 10th anniversary edition. Reissue. Includes new introduction contextualizing the work's importance with the original pamphlet covers collected and reproduced in full colour.
ISBN 978-1-77046-130-7 (pbk.)
    1. Riel, Louis, 1844-1885--Comic books, strips, etc. 2. Métis--Prairie Provinces--
Biography--Comic books, strips, etc. 3. Graphic novels. I. Title.
FC3217.1.R53B76 2013   971.051092   C2013-902357-7

Drawn & Quarterly acknowledges the financial contribution of the Government of Canada through the Canada Book Fund and the Canada Council for the Arts for our publishing activities and for support of this edition.

Published in the USA by Drawn & Quarterly, a client publisher of
Farrar, Straus and Giroux
Orders: 888.330.8477

Published in Canada by Drawn & Quarterly, a client publisher of
Raincoast Books
Orders: 800.663.5714

Published in the United Kingdom by Drawn & Quarterly, a client publisher of
Publishers Group UK
info@pguk.co.uk

For Gord

FOREWORD

Because it's unusual for a comic-book to have one, I want to point out that this book does have an index, even if it is a bit limited in scope. (It only lists 19th century individuals.)

This "comic-strip biography" is not a full biographical treatment of Riel's story. Long periods of time are skipped over, and many aspects of his life are completely ignored. I've mostly concentrated on Riel's antagonistic relationship with the Canadian government, and even that has been simplified and distorted in order to make it fit into a 241-page comic-strip narrative. In the end-notes I point out many of my distortions, as well as other stuff that I think may be of interest.

In case this book triggers a desire in you to read further, here are a few recommendations:
In my opinion, the best, most comprehensive biography is RIEL: A LIFE OF REVOLUTION by Maggie Siggins. She presents the Métis rebel as a heroic figure.
For a less sympathetic judgement of the man, try Thomas Flanagan's RIEL AND THE REBELLION: 1885 RECONSIDERED. Also worth reading by Flanagan is LOUIS 'DAVID' RIEL: 'PROPHET OF THE NEW WORLD', a fascinating study of the development of Riel's religious thinking. (I'm familiar with the two Flanagan books in their revised editions.)
PRAIRIE FIRE: THE 1885 NORTH-WEST REBELLION, by Bob Beal and Rod Macleod, is a good book that doesn't just focus on Riel.
I don't want this list to get too long, so I'm going to cut it off there, even though several other books that helped me in the creation of this strip were as enjoyable to read as the above ones. See the bibliography for a more complete list.

Several people have asked me if Hergé influenced the artwork in LOUIS RIEL. I love Hergé -- his Tintin books have probably affected my drawing-style to some degree -- but my main visual inspiration here was Harold Gray's work on Little Orphan Annie. I hesitate to acknowledge this because I'm well aware that my scratchings fall far short of the beauty of Gray's imagery.

My thanks to the following people for various forms of assistance or encouragement while I worked on this project: Peter Birkemoe, Jacques Boivin, Gordon Brown, Jeet Heer, Sook-Yin Lee, Marina Lesenko, Joe Matt, Akemi Nakamura, Chris Oliveros, Seth, Dave Sim, Colin Upton, and Elizabeth Walker.
Thanks also to THE CANADA COUNCIL FOR THE ARTS for providing me with financial assistance.

Chester
Brown
June 2003

FIRST
MAP SECTION

In 1670 the king of England granted Rupert's Land to a fur-trading enterprise called the Hudson's Bay Company.

In 1812 the company started the first agricultural settlement in Rupert's Land when it brought 170 people over from Scotland and placed them by the Red River.

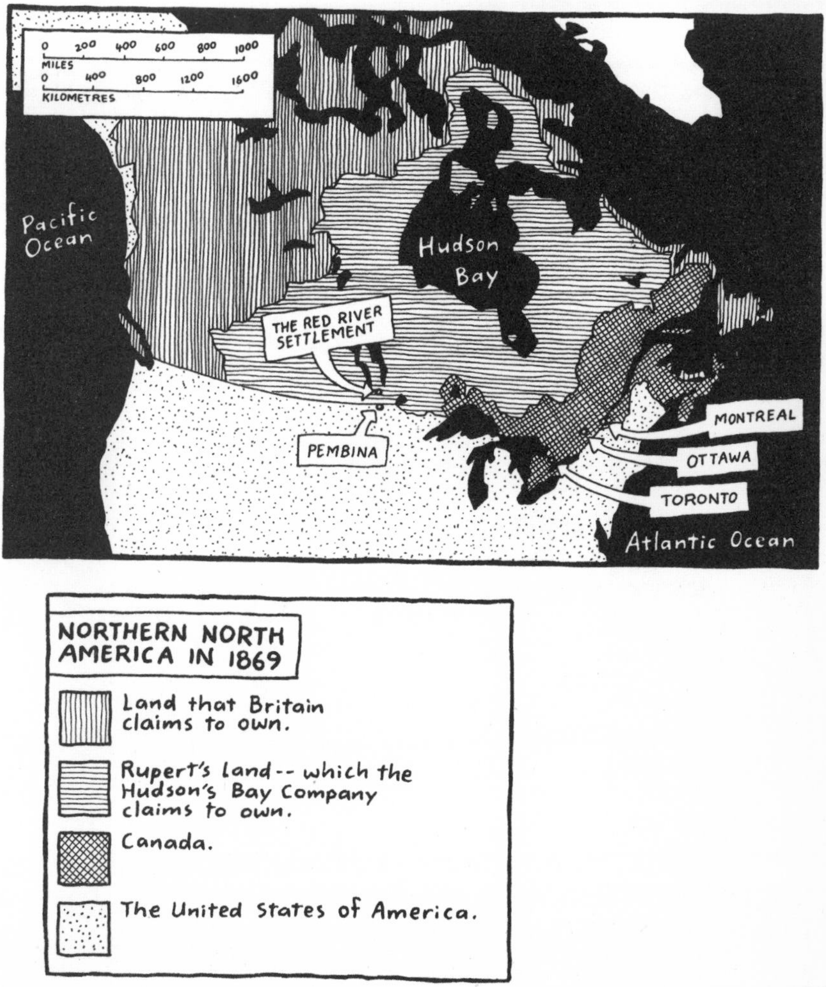
0 200 400 600 800 1000
MILES
0 400 800 1200 1600
KILOMETRES
Pacific Ocean
Hudson Bay
THE RED RIVER SETTLEMENT
PEMBINA
MONTREAL
OTTAWA
TORONTO
Atlantic Ocean
NORTHERN NORTH AMERICA IN 1869
Land that Britain claims to own.
Rupert's Land -- which the Hudson's Bay Company claims to own.
Canada.
The United States of America.

The Red River Settlement grew, and by 1869 almost 12,000 people lived there. More than 80 percent of this population were Métis -- people who have both Indians and whites in their family background. A large number of the whites who had come into the area had been French fur-traders, so a majority of the Red River Métis spoke French.

Canada in 1869 consisted of four provinces: Ontario, Quebec, New Brunswick, and Nova Scotia. Both Canada and the United States were eager to expand their borders.

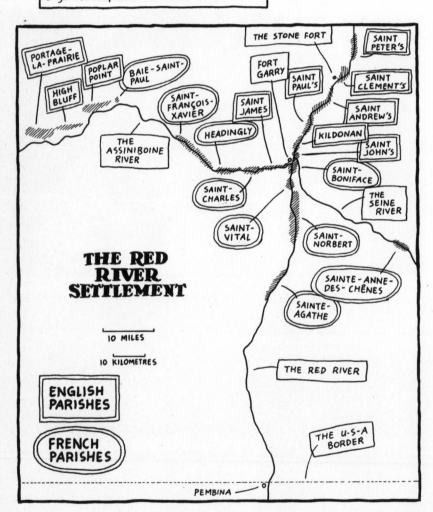

THE STONE FORT
SAINT PETER'S
PORTAGE-LA-PRAIRIE
POPLAR POINT
BAIE-SAINT-PAUL
FORT GARRY
SAINT PAUL'S
SAINT CLEMENT'S
HIGH BLUFF
SAINT-FRANÇOIS-XAVIER
SAINT JAMES
SAINT ANDREW'S
HEADINGLY
KILDONAN
THE ASSINIBOINE RIVER
SAINT JOHN'S
SAINT-BONIFACE
SAINT-CHARLES
THE SEINE RIVER
SAINT-VITAL
SAINT-NORBERT
THE RED RIVER SETTLEMENT
SAINTE-ANNE-DES-CHÊNES
SAINTE-AGATHE
10 MILES
10 KILOMETRES
THE RED RIVER
ENGLISH PARISHES
FRENCH PARISHES
THE U-S-A BORDER
PEMBINA

PART ONE

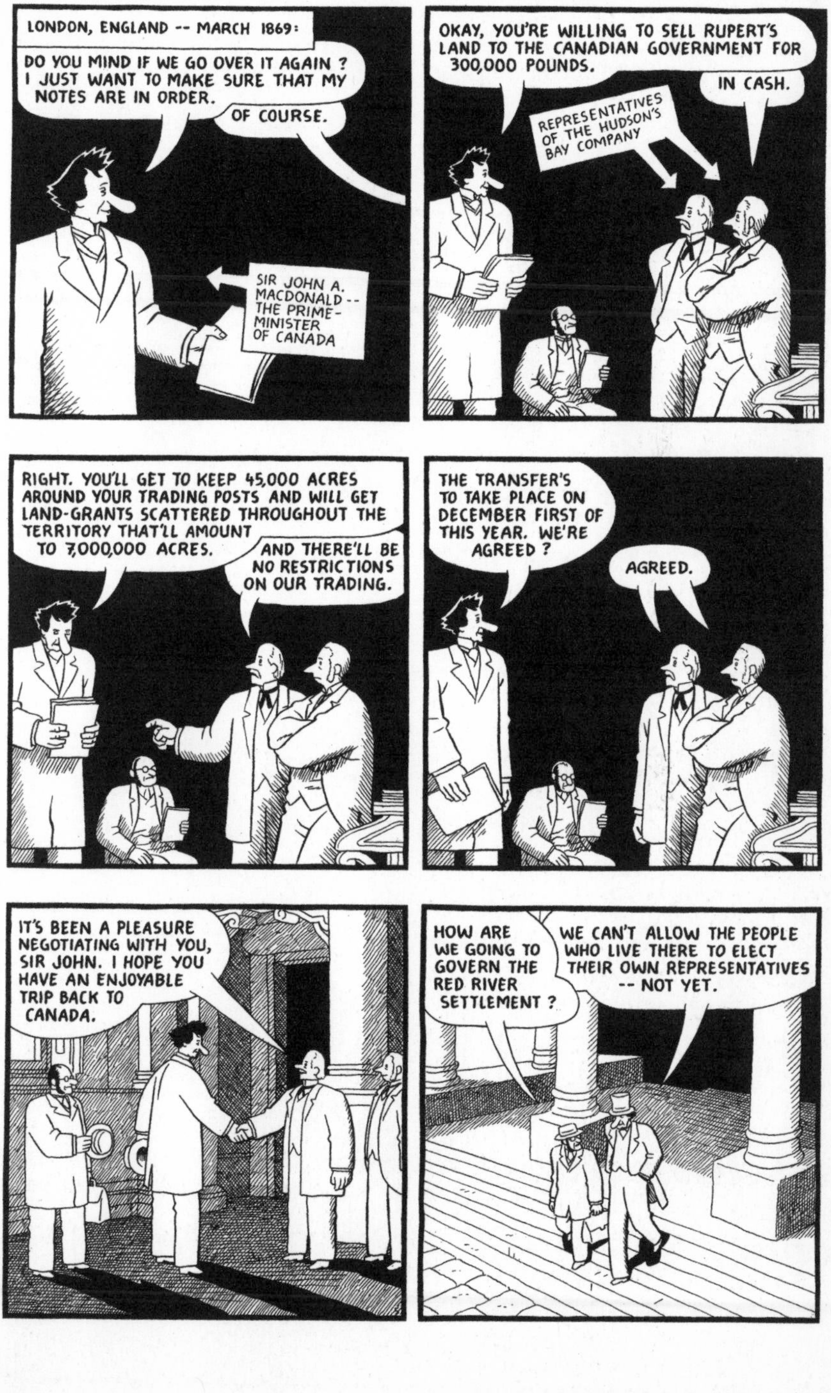
LONDON, ENGLAND -- MARCH 1869:
DO YOU MIND IF WE GO OVER IT AGAIN? I JUST WANT TO MAKE SURE THAT MY NOTES ARE IN ORDER.
OF COURSE.
SIR JOHN A. MACDONALD -- THE PRIME-MINISTER OF CANADA
OKAY, YOU'RE WILLING TO SELL RUPERT'S LAND TO THE CANADIAN GOVERNMENT FOR 300,000 POUNDS.
IN CASH.
REPRESENTATIVES OF THE HUDSON'S BAY COMPANY
RIGHT. YOU'LL GET TO KEEP 45,000 ACRES AROUND YOUR TRADING POSTS AND WILL GET LAND-GRANTS SCATTERED THROUGHOUT THE TERRITORY THAT'LL AMOUNT TO 7,000,000 ACRES.
AND THERE'LL BE NO RESTRICTIONS ON OUR TRADING.
THE TRANSFER'S TO TAKE PLACE ON DECEMBER FIRST OF THIS YEAR. WE'RE AGREED?
AGREED.
IT'S BEEN A PLEASURE NEGOTIATING WITH YOU, SIR JOHN. I HOPE YOU HAVE AN ENJOYABLE TRIP BACK TO CANADA.
HOW ARE WE GOING TO GOVERN THE RED RIVER SETTLEMENT?
WE CAN'T ALLOW THE PEOPLE WHO LIVE THERE TO ELECT THEIR OWN REPRESENTATIVES -- NOT YET.

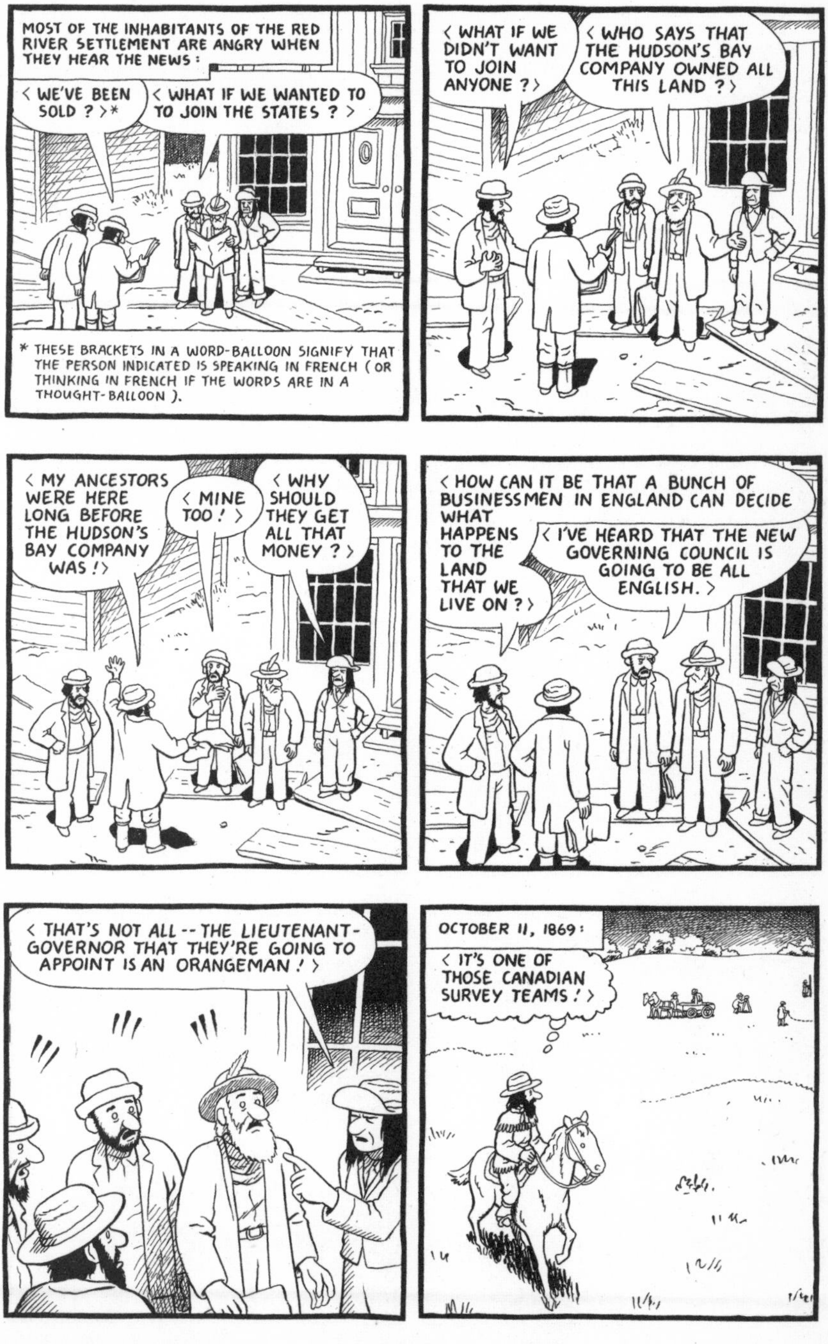
MOST OF THE INHABITANTS OF THE RED RIVER SETTLEMENT ARE ANGRY WHEN THEY HEAR THE NEWS :
< WE'VE BEEN SOLD ? >*
< WHAT IF WE WANTED TO TO JOIN THE STATES ? >
* THESE BRACKETS IN A WORD-BALLOON SIGNIFY THAT THE PERSON INDICATED IS SPEAKING IN FRENCH (OR THINKING IN FRENCH IF THE WORDS ARE IN A THOUGHT-BALLOON).
< WHAT IF WE DIDN'T WANT TO JOIN ANYONE ? >
< WHO SAYS THAT THE HUDSON'S BAY COMPANY OWNED ALL THIS LAND ? >
< MY ANCESTORS WERE HERE LONG BEFORE THE HUDSON'S BAY COMPANY WAS ! >
< MINE TOO ! >
< WHY SHOULD THEY GET ALL THAT MONEY ? >
< HOW CAN IT BE THAT A BUNCH OF BUSINESSMEN IN ENGLAND CAN DECIDE WHAT HAPPENS TO THE LAND THAT WE LIVE ON ? >
< I'VE HEARD THAT THE NEW GOVERNING COUNCIL IS GOING TO BE ALL ENGLISH. >
< THAT'S NOT ALL -- THE LIEUTENANT-GOVERNOR THAT THEY'RE GOING TO APPOINT IS AN ORANGEMAN ! >
!!!
!!!
!!!
OCTOBER 11, 1869 :
< IT'S ONE OF THOSE CANADIAN SURVEY TEAMS ! >

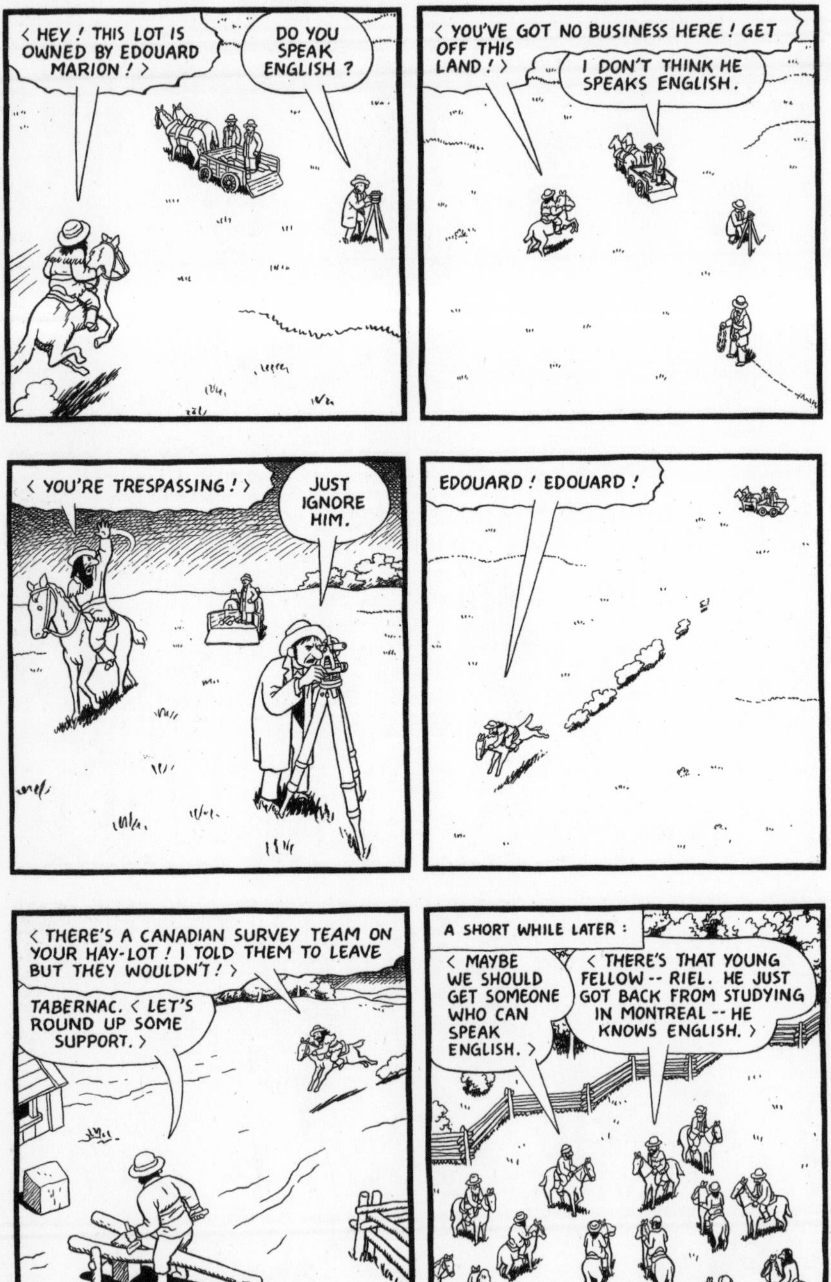
< HEY ! THIS LOT IS OWNED BY EDOUARD MARION ! >
DO YOU SPEAK ENGLISH ?
< YOU'VE GOT NO BUSINESS HERE ! GET OFF THIS LAND ! >
I DON'T THINK HE SPEAKS ENGLISH.
< YOU'RE TRESPASSING ! >
JUST IGNORE HIM.
EDOUARD ! EDOUARD !
< THERE'S A CANADIAN SURVEY TEAM ON YOUR HAY-LOT ! I TOLD THEM TO LEAVE BUT THEY WOULDN'T ! >
TABERNAC. < LET'S ROUND UP SOME SUPPORT. >
A SHORT WHILE LATER :
< MAYBE WE SHOULD GET SOMEONE WHO CAN SPEAK ENGLISH. >
< THERE'S THAT YOUNG FELLOW -- RIEL. HE JUST GOT BACK FROM STUDYING IN MONTREAL -- HE KNOWS ENGLISH. >

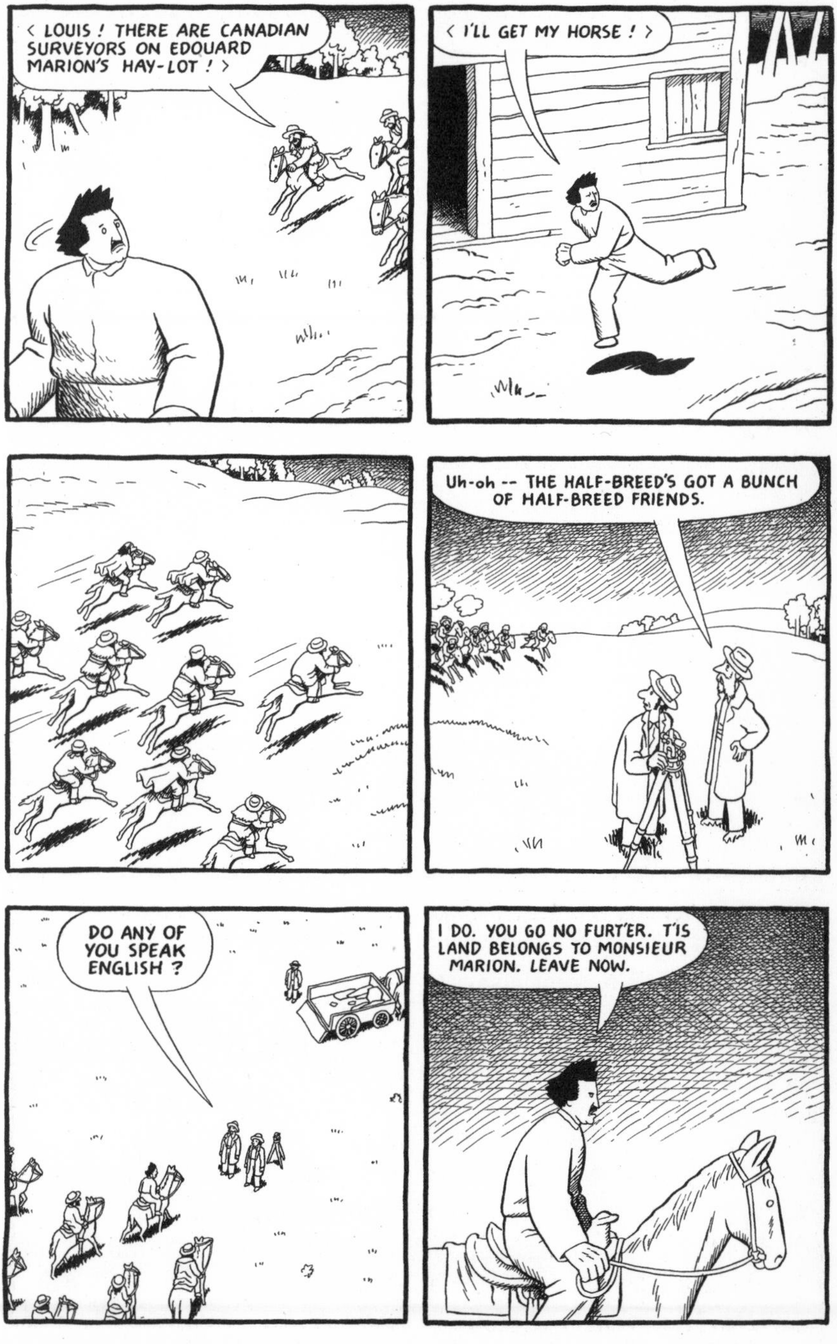
< LOUIS ! THERE ARE CANADIAN SURVEYORS ON EDOUARD MARION'S HAY-LOT ! >
< I'LL GET MY HORSE ! >
Uh-oh -- THE HALF-BREED'S GOT A BUNCH OF HALF-BREED FRIENDS.
DO ANY OF YOU SPEAK ENGLISH ?
I DO. YOU GO NO FURT'ER. T'IS LAND BELONGS TO MONSIEUR MARION. LEAVE NOW.

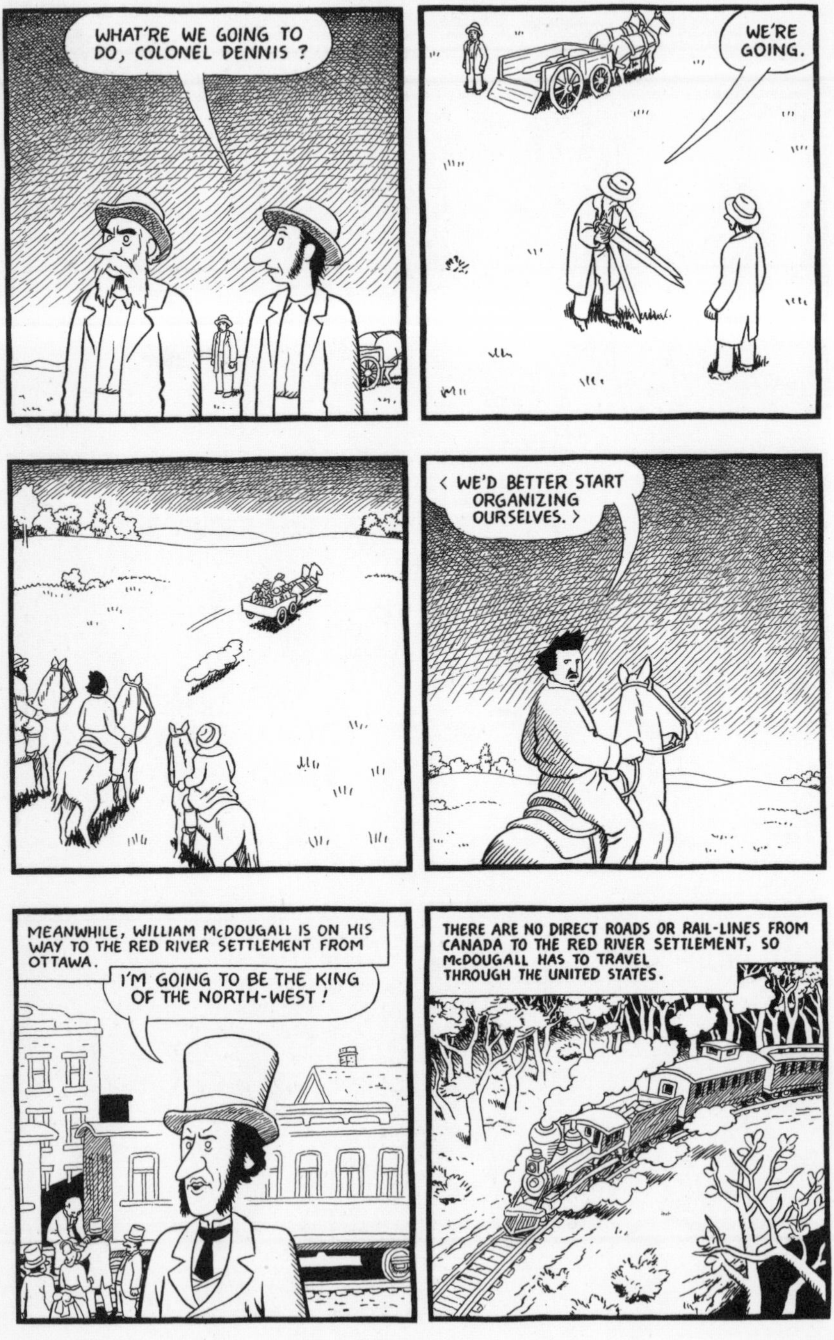
WHAT'RE WE GOING TO DO, COLONEL DENNIS ?
WE'RE GOING.
< WE'D BETTER START ORGANIZING OURSELVES. >
MEANWHILE, WILLIAM McDOUGALL IS ON HIS WAY TO THE RED RIVER SETTLEMENT FROM OTTAWA.
I'M GOING TO BE THE KING OF THE NORTH-WEST !
THERE ARE NO DIRECT ROADS OR RAIL-LINES FROM CANADA TO THE RED RIVER SETTLEMENT, SO McDOUGALL HAS TO TRAVEL THROUGH THE UNITED STATES.

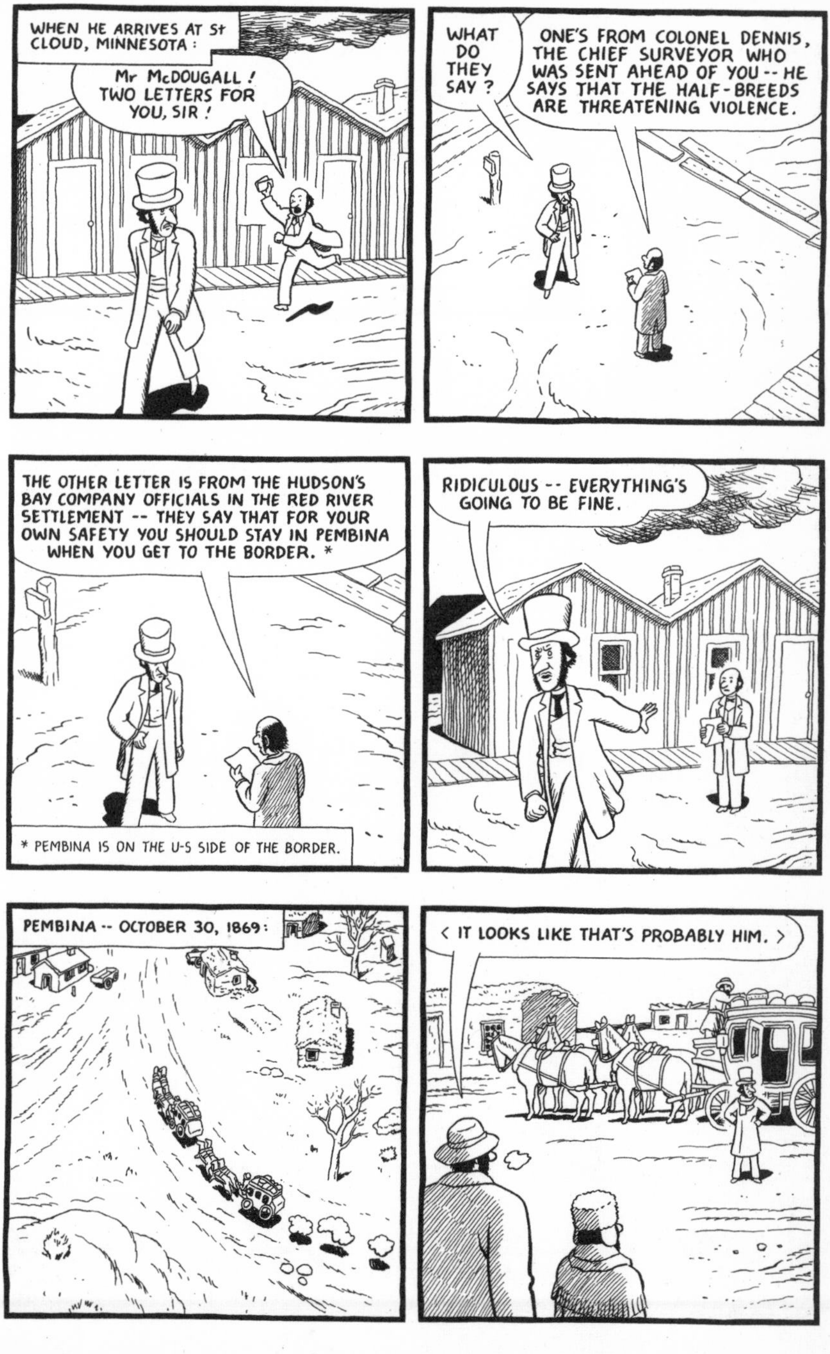
WHEN HE ARRIVES AT St CLOUD, MINNESOTA:
Mr McDOUGALL! TWO LETTERS FOR YOU, SIR!
WHAT DO THEY SAY?
ONE'S FROM COLONEL DENNIS, THE CHIEF SURVEYOR WHO WAS SENT AHEAD OF YOU -- HE SAYS THAT THE HALF-BREEDS ARE THREATENING VIOLENCE.
THE OTHER LETTER IS FROM THE HUDSON'S BAY COMPANY OFFICIALS IN THE RED RIVER SETTLEMENT -- THEY SAY THAT FOR YOUR OWN SAFETY YOU SHOULD STAY IN PEMBINA WHEN YOU GET TO THE BORDER. *
* PEMBINA IS ON THE U-S SIDE OF THE BORDER.
RIDICULOUS -- EVERYTHING'S GOING TO BE FINE.
PEMBINA -- OCTOBER 30, 1869:
< IT LOOKS LIKE THAT'S PROBABLY HIM. >

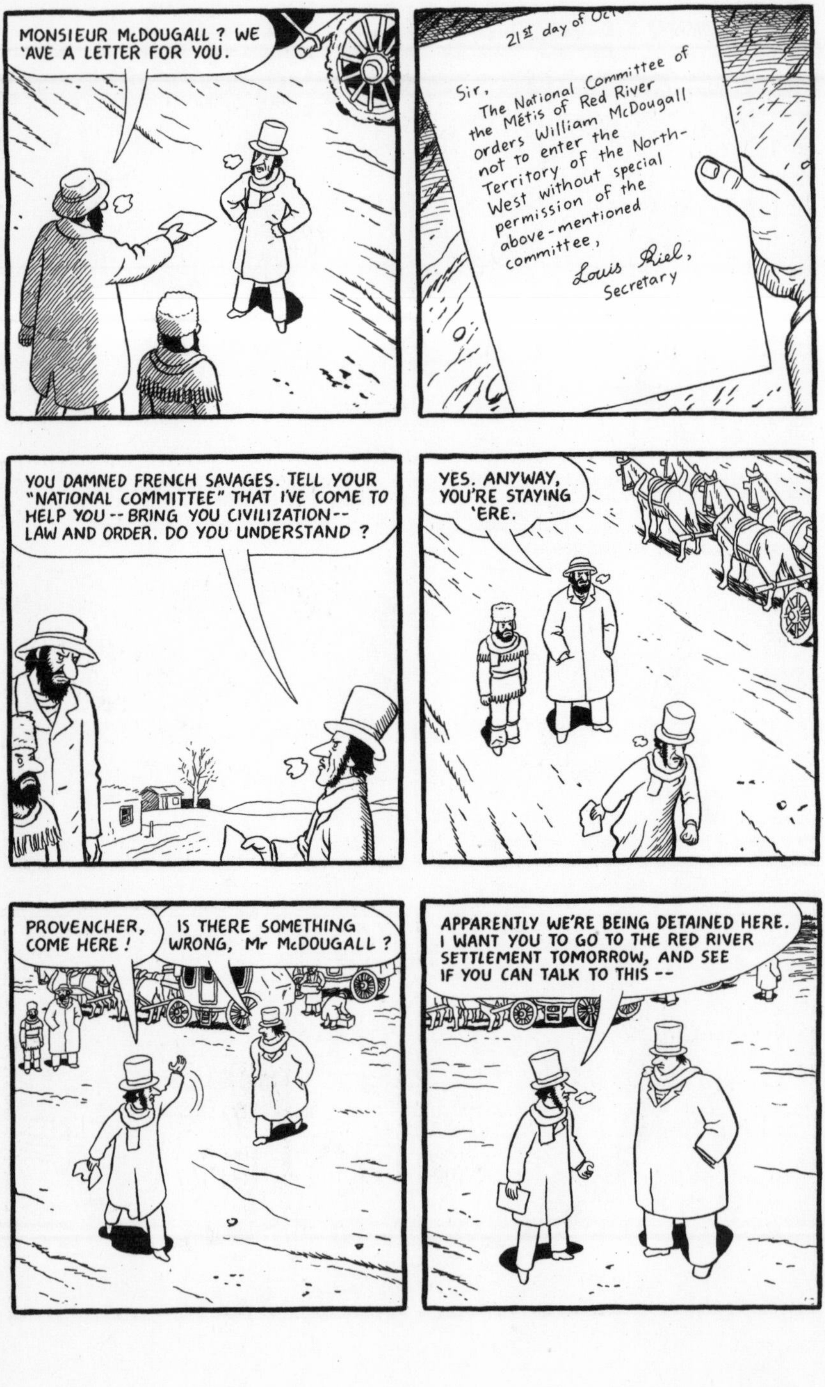
MONSIEUR McDOUGALL ? WE 'AVE A LETTER FOR YOU.
21st day of Oc
Sir,
The National Committee of the Métis of Red River orders William McDougall not to enter the North-West Territory without special permission of the above-mentioned committee,
Louis Riel,
Secretary
YOU DAMNED FRENCH SAVAGES. TELL YOUR "NATIONAL COMMITTEE" THAT I'VE COME TO HELP YOU -- BRING YOU CIVILIZATION -- LAW AND ORDER. DO YOU UNDERSTAND ?
YES. ANYWAY, YOU'RE STAYING 'ERE.
PROVENCHER, COME HERE !
IS THERE SOMETHING WRONG, Mr McDOUGALL ?
APPARENTLY WE'RE BEING DETAINED HERE. I WANT YOU TO GO TO THE RED RIVER SETTLEMENT TOMORROW, AND SEE IF YOU CAN TALK TO THIS --

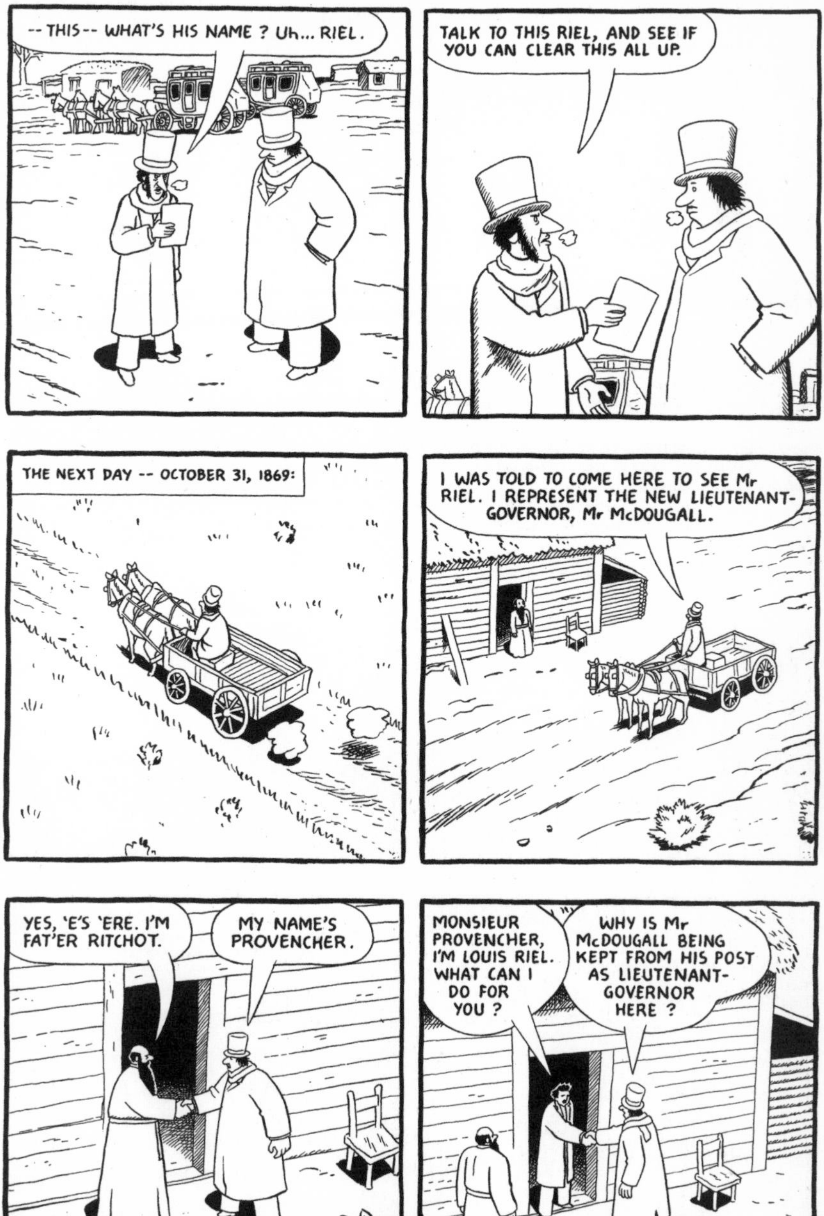
-- THIS -- WHAT'S HIS NAME ? Uh... RIEL.
TALK TO THIS RIEL, AND SEE IF YOU CAN CLEAR THIS ALL UP.
THE NEXT DAY -- OCTOBER 31, 1869:
I WAS TOLD TO COME HERE TO SEE Mr RIEL. I REPRESENT THE NEW LIEUTENANT-GOVERNOR, Mr McDOUGALL.
YES, 'E'S 'ERE. I'M FAT'ER RITCHOT.
MY NAME'S PROVENCHER.
MONSIEUR PROVENCHER, I'M LOUIS RIEL. WHAT CAN I DO FOR YOU ?
WHY IS Mr McDOUGALL BEING KEPT FROM HIS POST AS LIEUTENANT-GOVERNOR HERE ?

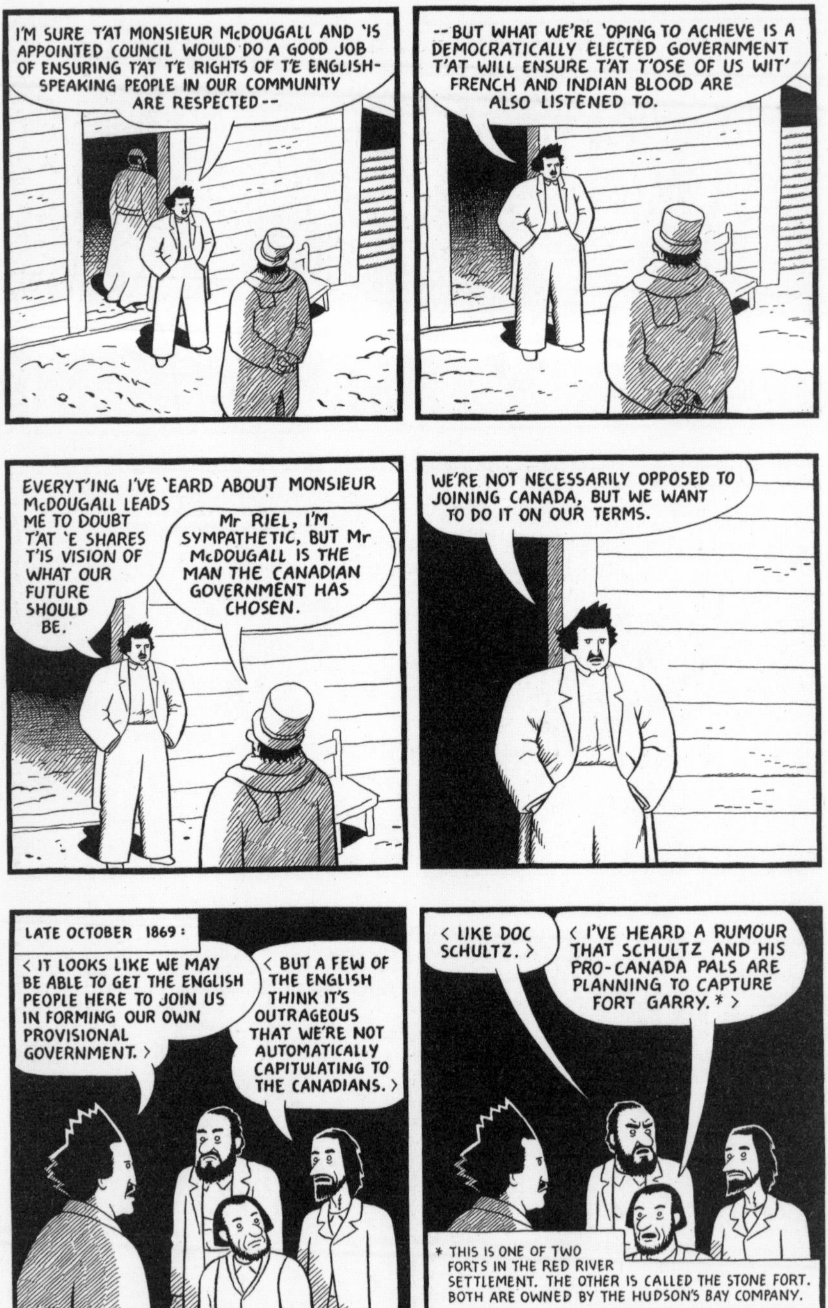
I'M SURE T'AT MONSIEUR McDOUGALL AND 'IS APPOINTED COUNCIL WOULD DO A GOOD JOB OF ENSURING T'AT T'E RIGHTS OF T'E ENGLISH-SPEAKING PEOPLE IN OUR COMMUNITY ARE RESPECTED--
--BUT WHAT WE'RE 'OPING TO ACHIEVE IS A DEMOCRATICALLY ELECTED GOVERNMENT T'AT WILL ENSURE T'AT T'OSE OF US WIT' FRENCH AND INDIAN BLOOD ARE ALSO LISTENED TO.
EVERYT'ING I'VE 'EARD ABOUT MONSIEUR McDOUGALL LEADS ME TO DOUBT T'AT 'E SHARES T'IS VISION OF WHAT OUR FUTURE SHOULD BE.
Mr RIEL, I'M SYMPATHETIC, BUT Mr McDOUGALL IS THE MAN THE CANADIAN GOVERNMENT HAS CHOSEN.
WE'RE NOT NECESSARILY OPPOSED TO JOINING CANADA, BUT WE WANT TO DO IT ON OUR TERMS.
LATE OCTOBER 1869:
< IT LOOKS LIKE WE MAY BE ABLE TO GET THE ENGLISH PEOPLE HERE TO JOIN US IN FORMING OUR OWN PROVISIONAL GOVERNMENT. >
< BUT A FEW OF THE ENGLISH THINK IT'S OUTRAGEOUS THAT WE'RE NOT AUTOMATICALLY CAPITULATING TO THE CANADIANS. >
< LIKE DOC SCHULTZ. >
< I'VE HEARD A RUMOUR THAT SCHULTZ AND HIS PRO-CANADA PALS ARE PLANNING TO CAPTURE FORT GARRY. * >
* THIS IS ONE OF TWO FORTS IN THE RED RIVER SETTLEMENT. THE OTHER IS CALLED THE STONE FORT. BOTH ARE OWNED BY THE HUDSON'S BAY COMPANY.

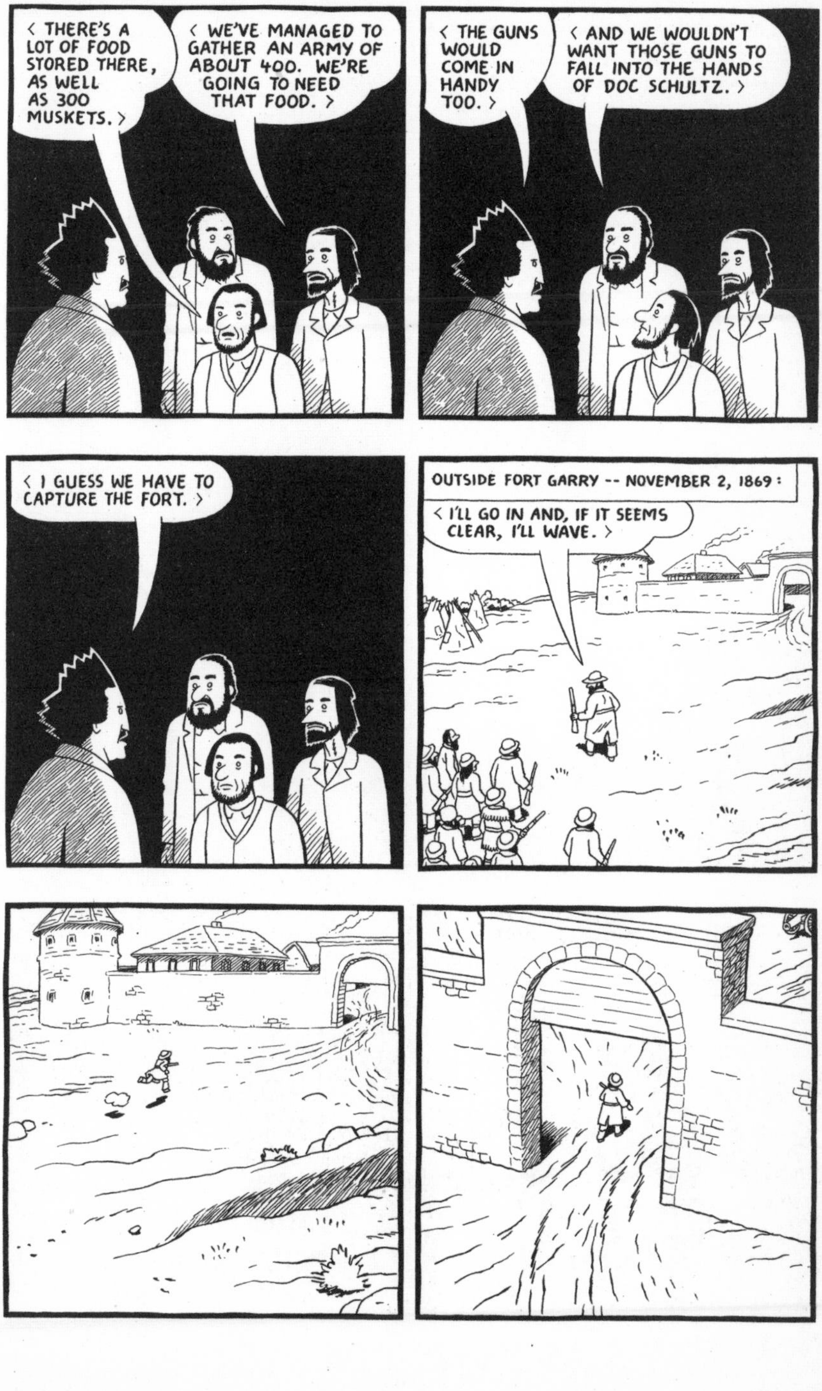

< THERE'S A LOT OF FOOD STORED THERE, AS WELL AS 300 MUSKETS. >
< WE'VE MANAGED TO GATHER AN ARMY OF ABOUT 400. WE'RE GOING TO NEED THAT FOOD. >
< THE GUNS WOULD COME IN HANDY TOO. >
< AND WE WOULDN'T WANT THOSE GUNS TO FALL INTO THE HANDS OF DOC SCHULTZ. >
< I GUESS WE HAVE TO CAPTURE THE FORT. >
OUTSIDE FORT GARRY -- NOVEMBER 2, 1869:
< I'LL GO IN AND, IF IT SEEMS CLEAR, I'LL WAVE. >

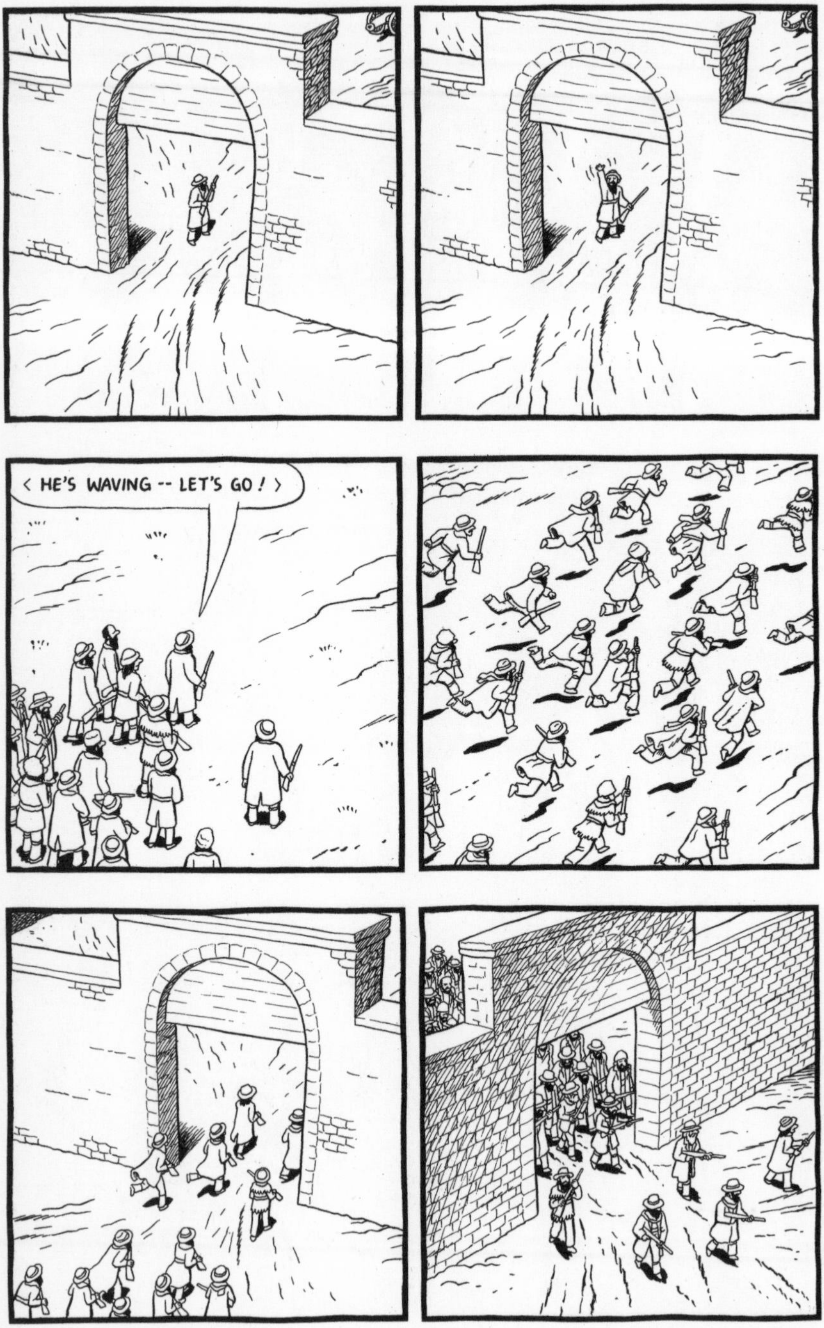
< HE'S WAVING -- LET'S GO! >

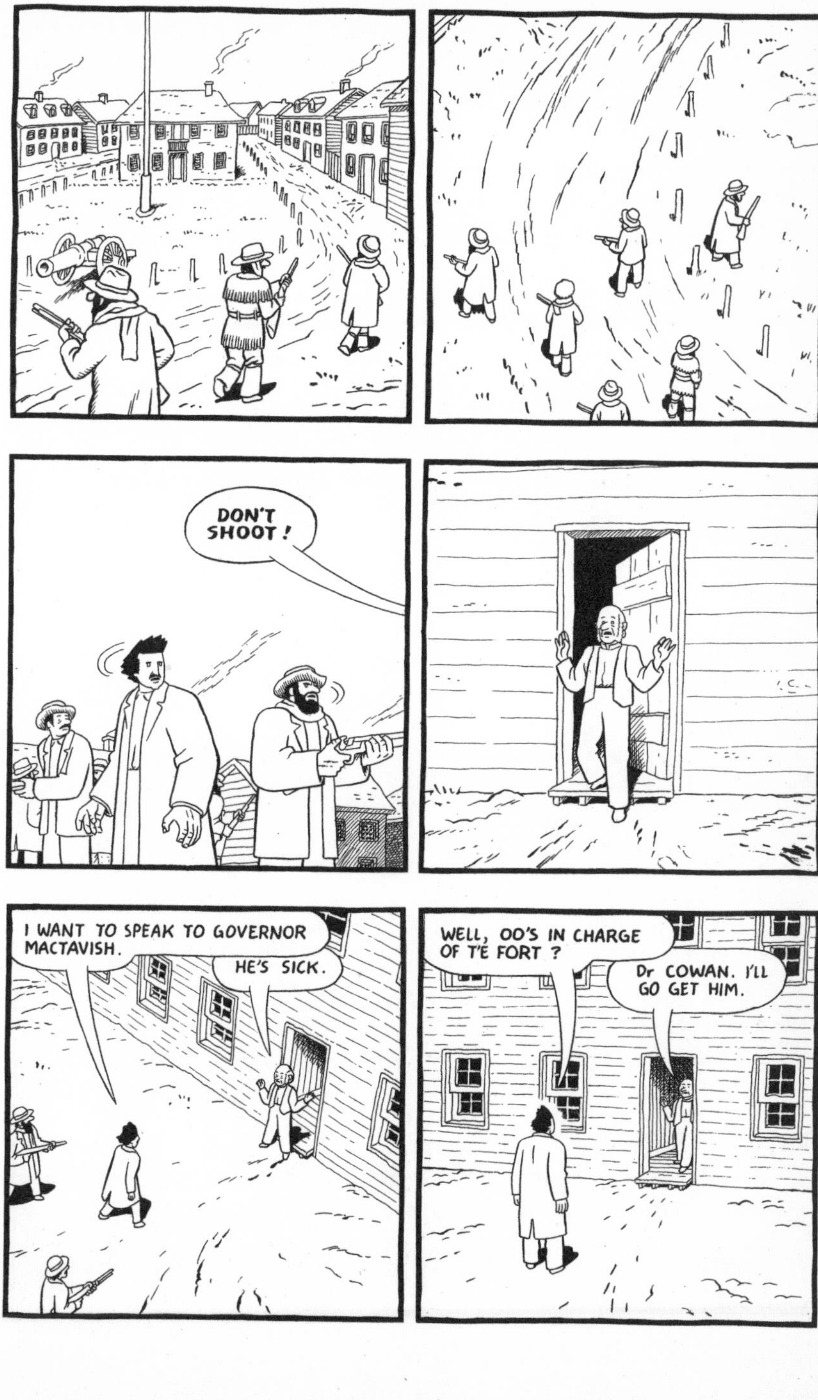
DON'T SHOOT!
I WANT TO SPEAK TO GOVERNOR MACTAVISH.
HE'S SICK.
WELL, OO'S IN CHARGE OF T'E FORT ?
Dr COWAN. I'LL GO GET HIM.

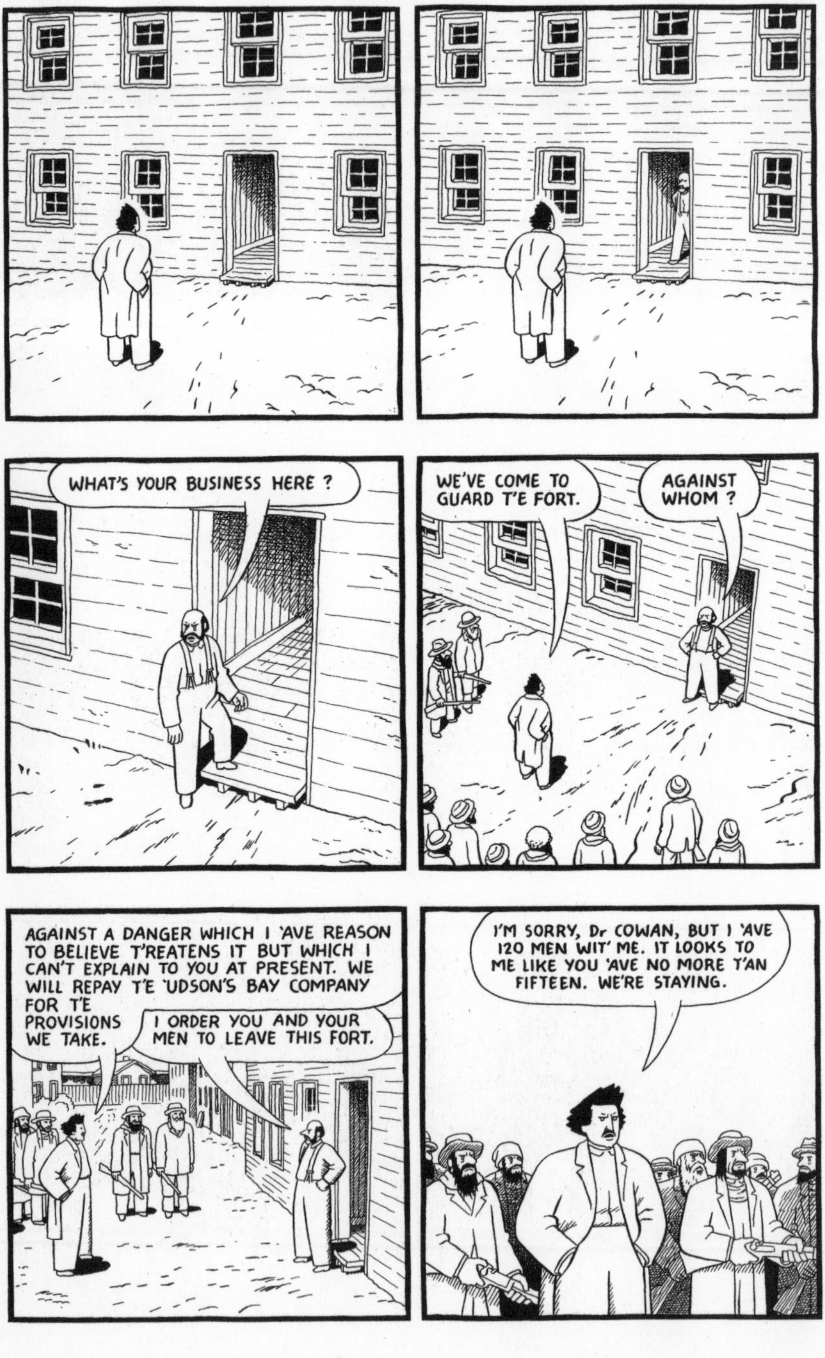

WHAT'S YOUR BUSINESS HERE ?
WE'VE COME TO GUARD T'E FORT.
AGAINST WHOM ?
AGAINST A DANGER WHICH I 'AVE REASON TO BELIEVE T'REATENS IT BUT WHICH I CAN'T EXPLAIN TO YOU AT PRESENT. WE WILL REPAY T'E 'UDSON'S BAY COMPANY FOR T'E PROVISIONS WE TAKE.
I ORDER YOU AND YOUR MEN TO LEAVE THIS FORT.
I'M SORRY, Dr COWAN, BUT I 'AVE 120 MEN WIT' ME. IT LOOKS TO ME LIKE YOU 'AVE NO MORE T'AN FIFTEEN. WE'RE STAYING.

21

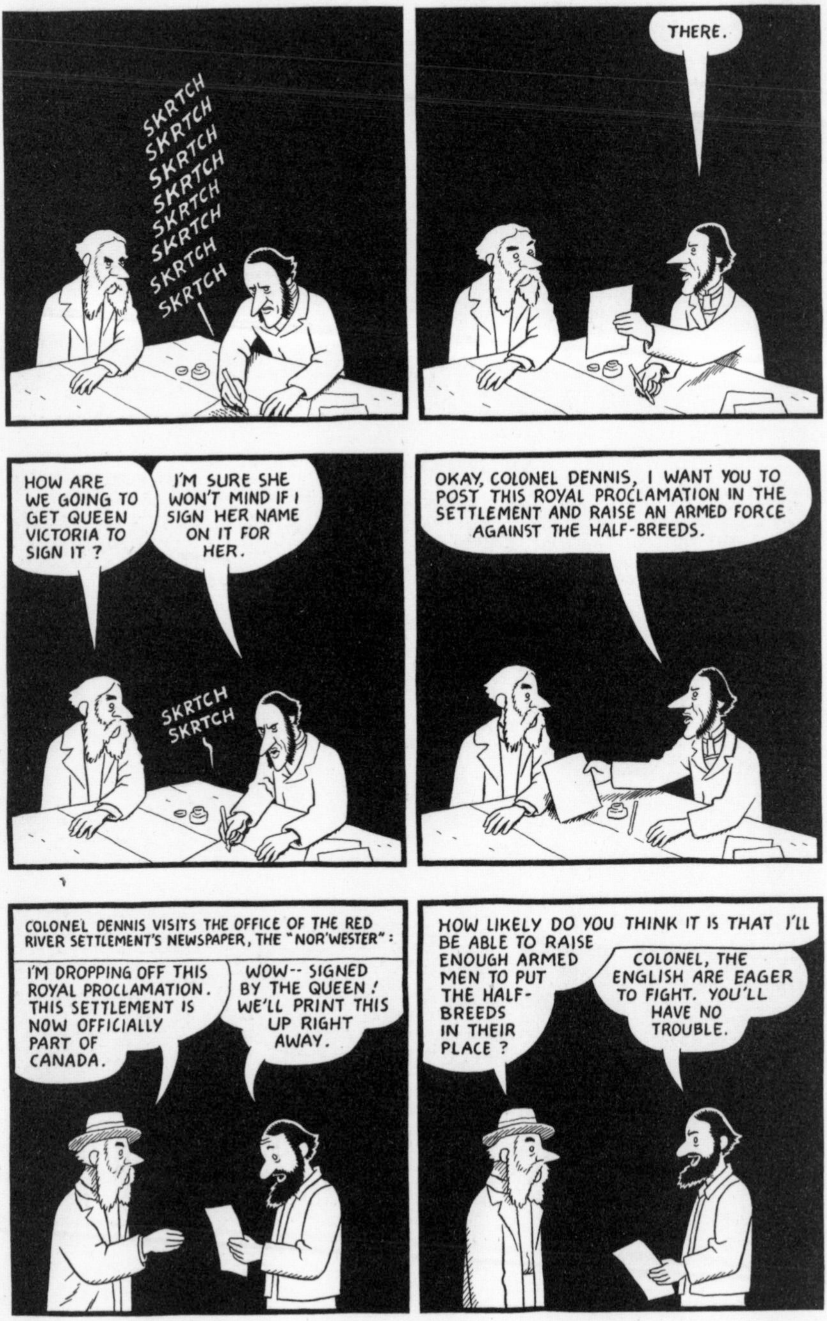
SKRTCH SKRTCH SKRTCH SKRTCH SKRTCH SKRTCH SKRTCH SKRTCH
THERE.
HOW ARE WE GOING TO GET QUEEN VICTORIA TO SIGN IT ?
I'M SURE SHE WON'T MIND IF I SIGN HER NAME ON IT FOR HER.
SKRTCH SKRTCH
OKAY, COLONEL DENNIS, I WANT YOU TO POST THIS ROYAL PROCLAMATION IN THE SETTLEMENT AND RAISE AN ARMED FORCE AGAINST THE HALF-BREEDS.
COLONEL DENNIS VISITS THE OFFICE OF THE RED RIVER SETTLEMENT'S NEWSPAPER, THE "NOR'WESTER":
I'M DROPPING OFF THIS ROYAL PROCLAMATION. THIS SETTLEMENT IS NOW OFFICIALLY PART OF CANADA.
WOW-- SIGNED BY THE QUEEN! WE'LL PRINT THIS UP RIGHT AWAY.
HOW LIKELY DO YOU THINK IT IS THAT I'LL BE ABLE TO RAISE ENOUGH ARMED MEN TO PUT THE HALF-BREEDS IN THEIR PLACE ?
COLONEL, THE ENGLISH ARE EAGER TO FIGHT. YOU'LL HAVE NO TROUBLE.

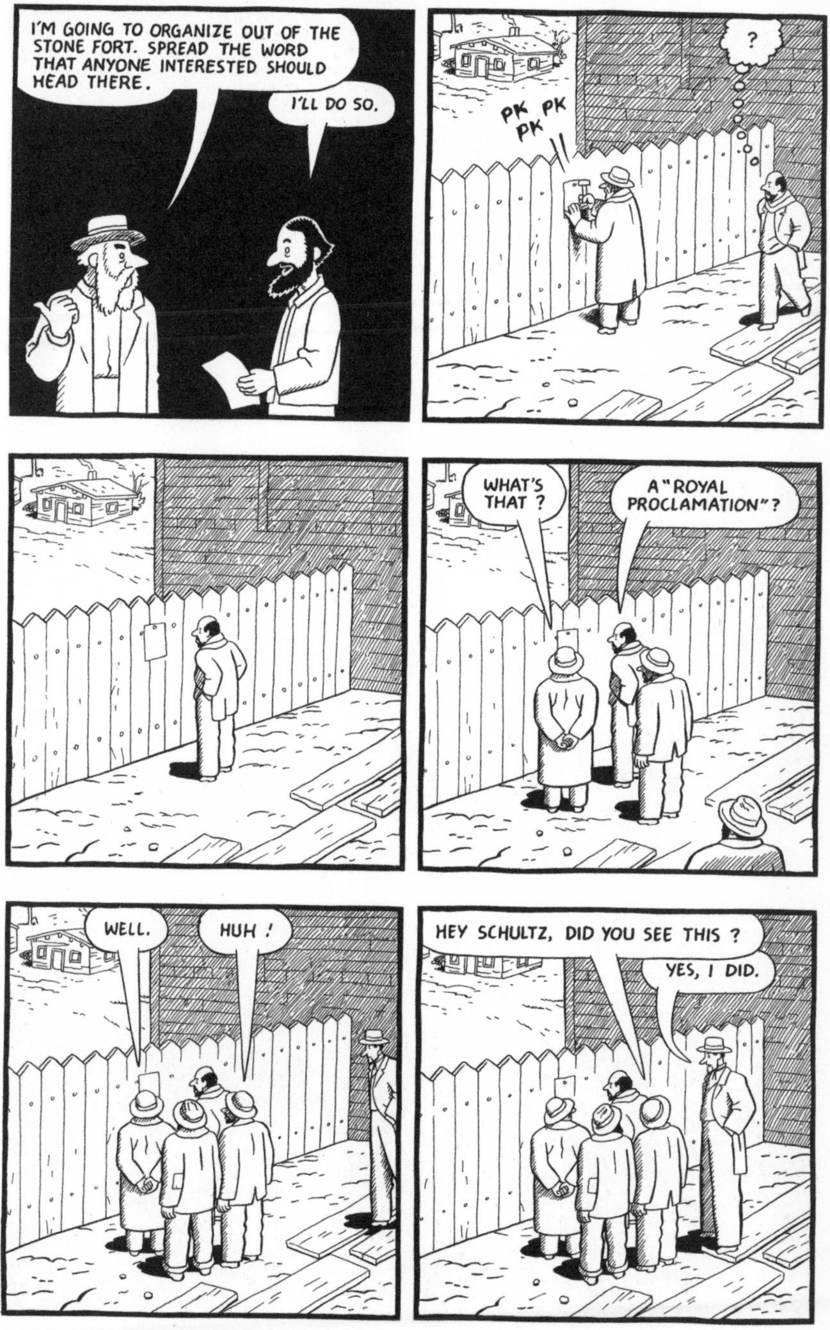
I'M GOING TO ORGANIZE OUT OF THE STONE FORT. SPREAD THE WORD THAT ANYONE INTERESTED SHOULD HEAD THERE.
I'LL DO SO.
?
PK PK PK
WHAT'S THAT ?
A "ROYAL PROCLAMATION"?
WELL.
HUH !
HEY SCHULTZ, DID YOU SEE THIS ?
YES, I DID.

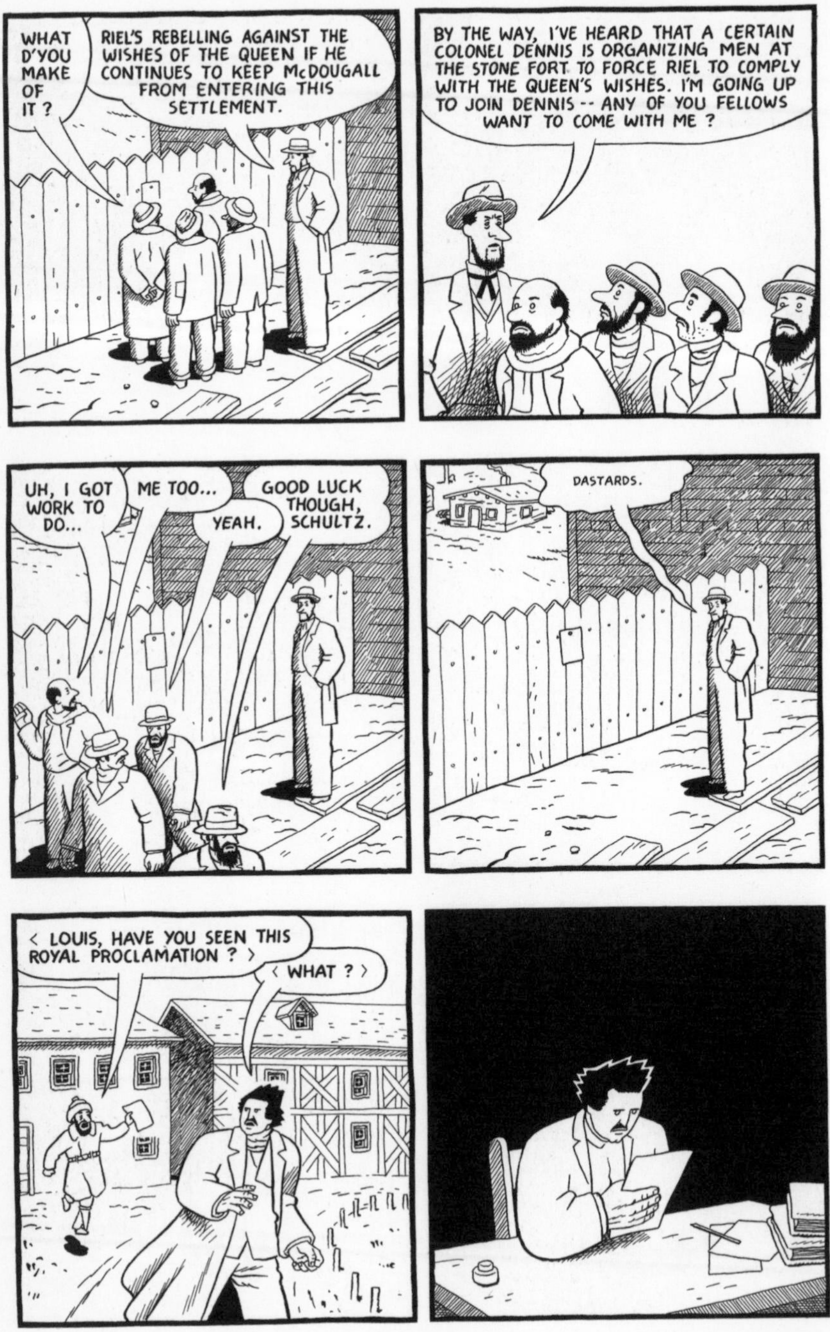
WHAT D'YOU MAKE OF IT ?
RIEL'S REBELLING AGAINST THE WISHES OF THE QUEEN IF HE CONTINUES TO KEEP McDOUGALL FROM ENTERING THIS SETTLEMENT.
BY THE WAY, I'VE HEARD THAT A CERTAIN COLONEL DENNIS IS ORGANIZING MEN AT THE STONE FORT TO FORCE RIEL TO COMPLY WITH THE QUEEN'S WISHES. I'M GOING UP TO JOIN DENNIS -- ANY OF YOU FELLOWS WANT TO COME WITH ME ?
UH, I GOT WORK TO DO...
ME TOO...
YEAH.
GOOD LUCK THOUGH, SCHULTZ.
DASTARDS.
< LOUIS, HAVE YOU SEEN THIS ROYAL PROCLAMATION ? >
< WHAT ? >

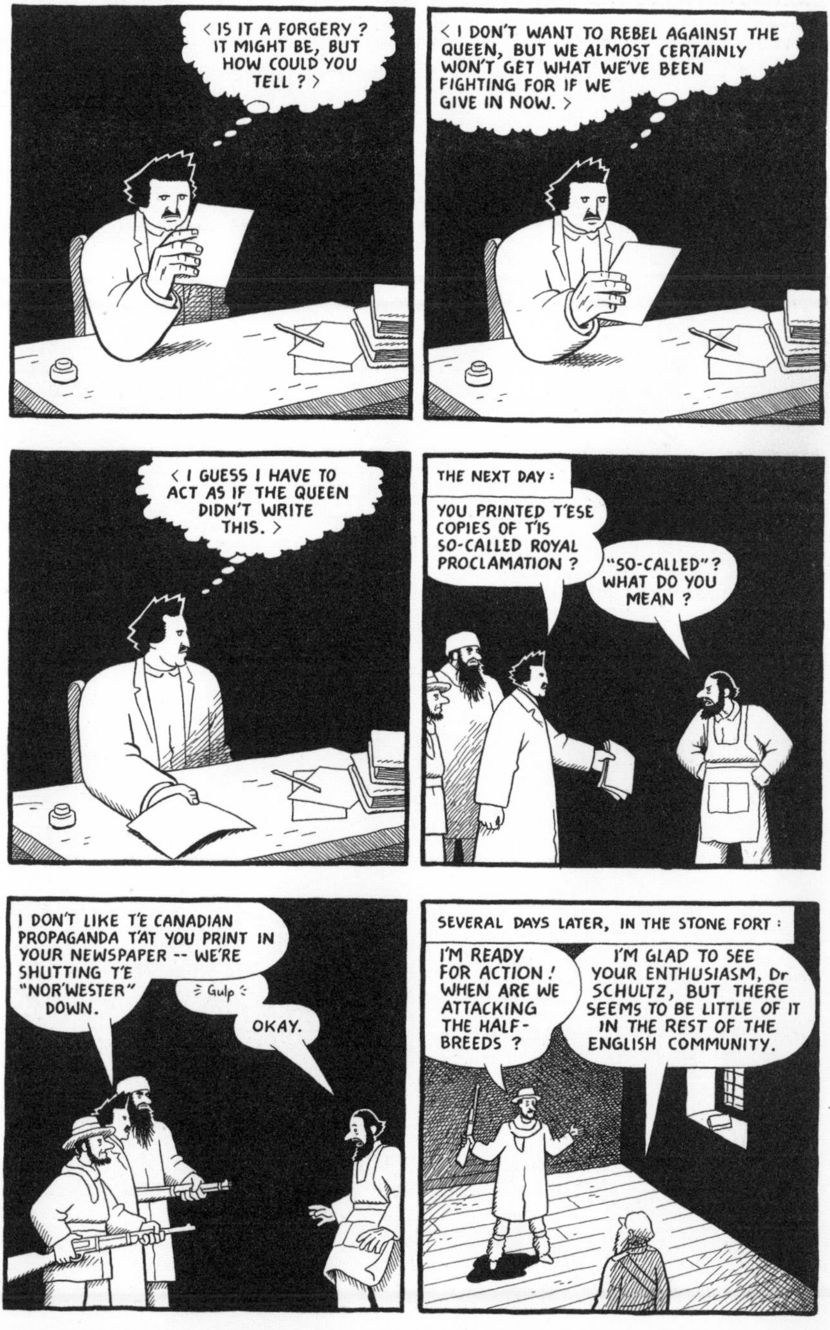
< IS IT A FORGERY ? IT MIGHT BE, BUT HOW COULD YOU TELL ? >
< I DON'T WANT TO REBEL AGAINST THE QUEEN, BUT WE ALMOST CERTAINLY WON'T GET WHAT WE'VE BEEN FIGHTING FOR IF WE GIVE IN NOW. >
< I GUESS I HAVE TO ACT AS IF THE QUEEN DIDN'T WRITE THIS. >
THE NEXT DAY :
YOU PRINTED T'ESE COPIES OF T'IS SO-CALLED ROYAL PROCLAMATION ?
"SO-CALLED"? WHAT DO YOU MEAN ?
I DON'T LIKE T'E CANADIAN PROPAGANDA T'AT YOU PRINT IN YOUR NEWSPAPER -- WE'RE SHUTTING T'E "NOR'WESTER" DOWN.
Gulp
OKAY.
SEVERAL DAYS LATER, IN THE STONE FORT :
I'M READY FOR ACTION ! WHEN ARE WE ATTACKING THE HALF-BREEDS ?
I'M GLAD TO SEE YOUR ENTHUSIASM, Dr SCHULTZ, BUT THERE SEEMS TO BE LITTLE OF IT IN THE REST OF THE ENGLISH COMMUNITY.

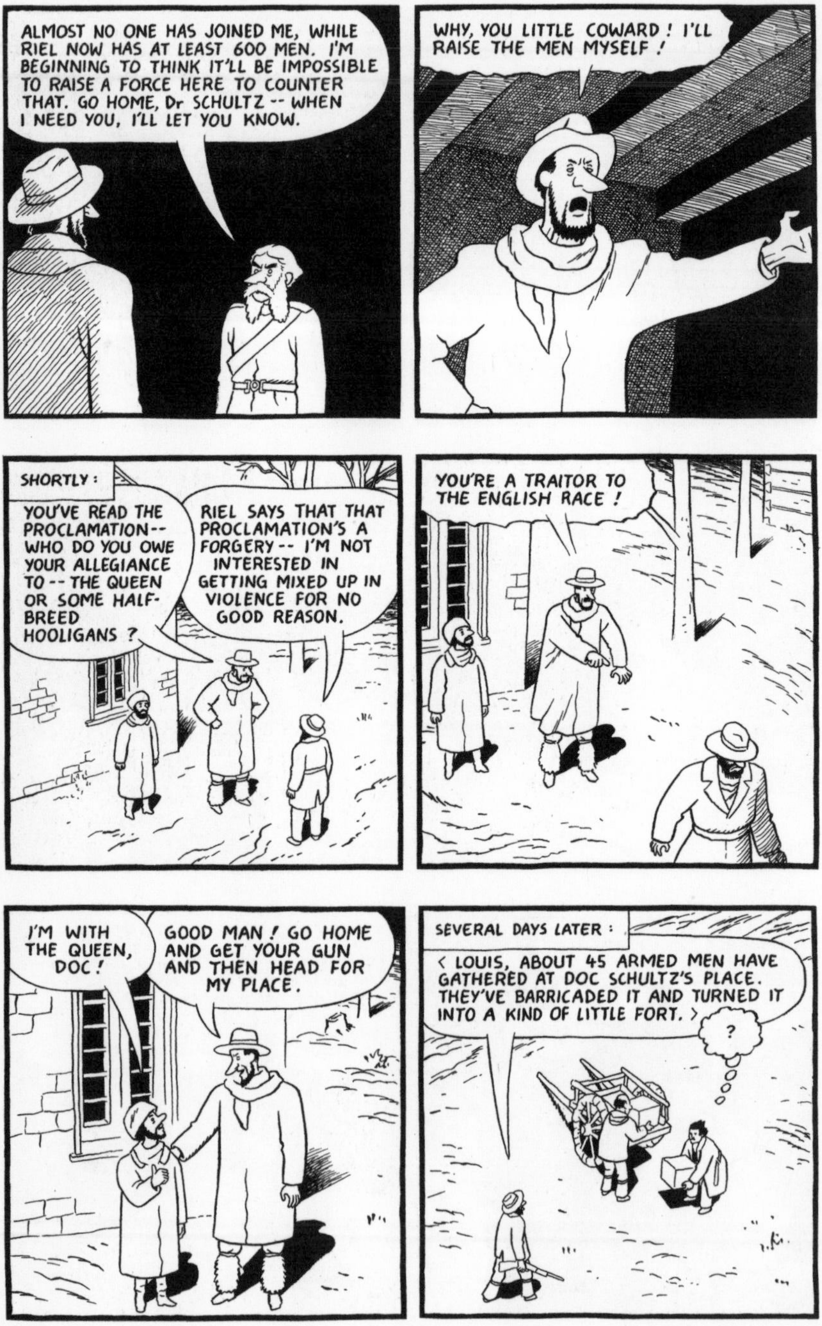
ALMOST NO ONE HAS JOINED ME, WHILE RIEL NOW HAS AT LEAST 600 MEN. I'M BEGINNING TO THINK IT'LL BE IMPOSSIBLE TO RAISE A FORCE HERE TO COUNTER THAT. GO HOME, Dr SCHULTZ -- WHEN I NEED YOU, I'LL LET YOU KNOW.
WHY, YOU LITTLE COWARD! I'LL RAISE THE MEN MYSELF!
SHORTLY:
YOU'VE READ THE PROCLAMATION-- WHO DO YOU OWE YOUR ALLEGIANCE TO -- THE QUEEN OR SOME HALF-BREED HOOLIGANS?
RIEL SAYS THAT THAT PROCLAMATION'S A FORGERY -- I'M NOT INTERESTED IN GETTING MIXED UP IN VIOLENCE FOR NO GOOD REASON.
YOU'RE A TRAITOR TO THE ENGLISH RACE!
I'M WITH THE QUEEN, DOC!
GOOD MAN! GO HOME AND GET YOUR GUN AND THEN HEAD FOR MY PLACE.
SEVERAL DAYS LATER:
< LOUIS, ABOUT 45 ARMED MEN HAVE GATHERED AT DOC SCHULTZ'S PLACE. THEY'VE BARRICADED IT AND TURNED IT INTO A KIND OF LITTLE FORT. >
?

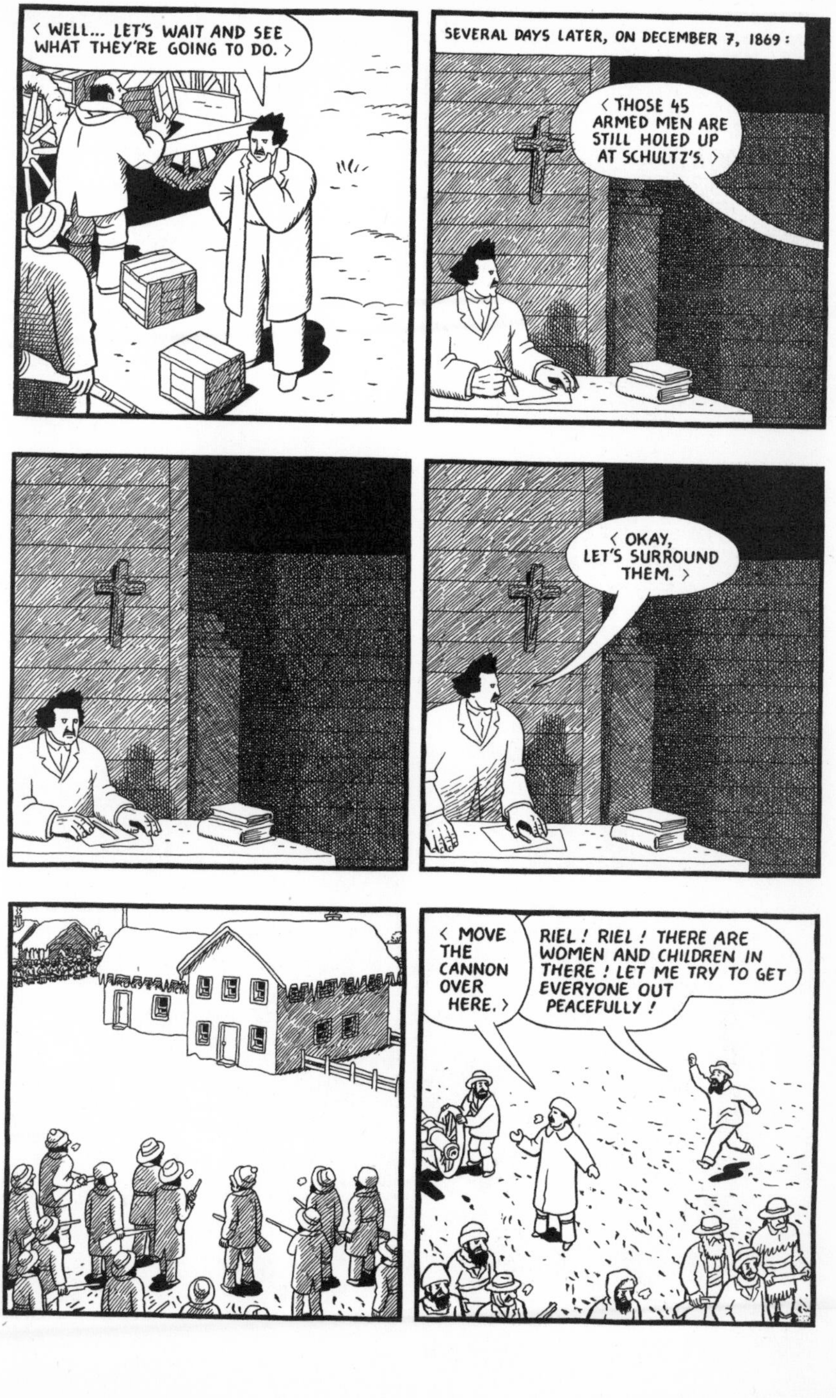
< WELL... LET'S WAIT AND SEE WHAT THEY'RE GOING TO DO. >
SEVERAL DAYS LATER, ON DECEMBER 7, 1869:
< THOSE 45 ARMED MEN ARE STILL HOLED UP AT SCHULTZ'S. >
< OKAY, LET'S SURROUND THEM. >
< MOVE THE CANNON OVER HERE. >
RIEL! RIEL! THERE ARE WOMEN AND CHILDREN IN THERE! LET ME TRY TO GET EVERYONE OUT PEACEFULLY!

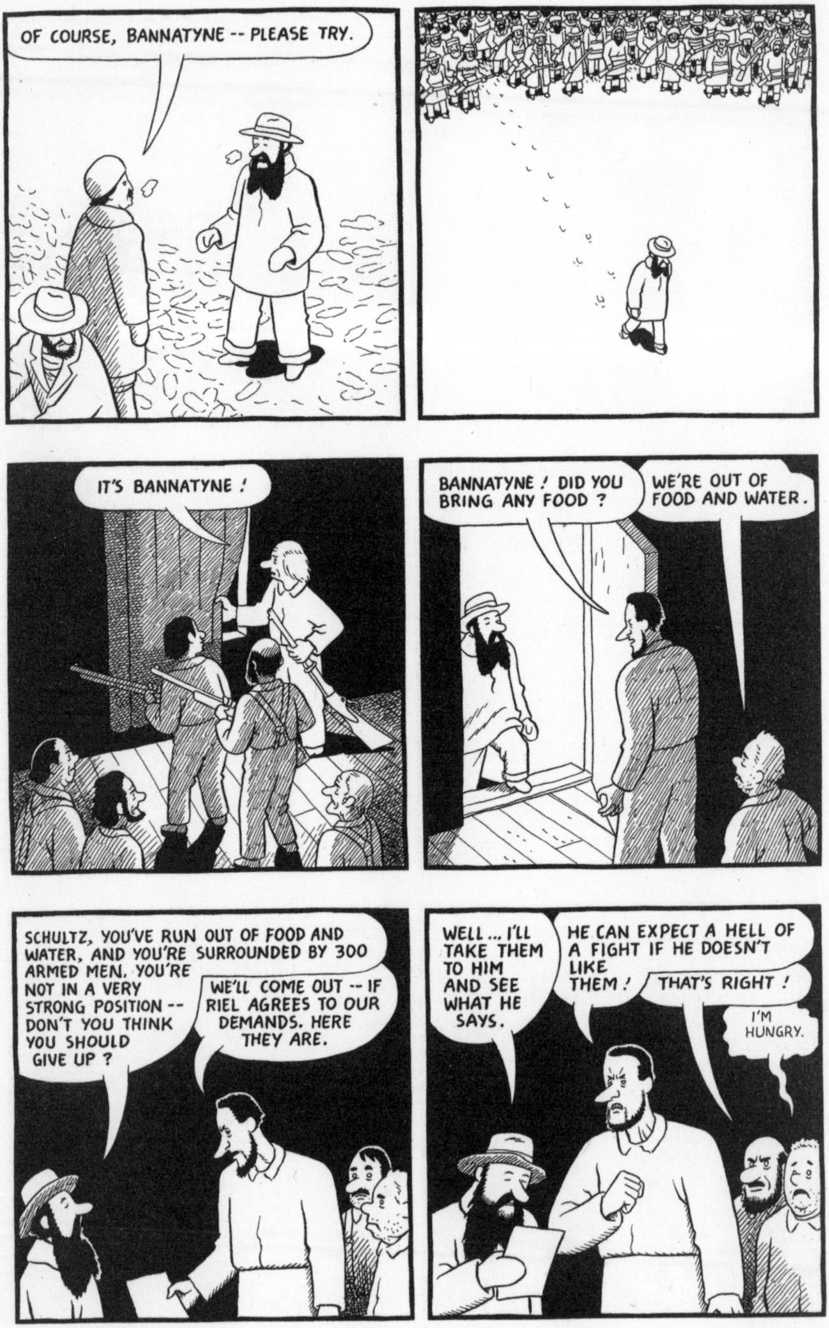
OF COURSE, BANNATYNE -- PLEASE TRY.
IT'S BANNATYNE !
BANNATYNE ! DID YOU BRING ANY FOOD ?
WE'RE OUT OF FOOD AND WATER.
SCHULTZ, YOU'VE RUN OUT OF FOOD AND WATER, AND YOU'RE SURROUNDED BY 300 ARMED MEN. YOU'RE NOT IN A VERY STRONG POSITION -- DON'T YOU THINK YOU SHOULD GIVE UP ?
WE'LL COME OUT -- IF RIEL AGREES TO OUR DEMANDS. HERE THEY ARE.
WELL ... I'LL TAKE THEM TO HIM AND SEE WHAT HE SAYS.
HE CAN EXPECT A HELL OF A FIGHT IF HE DOESN'T LIKE THEM !
THAT'S RIGHT !
I'M HUNGRY.

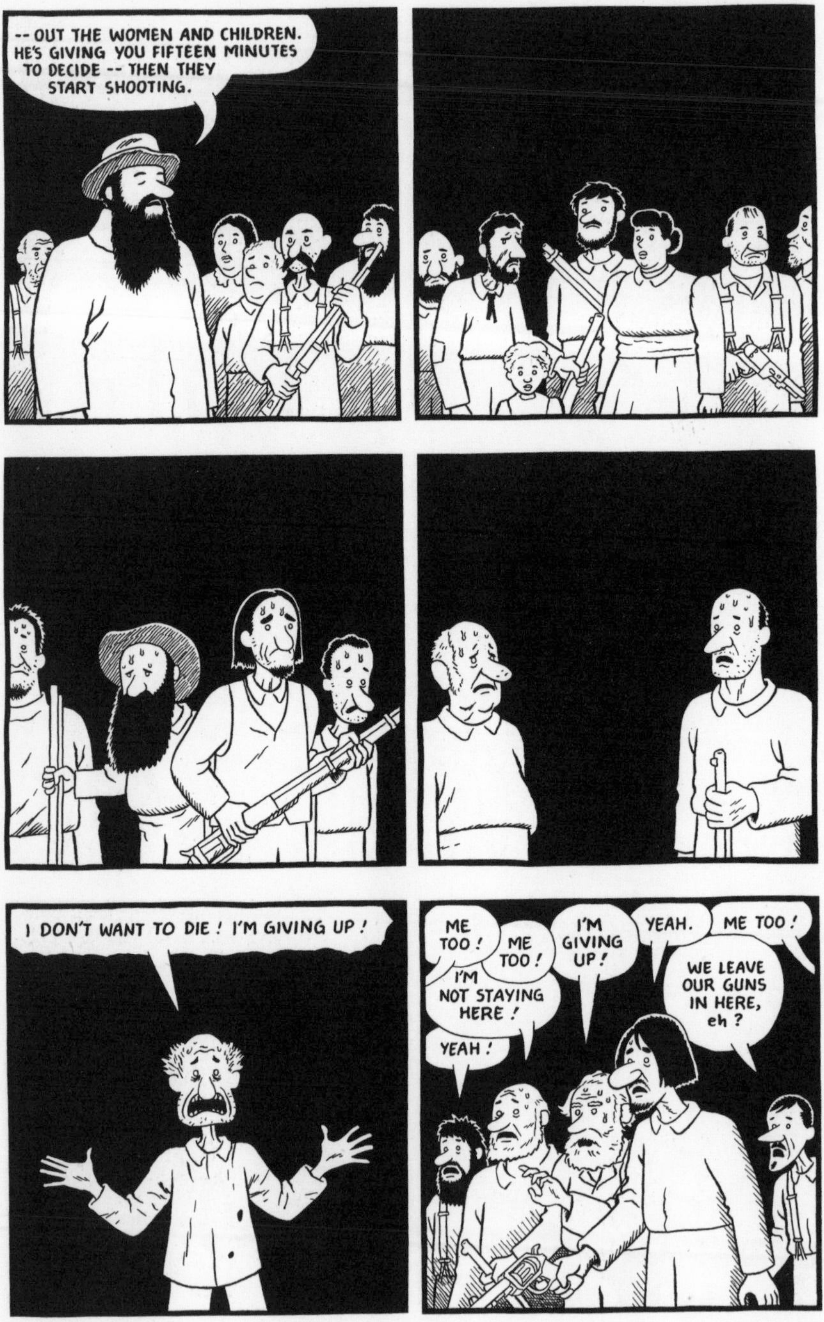
-- OUT THE WOMEN AND CHILDREN. HE'S GIVING YOU FIFTEEN MINUTES TO DECIDE -- THEN THEY START SHOOTING.
I DON'T WANT TO DIE! I'M GIVING UP!
ME TOO!
ME TOO!
I'M GIVING UP!
YEAH.
ME TOO!
I'M NOT STAYING HERE!
WE LEAVE OUR GUNS IN HERE, eh?
YEAH!

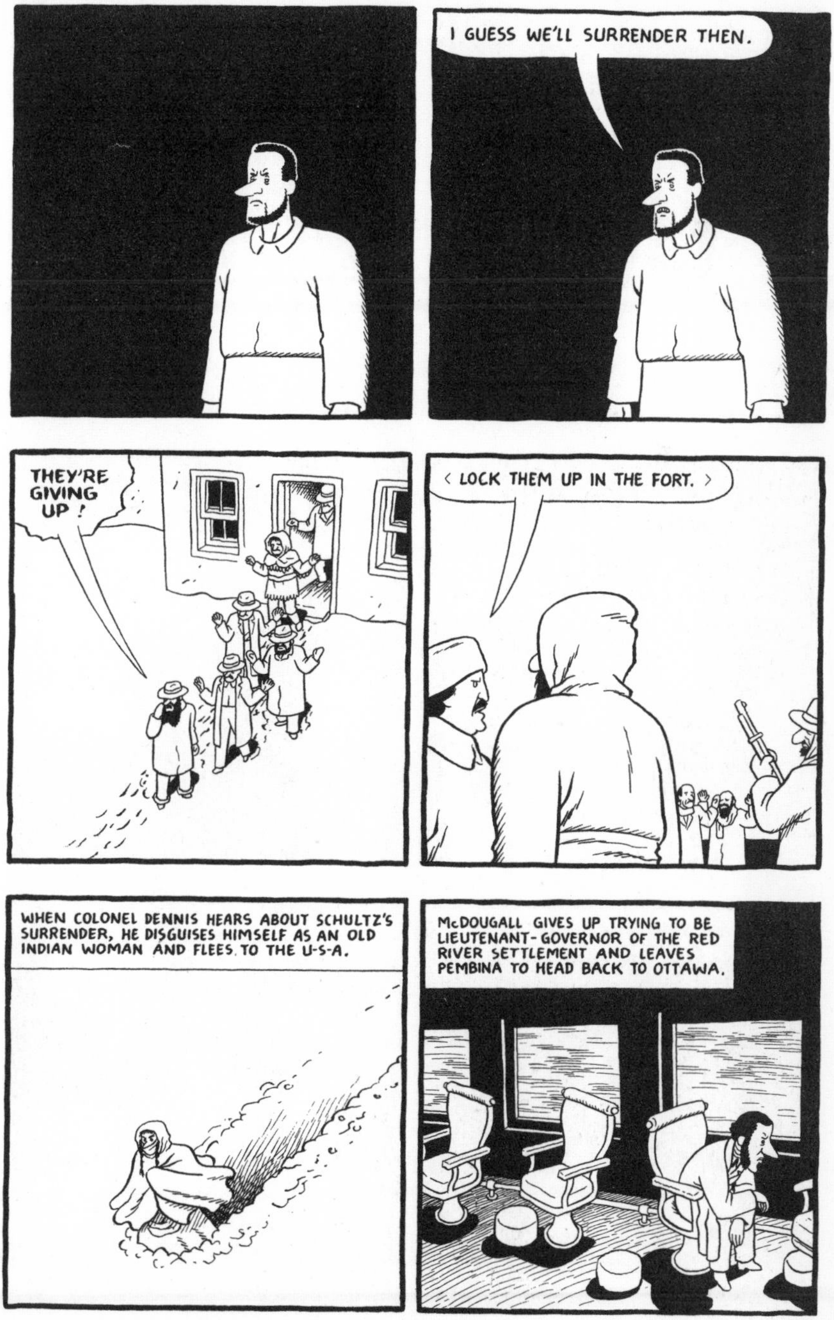
I GUESS WE'LL SURRENDER THEN.
THEY'RE GIVING UP!
< LOCK THEM UP IN THE FORT. >
WHEN COLONEL DENNIS HEARS ABOUT SCHULTZ'S SURRENDER, HE DISGUISES HIMSELF AS AN OLD INDIAN WOMAN AND FLEES TO THE U-S-A.
McDOUGALL GIVES UP TRYING TO BE LIEUTENANT-GOVERNOR OF THE RED RIVER SETTLEMENT AND LEAVES PEMBINA TO HEAD BACK TO OTTAWA.

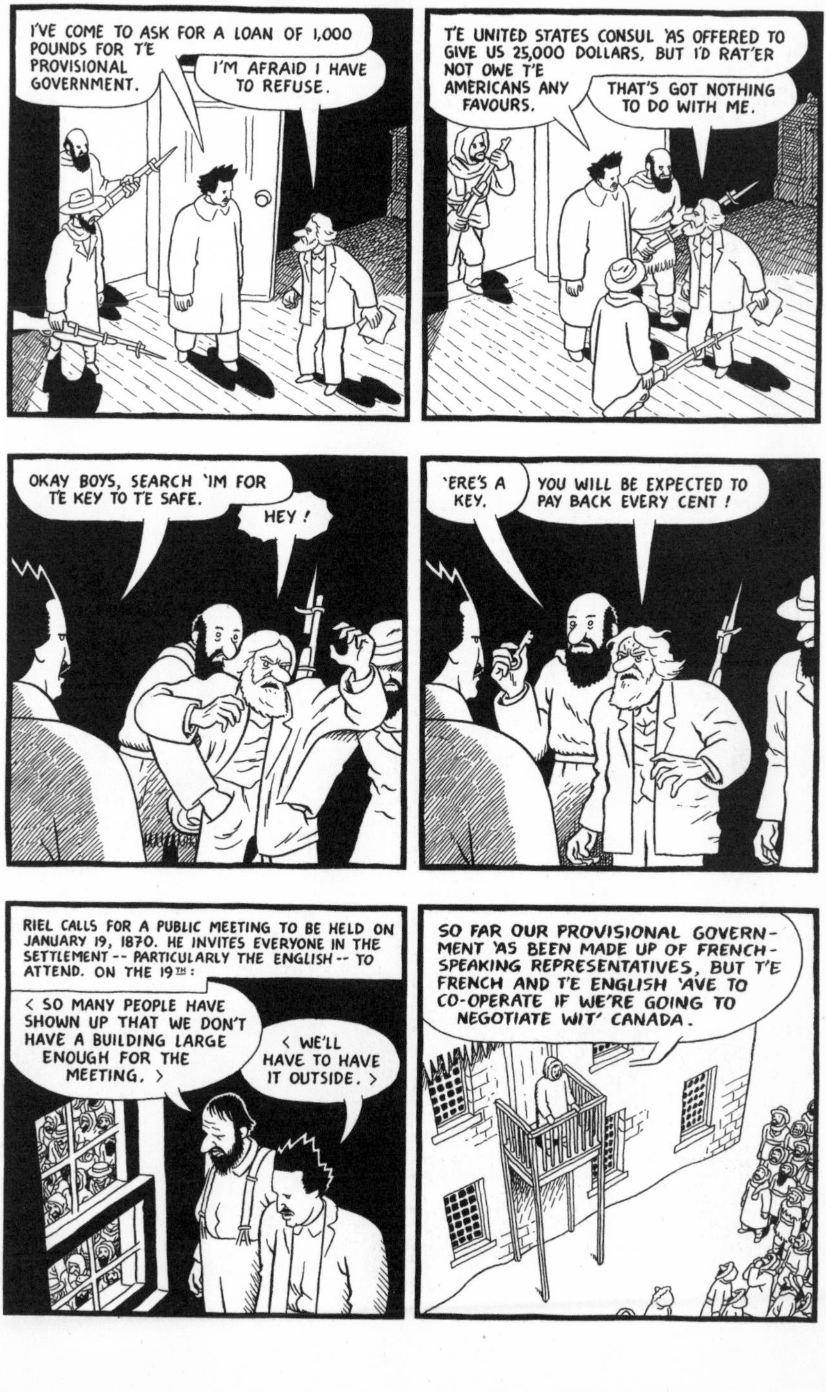
I'VE COME TO ASK FOR A LOAN OF 1,000 POUNDS FOR T'E PROVISIONAL GOVERNMENT.
I'M AFRAID I HAVE TO REFUSE.
T'E UNITED STATES CONSUL 'AS OFFERED TO GIVE US 25,000 DOLLARS, BUT I'D RAT'ER NOT OWE T'E AMERICANS ANY FAVOURS.
THAT'S GOT NOTHING TO DO WITH ME.
OKAY BOYS, SEARCH 'IM FOR T'E KEY TO T'E SAFE.
HEY !
'ERE'S A KEY.
YOU WILL BE EXPECTED TO PAY BACK EVERY CENT !
RIEL CALLS FOR A PUBLIC MEETING TO BE HELD ON JANUARY 19, 1870. HE INVITES EVERYONE IN THE SETTLEMENT -- PARTICULARLY THE ENGLISH -- TO ATTEND. ON THE 19TH:
< SO MANY PEOPLE HAVE SHOWN UP THAT WE DON'T HAVE A BUILDING LARGE ENOUGH FOR THE MEETING. >
< WE'LL HAVE TO HAVE IT OUTSIDE. >
SO FAR OUR PROVISIONAL GOVERNMENT 'AS BEEN MADE UP OF FRENCH-SPEAKING REPRESENTATIVES, BUT T'E FRENCH AND T'E ENGLISH 'AVE TO CO-OPERATE IF WE'RE GOING TO NEGOTIATE WIT' CANADA.

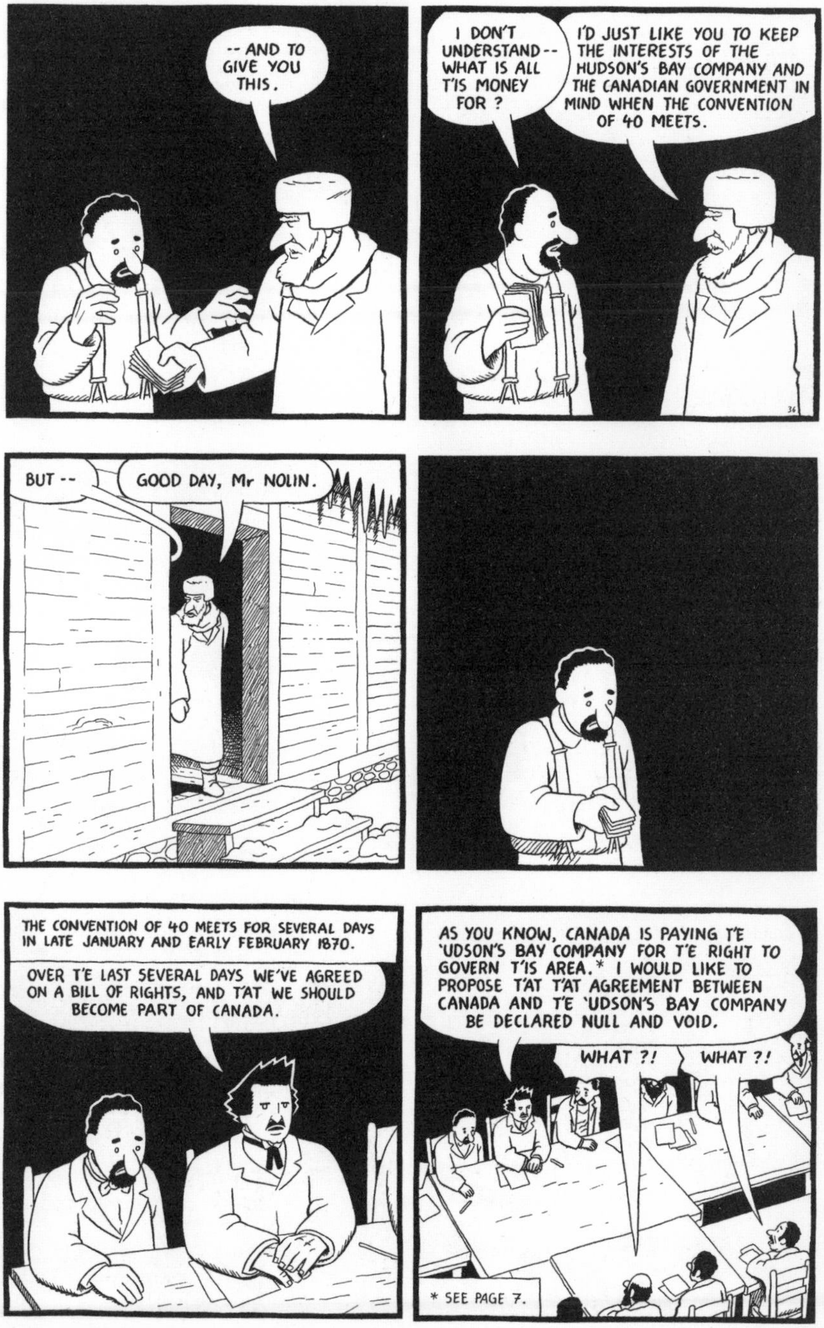
-- AND TO GIVE YOU THIS.
I DON'T UNDERSTAND -- WHAT IS ALL T'IS MONEY FOR ?
I'D JUST LIKE YOU TO KEEP THE INTERESTS OF THE HUDSON'S BAY COMPANY AND THE CANADIAN GOVERNMENT IN MIND WHEN THE CONVENTION OF 40 MEETS.
36
BUT --
GOOD DAY, Mr NOLIN.
THE CONVENTION OF 40 MEETS FOR SEVERAL DAYS IN LATE JANUARY AND EARLY FEBRUARY 1870.
OVER T'E LAST SEVERAL DAYS WE'VE AGREED ON A BILL OF RIGHTS, AND T'AT WE SHOULD BECOME PART OF CANADA.
AS YOU KNOW, CANADA IS PAYING T'E 'UDSON'S BAY COMPANY FOR T'E RIGHT TO GOVERN T'IS AREA.* I WOULD LIKE TO PROPOSE T'AT T'AT AGREEMENT BETWEEN CANADA AND T'E 'UDSON'S BAY COMPANY BE DECLARED NULL AND VOID.
WHAT ?!
WHAT ?!
* SEE PAGE 7.

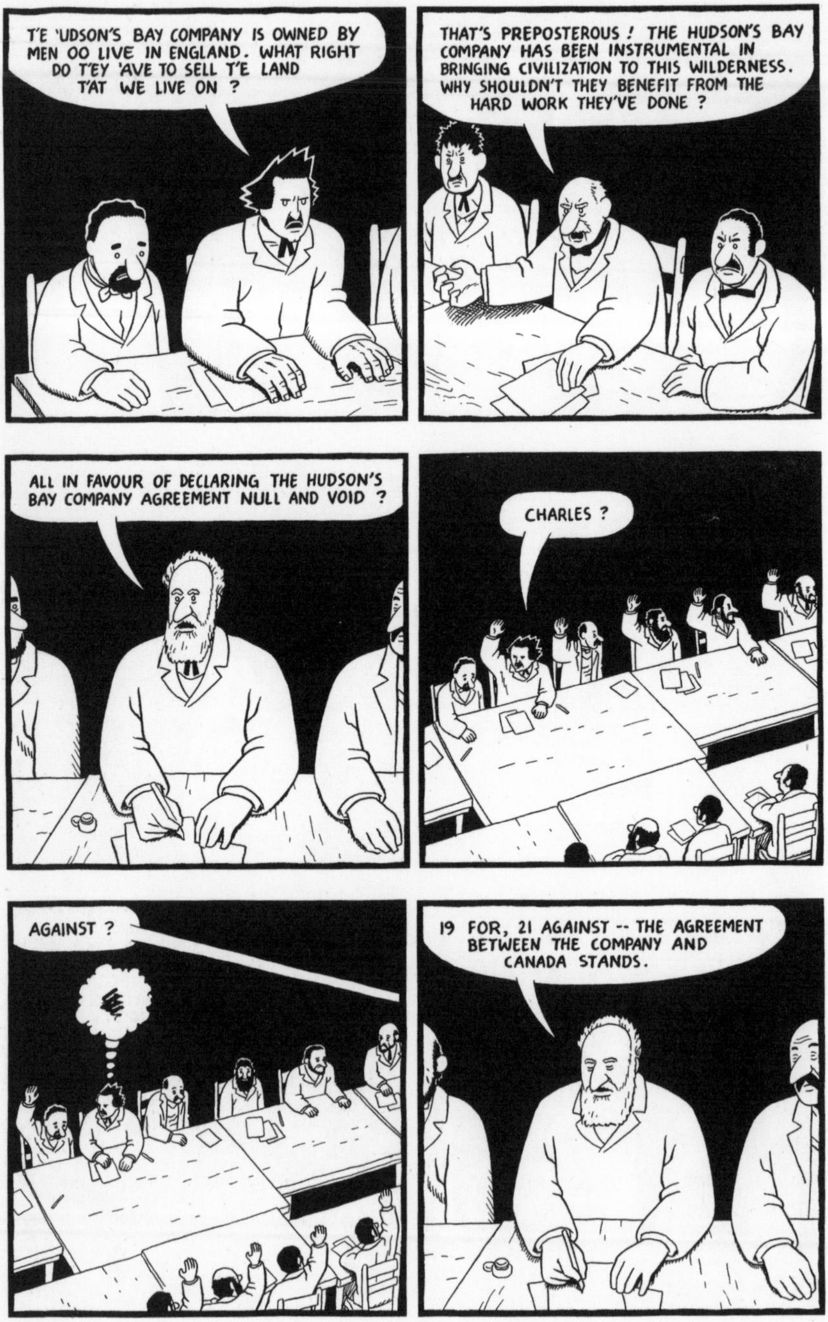
T'E 'UDSON'S BAY COMPANY IS OWNED BY MEN OO LIVE IN ENGLAND. WHAT RIGHT DO T'EY 'AVE TO SELL T'E LAND T'AT WE LIVE ON ?
THAT'S PREPOSTEROUS ! THE HUDSON'S BAY COMPANY HAS BEEN INSTRUMENTAL IN BRINGING CIVILIZATION TO THIS WILDERNESS. WHY SHOULDN'T THEY BENEFIT FROM THE HARD WORK THEY'VE DONE ?
ALL IN FAVOUR OF DECLARING THE HUDSON'S BAY COMPANY AGREEMENT NULL AND VOID ?
CHARLES ?
AGAINST ?
19 FOR, 21 AGAINST -- THE AGREEMENT BETWEEN THE COMPANY AND CANADA STANDS.

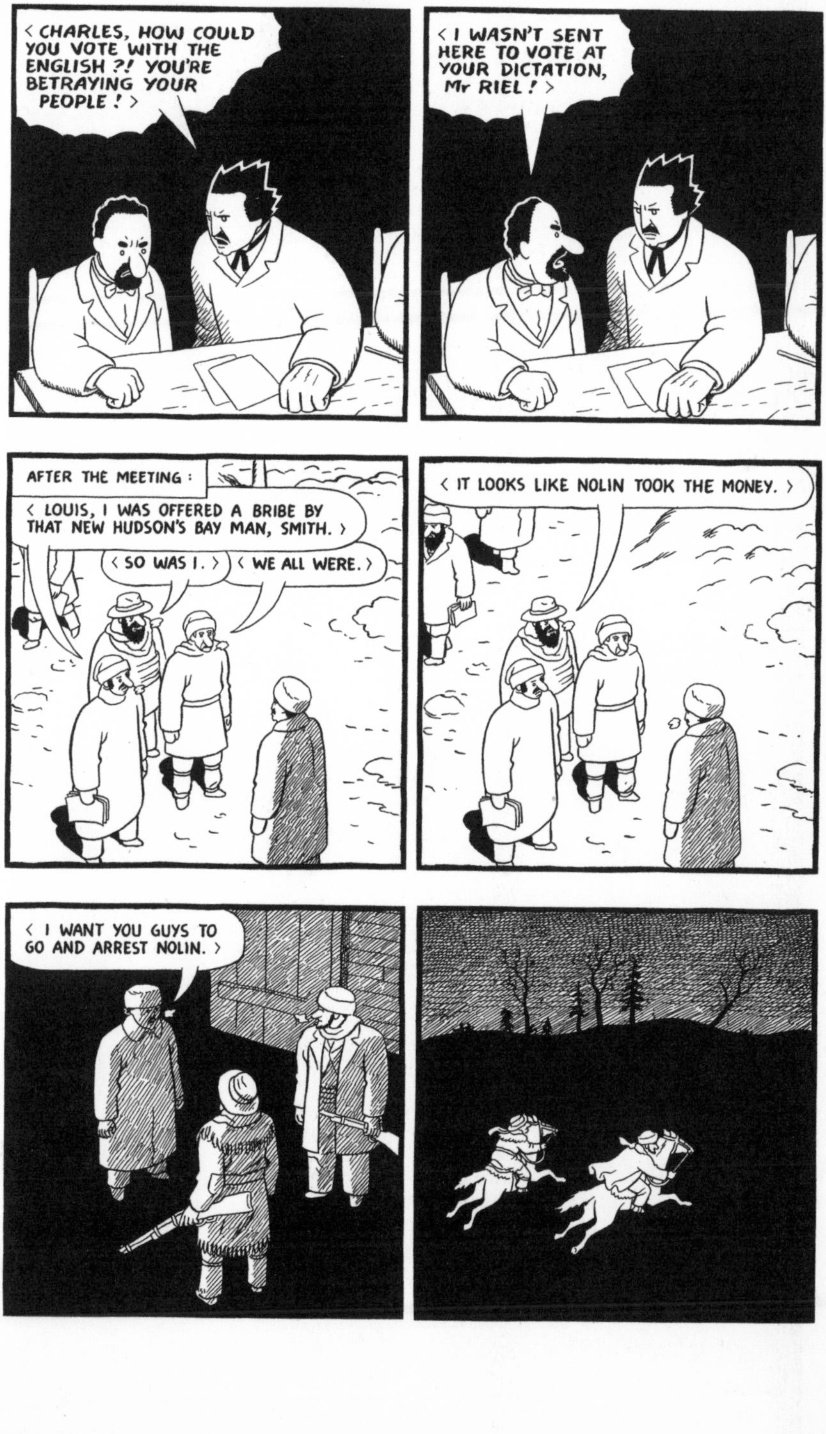
< CHARLES, HOW COULD YOU VOTE WITH THE ENGLISH ?! YOU'RE BETRAYING YOUR PEOPLE ! >
< I WASN'T SENT HERE TO VOTE AT YOUR DICTATION, Mr RIEL ! >
AFTER THE MEETING :
< LOUIS, I WAS OFFERED A BRIBE BY THAT NEW HUDSON'S BAY MAN, SMITH. >
< SO WAS I. >
< WE ALL WERE. >
< IT LOOKS LIKE NOLIN TOOK THE MONEY. >
< I WANT YOU GUYS TO GO AND ARREST NOLIN. >

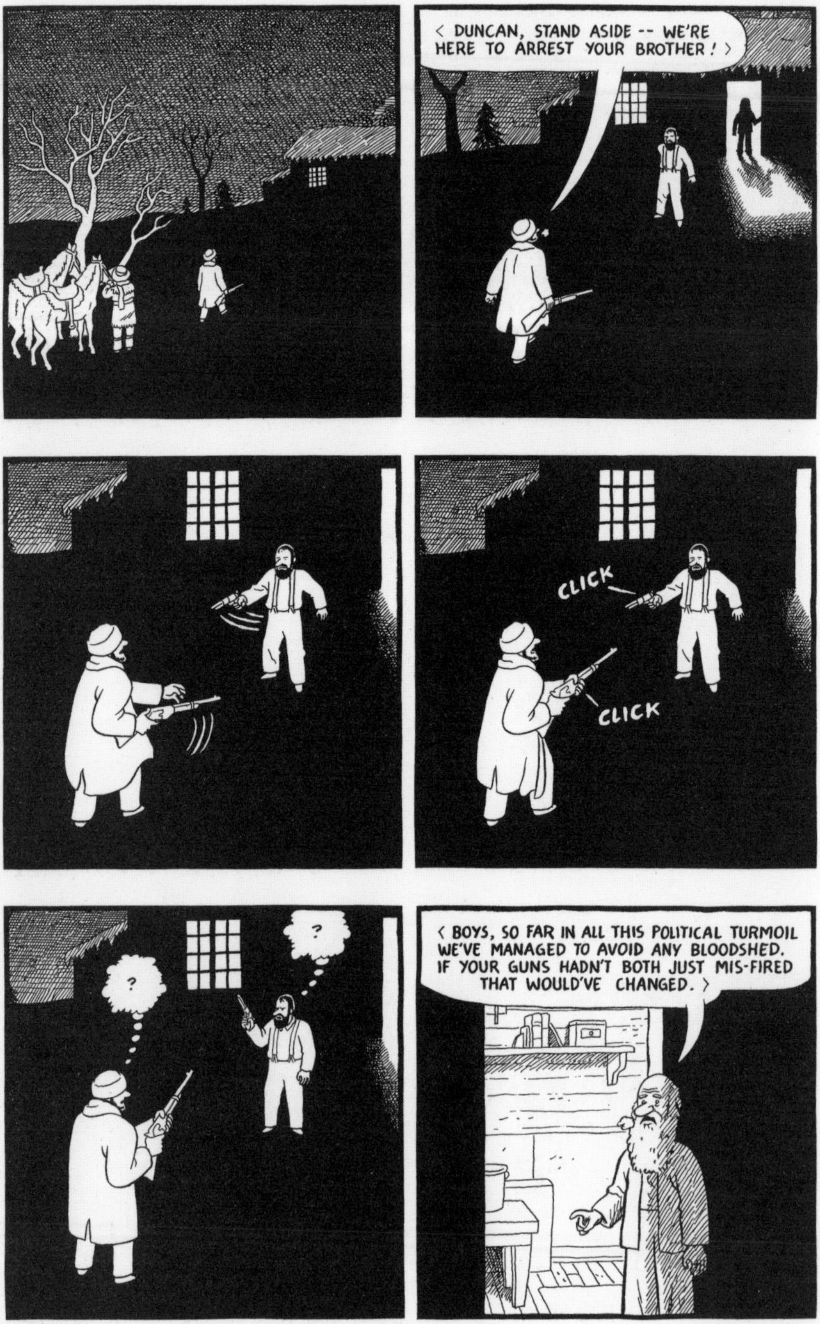
< DUNCAN, STAND ASIDE -- WE'RE HERE TO ARREST YOUR BROTHER! >
CLICK
CLICK
?
?
< BOYS, SO FAR IN ALL THIS POLITICAL TURMOIL WE'VE MANAGED TO AVOID ANY BLOODSHED. IF YOUR GUNS HADN'T BOTH JUST MIS-FIRED THAT WOULD'VE CHANGED. >

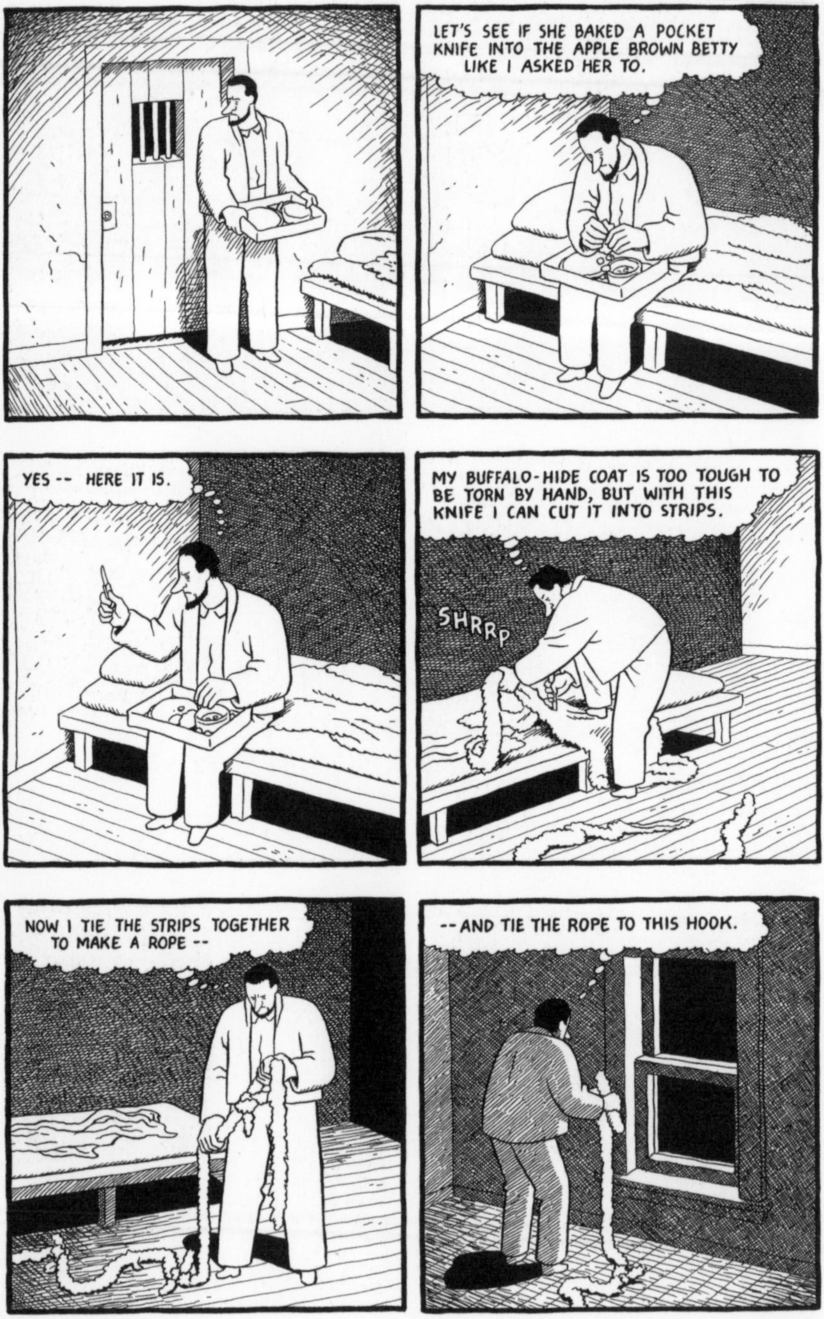
LET'S SEE IF SHE BAKED A POCKET KNIFE INTO THE APPLE BROWN BETTY LIKE I ASKED HER TO.
YES -- HERE IT IS.
MY BUFFALO-HIDE COAT IS TOO TOUGH TO BE TORN BY HAND, BUT WITH THIS KNIFE I CAN CUT IT INTO STRIPS.
SHRRP
NOW I TIE THE STRIPS TOGETHER TO MAKE A ROPE --
-- AND TIE THE ROPE TO THIS HOOK.

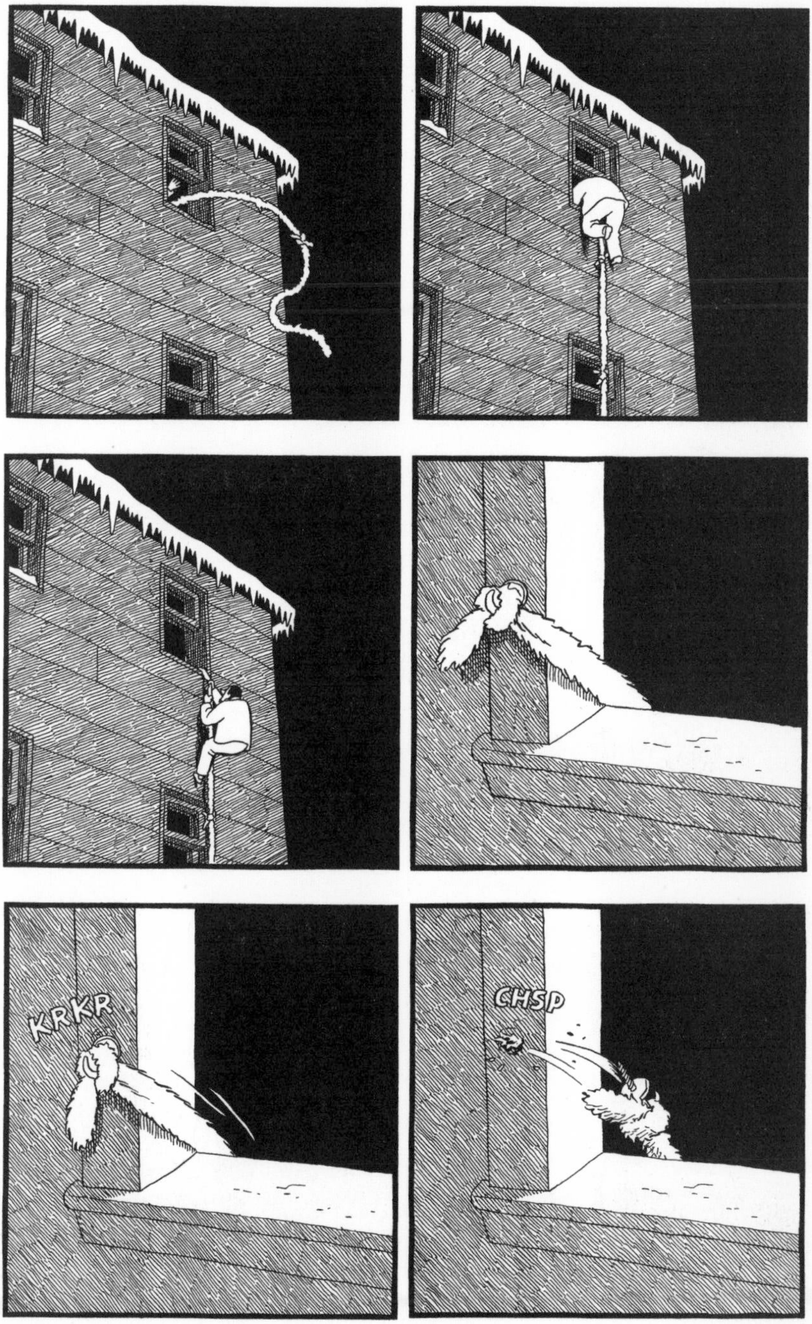
KRKR
CHSP

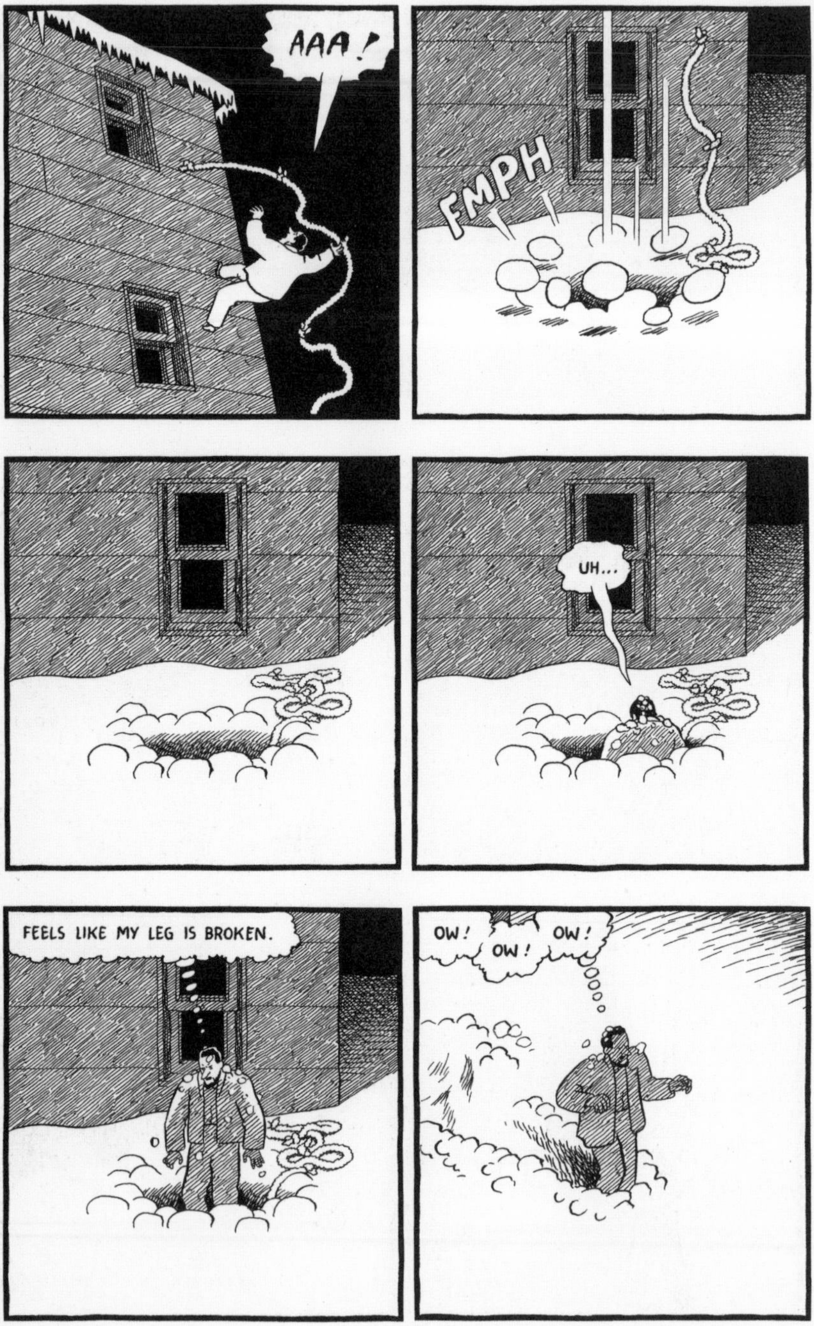
AAA!
FMPH
UH...
FEELS LIKE MY LEG IS BROKEN.
OW!
OW!
OW!

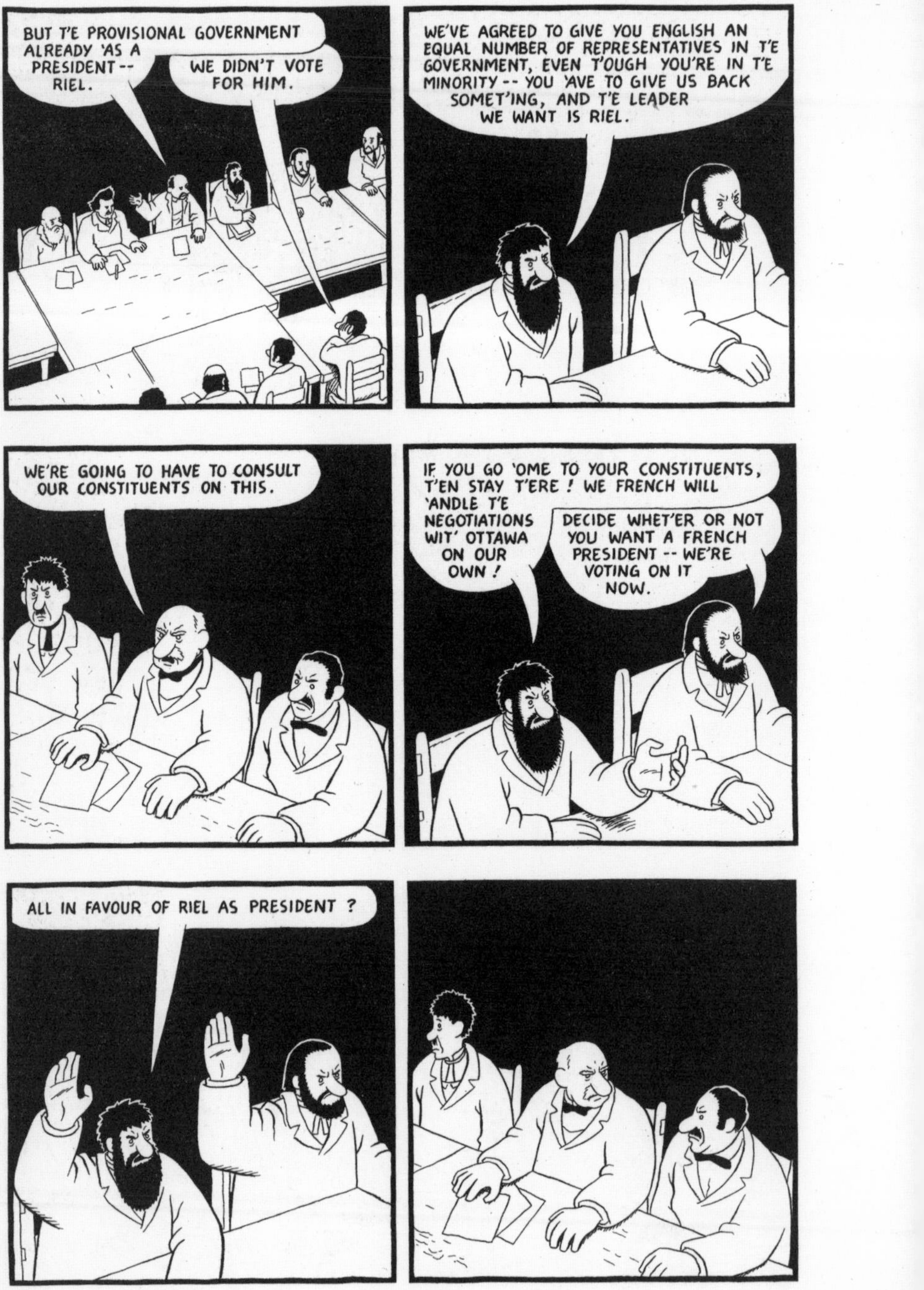
BUT T'E PROVISIONAL GOVERNMENT ALREADY 'AS A PRESIDENT -- RIEL.
WE DIDN'T VOTE FOR HIM.
WE'VE AGREED TO GIVE YOU ENGLISH AN EQUAL NUMBER OF REPRESENTATIVES IN T'E GOVERNMENT, EVEN T'OUGH YOU'RE IN T'E MINORITY -- YOU 'AVE TO GIVE US BACK SOMET'ING, AND T'E LEADER WE WANT IS RIEL.
WE'RE GOING TO HAVE TO CONSULT OUR CONSTITUENTS ON THIS.
IF YOU GO 'OME TO YOUR CONSTITUENTS, T'EN STAY T'ERE ! WE FRENCH WILL 'ANDLE T'E NEGOTIATIONS WIT' OTTAWA ON OUR OWN !
DECIDE WHET'ER OR NOT YOU WANT A FRENCH PRESIDENT -- WE'RE VOTING ON IT NOW.
ALL IN FAVOUR OF RIEL AS PRESIDENT ?

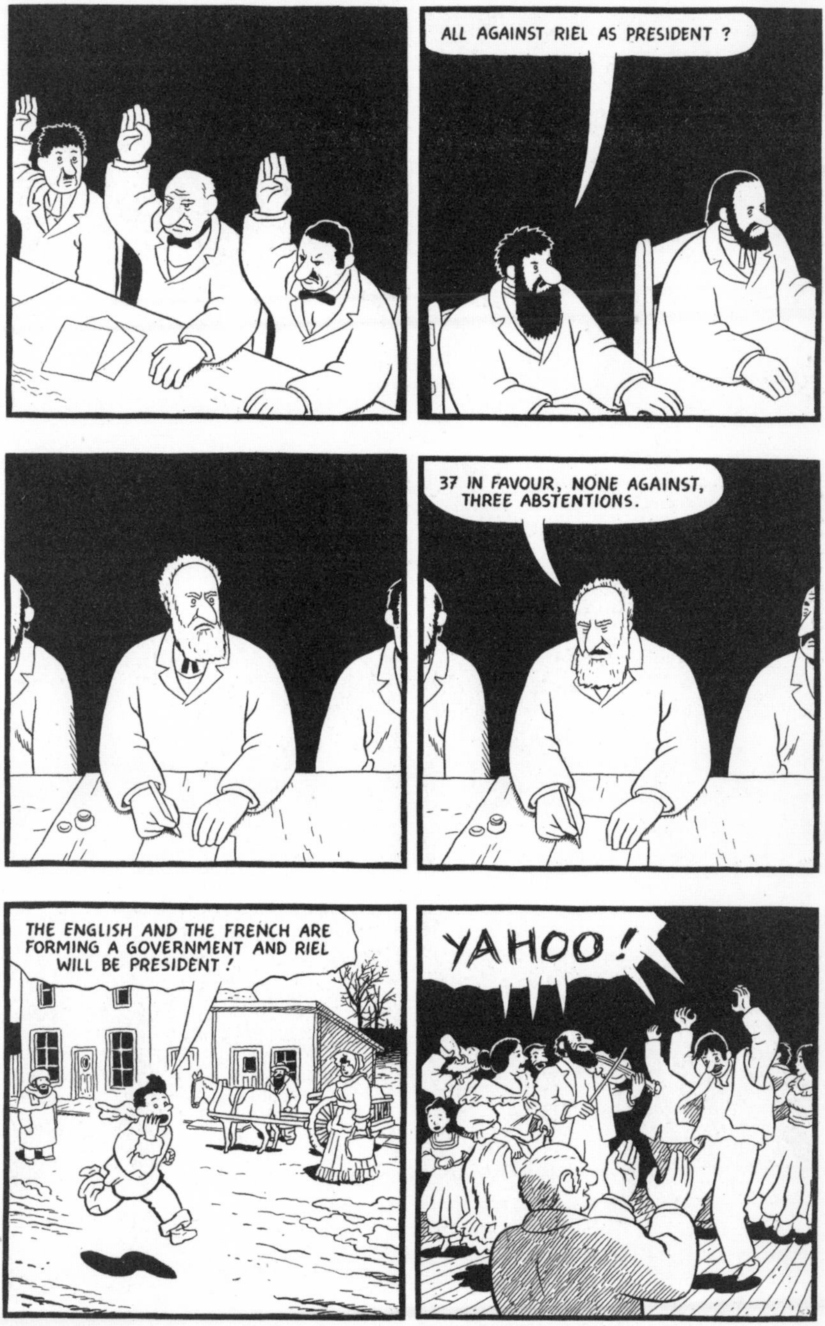
ALL AGAINST RIEL AS PRESIDENT ?
37 IN FAVOUR, NONE AGAINST, THREE ABSTENTIONS.
THE ENGLISH AND THE FRENCH ARE FORMING A GOVERNMENT AND RIEL WILL BE PRESIDENT !
YAHOO !

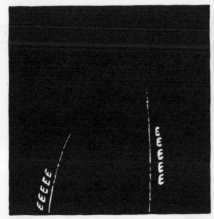

RIEL, IT MIGHT BE TIME TO START THINKING ABOUT LETTING THOSE PRISONERS IN FORT GARRY GO FREE.

NOT YET.

JOHN SUTHERLAND -- AN ENGLISH SETTLER

I'VE HEARD A RUMOUR THAT SCHULTZ IS NOW IN KILDONAN AND HAS MANAGED TO PUT TOGETHER AN ARMY OF OVER 300 MEN TO FREE THE PRISONERS.

SCHULTZ COULDN'T HAVE GOTTEN THAT MANY MEN MOTIVATED IF YOU DIDN'T HAVE ANY PRISONERS -- IT GIVES HIM A CAUSE TO RALLY AROUND.

LET ME T'INK ABOUT IT.

ON FEBRUARY 15, 1870, A MÉTIS NAMED NORBERT PARISIEN WANDERS THROUGH KILDONAN:

< SEEMS TO BE A BIG COMMOTION GOING ON HERE. >

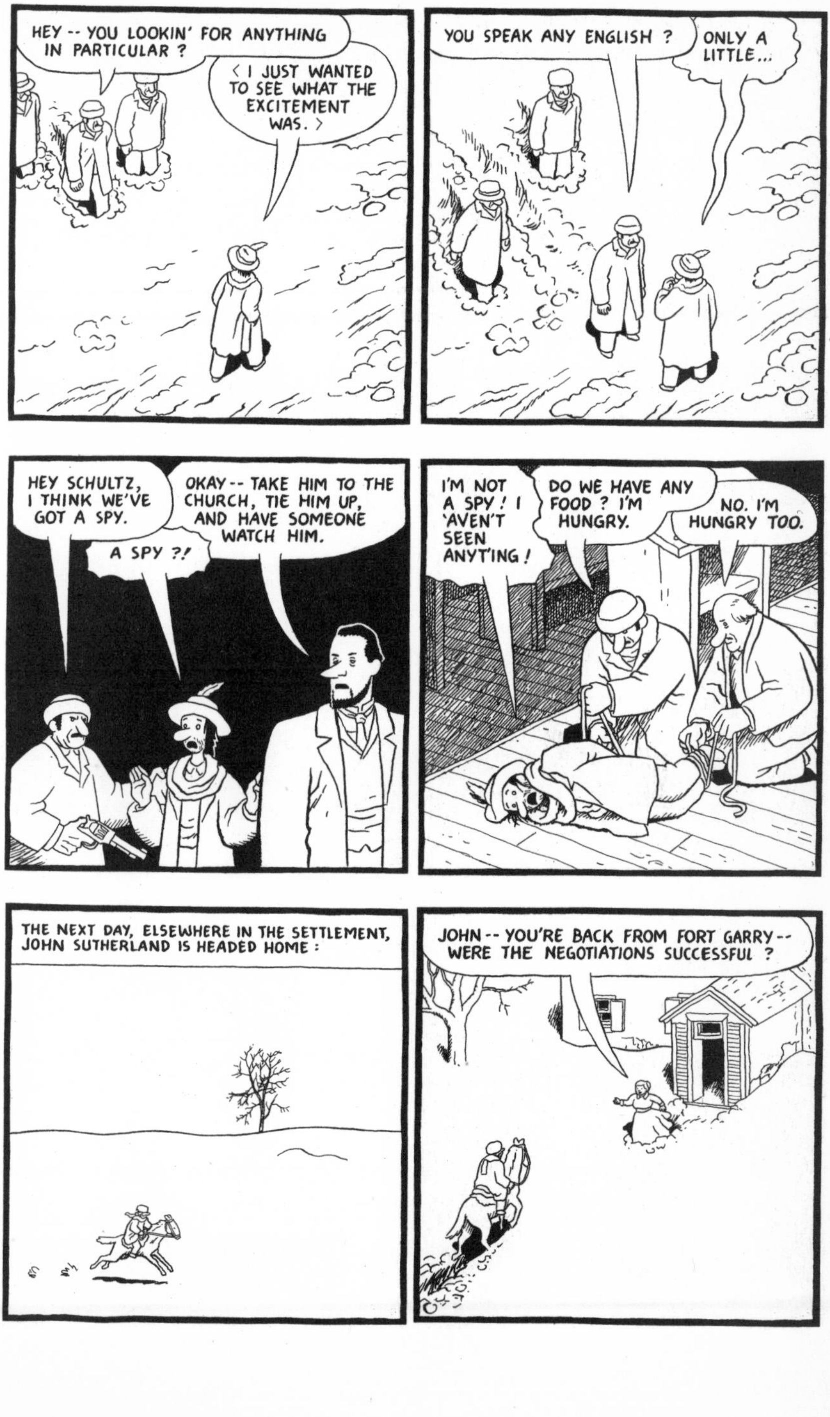
HEY -- YOU LOOKIN' FOR ANYTHING IN PARTICULAR ?
< I JUST WANTED TO SEE WHAT THE EXCITEMENT WAS. >
YOU SPEAK ANY ENGLISH ?
ONLY A LITTLE...
HEY SCHULTZ, I THINK WE'VE GOT A SPY.
A SPY ?!
OKAY -- TAKE HIM TO THE CHURCH, TIE HIM UP, AND HAVE SOMEONE WATCH HIM.
I'M NOT A SPY ! I 'AVEN'T SEEN ANYT'ING !
DO WE HAVE ANY FOOD ? I'M HUNGRY.
NO. I'M HUNGRY TOO.
THE NEXT DAY, ELSEWHERE IN THE SETTLEMENT, JOHN SUTHERLAND IS HEADED HOME :
JOHN -- YOU'RE BACK FROM FORT GARRY -- WERE THE NEGOTIATIONS SUCCESSFUL ?

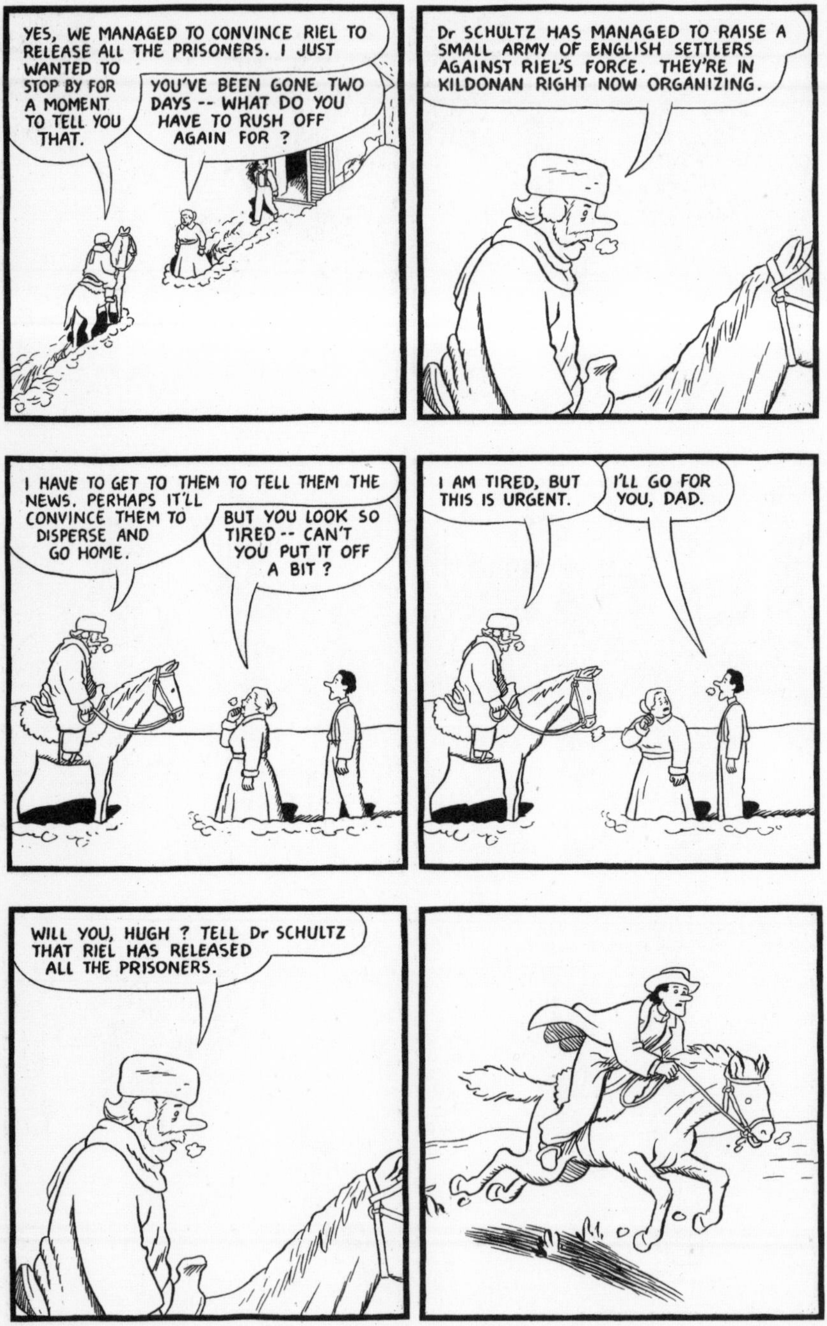
YES, WE MANAGED TO CONVINCE RIEL TO RELEASE ALL THE PRISONERS. I JUST WANTED TO STOP BY FOR A MOMENT TO TELL YOU THAT.
YOU'VE BEEN GONE TWO DAYS -- WHAT DO YOU HAVE TO RUSH OFF AGAIN FOR ?
Dr SCHULTZ HAS MANAGED TO RAISE A SMALL ARMY OF ENGLISH SETTLERS AGAINST RIEL'S FORCE. THEY'RE IN KILDONAN RIGHT NOW ORGANIZING.
I HAVE TO GET TO THEM TO TELL THEM THE NEWS. PERHAPS IT'LL CONVINCE THEM TO DISPERSE AND GO HOME.
BUT YOU LOOK SO TIRED -- CAN'T YOU PUT IT OFF A BIT ?
I AM TIRED, BUT THIS IS URGENT.
I'LL GO FOR YOU, DAD.
WILL YOU, HUGH ? TELL Dr SCHULTZ THAT RIEL HAS RELEASED ALL THE PRISONERS.

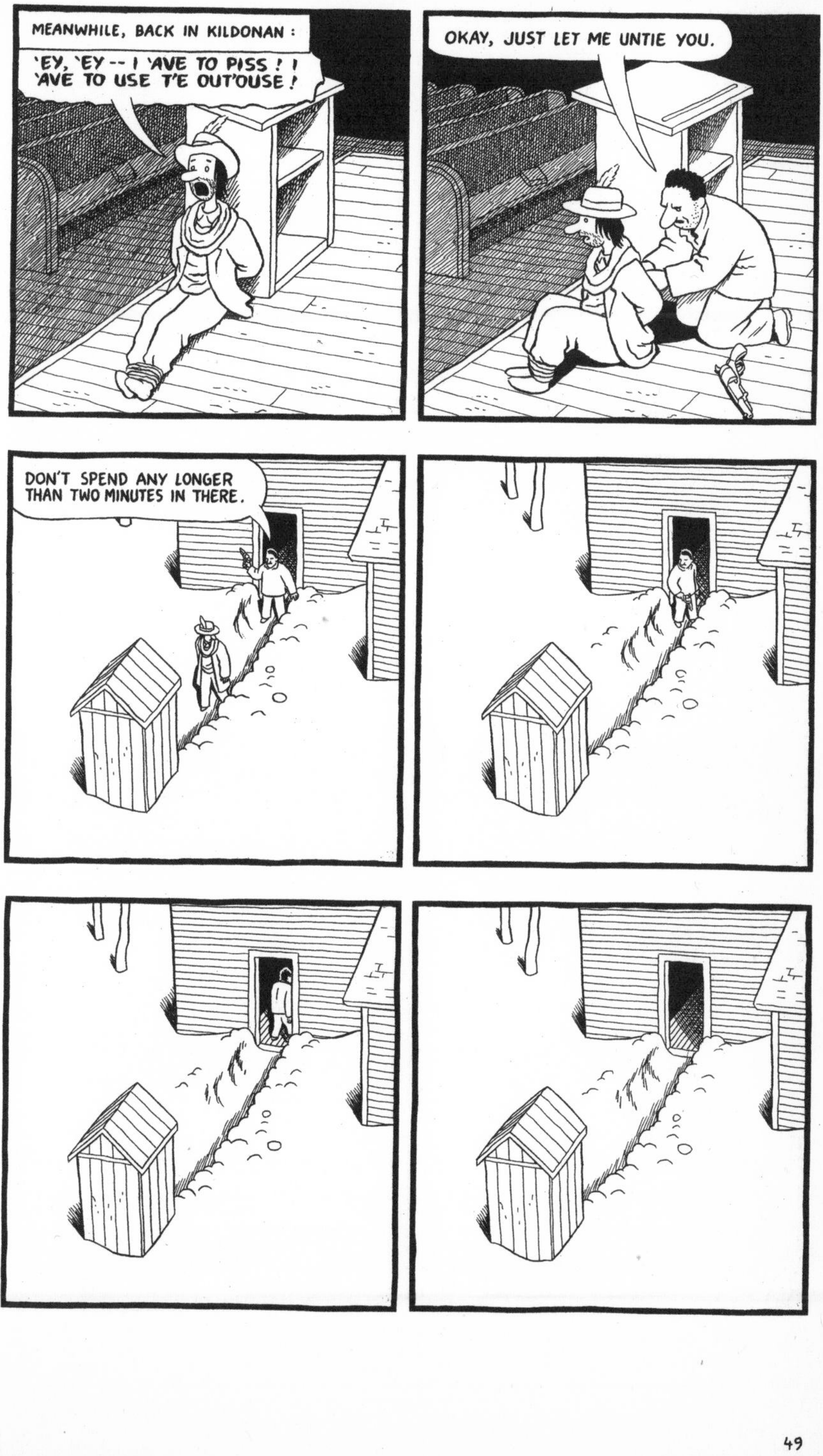
MEANWHILE, BACK IN KILDONAN :
'EY, 'EY -- I 'AVE TO PISS ! I 'AVE TO USE T'E OUT'OUSE !
OKAY, JUST LET ME UNTIE YOU.
DON'T SPEND ANY LONGER THAN TWO MINUTES IN THERE.

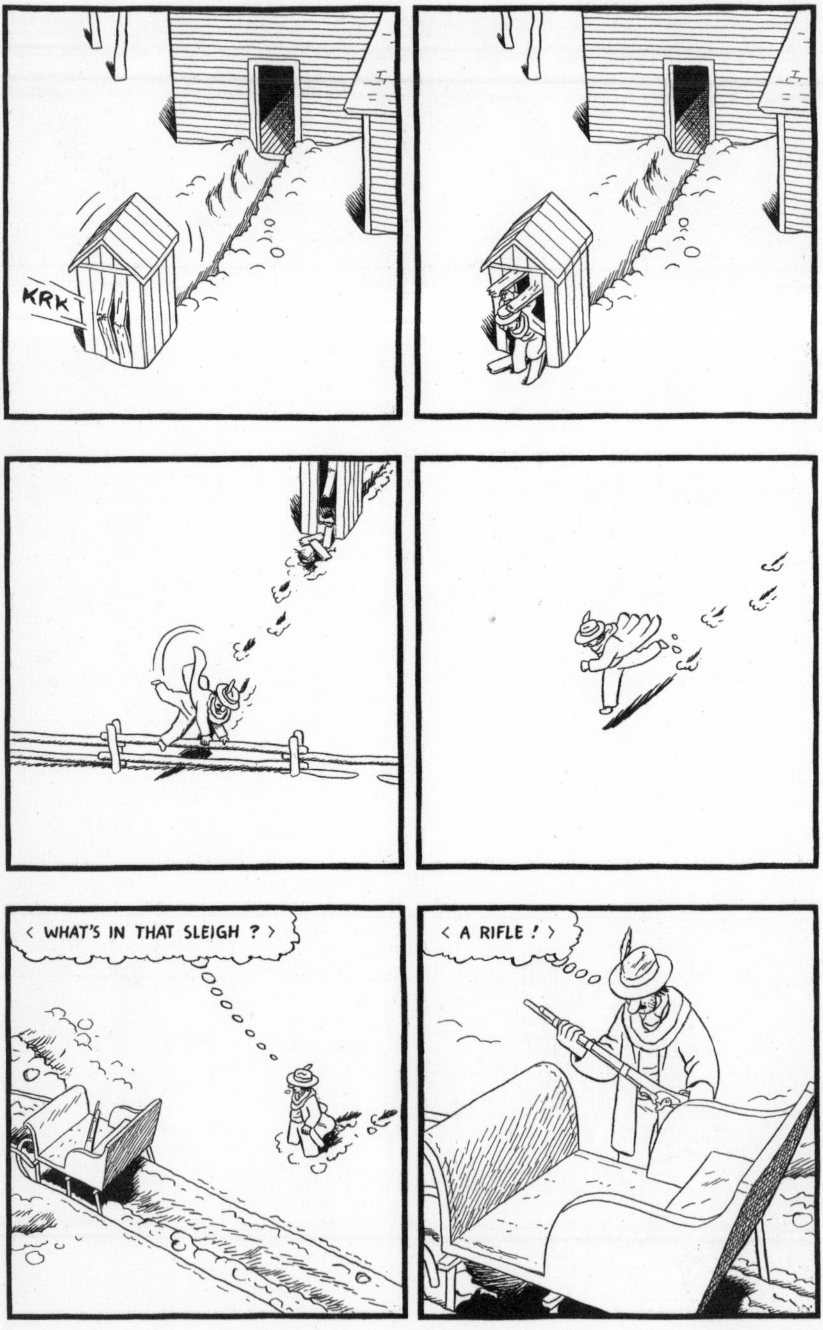
KRK
< WHAT'S IN THAT SLEIGH ? >
< A RIFLE ! >

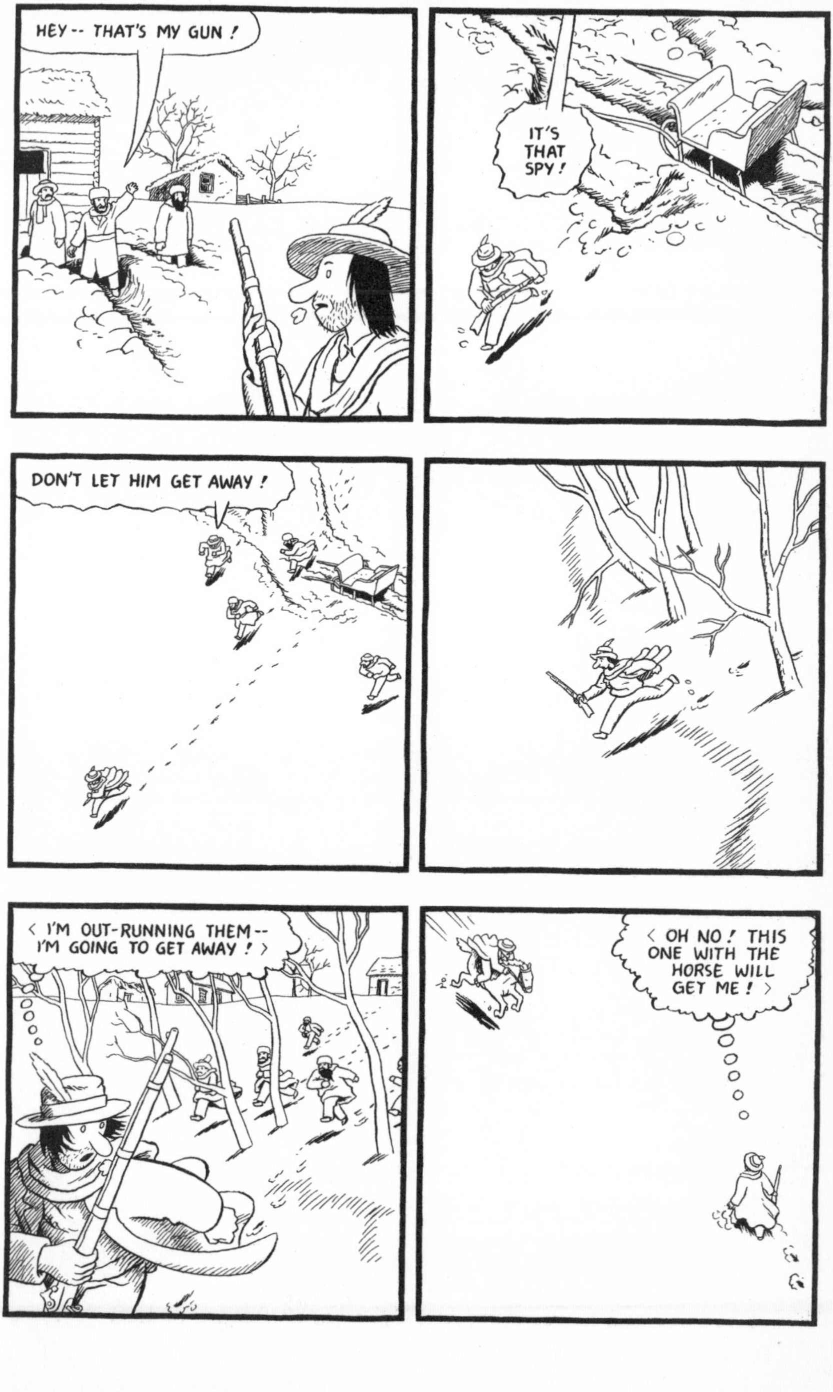
HEY -- THAT'S MY GUN !
IT'S THAT SPY !
DON'T LET HIM GET AWAY !
< I'M OUT-RUNNING THEM -- I'M GOING TO GET AWAY ! >
< OH NO ! THIS ONE WITH THE HORSE WILL GET ME ! >

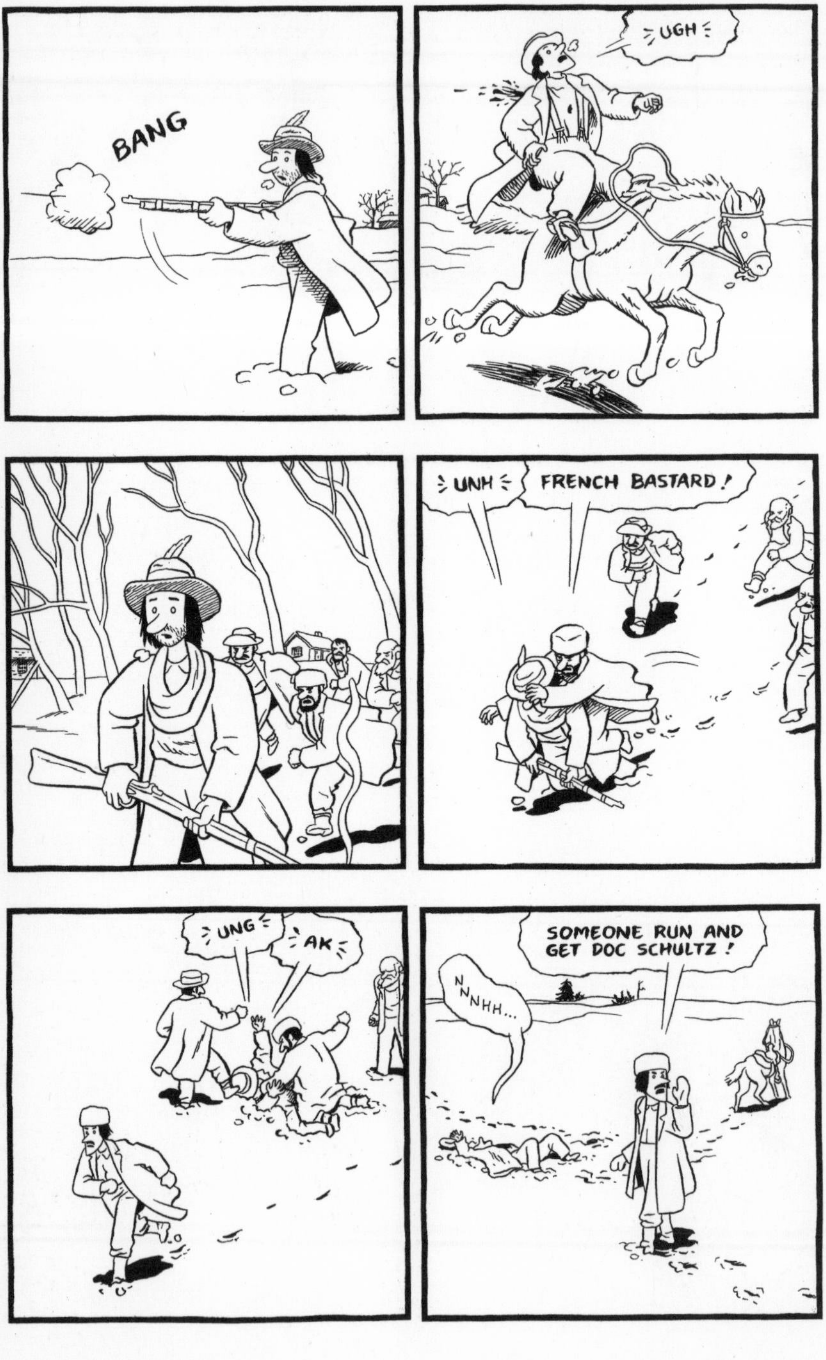
BANG
UGH
UNH
FRENCH BASTARD!
UNG
AK
SOMEONE RUN AND GET DOC SCHULTZ!
NNNHH...

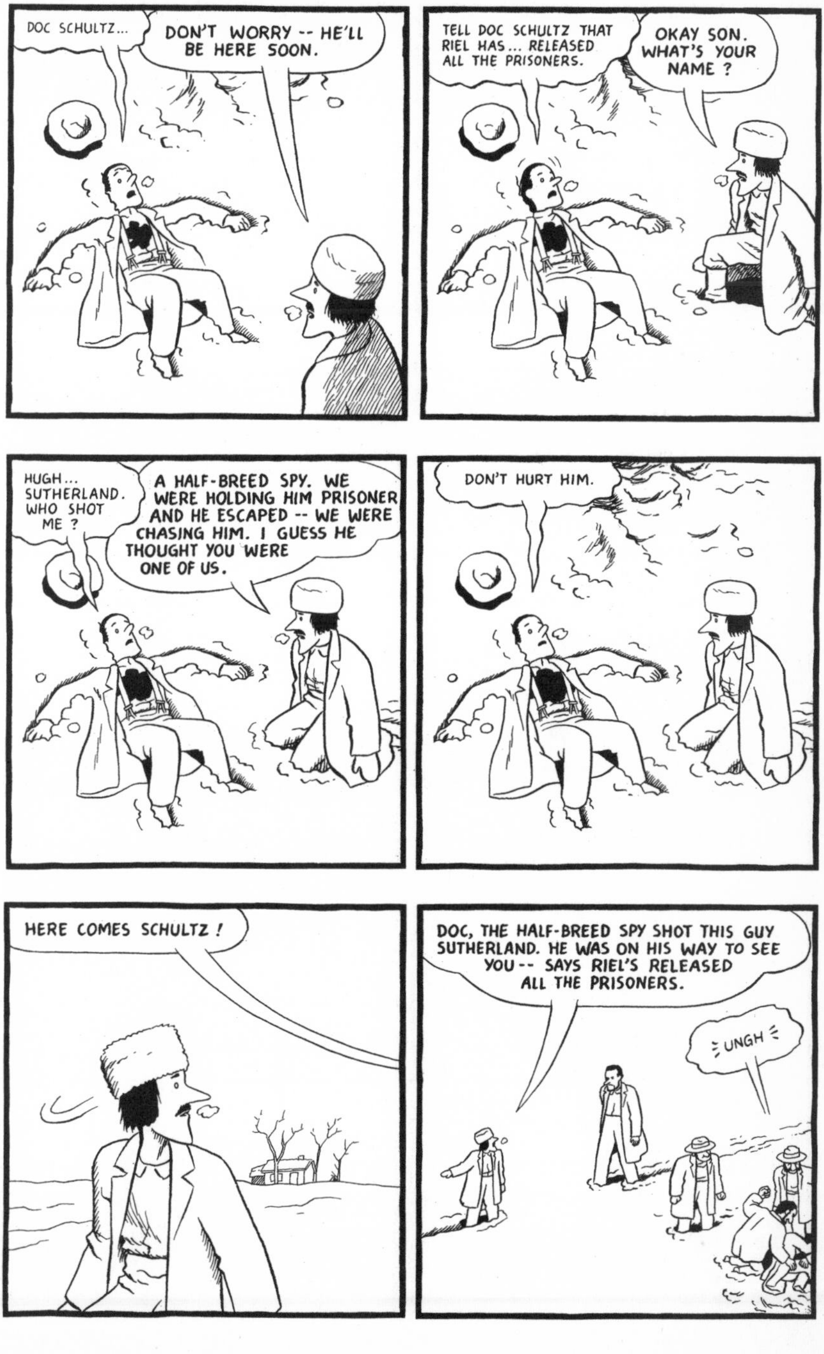
DOC SCHULTZ...
DON'T WORRY -- HE'LL BE HERE SOON.
TELL DOC SCHULTZ THAT RIEL HAS... RELEASED ALL THE PRISONERS.
OKAY SON. WHAT'S YOUR NAME ?
HUGH... SUTHERLAND. WHO SHOT ME ?
A HALF-BREED SPY. WE WERE HOLDING HIM PRISONER AND HE ESCAPED -- WE WERE CHASING HIM. I GUESS HE THOUGHT YOU WERE ONE OF US.
DON'T HURT HIM.
HERE COMES SCHULTZ !
DOC, THE HALF-BREED SPY SHOT THIS GUY SUTHERLAND. HE WAS ON HIS WAY TO SEE YOU -- SAYS RIEL'S RELEASED ALL THE PRISONERS.
UNGH

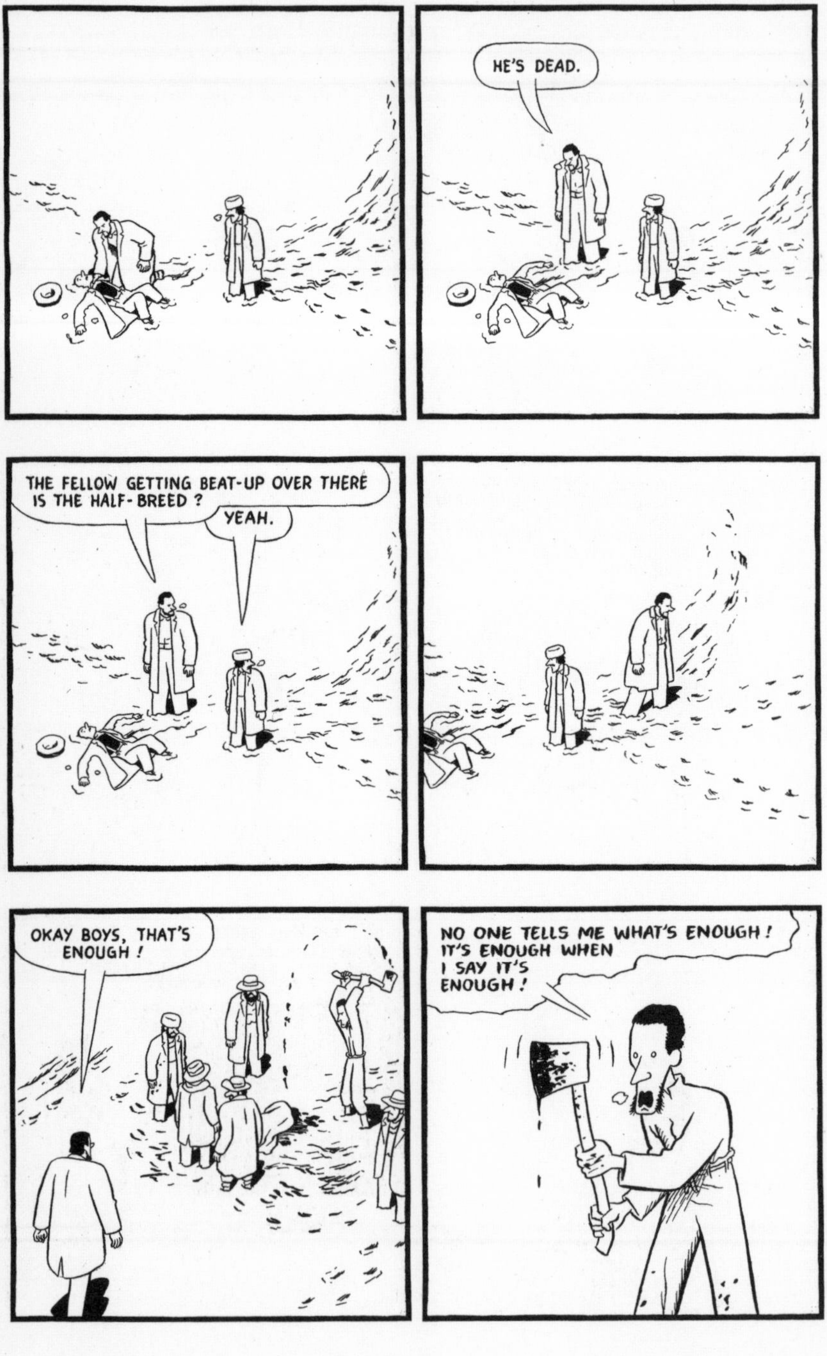
HE'S DEAD.
THE FELLOW GETTING BEAT-UP OVER THERE IS THE HALF-BREED ?
YEAH.
OKAY BOYS, THAT'S ENOUGH !
NO ONE TELLS ME WHAT'S ENOUGH ! IT'S ENOUGH WHEN I SAY IT'S ENOUGH !

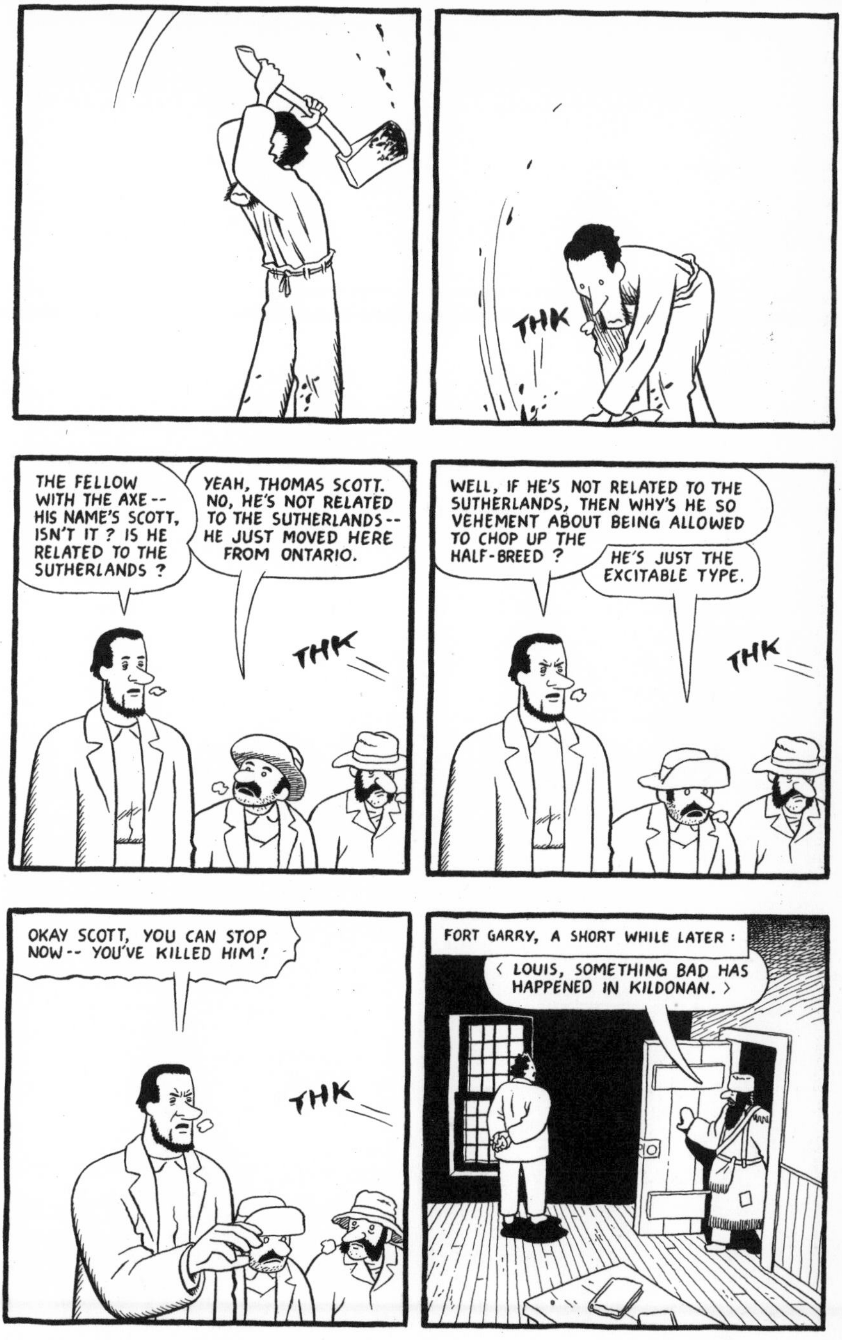
THK
THE FELLOW WITH THE AXE -- HIS NAME'S SCOTT, ISN'T IT ? IS HE RELATED TO THE SUTHERLANDS ?
YEAH, THOMAS SCOTT. NO, HE'S NOT RELATED TO THE SUTHERLANDS -- HE JUST MOVED HERE FROM ONTARIO.
THK
WELL, IF HE'S NOT RELATED TO THE SUTHERLANDS, THEN WHY'S HE SO VEHEMENT ABOUT BEING ALLOWED TO CHOP UP THE HALF-BREED ?
HE'S JUST THE EXCITABLE TYPE.
THK
OKAY SCOTT, YOU CAN STOP NOW -- YOU'VE KILLED HIM !
THK
FORT GARRY, A SHORT WHILE LATER :
‹ LOUIS, SOMETHING BAD HAS HAPPENED IN KILDONAN. ›

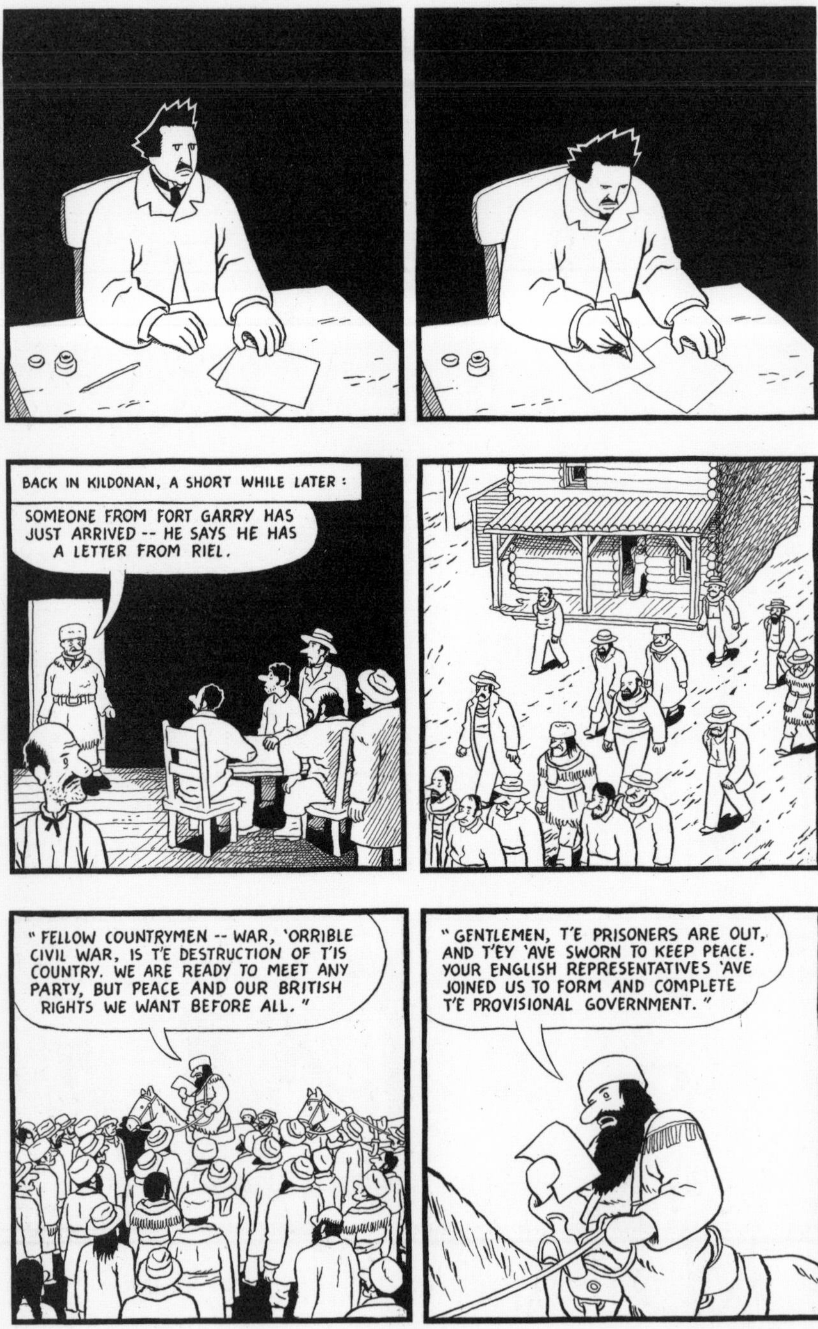
BACK IN KILDONAN, A SHORT WHILE LATER:
SOMEONE FROM FORT GARRY HAS JUST ARRIVED -- HE SAYS HE HAS A LETTER FROM RIEL.
" FELLOW COUNTRYMEN -- WAR, 'ORRIBLE CIVIL WAR, IS T'E DESTRUCTION OF T'IS COUNTRY. WE ARE READY TO MEET ANY PARTY, BUT PEACE AND OUR BRITISH RIGHTS WE WANT BEFORE ALL."
" GENTLEMEN, T'E PRISONERS ARE OUT, AND T'EY 'AVE SWORN TO KEEP PEACE. YOUR ENGLISH REPRESENTATIVES 'AVE JOINED US TO FORM AND COMPLETE T'E PROVISIONAL GOVERNMENT."

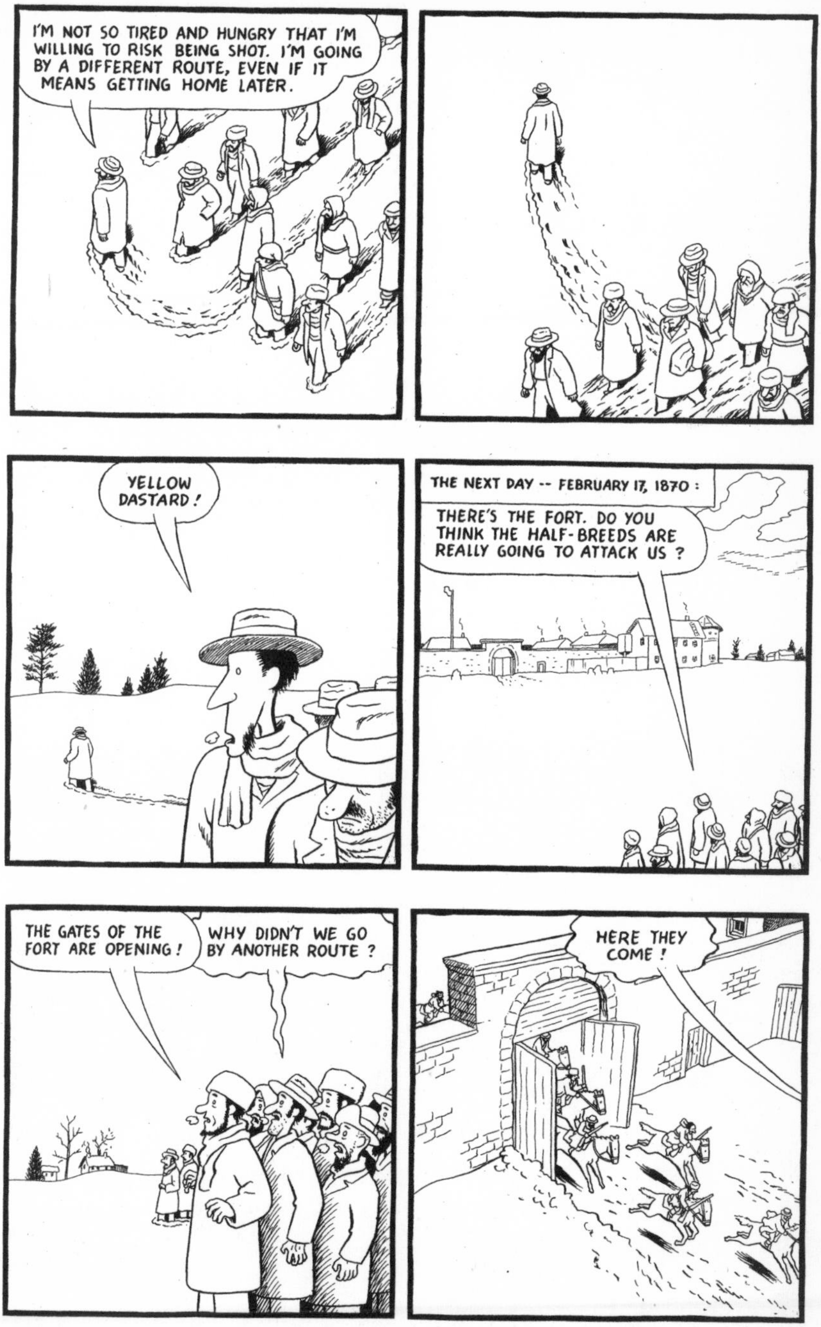
I'M NOT SO TIRED AND HUNGRY THAT I'M WILLING TO RISK BEING SHOT. I'M GOING BY A DIFFERENT ROUTE, EVEN IF IT MEANS GETTING HOME LATER.
YELLOW DASTARD!
THE NEXT DAY -- FEBRUARY 17, 1870:
THERE'S THE FORT. DO YOU THINK THE HALF-BREEDS ARE REALLY GOING TO ATTACK US?
THE GATES OF THE FORT ARE OPENING!
WHY DIDN'T WE GO BY ANOTHER ROUTE?
HERE THEY COME!

OUR LEADER, LOUIS RIEL, AND 'IS OFFICERS WISH YOU ALL TO COME INTO T'E FORT AND 'AVE DINNER.

I'M PRETTY HUNGRY.

ME TOO.

HAVEN'T HAD A GOOD MEAL IN DAYS.

AND SO:

MMM... TASTES PRETTY GOOD.

* THE LETTER X IS USED HERE TO INDICATE RACIST COMMENTS AND PROFANITY.

BUT SCHULTZ MANAGES TO ESCAPE BY DOGSLED TO THE UNITED STATES.

CAN YOU PUT SCOTT IN ANOTHER ROOM ? HE'S DRIVING THE REST OF US PRISONERS CRAZY.

'E'S DRIVING **YOU** CRAZY.

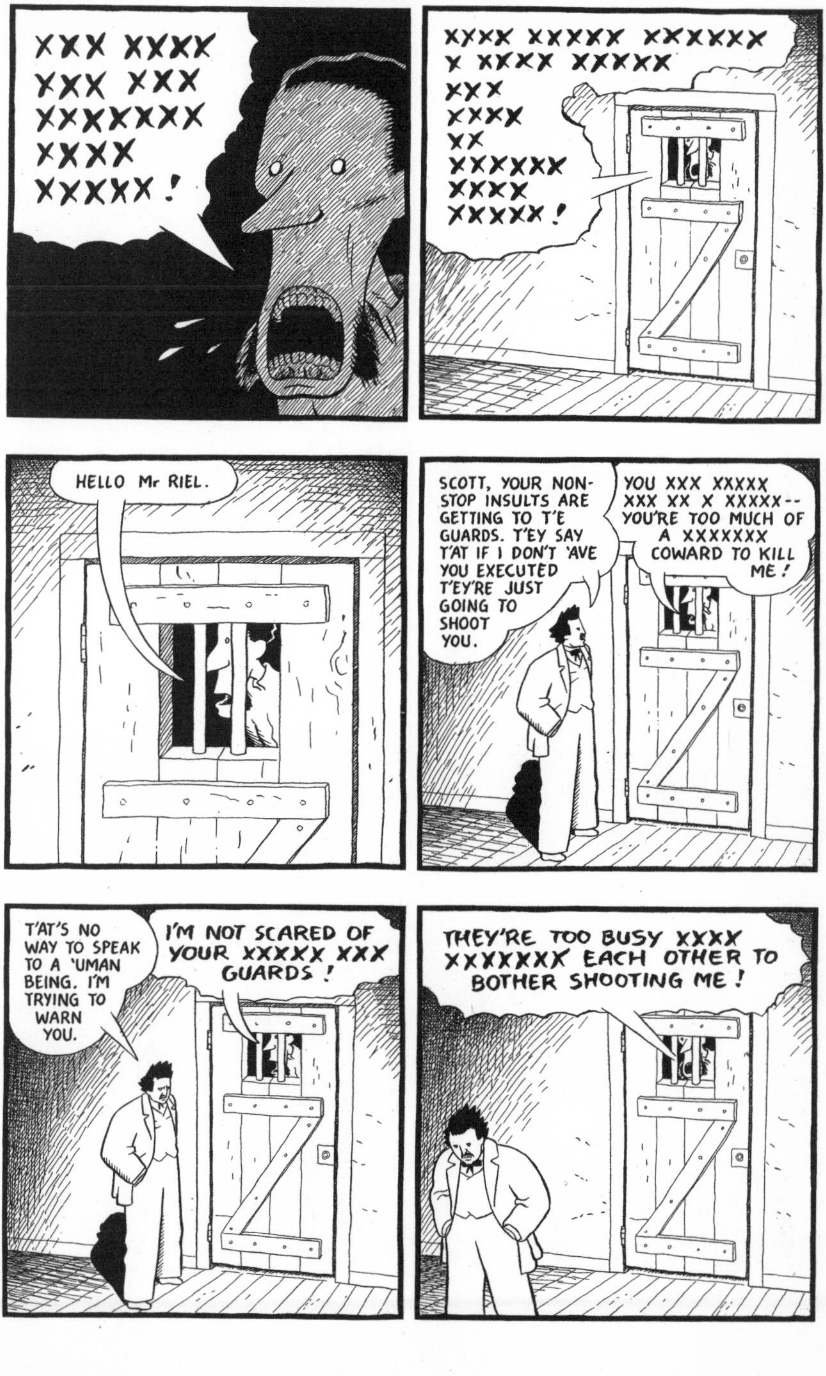
XXX XXXX XXX XXX XXXXXXX XXXX XXXXX!
XXXX XXXXX XXXXXX X XXXX XXXXX XXX XXXX XX XXXXXX XXXX XXXXX!
HELLO Mr RIEL.
SCOTT, YOUR NON-STOP INSULTS ARE GETTING TO T'E GUARDS. T'EY SAY T'AT IF I DON'T 'AVE YOU EXECUTED T'EY'RE JUST GOING TO SHOOT YOU.
YOU XXX XXXXX XXX XX X XXXXX-- YOU'RE TOO MUCH OF A XXXXXXX COWARD TO KILL ME!
T'AT'S NO WAY TO SPEAK TO A 'UMAN BEING. I'M TRYING TO WARN YOU.
I'M NOT SCARED OF YOUR XXXXX XXX GUARDS!
THEY'RE TOO BUSY XXXX XXXXXXX EACH OTHER TO BOTHER SHOOTING ME!

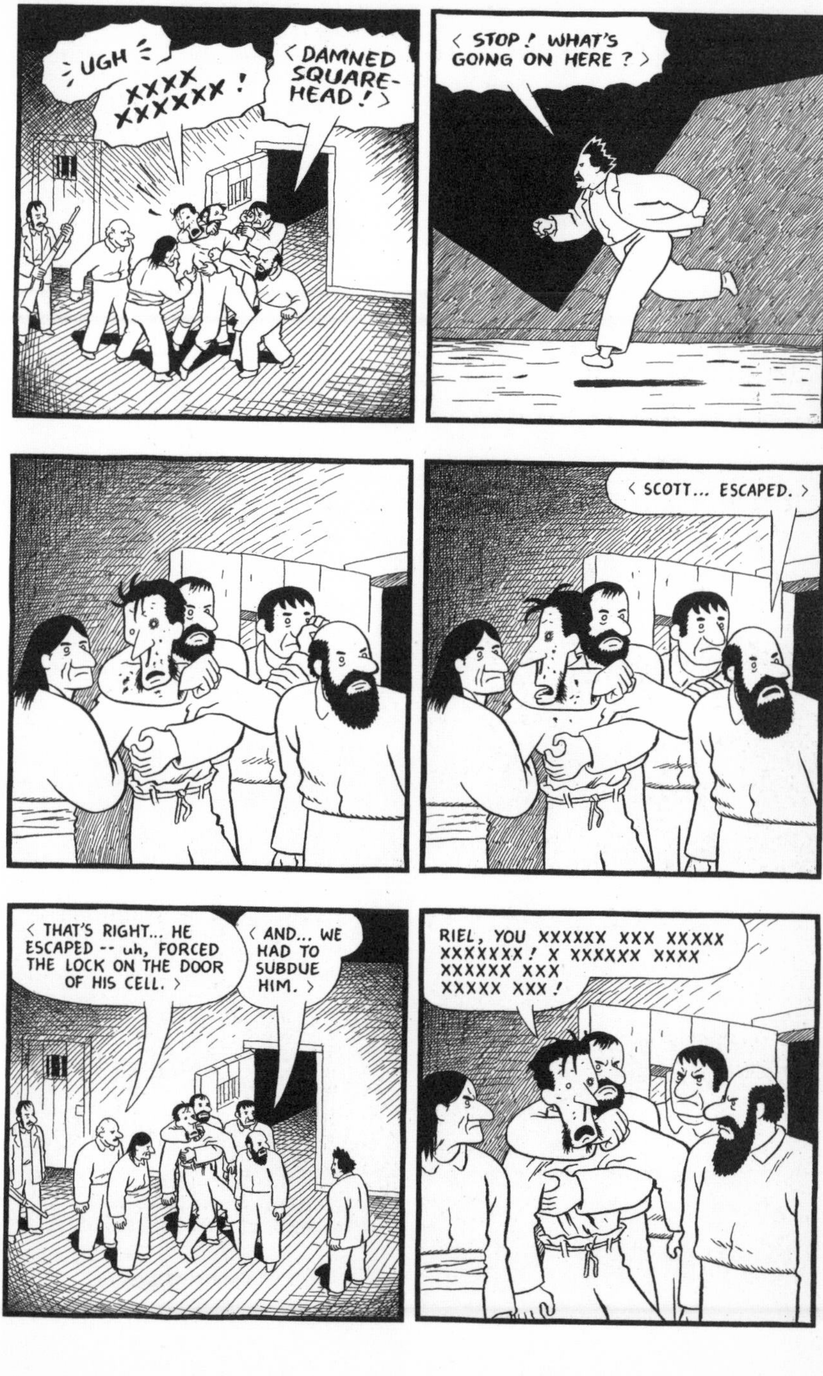
UGH
XXXX XXXXXX!
< DAMNED SQUAREHEAD! >
< STOP! WHAT'S GOING ON HERE? >
< SCOTT... ESCAPED. >
< THAT'S RIGHT... HE ESCAPED -- uh, FORCED THE LOCK ON THE DOOR OF HIS CELL. >
< AND... WE HAD TO SUBDUE HIM. >
RIEL, YOU XXXXXX XXX XXXXX XXXXXXX! X XXXXXX XXXX XXXXXX XXX XXXXX XXX!

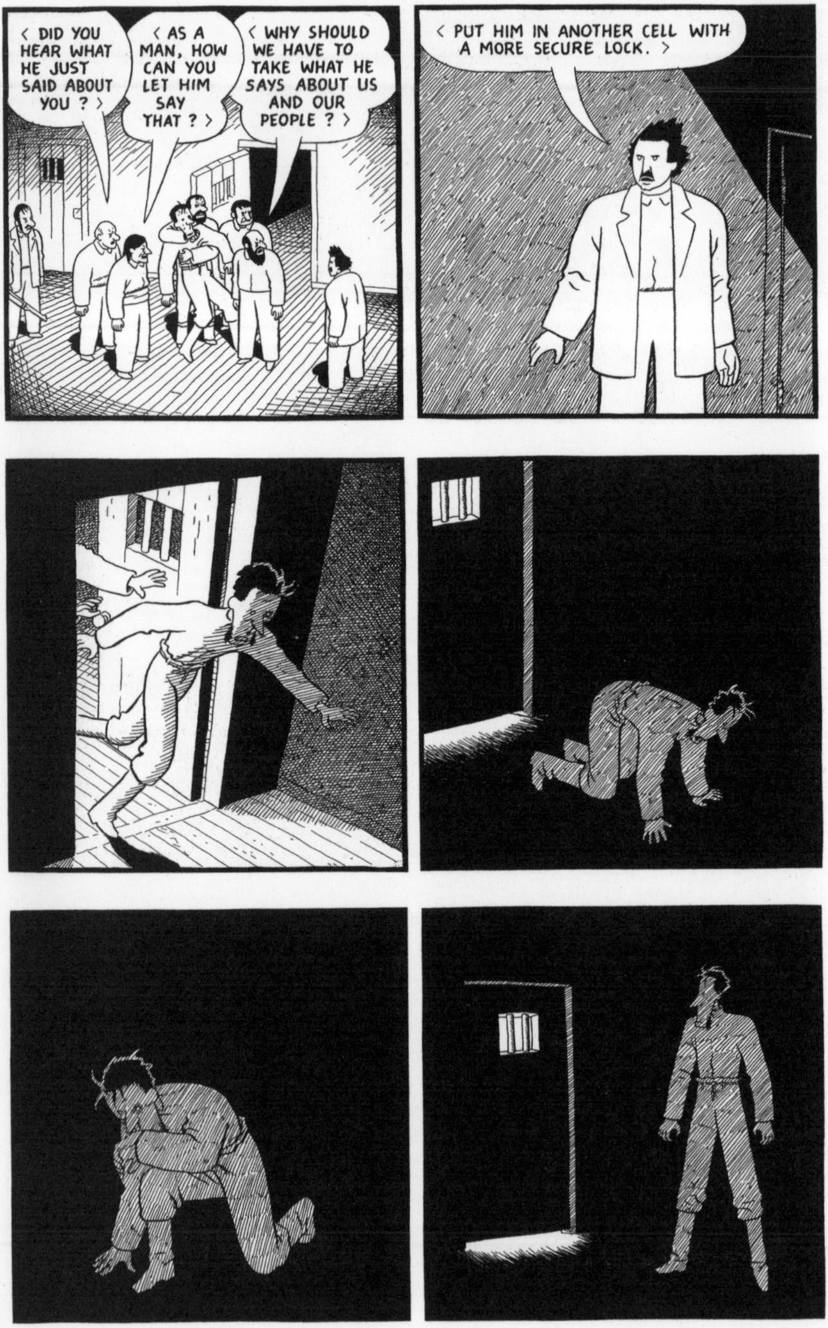
< DID YOU HEAR WHAT HE JUST SAID ABOUT YOU ? >
< AS A MAN, HOW CAN YOU LET HIM SAY THAT ? >
< WHY SHOULD WE HAVE TO TAKE WHAT HE SAYS ABOUT US AND OUR PEOPLE ? >
< PUT HIM IN ANOTHER CELL WITH A MORE SECURE LOCK. >

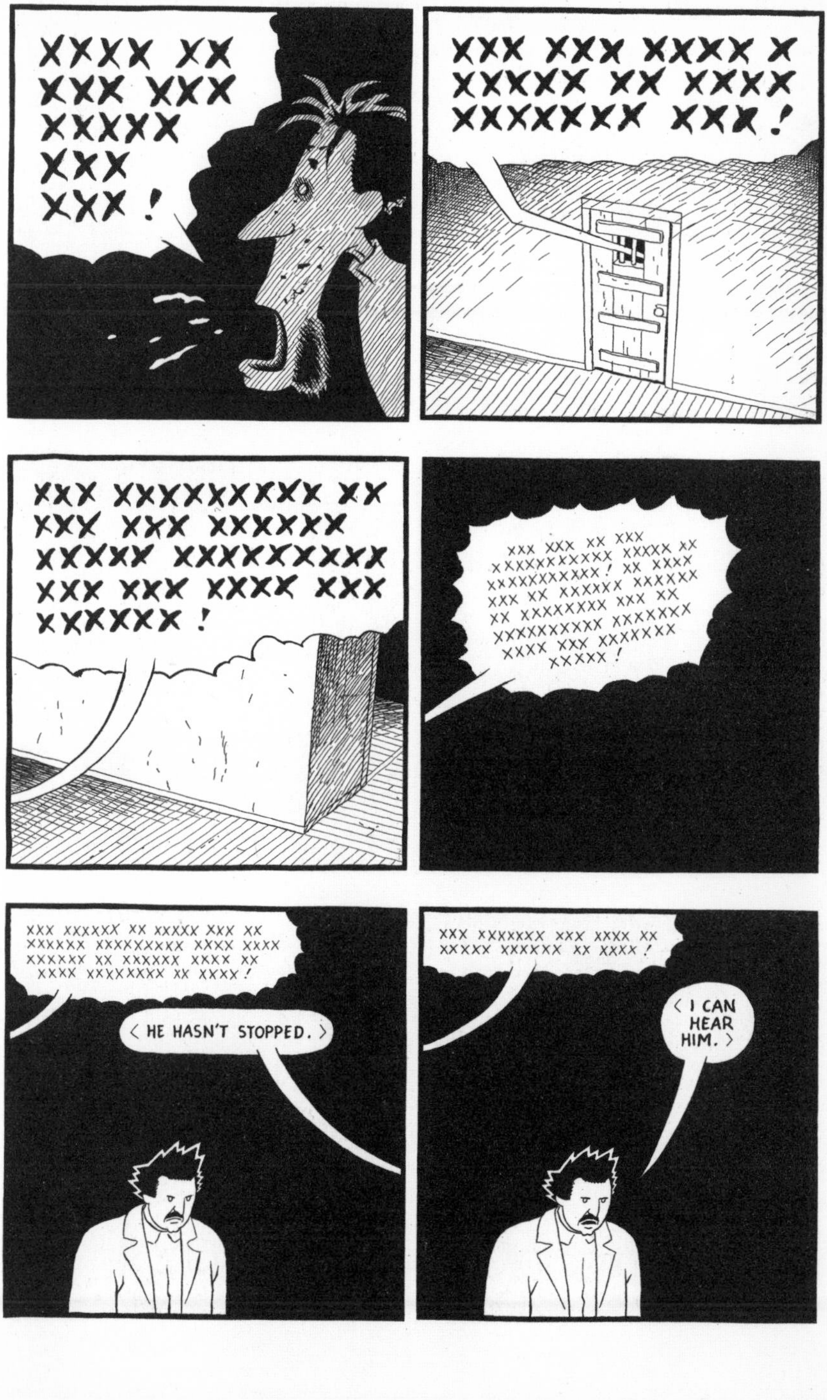
XXXX XX XXX XXX XXXXX XXX XXX !
XXX XXX XXXX X XXXXX XX XXXX XXXXXXX XXX !
XXX XXXXXXXXX XX XXX XXX XXXXXX XXXXX XXXXXXXXX XXX XXX XXXX XXX XXXXXX !
< HE HASN'T STOPPED. >
< I CAN HEAR HIM. >

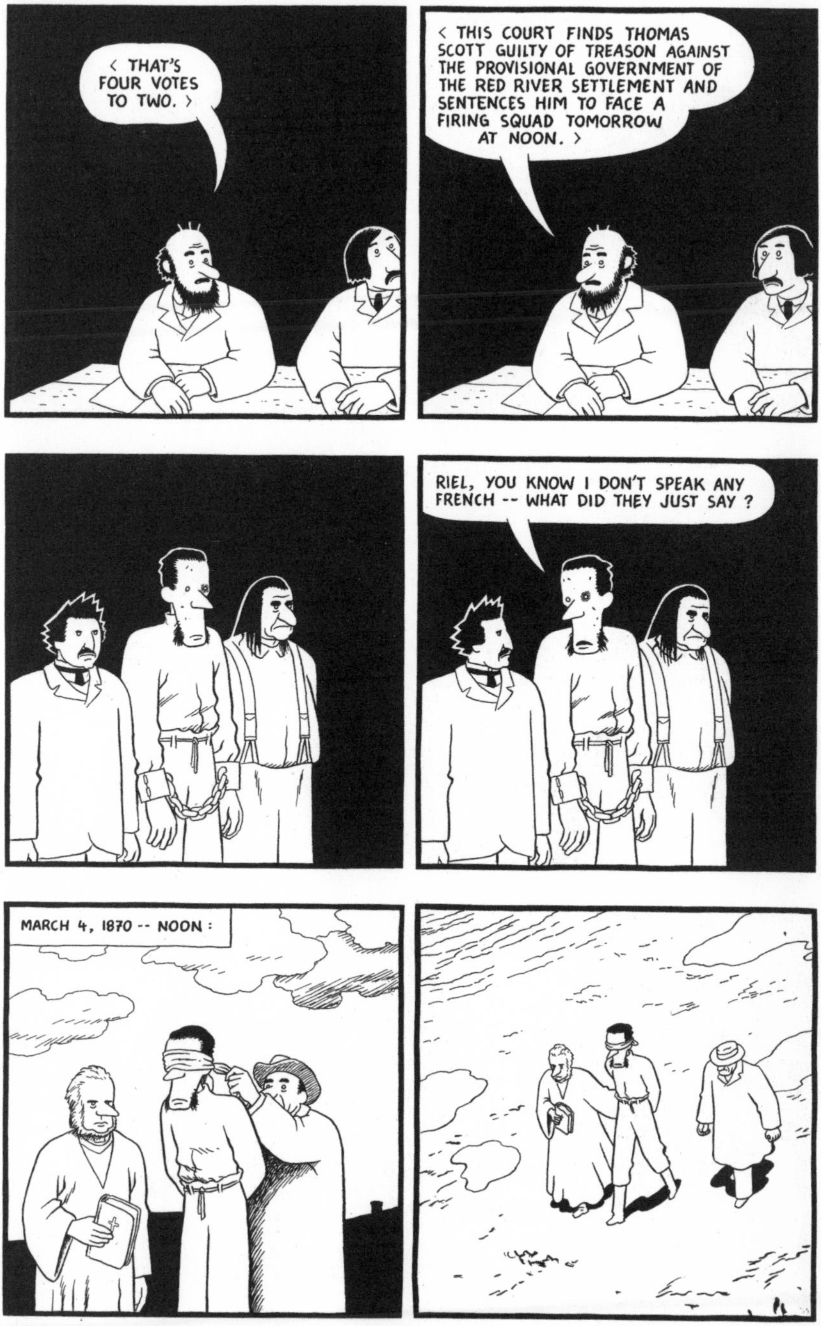
< THAT'S FOUR VOTES TO TWO. >
< THIS COURT FINDS THOMAS SCOTT GUILTY OF TREASON AGAINST THE PROVISIONAL GOVERNMENT OF THE RED RIVER SETTLEMENT AND SENTENCES HIM TO FACE A FIRING SQUAD TOMORROW AT NOON. >
RIEL, YOU KNOW I DON'T SPEAK ANY FRENCH -- WHAT DID THEY JUST SAY ?
MARCH 4, 1870 -- NOON :

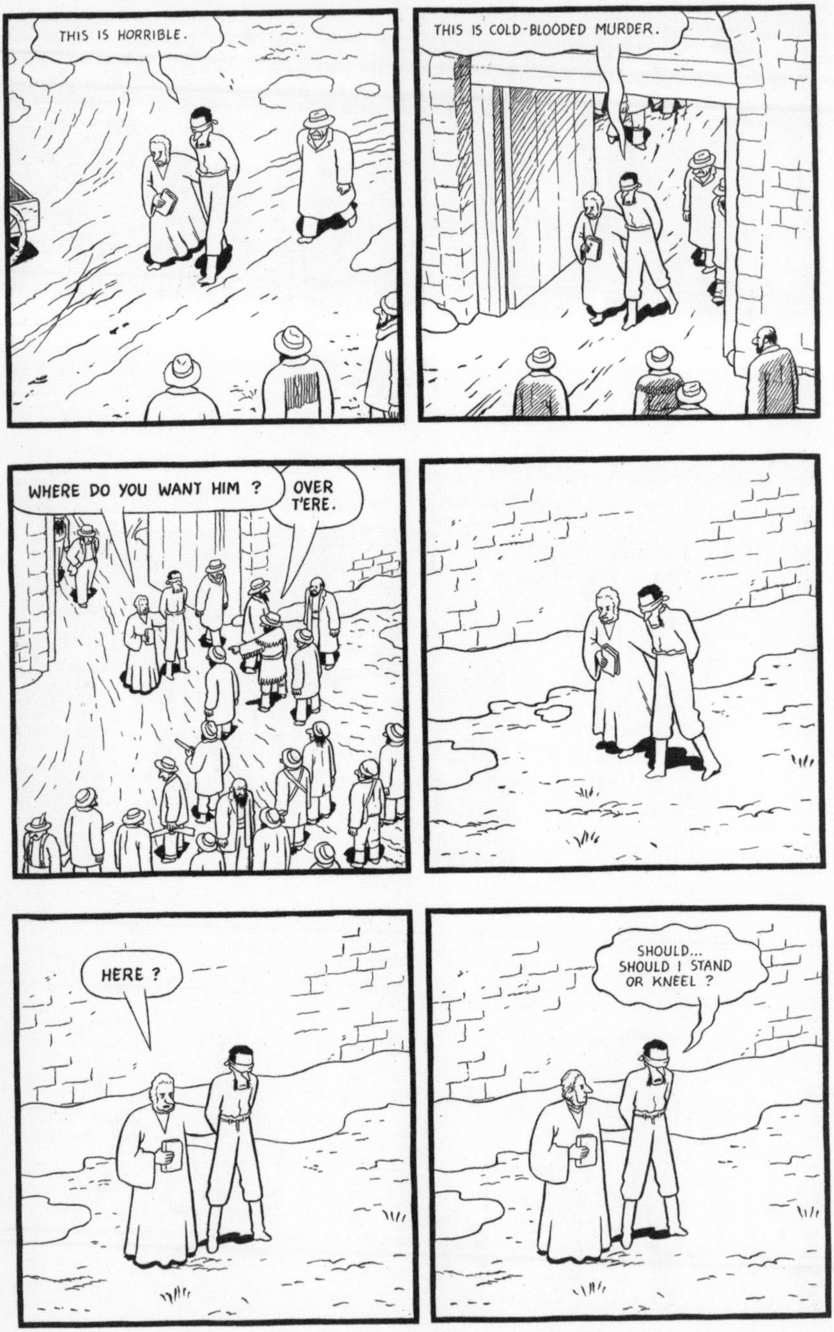
THIS IS HORRIBLE.
THIS IS COLD-BLOODED MURDER.
WHERE DO YOU WANT HIM ?
OVER T'ERE.
HERE ?
SHOULD... SHOULD I STAND OR KNEEL ?

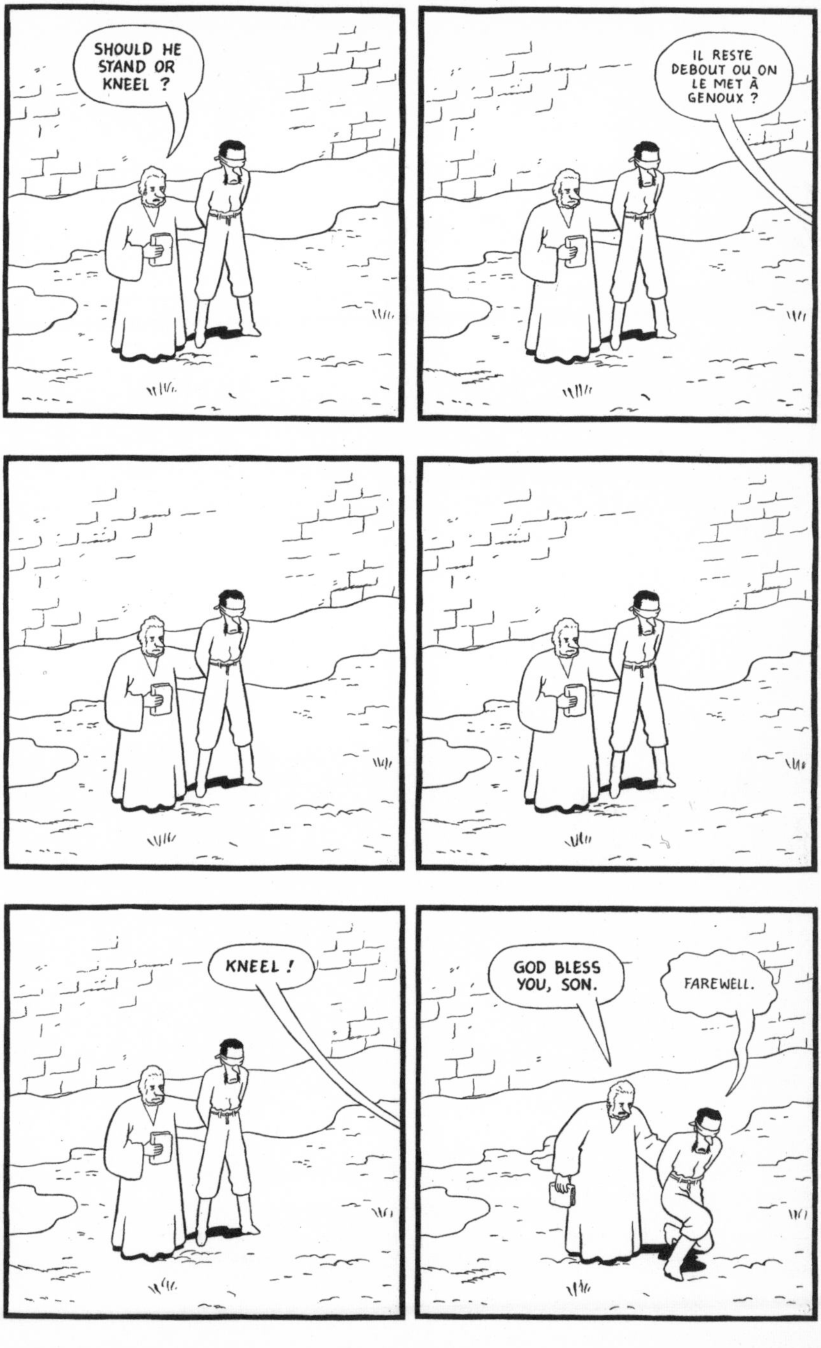
SHOULD HE STAND OR KNEEL ?
IL RESTE DEBOUT OU ON LE MET À GENOUX ?
KNEEL !
GOD BLESS YOU, SON.
FAREWELL.

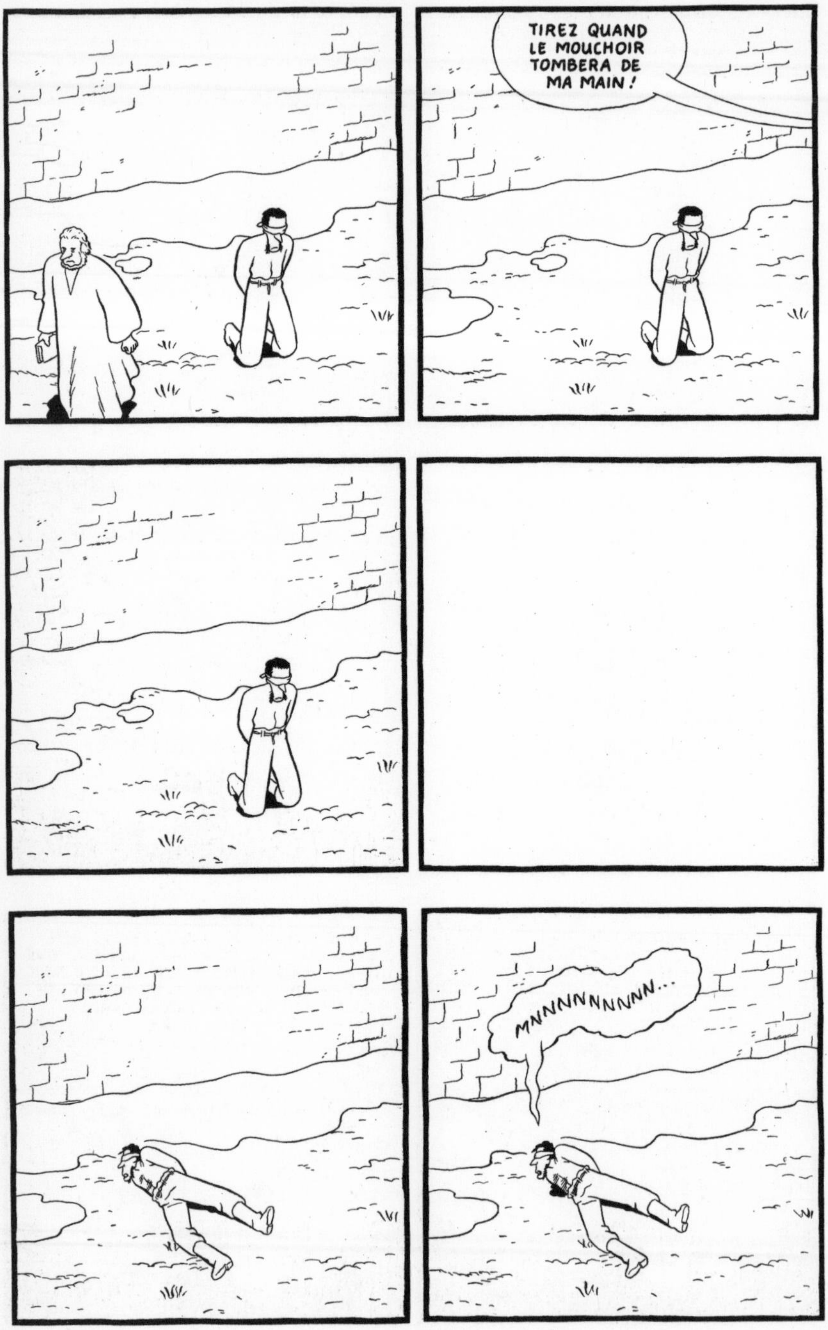
TIREZ QUAND LE MOUCHOIR TOMBERA DE MA MAIN !
MNNNNNNNNN...

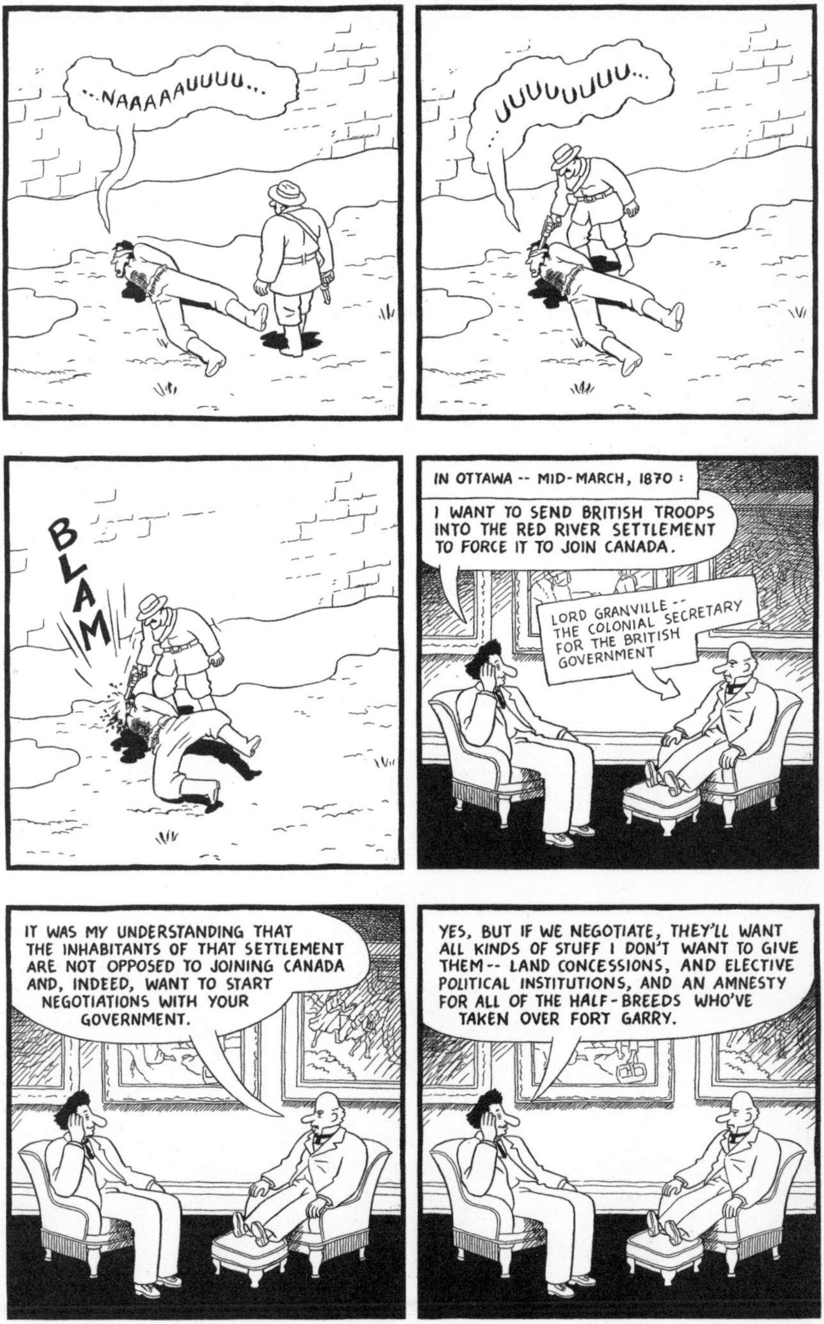
...NAAAAAUUUU...
UUUUUUUU...
BLAM
IN OTTAWA -- MID-MARCH, 1870 :
I WANT TO SEND BRITISH TROOPS INTO THE RED RIVER SETTLEMENT TO FORCE IT TO JOIN CANADA.
LORD GRANVILLE -- THE COLONIAL SECRETARY FOR THE BRITISH GOVERNMENT
IT WAS MY UNDERSTANDING THAT THE INHABITANTS OF THAT SETTLEMENT ARE NOT OPPOSED TO JOINING CANADA AND, INDEED, WANT TO START NEGOTIATIONS WITH YOUR GOVERNMENT.
YES, BUT IF WE NEGOTIATE, THEY'LL WANT ALL KINDS OF STUFF I DON'T WANT TO GIVE THEM -- LAND CONCESSIONS, AND ELECTIVE POLITICAL INSTITUTIONS, AND AN AMNESTY FOR ALL OF THE HALF-BREEDS WHO'VE TAKEN OVER FORT GARRY.

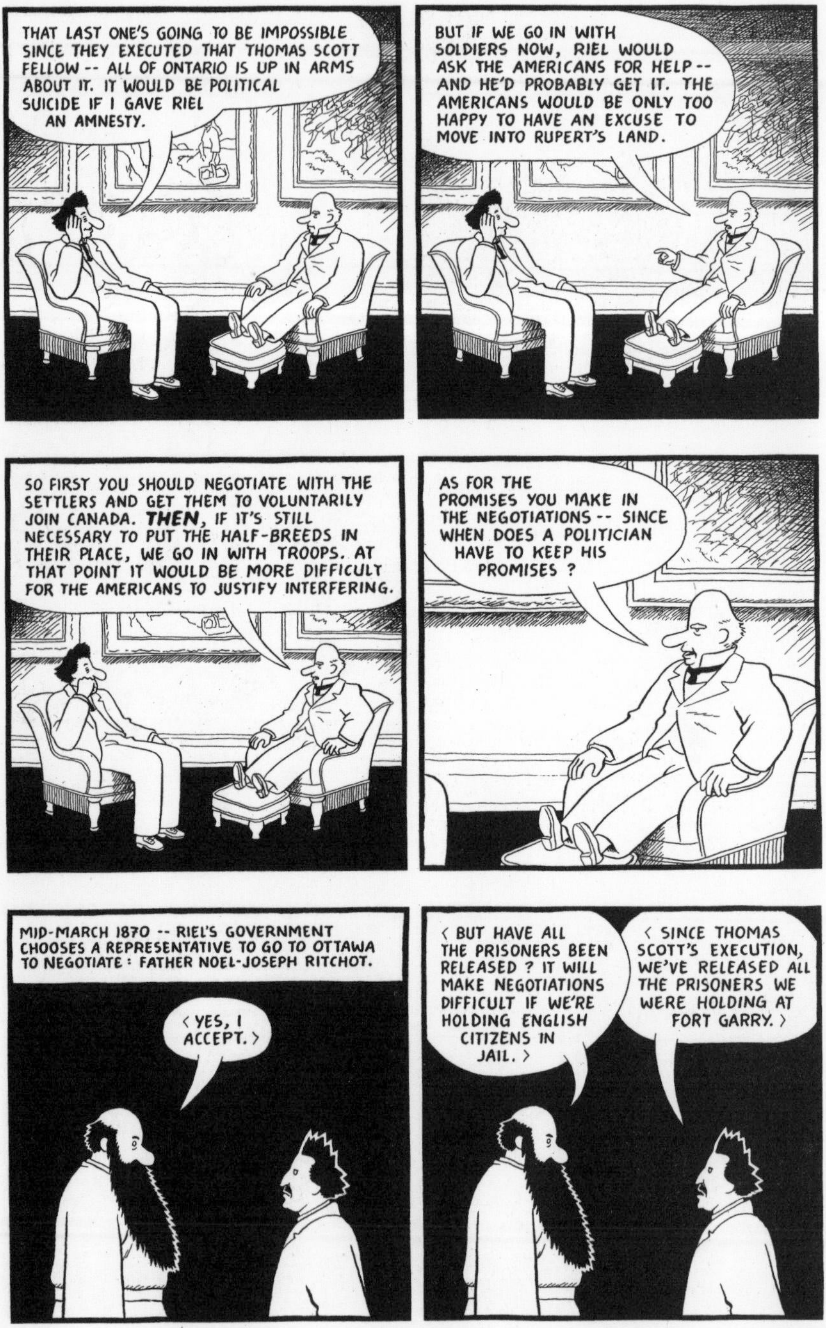

THAT LAST ONE'S GOING TO BE IMPOSSIBLE SINCE THEY EXECUTED THAT THOMAS SCOTT FELLOW -- ALL OF ONTARIO IS UP IN ARMS ABOUT IT. IT WOULD BE POLITICAL SUICIDE IF I GAVE RIEL AN AMNESTY.
BUT IF WE GO IN WITH SOLDIERS NOW, RIEL WOULD ASK THE AMERICANS FOR HELP -- AND HE'D PROBABLY GET IT. THE AMERICANS WOULD BE ONLY TOO HAPPY TO HAVE AN EXCUSE TO MOVE INTO RUPERT'S LAND.
SO FIRST YOU SHOULD NEGOTIATE WITH THE SETTLERS AND GET THEM TO VOLUNTARILY JOIN CANADA. **THEN**, IF IT'S STILL NECESSARY TO PUT THE HALF-BREEDS IN THEIR PLACE, WE GO IN WITH TROOPS. AT THAT POINT IT WOULD BE MORE DIFFICULT FOR THE AMERICANS TO JUSTIFY INTERFERING.
AS FOR THE PROMISES YOU MAKE IN THE NEGOTIATIONS -- SINCE WHEN DOES A POLITICIAN HAVE TO KEEP HIS PROMISES ?
MID-MARCH 1870 -- RIEL'S GOVERNMENT CHOOSES A REPRESENTATIVE TO GO TO OTTAWA TO NEGOTIATE : FATHER NOEL-JOSEPH RITCHOT.
〈 YES, I ACCEPT. 〉
〈 BUT HAVE ALL THE PRISONERS BEEN RELEASED ? IT WILL MAKE NEGOTIATIONS DIFFICULT IF WE'RE HOLDING ENGLISH CITIZENS IN JAIL. 〉
〈 SINCE THOMAS SCOTT'S EXECUTION, WE'VE RELEASED ALL THE PRISONERS WE WERE HOLDING AT FORT GARRY. 〉

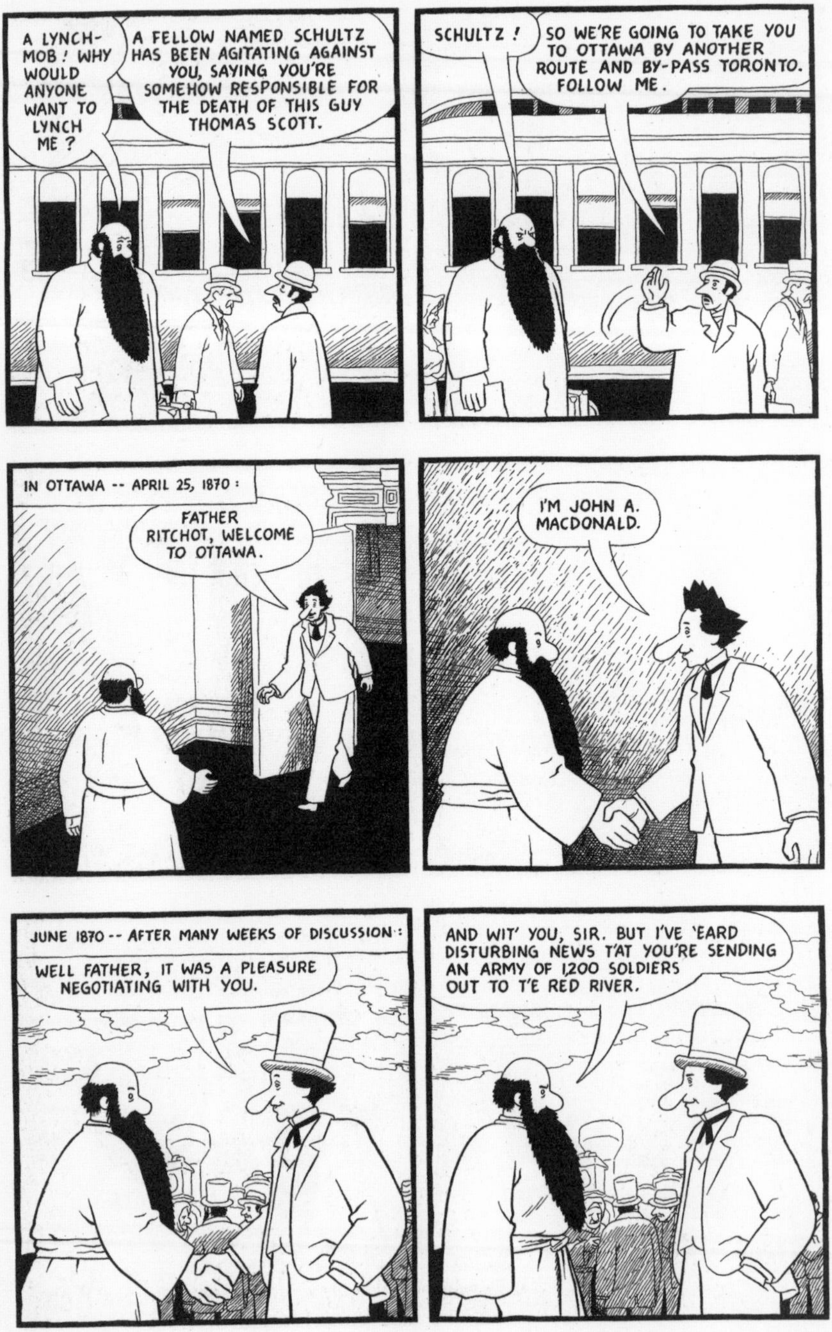
A LYNCH-MOB! WHY WOULD ANYONE WANT TO LYNCH ME?
A FELLOW NAMED SCHULTZ HAS BEEN AGITATING AGAINST YOU, SAYING YOU'RE SOMEHOW RESPONSIBLE FOR THE DEATH OF THIS GUY THOMAS SCOTT.
SCHULTZ!
SO WE'RE GOING TO TAKE YOU TO OTTAWA BY ANOTHER ROUTE AND BY-PASS TORONTO. FOLLOW ME.
IN OTTAWA -- APRIL 25, 1870:
FATHER RITCHOT, WELCOME TO OTTAWA.
I'M JOHN A. MACDONALD.
JUNE 1870 -- AFTER MANY WEEKS OF DISCUSSION:
WELL FATHER, IT WAS A PLEASURE NEGOTIATING WITH YOU.
AND WIT' YOU, SIR. BUT I'VE 'EARD DISTURBING NEWS T'AT YOU'RE SENDING AN ARMY OF 1,200 SOLDIERS OUT TO T'E RED RIVER.

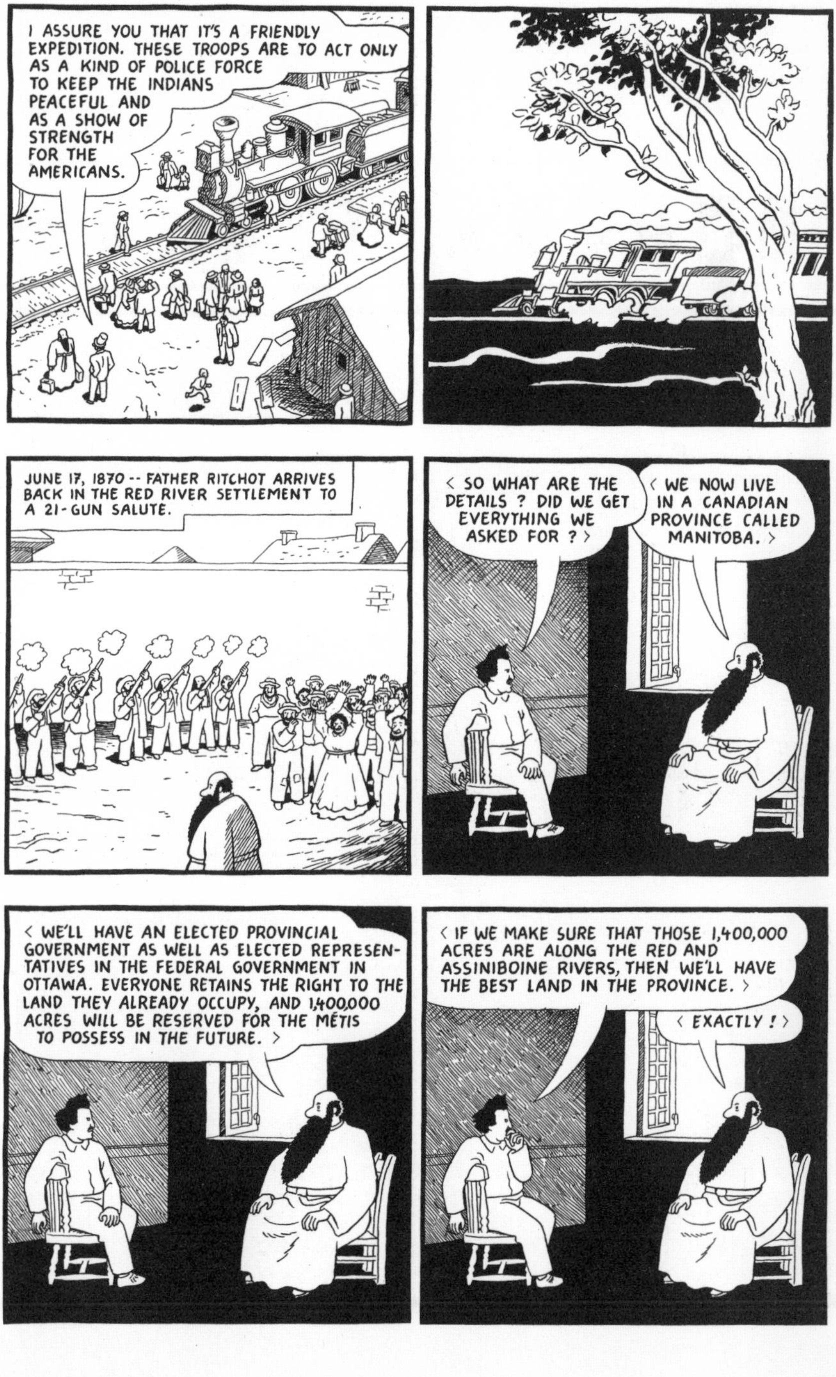
I ASSURE YOU THAT IT'S A FRIENDLY EXPEDITION. THESE TROOPS ARE TO ACT ONLY AS A KIND OF POLICE FORCE TO KEEP THE INDIANS PEACEFUL AND AS A SHOW OF STRENGTH FOR THE AMERICANS.
JUNE 17, 1870 -- FATHER RITCHOT ARRIVES BACK IN THE RED RIVER SETTLEMENT TO A 21-GUN SALUTE.
< SO WHAT ARE THE DETAILS ? DID WE GET EVERYTHING WE ASKED FOR ? >
< WE NOW LIVE IN A CANADIAN PROVINCE CALLED MANITOBA. >
< WE'LL HAVE AN ELECTED PROVINCIAL GOVERNMENT AS WELL AS ELECTED REPRESENTATIVES IN THE FEDERAL GOVERNMENT IN OTTAWA. EVERYONE RETAINS THE RIGHT TO THE LAND THEY ALREADY OCCUPY, AND 1,400,000 ACRES WILL BE RESERVED FOR THE MÉTIS TO POSSESS IN THE FUTURE. >
< IF WE MAKE SURE THAT THOSE 1,400,000 ACRES ARE ALONG THE RED AND ASSINIBOINE RIVERS, THEN WE'LL HAVE THE BEST LAND IN THE PROVINCE. >
< EXACTLY ! >

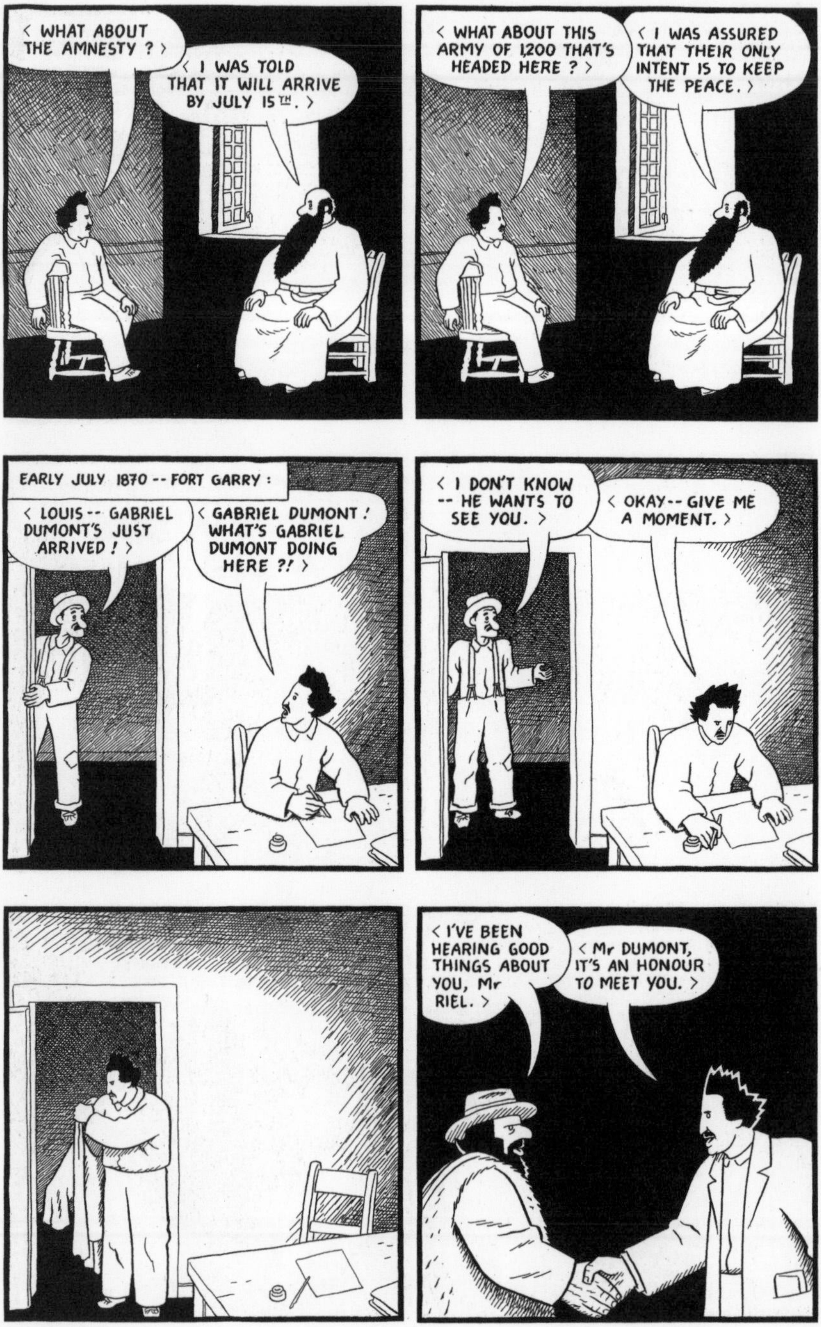

< WHAT ABOUT THE AMNESTY ? >
< I WAS TOLD THAT IT WILL ARRIVE BY JULY 15TH. >
< WHAT ABOUT THIS ARMY OF 1,200 THAT'S HEADED HERE ? >
< I WAS ASSURED THAT THEIR ONLY INTENT IS TO KEEP THE PEACE. >
EARLY JULY 1870 -- FORT GARRY :
< LOUIS -- GABRIEL DUMONT'S JUST ARRIVED ! >
< GABRIEL DUMONT ! WHAT'S GABRIEL DUMONT DOING HERE ?! >
< I DON'T KNOW -- HE WANTS TO SEE YOU. >
< OKAY -- GIVE ME A MOMENT. >
< I'VE BEEN HEARING GOOD THINGS ABOUT YOU, Mr RIEL. >
< Mr DUMONT, IT'S AN HONOUR TO MEET YOU. >

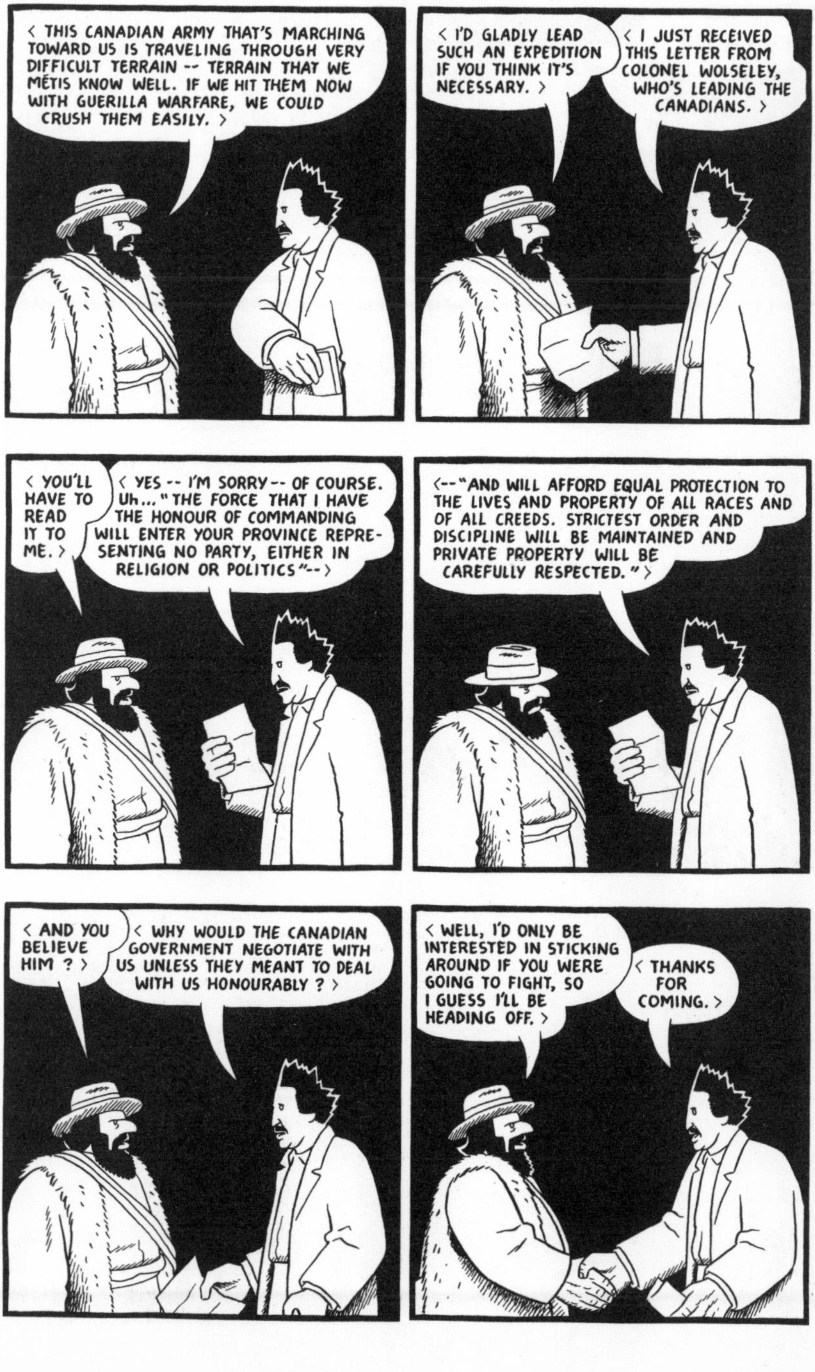
< THIS CANADIAN ARMY THAT'S MARCHING TOWARD US IS TRAVELING THROUGH VERY DIFFICULT TERRAIN -- TERRAIN THAT WE MÉTIS KNOW WELL. IF WE HIT THEM NOW WITH GUERILLA WARFARE, WE COULD CRUSH THEM EASILY. >
< I'D GLADLY LEAD SUCH AN EXPEDITION IF YOU THINK IT'S NECESSARY. >
< I JUST RECEIVED THIS LETTER FROM COLONEL WOLSELEY, WHO'S LEADING THE CANADIANS. >
< YOU'LL HAVE TO READ IT TO ME. >
< YES -- I'M SORRY -- OF COURSE. Uh... "THE FORCE THAT I HAVE THE HONOUR OF COMMANDING WILL ENTER YOUR PROVINCE REPRESENTING NO PARTY, EITHER IN RELIGION OR POLITICS"-- >
<-- "AND WILL AFFORD EQUAL PROTECTION TO THE LIVES AND PROPERTY OF ALL RACES AND OF ALL CREEDS. STRICTEST ORDER AND DISCIPLINE WILL BE MAINTAINED AND PRIVATE PROPERTY WILL BE CAREFULLY RESPECTED." >
< AND YOU BELIEVE HIM ? >
< WHY WOULD THE CANADIAN GOVERNMENT NEGOTIATE WITH US UNLESS THEY MEANT TO DEAL WITH US HONOURABLY ? >
< WELL, I'D ONLY BE INTERESTED IN STICKING AROUND IF YOU WERE GOING TO FIGHT, SO I GUESS I'LL BE HEADING OFF. >
< THANKS FOR COMING. >

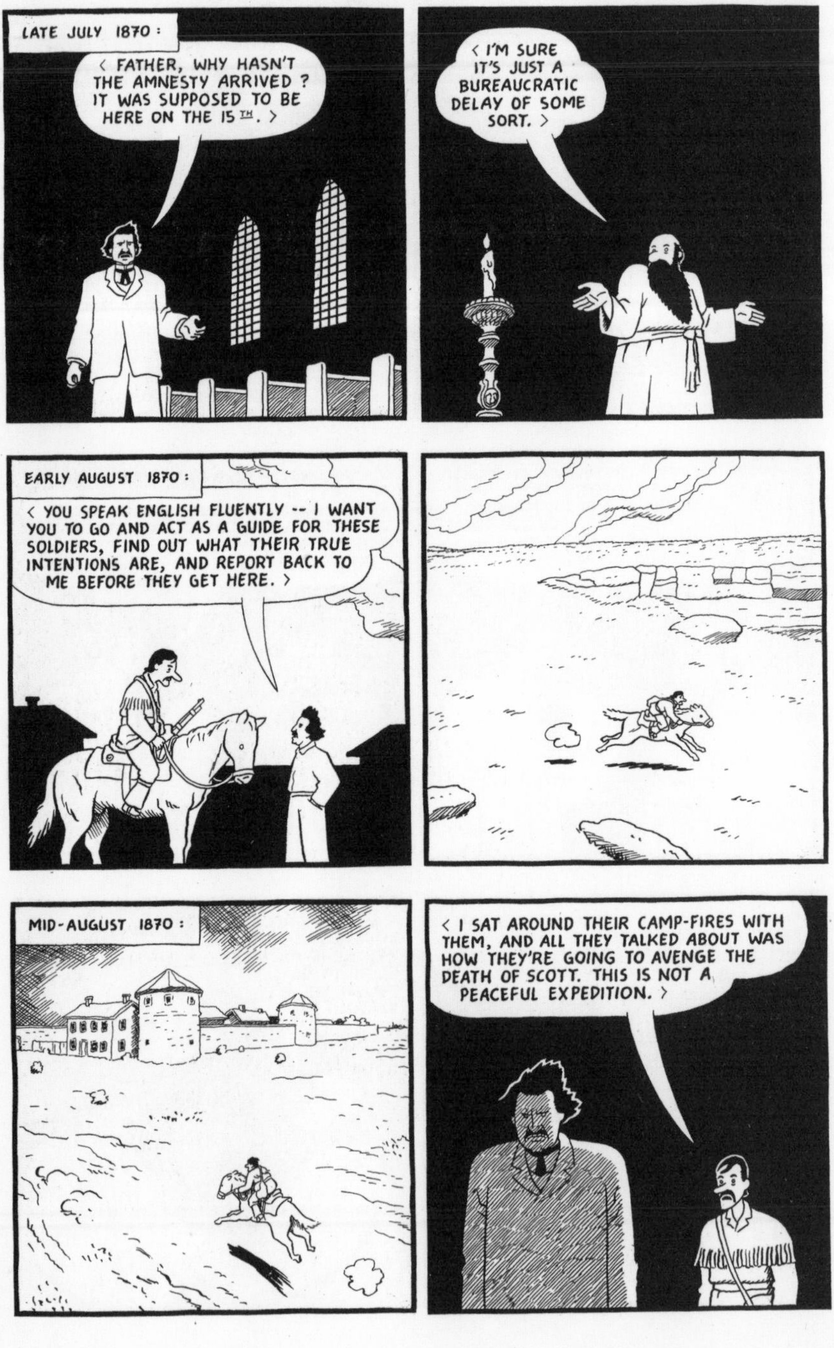
LATE JULY 1870 :
< FATHER, WHY HASN'T THE AMNESTY ARRIVED ? IT WAS SUPPOSED TO BE HERE ON THE 15TH. >
< I'M SURE IT'S JUST A BUREAUCRATIC DELAY OF SOME SORT. >
EARLY AUGUST 1870 :
< YOU SPEAK ENGLISH FLUENTLY -- I WANT YOU TO GO AND ACT AS A GUIDE FOR THESE SOLDIERS, FIND OUT WHAT THEIR TRUE INTENTIONS ARE, AND REPORT BACK TO ME BEFORE THEY GET HERE. >
MID-AUGUST 1870 :
< I SAT AROUND THEIR CAMP-FIRES WITH THEM, AND ALL THEY TALKED ABOUT WAS HOW THEY'RE GOING TO AVENGE THE DEATH OF SCOTT. THIS IS NOT A PEACEFUL EXPEDITION. >

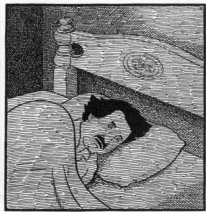

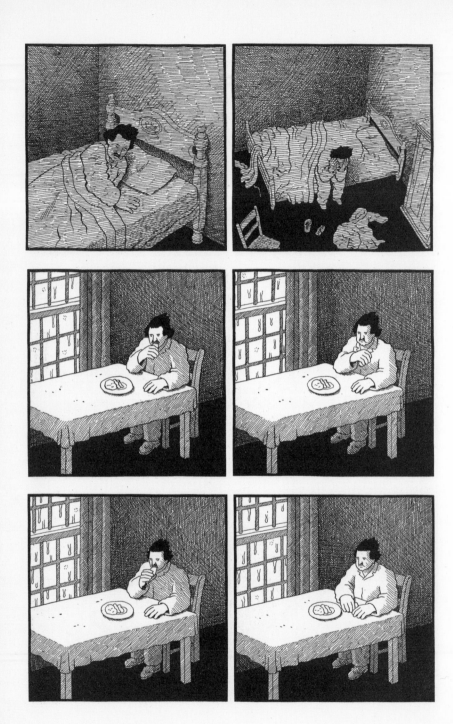

IS ANYONE HERE ?!
IS ANYONE HERE ?!
48
HELLO ?!
ANYONE STILL HERE ?!

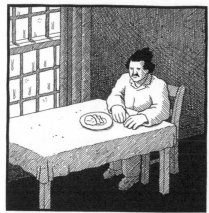

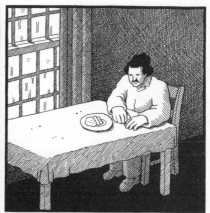

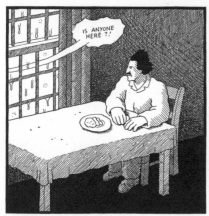

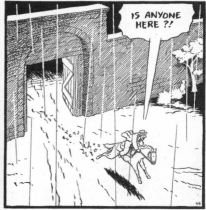

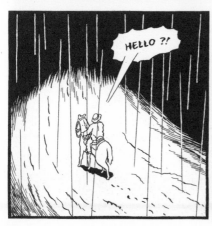

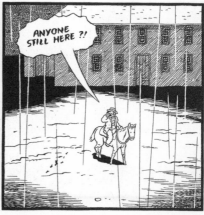

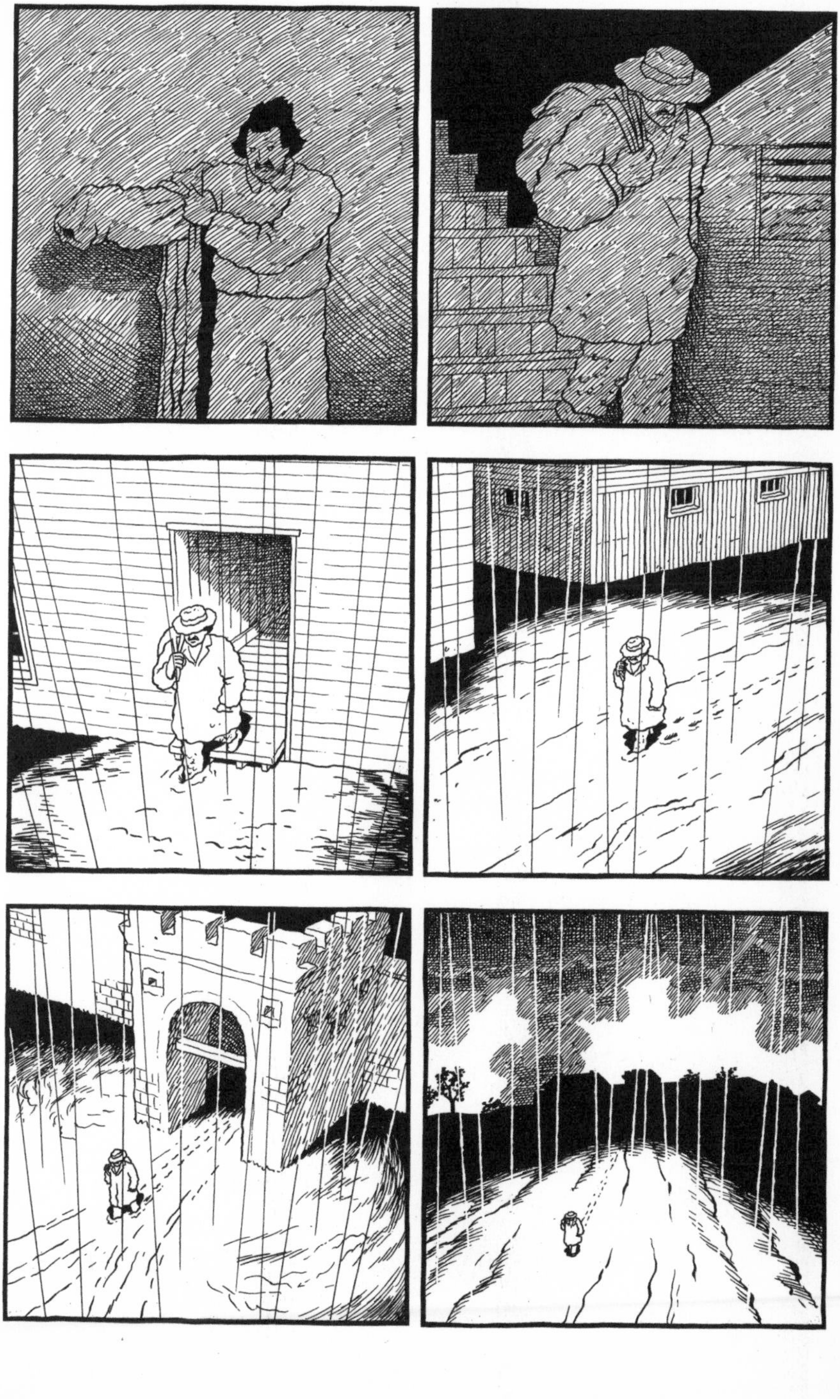

PART TWO

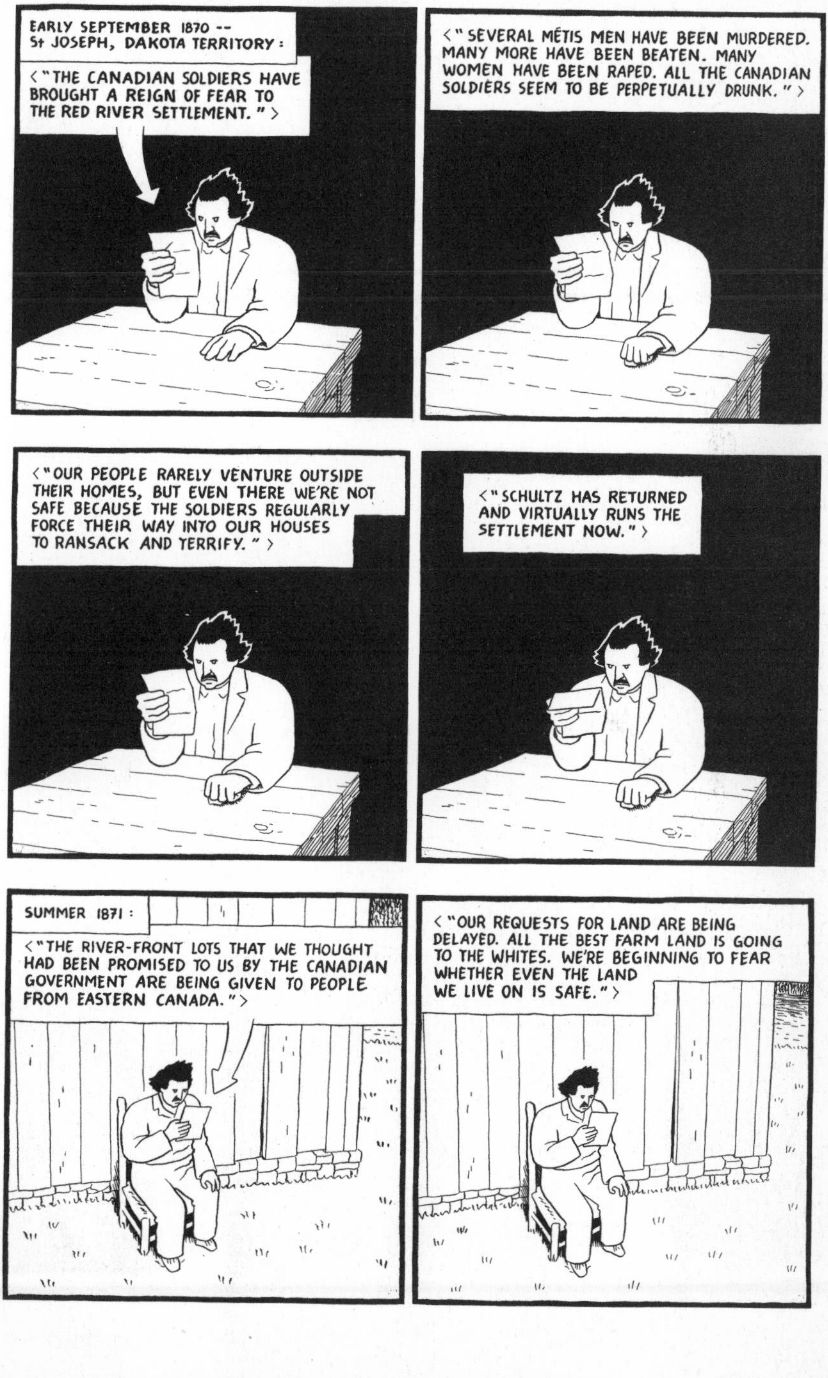
EARLY SEPTEMBER 1870 -- St JOSEPH, DAKOTA TERRITORY:
<"THE CANADIAN SOLDIERS HAVE BROUGHT A REIGN OF FEAR TO THE RED RIVER SETTLEMENT.">
<"SEVERAL MÉTIS MEN HAVE BEEN MURDERED. MANY MORE HAVE BEEN BEATEN. MANY WOMEN HAVE BEEN RAPED. ALL THE CANADIAN SOLDIERS SEEM TO BE PERPETUALLY DRUNK.">
<"OUR PEOPLE RARELY VENTURE OUTSIDE THEIR HOMES, BUT EVEN THERE WE'RE NOT SAFE BECAUSE THE SOLDIERS REGULARLY FORCE THEIR WAY INTO OUR HOUSES TO RANSACK AND TERRIFY.">
<"SCHULTZ HAS RETURNED AND VIRTUALLY RUNS THE SETTLEMENT NOW.">
SUMMER 1871:
<"THE RIVER-FRONT LOTS THAT WE THOUGHT HAD BEEN PROMISED TO US BY THE CANADIAN GOVERNMENT ARE BEING GIVEN TO PEOPLE FROM EASTERN CANADA.">
<"OUR REQUESTS FOR LAND ARE BEING DELAYED. ALL THE BEST FARM LAND IS GOING TO THE WHITES. WE'RE BEGINNING TO FEAR WHETHER EVEN THE LAND WE LIVE ON IS SAFE.">

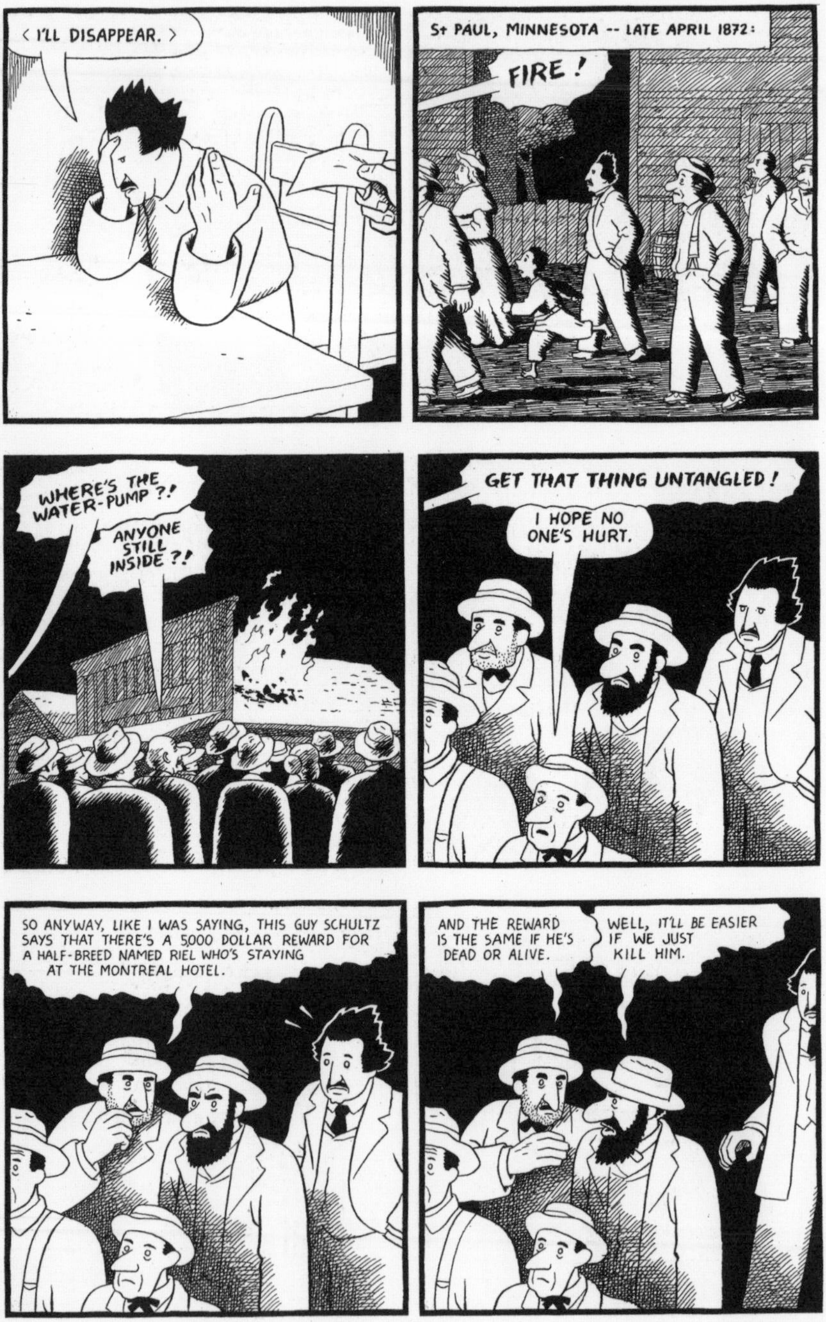

< I'LL DISAPPEAR. >
St PAUL, MINNESOTA -- LATE APRIL 1872:
FIRE !
WHERE'S THE WATER-PUMP ?!
ANYONE STILL INSIDE ?!
GET THAT THING UNTANGLED !
I HOPE NO ONE'S HURT.
SO ANYWAY, LIKE I WAS SAYING, THIS GUY SCHULTZ SAYS THAT THERE'S A 5,000 DOLLAR REWARD FOR A HALF-BREED NAMED RIEL WHO'S STAYING AT THE MONTREAL HOTEL.
AND THE REWARD IS THE SAME IF HE'S DEAD OR ALIVE.
WELL, IT'LL BE EASIER IF WE JUST KILL HIM.

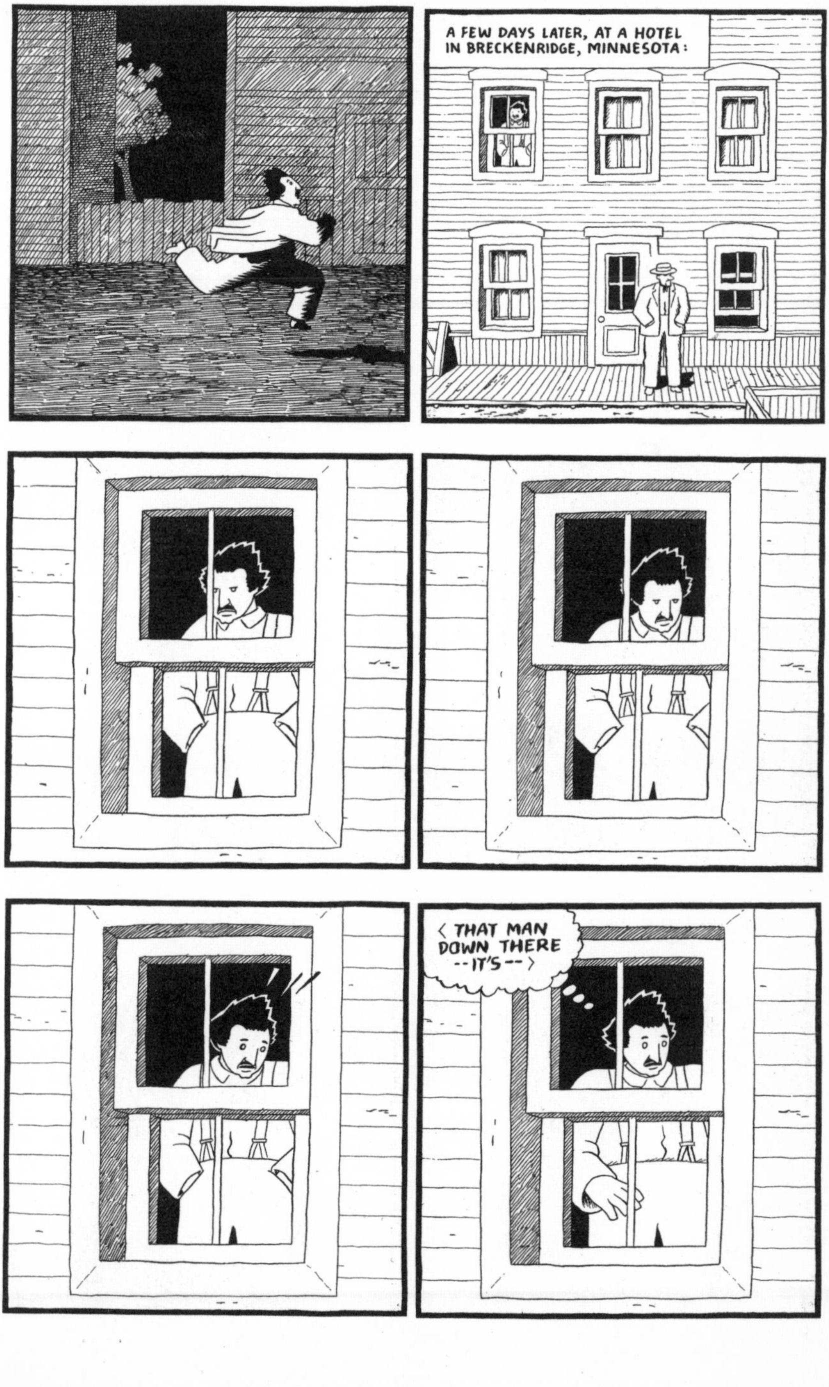
A FEW DAYS LATER, AT A HOTEL IN BRECKENRIDGE, MINNESOTA:
< THAT MAN DOWN THERE --IT'S-- >

96

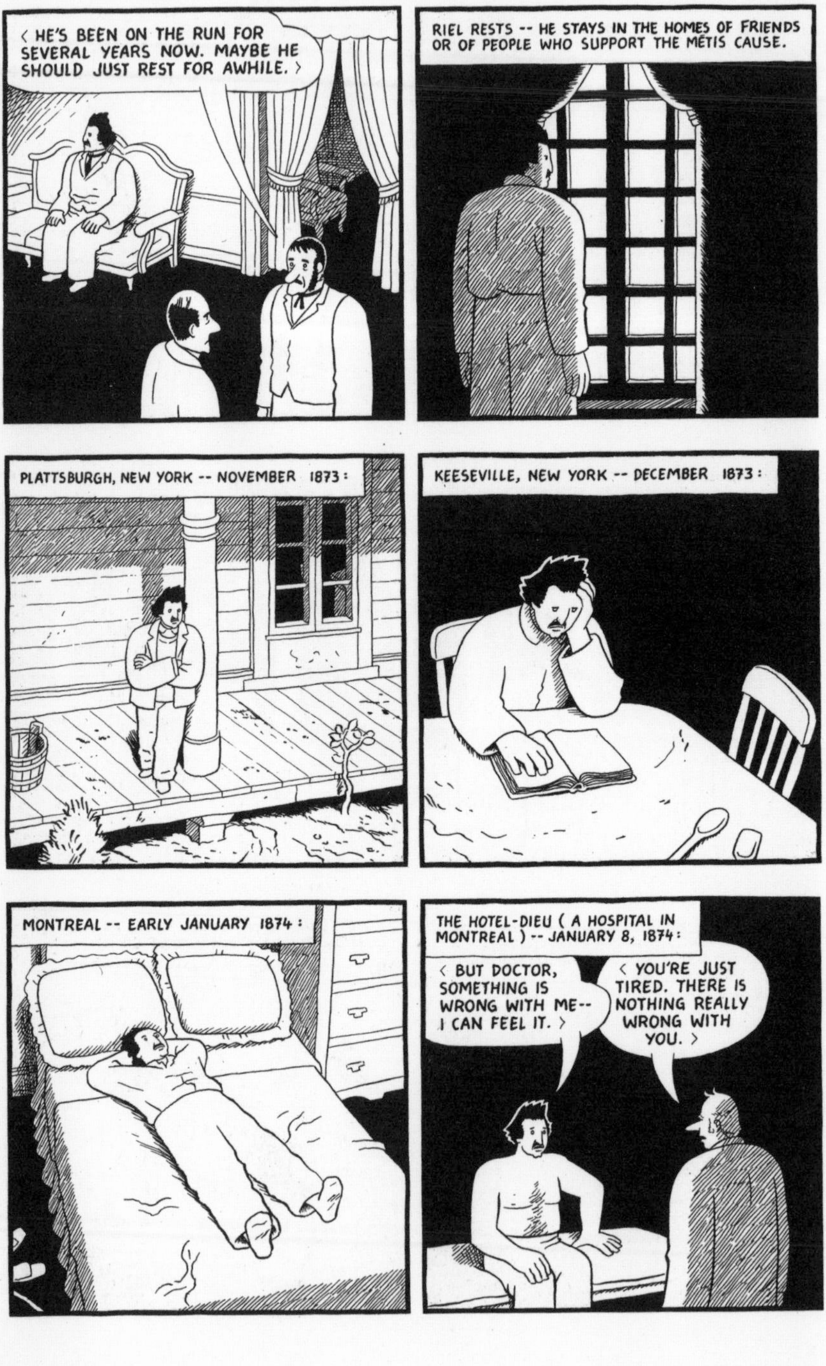
< HE'S BEEN ON THE RUN FOR SEVERAL YEARS NOW. MAYBE HE SHOULD JUST REST FOR AWHILE. >
RIEL RESTS -- HE STAYS IN THE HOMES OF FRIENDS OR OF PEOPLE WHO SUPPORT THE MÉTIS CAUSE.
PLATTSBURGH, NEW YORK -- NOVEMBER 1873:
KEESEVILLE, NEW YORK -- DECEMBER 1873:
MONTREAL -- EARLY JANUARY 1874:
THE HOTEL-DIEU (A HOSPITAL IN MONTREAL) -- JANUARY 8, 1874:
< BUT DOCTOR, SOMETHING IS WRONG WITH ME-- I CAN FEEL IT. >
< YOU'RE JUST TIRED. THERE IS NOTHING REALLY WRONG WITH YOU. >

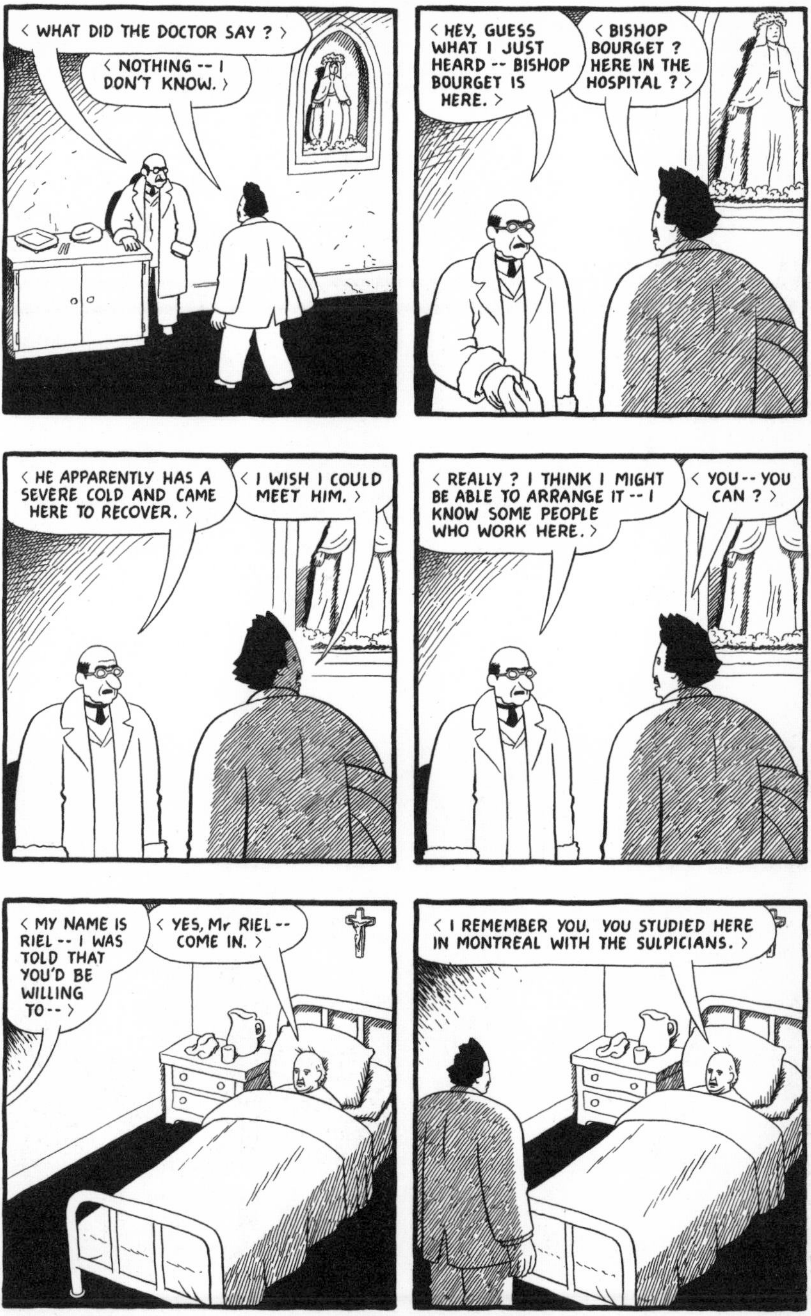
< WHAT DID THE DOCTOR SAY ? >
< NOTHING -- I DON'T KNOW. >
< HEY, GUESS WHAT I JUST HEARD -- BISHOP BOURGET IS HERE. >
< BISHOP BOURGET ? HERE IN THE HOSPITAL ? >
< HE APPARENTLY HAS A SEVERE COLD AND CAME HERE TO RECOVER. >
< I WISH I COULD MEET HIM. >
< REALLY ? I THINK I MIGHT BE ABLE TO ARRANGE IT -- I KNOW SOME PEOPLE WHO WORK HERE. >
< YOU -- YOU CAN ? >
< MY NAME IS RIEL -- I WAS TOLD THAT YOU'D BE WILLING TO -- >
< YES, Mr RIEL -- COME IN. >
< I REMEMBER YOU. YOU STUDIED HERE IN MONTREAL WITH THE SULPICIANS. >

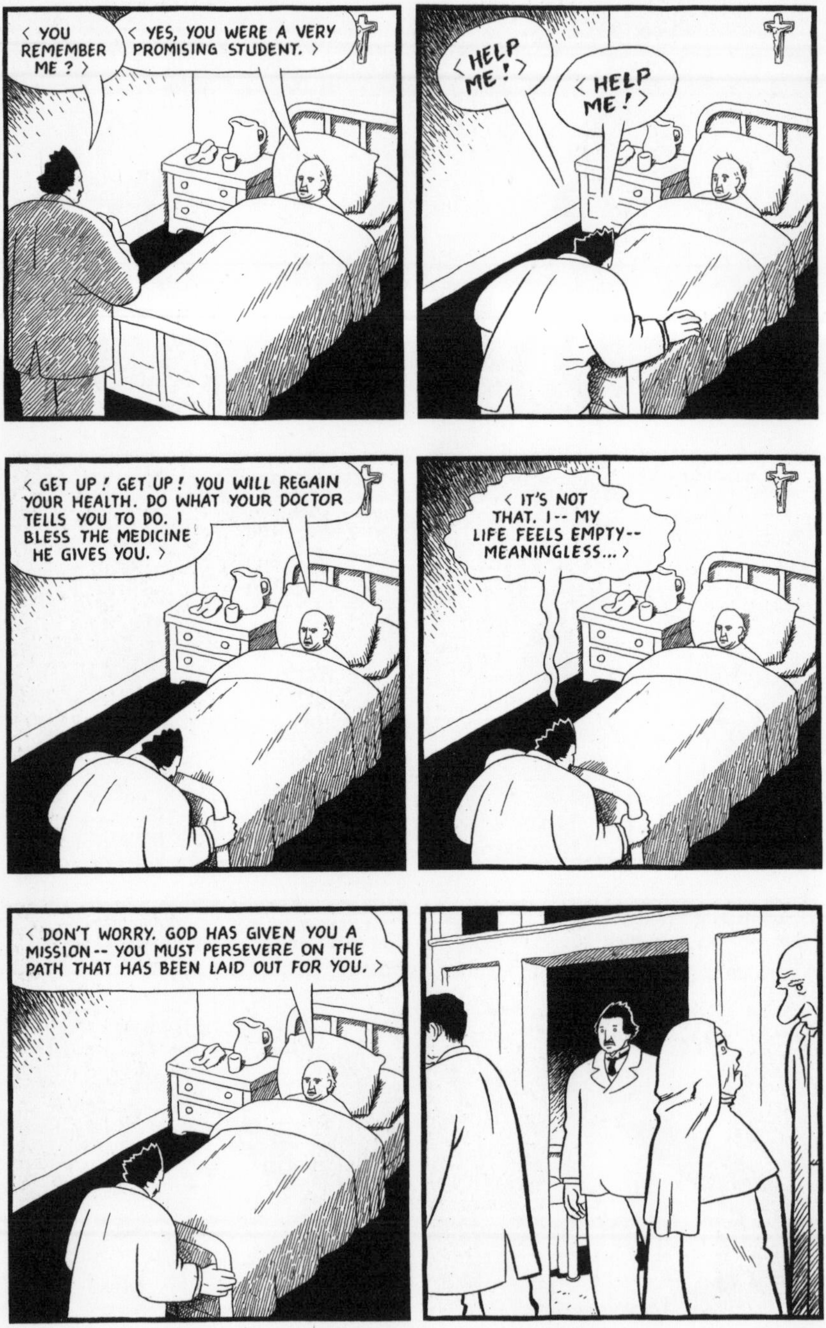
< YOU REMEMBER ME ? >
< YES, YOU WERE A VERY PROMISING STUDENT. >
< HELP ME ! >
< HELP ME ! >
< GET UP ! GET UP ! YOU WILL REGAIN YOUR HEALTH. DO WHAT YOUR DOCTOR TELLS YOU TO DO. I BLESS THE MEDICINE HE GIVES YOU. >
< IT'S NOT THAT. I -- MY LIFE FEELS EMPTY-- MEANINGLESS... >
< DON'T WORRY. GOD HAS GIVEN YOU A MISSION -- YOU MUST PERSEVERE ON THE PATH THAT HAS BEEN LAID OUT FOR YOU. >

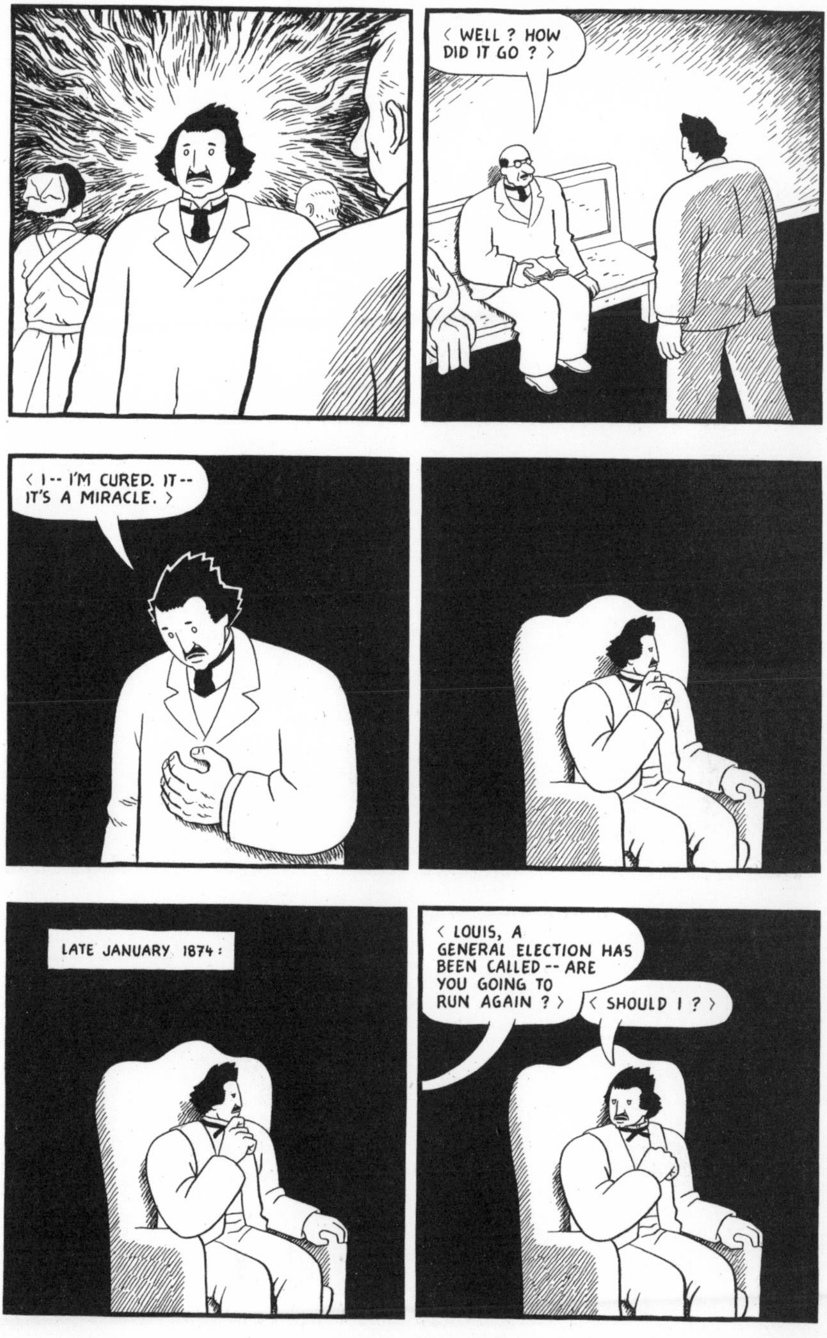

< WELL ? HOW DID IT GO ? >
< I-- I'M CURED. IT -- IT'S A MIRACLE. >
LATE JANUARY 1874 :
< LOUIS, A GENERAL ELECTION HAS BEEN CALLED -- ARE YOU GOING TO RUN AGAIN ? >
< SHOULD I ? >

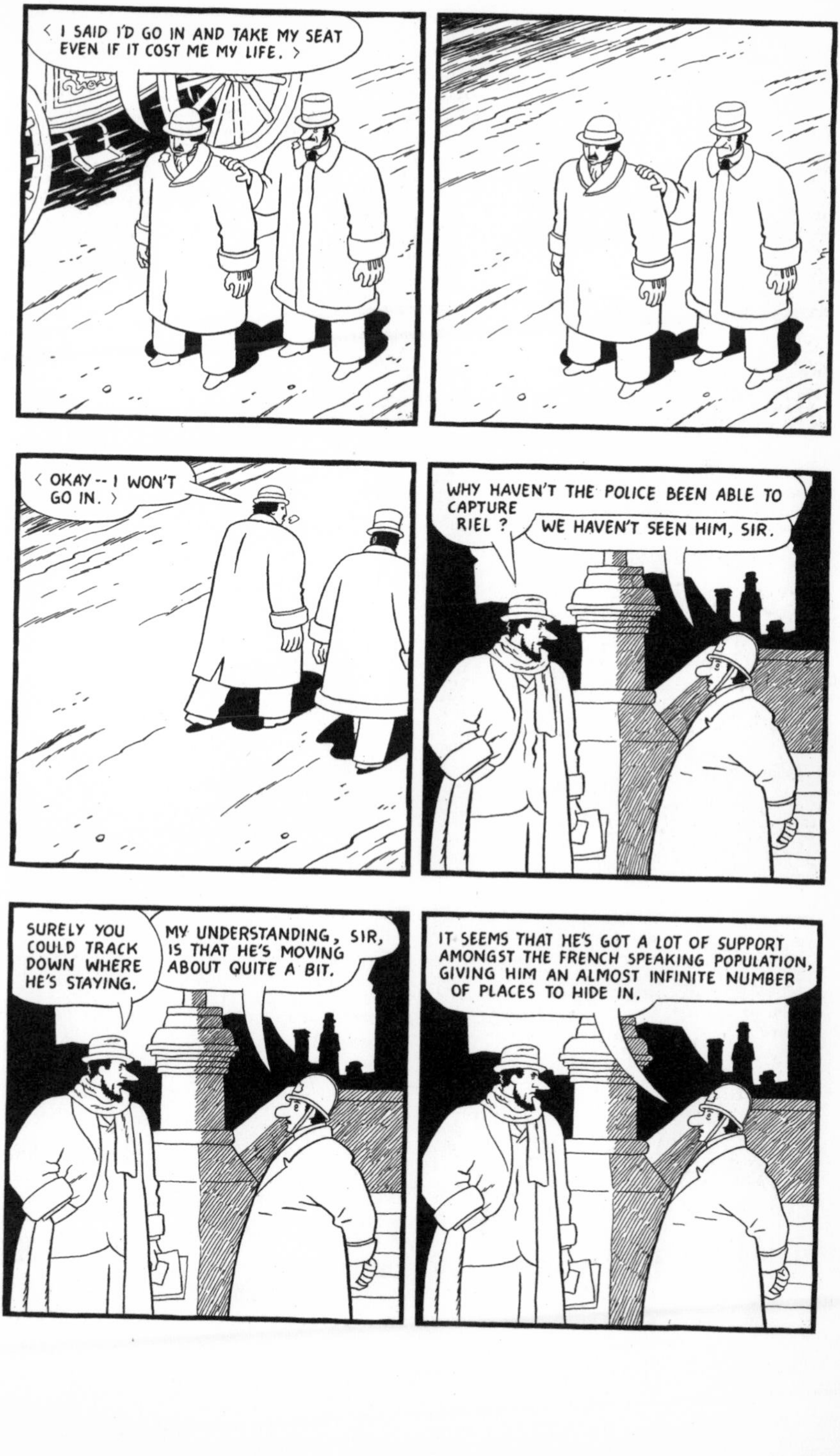
< I SAID I'D GO IN AND TAKE MY SEAT EVEN IF IT COST ME MY LIFE. >
< OKAY -- I WON'T GO IN. >
WHY HAVEN'T THE POLICE BEEN ABLE TO CAPTURE RIEL ?
WE HAVEN'T SEEN HIM, SIR.
SURELY YOU COULD TRACK DOWN WHERE HE'S STAYING.
MY UNDERSTANDING, SIR, IS THAT HE'S MOVING ABOUT QUITE A BIT.
IT SEEMS THAT HE'S GOT A LOT OF SUPPORT AMONGST THE FRENCH SPEAKING POPULATION, GIVING HIM AN ALMOST INFINITE NUMBER OF PLACES TO HIDE IN.

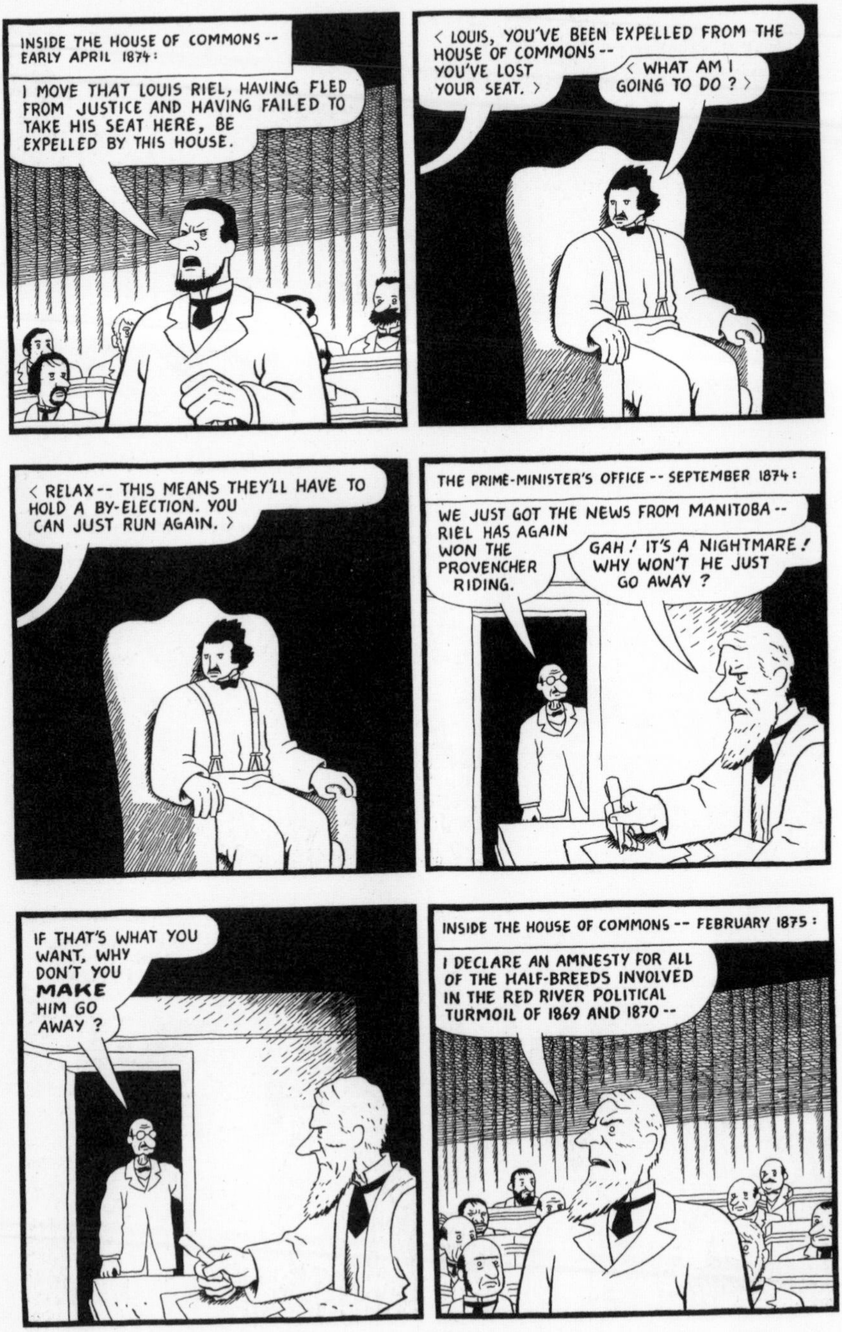
INSIDE THE HOUSE OF COMMONS -- EARLY APRIL 1874:
I MOVE THAT LOUIS RIEL, HAVING FLED FROM JUSTICE AND HAVING FAILED TO TAKE HIS SEAT HERE, BE EXPELLED BY THIS HOUSE.
< LOUIS, YOU'VE BEEN EXPELLED FROM THE HOUSE OF COMMONS -- YOU'VE LOST YOUR SEAT. >
< WHAT AM I GOING TO DO ? >
< RELAX -- THIS MEANS THEY'LL HAVE TO HOLD A BY-ELECTION. YOU CAN JUST RUN AGAIN. >
THE PRIME-MINISTER'S OFFICE -- SEPTEMBER 1874:
WE JUST GOT THE NEWS FROM MANITOBA -- RIEL HAS AGAIN WON THE PROVENCHER RIDING.
GAH! IT'S A NIGHTMARE! WHY WON'T HE JUST GO AWAY ?
IF THAT'S WHAT YOU WANT, WHY DON'T YOU **MAKE** HIM GO AWAY ?
INSIDE THE HOUSE OF COMMONS -- FEBRUARY 1875:
I DECLARE AN AMNESTY FOR ALL OF THE HALF-BREEDS INVOLVED IN THE RED RIVER POLITICAL TURMOIL OF 1869 AND 1870 --

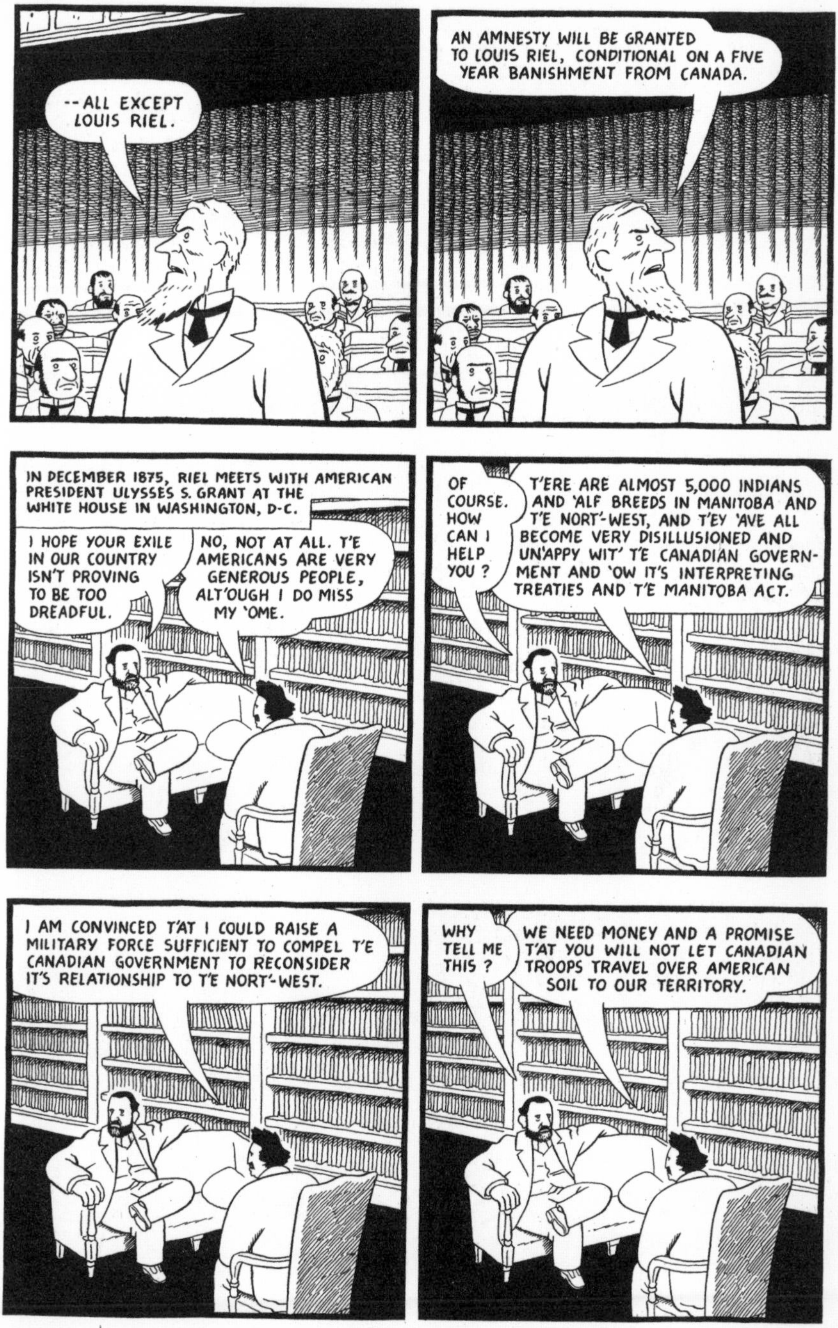
--ALL EXCEPT LOUIS RIEL.
AN AMNESTY WILL BE GRANTED TO LOUIS RIEL, CONDITIONAL ON A FIVE YEAR BANISHMENT FROM CANADA.
IN DECEMBER 1875, RIEL MEETS WITH AMERICAN PRESIDENT ULYSSES S. GRANT AT THE WHITE HOUSE IN WASHINGTON, D-C.
I HOPE YOUR EXILE IN OUR COUNTRY ISN'T PROVING TO BE TOO DREADFUL.
NO, NOT AT ALL. T'E AMERICANS ARE VERY GENEROUS PEOPLE, ALT'OUGH I DO MISS MY 'OME.
OF COURSE. HOW CAN I HELP YOU ?
T'ERE ARE ALMOST 5,000 INDIANS AND 'ALF BREEDS IN MANITOBA AND T'E NORT'-WEST, AND T'EY 'AVE ALL BECOME VERY DISILLUSIONED AND UN'APPY WIT' T'E CANADIAN GOVERNMENT AND 'OW IT'S INTERPRETING TREATIES AND T'E MANITOBA ACT.
I AM CONVINCED T'AT I COULD RAISE A MILITARY FORCE SUFFICIENT TO COMPEL T'E CANADIAN GOVERNMENT TO RECONSIDER IT'S RELATIONSHIP TO T'E NORT'-WEST.
WHY TELL ME THIS ?
WE NEED MONEY AND A PROMISE T'AT YOU WILL NOT LET CANADIAN TROOPS TRAVEL OVER AMERICAN SOIL TO OUR TERRITORY.

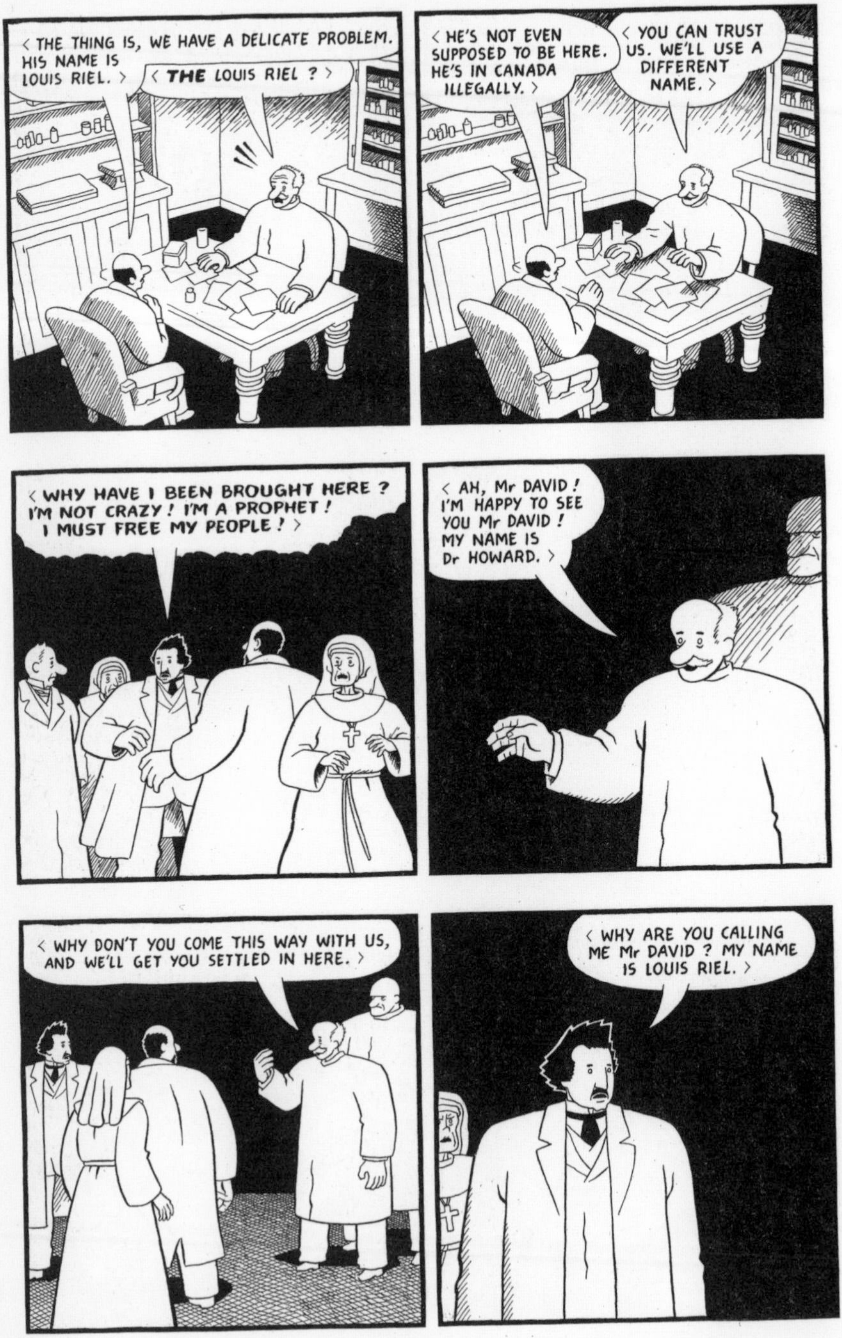

< THE THING IS, WE HAVE A DELICATE PROBLEM. HIS NAME IS LOUIS RIEL. >
< **THE** LOUIS RIEL ? >
< HE'S NOT EVEN SUPPOSED TO BE HERE. HE'S IN CANADA ILLEGALLY. >
< YOU CAN TRUST US. WE'LL USE A DIFFERENT NAME. >
< WHY HAVE I BEEN BROUGHT HERE ? I'M NOT CRAZY ! I'M A PROPHET ! I MUST FREE MY PEOPLE ! >
< AH, Mr DAVID ! I'M HAPPY TO SEE YOU Mr DAVID ! MY NAME IS Dr HOWARD. >
< WHY DON'T YOU COME THIS WAY WITH US, AND WE'LL GET YOU SETTLED IN HERE. >
< WHY ARE YOU CALLING ME Mr DAVID ? MY NAME IS LOUIS RIEL. >

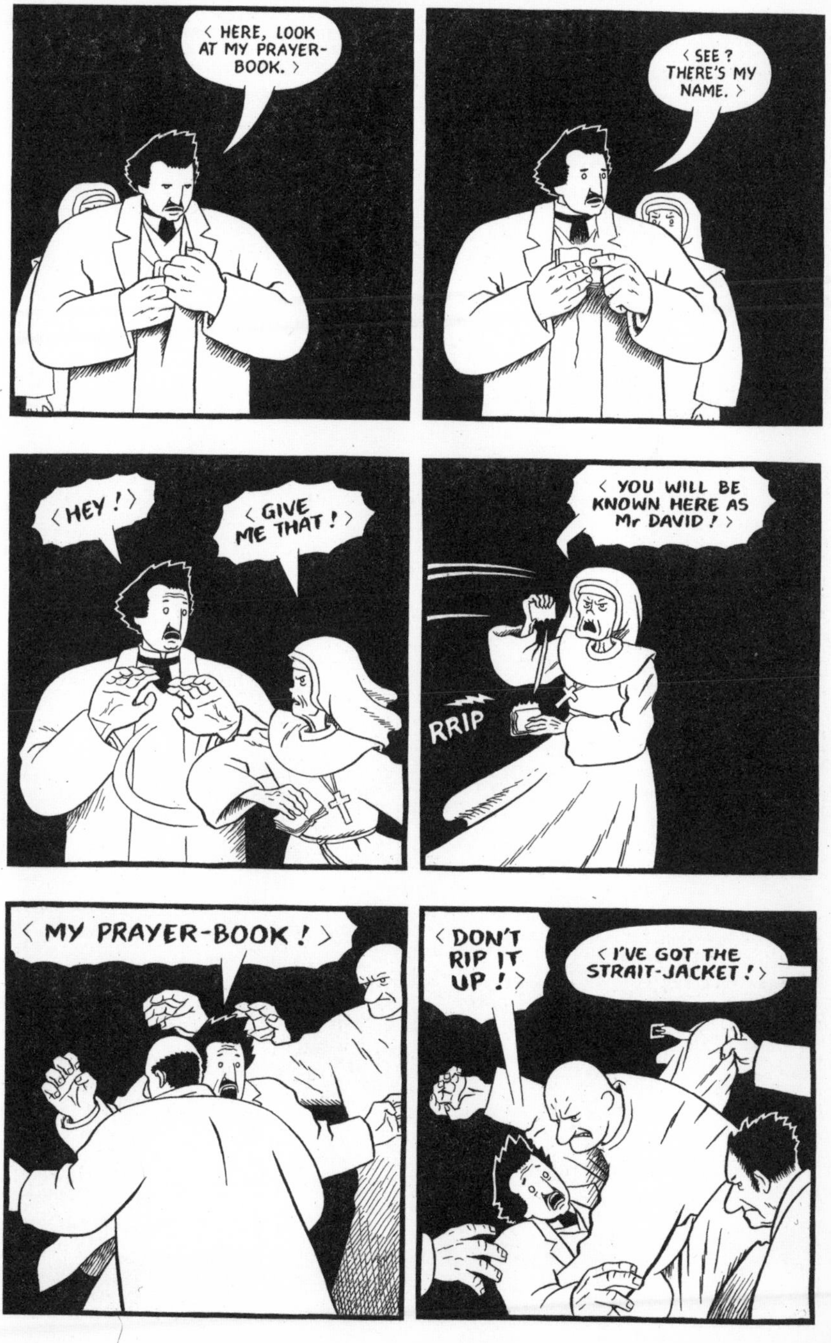

< HERE, LOOK AT MY PRAYER-BOOK. >
< SEE ? THERE'S MY NAME. >
< HEY ! >
< GIVE ME THAT ! >
< YOU WILL BE KNOWN HERE AS Mr DAVID ! >
RRIP
< MY PRAYER-BOOK ! >
< DON'T RIP IT UP ! >
< I'VE GOT THE STRAIT-JACKET ! >

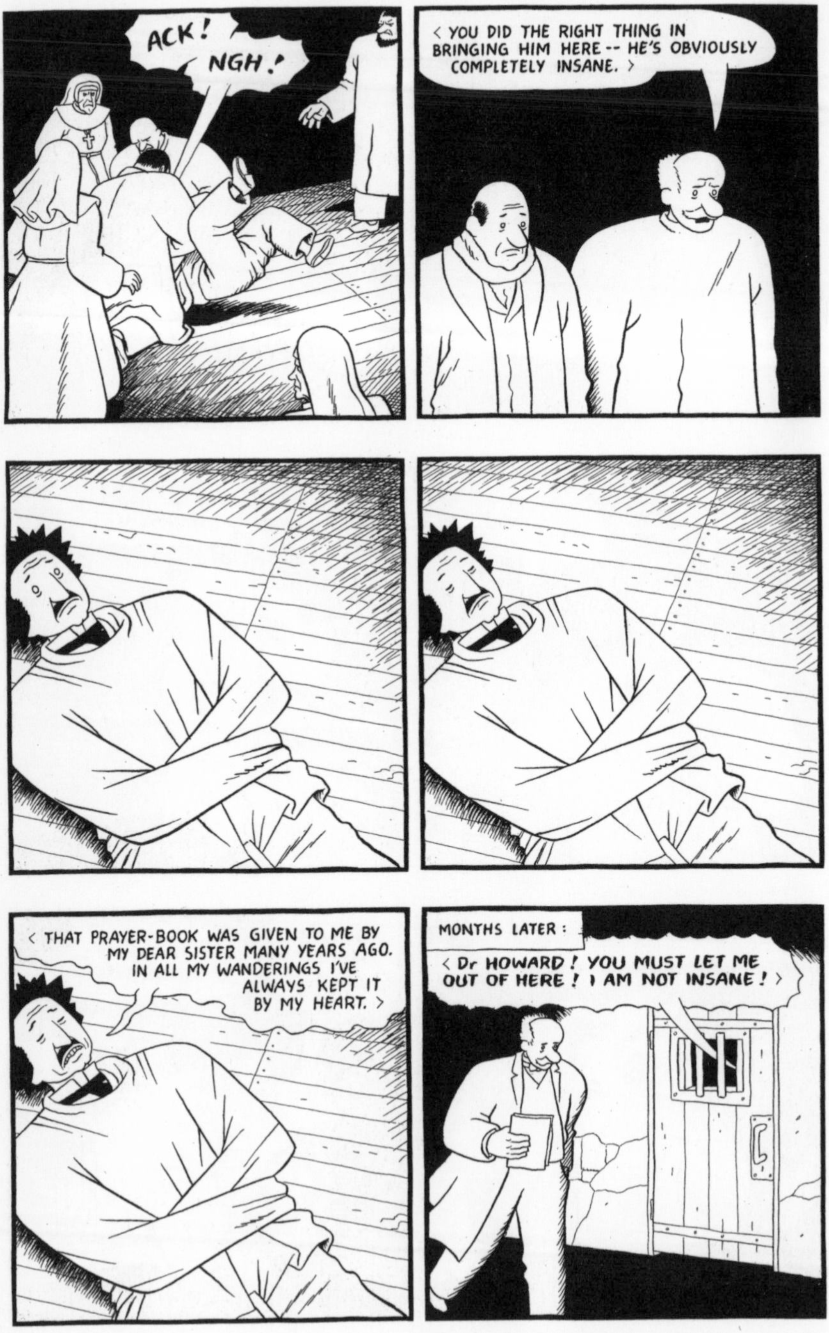
ACK! NGH!
< YOU DID THE RIGHT THING IN BRINGING HIM HERE -- HE'S OBVIOUSLY COMPLETELY INSANE. >
< THAT PRAYER-BOOK WAS GIVEN TO ME BY MY DEAR SISTER MANY YEARS AGO. IN ALL MY WANDERINGS I'VE ALWAYS KEPT IT BY MY HEART. >
MONTHS LATER :
< Dr HOWARD ! YOU MUST LET ME OUT OF HERE ! I AM NOT INSANE ! >

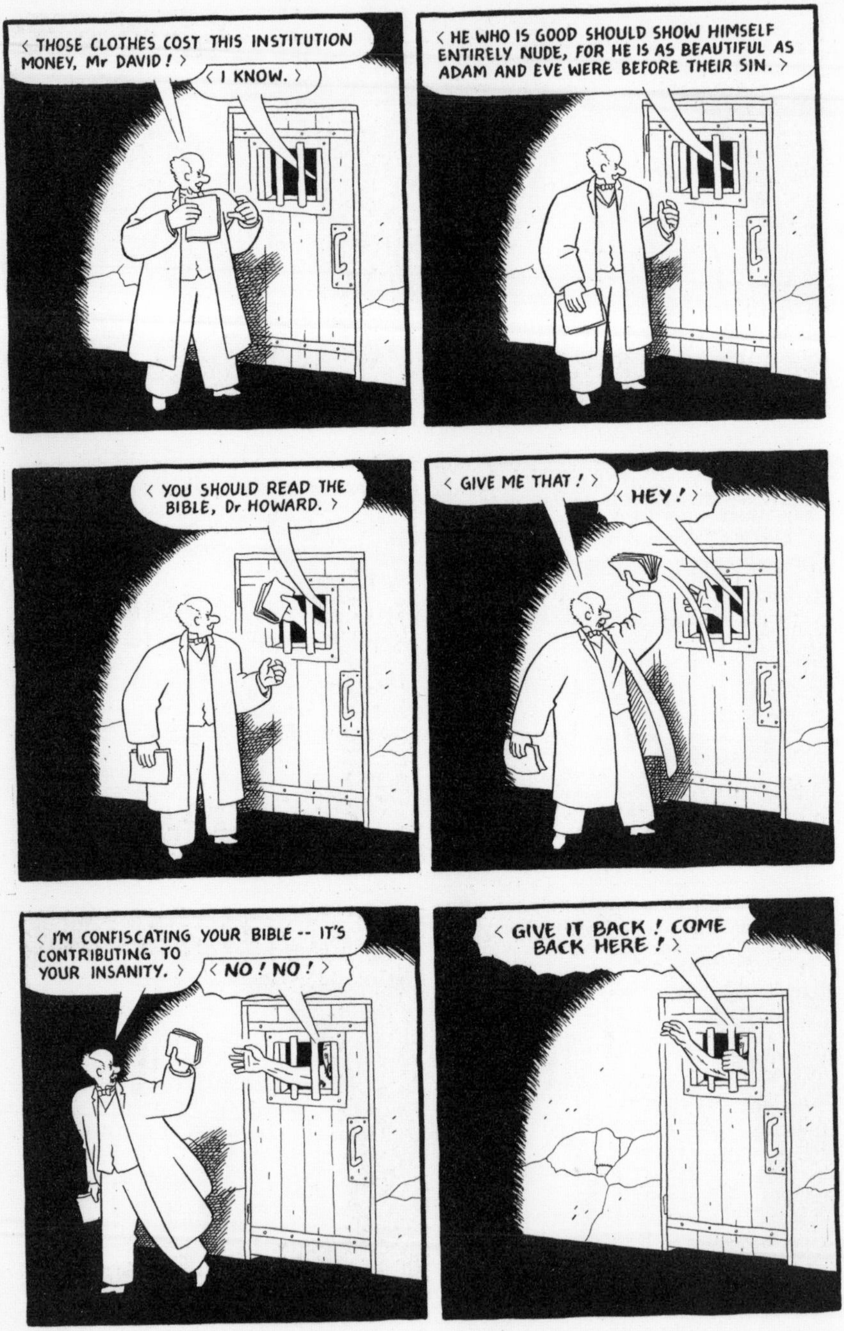
< THOSE CLOTHES COST THIS INSTITUTION MONEY, Mr DAVID! >
< I KNOW. >
< HE WHO IS GOOD SHOULD SHOW HIMSELF ENTIRELY NUDE, FOR HE IS AS BEAUTIFUL AS ADAM AND EVE WERE BEFORE THEIR SIN. >
< YOU SHOULD READ THE BIBLE, Dr HOWARD. >
< GIVE ME THAT! >
< HEY! >
< I'M CONFISCATING YOUR BIBLE -- IT'S CONTRIBUTING TO YOUR INSANITY. >
< NO! NO! >
< GIVE IT BACK! COME BACK HERE! >

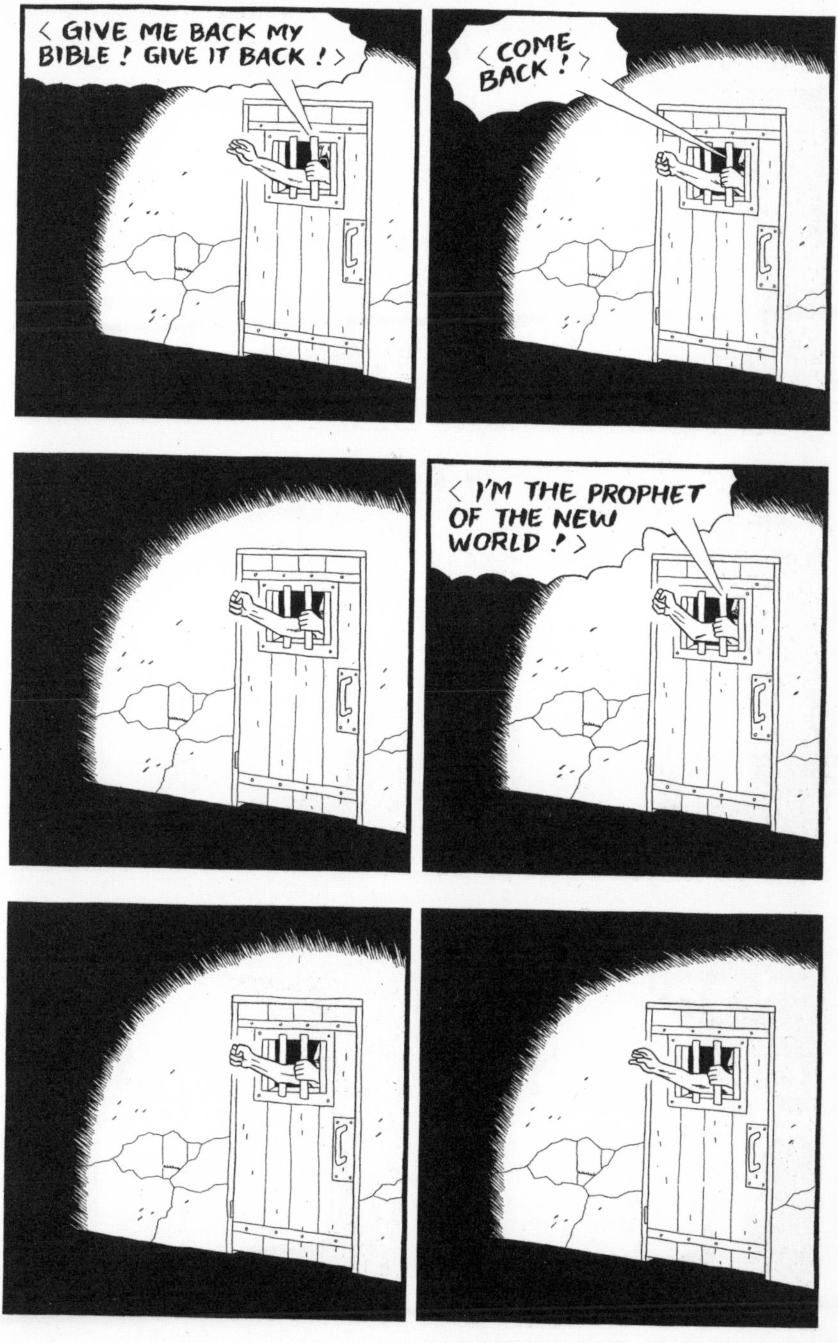
< GIVE ME BACK MY BIBLE ! GIVE IT BACK ! >
< COME BACK ! >
< I'M THE PROPHET OF THE NEW WORLD ! >

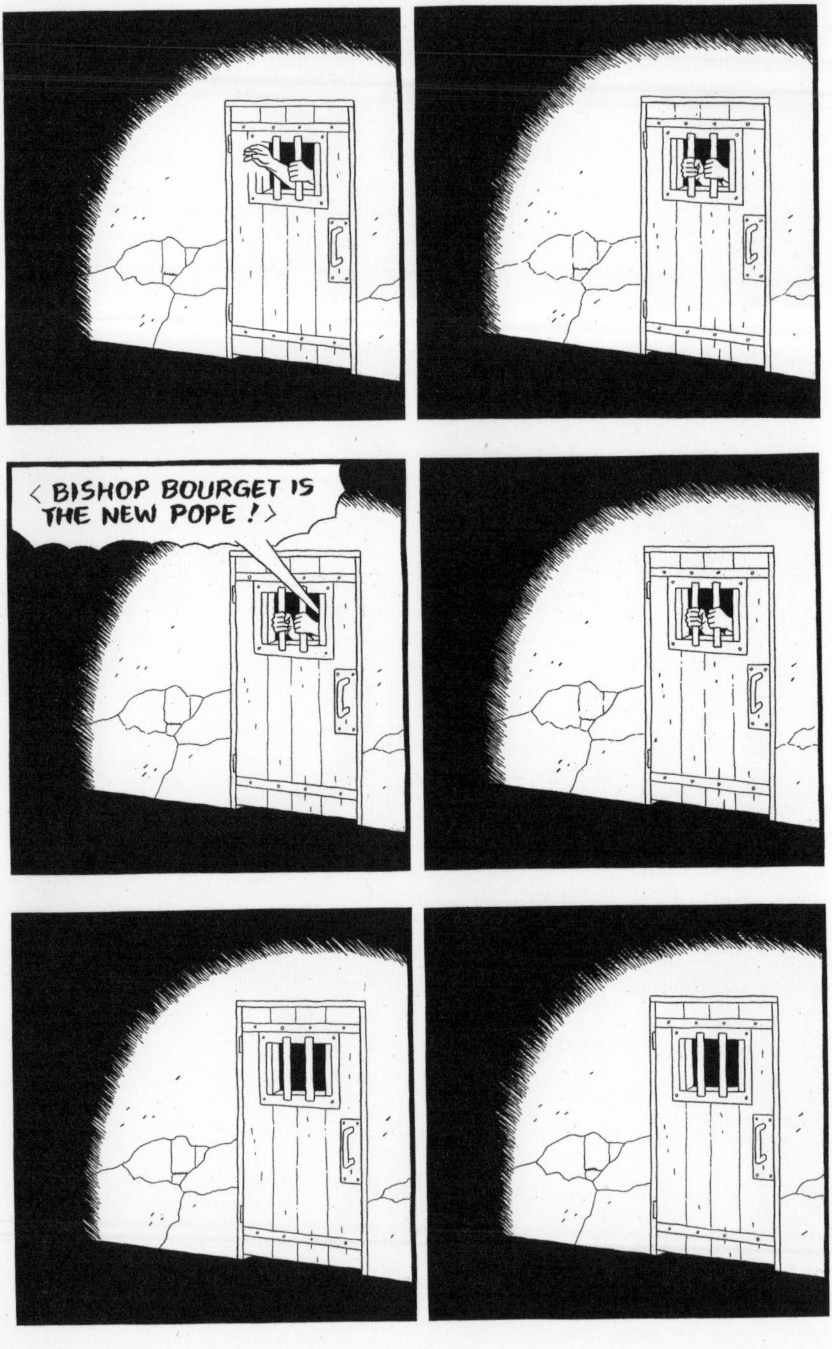
< BISHOP BOURGET IS THE NEW POPE ! >

SECOND
MAP SECTION

In the 1870 Manitoba Act, the Canadian government had promised to give 1,400,000 acres to the Mētis. Riel and Father Ritchot had hoped that this land would be along the Red and Assiniboine Rivers, ensuring the development of a strong and prosperous Mētis community, and had expected that the Mētis would be allowed to select their own lots. The government at first appeared undecided about how to hand out the land and delayed the distribution. During this period of delay, many of the river-front lots that the Mētis would have wanted were given to immigrants from Ontario. After a few years, the government finally settled on a distribution scheme for the 1,400,000 acres. Instead of letting the Mētis choose the land that they wanted, the government chose the lots, which, rather than being river-front lots, ended up being interior prarie-land unconnected to waterways -- land that the Mētis considered to be inferior. These lots were then distributed by lottery. Since this land wasn't suited to the form of agriculture that they were used to, the Mētis had no interest in it and sold it to land-speculators.

0 200 400 600 800 1000
MILES
0 400 800 1200 1600
KILOMETRES
Pacific Ocean
Batoche
Regina
Winnipeg (the Red River settlement)
St. Peter's Mission (Montana)
Montreal
Ottawa
Toronto
Atlantic Ocean
Canada
Not Canada

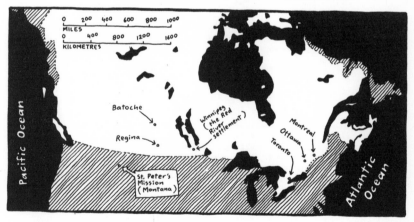

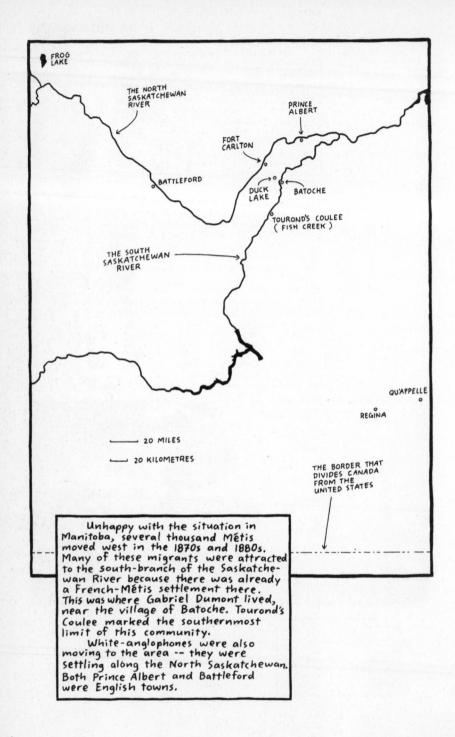

FROG LAKE

THE NORTH SASKATCHEWAN RIVER

PRINCE ALBERT

FORT CARLTON

BATTLEFORD

DUCK LAKE

BATOCHE

TOUROND'S COULEE (FISH CREEK)

THE SOUTH SASKATCHEWAN RIVER

QU'APPELLE

REGINA

20 MILES

20 KILOMETRES

THE BORDER THAT DIVIDES CANADA FROM THE UNITED STATES

Unhappy with the situation in Manitoba, several thousand Métis moved west in the 1870s and 1880s. Many of these migrants were attracted to the south-branch of the Saskatchewan River because there was already a French-Métis settlement there. This was where Gabriel Dumont lived, near the village of Batoche. Tourond's Coulee marked the southernmost limit of this community.

White-anglophones were also moving to the area -- they were settling along the North Saskatchewan. Both Prince Albert and Battleford were English towns.

PART THREE

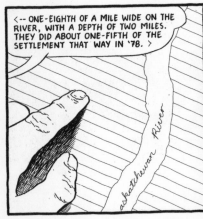

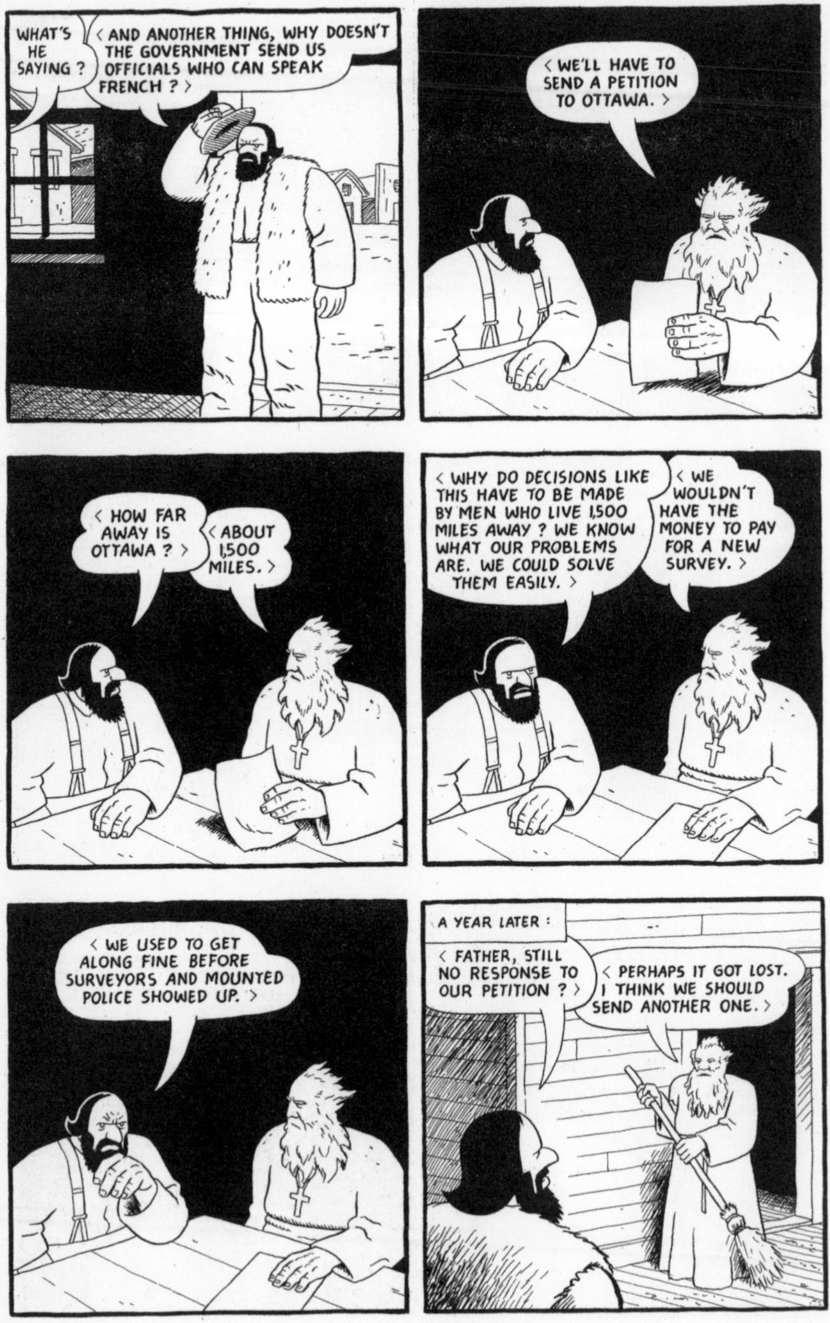
WHAT'S HE SAYING ?
< AND ANOTHER THING, WHY DOESN'T THE GOVERNMENT SEND US OFFICIALS WHO CAN SPEAK FRENCH ? >
< WE'LL HAVE TO SEND A PETITION TO OTTAWA. >
< HOW FAR AWAY IS OTTAWA ? >
< ABOUT 1,500 MILES. >
< WHY DO DECISIONS LIKE THIS HAVE TO BE MADE BY MEN WHO LIVE 1,500 MILES AWAY ? WE KNOW WHAT OUR PROBLEMS ARE. WE COULD SOLVE THEM EASILY. >
< WE WOULDN'T HAVE THE MONEY TO PAY FOR A NEW SURVEY. >
< WE USED TO GET ALONG FINE BEFORE SURVEYORS AND MOUNTED POLICE SHOWED UP. >
A YEAR LATER :
< FATHER, STILL NO RESPONSE TO OUR PETITION ? >
< PERHAPS IT GOT LOST. I THINK WE SHOULD SEND ANOTHER ONE. >

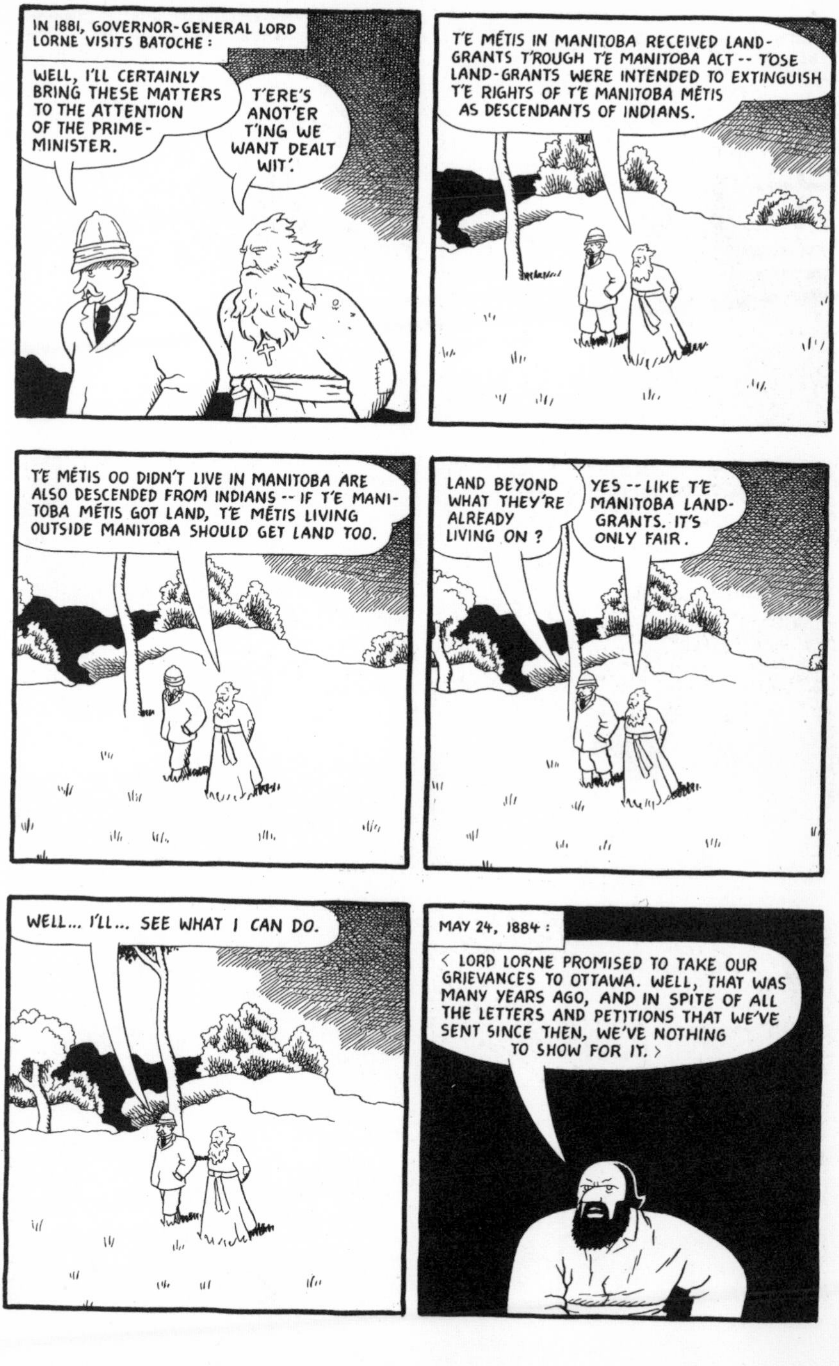
IN 1881, GOVERNOR-GENERAL LORD LORNE VISITS BATOCHE :
WELL, I'LL CERTAINLY BRING THESE MATTERS TO THE ATTENTION OF THE PRIME-MINISTER.
T'ERE'S ANOT'ER T'ING WE WANT DEALT WIT'.
T'E MÉTIS IN MANITOBA RECEIVED LAND-GRANTS T'ROUGH T'E MANITOBA ACT -- T'OSE LAND-GRANTS WERE INTENDED TO EXTINGUISH T'E RIGHTS OF T'E MANITOBA MÉTIS AS DESCENDANTS OF INDIANS.
T'E MÉTIS OO DIDN'T LIVE IN MANITOBA ARE ALSO DESCENDED FROM INDIANS -- IF T'E MANITOBA MÉTIS GOT LAND, T'E MÉTIS LIVING OUTSIDE MANITOBA SHOULD GET LAND TOO.
LAND BEYOND WHAT THEY'RE ALREADY LIVING ON ?
YES -- LIKE T'E MANITOBA LAND-GRANTS. IT'S ONLY FAIR.
WELL... I'LL... SEE WHAT I CAN DO.
MAY 24, 1884 :
< LORD LORNE PROMISED TO TAKE OUR GRIEVANCES TO OTTAWA. WELL, THAT WAS MANY YEARS AGO, AND IN SPITE OF ALL THE LETTERS AND PETITIONS THAT WE'VE SENT SINCE THEN, WE'VE NOTHING TO SHOW FOR IT. >

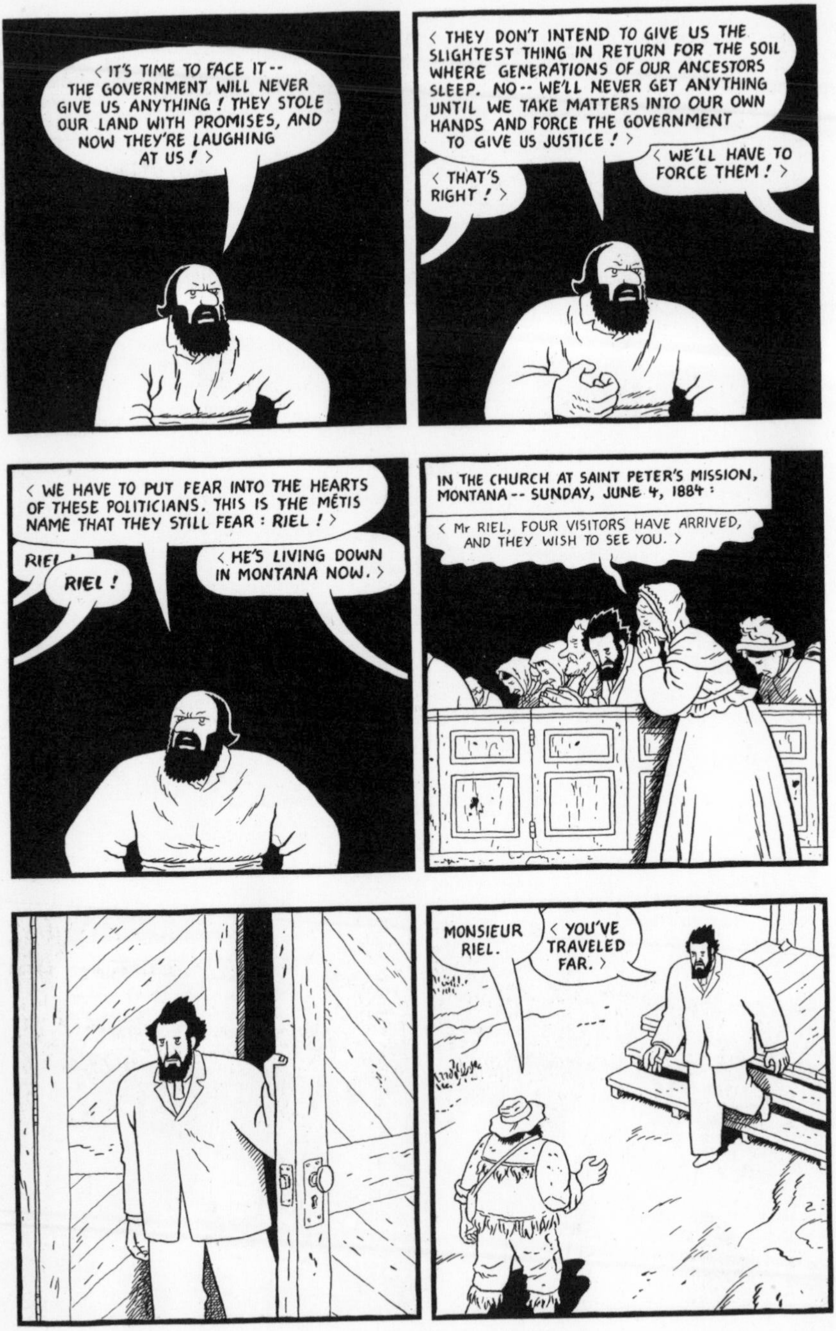
< IT'S TIME TO FACE IT -- THE GOVERNMENT WILL NEVER GIVE US ANYTHING ! THEY STOLE OUR LAND WITH PROMISES, AND NOW THEY'RE LAUGHING AT US ! >
< THEY DON'T INTEND TO GIVE US THE SLIGHTEST THING IN RETURN FOR THE SOIL WHERE GENERATIONS OF OUR ANCESTORS SLEEP. NO -- WE'LL NEVER GET ANYTHING UNTIL WE TAKE MATTERS INTO OUR OWN HANDS AND FORCE THE GOVERNMENT TO GIVE US JUSTICE ! >
< THAT'S RIGHT ! >
< WE'LL HAVE TO FORCE THEM ! >
< WE HAVE TO PUT FEAR INTO THE HEARTS OF THESE POLITICIANS. THIS IS THE MÉTIS NAME THAT THEY STILL FEAR : RIEL ! >
RIEL !
RIEL !
< HE'S LIVING DOWN IN MONTANA NOW. >
IN THE CHURCH AT SAINT PETER'S MISSION, MONTANA -- SUNDAY, JUNE 4, 1884 :
< Mr RIEL, FOUR VISITORS HAVE ARRIVED, AND THEY WISH TO SEE YOU. >
MONSIEUR RIEL.
< YOU'VE TRAVELED FAR. >

< ALMOST 700 MILES. IT'S TAKEN US SEVENTEEN DAYS. >
< I DON'T KNOW YOU, BUT YOU SEEM TO KNOW ME. >
< DON'T YOU REMEMBER MEETING ME ? GABRIEL DUMONT. >
< OF COURSE ! IT'S BEEN SO MANY YEARS. IT'S GOOD TO SEE YOU. IF YOU'LL EXCUSE ME, THOUGH, I'D LIKE TO HEAR THE REST OF THE MASS. >
< PLEASE FEEL FREE TO WAIT FOR ME AT MY HOME. IT'S THE HOUSE OVER THERE BY THE SMALL BRIDGE. MY WIFE IS THERE, AND I'LL JOIN YOU SHORTLY. >
AFTER THE MASS :
< THIS IS MY BROTHER-IN-LAW, MOISE OUELLETTE -- >
< IT-IT'S AN HONOUR. >
< THANK YOU. >
< --THIS IS JAMES ISBISTER-- >
< A **GREAT** HONOUR, Mr RIEL. >
< A PLEASURE TO MEET YOU. >

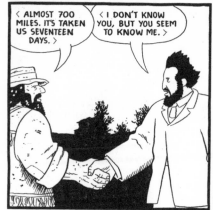

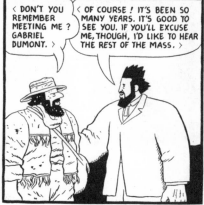

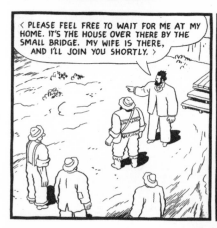

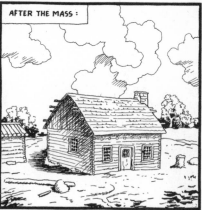

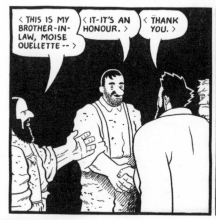

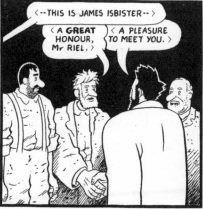

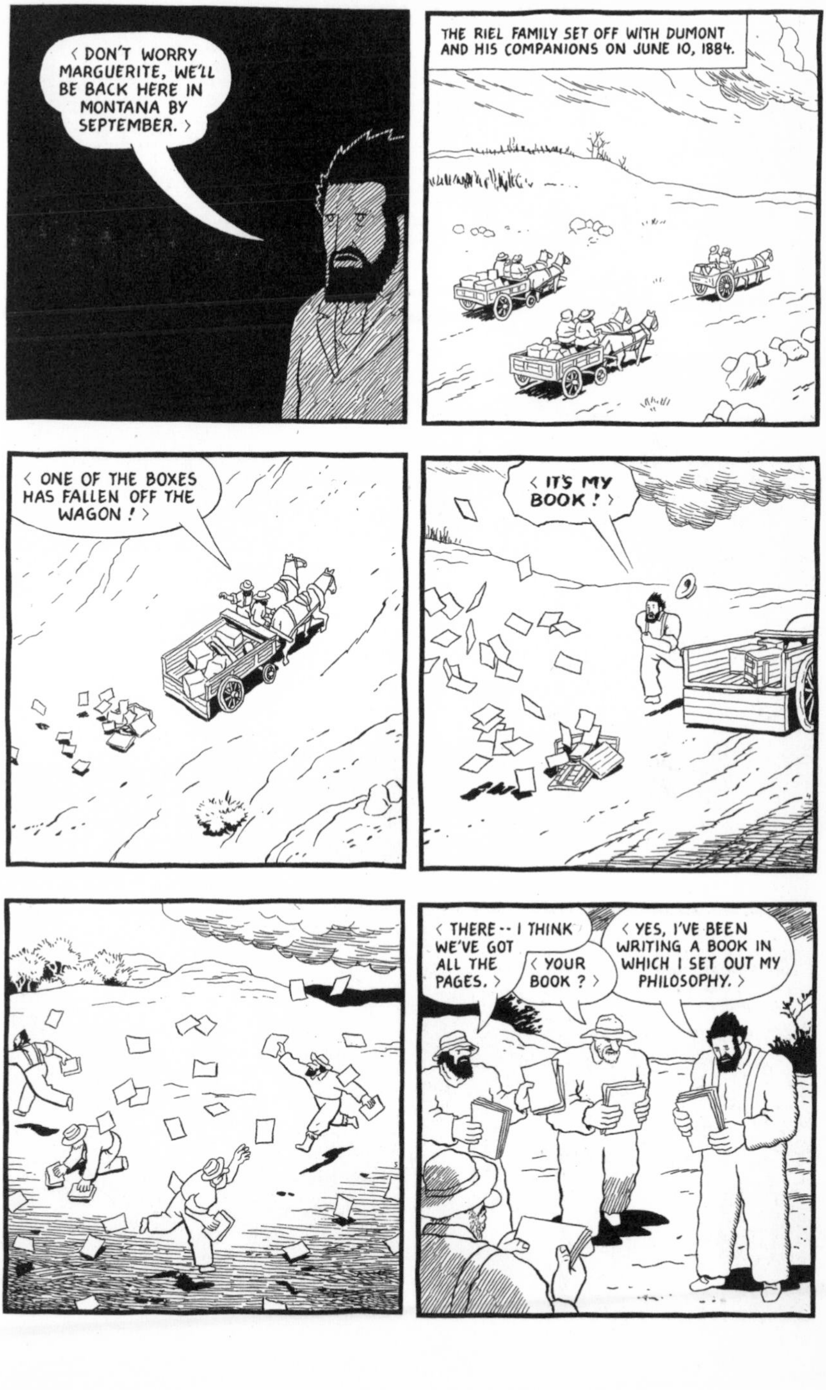
< DON'T WORRY MARGUERITE, WE'LL BE BACK HERE IN MONTANA BY SEPTEMBER. >
THE RIEL FAMILY SET OFF WITH DUMONT AND HIS COMPANIONS ON JUNE 10, 1884.
< ONE OF THE BOXES HAS FALLEN OFF THE WAGON ! >
< IT'S MY BOOK ! >
< THERE -- I THINK WE'VE GOT ALL THE PAGES. >
< YOUR BOOK ? >
< YES, I'VE BEEN WRITING A BOOK IN WHICH I SET OUT MY PHILOSOPHY. >

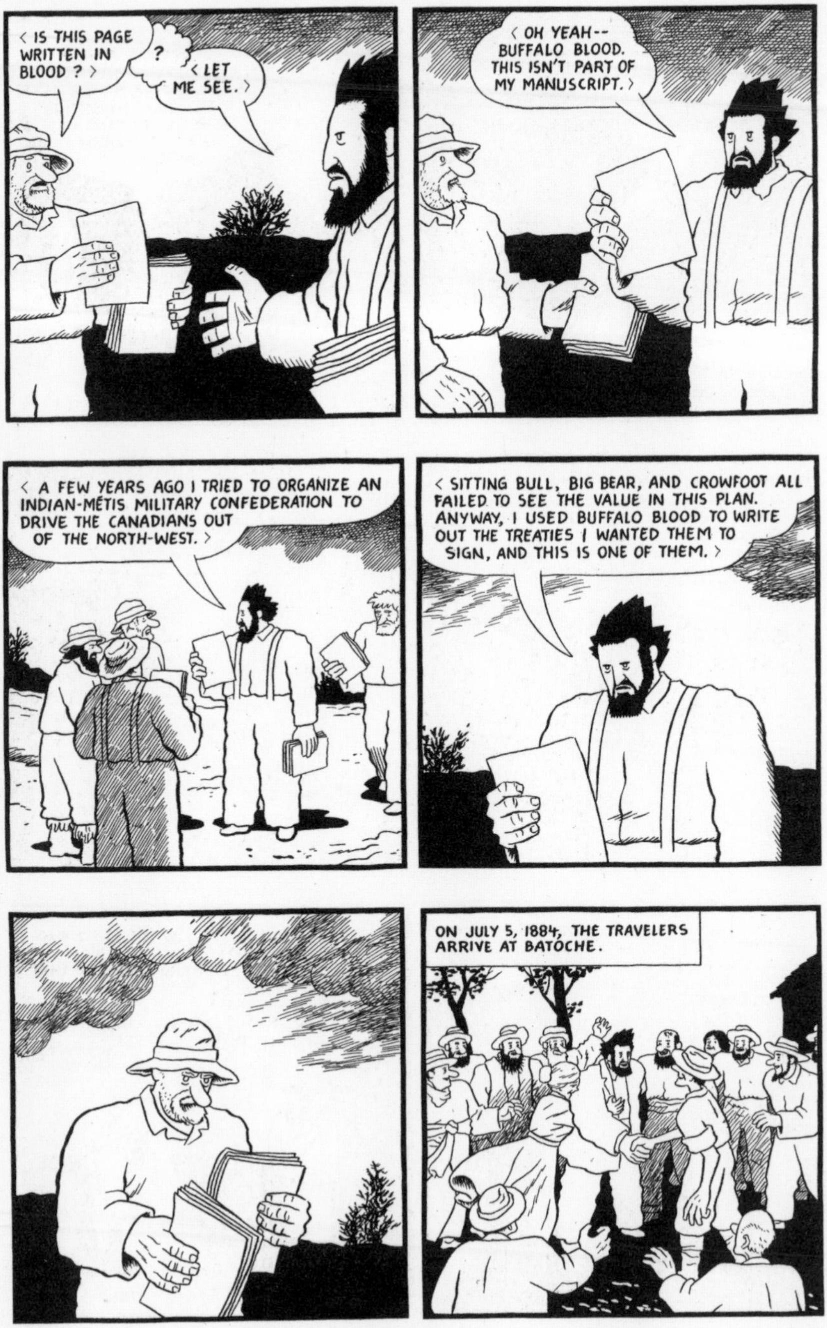
< IS THIS PAGE WRITTEN IN BLOOD ? >
?
< LET ME SEE. >
< OH YEAH-- BUFFALO BLOOD. THIS ISN'T PART OF MY MANUSCRIPT. >
< A FEW YEARS AGO I TRIED TO ORGANIZE AN INDIAN-MÉTIS MILITARY CONFEDERATION TO DRIVE THE CANADIANS OUT OF THE NORTH-WEST. >
< SITTING BULL, BIG BEAR, AND CROWFOOT ALL FAILED TO SEE THE VALUE IN THIS PLAN. ANYWAY, I USED BUFFALO BLOOD TO WRITE OUT THE TREATIES I WANTED THEM TO SIGN, AND THIS IS ONE OF THEM. >
ON JULY 5, 1884, THE TRAVELERS ARRIVE AT BATOCHE.

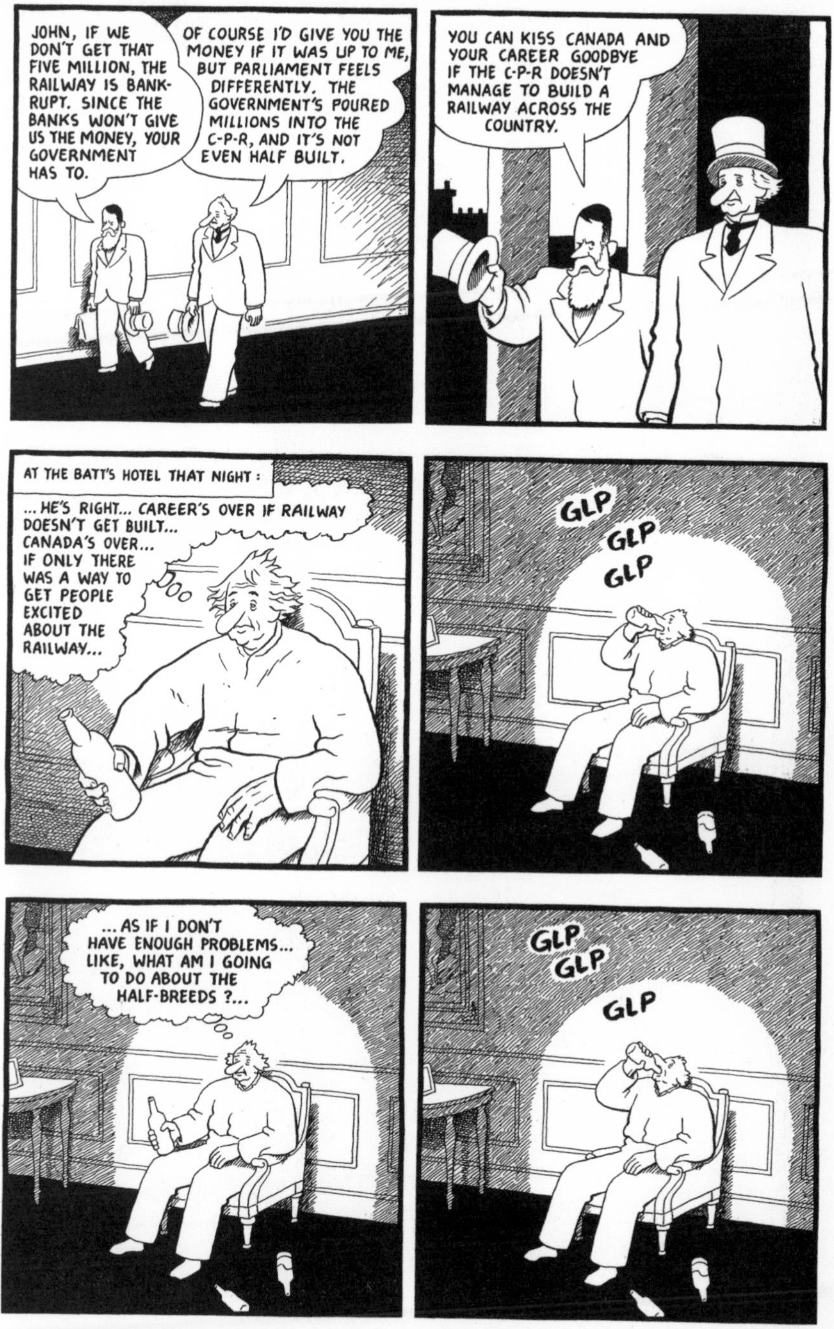
JOHN, IF WE DON'T GET THAT FIVE MILLION, THE RAILWAY IS BANK-RUPT. SINCE THE BANKS WON'T GIVE US THE MONEY, YOUR GOVERNMENT HAS TO.
OF COURSE I'D GIVE YOU THE MONEY IF IT WAS UP TO ME, BUT PARLIAMENT FEELS DIFFERENTLY. THE GOVERNMENT'S POURED MILLIONS INTO THE C-P-R, AND IT'S NOT EVEN HALF BUILT.
YOU CAN KISS CANADA AND YOUR CAREER GOODBYE IF THE C-P-R DOESN'T MANAGE TO BUILD A RAILWAY ACROSS THE COUNTRY.
AT THE BATT'S HOTEL THAT NIGHT:
... HE'S RIGHT... CAREER'S OVER IF RAILWAY DOESN'T GET BUILT... CANADA'S OVER... IF ONLY THERE WAS A WAY TO GET PEOPLE EXCITED ABOUT THE RAILWAY...
GLP
GLP
GLP
... AS IF I DON'T HAVE ENOUGH PROBLEMS... LIKE, WHAT AM I GOING TO DO ABOUT THE HALF-BREEDS ?...
GLP
GLP
GLP

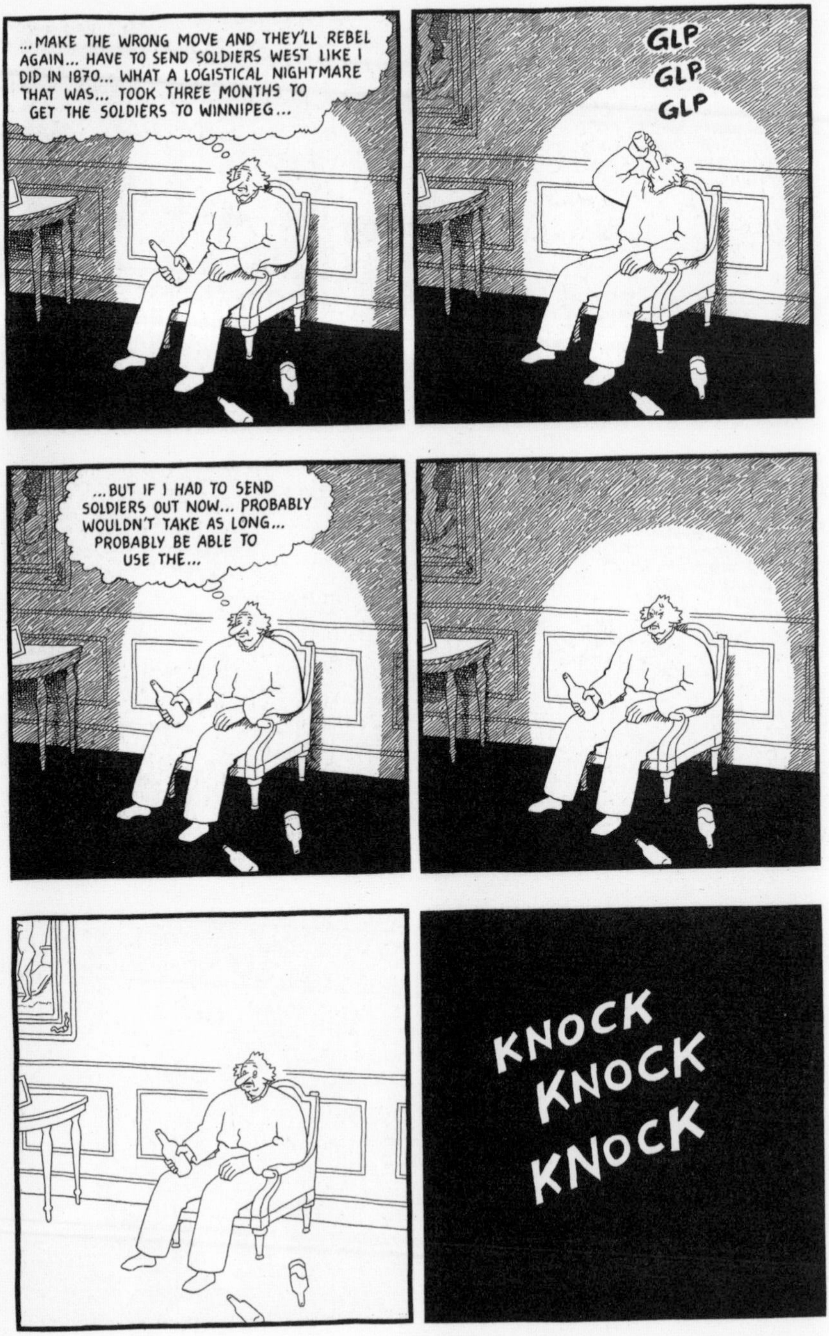
...MAKE THE WRONG MOVE AND THEY'LL REBEL AGAIN... HAVE TO SEND SOLDIERS WEST LIKE I DID IN 1870... WHAT A LOGISTICAL NIGHTMARE THAT WAS... TOOK THREE MONTHS TO GET THE SOLDIERS TO WINNIPEG...
GLP
GLP
GLP
...BUT IF I HAD TO SEND SOLDIERS OUT NOW... PROBABLY WOULDN'T TAKE AS LONG... PROBABLY BE ABLE TO USE THE...
KNOCK
KNOCK
KNOCK

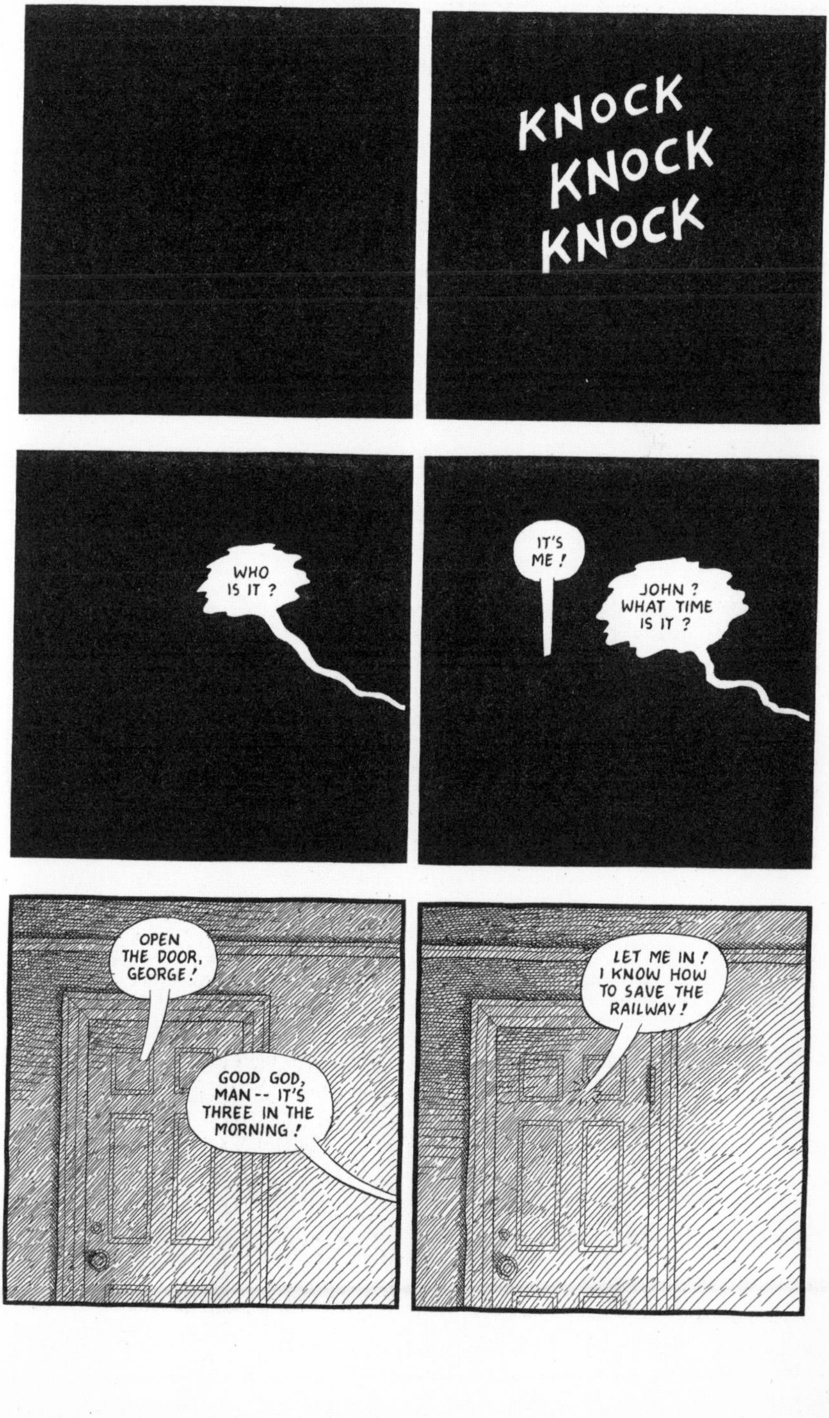
KNOCK
KNOCK
KNOCK
WHO IS IT ?
IT'S ME !
JOHN ? WHAT TIME IS IT ?
OPEN THE DOOR, GEORGE !
GOOD GOD, MAN -- IT'S THREE IN THE MORNING !
LET ME IN ! I KNOW HOW TO SAVE THE RAILWAY !

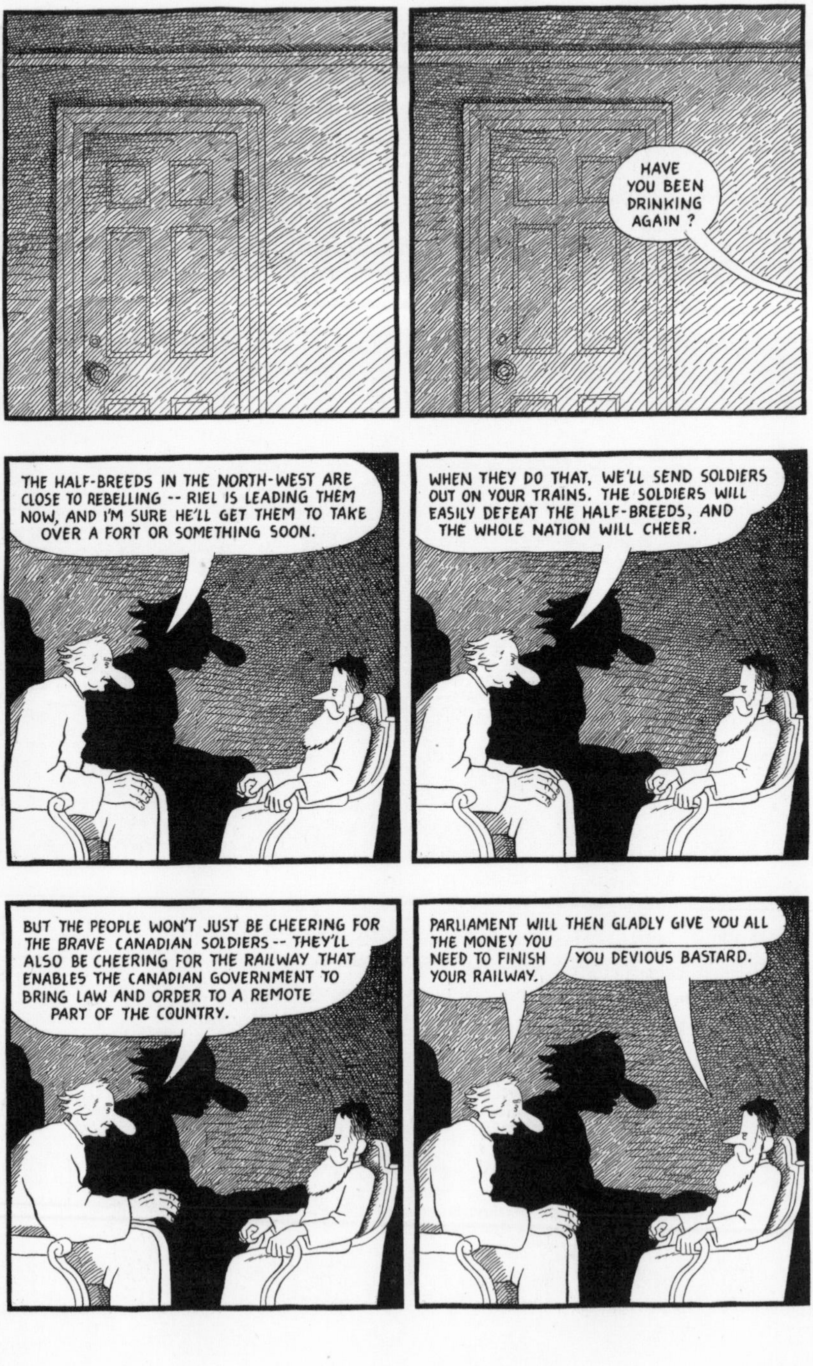
HAVE YOU BEEN DRINKING AGAIN ?
THE HALF-BREEDS IN THE NORTH-WEST ARE CLOSE TO REBELLING -- RIEL IS LEADING THEM NOW, AND I'M SURE HE'LL GET THEM TO TAKE OVER A FORT OR SOMETHING SOON.
WHEN THEY DO THAT, WE'LL SEND SOLDIERS OUT ON YOUR TRAINS. THE SOLDIERS WILL EASILY DEFEAT THE HALF-BREEDS, AND THE WHOLE NATION WILL CHEER.
BUT THE PEOPLE WON'T JUST BE CHEERING FOR THE BRAVE CANADIAN SOLDIERS -- THEY'LL ALSO BE CHEERING FOR THE RAILWAY THAT ENABLES THE CANADIAN GOVERNMENT TO BRING LAW AND ORDER TO A REMOTE PART OF THE COUNTRY.
PARLIAMENT WILL THEN GLADLY GIVE YOU ALL THE MONEY YOU NEED TO FINISH YOUR RAILWAY.
YOU DEVIOUS BASTARD.

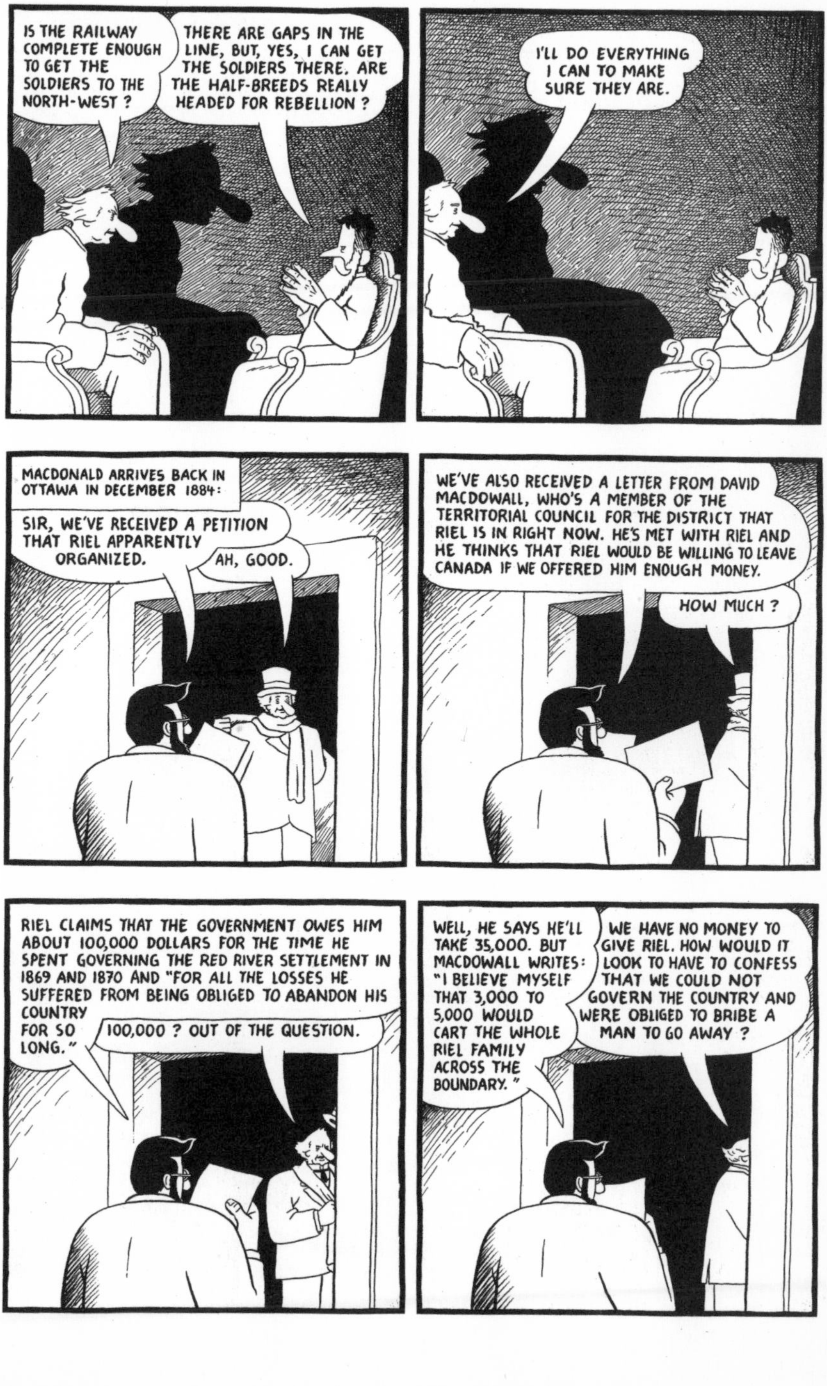
IS THE RAILWAY COMPLETE ENOUGH TO GET THE SOLDIERS TO THE NORTH-WEST ?
THERE ARE GAPS IN THE LINE, BUT, YES, I CAN GET THE SOLDIERS THERE. ARE THE HALF-BREEDS REALLY HEADED FOR REBELLION ?
I'LL DO EVERYTHING I CAN TO MAKE SURE THEY ARE.
MACDONALD ARRIVES BACK IN OTTAWA IN DECEMBER 1884:
SIR, WE'VE RECEIVED A PETITION THAT RIEL APPARENTLY ORGANIZED.
AH, GOOD.
WE'VE ALSO RECEIVED A LETTER FROM DAVID MACDOWALL, WHO'S A MEMBER OF THE TERRITORIAL COUNCIL FOR THE DISTRICT THAT RIEL IS IN RIGHT NOW. HE'S MET WITH RIEL AND HE THINKS THAT RIEL WOULD BE WILLING TO LEAVE CANADA IF WE OFFERED HIM ENOUGH MONEY.
HOW MUCH ?
RIEL CLAIMS THAT THE GOVERNMENT OWES HIM ABOUT 100,000 DOLLARS FOR THE TIME HE SPENT GOVERNING THE RED RIVER SETTLEMENT IN 1869 AND 1870 AND "FOR ALL THE LOSSES HE SUFFERED FROM BEING OBLIGED TO ABANDON HIS COUNTRY FOR SO LONG."
100,000 ? OUT OF THE QUESTION.
WELL, HE SAYS HE'LL TAKE 35,000. BUT MACDOWALL WRITES: "I BELIEVE MYSELF THAT 3,000 TO 5,000 WOULD CART THE WHOLE RIEL FAMILY ACROSS THE BOUNDARY."
WE HAVE NO MONEY TO GIVE RIEL. HOW WOULD IT LOOK TO HAVE TO CONFESS THAT WE COULD NOT GOVERN THE COUNTRY AND WERE OBLIGED TO BRIBE A MAN TO GO AWAY ?

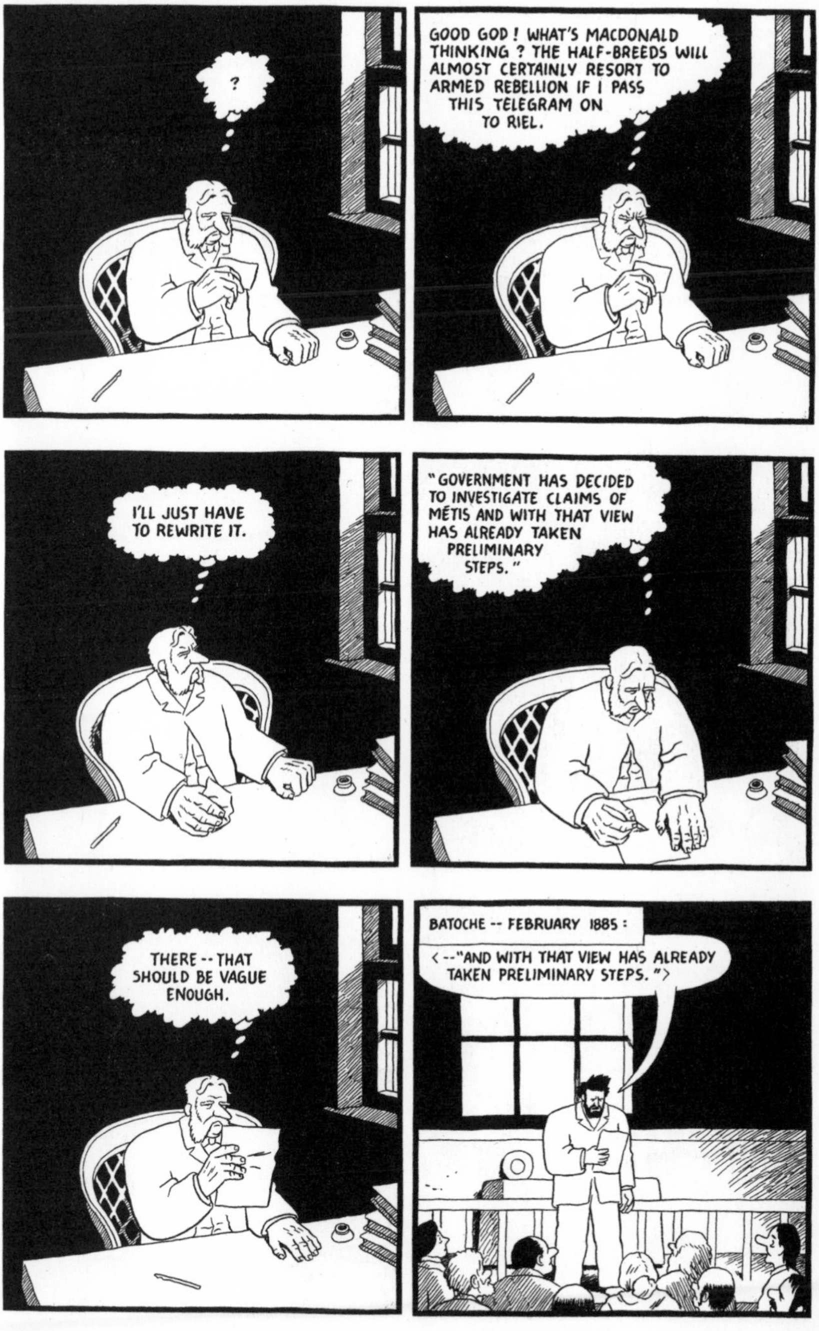
?
GOOD GOD! WHAT'S MACDONALD THINKING? THE HALF-BREEDS WILL ALMOST CERTAINLY RESORT TO ARMED REBELLION IF I PASS THIS TELEGRAM ON TO RIEL.
I'LL JUST HAVE TO REWRITE IT.
"GOVERNMENT HAS DECIDED TO INVESTIGATE CLAIMS OF MÉTIS AND WITH THAT VIEW HAS ALREADY TAKEN PRELIMINARY STEPS."
THERE -- THAT SHOULD BE VAGUE ENOUGH.
BATOCHE -- FEBRUARY 1885:
< --"AND WITH THAT VIEW HAS ALREADY TAKEN PRELIMINARY STEPS.">

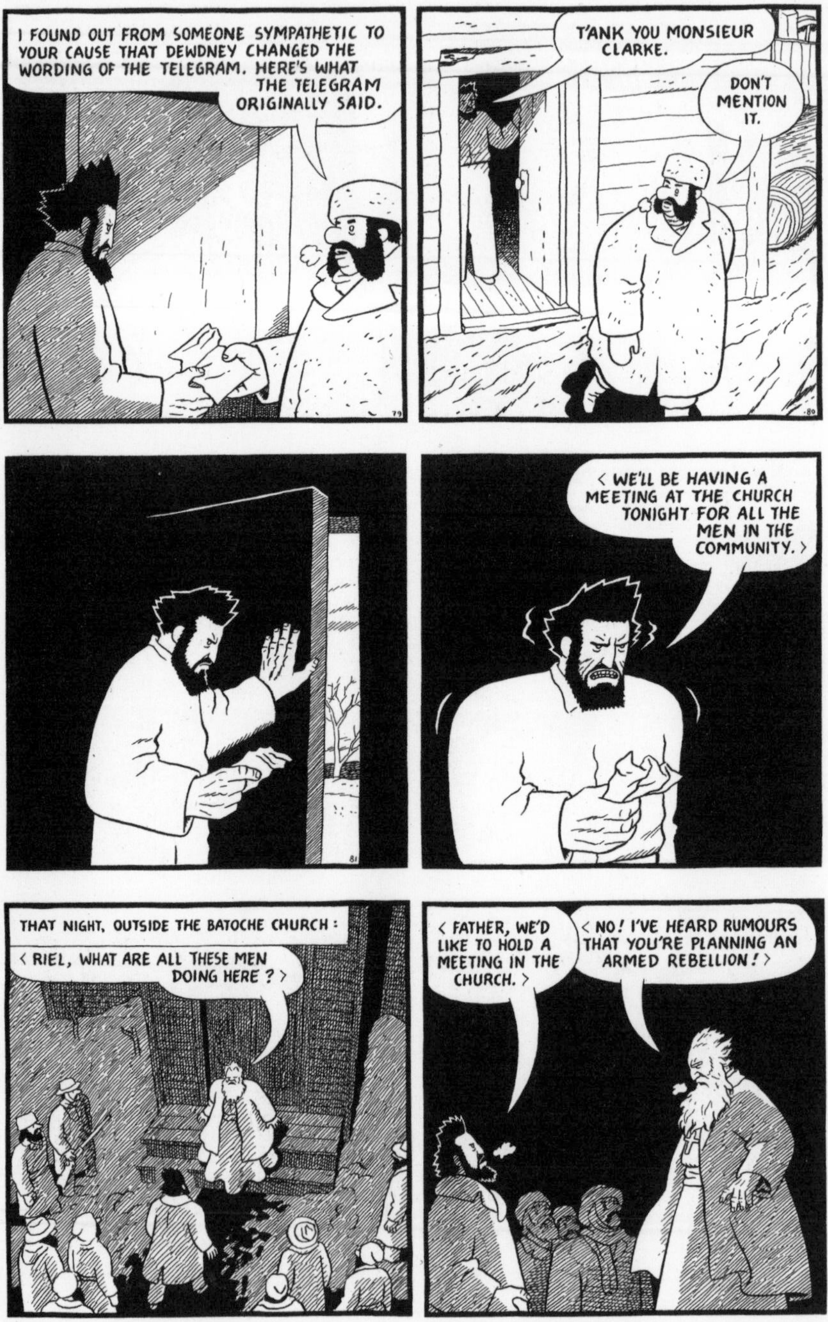
I FOUND OUT FROM SOMEONE SYMPATHETIC TO YOUR CAUSE THAT DEWDNEY CHANGED THE WORDING OF THE TELEGRAM. HERE'S WHAT THE TELEGRAM ORIGINALLY SAID.
T'ANK YOU MONSIEUR CLARKE.
DON'T MENTION IT.
< WE'LL BE HAVING A MEETING AT THE CHURCH TONIGHT FOR ALL THE MEN IN THE COMMUNITY. >
THAT NIGHT, OUTSIDE THE BATOCHE CHURCH:
< RIEL, WHAT ARE ALL THESE MEN DOING HERE? >
< FATHER, WE'D LIKE TO HOLD A MEETING IN THE CHURCH. >
< NO! I'VE HEARD RUMOURS THAT YOU'RE PLANNING AN ARMED REBELLION! >

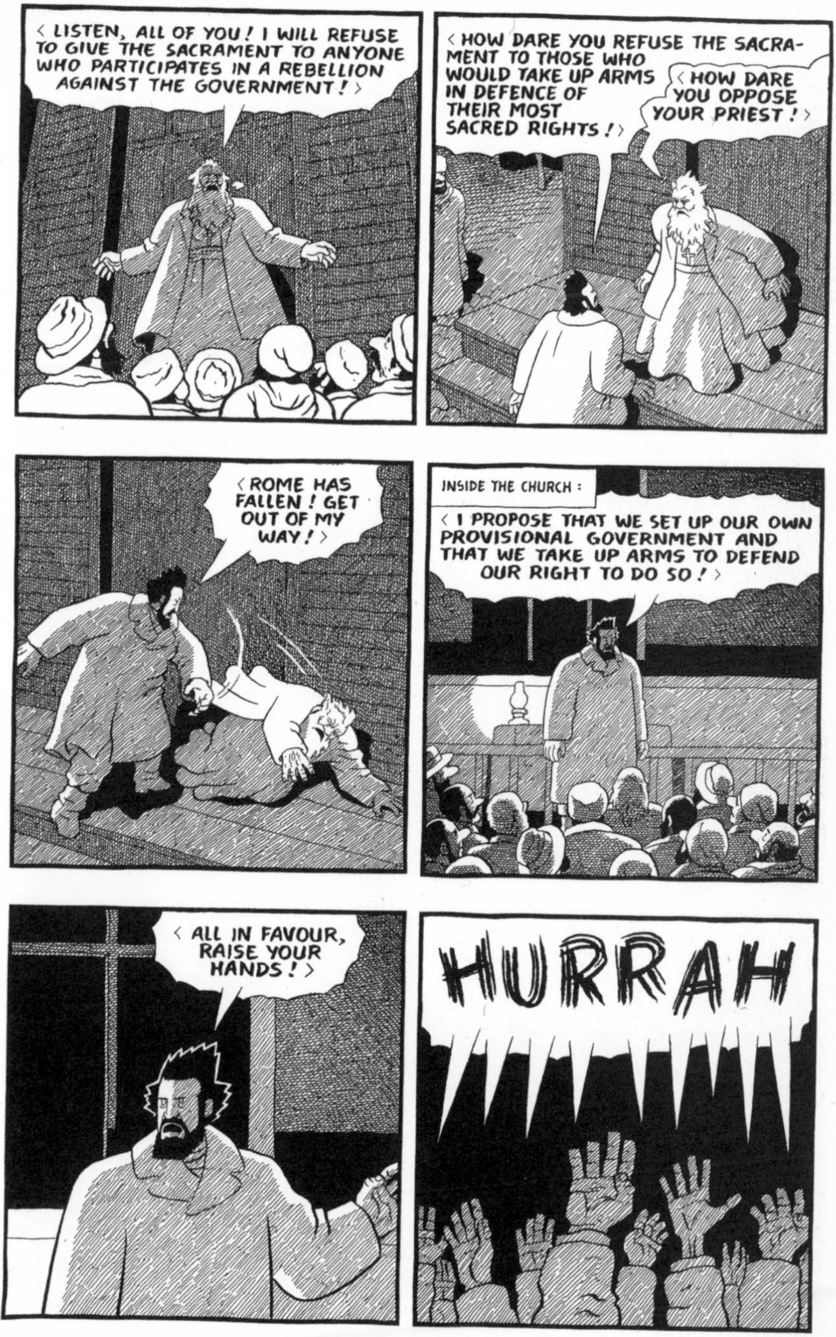

< LISTEN, ALL OF YOU! I WILL REFUSE TO GIVE THE SACRAMENT TO ANYONE WHO PARTICIPATES IN A REBELLION AGAINST THE GOVERNMENT! >
< HOW DARE YOU REFUSE THE SACRAMENT TO THOSE WHO WOULD TAKE UP ARMS IN DEFENCE OF THEIR MOST SACRED RIGHTS! >
< HOW DARE YOU OPPOSE YOUR PRIEST! >
< ROME HAS FALLEN! GET OUT OF MY WAY! >
INSIDE THE CHURCH:
< I PROPOSE THAT WE SET UP OUR OWN PROVISIONAL GOVERNMENT AND THAT WE TAKE UP ARMS TO DEFEND OUR RIGHT TO DO SO! >
< ALL IN FAVOUR, RAISE YOUR HANDS! >
HURRAH

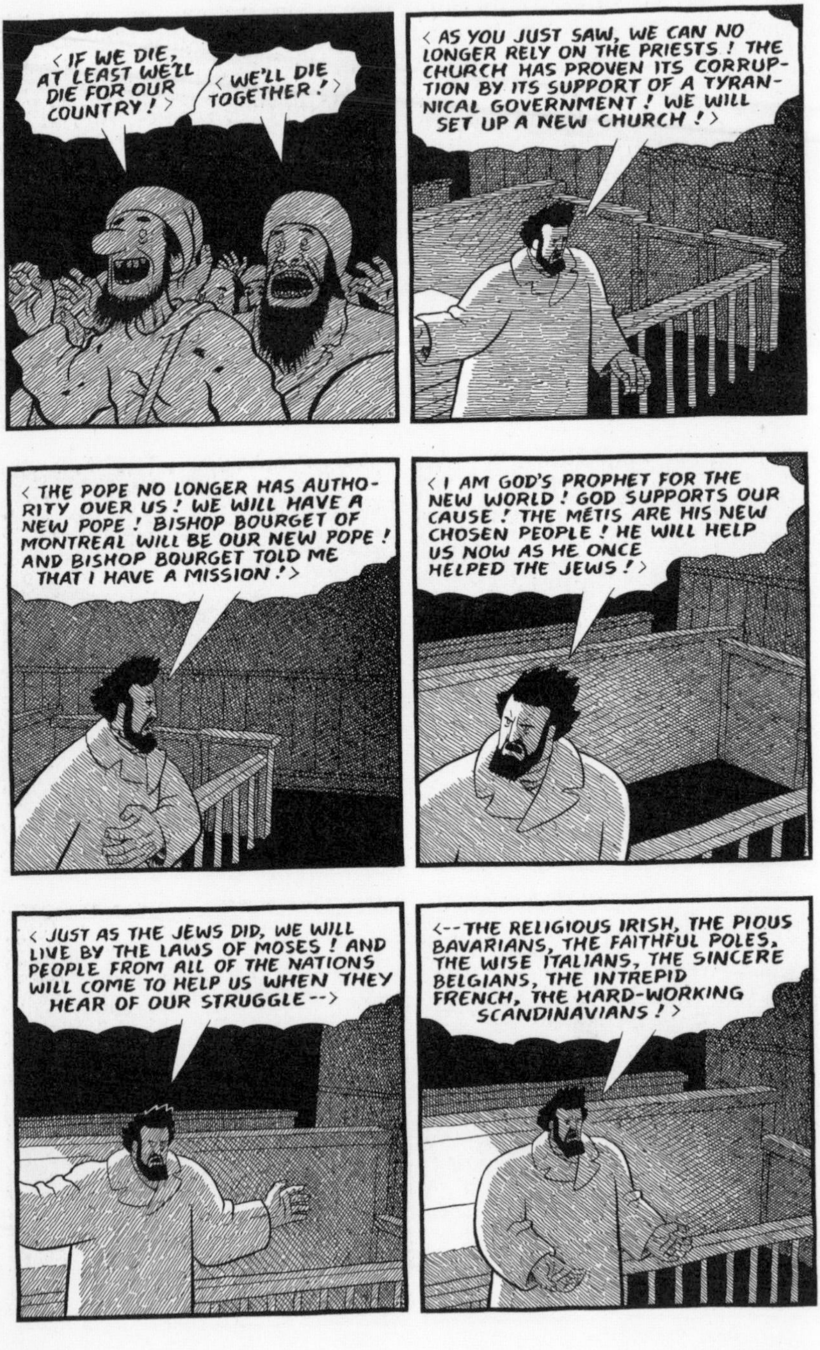
< IF WE DIE, AT LEAST WE'LL DIE FOR OUR COUNTRY! >
< WE'LL DIE TOGETHER! >
< AS YOU JUST SAW, WE CAN NO LONGER RELY ON THE PRIESTS! THE CHURCH HAS PROVEN ITS CORRUPTION BY ITS SUPPORT OF A TYRANNICAL GOVERNMENT! WE WILL SET UP A NEW CHURCH! >
< THE POPE NO LONGER HAS AUTHORITY OVER US! WE WILL HAVE A NEW POPE! BISHOP BOURGET OF MONTREAL WILL BE OUR NEW POPE! AND BISHOP BOURGET TOLD ME THAT I HAVE A MISSION! >
< I AM GOD'S PROPHET FOR THE NEW WORLD! GOD SUPPORTS OUR CAUSE! THE MÉTIS ARE HIS NEW CHOSEN PEOPLE! HE WILL HELP US NOW AS HE ONCE HELPED THE JEWS! >
< JUST AS THE JEWS DID, WE WILL LIVE BY THE LAWS OF MOSES! AND PEOPLE FROM ALL OF THE NATIONS WILL COME TO HELP US WHEN THEY HEAR OF OUR STRUGGLE-->
<--THE RELIGIOUS IRISH, THE PIOUS BAVARIANS, THE FAITHFUL POLES, THE WISE ITALIANS, THE SINCERE BELGIANS, THE INTREPID FRENCH, THE HARD-WORKING SCANDINAVIANS! >

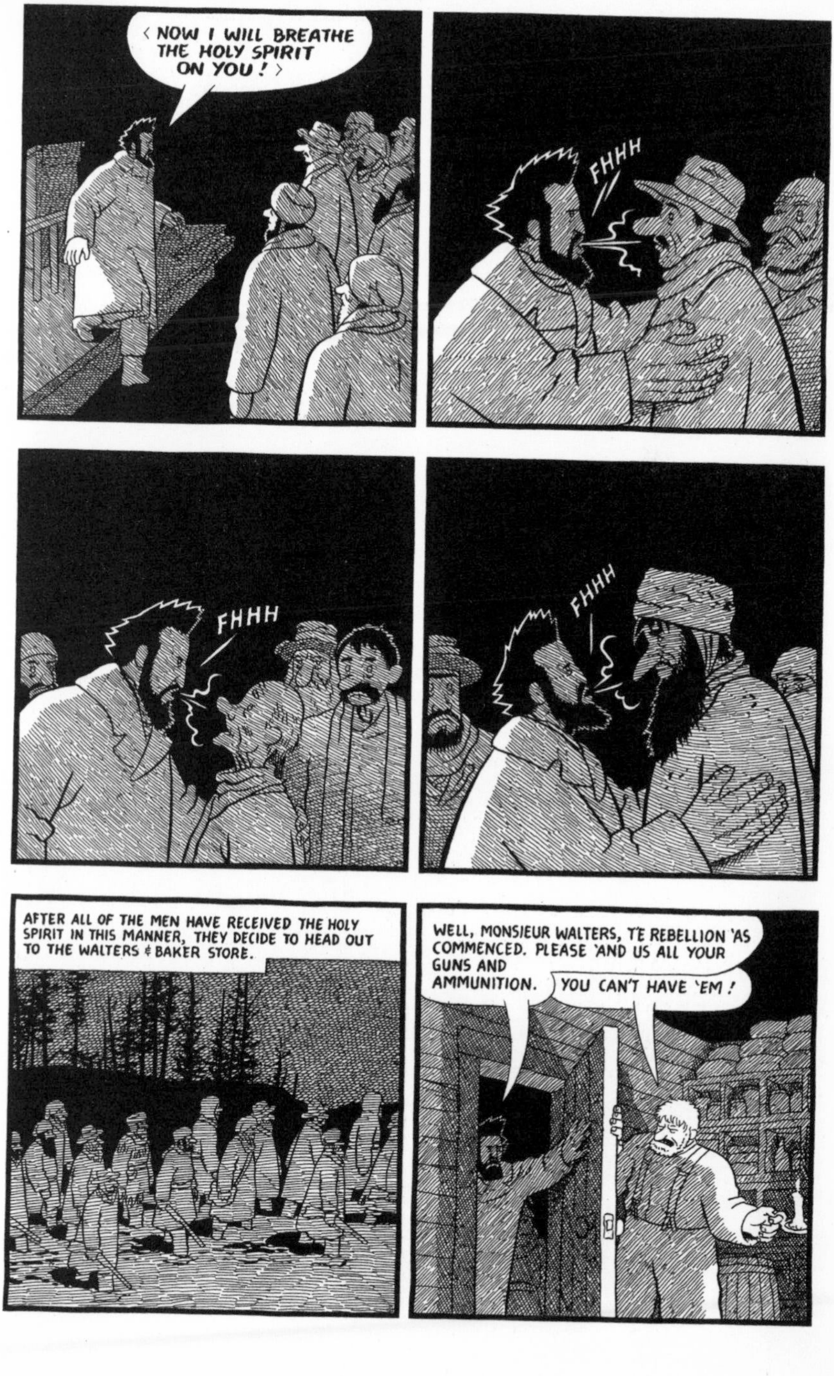
< NOW I WILL BREATHE THE HOLY SPIRIT ON YOU ! >
FHHH
FHHH
FHHH
AFTER ALL OF THE MEN HAVE RECEIVED THE HOLY SPIRIT IN THIS MANNER, THEY DECIDE TO HEAD OUT TO THE WALTERS & BAKER STORE.
WELL, MONSIEUR WALTERS, T'E REBELLION 'AS COMMENCED. PLEASE 'AND US ALL YOUR GUNS AND AMMUNITION.
YOU CAN'T HAVE 'EM !

MARCH 25, 1885:

KNOCK KNOCK

< YEAH ? >

< CHARLES NOLIN, YOU'RE UNDER ARREST IN THE NAME OF THE EXOVEDATE. YOU MUST COME WITH US NOW. >

< HERE HE IS. >

< WHAT'S THIS ABOUT NOT WANTING TO BE PART OF THE EXOVEDATE ? >

< WHAT'S THE EXOVEDATE ? >

< IT'S THE NAME OF OUR GOVERNMENT -- IT MEANS "OUT OF THE FLOCK" IN LATIN. WE DECIDED ON IT YESTERDAY. >

< I DON'T WANT TO BE INVOLVED IN YOUR REBELLION. I'VE BECOME SOMEWHAT WEALTHY IN THE LAST FEW YEARS, AND I'VE GOT NO INTEREST IN LOSING IT ALL. >

< CHARLES, YOU'RE EITHER WITH US OR YOU'RE AGAINST US. IF YOU'RE AGAINST US, WE'LL HAVE TO TRY YOU FOR TREASON, AND THE PUNISHMENT IS DEATH IF YOU'RE FOUND GUILTY. >

< WELL... uh... I GUESS I'M WITH YOU THEN. >

< GENTLEMEN, WELCOME THE NEWEST MEMBER OF THE EXOVEDATE. >

< HEY NOLIN. >

< THAT'S GREAT. >

≥ Heh ≤

< ANYWAY, WE NEED MORE GUNS AND AMMU-NITION. I WANT TO TAKE TEN MEN AND GO OVER TO MITCHELL'S STORE BY DUCK LAKE AND SEE IF THERE ARE ANY GUNS THERE. >

< DUCK LAKE IS CLOSE TO FORT CARLTON -- YOU MIGHT RUN INTO THE POLICE. >

< ARE WE REBELLING OR NOT ? SOONER OR LATER WE'RE GOING TO HAVE TO FACE THE POLICE. >

< OKAY, GO -- BUT, IF YOU DO COME ACROSS SOME MOUNTIES, DON'T FIRE UNLESS THEY SHOOT FIRST. >

THE NEXT MORNING -- MARCH 26, 1885 -- AT MITCHELL'S STORE :

< IT'S DESERTED. >

< NO AMMUNITION. >

< I DON'T SEE ANY GUNS. >

H. MITCHELL

< WORD THAT WE'RE REBELLING HAS GOTTEN OUT. MITCHELL'S PROBABLY HIDING OVER IN FORT CARLTON ALONG WITH HIS GUNS. >

GABRIEL...

< WHAT ? >

< TWO MOUNTIES ARE RIDING UP. I GUESS THEY SEE ALL THE HORSES AND ARE WONDERING WHO WE ARE AND WHAT WE'RE DOING HERE. >

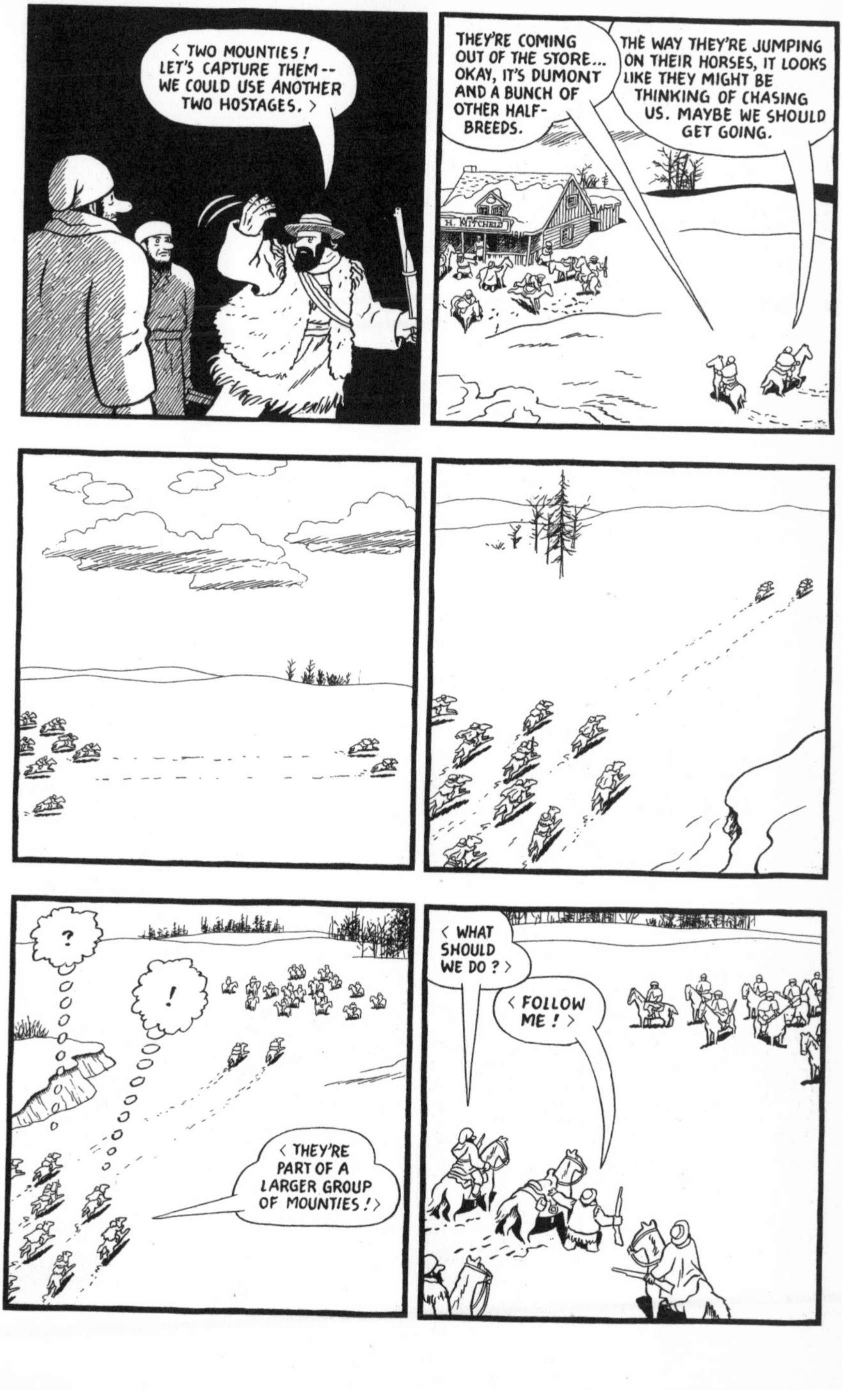
< TWO MOUNTIES! LET'S CAPTURE THEM -- WE COULD USE ANOTHER TWO HOSTAGES. >
THEY'RE COMING OUT OF THE STORE... OKAY, IT'S DUMONT AND A BUNCH OF OTHER HALF-BREEDS.
THE WAY THEY'RE JUMPING ON THEIR HORSES, IT LOOKS LIKE THEY MIGHT BE THINKING OF CHASING US. MAYBE WE SHOULD GET GOING.
H. MITCHELL
?
!
< THEY'RE PART OF A LARGER GROUP OF MOUNTIES! >
< WHAT SHOULD WE DO? >
< FOLLOW ME! >

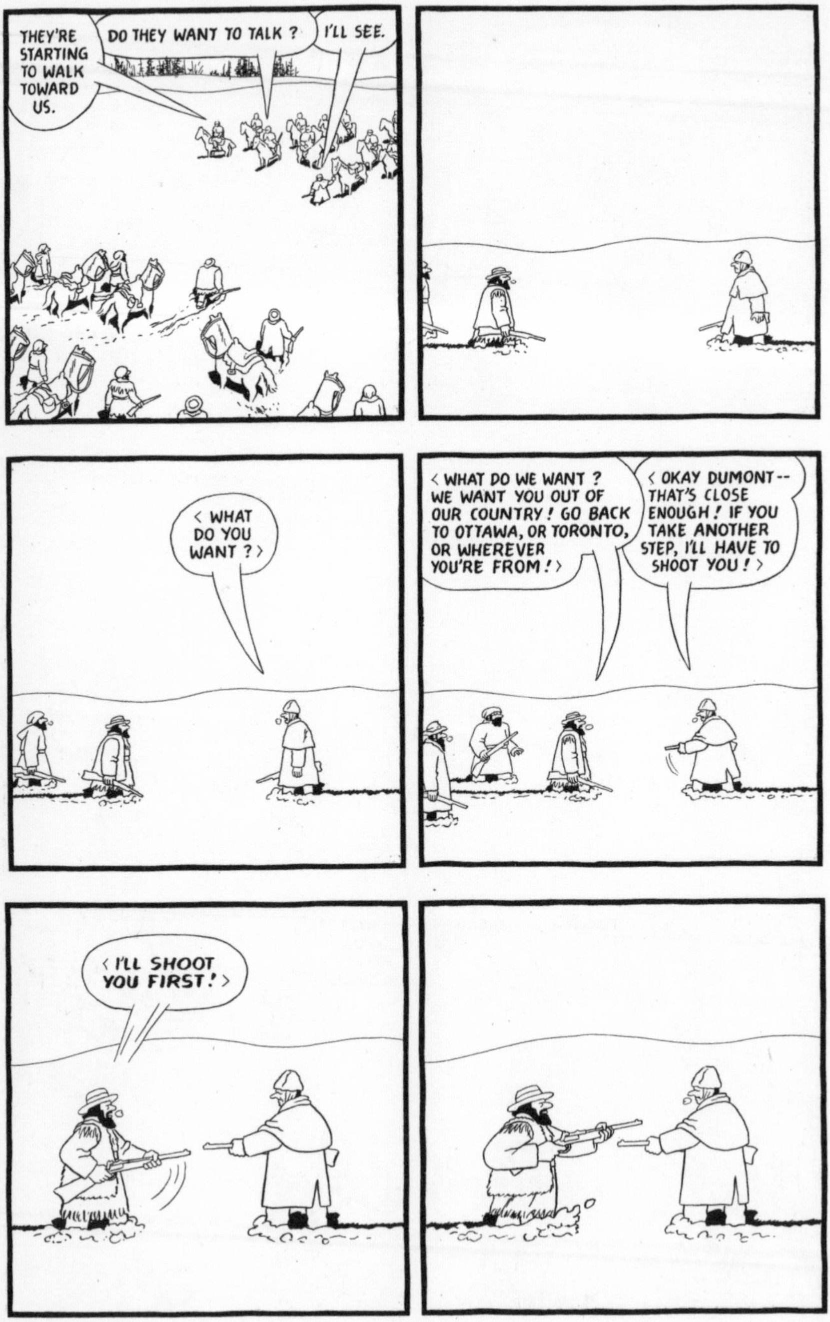
THEY'RE STARTING TO WALK TOWARD US.
DO THEY WANT TO TALK ?
I'LL SEE.
< WHAT DO YOU WANT ? >
< WHAT DO WE WANT ? WE WANT YOU OUT OF OUR COUNTRY ! GO BACK TO OTTAWA, OR TORONTO, OR WHEREVER YOU'RE FROM ! >
< OKAY DUMONT -- THAT'S CLOSE ENOUGH ! IF YOU TAKE ANOTHER STEP, I'LL HAVE TO SHOOT YOU ! >
< I'LL SHOOT YOU FIRST ! >

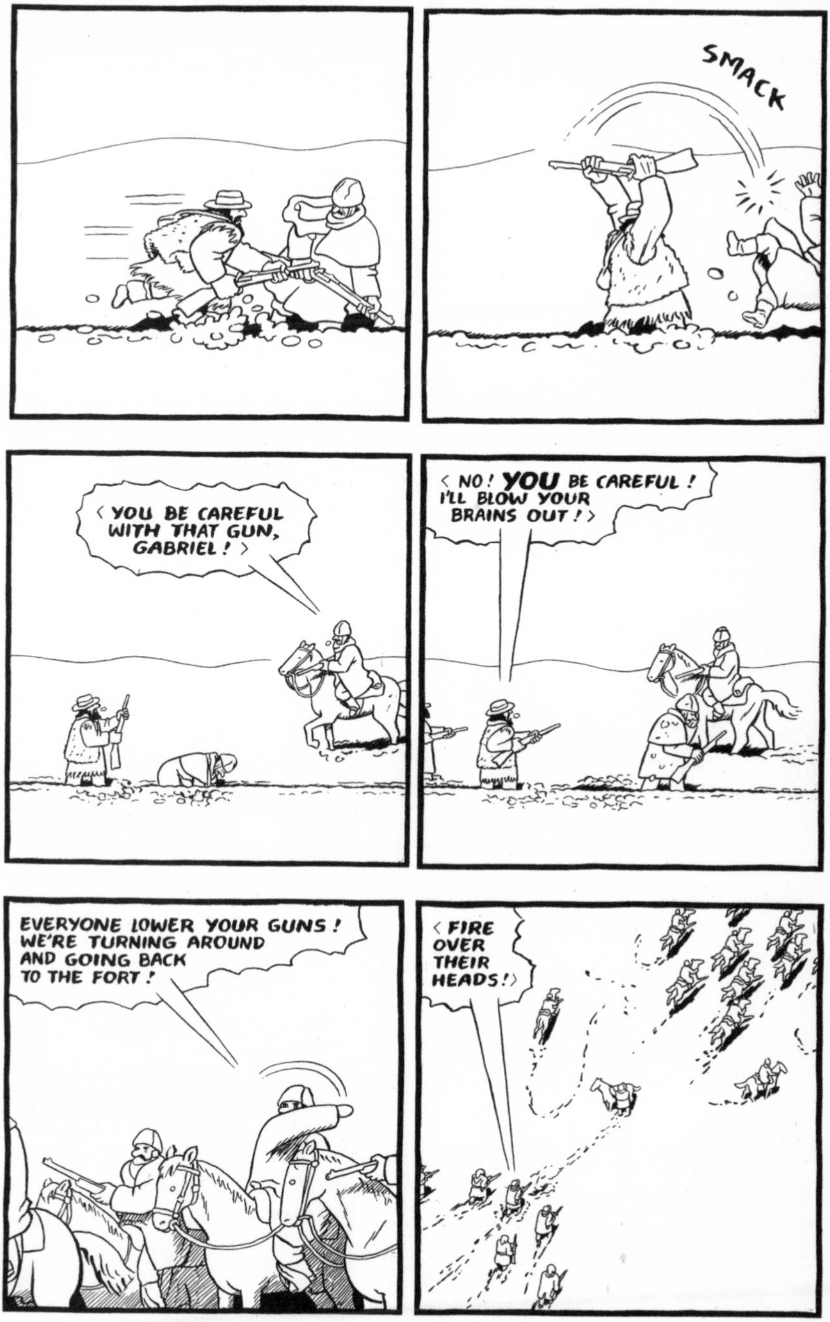
SMACK
< YOU BE CAREFUL WITH THAT GUN, GABRIEL! >
< NO! YOU BE CAREFUL! I'LL BLOW YOUR BRAINS OUT! >
EVERYONE LOWER YOUR GUNS! WE'RE TURNING AROUND AND GOING BACK TO THE FORT!
< FIRE OVER THEIR HEADS! >

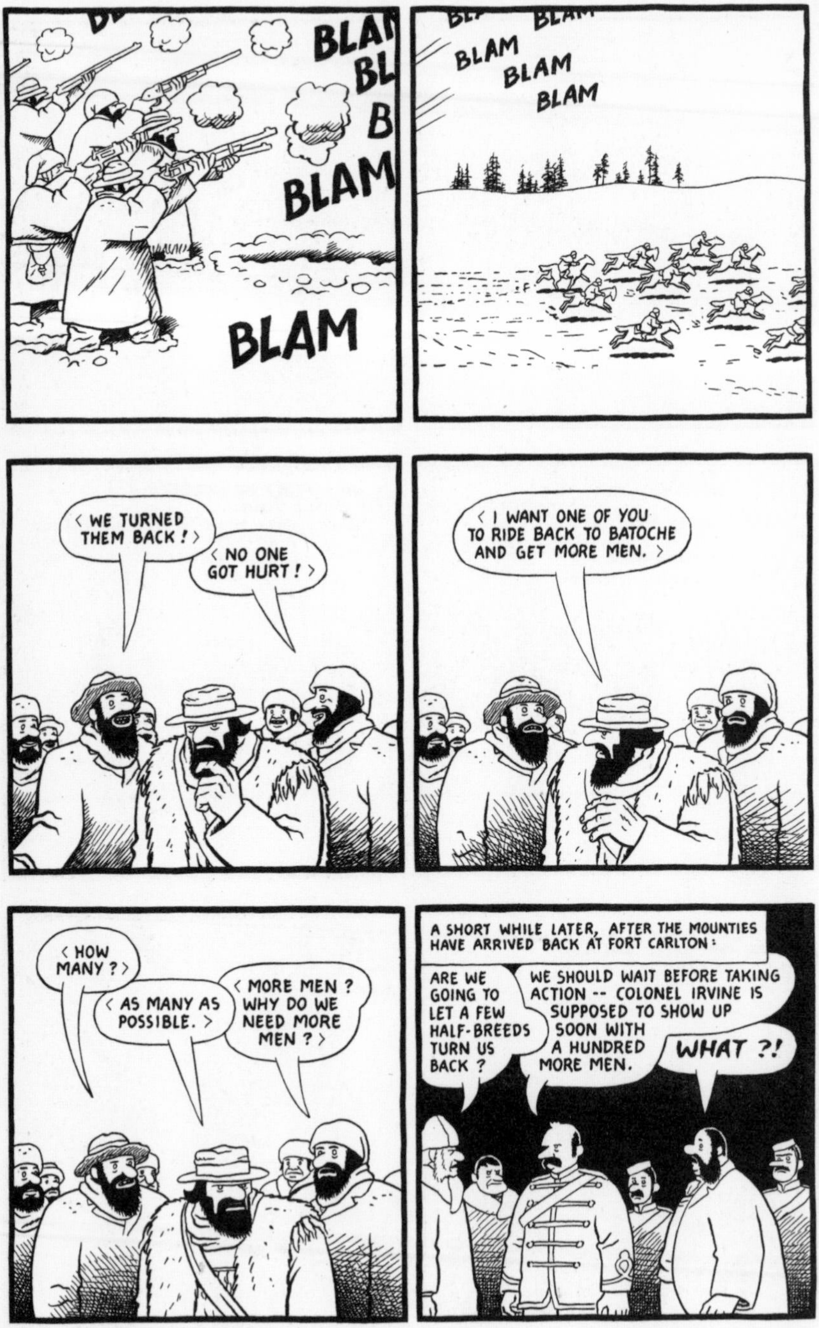
BLAM
BLAM
BLAM
BLAM
BLAM
< WE TURNED THEM BACK! >
< NO ONE GOT HURT! >
< I WANT ONE OF YOU TO RIDE BACK TO BATOCHE AND GET MORE MEN. >
< HOW MANY? >
< AS MANY AS POSSIBLE. >
< MORE MEN? WHY DO WE NEED MORE MEN? >
A SHORT WHILE LATER, AFTER THE MOUNTIES HAVE ARRIVED BACK AT FORT CARLTON:
ARE WE GOING TO LET A FEW HALF-BREEDS TURN US BACK?
WE SHOULD WAIT BEFORE TAKING ACTION -- COLONEL IRVINE IS SUPPOSED TO SHOW UP SOON WITH A HUNDRED MORE MEN.
WHAT?!

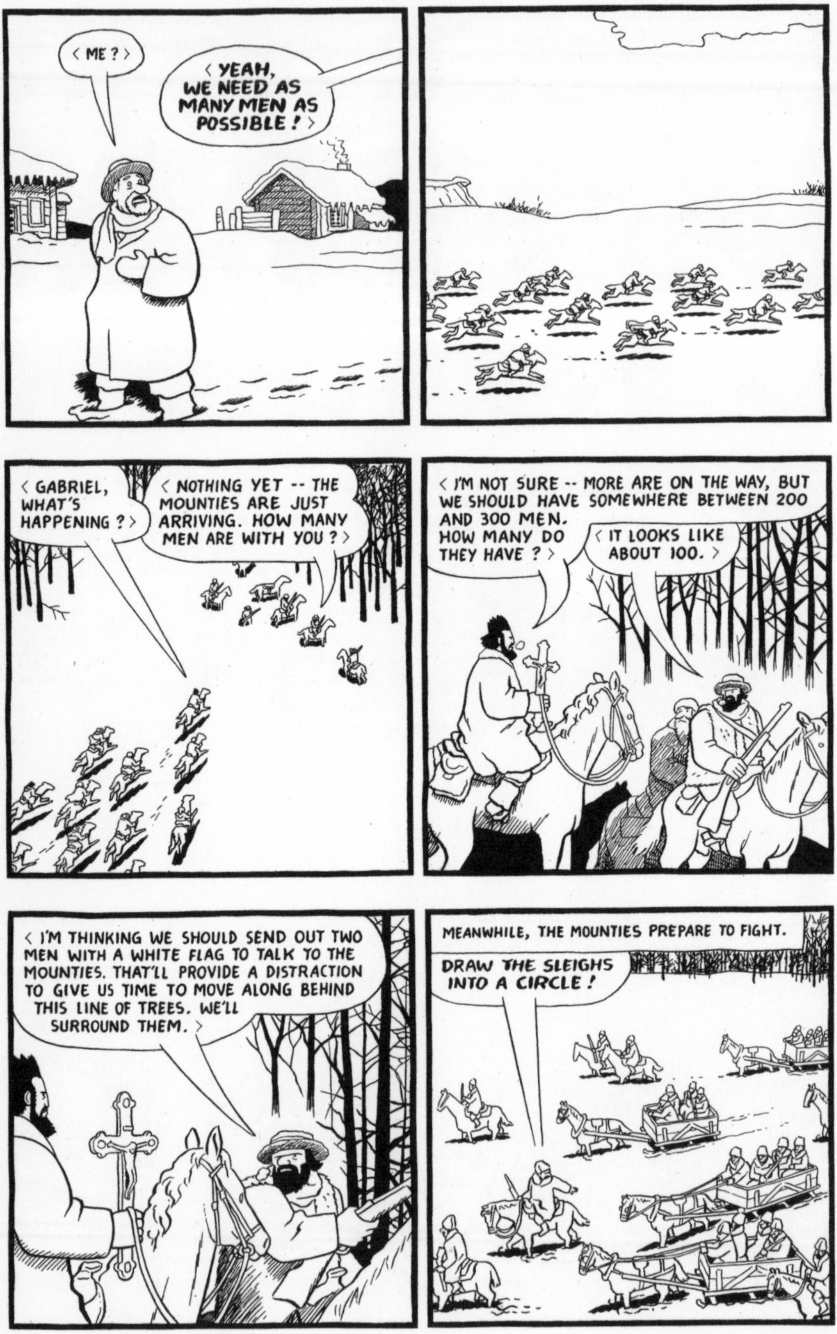
< ME ? >
< YEAH, WE NEED AS MANY MEN AS POSSIBLE ! >
< GABRIEL, WHAT'S HAPPENING ? >
< NOTHING YET -- THE MOUNTIES ARE JUST ARRIVING. HOW MANY MEN ARE WITH YOU ? >
< I'M NOT SURE -- MORE ARE ON THE WAY, BUT WE SHOULD HAVE SOMEWHERE BETWEEN 200 AND 300 MEN. HOW MANY DO THEY HAVE ? >
< IT LOOKS LIKE ABOUT 100. >
< I'M THINKING WE SHOULD SEND OUT TWO MEN WITH A WHITE FLAG TO TALK TO THE MOUNTIES. THAT'LL PROVIDE A DISTRACTION TO GIVE US TIME TO MOVE ALONG BEHIND THIS LINE OF TREES. WE'LL SURROUND THEM. >
MEANWHILE, THE MOUNTIES PREPARE TO FIGHT.
DRAW THE SLEIGHS INTO A CIRCLE !

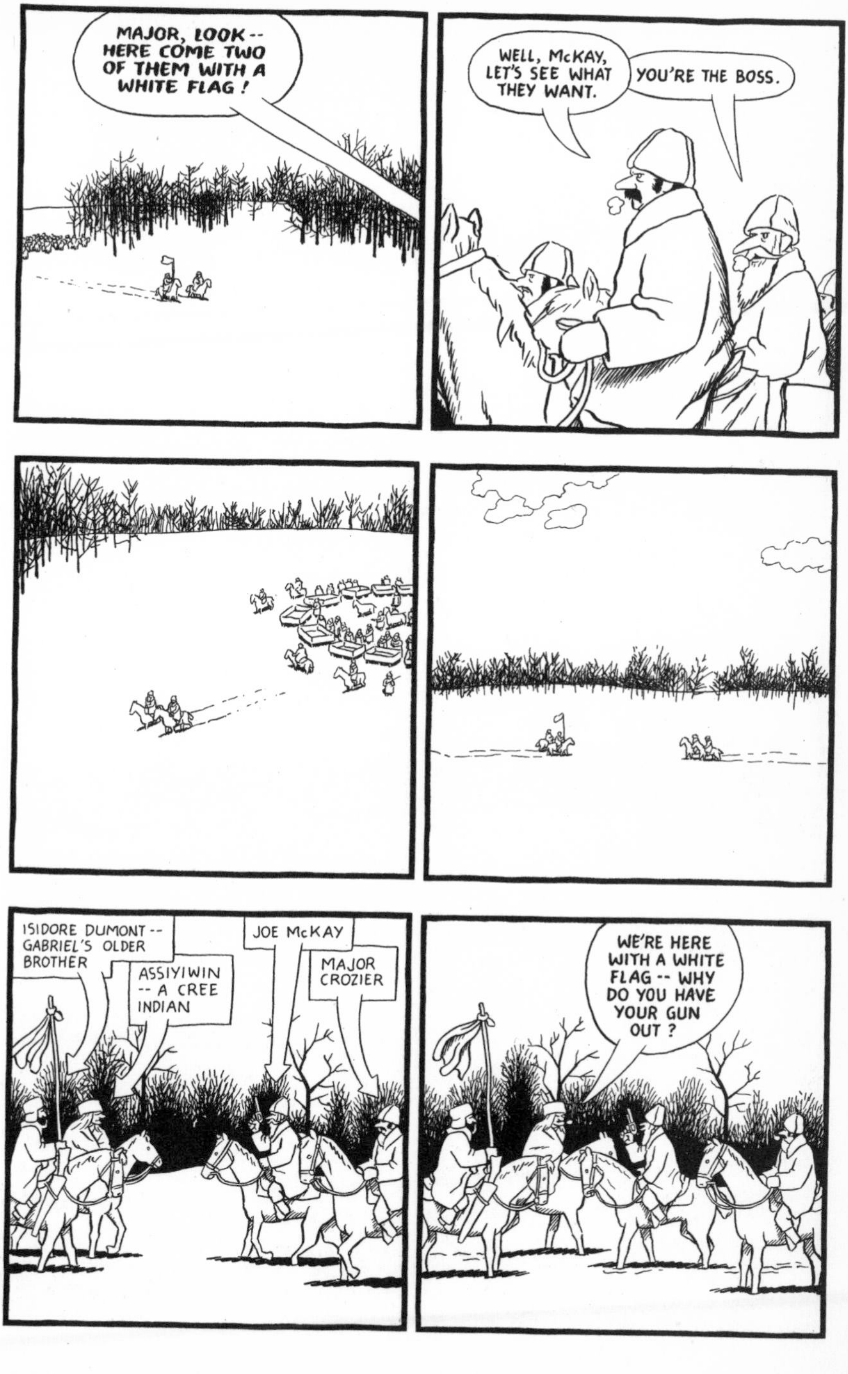
MAJOR, LOOK -- HERE COME TWO OF THEM WITH A WHITE FLAG !
WELL, McKAY, LET'S SEE WHAT THEY WANT.
YOU'RE THE BOSS.
ISIDORE DUMONT -- GABRIEL'S OLDER BROTHER
ASSIYIWIN -- A CREE INDIAN
JOE McKAY
MAJOR CROZIER
WE'RE HERE WITH A WHITE FLAG -- WHY DO YOU HAVE YOUR GUN OUT ?

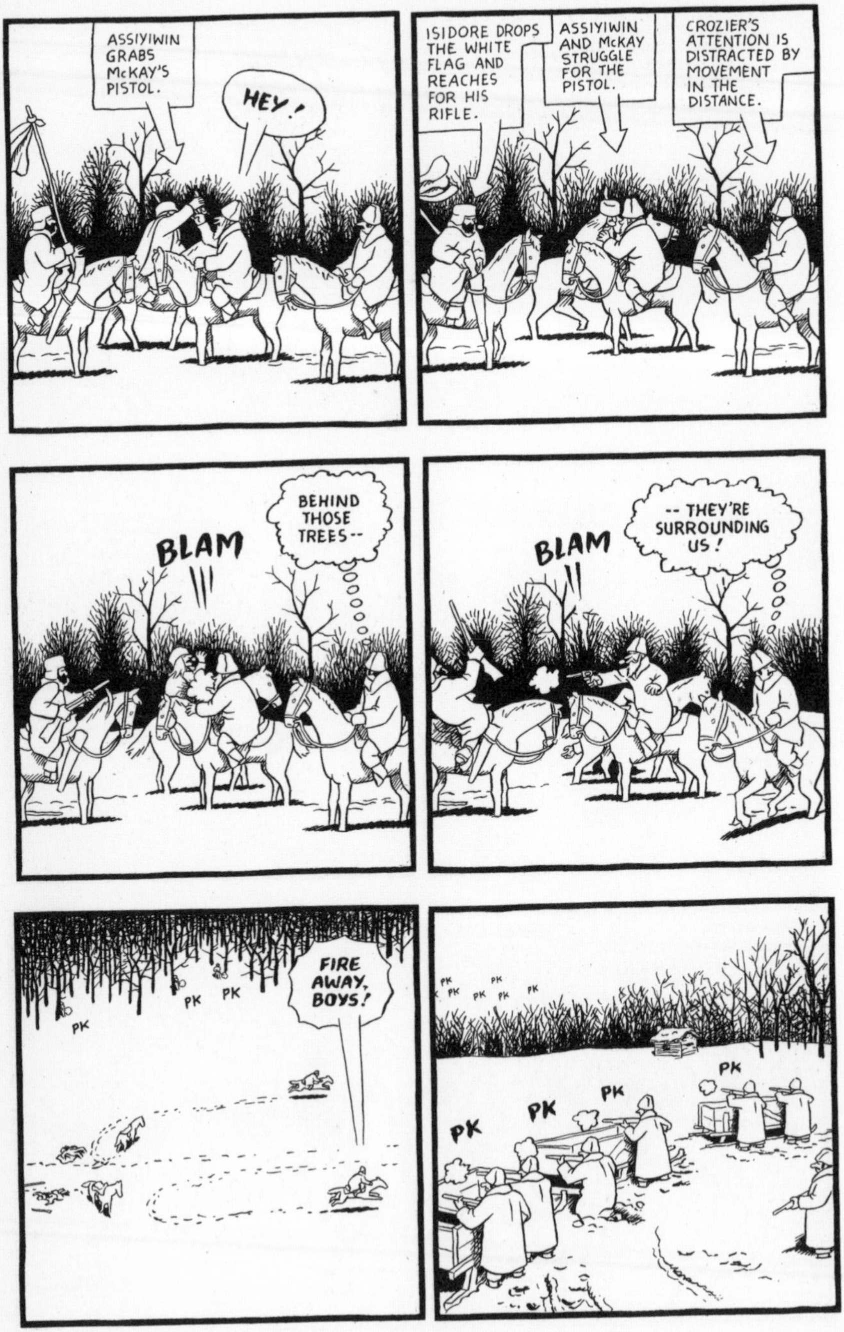
ASSIYIWIN GRABS McKAY'S PISTOL.
HEY!
ISIDORE DROPS THE WHITE FLAG AND REACHES FOR HIS RIFLE.
ASSIYIWIN AND McKAY STRUGGLE FOR THE PISTOL.
CROZIER'S ATTENTION IS DISTRACTED BY MOVEMENT IN THE DISTANCE.
BLAM
BEHIND THOSE TREES--
BLAM
-- THEY'RE SURROUNDING US!
PK
PK
PK
FIRE AWAY, BOYS!
PK PK PK PK PK PK PK
PK
PK
PK
PK

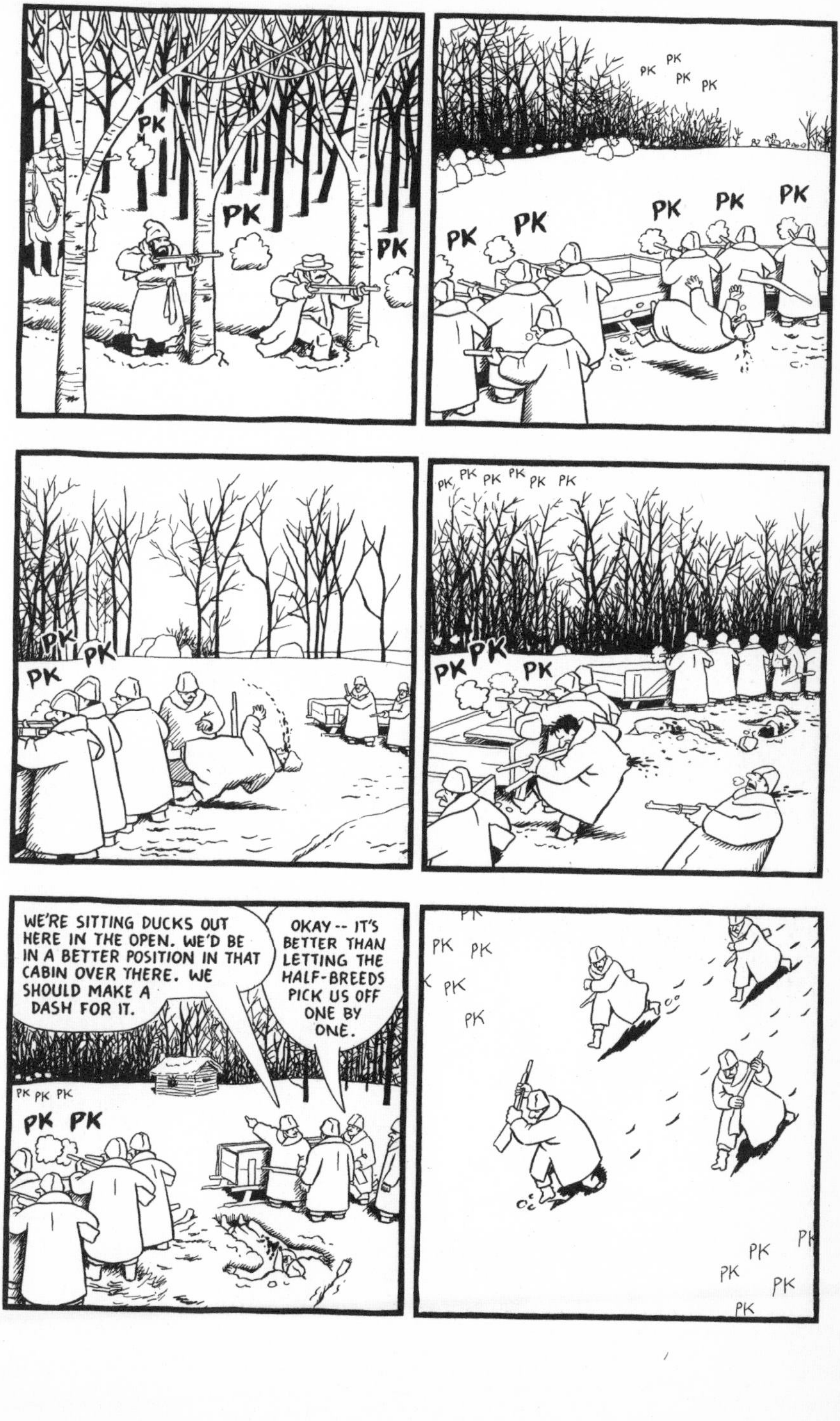
PK
PK
PK
PK PK PK PK
PK PK PK PK PK
PK PK
PK
PK
PK PK PK PK PK PK
PK PK
PK
WE'RE SITTING DUCKS OUT HERE IN THE OPEN. WE'D BE IN A BETTER POSITION IN THAT CABIN OVER THERE. WE SHOULD MAKE A DASH FOR IT.
OKAY -- IT'S BETTER THAN LETTING THE HALF-BREEDS PICK US OFF ONE BY ONE.
PK PK PK
PK PK
PK PK PK PK
PK PK PK PK PK

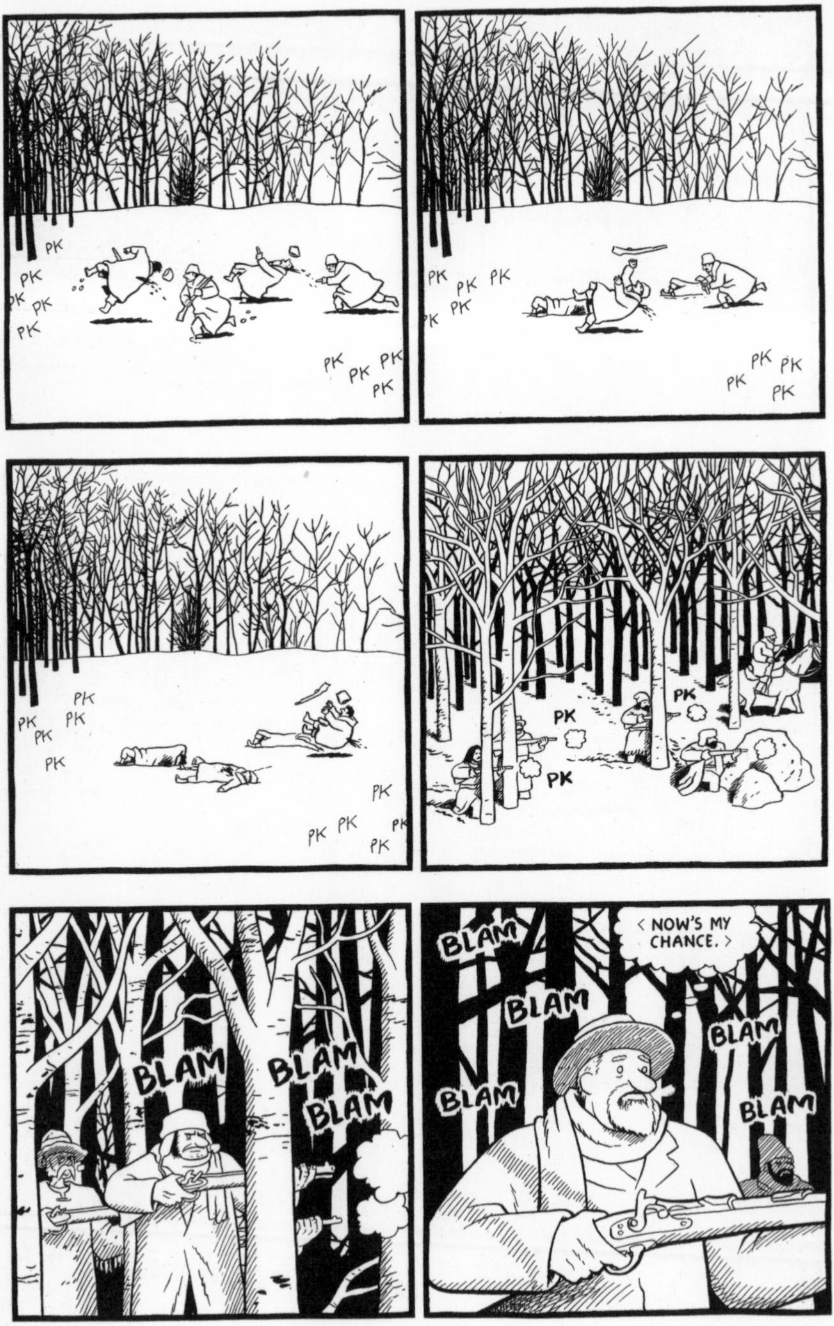
PK
PK
PK
PK
PK
PK
PK
PK
PK
PK
PK
PK
PK
PK
PK
PK
PK
PK
PK
PK
PK
PK
PK
PK
PK
PK
PK
PK
PK
PK
PK
BLAM
BLAM
BLAM
BLAM
BLAM
< NOW'S MY CHANCE. >
BLAM
BLAM
BLAM

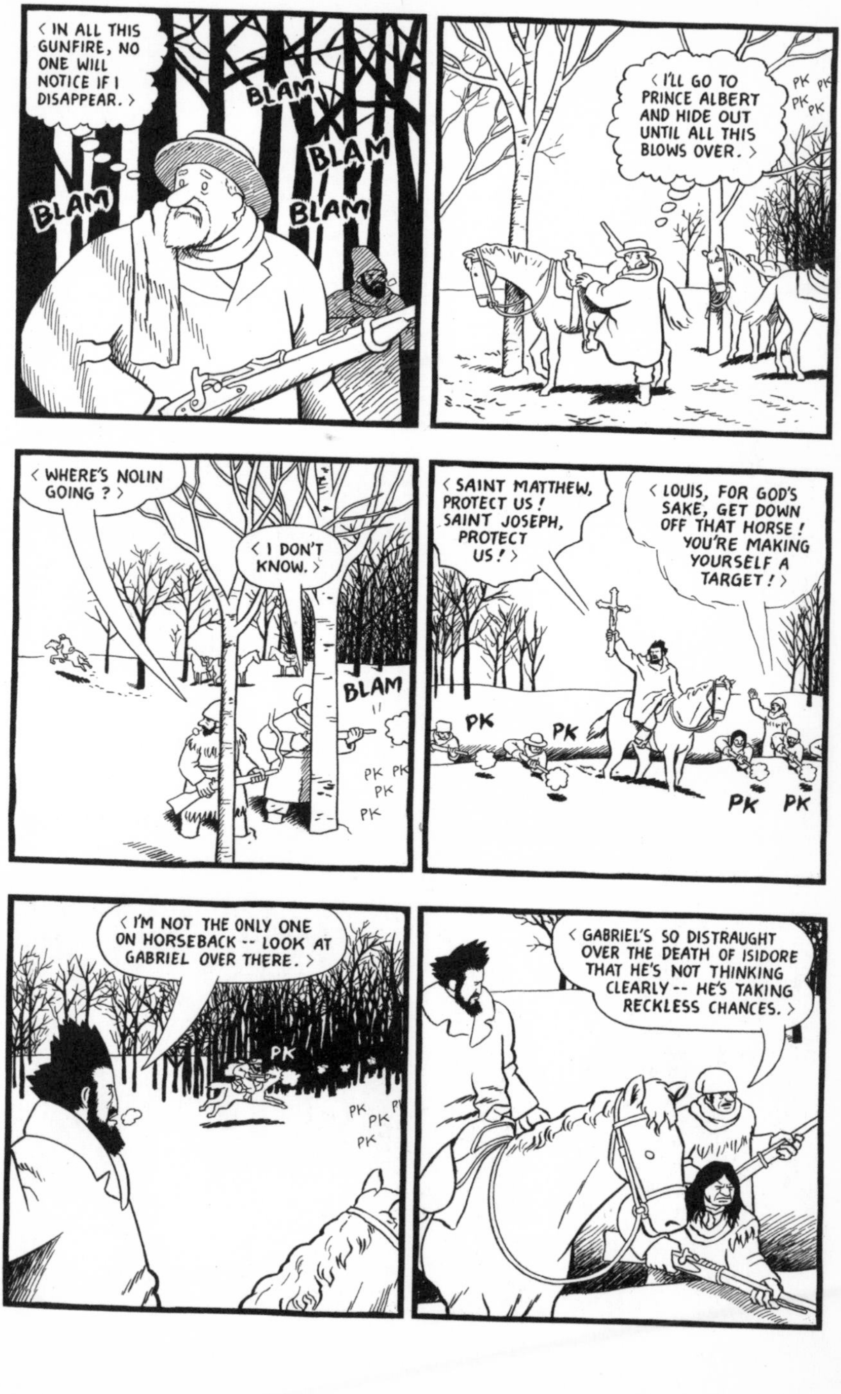
< IN ALL THIS GUNFIRE, NO ONE WILL NOTICE IF I DISAPPEAR. >
BLAM
BLAM
BLAM
BLAM
< I'LL GO TO PRINCE ALBERT AND HIDE OUT UNTIL ALL THIS BLOWS OVER. >
PK PK PK PK
< WHERE'S NOLIN GOING ? >
< I DON'T KNOW. >
BLAM
PK PK PK PK
< SAINT MATTHEW, PROTECT US ! SAINT JOSEPH, PROTECT US ! >
< LOUIS, FOR GOD'S SAKE, GET DOWN OFF THAT HORSE ! YOU'RE MAKING YOURSELF A TARGET ! >
PK PK PK PK
< I'M NOT THE ONLY ONE ON HORSEBACK -- LOOK AT GABRIEL OVER THERE. >
PK
PK PK PK
< GABRIEL'S SO DISTRAUGHT OVER THE DEATH OF ISIDORE THAT HE'S NOT THINKING CLEARLY -- HE'S TAKING RECKLESS CHANCES. >

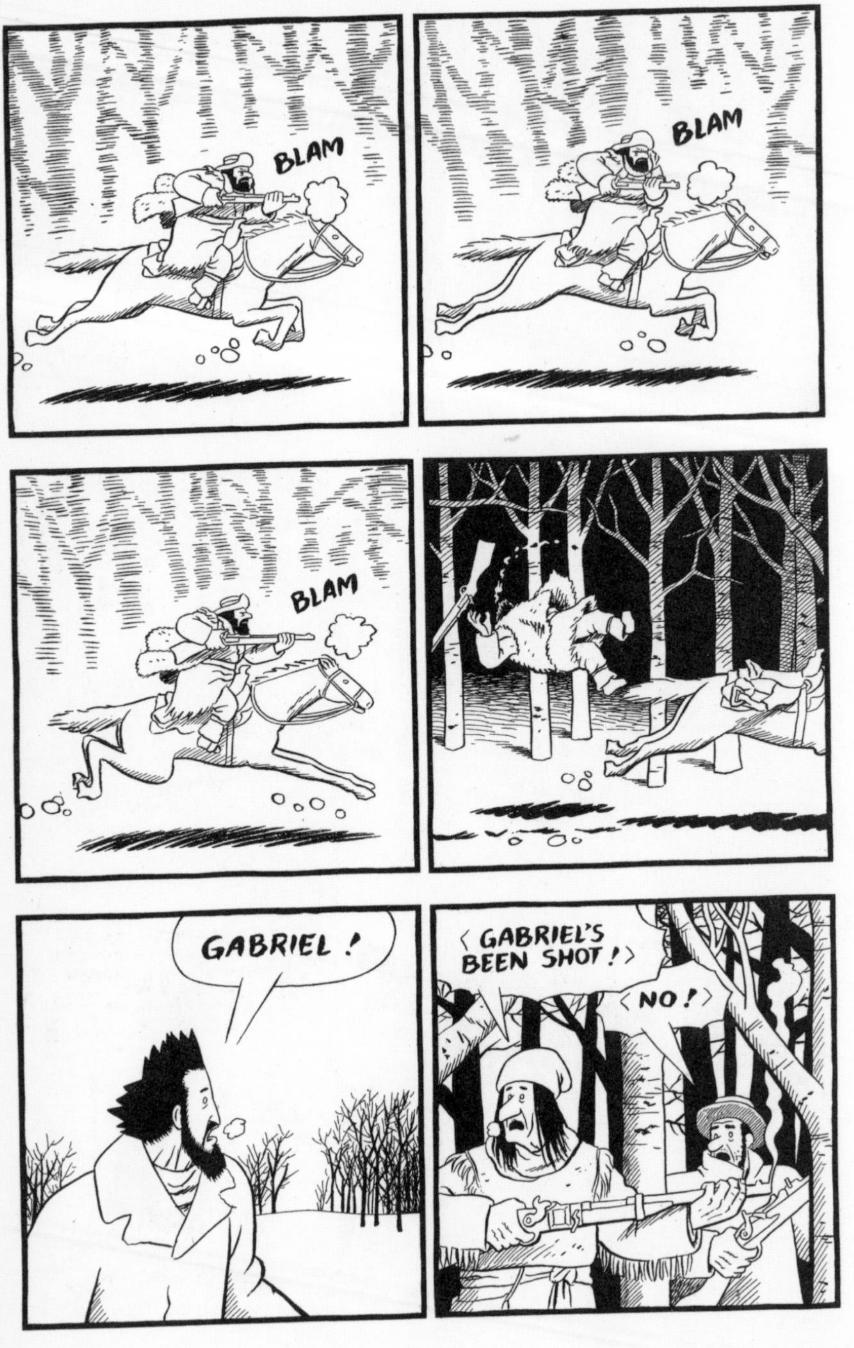
BLAM
BLAM
BLAM
GABRIEL !
⟨ GABRIEL'S BEEN SHOT ! ⟩
⟨ NO ! ⟩

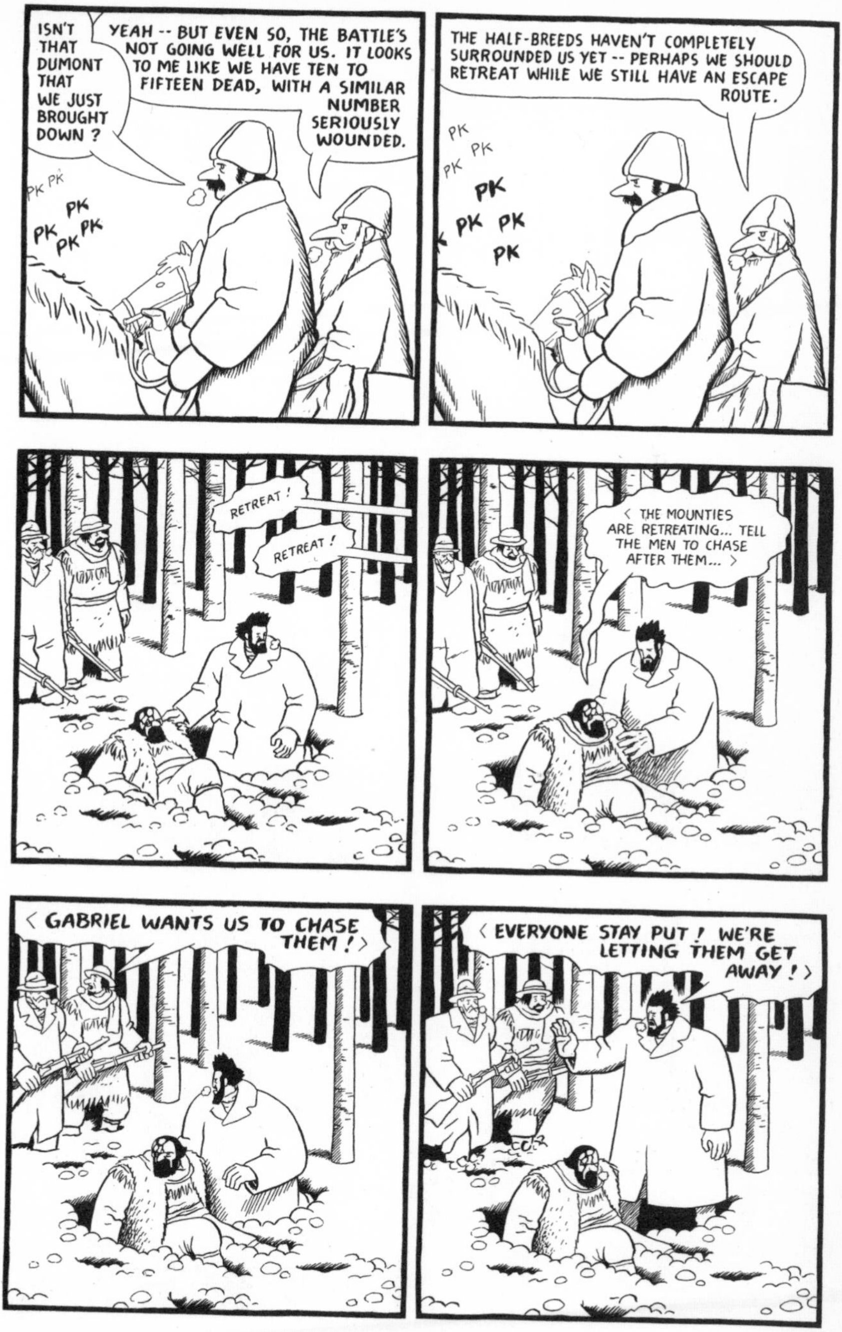
ISN'T THAT DUMONT THAT WE JUST BROUGHT DOWN ?
YEAH -- BUT EVEN SO, THE BATTLE'S NOT GOING WELL FOR US. IT LOOKS TO ME LIKE WE HAVE TEN TO FIFTEEN DEAD, WITH A SIMILAR NUMBER SERIOUSLY WOUNDED.
PK PK
PK
PK PK PK
THE HALF-BREEDS HAVEN'T COMPLETELY SURROUNDED US YET -- PERHAPS WE SHOULD RETREAT WHILE WE STILL HAVE AN ESCAPE ROUTE.
PK
PK PK
PK
PK PK
PK
RETREAT !
RETREAT !
< THE MOUNTIES ARE RETREATING... TELL THE MEN TO CHASE AFTER THEM... >
< GABRIEL WANTS US TO CHASE THEM ! >
< EVERYONE STAY PUT ! WE'RE LETTING THEM GET AWAY ! >

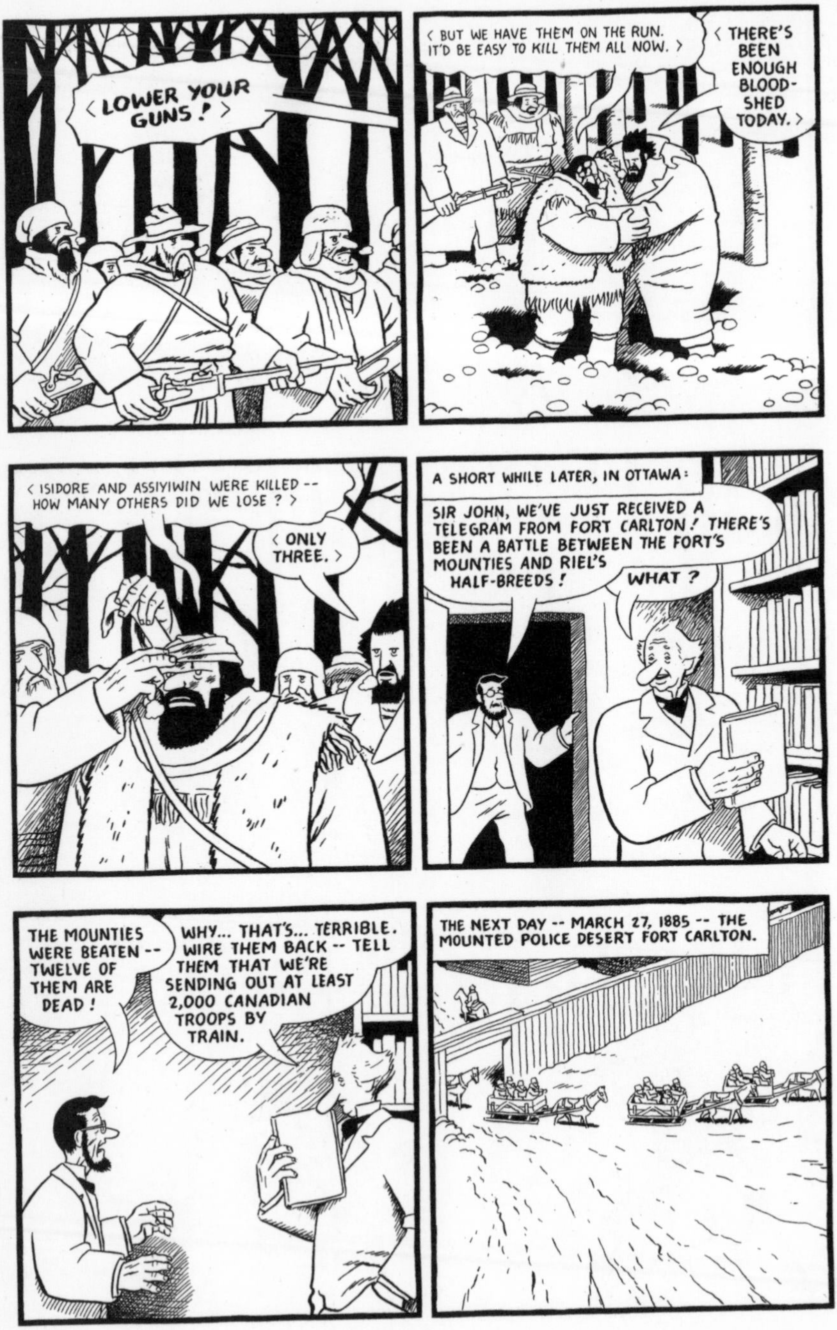

< LOWER YOUR GUNS ! >
< BUT WE HAVE THEM ON THE RUN. IT'D BE EASY TO KILL THEM ALL NOW. >
< THERE'S BEEN ENOUGH BLOOD-SHED TODAY. >
< ISIDORE AND ASSIYIWIN WERE KILLED -- HOW MANY OTHERS DID WE LOSE ? >
< ONLY THREE. >
A SHORT WHILE LATER, IN OTTAWA:
SIR JOHN, WE'VE JUST RECEIVED A TELEGRAM FROM FORT CARLTON! THERE'S BEEN A BATTLE BETWEEN THE FORT'S MOUNTIES AND RIEL'S HALF-BREEDS!
WHAT ?
THE MOUNTIES WERE BEATEN -- TWELVE OF THEM ARE DEAD!
WHY... THAT'S... TERRIBLE. WIRE THEM BACK -- TELL THEM THAT WE'RE SENDING OUT AT LEAST 2,000 CANADIAN TROOPS BY TRAIN.
THE NEXT DAY -- MARCH 27, 1885 -- THE MOUNTED POLICE DESERT FORT CARLTON.

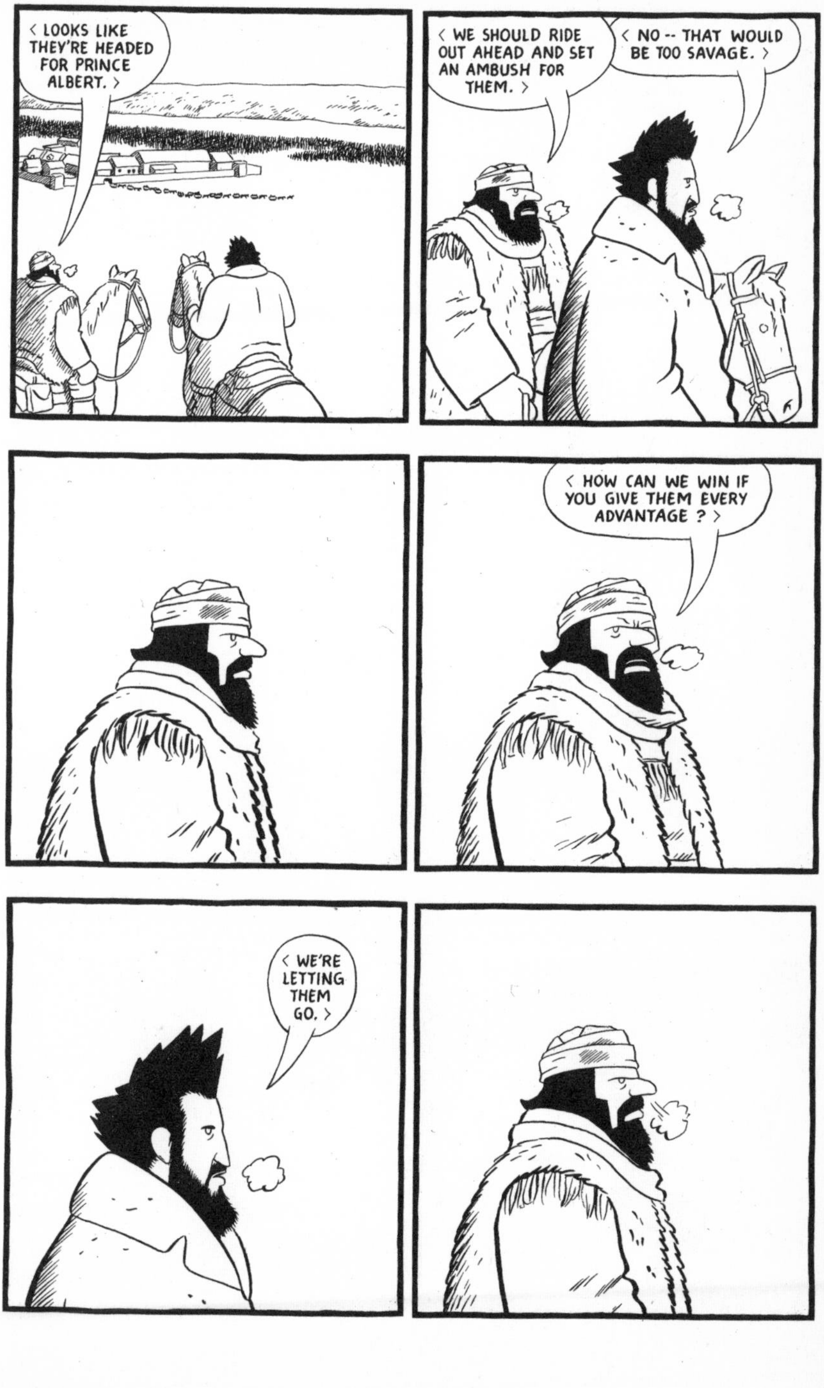
< LOOKS LIKE THEY'RE HEADED FOR PRINCE ALBERT. >
< WE SHOULD RIDE OUT AHEAD AND SET AN AMBUSH FOR THEM. >
< NO -- THAT WOULD BE TOO SAVAGE. >
< HOW CAN WE WIN IF YOU GIVE THEM EVERY ADVANTAGE ? >
< WE'RE LETTING THEM GO. >

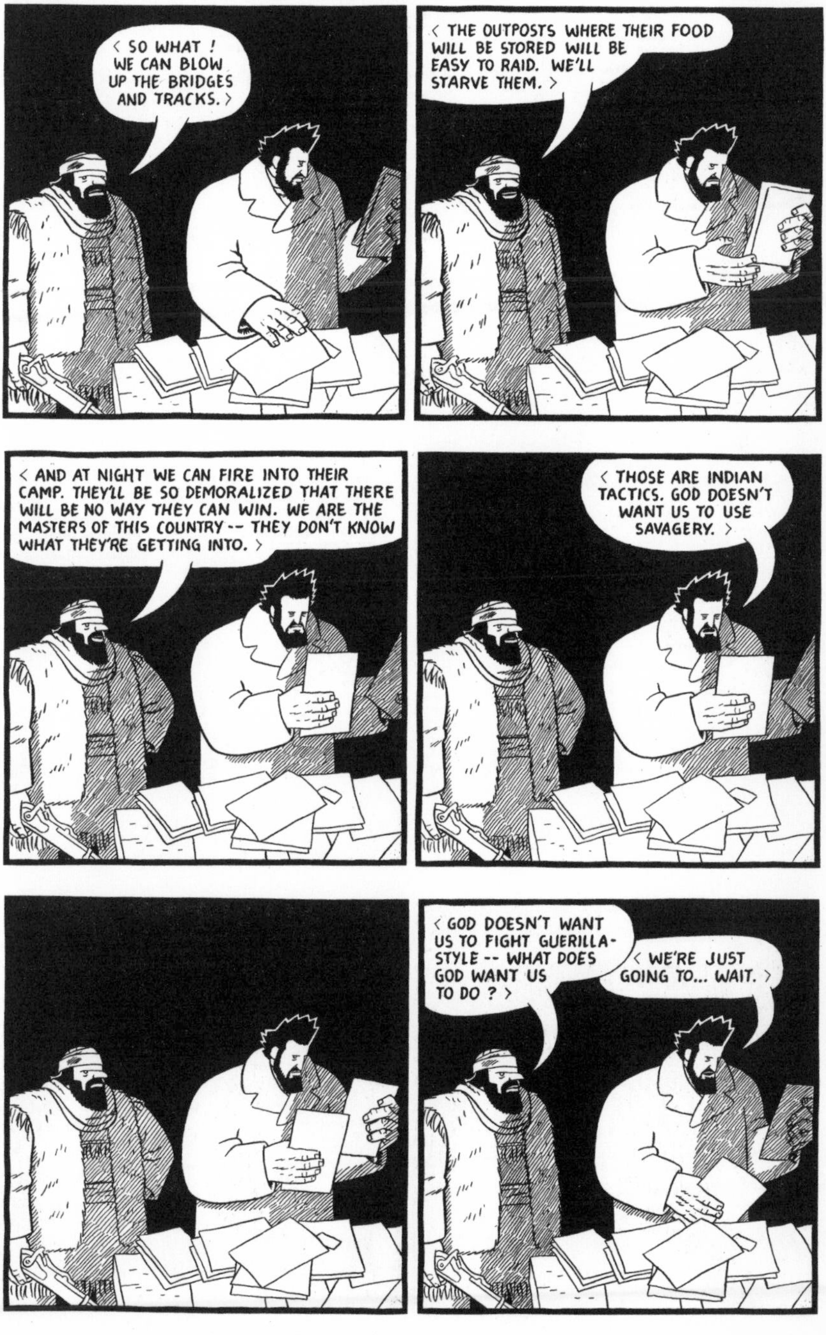

< SO WHAT ! WE CAN BLOW UP THE BRIDGES AND TRACKS. >
< THE OUTPOSTS WHERE THEIR FOOD WILL BE STORED WILL BE EASY TO RAID. WE'LL STARVE THEM. >
< AND AT NIGHT WE CAN FIRE INTO THEIR CAMP. THEY'LL BE SO DEMORALIZED THAT THERE WILL BE NO WAY THEY CAN WIN. WE ARE THE MASTERS OF THIS COUNTRY -- THEY DON'T KNOW WHAT THEY'RE GETTING INTO. >
< THOSE ARE INDIAN TACTICS. GOD DOESN'T WANT US TO USE SAVAGERY. >
< GOD DOESN'T WANT US TO FIGHT GUERILLA-STYLE -- WHAT DOES GOD WANT US TO DO ? >
< WE'RE JUST GOING TO... WAIT. >

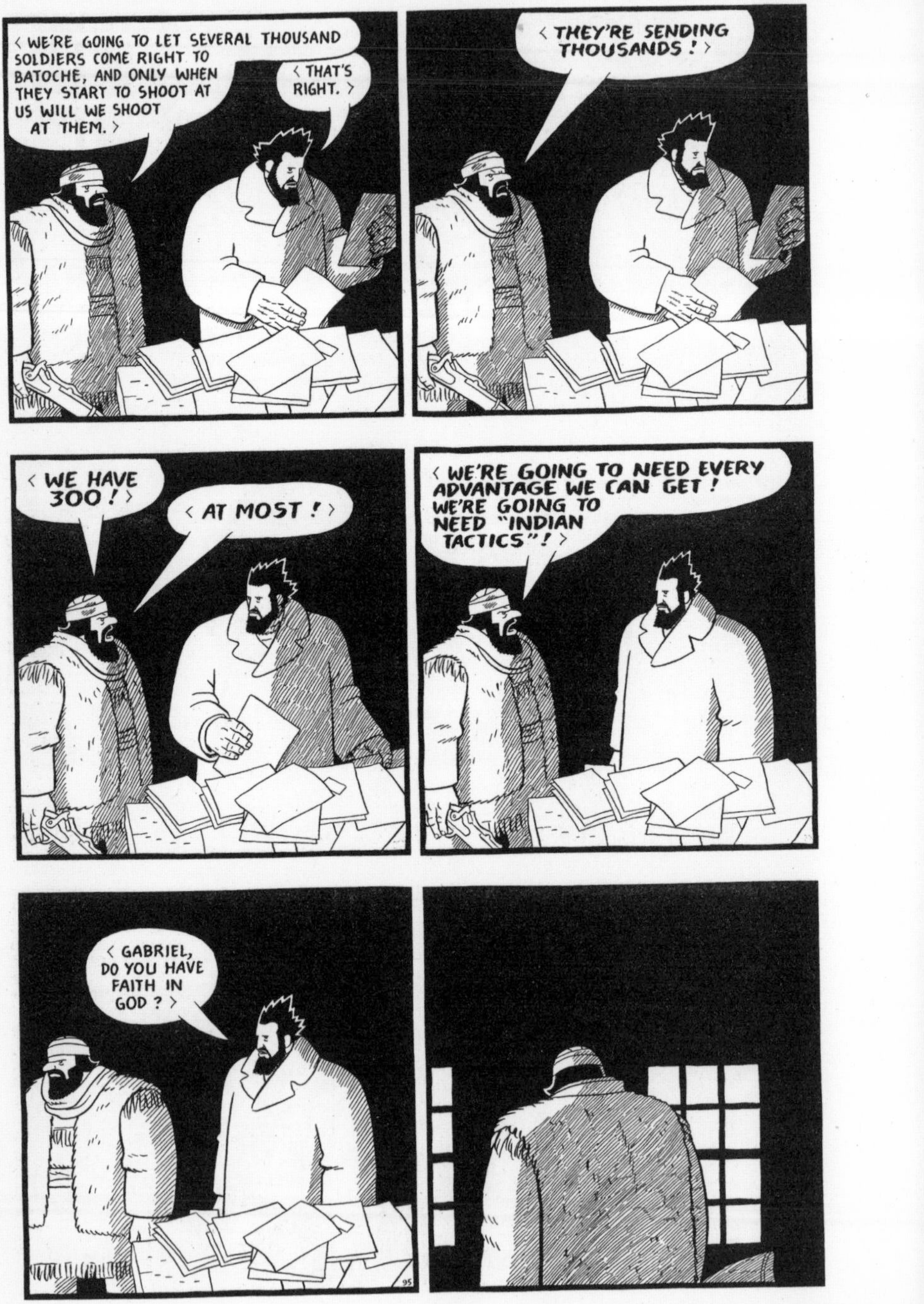
< WE'RE GOING TO LET SEVERAL THOUSAND SOLDIERS COME RIGHT TO BATOCHE, AND ONLY WHEN THEY START TO SHOOT AT US WILL WE SHOOT AT THEM. >
< THAT'S RIGHT. >
< THEY'RE SENDING THOUSANDS! >
< WE HAVE 300! >
< AT MOST! >
< WE'RE GOING TO NEED EVERY ADVANTAGE WE CAN GET! WE'RE GOING TO NEED "INDIAN TACTICS"! >
< GABRIEL, DO YOU HAVE FAITH IN GOD? >

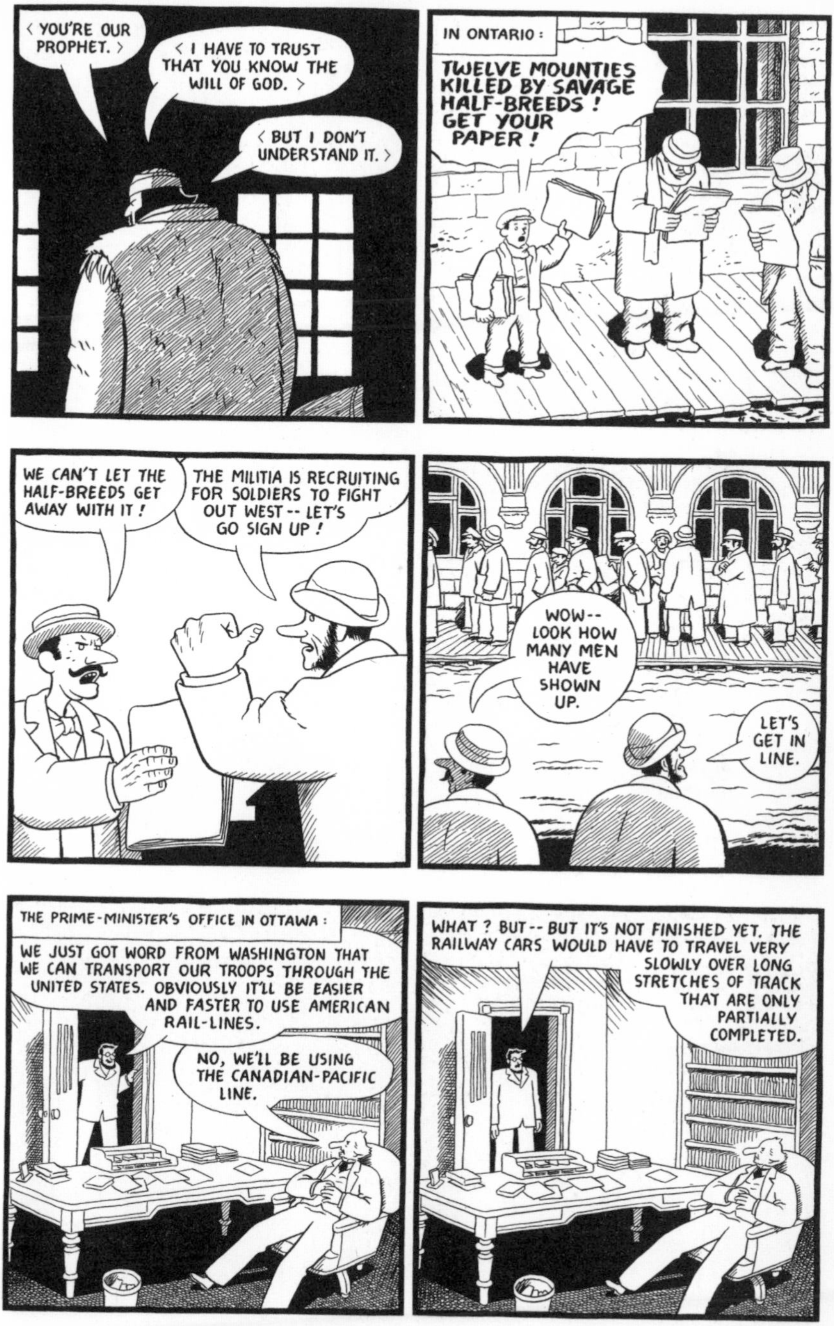
< YOU'RE OUR PROPHET. >
< I HAVE TO TRUST THAT YOU KNOW THE WILL OF GOD. >
< BUT I DON'T UNDERSTAND IT. >
IN ONTARIO :
TWELVE MOUNTIES KILLED BY SAVAGE HALF-BREEDS ! GET YOUR PAPER !
WE CAN'T LET THE HALF-BREEDS GET AWAY WITH IT !
THE MILITIA IS RECRUITING FOR SOLDIERS TO FIGHT OUT WEST -- LET'S GO SIGN UP !
WOW -- LOOK HOW MANY MEN HAVE SHOWN UP.
LET'S GET IN LINE.
THE PRIME-MINISTER'S OFFICE IN OTTAWA :
WE JUST GOT WORD FROM WASHINGTON THAT WE CAN TRANSPORT OUR TROOPS THROUGH THE UNITED STATES. OBVIOUSLY IT'LL BE EASIER AND FASTER TO USE AMERICAN RAIL-LINES.
NO, WE'LL BE USING THE CANADIAN-PACIFIC LINE.
WHAT ? BUT -- BUT IT'S NOT FINISHED YET. THE RAILWAY CARS WOULD HAVE TO TRAVEL VERY SLOWLY OVER LONG STRETCHES OF TRACK THAT ARE ONLY PARTIALLY COMPLETED.

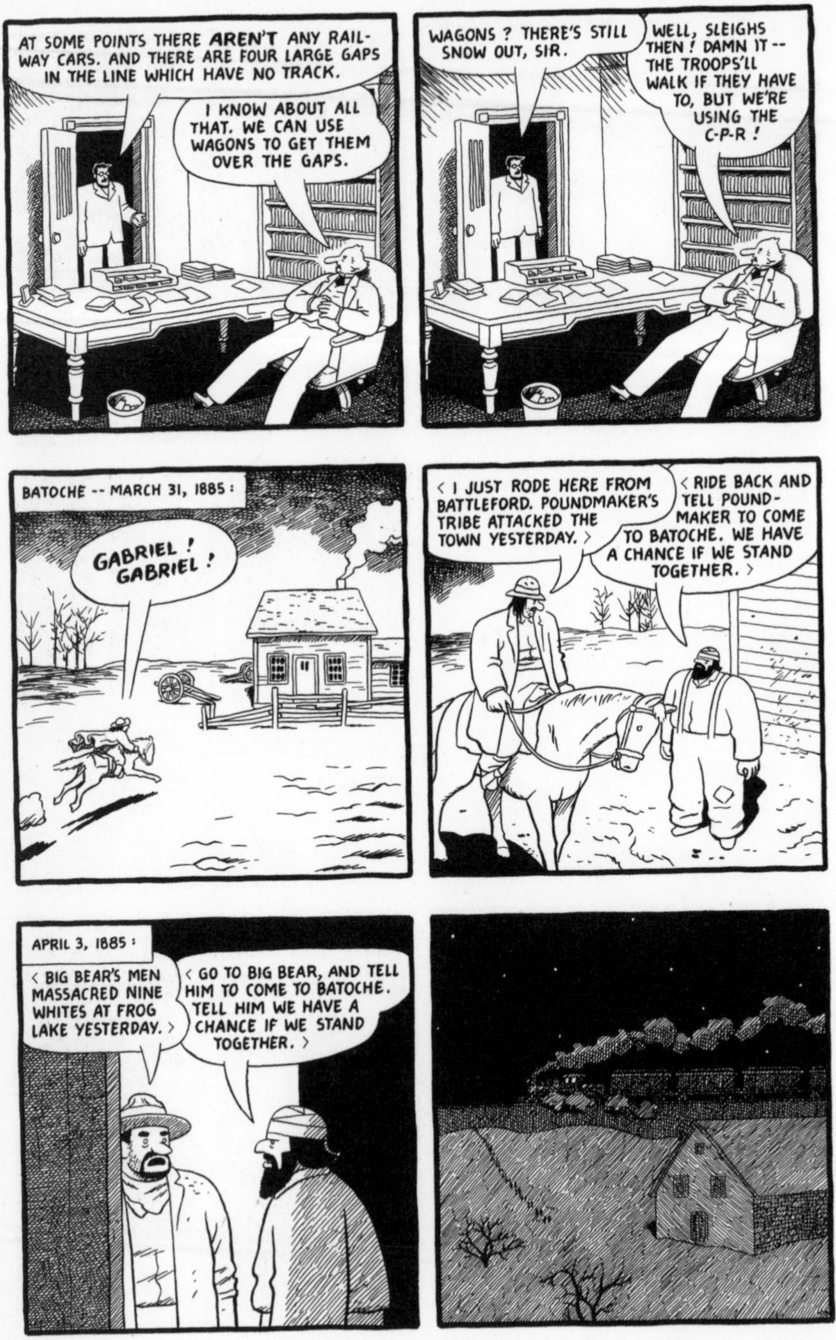
AT SOME POINTS THERE **AREN'T** ANY RAILWAY CARS. AND THERE ARE FOUR LARGE GAPS IN THE LINE WHICH HAVE NO TRACK.
I KNOW ABOUT ALL THAT. WE CAN USE WAGONS TO GET THEM OVER THE GAPS.
WAGONS ? THERE'S STILL SNOW OUT, SIR.
WELL, SLEIGHS THEN ! DAMN IT -- THE TROOPS'LL WALK IF THEY HAVE TO, BUT WE'RE USING THE C-P-R !
BATOCHE -- MARCH 31, 1885 :
GABRIEL ! GABRIEL !
< I JUST RODE HERE FROM BATTLEFORD. POUNDMAKER'S TRIBE ATTACKED THE TOWN YESTERDAY. >
< RIDE BACK AND TELL POUNDMAKER TO COME TO BATOCHE. WE HAVE A CHANCE IF WE STAND TOGETHER. >
APRIL 3, 1885 :
< BIG BEAR'S MEN MASSACRED NINE WHITES AT FROG LAKE YESTERDAY. >
< GO TO BIG BEAR, AND TELL HIM TO COME TO BATOCHE. TELL HIM WE HAVE A CHANCE IF WE STAND TOGETHER. >

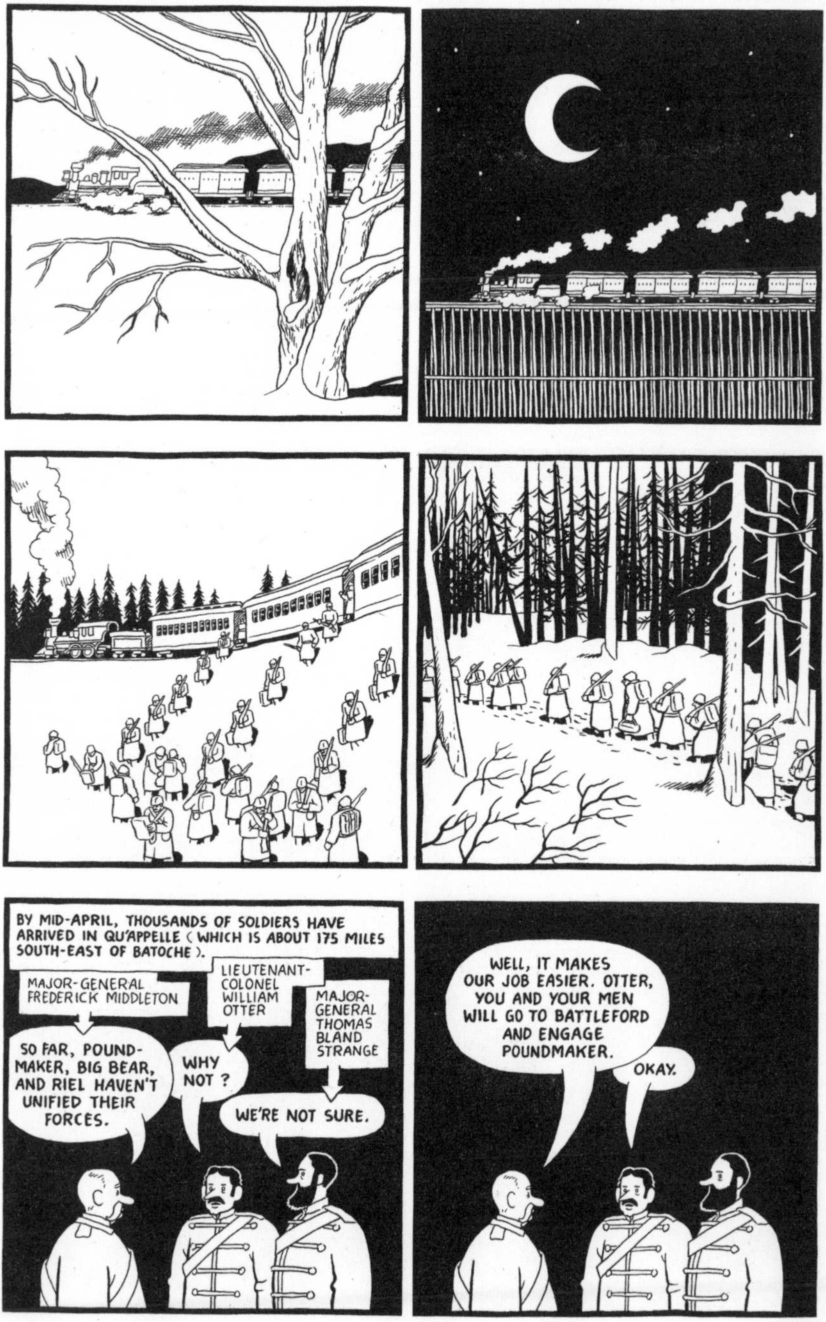
BY MID-APRIL, THOUSANDS OF SOLDIERS HAVE ARRIVED IN QU'APPELLE (WHICH IS ABOUT 175 MILES SOUTH-EAST OF BATOCHE).
MAJOR-GENERAL FREDERICK MIDDLETON
LIEUTENANT-COLONEL WILLIAM OTTER
MAJOR-GENERAL THOMAS BLAND STRANGE
SO FAR, POUND-MAKER, BIG BEAR, AND RIEL HAVEN'T UNIFIED THEIR FORCES.
WHY NOT ?
WE'RE NOT SURE.
WELL, IT MAKES OUR JOB EASIER. OTTER, YOU AND YOUR MEN WILL GO TO BATTLEFORD AND ENGAGE POUNDMAKER.
OKAY.

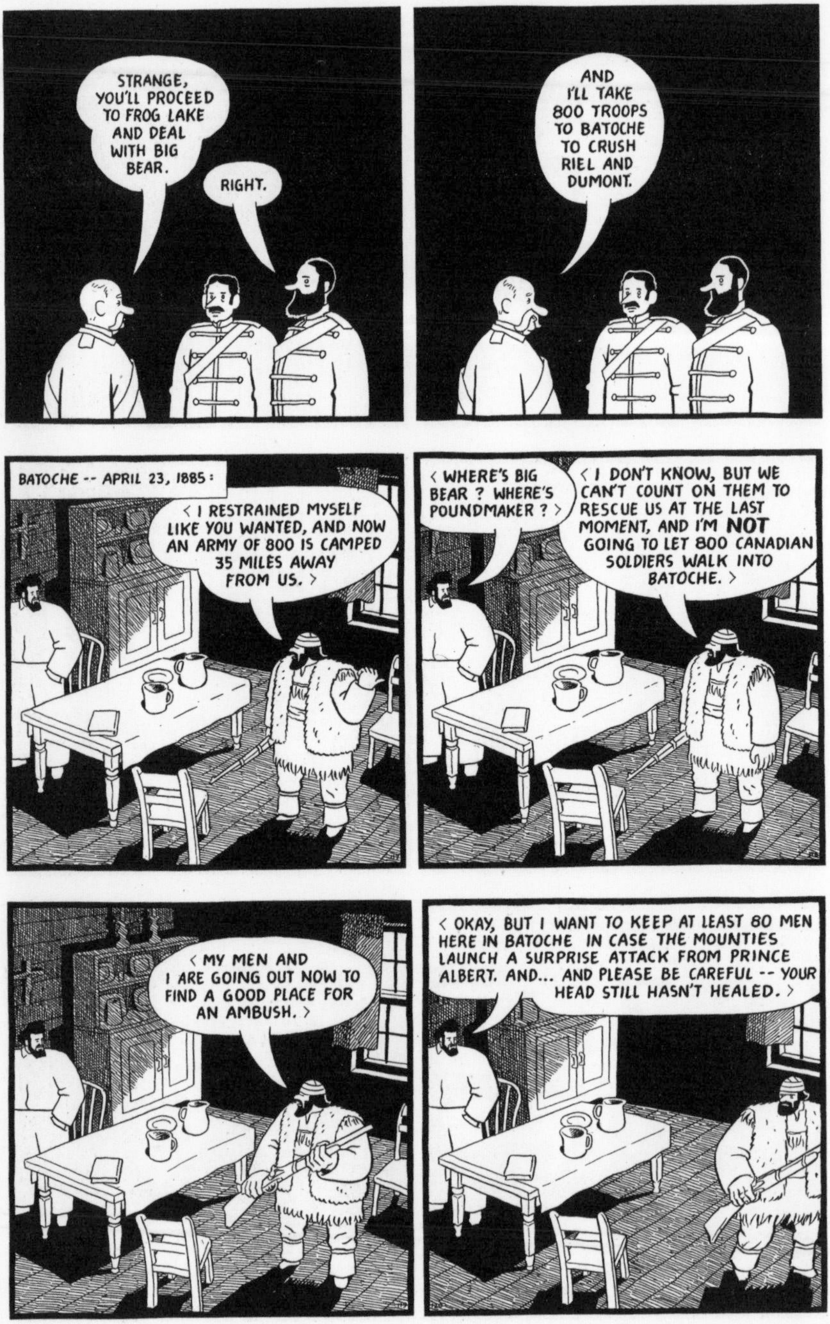
STRANGE, YOU'LL PROCEED TO FROG LAKE AND DEAL WITH BIG BEAR.
RIGHT.
AND I'LL TAKE 800 TROOPS TO BATOCHE TO CRUSH RIEL AND DUMONT.
BATOCHE -- APRIL 23, 1885:
< I RESTRAINED MYSELF LIKE YOU WANTED, AND NOW AN ARMY OF 800 IS CAMPED 35 MILES AWAY FROM US. >
< WHERE'S BIG BEAR ? WHERE'S POUNDMAKER ? >
< I DON'T KNOW, BUT WE CAN'T COUNT ON THEM TO RESCUE US AT THE LAST MOMENT, AND I'M **NOT** GOING TO LET 800 CANADIAN SOLDIERS WALK INTO BATOCHE. >
< MY MEN AND I ARE GOING OUT NOW TO FIND A GOOD PLACE FOR AN AMBUSH. >
< OKAY, BUT I WANT TO KEEP AT LEAST 80 MEN HERE IN BATOCHE IN CASE THE MOUNTIES LAUNCH A SURPRISE ATTACK FROM PRINCE ALBERT. AND... AND PLEASE BE CAREFUL -- YOUR HEAD STILL HASN'T HEALED. >

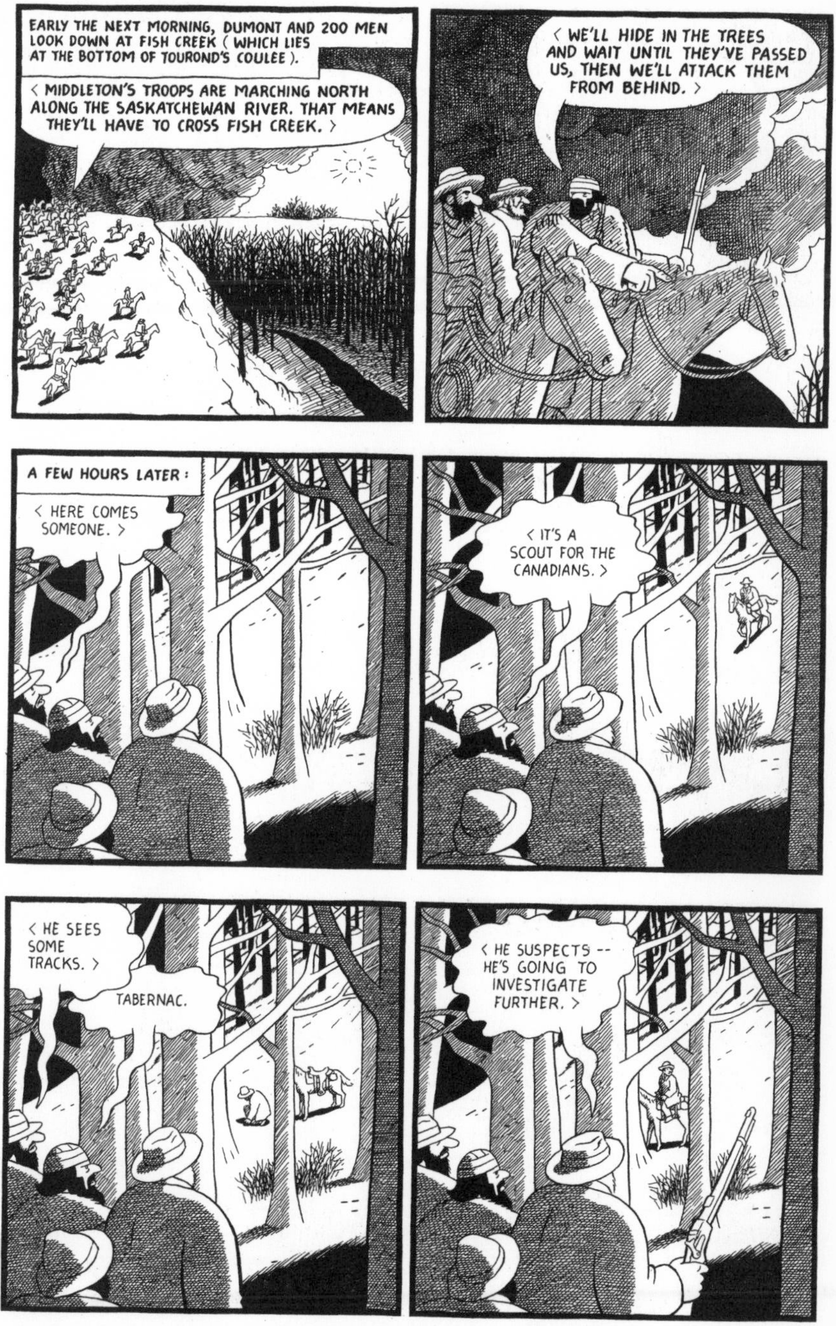
EARLY THE NEXT MORNING, DUMONT AND 200 MEN LOOK DOWN AT FISH CREEK (WHICH LIES AT THE BOTTOM OF TOUROND'S COULÉE).
< MIDDLETON'S TROOPS ARE MARCHING NORTH ALONG THE SASKATCHEWAN RIVER. THAT MEANS THEY'LL HAVE TO CROSS FISH CREEK. >
< WE'LL HIDE IN THE TREES AND WAIT UNTIL THEY'VE PASSED US, THEN WE'LL ATTACK THEM FROM BEHIND. >
A FEW HOURS LATER :
< HERE COMES SOMEONE. >
< IT'S A SCOUT FOR THE CANADIANS. >
< HE SEES SOME TRACKS. >
TABERNAC.
< HE SUSPECTS -- HE'S GOING TO INVESTIGATE FURTHER. >

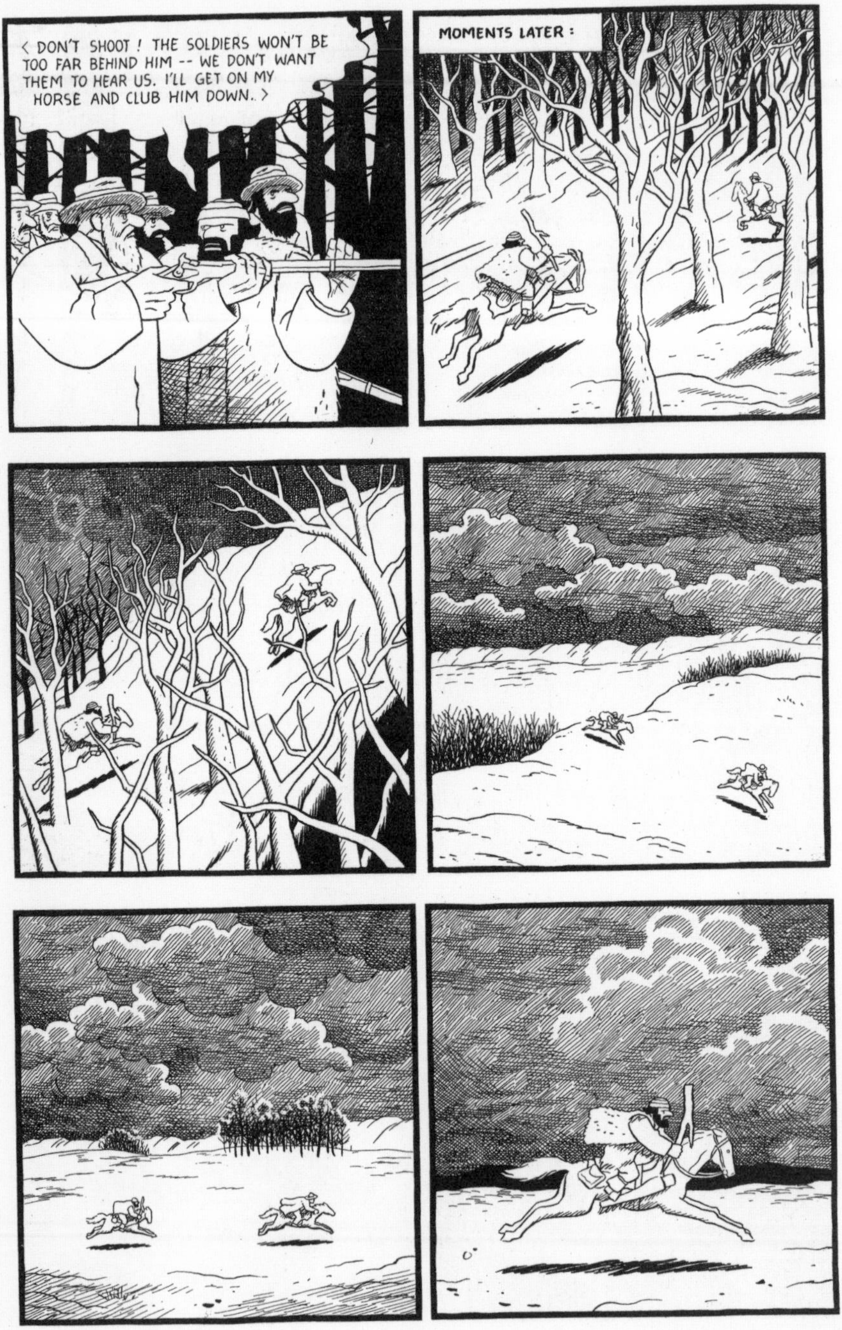
< DON'T SHOOT ! THE SOLDIERS WON'T BE TOO FAR BEHIND HIM -- WE DON'T WANT THEM TO HEAR US. I'LL GET ON MY HORSE AND CLUB HIM DOWN.. >
MOMENTS LATER :

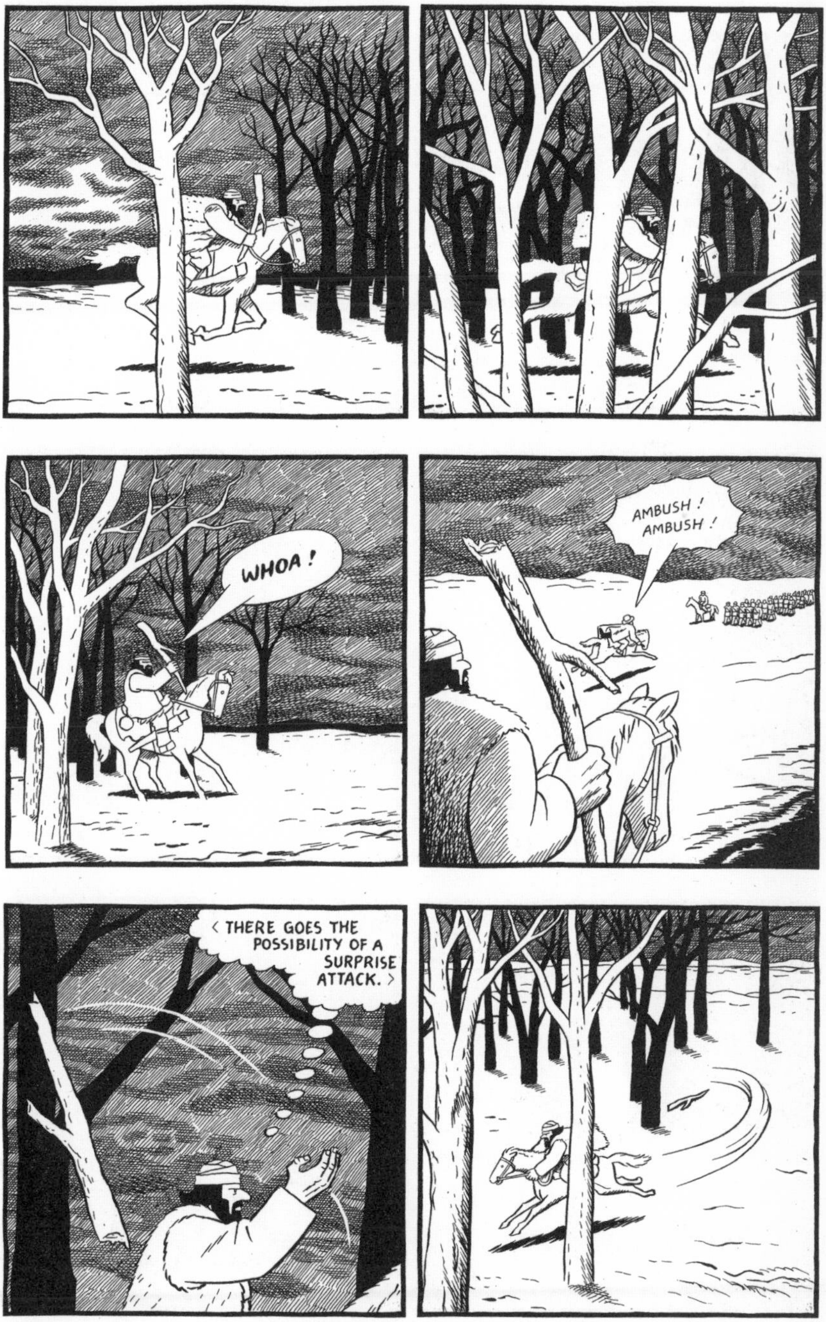
WHOA !
AMBUSH ! AMBUSH !
< THERE GOES THE POSSIBILITY OF A SURPRISE ATTACK. >

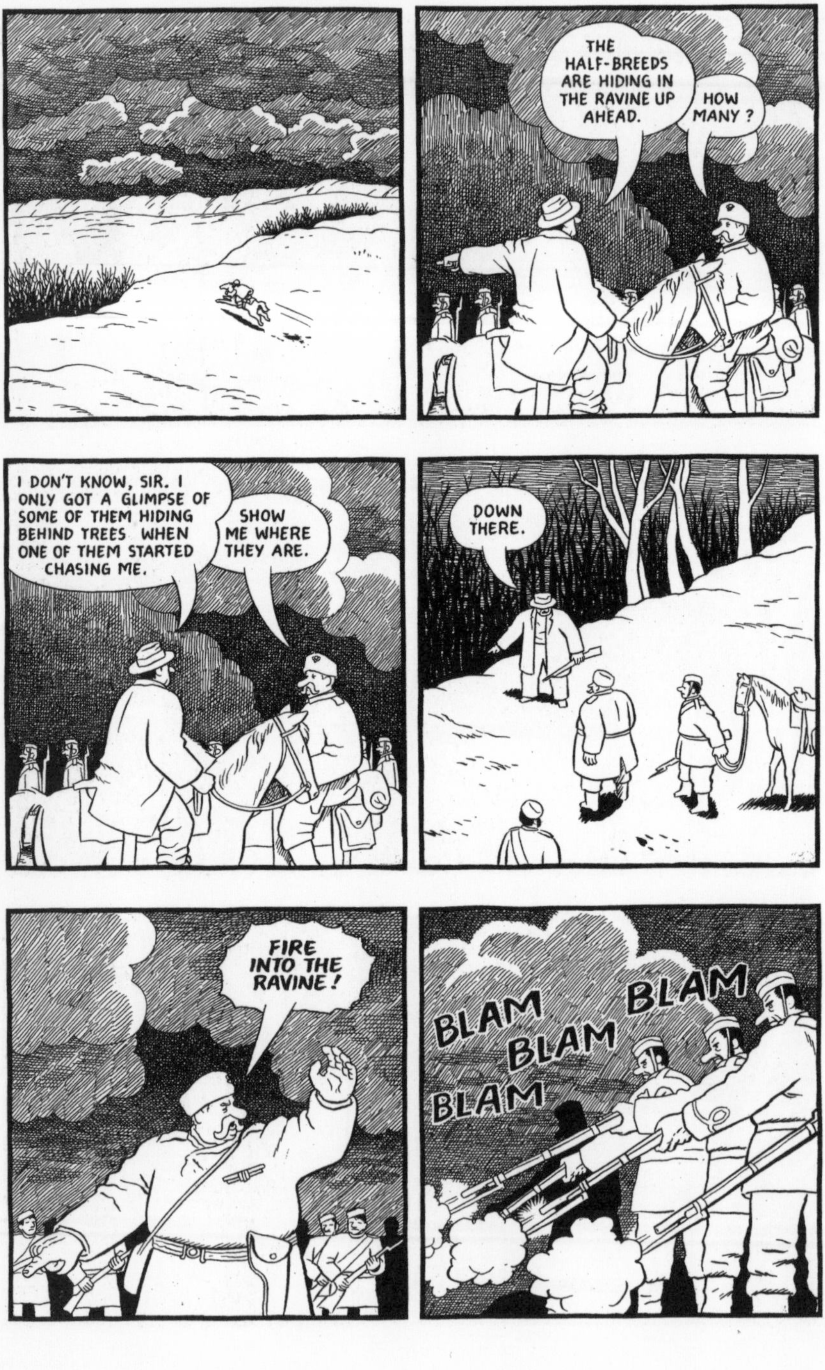
THE HALF-BREEDS ARE HIDING IN THE RAVINE UP AHEAD.
HOW MANY ?
I DON'T KNOW, SIR. I ONLY GOT A GLIMPSE OF SOME OF THEM HIDING BEHIND TREES WHEN ONE OF THEM STARTED CHASING ME.
SHOW ME WHERE THEY ARE.
DOWN THERE.
FIRE INTO THE RAVINE!
BLAM
BLAM
BLAM
BLAM

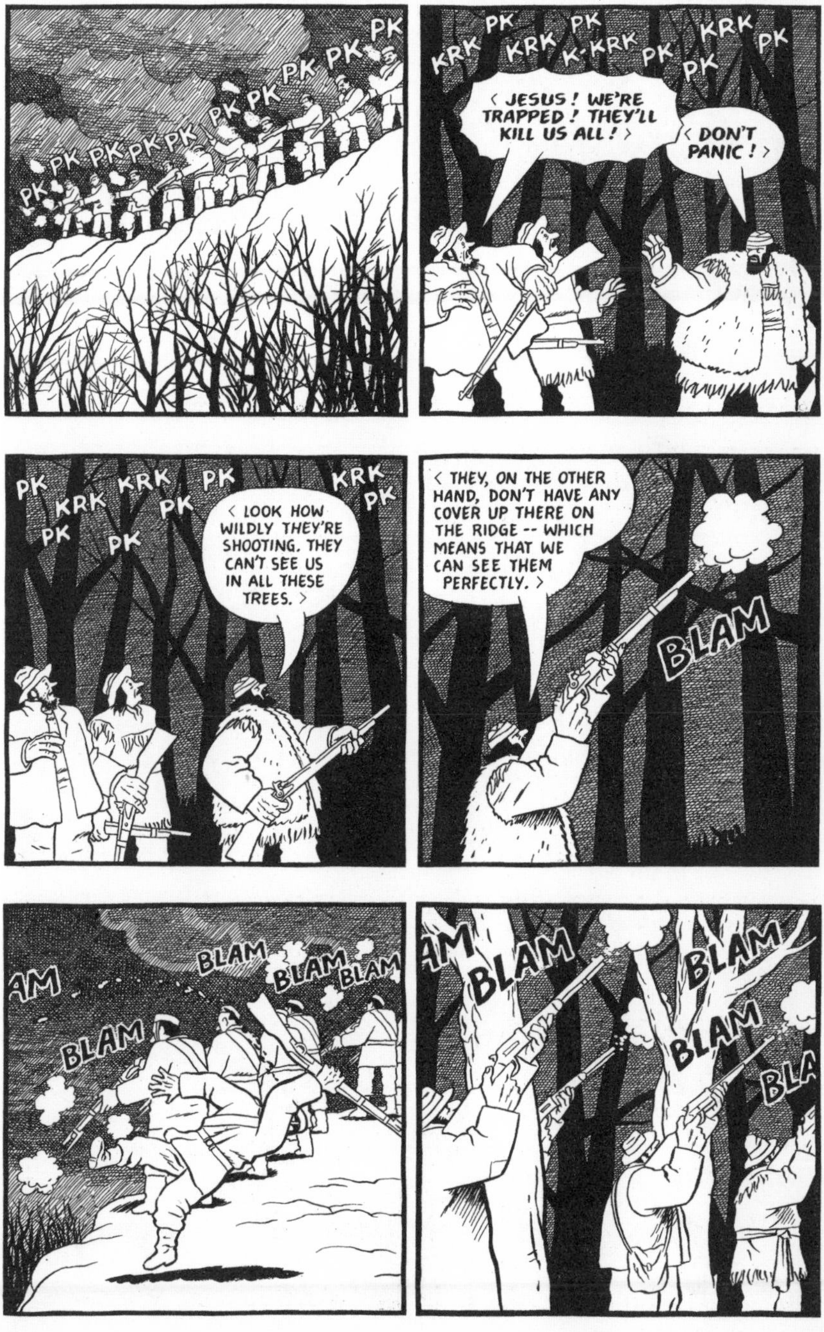
PK PK PK PK PK PK PK PK PK PK
KRK PK KRK PK K-KRK PK KRK PK PK
< JESUS! WE'RE TRAPPED! THEY'LL KILL US ALL! >
< DON'T PANIC! >
PK KRK PK PK KRK PK PK KRK PK
< LOOK HOW WILDLY THEY'RE SHOOTING. THEY CAN'T SEE US IN ALL THESE TREES. >
< THEY, ON THE OTHER HAND, DON'T HAVE ANY COVER UP THERE ON THE RIDGE -- WHICH MEANS THAT WE CAN SEE THEM PERFECTLY. >
BLAM
AM
BLAM BLAM BLAM
BLAM
AM
BLAM
BLAM
BLAM
BLA

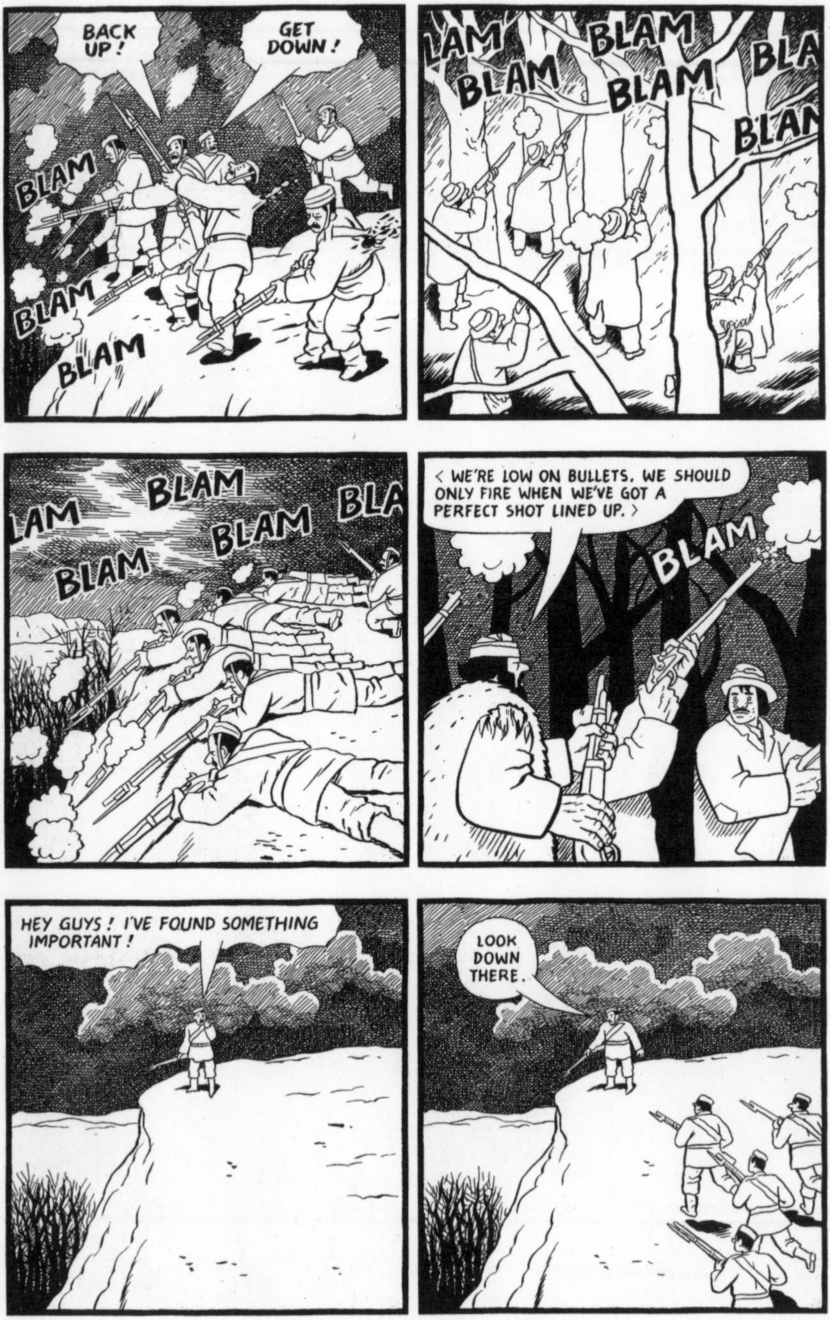
BACK UP!
GET DOWN!
BLAM
BLAM
BLAM
LAM
BLAM
BLAM
BLAM
BLA
BLAM
LAM
BLAM
BLAM
BLAM
BLA
< WE'RE LOW ON BULLETS. WE SHOULD ONLY FIRE WHEN WE'VE GOT A PERFECT SHOT LINED UP. >
BLAM
HEY GUYS! I'VE FOUND SOMETHING IMPORTANT!
LOOK DOWN THERE.

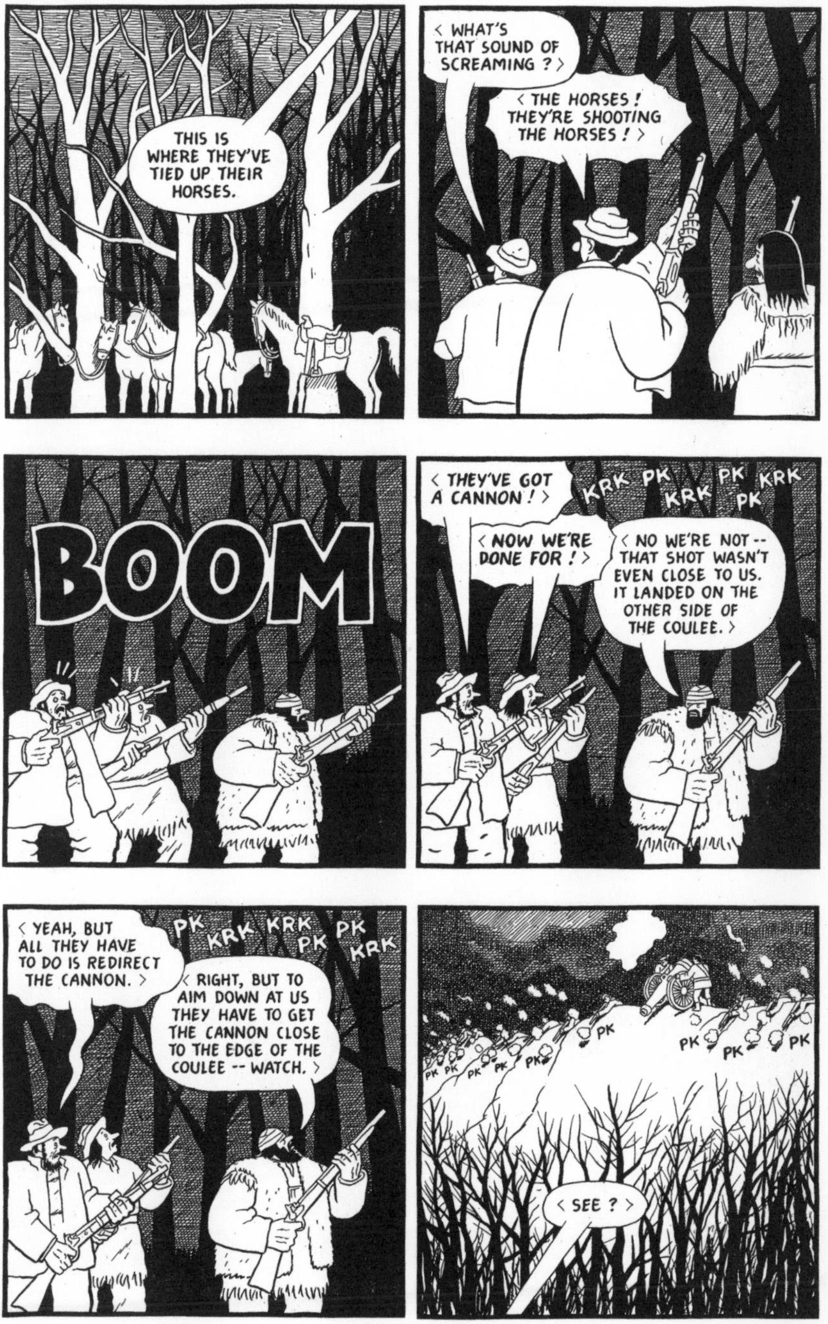
THIS IS WHERE THEY'VE TIED UP THEIR HORSES.
< WHAT'S THAT SOUND OF SCREAMING ? >
< THE HORSES ! THEY'RE SHOOTING THE HORSES ! >
BOOM
< THEY'VE GOT A CANNON ! >
KRK PK KRK PK KRK PK
< NOW WE'RE DONE FOR ! >
< NO WE'RE NOT -- THAT SHOT WASN'T EVEN CLOSE TO US. IT LANDED ON THE OTHER SIDE OF THE COULEE. >
< YEAH, BUT ALL THEY HAVE TO DO IS REDIRECT THE CANNON. >
PK KRK KRK PK PK KRK
< RIGHT, BUT TO AIM DOWN AT US THEY HAVE TO GET THE CANNON CLOSE TO THE EDGE OF THE COULEE -- WATCH. >
PK PK PK PK PK PK PK PK PK PK
< SEE ? >

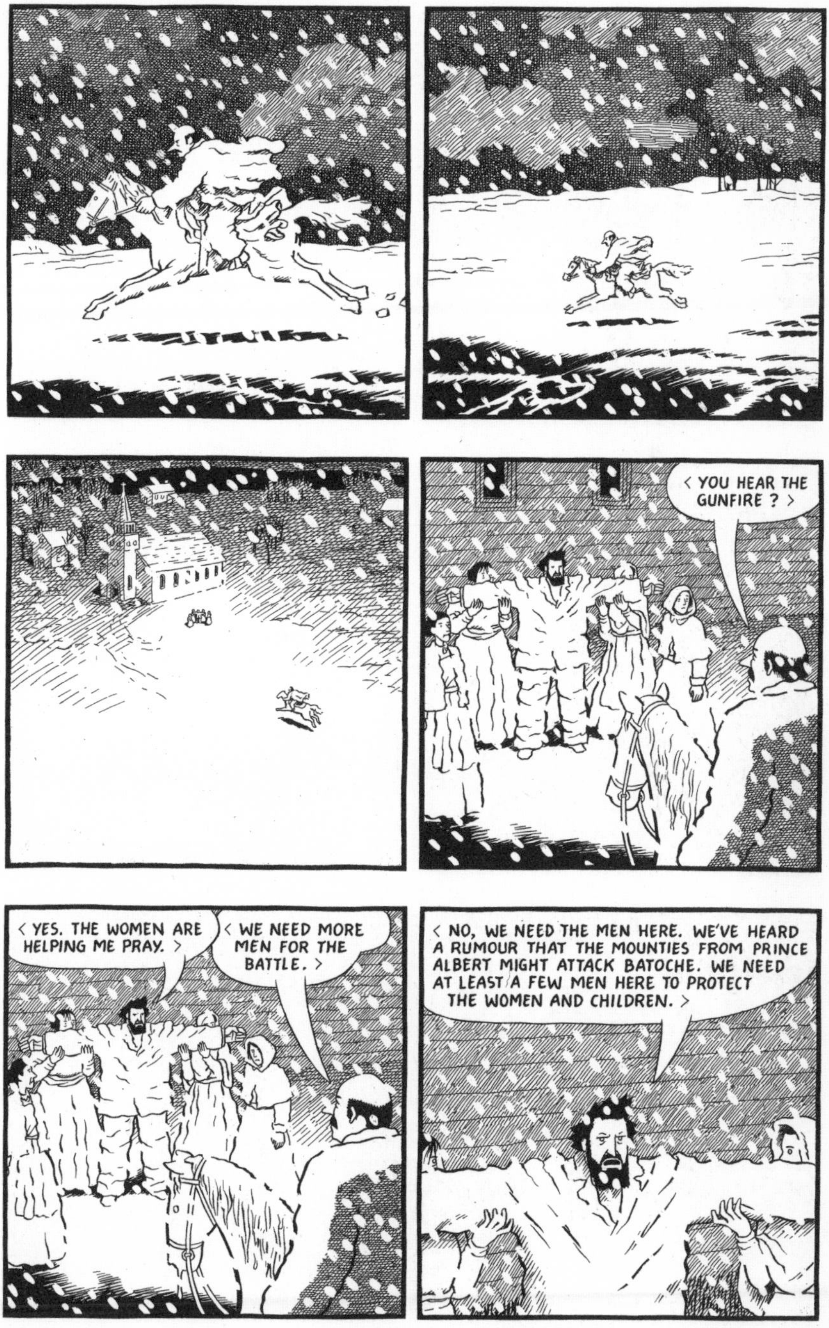
< YOU HEAR THE GUNFIRE ? >
< YES. THE WOMEN ARE HELPING ME PRAY. >
< WE NEED MORE MEN FOR THE BATTLE. >
< NO, WE NEED THE MEN HERE. WE'VE HEARD A RUMOUR THAT THE MOUNTIES FROM PRINCE ALBERT MIGHT ATTACK BATOCHE. WE NEED AT LEAST A FEW MEN HERE TO PROTECT THE WOMEN AND CHILDREN. >

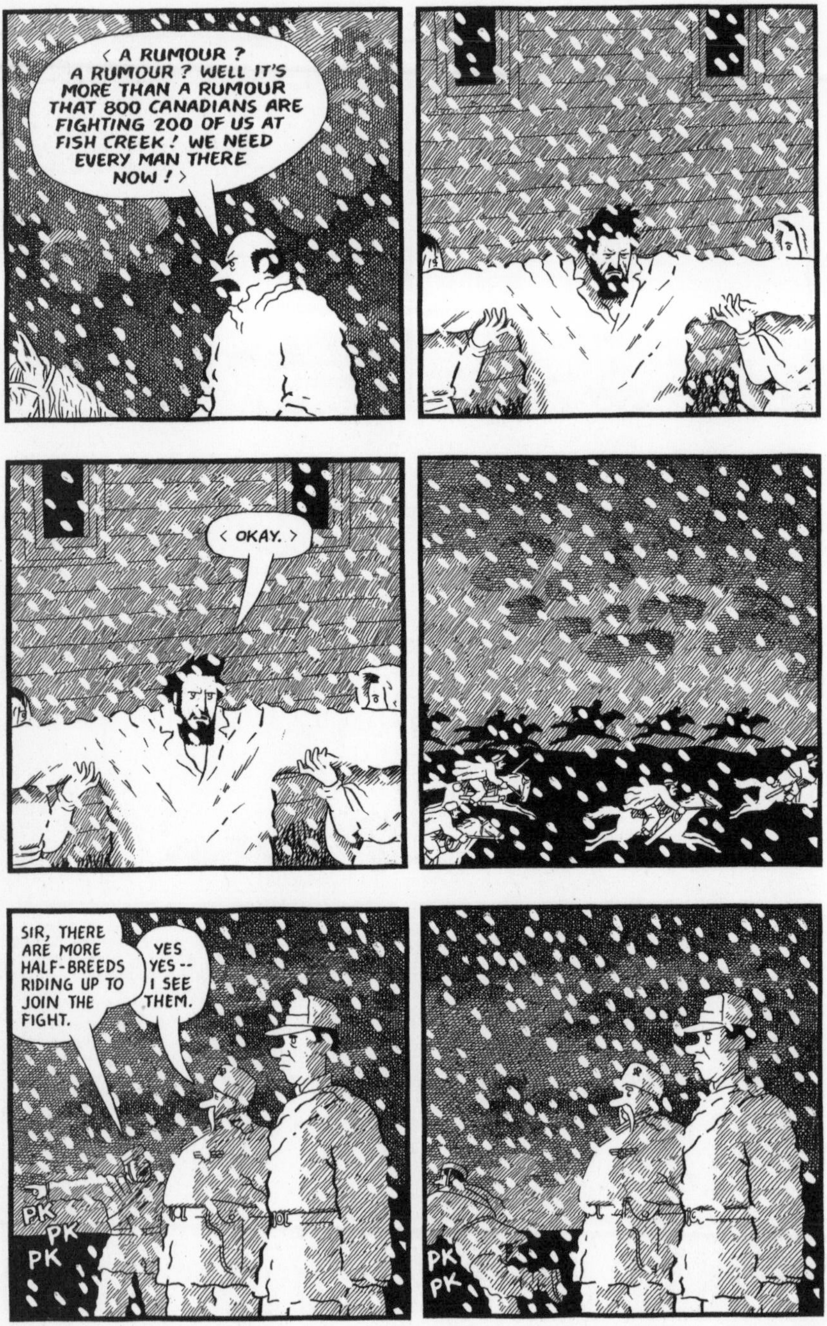

< A RUMOUR ? A RUMOUR ? WELL IT'S MORE THAN A RUMOUR THAT 800 CANADIANS ARE FIGHTING 200 OF US AT FISH CREEK ! WE NEED EVERY MAN THERE NOW ! >
< OKAY. >
SIR, THERE ARE MORE HALF-BREEDS RIDING UP TO JOIN THE FIGHT.
YES YES -- I SEE THEM.
PK PK PK
PK PK

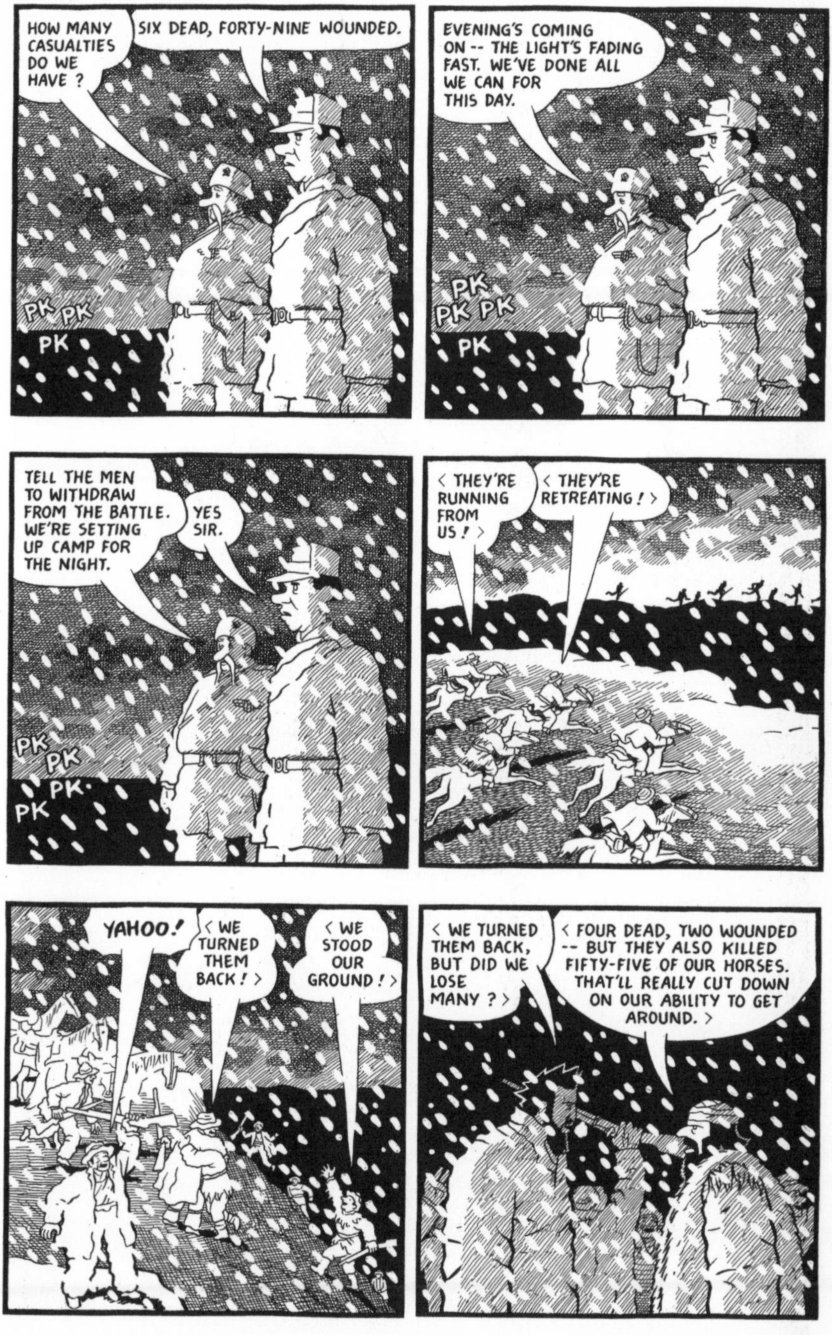

HOW MANY CASUALTIES DO WE HAVE ?
SIX DEAD, FORTY-NINE WOUNDED.
PK PK
PK
EVENING'S COMING ON -- THE LIGHT'S FADING FAST. WE'VE DONE ALL WE CAN FOR THIS DAY.
PK
PK PK
PK
TELL THE MEN TO WITHDRAW FROM THE BATTLE. WE'RE SETTING UP CAMP FOR THE NIGHT.
YES SIR.
PK
PK
PK
PK
< THEY'RE RUNNING FROM US ! >
< THEY'RE RETREATING ! >
YAHOO !
< WE TURNED THEM BACK ! >
< WE STOOD OUR GROUND ! >
< WE TURNED THEM BACK, BUT DID WE LOSE MANY ? >
< FOUR DEAD, TWO WOUNDED -- BUT THEY ALSO KILLED FIFTY-FIVE OF OUR HORSES. THAT'LL REALLY CUT DOWN ON OUR ABILITY TO GET AROUND. >

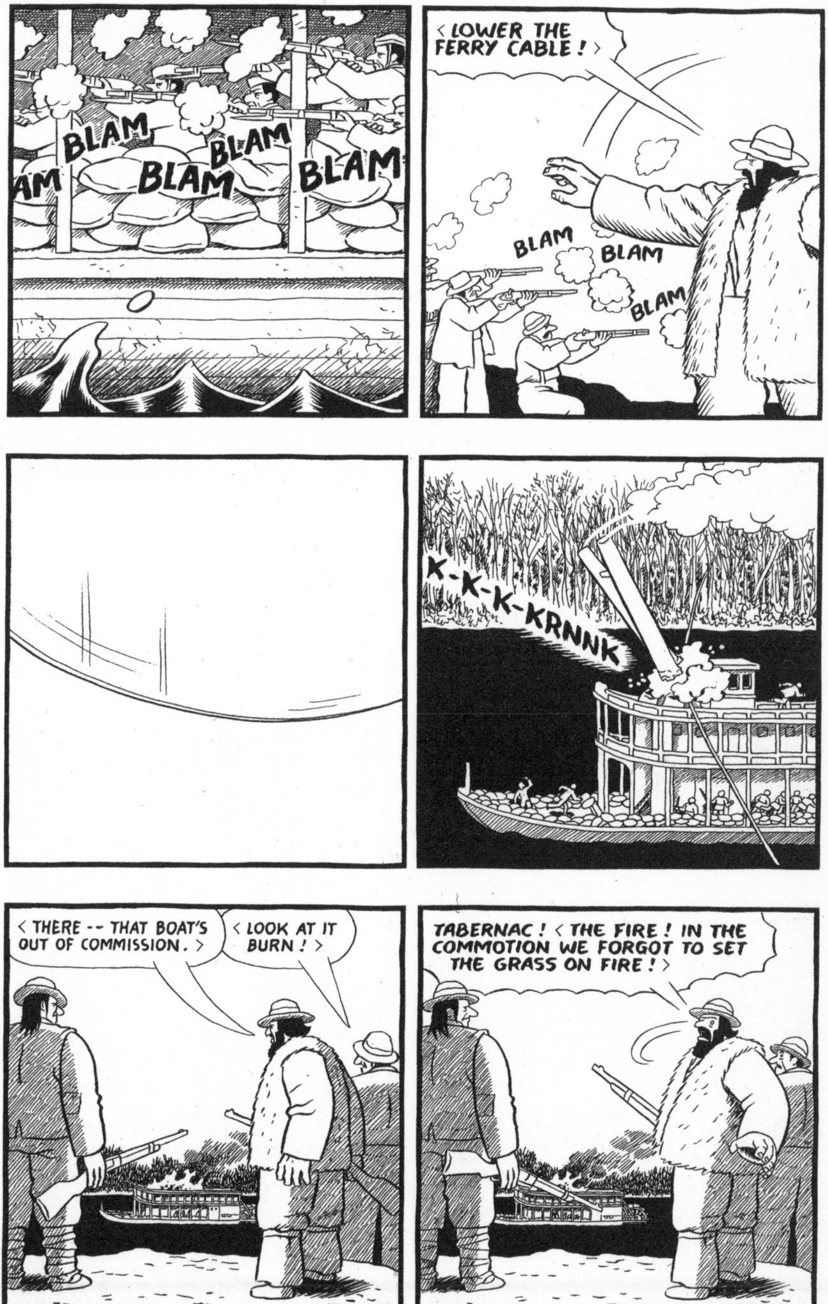
BLAM
BLAM
BLAM
BLAM
AM
< LOWER THE FERRY CABLE ! >
BLAM
BLAM
BLAM
K-K-K-KRNNK
< THERE -- THAT BOAT'S OUT OF COMMISSION. >
< LOOK AT IT BURN ! >
TABERNAC ! < THE FIRE ! IN THE COMMOTION WE FORGOT TO SET THE GRASS ON FIRE ! >

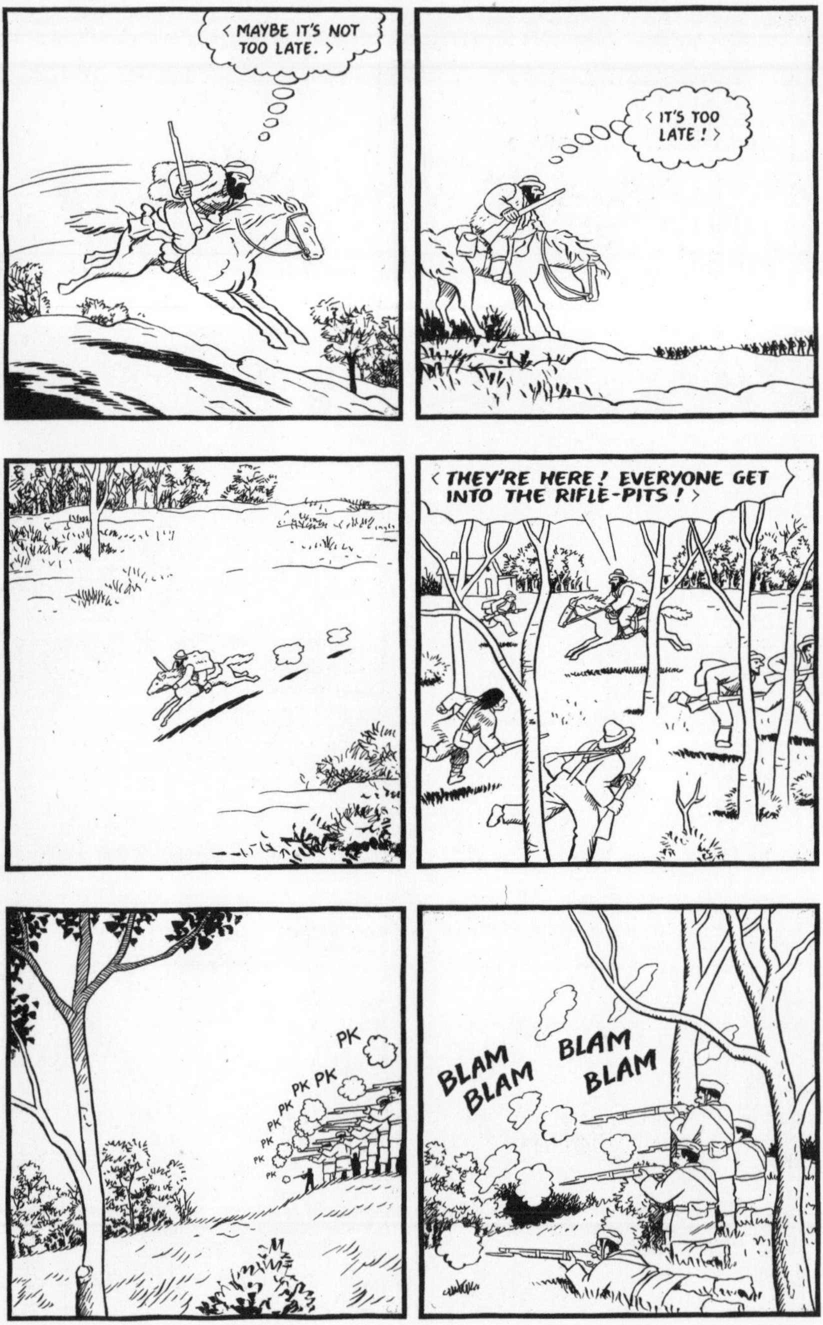
< MAYBE IT'S NOT TOO LATE. >
< IT'S TOO LATE! >
< THEY'RE HERE! EVERYONE GET INTO THE RIFLE-PITS! >
PK
PK PK
PK
PK
PK
PK
PK
BLAM
BLAM
BLAM
BLAM

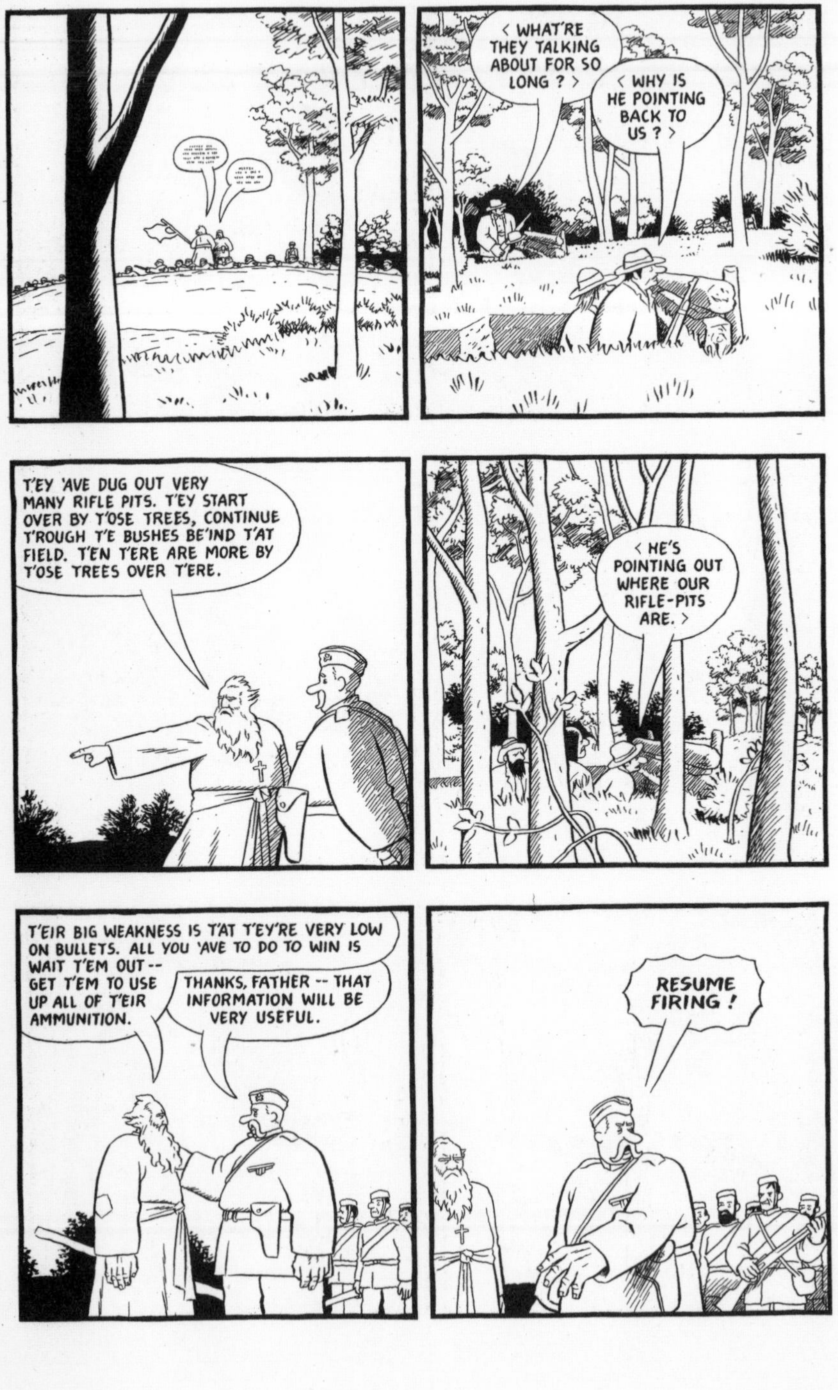

< WHAT'RE THEY TALKING ABOUT FOR SO LONG ? >
< WHY IS HE POINTING BACK TO US ? >
T'EY 'AVE DUG OUT VERY MANY RIFLE PITS. T'EY START OVER BY T'OSE TREES, CONTINUE T'ROUGH T'E BUSHES BE'IND T'AT FIELD. T'EN T'ERE ARE MORE BY T'OSE TREES OVER T'ERE.
< HE'S POINTING OUT WHERE OUR RIFLE-PITS ARE. >
T'EIR BIG WEAKNESS IS T'AT T'EY'RE VERY LOW ON BULLETS. ALL YOU 'AVE TO DO TO WIN IS WAIT T'EM OUT -- GET T'EM TO USE UP ALL OF T'EIR AMMUNITION.
THANKS, FATHER -- THAT INFORMATION WILL BE VERY USEFUL.
RESUME FIRING !

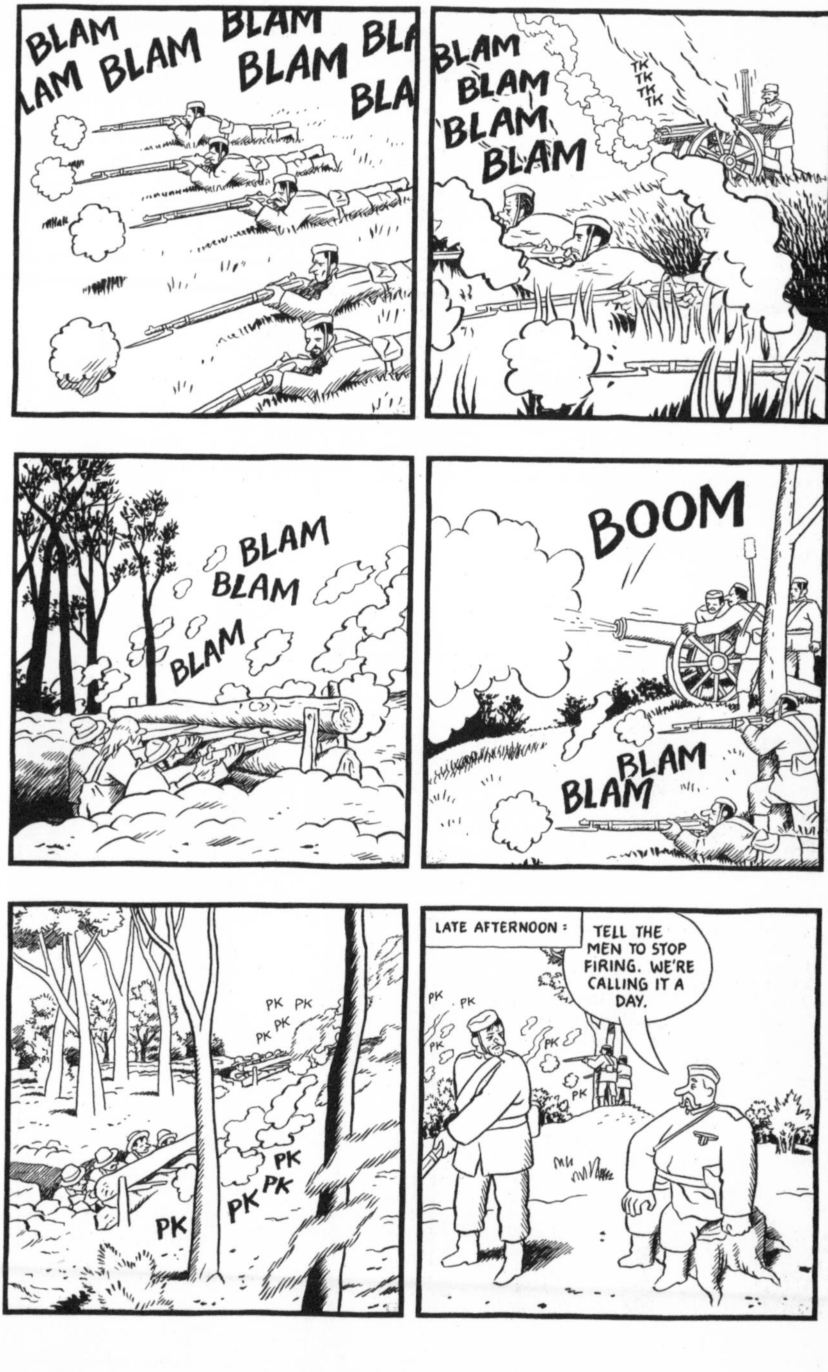
BLAM
LAM BLAM
BLAM
BLAM
BL
BLA
BLAM
BLAM
BLAM
BLAM
TK TK TK TK
BLAM
BLAM
BLAM
BOOM
BLAM
BLAM
PK PK
PK
PK
PK
PK
PK
PK
LATE AFTERNOON :
TELL THE MEN TO STOP FIRING. WE'RE CALLING IT A DAY.
PK PK
PK
PK
PK

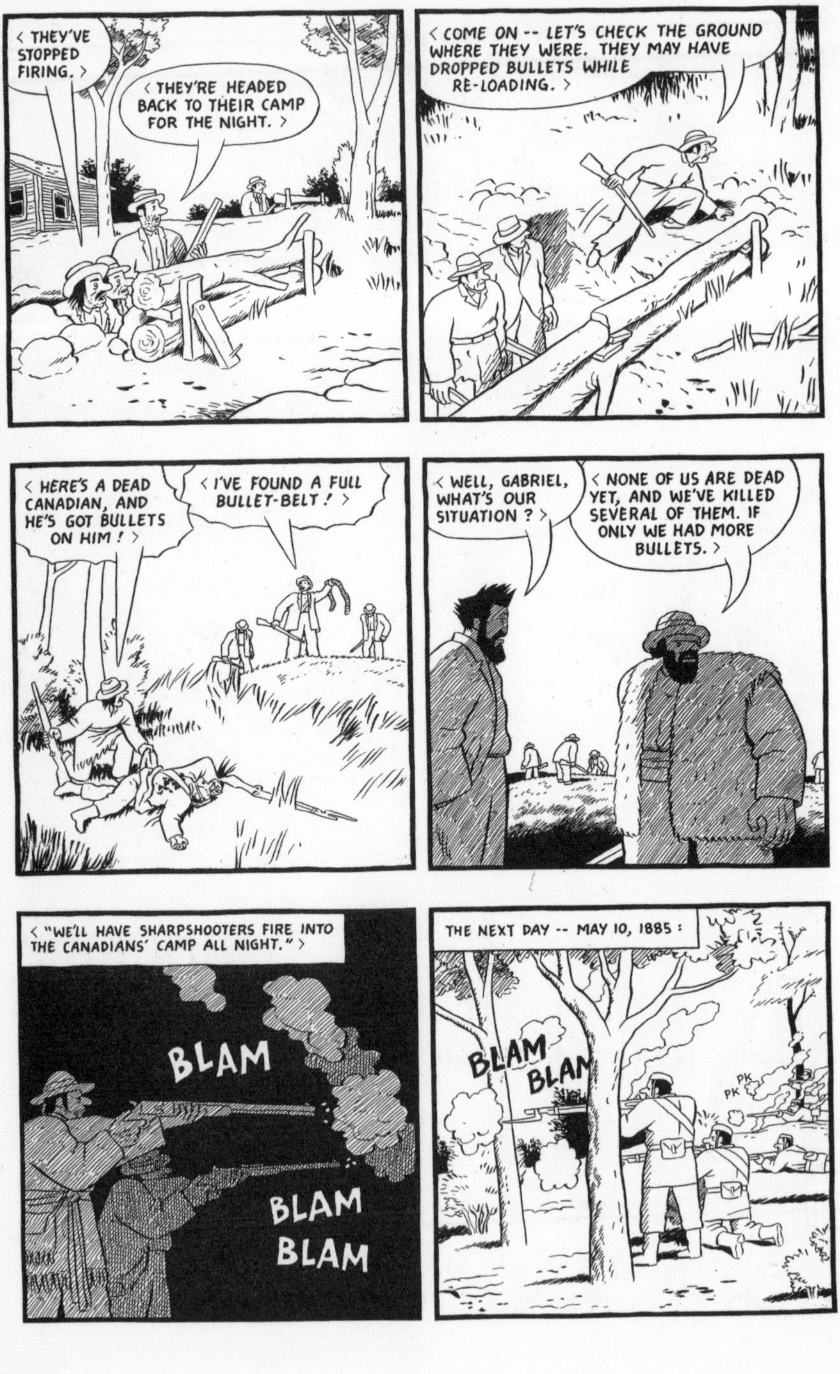

< THEY'VE STOPPED FIRING. >
< THEY'RE HEADED BACK TO THEIR CAMP FOR THE NIGHT. >
< COME ON -- LET'S CHECK THE GROUND WHERE THEY WERE. THEY MAY HAVE DROPPED BULLETS WHILE RE-LOADING. >
< HERE'S A DEAD CANADIAN, AND HE'S GOT BULLETS ON HIM! >
< I'VE FOUND A FULL BULLET-BELT! >
< WELL, GABRIEL, WHAT'S OUR SITUATION? >
< NONE OF US ARE DEAD YET, AND WE'VE KILLED SEVERAL OF THEM. IF ONLY WE HAD MORE BULLETS. >
< "WE'LL HAVE SHARPSHOOTERS FIRE INTO THE CANADIANS' CAMP ALL NIGHT." >
BLAM
BLAM
BLAM
THE NEXT DAY -- MAY 10, 1885:
BLAM
BLAM
PK
PK

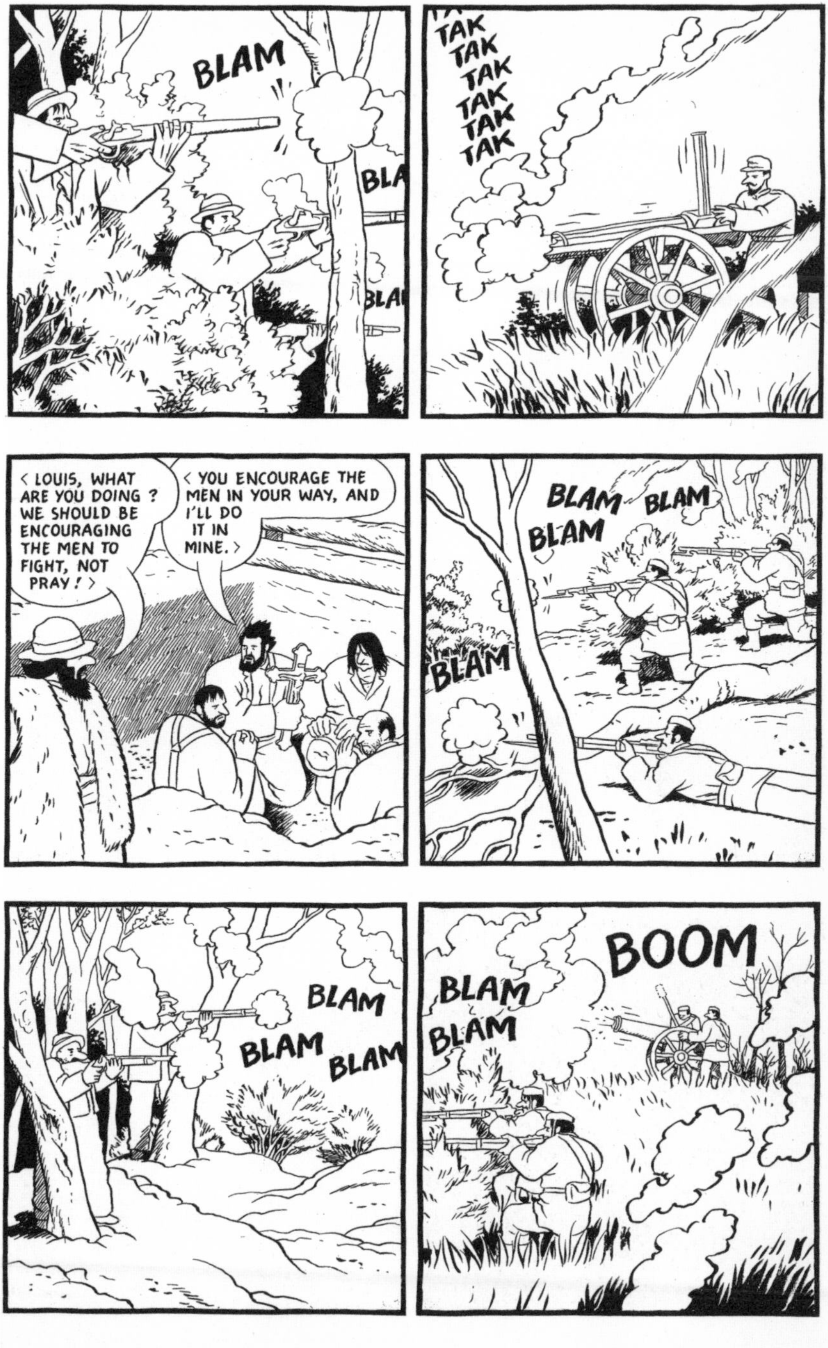
BLAM
BLA
BLA
TAK
TAK
TAK
TAK
TAK
TAK
< LOUIS, WHAT ARE YOU DOING ? WE SHOULD BE ENCOURAGING THE MEN TO FIGHT, NOT PRAY ! >
< YOU ENCOURAGE THE MEN IN YOUR WAY, AND I'LL DO IT IN MINE. >
BLAM
BLAM
BLAM
BLAM
BLAM
BLAM
BLAM
BOOM
BLAM
BLAM

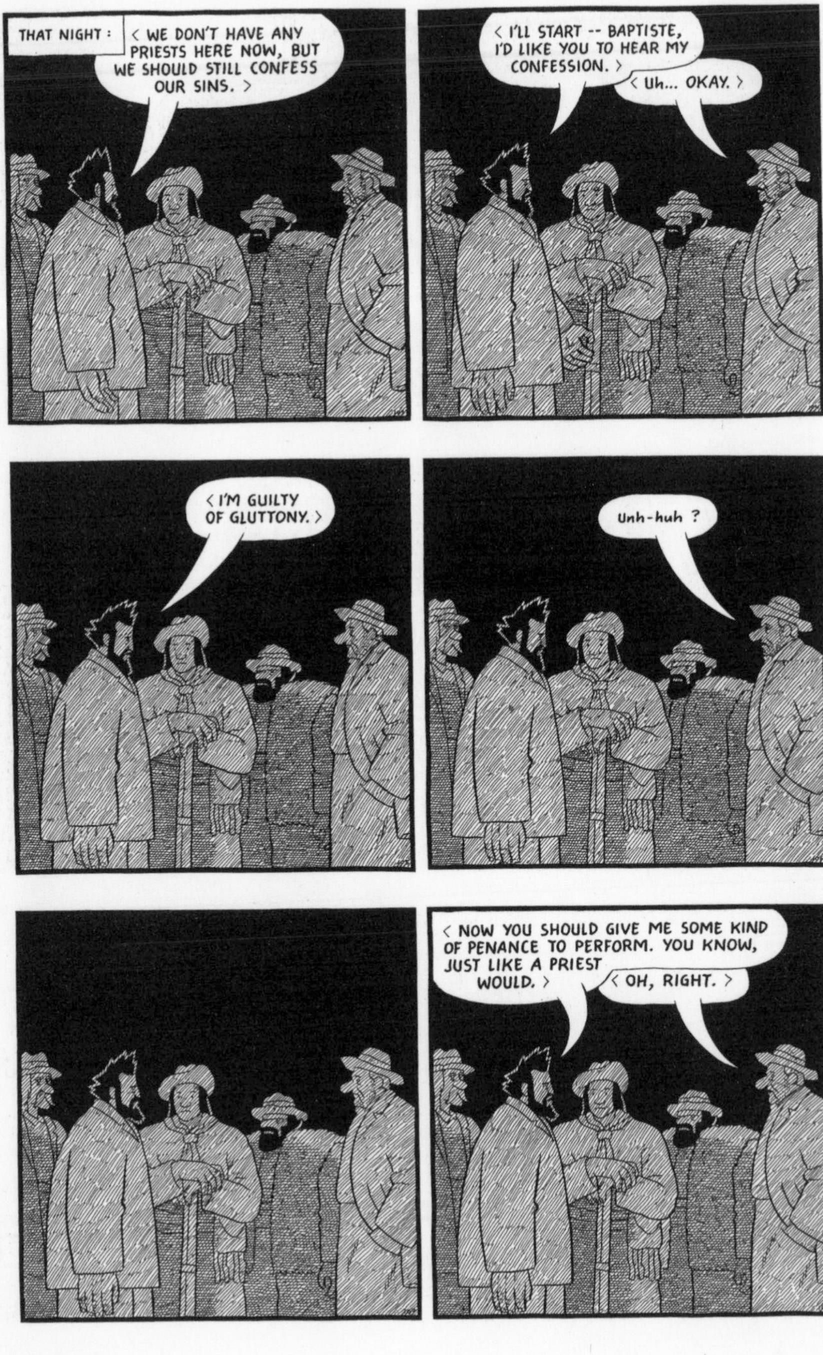
THAT NIGHT :
< WE DON'T HAVE ANY PRIESTS HERE NOW, BUT WE SHOULD STILL CONFESS OUR SINS. >
< I'LL START -- BAPTISTE, I'D LIKE YOU TO HEAR MY CONFESSION. >
< Uh... OKAY. >
< I'M GUILTY OF GLUTTONY. >
Unh-huh ?
< NOW YOU SHOULD GIVE ME SOME KIND OF PENANCE TO PERFORM. YOU KNOW, JUST LIKE A PRIEST WOULD. >
< OH, RIGHT. >

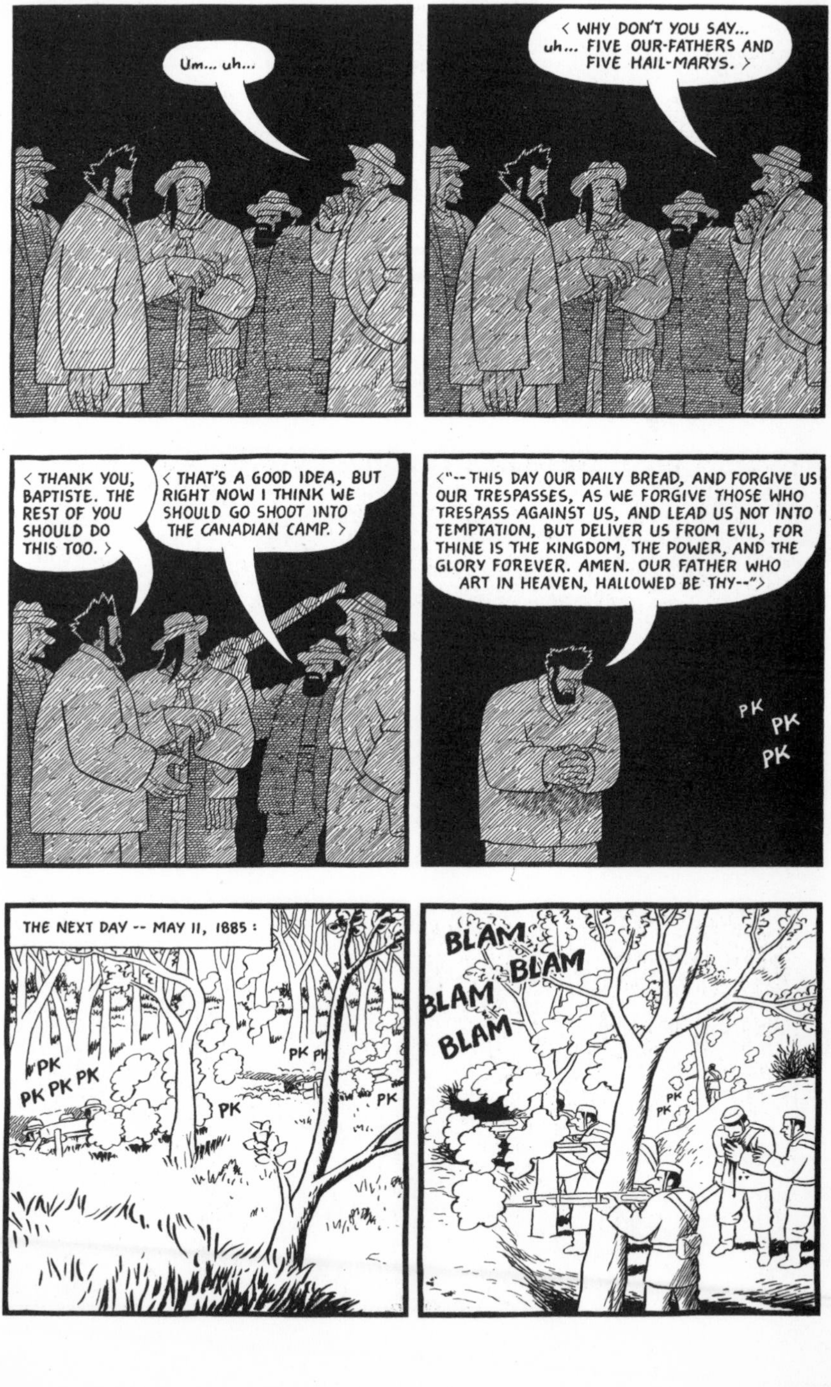
Um... uh...
< WHY DON'T YOU SAY... uh... FIVE OUR-FATHERS AND FIVE HAIL-MARYS. >
< THANK YOU, BAPTISTE. THE REST OF YOU SHOULD DO THIS TOO. >
< THAT'S A GOOD IDEA, BUT RIGHT NOW I THINK WE SHOULD GO SHOOT INTO THE CANADIAN CAMP. >
<"-- THIS DAY OUR DAILY BREAD, AND FORGIVE US OUR TRESPASSES, AS WE FORGIVE THOSE WHO TRESPASS AGAINST US, AND LEAD US NOT INTO TEMPTATION, BUT DELIVER US FROM EVIL, FOR THINE IS THE KINGDOM, THE POWER, AND THE GLORY FOREVER. AMEN. OUR FATHER WHO ART IN HEAVEN, HALLOWED BE THY--">
PK PK PK
THE NEXT DAY -- MAY 11, 1885 :
PK PK PK PK
PK PK
PK
PK
BLAM BLAM BLAM BLAM
PK PK

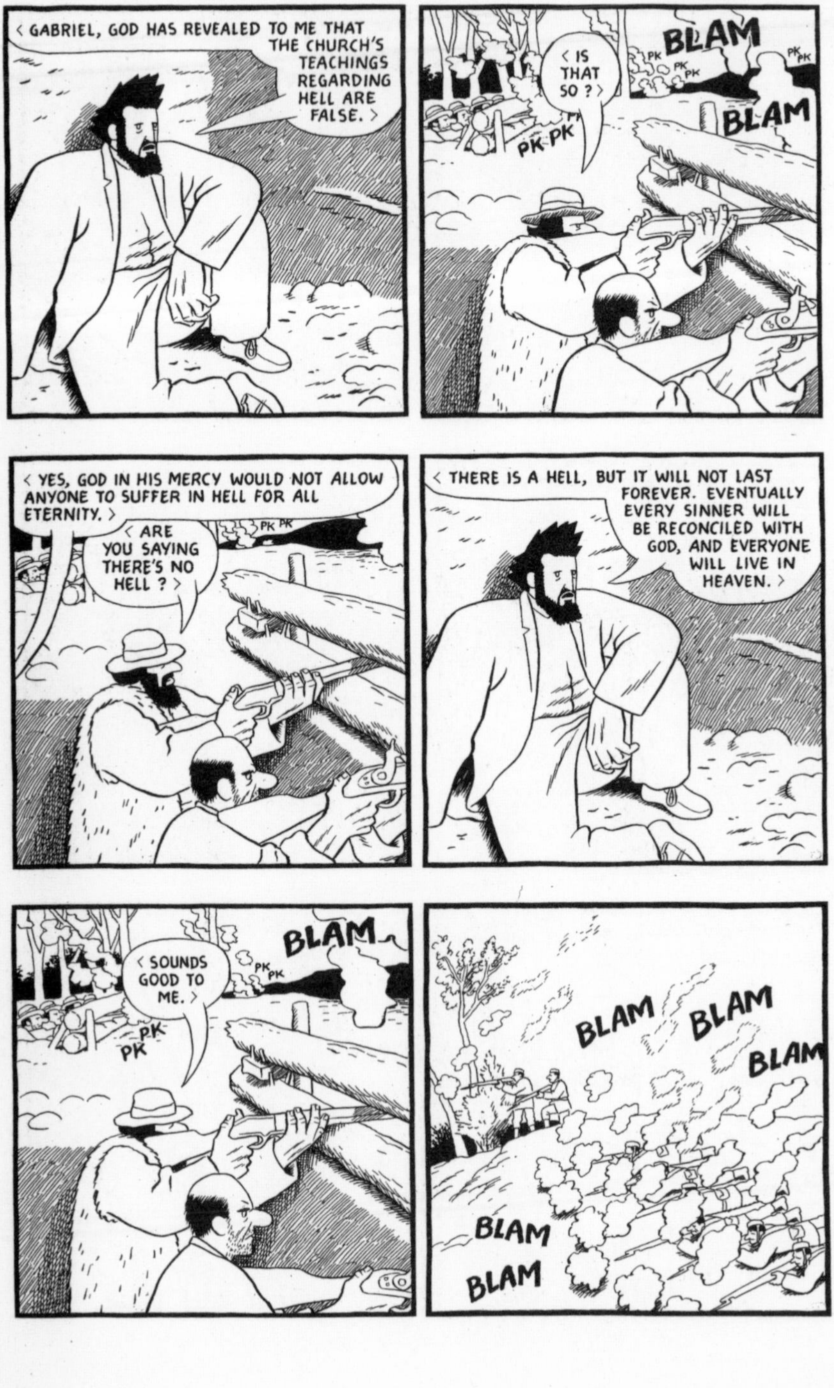
< GABRIEL, GOD HAS REVEALED TO ME THAT THE CHURCH'S TEACHINGS REGARDING HELL ARE FALSE. >
< IS THAT SO ? >
PK
BLAM
PK PK
PK PK
PK PK
BLAM
PK PK
< YES, GOD IN HIS MERCY WOULD NOT ALLOW ANYONE TO SUFFER IN HELL FOR ALL ETERNITY. >
PK PK
< ARE YOU SAYING THERE'S NO HELL ? >
< THERE IS A HELL, BUT IT WILL NOT LAST FOREVER. EVENTUALLY EVERY SINNER WILL BE RECONCILED WITH GOD, AND EVERYONE WILL LIVE IN HEAVEN. >
< SOUNDS GOOD TO ME. >
BLAM
PK PK
PK PK
BLAM
BLAM
BLAM
BLAM
BLAM

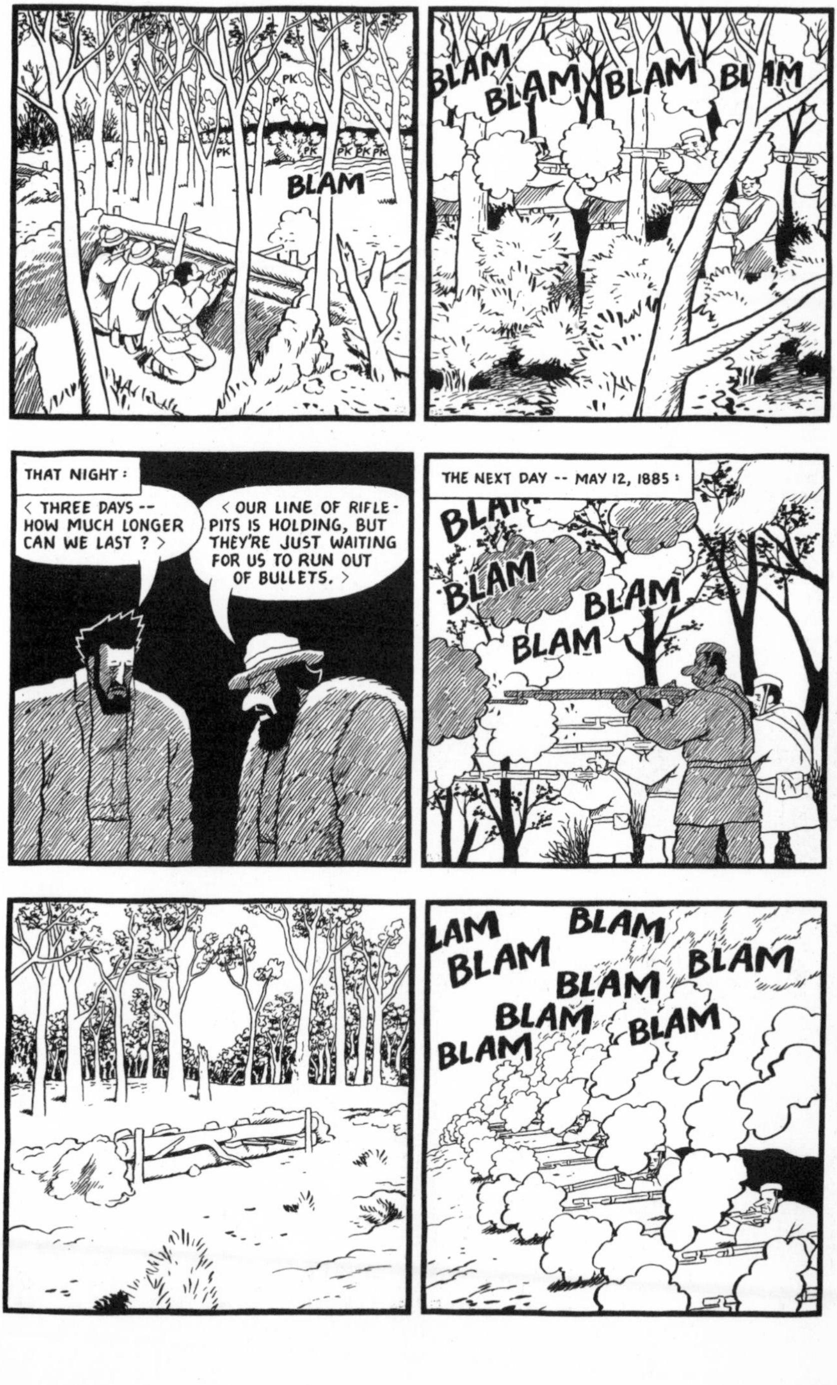
PK
PK
PK
PK PK PK PK
BLAM
BLAM BLAM BLAM BLAM
THAT NIGHT :
< THREE DAYS -- HOW MUCH LONGER CAN WE LAST ? >
< OUR LINE OF RIFLE-PITS IS HOLDING, BUT THEY'RE JUST WAITING FOR US TO RUN OUT OF BULLETS. >
THE NEXT DAY -- MAY 12, 1885 :
BLAM
BLAM
BLAM
LAM BLAM
BLAM BLAM BLAM
BLAM BLAM BLAM BLAM

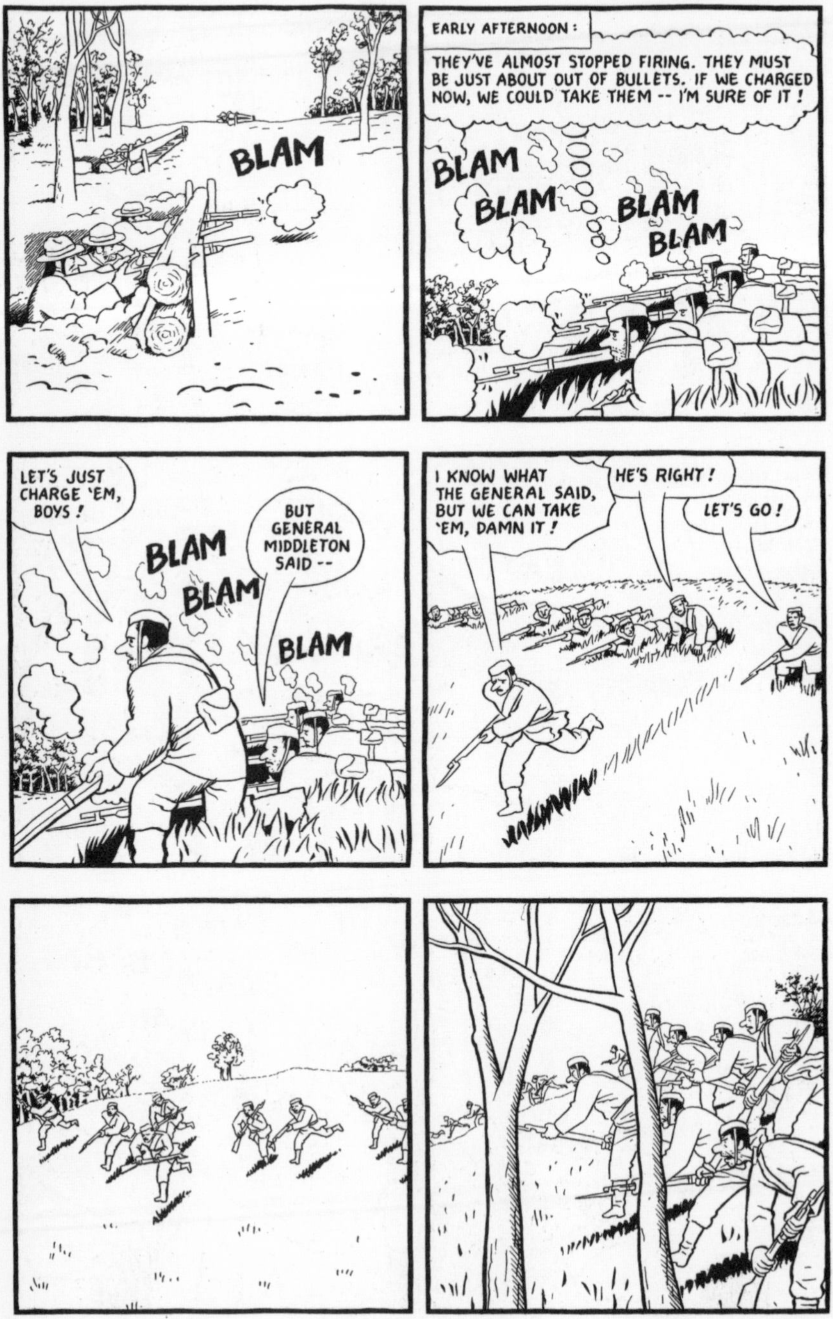
BLAM
EARLY AFTERNOON:
THEY'VE ALMOST STOPPED FIRING. THEY MUST BE JUST ABOUT OUT OF BULLETS. IF WE CHARGED NOW, WE COULD TAKE THEM -- I'M SURE OF IT!
BLAM
BLAM
BLAM
BLAM
LET'S JUST CHARGE 'EM, BOYS!
BLAM
BLAM
BUT GENERAL MIDDLETON SAID --
BLAM
I KNOW WHAT THE GENERAL SAID, BUT WE CAN TAKE 'EM, DAMN IT!
HE'S RIGHT!
LET'S GO!

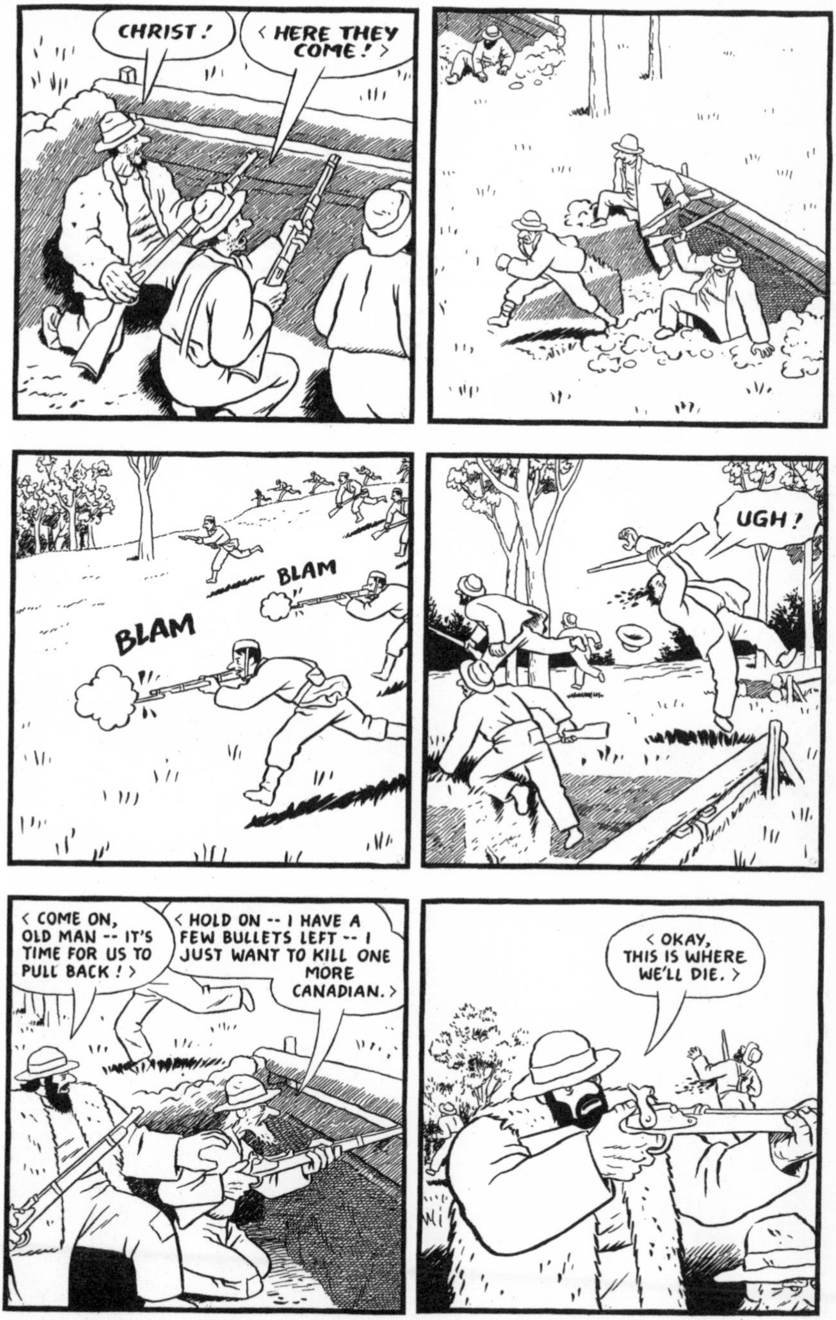
CHRIST!
< HERE THEY COME! >
BLAM
BLAM
UGH!
< COME ON, OLD MAN -- IT'S TIME FOR US TO PULL BACK! >
< HOLD ON -- I HAVE A FEW BULLETS LEFT -- I JUST WANT TO KILL ONE MORE CANADIAN. >
< OKAY, THIS IS WHERE WE'LL DIE. >

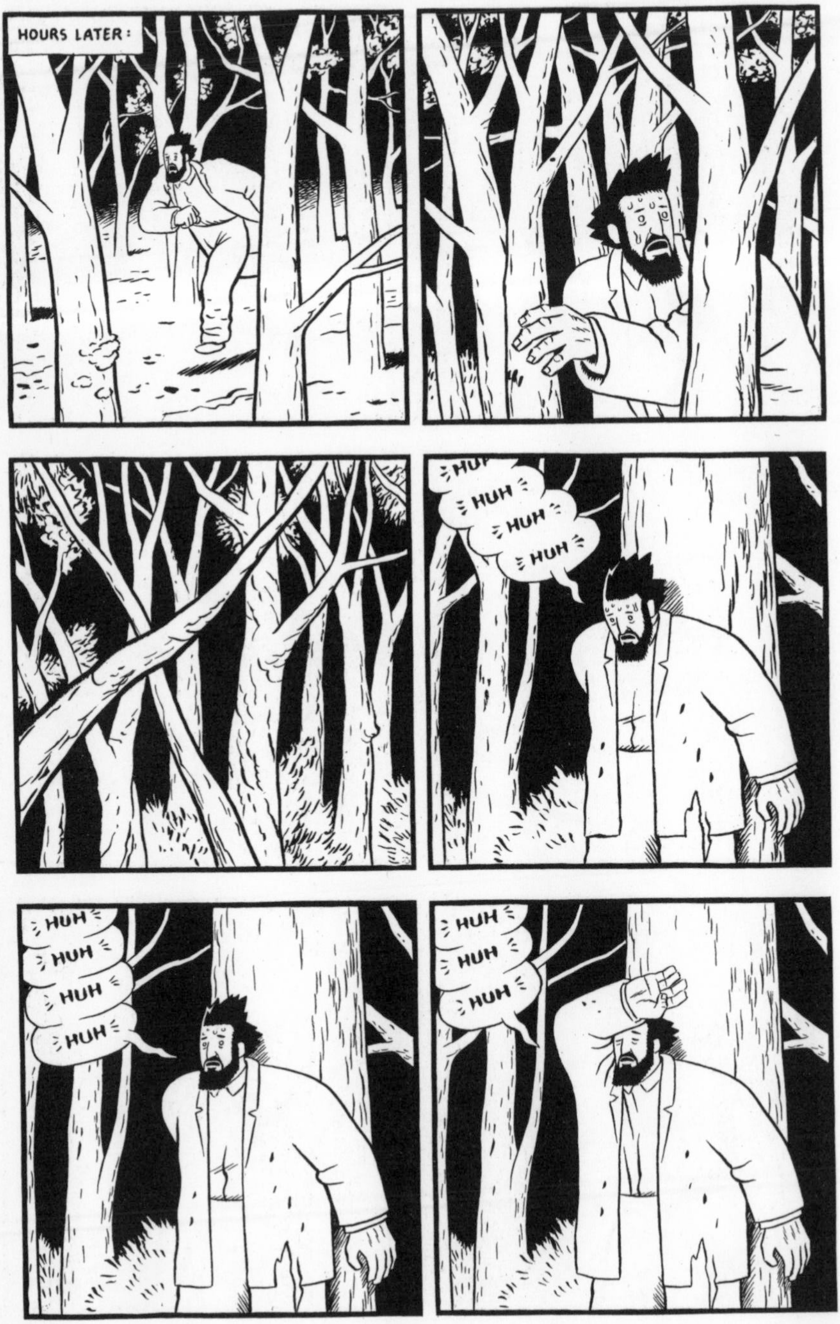
HOURS LATER:
HUH
HUH
HUH
HUH
HUH
HUH
HUH
HUH
HUH
HUH
HUH

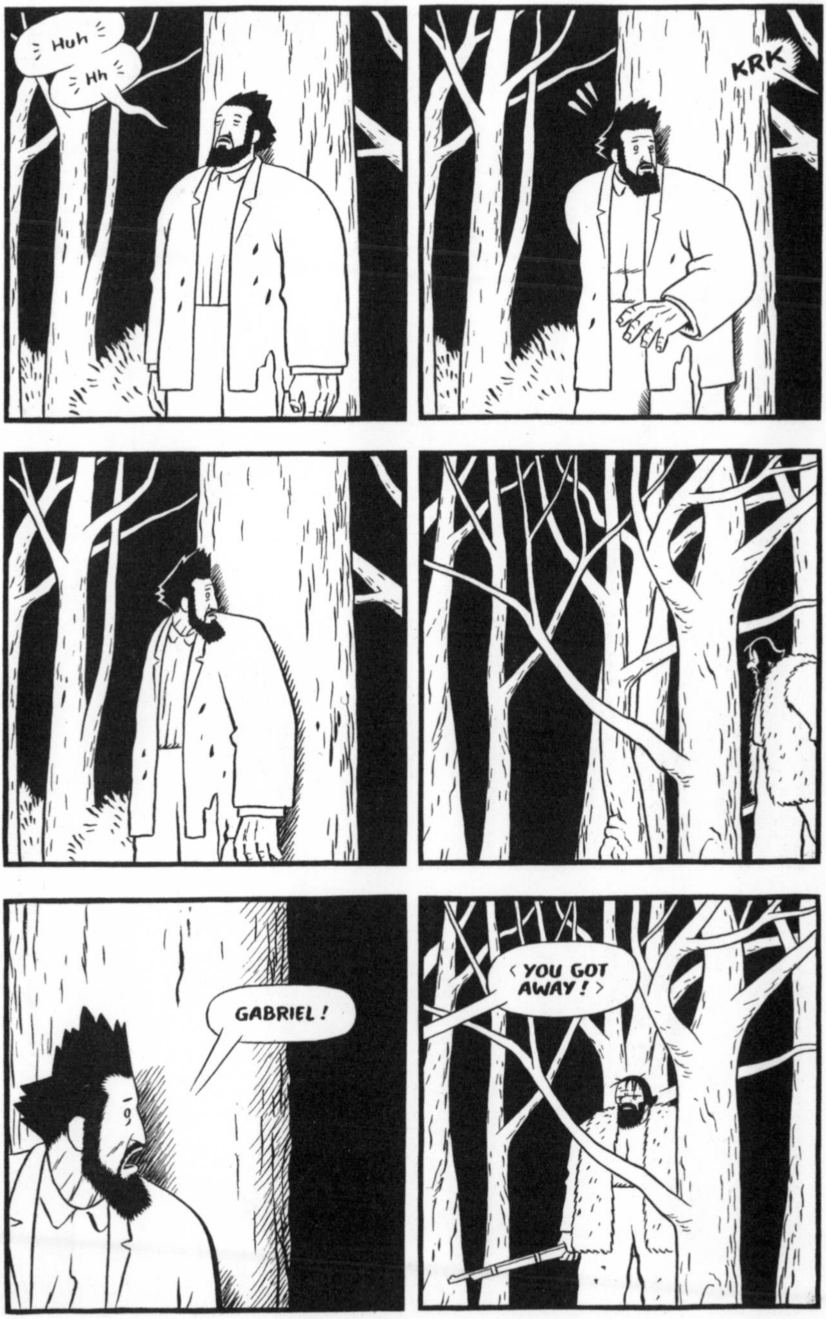
Huh
Hh
KRK
GABRIEL!
‹ YOU GOT AWAY! ›

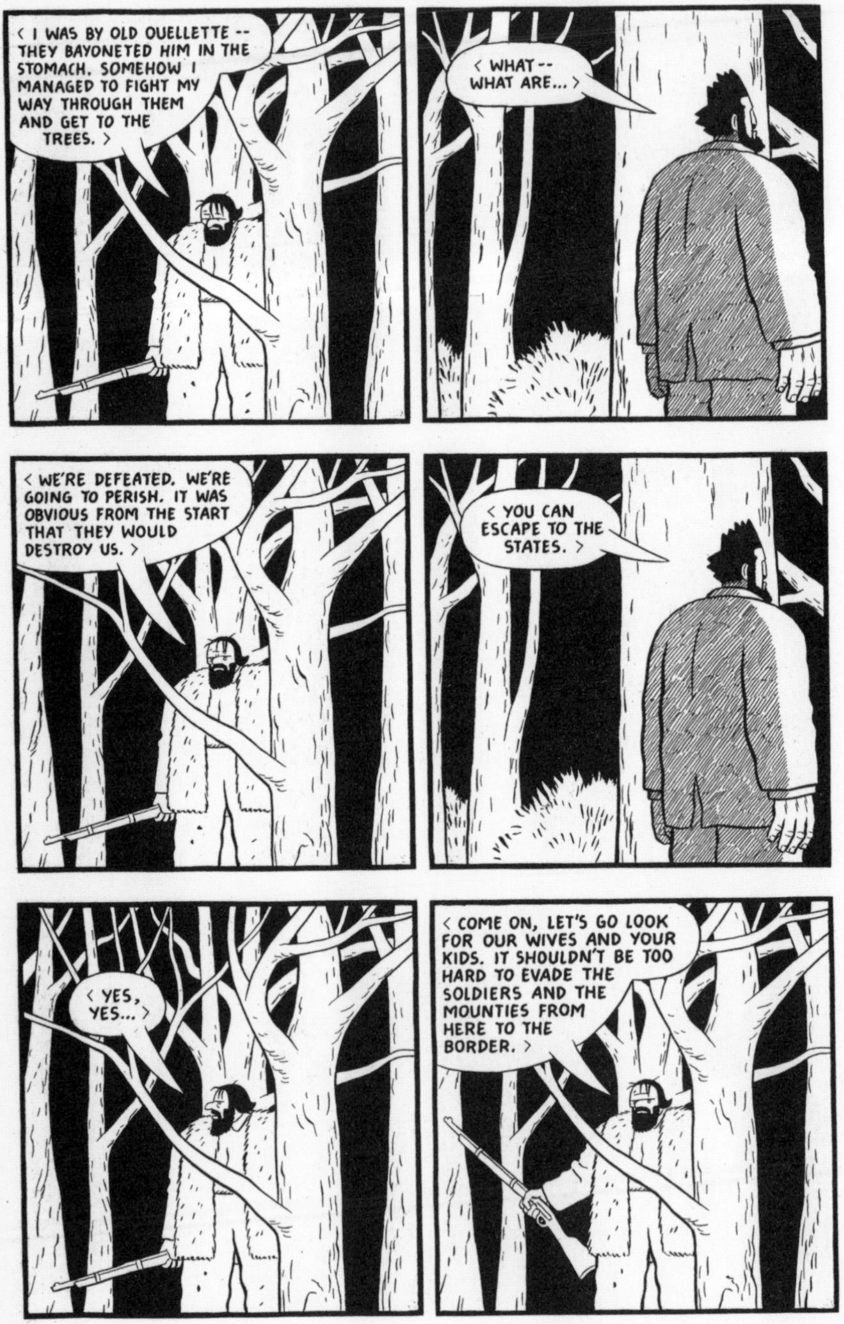
< I WAS BY OLD OUELLETTE -- THEY BAYONETED HIM IN THE STOMACH. SOMEHOW I MANAGED TO FIGHT MY WAY THROUGH THEM AND GET TO THE TREES. >
< WHAT -- WHAT ARE... >
< WE'RE DEFEATED. WE'RE GOING TO PERISH. IT WAS OBVIOUS FROM THE START THAT THEY WOULD DESTROY US. >
< YOU CAN ESCAPE TO THE STATES. >
< YES, YES... >
< COME ON, LET'S GO LOOK FOR OUR WIVES AND YOUR KIDS. IT SHOULDN'T BE TOO HARD TO EVADE THE SOLDIERS AND THE MOUNTIES FROM HERE TO THE BORDER. >

PART FOUR

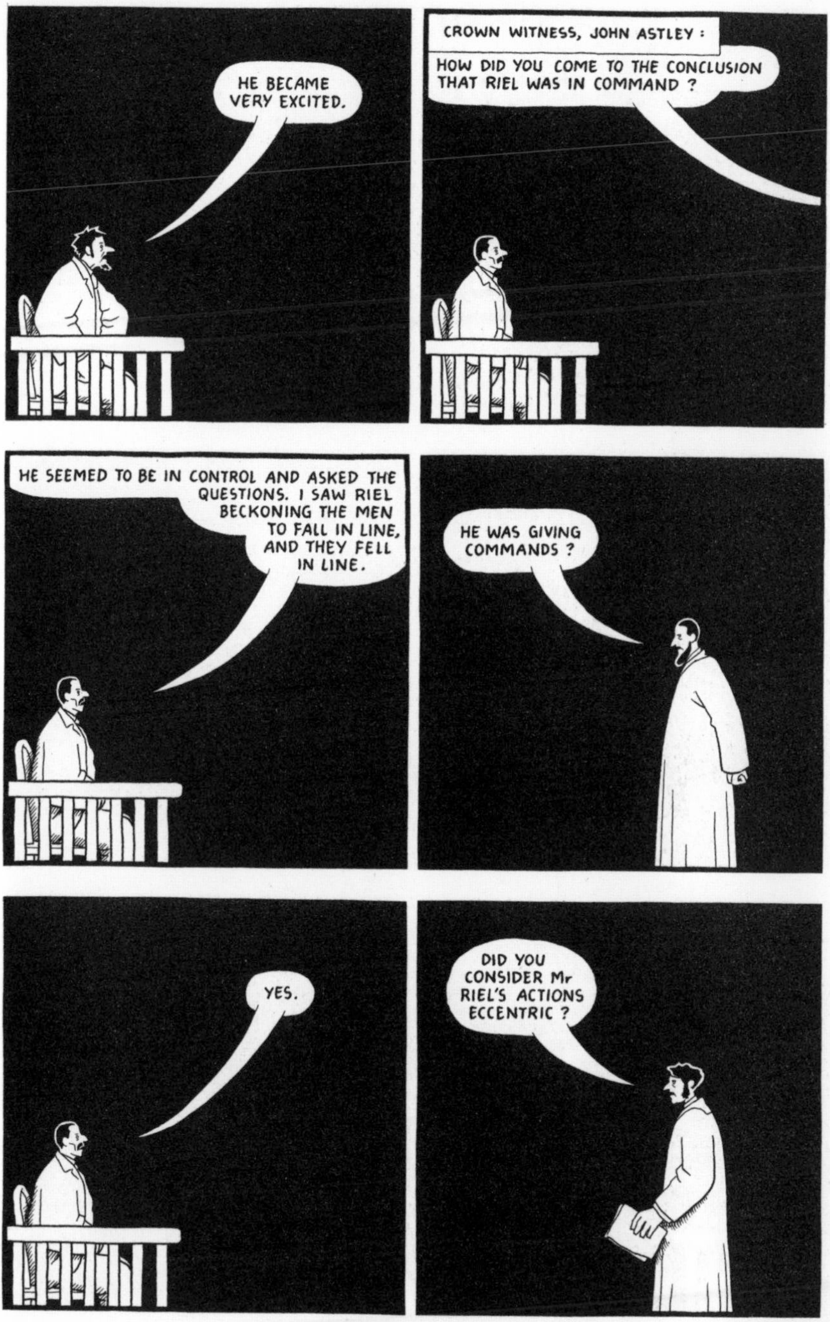
HE BECAME VERY EXCITED.
CROWN WITNESS, JOHN ASTLEY :
HOW DID YOU COME TO THE CONCLUSION THAT RIEL WAS IN COMMAND ?
HE SEEMED TO BE IN CONTROL AND ASKED THE QUESTIONS. I SAW RIEL BECKONING THE MEN TO FALL IN LINE, AND THEY FELL IN LINE.
HE WAS GIVING COMMANDS ?
YES.
DID YOU CONSIDER Mr RIEL'S ACTIONS ECCENTRIC ?

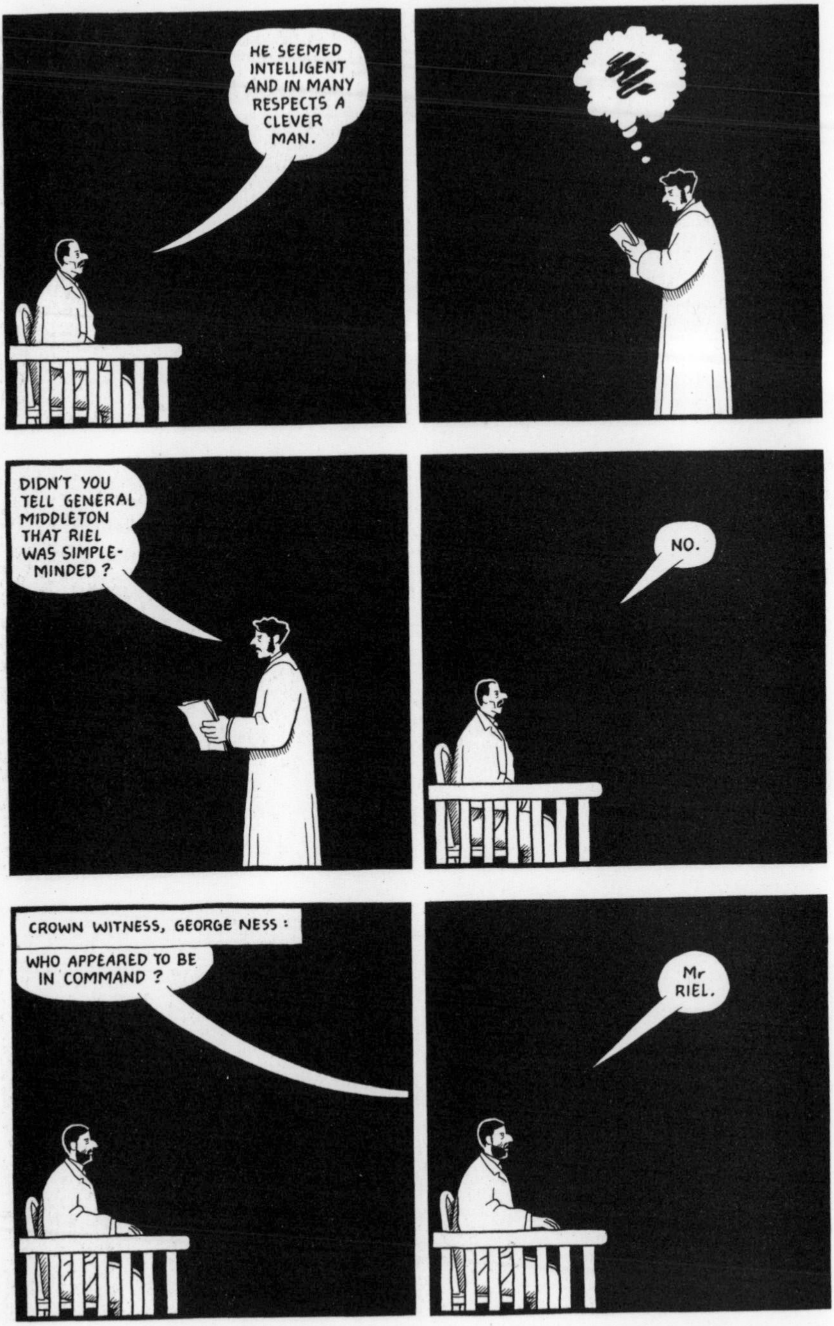
HE SEEMED INTELLIGENT AND IN MANY RESPECTS A CLEVER MAN.
DIDN'T YOU TELL GENERAL MIDDLETON THAT RIEL WAS SIMPLE-MINDED ?
NO.
CROWN WITNESS, GEORGE NESS :
WHO APPEARED TO BE IN COMMAND ?
Mr RIEL.

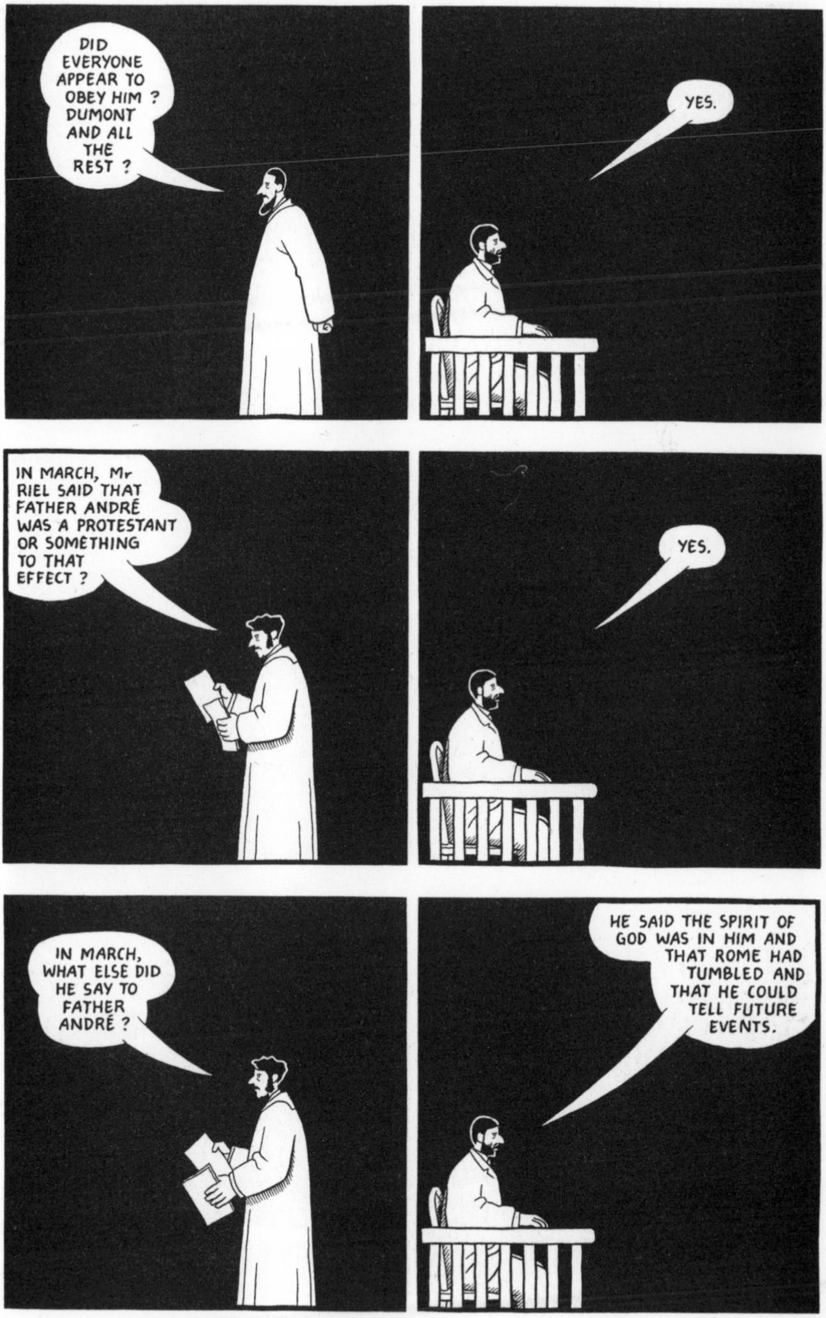
DID EVERYONE APPEAR TO OBEY HIM ? DUMONT AND ALL THE REST ?
YES.
IN MARCH, Mr RIEL SAID THAT FATHER ANDRÉ WAS A PROTESTANT OR SOMETHING TO THAT EFFECT ?
YES.
IN MARCH, WHAT ELSE DID HE SAY TO FATHER ANDRÉ ?
HE SAID THE SPIRIT OF GOD WAS IN HIM AND THAT ROME HAD TUMBLED AND THAT HE COULD TELL FUTURE EVENTS.

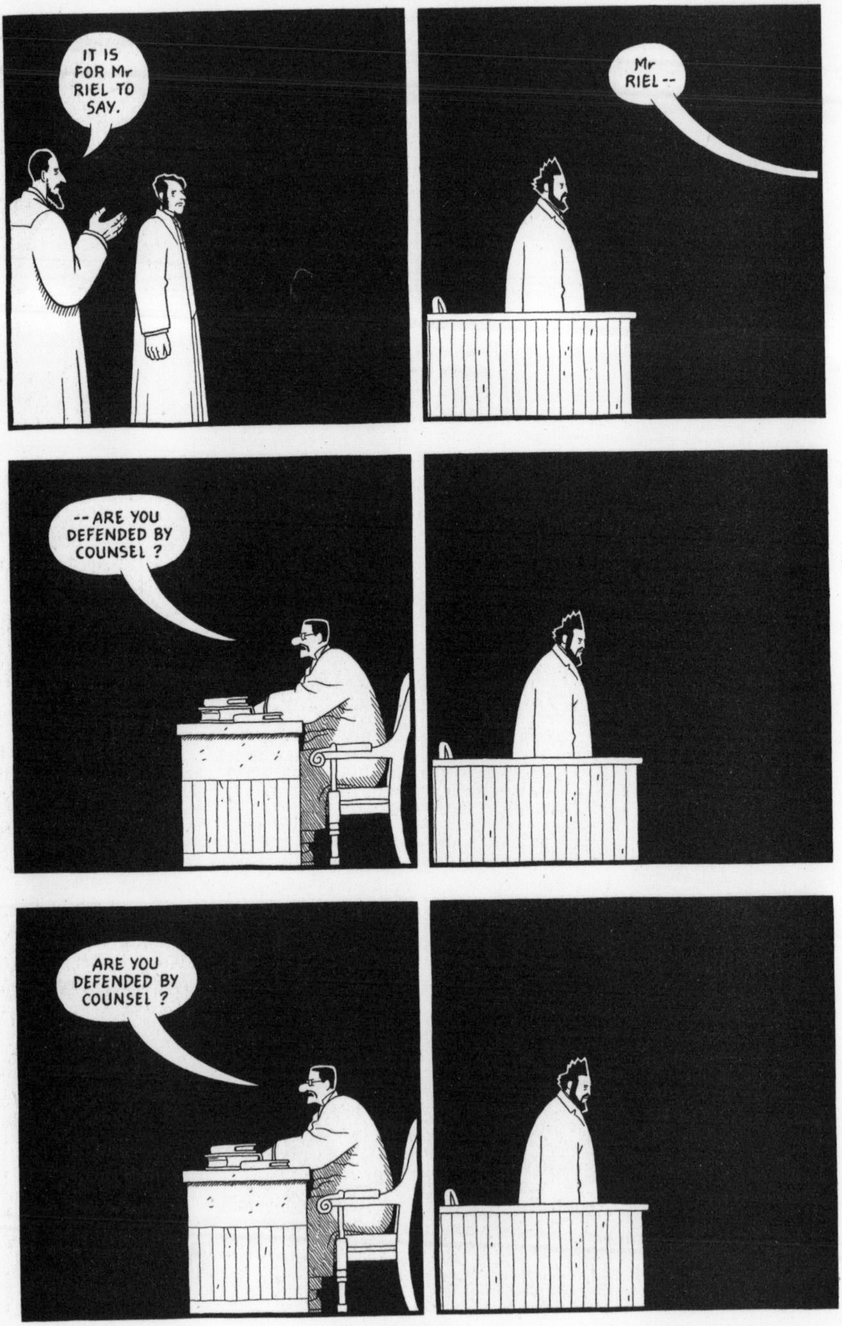
IT IS FOR Mr RIEL TO SAY.
Mr RIEL --
-- ARE YOU DEFENDED BY COUNSEL ?
ARE YOU DEFENDED BY COUNSEL ?

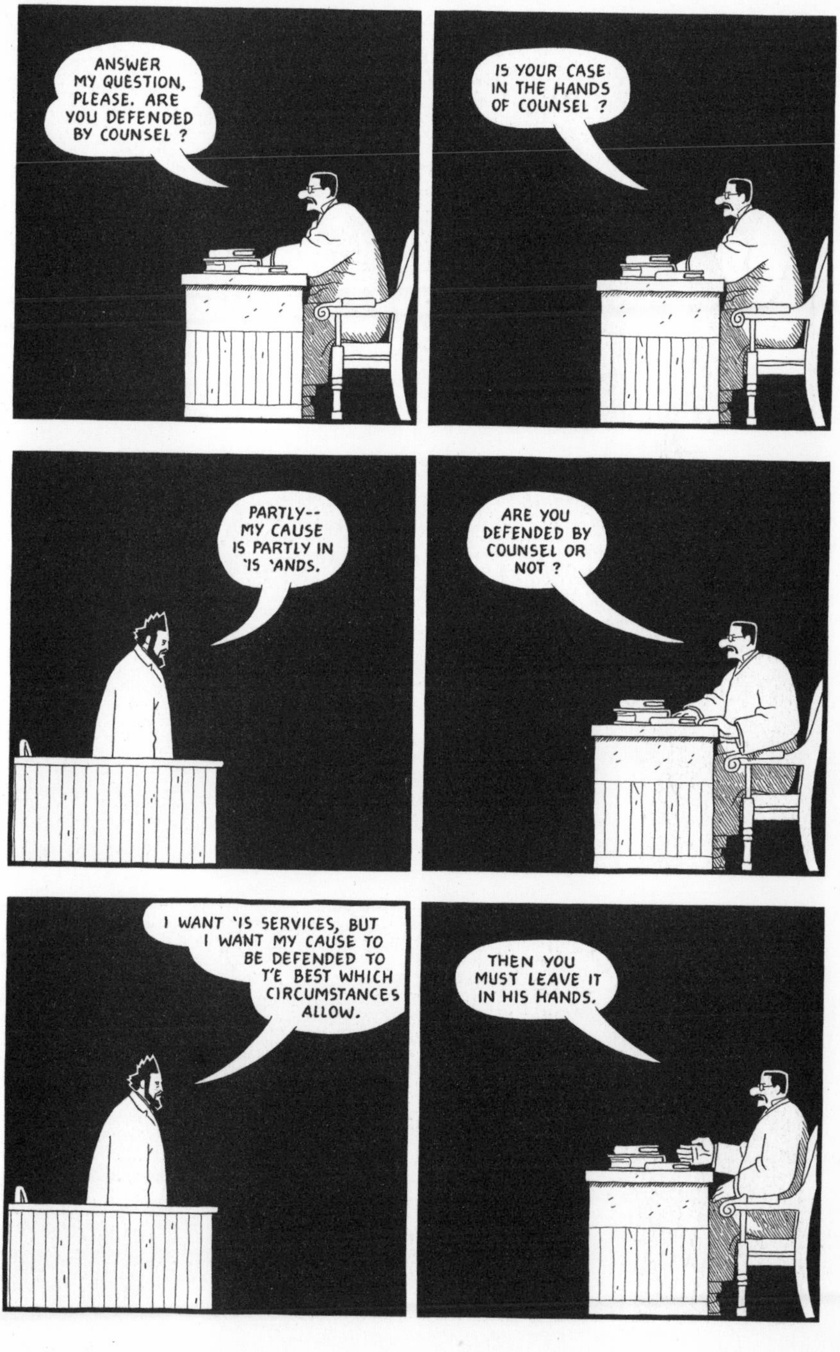
ANSWER MY QUESTION, PLEASE. ARE YOU DEFENDED BY COUNSEL ?
IS YOUR CASE IN THE HANDS OF COUNSEL ?
PARTLY-- MY CAUSE IS PARTLY IN 'IS 'ANDS.
ARE YOU DEFENDED BY COUNSEL OR NOT ?
I WANT 'IS SERVICES, BUT I WANT MY CAUSE TO BE DEFENDED TO T'E BEST WHICH CIRCUMSTANCES ALLOW.
THEN YOU MUST LEAVE IT IN HIS HANDS.

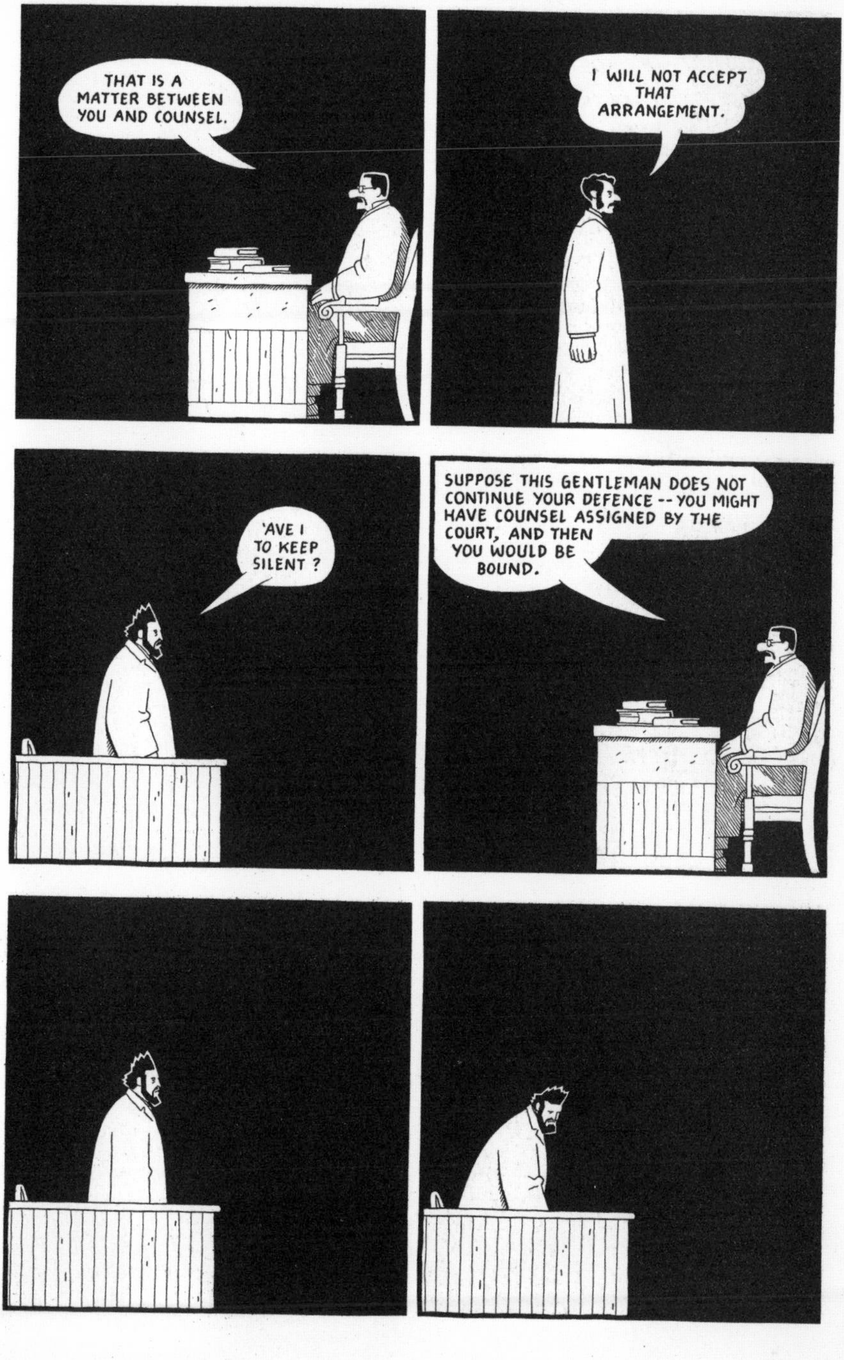
THAT IS A MATTER BETWEEN YOU AND COUNSEL.
I WILL NOT ACCEPT THAT ARRANGEMENT.
'AVE I TO KEEP SILENT ?
SUPPOSE THIS GENTLEMAN DOES NOT CONTINUE YOUR DEFENCE -- YOU MIGHT HAVE COUNSEL ASSIGNED BY THE COURT, AND THEN YOU WOULD BE BOUND.

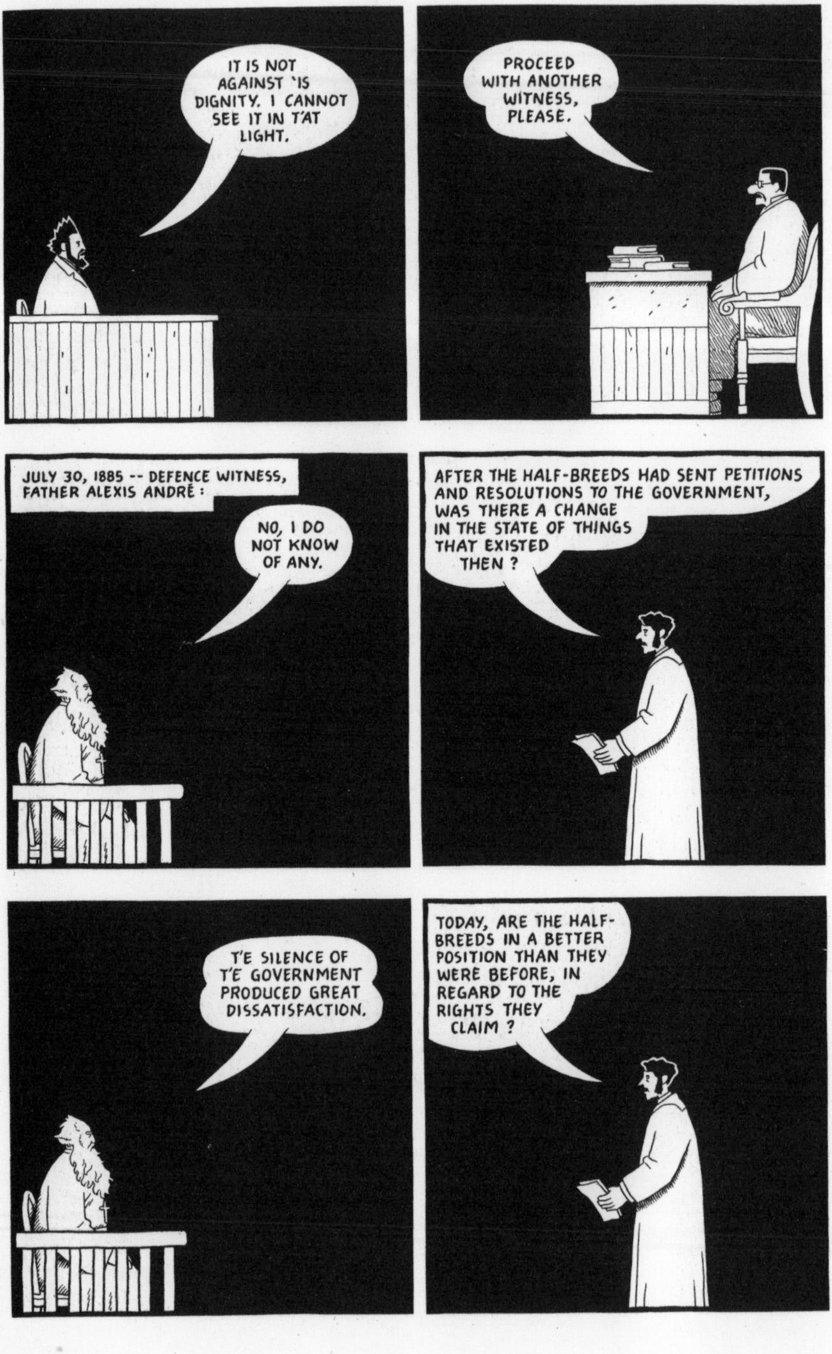
IT IS NOT AGAINST 'IS DIGNITY. I CANNOT SEE IT IN T'AT LIGHT.
PROCEED WITH ANOTHER WITNESS, PLEASE.
JULY 30, 1885 -- DEFENCE WITNESS, FATHER ALEXIS ANDRÉ :
NO, I DO NOT KNOW OF ANY.
AFTER THE HALF-BREEDS HAD SENT PETITIONS AND RESOLUTIONS TO THE GOVERNMENT, WAS THERE A CHANGE IN THE STATE OF THINGS THAT EXISTED THEN ?
T'E SILENCE OF T'E GOVERNMENT PRODUCED GREAT DISSATISFACTION.
TODAY, ARE THE HALF-BREEDS IN A BETTER POSITION THAN THEY WERE BEFORE, IN REGARD TO THE RIGHTS THEY CLAIM ?

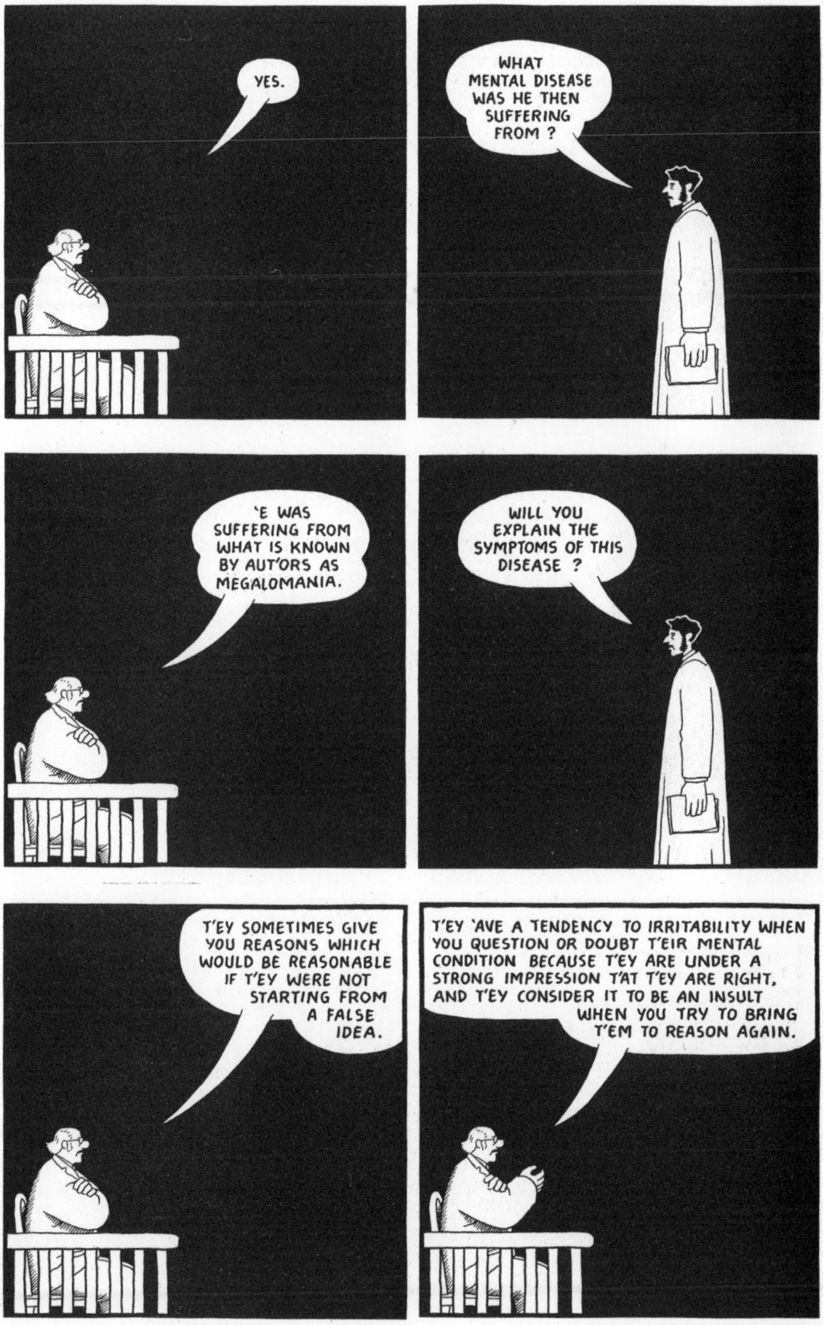
YES.
WHAT MENTAL DISEASE WAS HE THEN SUFFERING FROM ?
'E WAS SUFFERING FROM WHAT IS KNOWN BY AUT'ORS AS MEGALOMANIA.
WILL YOU EXPLAIN THE SYMPTOMS OF THIS DISEASE ?
T'EY SOMETIMES GIVE YOU REASONS WHICH WOULD BE REASONABLE IF T'EY WERE NOT STARTING FROM A FALSE IDEA.
T'EY 'AVE A TENDENCY TO IRRITABILITY WHEN YOU QUESTION OR DOUBT T'EIR MENTAL CONDITION BECAUSE T'EY ARE UNDER A STRONG IMPRESSION T'AT T'EY ARE RIGHT, AND T'EY CONSIDER IT TO BE AN INSULT WHEN YOU TRY TO BRING T'EM TO REASON AGAIN.

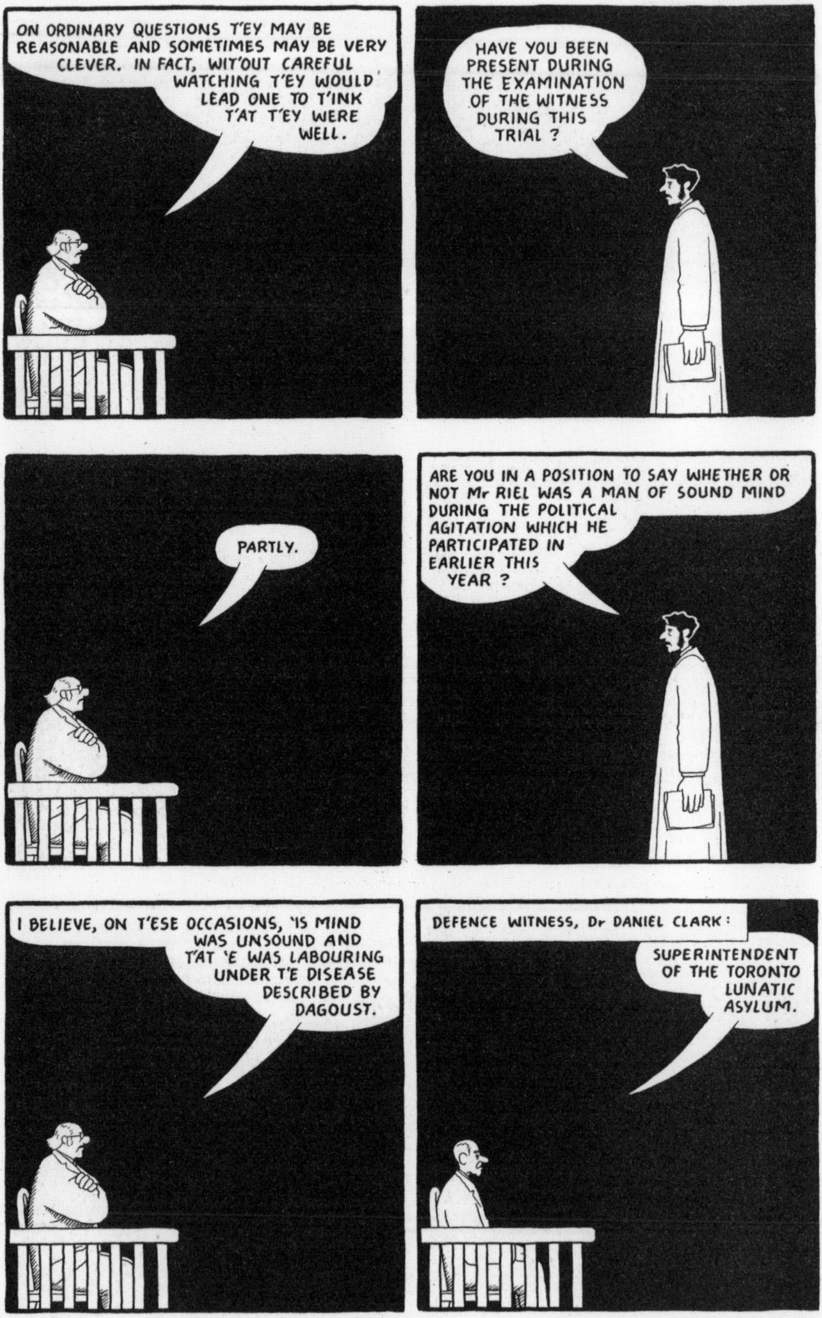
ON ORDINARY QUESTIONS T'EY MAY BE REASONABLE AND SOMETIMES MAY BE VERY CLEVER. IN FACT, WIT'OUT CAREFUL WATCHING T'EY WOULD LEAD ONE TO T'INK T'AT T'EY WERE WELL.
HAVE YOU BEEN PRESENT DURING THE EXAMINATION OF THE WITNESS DURING THIS TRIAL ?
PARTLY.
ARE YOU IN A POSITION TO SAY WHETHER OR NOT Mr RIEL WAS A MAN OF SOUND MIND DURING THE POLITICAL AGITATION WHICH HE PARTICIPATED IN EARLIER THIS YEAR ?
I BELIEVE, ON T'ESE OCCASIONS, 'IS MIND WAS UNSOUND AND T'AT 'E WAS LABOURING UNDER T'E DISEASE DESCRIBED BY DAGOUST.
DEFENCE WITNESS, Dr DANIEL CLARK :
SUPERINTENDENT OF THE TORONTO LUNATIC ASYLUM.

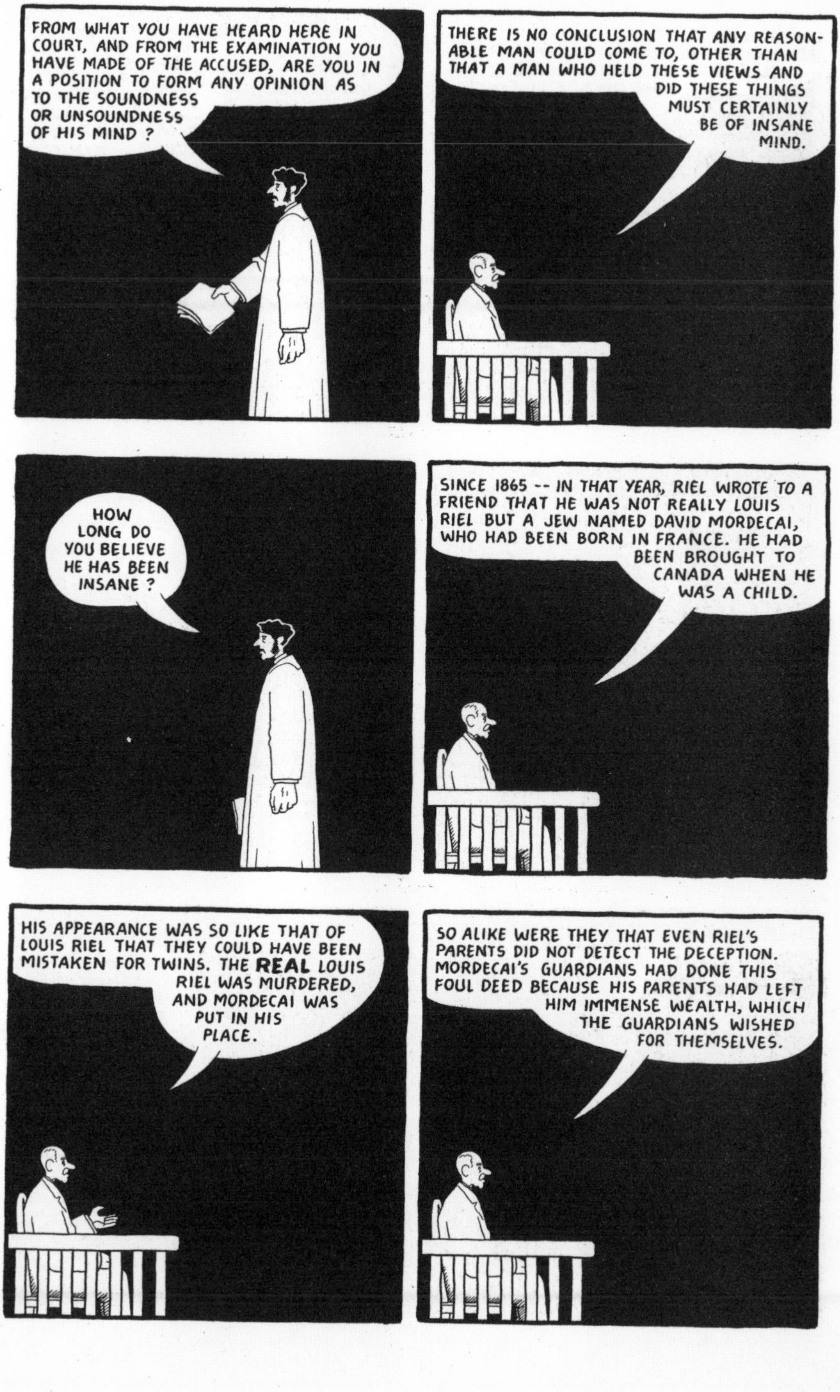
FROM WHAT YOU HAVE HEARD HERE IN COURT, AND FROM THE EXAMINATION YOU HAVE MADE OF THE ACCUSED, ARE YOU IN A POSITION TO FORM ANY OPINION AS TO THE SOUNDNESS OR UNSOUNDNESS OF HIS MIND ?
THERE IS NO CONCLUSION THAT ANY REASON-ABLE MAN COULD COME TO, OTHER THAN THAT A MAN WHO HELD THESE VIEWS AND DID THESE THINGS MUST CERTAINLY BE OF INSANE MIND.
HOW LONG DO YOU BELIEVE HE HAS BEEN INSANE ?
SINCE 1865 -- IN THAT YEAR, RIEL WROTE TO A FRIEND THAT HE WAS NOT REALLY LOUIS RIEL BUT A JEW NAMED DAVID MORDECAI, WHO HAD BEEN BORN IN FRANCE. HE HAD BEEN BROUGHT TO CANADA WHEN HE WAS A CHILD.
HIS APPEARANCE WAS SO LIKE THAT OF LOUIS RIEL THAT THEY COULD HAVE BEEN MISTAKEN FOR TWINS. THE **REAL** LOUIS RIEL WAS MURDERED, AND MORDECAI WAS PUT IN HIS PLACE.
SO ALIKE WERE THEY THAT EVEN RIEL'S PARENTS DID NOT DETECT THE DECEPTION. MORDECAI'S GUARDIANS HAD DONE THIS FOUL DEED BECAUSE HIS PARENTS HAD LEFT HIM IMMENSE WEALTH, WHICH THE GUARDIANS WISHED FOR THEMSELVES.

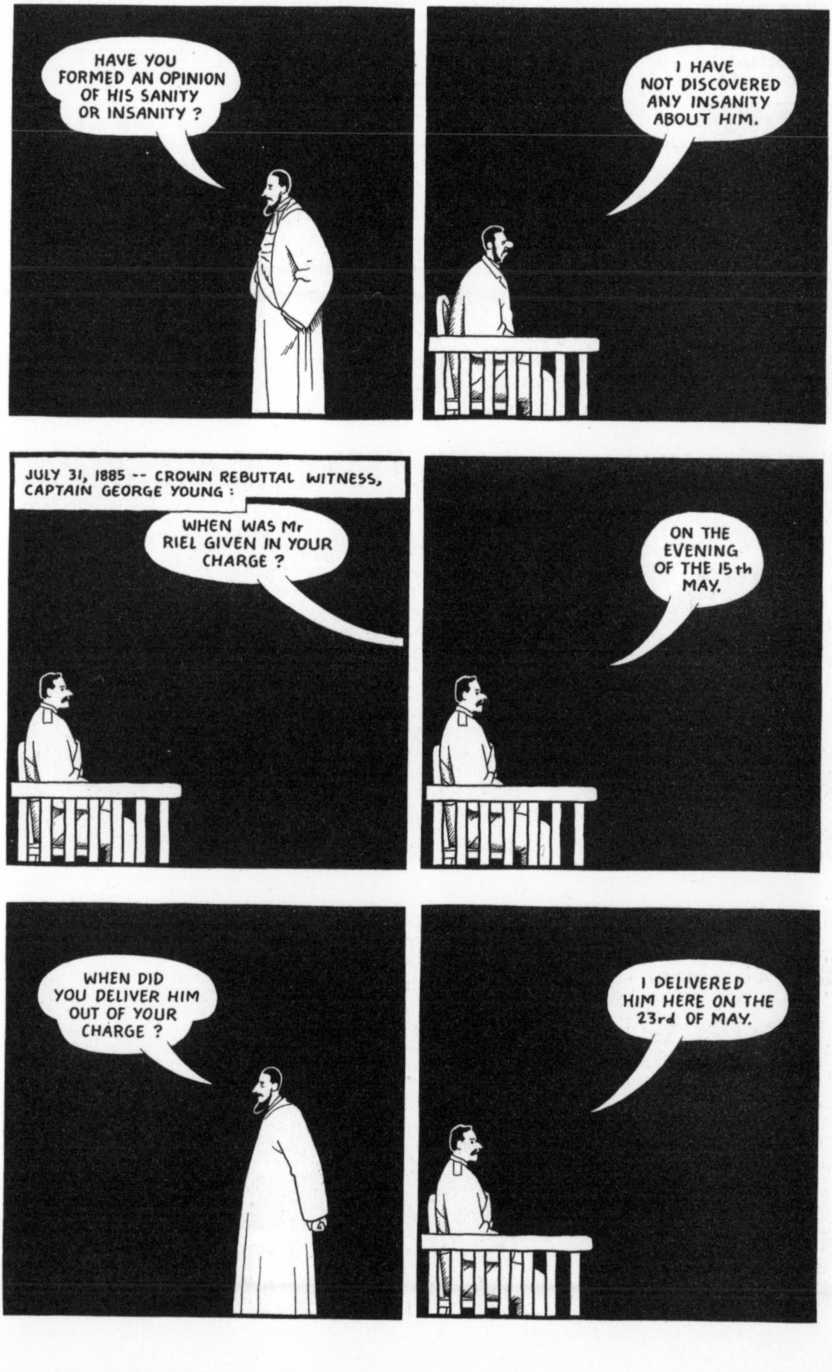
HAVE YOU FORMED AN OPINION OF HIS SANITY OR INSANITY ?
I HAVE NOT DISCOVERED ANY INSANITY ABOUT HIM.
JULY 31, 1885 -- CROWN REBUTTAL WITNESS, CAPTAIN GEORGE YOUNG :
WHEN WAS Mr RIEL GIVEN IN YOUR CHARGE ?
ON THE EVENING OF THE 15th MAY.
WHEN DID YOU DELIVER HIM OUT OF YOUR CHARGE ?
I DELIVERED HIM HERE ON THE 23rd OF MAY.

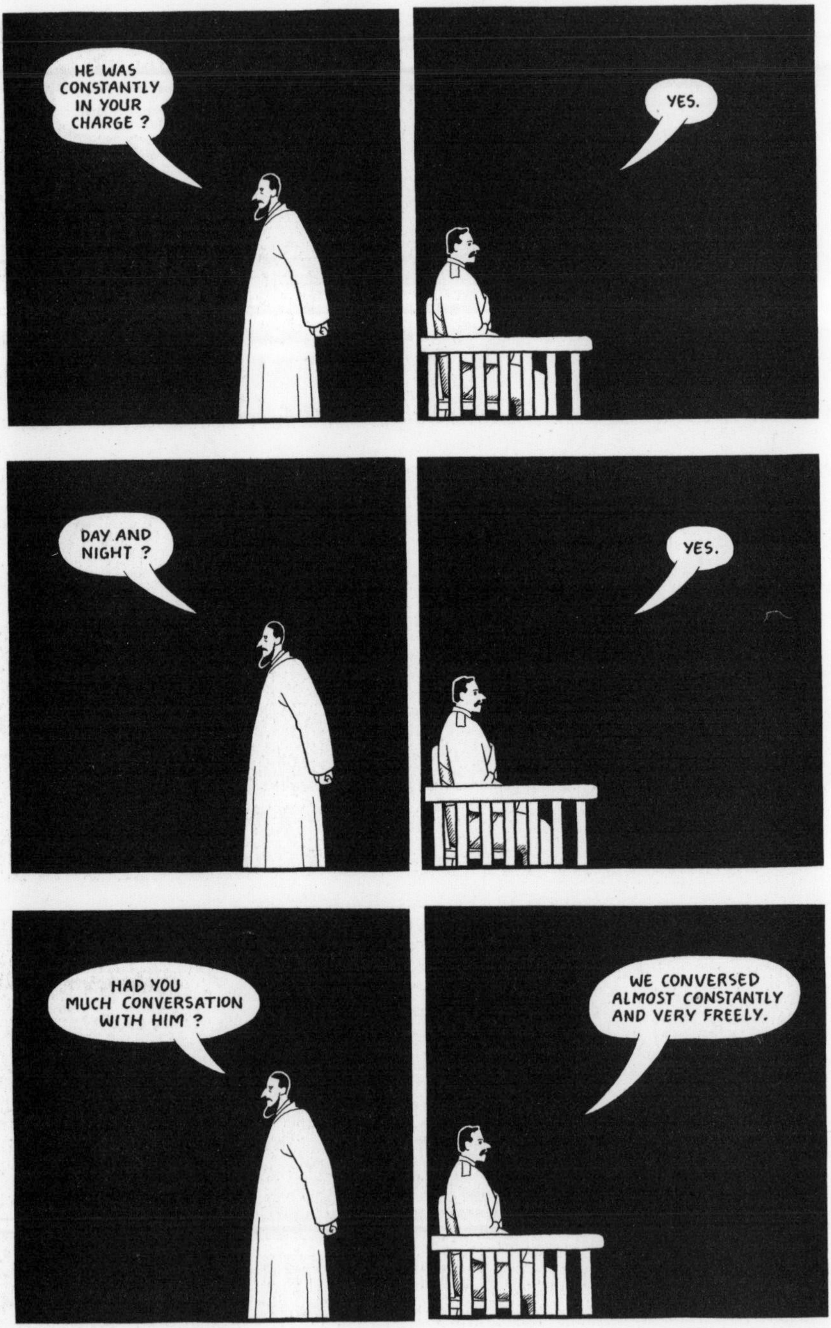
HE WAS CONSTANTLY IN YOUR CHARGE ?
YES.
DAY AND NIGHT ?
YES.
HAD YOU MUCH CONVERSATION WITH HIM ?
WE CONVERSED ALMOST CONSTANTLY AND VERY FREELY.

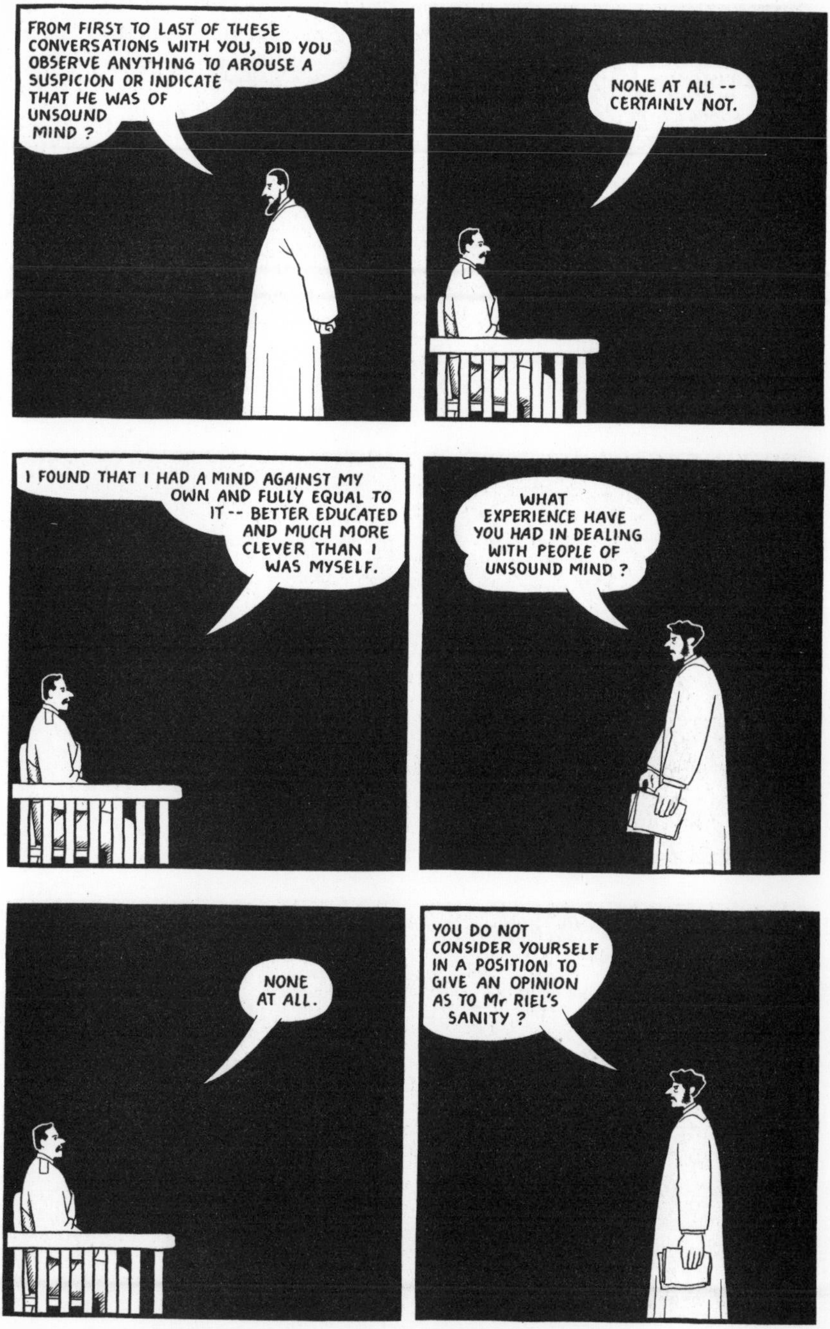
FROM FIRST TO LAST OF THESE CONVERSATIONS WITH YOU, DID YOU OBSERVE ANYTHING TO AROUSE A SUSPICION OR INDICATE THAT HE WAS OF UNSOUND MIND ?
NONE AT ALL -- CERTAINLY NOT.
I FOUND THAT I HAD A MIND AGAINST MY OWN AND FULLY EQUAL TO IT -- BETTER EDUCATED AND MUCH MORE CLEVER THAN I WAS MYSELF.
WHAT EXPERIENCE HAVE YOU HAD IN DEALING WITH PEOPLE OF UNSOUND MIND ?
NONE AT ALL.
YOU DO NOT CONSIDER YOURSELF IN A POSITION TO GIVE AN OPINION AS TO Mr RIEL'S SANITY ?

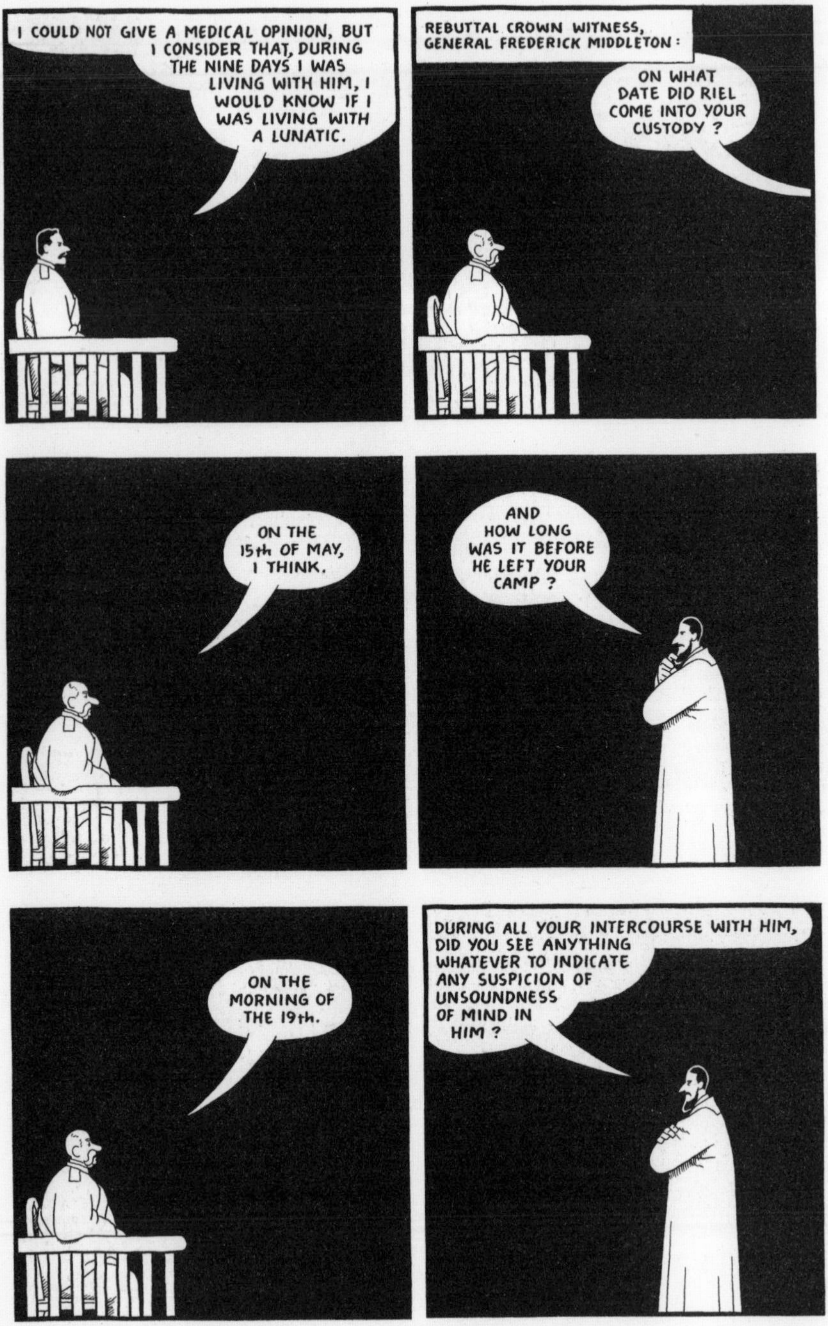
I COULD NOT GIVE A MEDICAL OPINION, BUT I CONSIDER THAT, DURING THE NINE DAYS I WAS LIVING WITH HIM, I WOULD KNOW IF I WAS LIVING WITH A LUNATIC.
REBUTTAL CROWN WITNESS, GENERAL FREDERICK MIDDLETON:
ON WHAT DATE DID RIEL COME INTO YOUR CUSTODY ?
ON THE 15th OF MAY, I THINK.
AND HOW LONG WAS IT BEFORE HE LEFT YOUR CAMP ?
ON THE MORNING OF THE 19th.
DURING ALL YOUR INTERCOURSE WITH HIM, DID YOU SEE ANYTHING WHATEVER TO INDICATE ANY SUSPICION OF UNSOUNDNESS OF MIND IN HIM ?

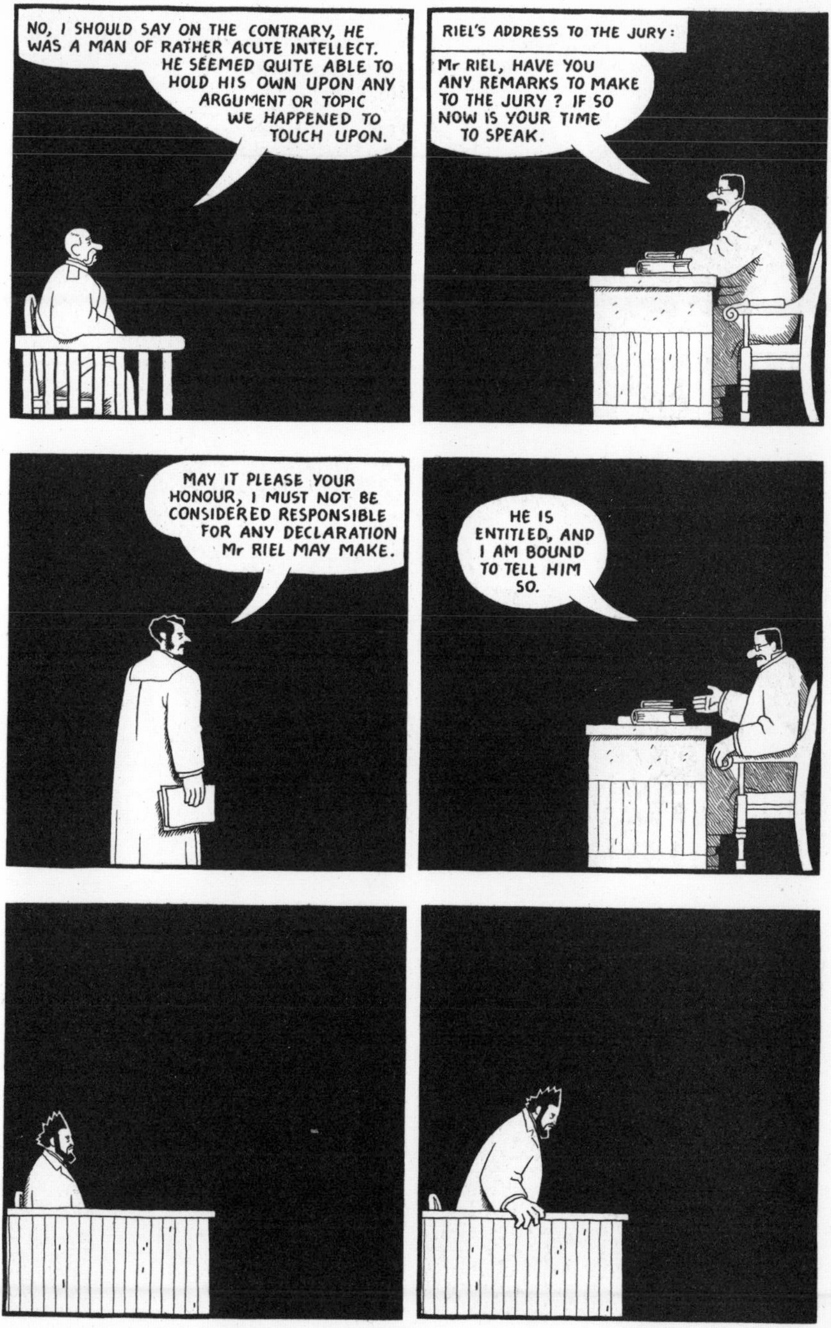
NO, I SHOULD SAY ON THE CONTRARY, HE WAS A MAN OF RATHER ACUTE INTELLECT. HE SEEMED QUITE ABLE TO HOLD HIS OWN UPON ANY ARGUMENT OR TOPIC WE HAPPENED TO TOUCH UPON.
RIEL'S ADDRESS TO THE JURY:
Mr RIEL, HAVE YOU ANY REMARKS TO MAKE TO THE JURY? IF SO NOW IS YOUR TIME TO SPEAK.
MAY IT PLEASE YOUR HONOUR, I MUST NOT BE CONSIDERED RESPONSIBLE FOR ANY DECLARATION Mr RIEL MAY MAKE.
HE IS ENTITLED, AND I AM BOUND TO TELL HIM SO.

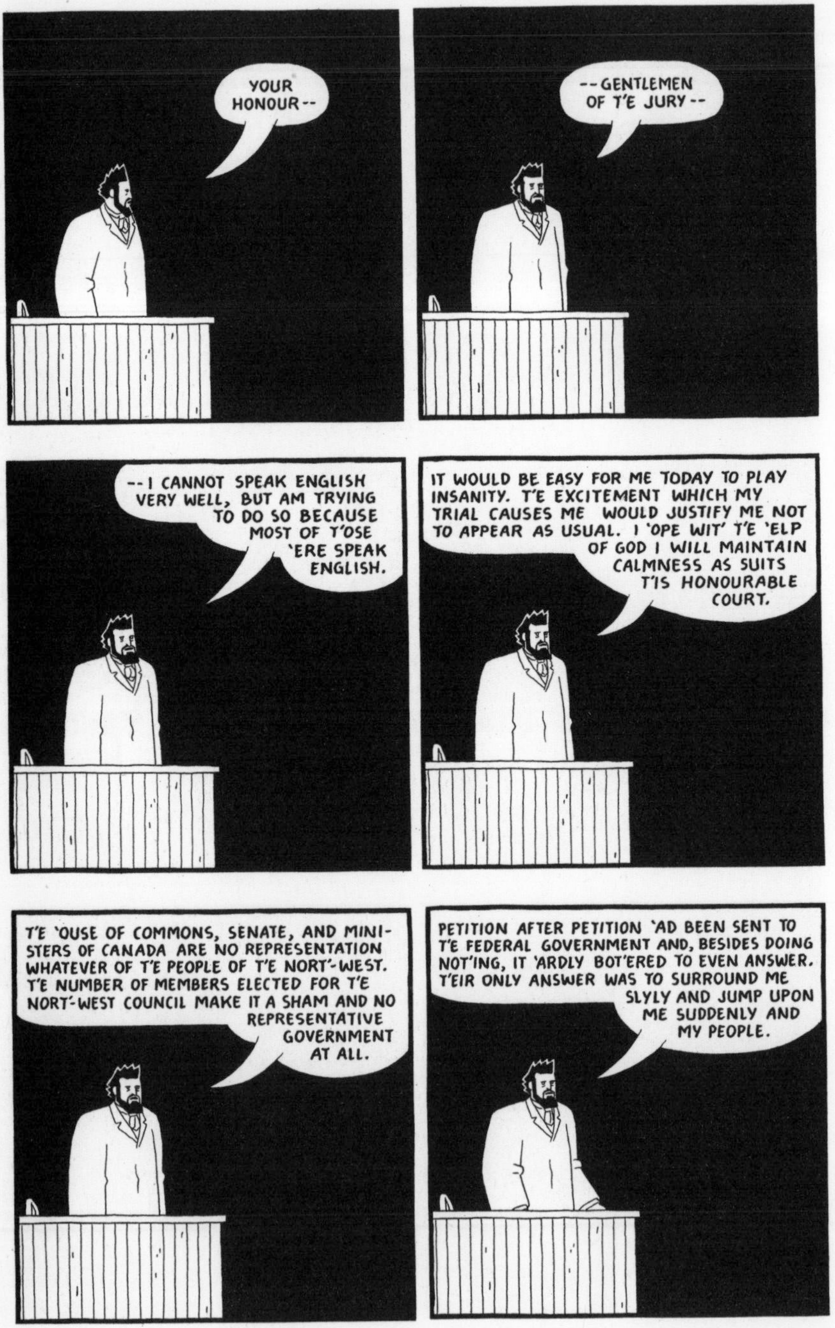
YOUR HONOUR--
--GENTLEMEN OF T'E JURY--
--I CANNOT SPEAK ENGLISH VERY WELL, BUT AM TRYING TO DO SO BECAUSE MOST OF T'OSE 'ERE SPEAK ENGLISH.
IT WOULD BE EASY FOR ME TODAY TO PLAY INSANITY. T'E EXCITEMENT WHICH MY TRIAL CAUSES ME WOULD JUSTIFY ME NOT TO APPEAR AS USUAL. I 'OPE WIT' T'E 'ELP OF GOD I WILL MAINTAIN CALMNESS AS SUITS T'IS HONOURABLE COURT.
T'E 'OUSE OF COMMONS, SENATE, AND MINISTERS OF CANADA ARE NO REPRESENTATION WHATEVER OF T'E PEOPLE OF T'E NORT'-WEST. T'E NUMBER OF MEMBERS ELECTED FOR T'E NORT'-WEST COUNCIL MAKE IT A SHAM AND NO REPRESENTATIVE GOVERNMENT AT ALL.
PETITION AFTER PETITION 'AD BEEN SENT TO T'E FEDERAL GOVERNMENT AND, BESIDES DOING NOT'ING, IT 'ARDLY BOT'ERED TO EVEN ANSWER. T'EIR ONLY ANSWER WAS TO SURROUND ME SLYLY AND JUMP UPON ME SUDDENLY AND MY PEOPLE.

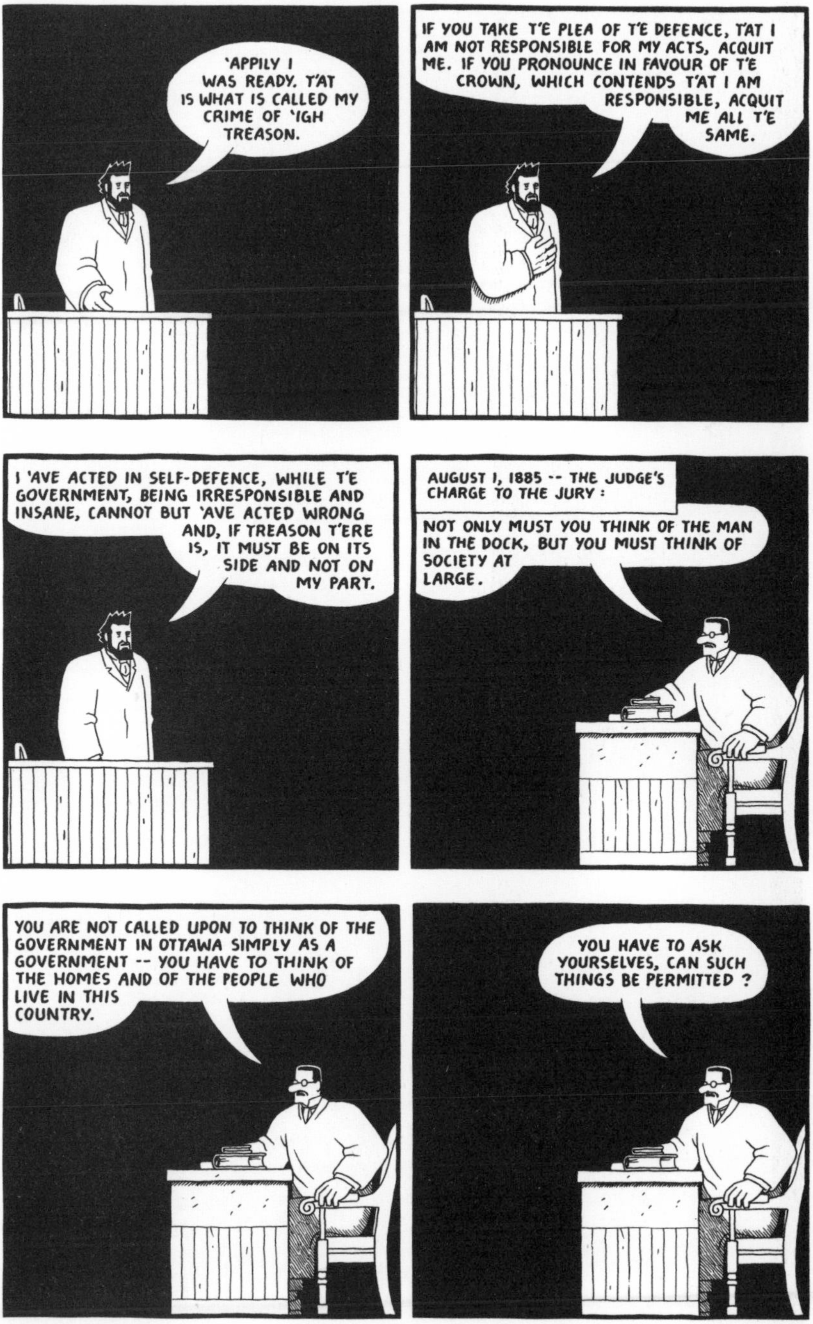
'APPILY I WAS READY. T'AT IS WHAT IS CALLED MY CRIME OF 'IGH TREASON.
IF YOU TAKE T'E PLEA OF T'E DEFENCE, T'AT I AM NOT RESPONSIBLE FOR MY ACTS, ACQUIT ME. IF YOU PRONOUNCE IN FAVOUR OF T'E CROWN, WHICH CONTENDS T'AT I AM RESPONSIBLE, ACQUIT ME ALL T'E SAME.
I 'AVE ACTED IN SELF-DEFENCE, WHILE T'E GOVERNMENT, BEING IRRESPONSIBLE AND INSANE, CANNOT BUT 'AVE ACTED WRONG AND, IF TREASON T'ERE IS, IT MUST BE ON ITS SIDE AND NOT ON MY PART.
AUGUST 1, 1885 -- THE JUDGE'S CHARGE TO THE JURY :
NOT ONLY MUST YOU THINK OF THE MAN IN THE DOCK, BUT YOU MUST THINK OF SOCIETY AT LARGE.
YOU ARE NOT CALLED UPON TO THINK OF THE GOVERNMENT IN OTTAWA SIMPLY AS A GOVERNMENT -- YOU HAVE TO THINK OF THE HOMES AND OF THE PEOPLE WHO LIVE IN THIS COUNTRY.
YOU HAVE TO ASK YOURSELVES, CAN SUCH THINGS BE PERMITTED ?

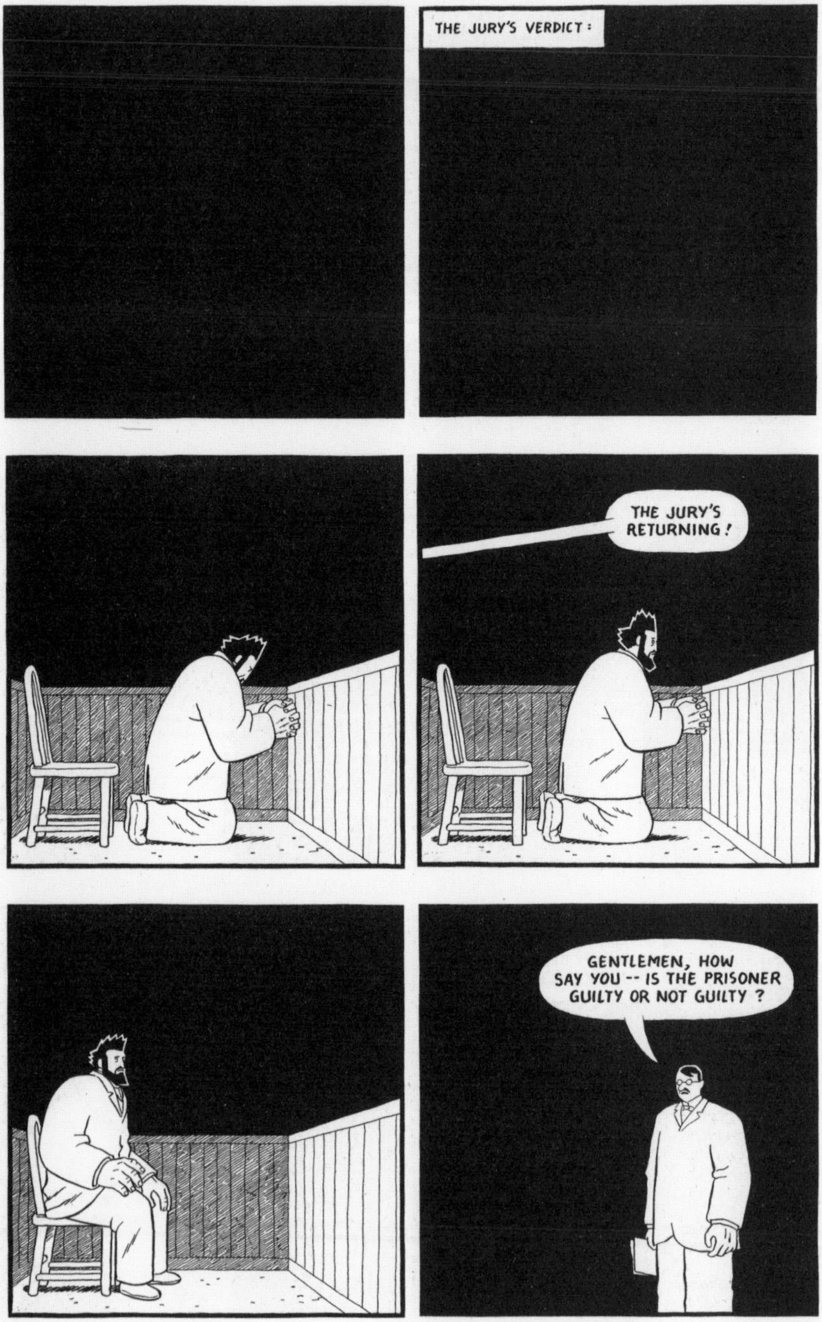
THE JURY'S VERDICT:
THE JURY'S RETURNING!
GENTLEMEN, HOW SAY YOU -- IS THE PRISONER GUILTY OR NOT GUILTY?

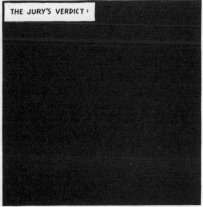

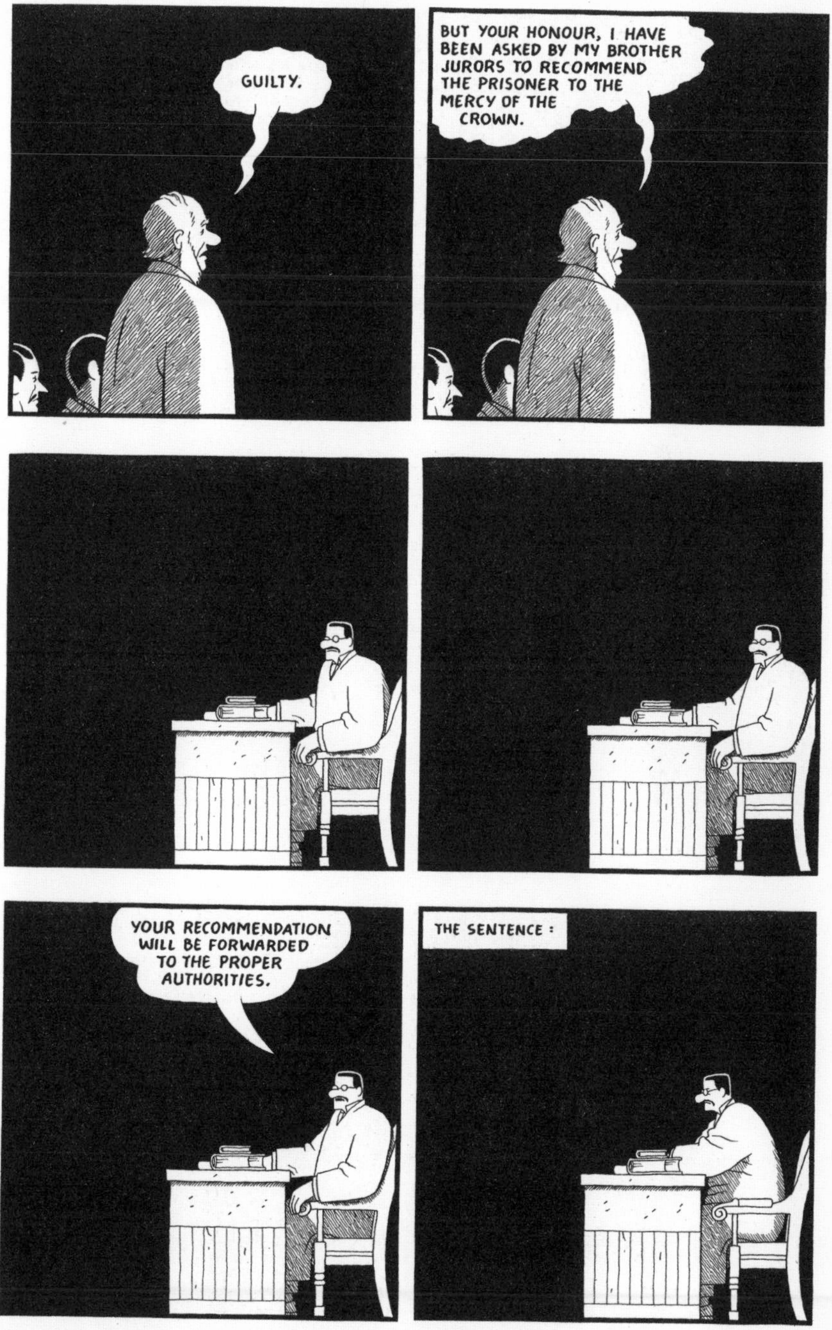
GUILTY.
BUT YOUR HONOUR, I HAVE BEEN ASKED BY MY BROTHER JURORS TO RECOMMEND THE PRISONER TO THE MERCY OF THE CROWN.
YOUR RECOMMENDATION WILL BE FORWARDED TO THE PROPER AUTHORITIES.
THE SENTENCE :

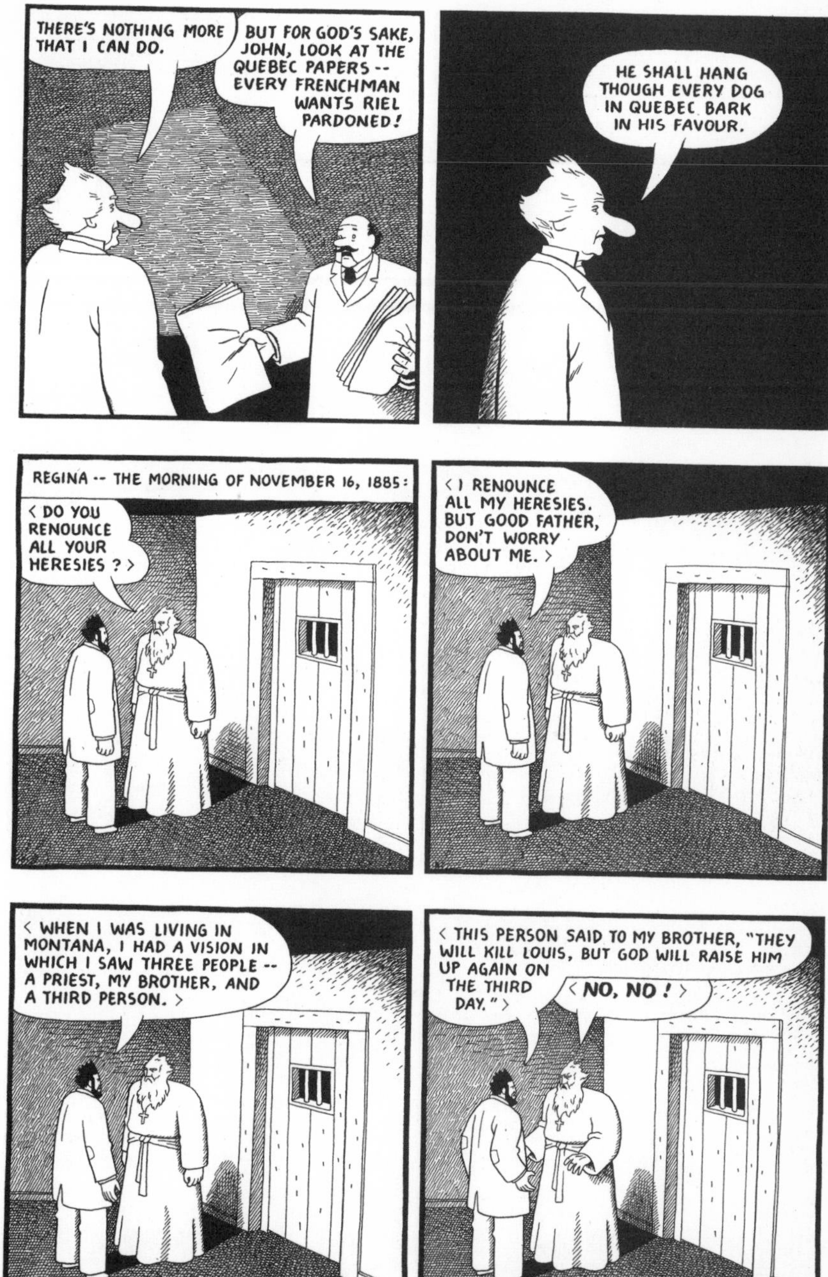
THERE'S NOTHING MORE THAT I CAN DO.
BUT FOR GOD'S SAKE, JOHN, LOOK AT THE QUEBEC PAPERS -- EVERY FRENCHMAN WANTS RIEL PARDONED!
HE SHALL HANG THOUGH EVERY DOG IN QUEBEC BARK IN HIS FAVOUR.
REGINA -- THE MORNING OF NOVEMBER 16, 1885:
< DO YOU RENOUNCE ALL YOUR HERESIES ? >
< I RENOUNCE ALL MY HERESIES. BUT GOOD FATHER, DON'T WORRY ABOUT ME. >
< WHEN I WAS LIVING IN MONTANA, I HAD A VISION IN WHICH I SAW THREE PEOPLE -- A PRIEST, MY BROTHER, AND A THIRD PERSON. >
< THIS PERSON SAID TO MY BROTHER, "THEY WILL KILL LOUIS, BUT GOD WILL RAISE HIM UP AGAIN ON THE THIRD DAY." >
< NO, NO ! >

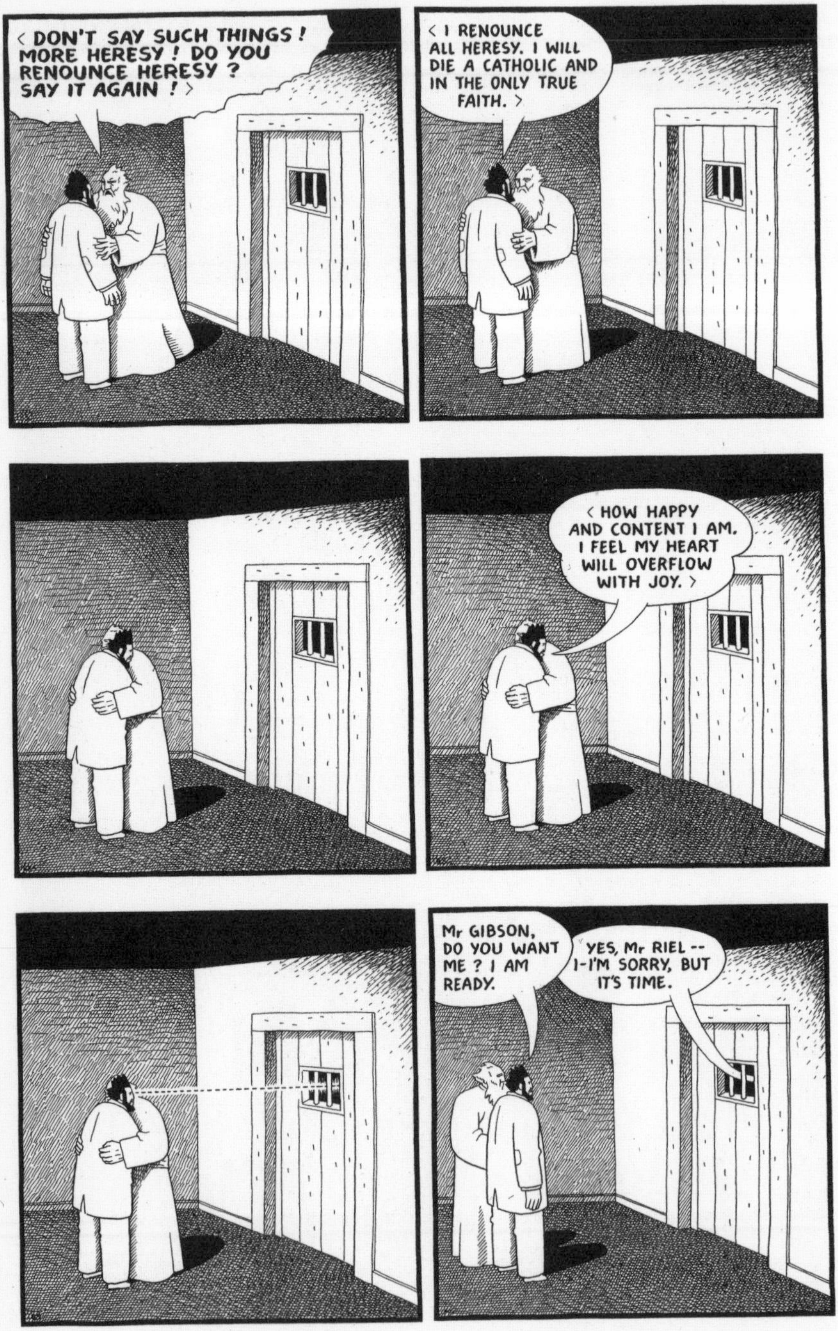
< DON'T SAY SUCH THINGS ! MORE HERESY ! DO YOU RENOUNCE HERESY ? SAY IT AGAIN ! >
< I RENOUNCE ALL HERESY. I WILL DIE A CATHOLIC AND IN THE ONLY TRUE FAITH. >
< HOW HAPPY AND CONTENT I AM. I FEEL MY HEART WILL OVERFLOW WITH JOY. >
Mr GIBSON, DO YOU WANT ME ? I AM READY.
YES, Mr RIEL -- I-I'M SORRY, BUT IT'S TIME.

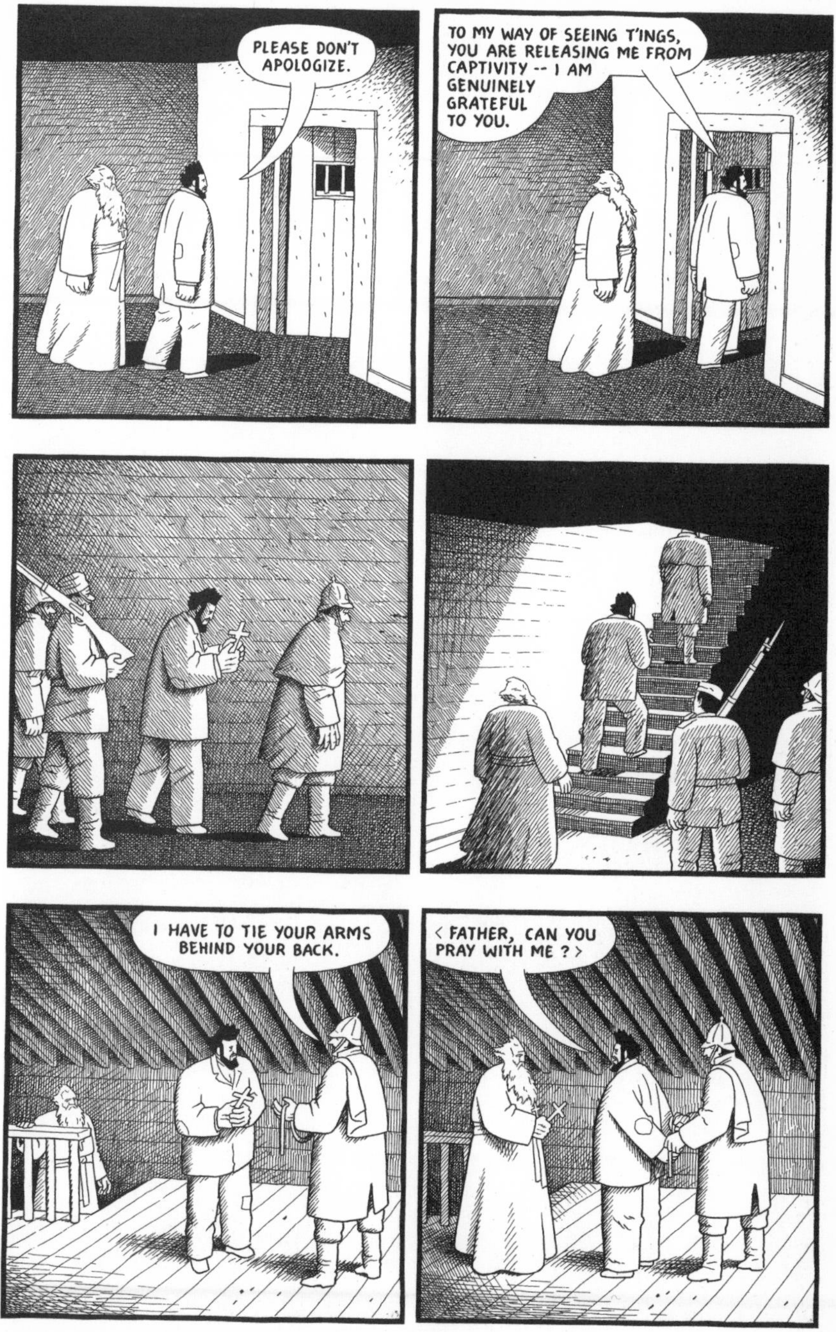
PLEASE DON'T APOLOGIZE.
TO MY WAY OF SEEING T'INGS, YOU ARE RELEASING ME FROM CAPTIVITY -- I AM GENUINELY GRATEFUL TO YOU.
I HAVE TO TIE YOUR ARMS BEHIND YOUR BACK.
< FATHER, CAN YOU PRAY WITH ME ? >

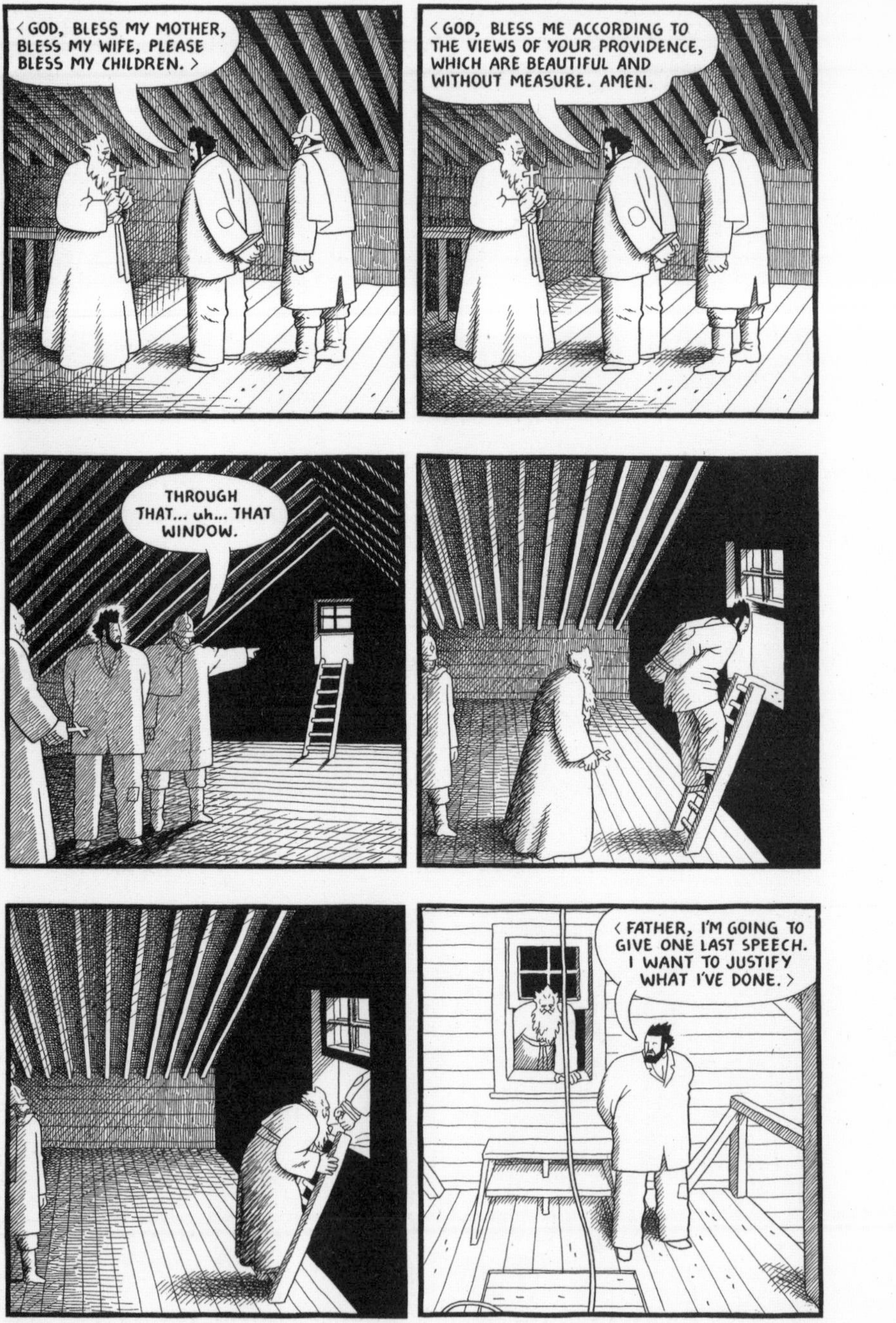
< GOD, BLESS MY MOTHER, BLESS MY WIFE, PLEASE BLESS MY CHILDREN. >
< GOD, BLESS ME ACCORDING TO THE VIEWS OF YOUR PROVIDENCE, WHICH ARE BEAUTIFUL AND WITHOUT MEASURE. AMEN.
THROUGH THAT... uh... THAT WINDOW.
< FATHER, I'M GOING TO GIVE ONE LAST SPEECH. I WANT TO JUSTIFY WHAT I'VE DONE. >

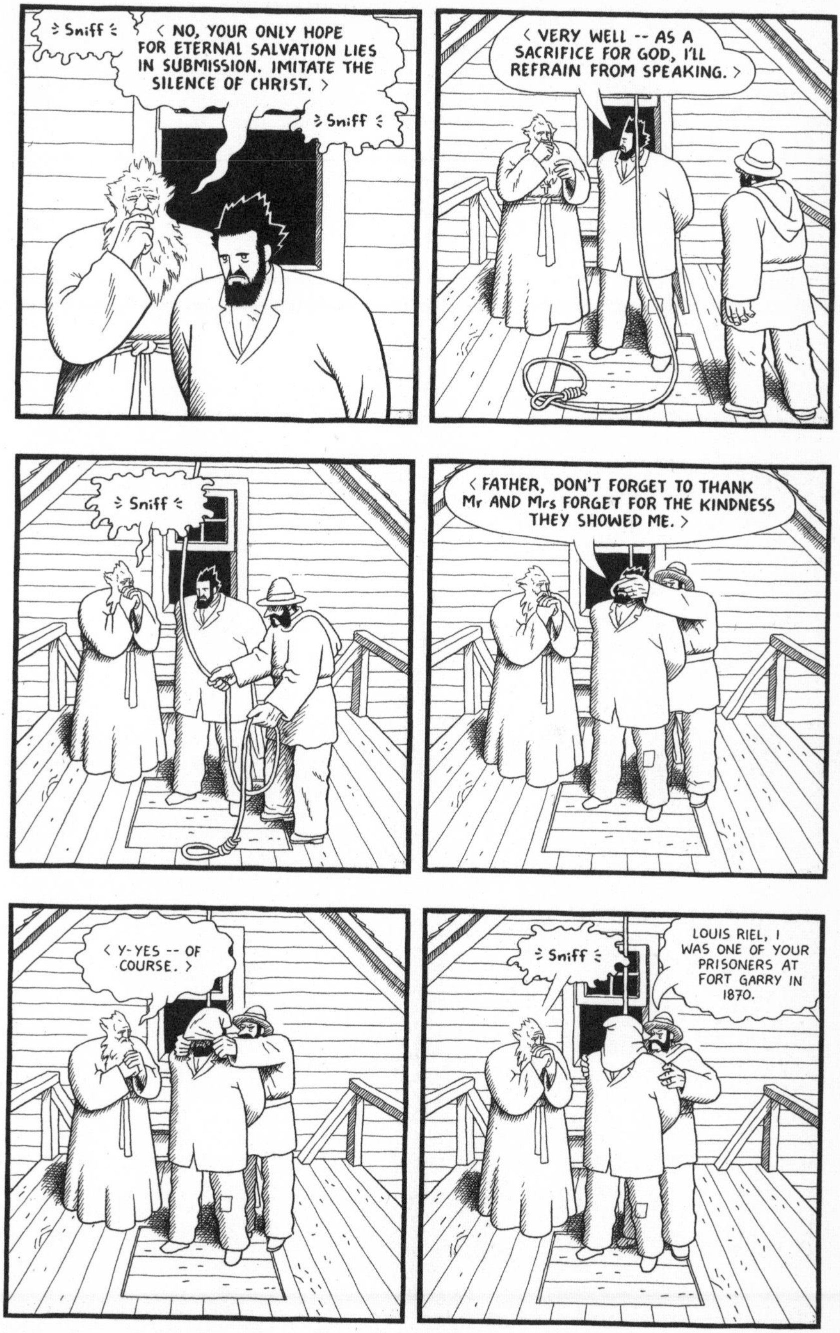

Sniff
< NO, YOUR ONLY HOPE FOR ETERNAL SALVATION LIES IN SUBMISSION. IMITATE THE SILENCE OF CHRIST. >
Sniff
< VERY WELL -- AS A SACRIFICE FOR GOD, I'LL REFRAIN FROM SPEAKING. >
Sniff
< FATHER, DON'T FORGET TO THANK Mr AND Mrs FORGET FOR THE KINDNESS THEY SHOWED ME. >
< Y-YES -- OF COURSE. >
Sniff
LOUIS RIEL, I WAS ONE OF YOUR PRISONERS AT FORT GARRY IN 1870.

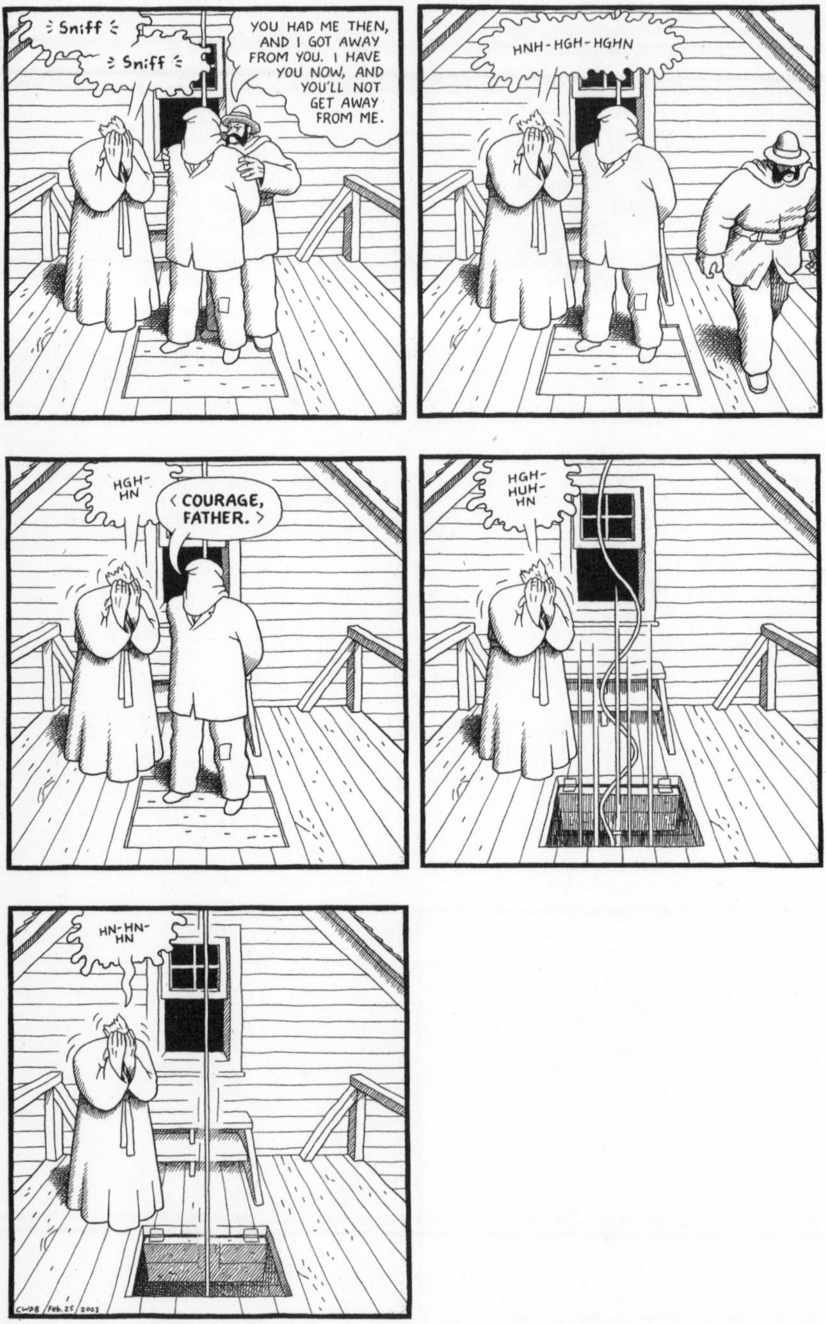

Sniff
Sniff
YOU HAD ME THEN, AND I GOT AWAY FROM YOU. I HAVE YOU NOW, AND YOU'LL NOT GET AWAY FROM ME.
HNH-HGH-HGHN
HGH-HN
< COURAGE, FATHER. >
HGH-HUH-HN
HN-HN-HN
CWDB Feb. 25 2003

EPILOGUE

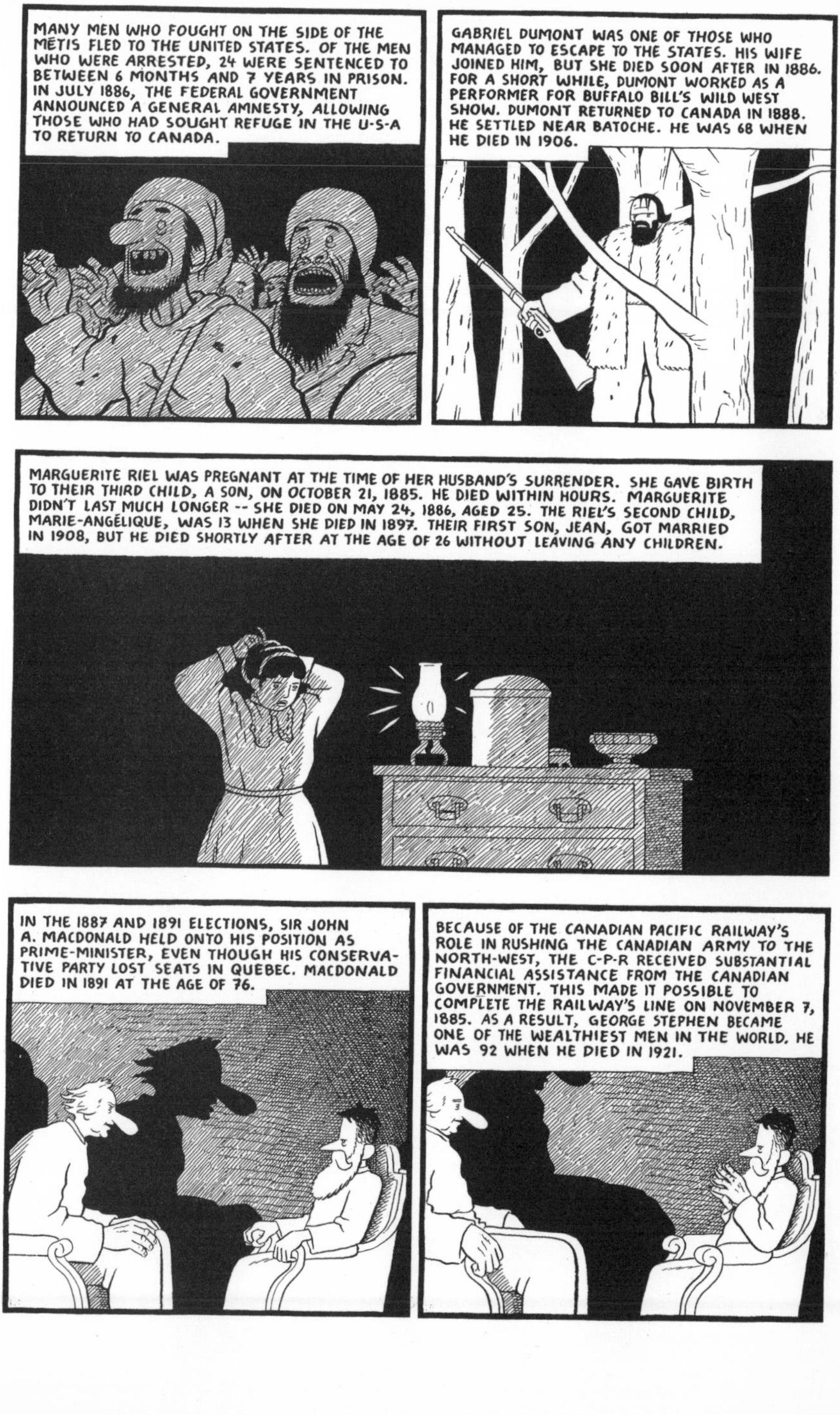
MANY MEN WHO FOUGHT ON THE SIDE OF THE MÉTIS FLED TO THE UNITED STATES. OF THE MEN WHO WERE ARRESTED, 24 WERE SENTENCED TO BETWEEN 6 MONTHS AND 7 YEARS IN PRISON. IN JULY 1886, THE FEDERAL GOVERNMENT ANNOUNCED A GENERAL AMNESTY, ALLOWING THOSE WHO HAD SOUGHT REFUGE IN THE U-S-A TO RETURN TO CANADA.
GABRIEL DUMONT WAS ONE OF THOSE WHO MANAGED TO ESCAPE TO THE STATES. HIS WIFE JOINED HIM, BUT SHE DIED SOON AFTER IN 1886. FOR A SHORT WHILE, DUMONT WORKED AS A PERFORMER FOR BUFFALO BILL'S WILD WEST SHOW. DUMONT RETURNED TO CANADA IN 1888. HE SETTLED NEAR BATOCHE. HE WAS 68 WHEN HE DIED IN 1906.
MARGUERITE RIEL WAS PREGNANT AT THE TIME OF HER HUSBAND'S SURRENDER. SHE GAVE BIRTH TO THEIR THIRD CHILD, A SON, ON OCTOBER 21, 1885. HE DIED WITHIN HOURS. MARGUERITE DIDN'T LAST MUCH LONGER -- SHE DIED ON MAY 24, 1886, AGED 25. THE RIEL'S SECOND CHILD, MARIE-ANGÉLIQUE, WAS 13 WHEN SHE DIED IN 1897. THEIR FIRST SON, JEAN, GOT MARRIED IN 1908, BUT HE DIED SHORTLY AFTER AT THE AGE OF 26 WITHOUT LEAVING ANY CHILDREN.
IN THE 1887 AND 1891 ELECTIONS, SIR JOHN A. MACDONALD HELD ONTO HIS POSITION AS PRIME-MINISTER, EVEN THOUGH HIS CONSERVATIVE PARTY LOST SEATS IN QUEBEC. MACDONALD DIED IN 1891 AT THE AGE OF 76.
BECAUSE OF THE CANADIAN PACIFIC RAILWAY'S ROLE IN RUSHING THE CANADIAN ARMY TO THE NORTH-WEST, THE C-P-R RECEIVED SUBSTANTIAL FINANCIAL ASSISTANCE FROM THE CANADIAN GOVERNMENT. THIS MADE IT POSSIBLE TO COMPLETE THE RAILWAY'S LINE ON NOVEMBER 7, 1885. AS A RESULT, GEORGE STEPHEN BECAME ONE OF THE WEALTHIEST MEN IN THE WORLD. HE WAS 92 WHEN HE DIED IN 1921.

NOTES

PAGE 3

Historian Stanley Ryerson observes that the Hudson's Bay Company charter that was signed by Charles II ignored "the rights of the native peoples dwelling there". (Ryerson, 1960, p. 138.)

PAGE 4

The 1869 population figures that I give on this page are actually from a census conducted in 1870.

PAGE 7 : PANEL 1

Macdonald was not in London in March 1869 and did not participate directly in the negotiations with the Hudson's Bay Company. The Canadian negotiators were William McDougall and George-Étienne Cartier. McDougall was then the Canadian government's Minister of Public Works, and Cartier was the deputy prime-minister. They left for London in either June 1868 (Bumsted, p. 40) or in the autumn of that year. (Sprague, p. 28.) Either way, the deal was concluded in March 1869.

7 : 3

The 7,000,000 acre figure was not mentioned in the March 1869 deal.

What was specified was that "the HBC would receive one-twentieth of all township land opened for settlement " (Siggins, p. 90) which "eventually amounted to 7,000,000 acres scattered through the West". (Bumsted, p. 40.)

8 : 2

The Orange Order was founded in 1795 in Ireland and grew out of that island's religious and political struggles with England.

> The lodges adopted a Masonic-type ritual and organization, providing for mutual aid and organizing social events. Orangemen who migrated to Britain and the colonies found the lodges useful in their adjustment to new environments.
> The Grand Lodge of British North America was founded 1 January 1830 in Brockville, UC [ie. Upper Canada, now known as Ontario] [....] By 1844 the power of the Orange vote induced John A. Macdonald to become an Orangeman. [Senior.]

8 : 3, 8 : 4

> Macdonald took it for granted that representative institutions were admissible for a British majority only ; and until a satisfactory ethnic composition was obtained, the majority must be "kept down." [Ryerson, 1968, p. 389.]

The opinions that I have some of the inhabitants of the Red River Settlement expressing here were also expressed by at least one person outside of that community. In 1868 the Canadian government asked A.J. Russel (who was the Crown Lands Inspector) to look into the legal title of Rupert's Land. He wrote:

[A]re we to be compelled to recognize the rights of the Hudson's Bay Company to lands which it has never bought or paid for? And is it in conformity with justice to the Indians, so loudly proclaimed in Britain, that in taking possession of their lands, instead of paying them full value for it, we should make a gift of the greater part of this sum to the H.B.Co., which never acquired from the true proprietors the slightest right to these territories? [Ryerson, 1968, p. 382.]

9:6

André Nault was the name of the Métis who spotted the Canadian surveyors on Edouard Marion's land. Nault was tending his cattle at the time -- a detail that I, for some reason, neglected to draw.

10:6

This is probably an exageration of the linguistic divide. In a group this large (sixteen or seventeen horsemen) there almost certainly would have been at least a few individuals with the ability to speak English.

11:5

During the confrontation, the Métis, or at least some of them, dismounted and stepped on the surveyor's chain.

12:5

I based my drawings of McDougall on an 1867 photograph of him (Sprague, p. 32) and an 1869 sketch. (Charlebois, p. 40.) After I'd drawn most of the scenes that feature him, I came across a passage in Charlebois's book that describes McDougall as "portly". (Ibid, p. 36.) I turned to Siggins' RIEL for confirmation, and read there that McDougall was a "tall, heavily built man". (Siggins, p. 99.) As you can see, he doesn't come across as a large man in my strip. I considered redrawing all of the panels that feature him, but then decided that I could live with that level of inaccuracy.

13:5

McDougall arrived in Pembina by

ox-cart, not stage-coach. I'm not sure why I drew stage-coaches -- there is a note in my script specifying ox-cart.

14:2

This letter was actually signed: "By order of the President, John Bruce. Louis Riel, Secretary". I didn't draw Bruce into the story.

[The Métis] elected as their president an ill-educated, weak man, named John Bruce, and as their secretary, Louis Riel. [...] Everyone knew that Bruce would be only a figurehead and that it was Riel who possessed the necessary education, sense of mission and power to direct that Bruce lacked. Riel [...] probably felt that, in view of the short time he had been back in the Settlement, it would be better for him to [take] a subordinate role, at least for the time being. [Stanley, p. 61.]

Bruce officially stepped down as president in mid-December 1869.

14:6

McDougall did spend the night in Pembina on October 30th. However, the next day he and his entourage ventured a mile and a half north beyond the U-S border, stopping at a Hudson's Bay Company post. McDougall hoped to stay there until being allowed into the Red River Settlement, but Métis horsemen forced him back to Pembina within days.

15:4 - 16:4

The way I've drawn this scene makes the conversation seem more casual than it probably was.

[Provencher] was stopped at the Métis barricades at St. Norbert by some thirty to forty armed guards. Nearby a virtual army camp for two hundred men had sprung up [...]. Provencher was escorted into Ritchot's residence. It was only a few moments before services for All Saints' Day were to begin, and Provencher was invited to attend mass. He told his friends later that he had never prayed with such fervor as he did that morning. Later he met with Riel, John Bruce and other Métis [. Siggins, p. 107.]

15:5

Father Noel-Joseph Ritchot (1825-1905) was born in Lower Canada (now known as Quebec) and moved to the Red River in 1862.

20:6

Riel "confined the Company men to their quarters and posted guards." (Howard, p. 108.) I'm guessing that they weren't held as prisoners for very long because their confinement never became an issue the way it did for the men who the

Métis imprisoned on December 7, 1869, (panels 31:3 and 31:4) and February 17, 1870 (panels 60:1 to 61:1).

21:2, 21:3

I should add a few more details to this brief sketch of Riel's early years.

He was born on October 22 or 23, 1844, and was his parent's first child.

> Two babies died in infancy, but eight more survived. It was a close family, and Louis seems to have been deeply attatched to his brothers and sisters. [Flanagan, 1996, p.4.]

In 1858 he was sent east to the Collège de Montréal, which was run by the Sulpician priests. His father died in early 1864. Shortly after, Riel became romantically involved with a young woman, Marie-Julie Guernon. He began to skip classes and, in early 1865, he either quit the college (Siggins, p.62) or was dismissed. (Flanagan, 1996, p. 20.) Riel ended up working in the law office of Rodolphe Laflamme, but by June 1886 it became clear that Marie-Julie's parents were going to keep their daughter from marrying the young Métis.

> We know almost nothing of Riel's life between his departure from Montreal on 19 June 1866 and his return to Red River on 26 July 1868. [...] Riel's own description of these years is anything but informative: "Left Montreal 19th June 1866. Came to St Paul, lived in Minneapolis, St Anthony and Saint Paul 2 years. Left St Anthony in July 68 and came to St Joe, Dakota." Nothing further is known for certain. [Ibid, p.27.]

Riel returned to the Red River Settlement to help run the family farm.

22:5 - 22:6, 25:4, 25:5

I've followed the sequence of events that Siggins gives, with the NOR'WESTER's press being used to print up copies of the "royal" proclamation and Riel putting a stop to the publication of the newspaper on December 2nd. (Siggins, pp. 121, 122.) But Bumsted claims that Riel took control of the NOR'WESTER's press in early November and that McDougall's proclamation then had to be copied out by hand for distribution in the settlement. (Bumsted, pp. 71, 91.)

Riel also shut down the Settlement's other newspaper, the RED RIVER PIONEER.

23:6

Dr John Schultz (1840-1896) was born in Amherstburg, Upper Canada (Ontario). He moved to the Red River Settlement to set up his medical practice in 1861. "[T]here is no record of his having received a medical degree." (Bumsted, p. 322.)

25:6, 26:1

Despite what I have Dennis saying in these panels, he was able to enlist about 380 men to fight the Métis, but "almost all the long-time English-speaking settlers refused point blank to have anything to do with his 'inglorious schemes'." (Siggins, p. 122.) A large number of Dennis's men were Salteaux and Sioux, and Dennis was heavily criticized at the time for arming Indians. Arming his recruits was another problem: "He had only two hundred guns, many of them old and dysfunctional". (Ibid.)

28:5

While I don't know what was on this list of demands, it's probably a safe guess that the primary one was that McDougall be allowed into the settlement.

33:1

According to Siggins, Riel asked for £1,000 and found £1,090 in the safe. (Siggins, p. 129.) Bumsted claims that the requested amount was £10,000 and that the Métis left with "all the cash in the coffers of the HBC." (Bumsted, pp. 105,106.)

33:5 - 35:3

In late 1869 Prime-Minister Macdonald sent Donald Smith as a "special commissioner" to the Red River settlement. Smith was at that time the Hudson's Bay Company's chief factor for the Montreal district. He arrived in the settlement in December, claiming that his mission was to make "the people both French and English fully acquainted with the liberal views of the Canadian Government so that a peaceful transfer of the Territory might be affected." (Bumsted, p. 121.) Another (not publicly stated) part of his role as "special commissioner" was handing out bribes.

Suspicious of the man, Riel tried to have Smith's papers seized in the hope that they would contain incriminating information, or at least state exactly how much power Macdonald had given him. Riel failed to get ahold of the papers, but Smith said that he would publicly read them if the Métis leader called a general meeting for the whole settlement. This was the outdoor January 19th meeting. My statement in panel 33:5 that this meeting was "particularly [for] the English" is untrue -- Smith wanted to win over the French as much as the English. He spoke for five hours, and then it was agreed that the meeting would reconvene on the next day. Smith again spoke for several hours on the 20th. Both days he mostly read from boring letters written by Canadian politicians who proposed nothing concrete. Sensing that Smith was failing to win over the audience, Riel got up during the second meeting and made his suggestion for the Convention of Forty. As the strip indicates, this was met with cheers of approval. Unlike Smith, Riel was apparently a charismatic speaker.

36:6

The vote on this issue was actually 23 to 16. The chair -- who was English -- didn't vote, which means that four French Métis voted against Riel's proposal.

37:5-39:2

Riel sent out twelve men to arrest Nolin, but two got to the Nolin residence ahead of the other ten. Charles Nolin had four brothers, and most or all of them were guarding him that night.

39:4-43:3

Schultz was not the only December 7th prisoner who escaped from the Métis. After spending several weeks in Fort Garry, most of the prisoners were moved from the fort "to a common jail outside the walls, where six cells held forty prisoners." (Siggins, p. 135.) Only Schultz was kept in the fort, because he was considered to be the most dangerous. On January 9th, eight men escaped from the common jail, though five of them were recaptured the next day.
I have Mrs Schultz smuggling in the pocket knife to her husband on January 23rd and show him escaping that night. While Schultz did escape on the 23rd, the apple-brown-betty-with-the-knife was probably delivered to him several days before, since Siggins implies that it took Schultz that amount of time to cut up the buffalo robe. (Ibid. pp. 150, 151.)

42:5

Schultz did not break his leg, but it was twisted so badly that he walked with a limp for the rest of his life.

46:3

Sutherland was a member of the Convention of Forty.

46:4

Crediting Schultz alone with raising the 300 men is a bit of an oversimplification. Charles Mair and Thomas Scott were two of the men who escaped from the Métis on January 9th. (See the note for panels 39:4 to 43:3.) They fled to Portage-la-Prairie and managed to convince Major Charles Boulton (who'd had ten years of service in the British Army) to help them. "Of all of Riel's opponents, Boulton was the one who wore a sheen of respectability -- so much so that he began to win converts among the English-speaking settlers." (Siggins, p. 149.) Boulton was able to gather together about 100 fighting men. Meanwhile, Schultz was in St Andrew rounding up about 200 men. (A lot of the men Schultz mobilized were the Salteaux and Sioux who'd been ready to fight for Colonel Dennis -- see the note for panels 25:6 and 26:1.) The Boulton and Schultz forces met in Kildonan.

48:4

Hugh didn't volunteer to ride to Kildonan -- his father had to ask him to.

54:5-55:5

Scott was born in 1842 and

was a native of Northern Ireland who emigrated to Canada West [Ontario] in the early 1860s. Of Scots-Irish descent, he was a member of [...] the Orange Order. He was also, contemporaries who knew him for the most part agreed, a "violent and boisterous man" who made his opinions known in a loud voice and a rude manner. [Bumsted, p. 163.]

During the beating of Parisien, "Thomas Scott was particularly vicious; he struck Parisien on the head with an axe" (Siggins, p. 154). Still, my depiction probably exaggerates Scott's viciousness. I don't know whether his axe hit Parisien once or many times. The way I've written the scene virtually implies that Scott alone killed Parisien, and in reality it's likely that the murder was more of a group effort.

Neither Sutherland nor Parisien died immediately. Sutherland passed on the next morning (February 17th), while Parisien lingered for "a few days" (Howard, p. 159), "several weeks" (Bumsted, p. 153), or a "month and a half" (Siggins, p. 154) before expiring. (Stanley (p. 106) agrees with Howard, while Siggins is corroborated by Charlebois (p. 64), who gives Parisien's date of death as April 4th.)

53:4

Before dying, Sutherland "begged that Norbert Parisien not be punished." (Siggins, p. 154.)

58:2

I show the men on foot. William Sanderson (who was one of this group) said that they were all walking as they approached Fort Garry (Spry, p. 129), but Stanley seems to think that they were all in sleighs. (Stanley, pp. 106, 107.) "Alexander Begg, who claimed to be able to see events from the village, insisted that there were carrioles, as well as men on foot." (Bumsted, p. 155.)

58:5

Were the men armed? Sanderson stated that "Each of us was given [...] a muzzle loader [...] and only three bullets". (Spry, p. 128.) But Boulton remembered that "We were not armed". (Bumsted, p. 156.) When the men were led into the fort, they were described as having "empty holsters, looking as if they had thrown away their weapons. A Métis party was detailed to find the weapons. It failed to discover any". (Ibid.)

59:2

In panel 6:6 I said that there were 50 men, and I here show one walking away, which would leave 49. Actually, 48 men ended up at Fort Garry.

59:4

And the day they ended up at Fort Garry was either February 17, 1870 (Bumsted, p. 154, and Howard, p. 160), or February 18th. (Charlebois, p. 64, Siggins, p. 155, and Stanley, p. 107.)

60:3 - 60:6

My depiction of a peaceful surrender is based on Sanderson's account. Of the question asked in panel 9:1, Sanderson wrote, "we wouldn't dream of refusing such an invitation as we had not had too much to eat since we left home." (Spry, p. 129.) According to Bumsted, as the horsemen drew near to Boulton's men, a fight started between a Métis and one of the English. Boulton quickly put a stop to it and then surrendered. (Bumsted, p. 156.)

62:1

I show Schultz fleeing alone, but he was accompanied by a friend and a guide.

After it was determined that Schultz was not among the prisoners, five of them -- including Boulton and Scott -- were judged to be the leaders of the group. A Métis tribunal sentenced these five to be killed. Hearing about the proposed execution, the mother of Hugh Sutherland rushed to the fort and pleaded for the lives of the condemned men. Riel agreed to spare four of them but insisted that Boulton must die. Donald Smith showed up and begged that mercy be shown to Boulton. The elections for Riel's provisional government were coming up, and many in the English community were starting to rethink whether they wanted to participate. Riel said that he would forego executing Boulton if Smith convinced the English parishes to elect representatives. Over the next few days, Smith did, and Boulton was allowed to live.

62:5

William Sanderson on Thomas Scott:

> We were all put into a large room [...]. We would have been quite comfortable had it not been for that man Scott making such a racket [...]. This Scott was so obnoxious and made so much trouble that some of our men asked the guard to have him removed. He was put into a room next to the one we occupied [.]
> [Spry, pp. 129, 130.]

William Sanderson on his imprisonment:

> Some years ago I picked up and began to read a history of the Manitoba Rebellion, the story told of great hardships we endured as prisoners and how we were starved.

It must have been written by
someone who knew nothing about
it for it was nothing but a lot of
damn lies, we were well treated.
[Ibid, p. 130.]

64:3, 64:4

Racette has been able to find
references to nine Métis flags from
the 1869-70 period. (Racette, pp. 13-
17.) Most of these included at least
one fleur-de-lis and one shamrock in
their design. In North America the
fleur-de-lis is the primary symbol of
French cultural identity, much as the
shamrock is to the Irish. So what was
an Irish symbol doing on Métis flags?
A small but significant number of
Riel's supporters were Fenians --
anti-British Irish-Catholics. Chief
among these was William O'Donoghue,
who was Riel's right-hand man for
awhile. The Fenians wanted the
settlement to join the United States
and, as it became clear that the
sympathies of the provisional government's president were with Britain,
the relationship between the two
men soured.
Why did Riel favour British
political ties over American ones?
Siggins speculates that he was
concerned that "the French language
and culture would be diluted in the
American melting-pot." (Siggins, p.95.)

65:1 - 66:2

On March 1, Scott and Murdoch
McLeod forced the door of their cell
and jumped two guards, shouting
that the other prisoners should do
the same. This outrage by Scott was
the last straw. The guards dragged
the big man, cursing and screaming,
into the courtyard, and were just
starting to beat him when a
member of the provisional government heard the noise and
intervened. [Siggins, p.161.]

65:1

A "tête-carrée" (square-head)
is an English person. This French
expression is used in Quebec today --
I don't know if it would have been
used in the 19th century.

69:2

I didn't address this in the strip
(and no one I've read on the subject
has either) but I couldn't help but
wonder if revenge wasn't a possible
motive for Scott's execution. It would
depend on whether the Métis knew of
Scott's role in the beating of Parisien.
While several men had participated
in the beating, it seems possible that

The Guy Who Used The Axe might
have been singled out for payback.
Perhaps Parisien could have given
enough of a physical description
(young, tall, Irish accent, side-
whiskers) that when Scott called
attention to himself in Fort Garry, he
was either recognized or suspected.

69:5 - 73:3

Reports varied as to whether [Scott]
emerged blindfolded or was blindfolded
later. Scott apparently prayed contin-
ually while in the open air. [...]
Reverend Young's much later report
was that Scott said, "This is
horrible! This is cold-blooded
murder. Be sure to make a true
statement." Scott then asked Reverend Young whether he should stand
or kneel. He then knelt in the snow
and said, "Farewell." [Bumsted,
p. 165.]

Donald Smith and others asked
Riel not to go through with the
execution, but the Métis leader was
adamant. James Taylor, the American consul in the Red River Settlement, wrote:

Riel firmly believed the execution
necessary not only to prevent bloodshed within the walls of the prison
itself but to check further attempts
at insurrection with the possible
contingency of an Indian war. "I
take a life to save lives," was his
reply to an appeal for mercy.
[Siggins, p. 163.]

71:2

"He stays standing or we put him
on his knees?"

72:2

"Fire when the handkerchief
falls from my hand."

73:4 - 74:2

Why did Macdonald have to ask
the British government for soldiers?
Why not just send in Canadian militiamen? "[A]ny such expedition would have
to be undertaken under British auspices,
since Canada had 'no authority beyond
her own limits.'" (Bumsted, p.146.)
Granville was not in Ottawa in
March, 1870, and for all I know he
may never have visited Canada. The
conversation between the two men
was conducted, not in person, but
through telegrams and letters.

74:5

There were actually three men

chosen to represent the Red River Settlement in Ottawa: Ritchot, a saloon barkeeper named Alfred Scott (no relation to Thomas Scott), and Judge John Black. Scott and Black contributed almost nothing to the negotiations, so I've dropped them from the story.

75:4 - 76:2

Ritchot and Alfred Scott traveled together and had to avoid Toronto as I show here. With Schultz encouraging him to do so,

> Thomas Scott's brother, Hugh, [...] went to the police magistrate in Toronto and applied for a warrant charging Father Ritchot and Alfred Scott with aiding and abetting the murder of Thomas Scott. This was granted and then sent on to the Ottawa police department. [Siggins, p. 177.]

Ritchot and Alfred Scott arrived in Ottawa on April 11th. Alfred was arrested by Ottawa police on the 12th and Ritchot gave himself up to the authorities on the 13th. Although an Ottawa judge deemed the Toronto warrant to be invalid in Ottawa and freed the two men, Hugh Scott immediately filed a warrant in Ottawa and Ritchot and Alfred were re-arrested. "[T]hey remained under guard [at their lodgings] in a kind of house arrest." (Ibid.) On April 23rd the charges were dismissed for lack of evidence. The negotiations between the Red River delegates (Ritchot, Alfred Scott, and Black) and the Canadian government (represented by the prime-minister, Sir John A. Macdonald, and the deputy prime-minister, Sir George-Étienne Cartier) started on April 25th.

76:3 - 77:1

Ritchot could not speak English. (Bumsted, p. 318.)

77:4 - 78:2

Riel and Ritchot had been in contact by letter, and Riel would have known all the details of the agreement -- which was called the Manitoba Act -- by the time that Ritchot arrived back in the settlement, so the two men would not have had this conversation. I have Riel and Ritchot talking as if the Act was a done deal, but it still had to be voted on by the Legislative Assembly of Riel's provisional government. This happened on June 24th, with the act passing unanimously.

77:5

1,400,000 acres was "about one-seventh of the total area of Manitoba as it then was." (Flanagan, 1996, p. 138.) Manitoba in 1870 was "roughly 11,000 square miles". (Bumsted,

p. 179.) The province has been expanded on three occasions. (1881, 1884, and 1912.) Its present size is 250,934 square miles.

To clarify what the 1,400,000 acres were intended for: The Red River Métis in 1870 already had their river-front farms. Ritchot proposed that 1,400,000 acres be set aside for the Métis, not because they needed more land at that point, but because the next generation would need land to settle on -- the 1,400,000 acres were intended for the Métis who would have been children in 1870.

> Manitoba statutes were changed on a number of occasions in order to allow Metis children to sell their land -- this at a time when the law made it clear that non-Metis children had no right to sell land. [...] In 1881 Manitoba legislation allowed Metis children of any age to sell their land without parental consent. [Purich, p. 69.]

77:6

Alert readers will note the crucial word "if" in this sentence. The act did not specify what land the Métis would get or how or when it would be distributed.

78:3 - 79:6

Dumont was born in 1837.

Gabriel Dumont was a frontiersman's frontiersman, the stuff of legends. He was the best shot in the North-West, the best rider, the best gambler among a people who gambled for days on end, the best buffalo hunter, the greatest leader. He was a good canoeist and swimmer, unusual talents on the plains, and a better-than-average billiards player. He owned the fastest horses in a society that loved horse-racing. He was fluent in French and several Indian languages but never bothered to learn much English. He was a shrewd trader and businessman. To his friends he was the most gracious, most generous person in the North-West; to his enemies he was a dangerous foe. [Beal & Macleod, p. 37.]

Some writers have cast doubt on Dumont's presence at the Red River, but the evidence suggests that he went at least once. Dumont himself said that he met Riel at Fort Garry on 17 June 1870 [.] [Woodcock, p. 81.]

79:1

With marksmen placed in strategic spots, the Métis could destroy a force of Canadians and Brits who had no experience whatsoever of the wilderness. At first Riel was tempted, especially since the long-promised amnesty had not arrived, but Bishop Taché talked him out of it. [Siggins, p. 186.]

79:2 - 79:4

Wolseley's letter arrived in the settlement on July 22nd (not in early July).

[Riel] sent four boatloads of Métis to help guide the troops and clear the road to the Winnipeg River. The word these men sent back caused the entire Red River Valley to shudder. Around the campfires at night, the Canadian soldiers talked of little but revenge. [Siggins, p. 186]

81:1 - 81:3

Bishop Alexandre-Antonin Taché was a Red River settlement priest with political connections in Ottawa. In February 1870 he traveled to that city and recieved from Macdonald, Cartier, and Secretary of State Joseph Howe a verbal promise of an amnesty for everyone involved in the settlement's political turmoil. It doesn't seem to have occured to him to get this in writing. Father Ritchot, on the other hand, definitely tried -- without success -- to get the amnesty promise in writing while he negotiated the Manitoba Act. (Macdonald's deviousness in this matter is probably best recounted by Sprague. The prime-minister not only lied to the priests but also to Cartier, who was able to convincingly assure the priests that an amnesty was coming because he actually believed it himself. See Sprague pp. 56, 57, 69-74.)
The exchange in these panels would seem to imply that hostile feelings had developed between Ritchot and Riel, but that wasn't the case -- it was between Taché and Riel that antagonism grew. I've combined the two priests into one character.

81:4 - 85:6

On the evening of August 23ʳᵈ, Riel did tell all of his followers in the Fort to get their personal belongings to safety, but not themselves. There were still many Métis in the fort as dawn broke on the 24ᵗʰ. It wasn't until the English settler James G. Stewart rode into the fort with his warning that

[m]embers of the old Métis council began to lose courage and drift away [...]. Riel went down to the courtyard and dismissed the guards. He and O'Donoghue were alone in Fort Garry. [Howard, p.181.]

For awhile the two men watched the British-Canadian force moving toward them. When the soldiers drew close, Riel and O'Donoghue walked out of the fort, down to the Assiniboine River, "and crossed on a raft they fashioned of fence posts lashed with their woven sashes." (Ibid., p.183.)

89:2

Two soldiers and a civilian chased [Elzéar] Goulet [a member of the court-martial that had tried Thomas Scott] to the Red River. Terrified, he leaped into the water to swim to the opposite shore and safety. The soldiers [...], and their companions, stoned him to death in the water. [...] François Guillemette, a member of the firing squad that had executed Scott, was murdered near Pembina. H.F. O'Lone, a friend of O'Donoghue's was murdered. An attempt was made on the life of Father Kavanaugh. [English Métis] James Tanner's horse was deliberately frightened in the dark causing it to rear and throw him to his death. Thomas Spence, editor of THE NEW NATION [a Red River Settlement newspaper], was horse-whipped by John Schultz's friends. André Nault was viciously beaten. [Charlebois, p. 89.]

Disorders in the first few weeks of Canadian administration claimed many times more casualties than had occurred in ten months of Métis rule, and the trouble continued for months. [Howard, p. 185.]

Regarding the reference to rape in this panel :

Standard histories seldom refer to this unsavoury crime against the civilian population because there is "little documentary evidence". But one of the few historians entirely sympathetic to the Métis cause, Auguste de Tremaudan, claims he was told by many "old-timers" about such rapes. [Siggins, p.193.]

89:5, 89:6

The government's first delaying tactic was to say that no lands could be registered until after a thorough land survey and census of the Manitoba population had been completed. That might have seemed logical enough, except that an Order-in-Council dated May 26, 1871, allowed all newcomers to stake land wherever they found it. [...T]he government officials ruled that the old settlers were not allowed this privilege because supposedly their lands were already protected under the Manitoba Act. [...I]n disputes between Métis and newly arrived homesteaders over ownership of land, the new settlers almost always won. Many Métis families were thrown off land they had occupied for decades [.] [Siggins, pp. 281, 282.]

90:1

Riel returned to the settlement on May 3, 1871.

90:2

The military force of 1,200 had consisted of 400 British soldiers and 800 Canadians. The British were sent home in September, 1870. 720 of the Canadians were freed from service in the spring of 1871 (Sprague, p. 98), but

Many of the Ontario soldiers had decided to remain permanently in Red River, mainly because they had been rewarded for their "valiant service" with 160-acre land grants. [Siggins, p. 202.]

In the summer and fall of 1871, William O'Donoghue tried to round up men in Minnesota and Dakota for a Fenian invasion of Manitoba. Hearing of this, Adams G. Archibald (Manitoba's new lieutenant-governor) was concerned. He knew that the Métis were unhappy with how things were going and feared that they would again join forces with the Fenians. He turned to Riel for help. Hoping that a show of loyalty to Canada would speed the arrival of his amnesty, Riel complied and urged his fellow Métis to fight for Canada should the Fenians actually attack. O'Donoghue's plans came to nothing, but Archibald was still grateful to Riel for his support, and in a public ceremony on October 8, 1871, he shook Riel's hand -- as well as the hand of Ambroise Lépine (a member of Riel's provisional government who had also participated in Thomas Scott's court-martial).

> The results of this dramatic scene were not at all what Archibald or Riel had anticipated. [...] A howl of rage issued forth from Orangemen across the land; how dare Her Majesty's representative actually grasp the "bloody hands" of Riel and Lépine ? The Ontario press lambasted the lieutenant-governor for his compliancy and Prime Minister Macdonald said he was "embarrassed" that Riel had been publicly recognized. Instead of receiving gratitude for their loyal devotion to the Canadian government, the Métis were accused of abetting the Fenian cause.[...] The long-promised amnesty receded even further into the background. [Siggins, p. 206.]

90:3 - 91:3

It was Bishop Taché, not Father Ritchot, who visited Ottawa in December 1871.

91:3

> On 27 December, Macdonald provided Taché with a sight draft on the Bank of Montreal for $1,000 for "the individual we have talked about." [...] After leaving Montreal in January of 1872, Taché received en route to Sarnia a letter from Cartier saying that Ambroise Lépine should also depart and that the money should be divided. [... Riel and Lépine] requested $1,000 each, plus eight to ten pounds' sterling every month for their families. [...] Bishop Taché had to go to Lieutenant-Governor Archibald for financial assistance. Archibald himself had no funds available, and so he called upon Donald A. Smith (as representative of the [Hudson's Bay Company] acting as bankers for the province) to furnish the money, on the understanding that it would eventually be reimbursed by Ottawa. Smith obliged, and the bishop gave Riel and Lépine $1,000 each, holding $1,000 back for their families. Although Sir John Macdonald and Sir George Cartier acknowledged Smith's advance, it was never repaid [. Bumsted, pp. 232, 233.]

Flanagan gives a different set of figures :

> In December 1871 Sir John A. Macdonald sent Archbishop Taché $5,000 for Riel and Ambroise Lépine to persuade them to leave the country for a year. Riel and Lépine took the money after Donald A. Smith, then MP for Selkirk, supplemented it with another $3,000.
> [Flanagan, 2000, pp. 117, 118.]

91:4

Taché and Riel had this conversation in February 1872. Riel went into exile in the United States with Ambrois Lépine.

91:5

> On March 9, the Ontario government [...] officially announced the $5,000 award for [Riel's] capture -- an incredible amount of money when the average working man made less than $ 500 a year." [Siggins, p. 210.]

92:2 - 93:1

Lépine was with Riel when this happened.

93:2 - 94:3

> Riel happened to glance out his window and spotted two suspicious-looking characters standing at the door of the hotel. He and Lépine fled out the back. It was later discovered that the two men had been hired by Schultz to kill Riel as he came out of the hotel. [Siggins, p. 211.]

94:4

Father Ritchot and others contacted Riel in the summer of 1872 -- there was a federal election coming up, and they believed that he could win if he ran. Riel was persuaded to move back to the Red River. The settlement was divided into four electoral ridings : Marquette, Selkirk, Lisgar, and Provencher. The latter had the highest number of French-speaking constituents, so that's where he ran as a Conservative candidate. (The two main parties in Canadian politics were the Conservatives and the Liberals. Prime-Minister Macdonald and Deputy Prime-Minister Cartier were Conservatives. "[T]he Liberals were considered friends of Schultz and his group". (Siggins, p. 212.)) For some reason Quebec electors voted several weeks ahead of their Manitoba counterparts and, as it turned out, Sir George-Étienne Cartier lost his seat in Montreal. Not wanting to lose his deputy prime-minister, Macdonald "frantically sent a coded telegram to Archibald -- 'get Sir George elected in your province.'" (Siggins, p.214.) Knowing that Provencher was the safest bet for Cartier (who was French), as long as Cartier didn't run against a strong French candidate like Riel, Archibald asked Riel to withdraw from the election. Hoping that this sacrifice would at last win him his amnesty, Riel stepped aside for Cartier, who won the election by acclamation in September 1872. Of course, no amnesty was forthcoming. Far from being grateful, Macdonald was angry that Riel had campaigned to begin with, since the money he'd given Taché in December 1871 had been intended to ensure Riel's "invisibility" during the election. (See panel 91:2.)

On May 20, 1873, Cartier died of Bright's disease, freeing up Provencher for the by-election that I show Riel winning.

94:5

So Riel didn't return to the Red River settlement in June 1873, as I claim in this panel -- he was already there.

96:5

It wasn't much of a race. "Since there were no Liberals who dared run in Provencher, Riel was elected by acclamation." (Siggins, p. 223.)

98:2

Riel had many friends in the east, thanks to his school days in Montreal.

99:2 - 100:5

In 1874 Bishop Ignace Bourget (1799-1885) "was nearing the end of a long, illustrious, and controversial career in the church. [... H]e was deeply involved in politics, both ecclesiastical and civil." (Flanagan, 1996, p.44.) Bourget was a vigorous promoter of French-Canadian interests.

100:5

Riel did fall to his knees in front of Bishop Bourget's bed on January 8, 1874, but the words I have Bourget saying in this panel come from a letter that he wrote to Riel on July 14, 1875. The relevant passage reads,

God who has up until the present directed you and assisted you will not abandon you in your most difficult of struggles, for He has given you a mission which you must accomplish step by step [and] with the Grace of God you must persevere on the path that has been laid out for you. [Siggins, p. 248.]

"Riel never parted with this letter. He carried it with him every day, next to his heart, and he placed it at the head of his bed every night." (Stanley, p. 222.)

101:6

In 1873, an incriminating telegram surfaced in which John A. [Macdonald] shamefully begged for more campaign money from [Canadian Pacific Railway] backers. The public was outraged, and the ensuing Pacific Scandal, as it was known, forced Macdonald to resign in

disgrace. [Ferguson, p. 241.]

Macdonald announced the resignation of his government in November, and the call for a new election came on January 7, 1874 (not "late January" as this panel implies).

102:6 - 103:3

On March 26, 1874, Riel did enter one of the parliament buildings. He wasn't recognized and walked into the chief clerk's office to register as a Member of Parliament. The clerk didn't realize who he was signing in until he saw the signature. He ran to inform the Minister of Justice, but Riel was already quickly retreating from the building.

104:1

It wasn't John Schultz who made this proposal, it was Conservative Member of Parliament Mackenzie Bowell (who later became prime-minister in 1894). Schultz, though, was quick to second the suggestion.

105:1, 105:2

Ambroise Lépine and William O'Donoghue were also banished from Canada at this time.

105:3 - 106:2

Riel spent most of 1875 planning and organizing an invasion of Manitoba. In October 1875 he met with American Senator Oliver P. Morton to discuss his proposed invasion. Morton was polite but uninterested. The senator's legs were paralysed, and after the meeting Riel tried unsuccessfully to cure, through prayer, at least one of his legs.

On December 8th, while in church, Riel had a mystical experience of intense joy followed by (what he called) "almost insupportable sadness [...]. Not long afterwards, only a few days, people began to treat me like a madman." (Flanagan, 1996, p.56.)

The meeting with Grant happened sometime between the 10th and the 15th of December.

Riel stayed at the home of his friend Edmond Mallet while in Washington. "Mallet thought that Riel had lost his mind from repeated disappointments culminating in the failure of President Grant to respond to his proposals." (Flanagan, 1996, p.59.)

106:3 - 107:4

This is a combination of two mystical experiences that Riel claimed to have had. On December 14th "the spirit of God comes upon him, [...] transports him to the fourth heaven and instructed him about the nations of the earth". (Riel referring to himself in the third person -- Flanagan, 1996, p. 57.) At an unknown date,

> While standing alone on a mountain top near Washington, DC, the same spirit that appeared to Moses in the midst of clouds of flame appeared to me in the same manner. [ibid.]

My use of pointed brackets in these panels would seem to indicate that this spirit spoke French, but according to Riel it spoke Latin.

107:5, 107:6

I searched through the various Riel biographies for specific behaviours (as opposed to beliefs) that led to his imprisonment in an asylum.

> He slept neither day nor night, he paced incessantly up and down, up and down, and he cried and howled so horribly that the priest's mother was terrified of him and wouldn't go near him. [...]
> "He continued to cry in the train. I told the travellers that he was a poor lunatic and to please excuse him. When they talked or laughed, Louis said, 'Keep still. Do not laugh, I beg you. I am a prophet.'" [...]
> For the first six days of his stay, Louis refused to sleep or be quiet, and "had contortions like a man in a rage". [...T]hree times he locked himself in his room, stripped naked and tore all his clothes and bed coverings to shreds. [...] He had to be re-dressed like a little child. [...]
> As the [...] sermon ended, Louis stood up and in a loud and dramatic voice sang out three times: "Hear the voice of the priest!" [Siggins, pp. 257 & 258.]

All of these examples come from Siggins' book -- the other bios describe the same behaviours and incidents without mentioning any additional ones. (Which isn't to say that there weren't any additional incidents-- I'm sure that there were others that Riel's friends and family neglected to record for posterity.)

109:3 - 110:5

Riel was upset when a nun tore the inscription-page out of his prayer-book, but he was not placed in a straitjacket on this occasion.

> Seven years after Riel had been confined [in St Jean de Dieu], Dr. Harold Tuke, a prominent British reformer advocating more humane treatment for the insane, made a tour of the asylums of North America. He said of [St Jean de Dieu], "In the course of seven and thirty years I have visited a large number of asylums in Europe, but I have rarely, if ever, seen anything more depressing....." It was horribly overcrowded, it stank, [...] and the food was disgusting. Each inmate was confined to a tiny, narrow room-- Tuke said it was more like an animal pen than a cell-- where there was hardly enough space for a bed. [Siggins, p. 259.]

111:1

Dr Henry Howard on Riel and murderers: "I believed him to be guilty of the murder he was accused of, and I believed every murderer to be either insane or a fool"(Flanagan, 1996, p.65.)

I don't believe that the behaviours that people associate with "mental illnesses" are caused by biological abnormalities or malfunctions in the brain. To put it more simply: "mental illnesses" are not illnesses. I was tempted to elaborate at length on why Riel's behaviours and beliefs in late 1875 and early 1876 weren't symptoms of an illness, but it would all just be a rehash of what I wrote in my strip "My Mom Was a Schizophrenic" (which can be found in my book THE LITTLE MAN). So instead I'll just quote a brief passage by historian Thomas Flanagan and urge any of you who are puzzled by my statement that "'mental illnesses' are not illnesses" to read my schizophrenia strip, or (even better) to read MADNESS, HERESY, AND THE RUMOUR OF ANGELS by Seth Farber and/or TOXIC PSYCHIATRY by Peter Breggin.

> Much of what strikes modern readers as incomprehensible and therefore insane makes sense in the context of Riel's ultramontane worldview, which included a God who controls human affairs, punishes the evil and rewards the good, works miracles in daily life, and speaks directly to men through revelation and prophecy. A hasty resort to medical labels rendering this phase of Riel's life meaningless, when in fact it is the key to understanding his character, and thus the overall pattern of his career. [Flanagan, 1996, p. 80.]

(The ultramontanes were Roman Catholics who placed papal authority over state authority and who desired the reunion of church and state. Bishop Bourget was an ultramontane.)

For unknown reasons, Riel was transferred from L'Hospice de St Jean de Dieu to the St Michel-Archange asylum at Beauport (near Quebec City) in May 1876. Conditions at St Michel-Archange were about the same as those at St Jean de Dieu.
In January 1878, Riel was released and was

> whisked to the American border. The last thing the officials of the asylum wanted was the scandal that would surely result if it was ever discovered he had been living in Canada illegally for two years. [Siggins, p. 271.]

I suspect that the worry that the authorities might find out the true identity of "Mr David" impelled the asylum officials to release Riel sooner than they would have if he had been an ordinary Canadian citizen.

> [H]e was having visions and receiving revelations within a few weeks of his discharge from Beauport. If he ever did repudiate his prophetic beliefs, it was not very deeply and not for very long. Riel's cure meant that he had learned how to conduct himself externally, not that he had undergone a deep internal transformation. [Flanagan, 1996, p.78.]

Riel went to Keesville and the home of Father Fabien Barnabé. With money borrowed from Barnabé, he rented a small farm and began working it. He also became engaged to the priest's 27 year-old sister Evelina. (Riel was then 33 and probably still a virgin.) The crop-yield at the end of the summer was disappointing, so Riel went to New York city to look for a job-- and also to try and raise support for an armed invasion of Manitoba. With no success achieved in either of those goals, he decided to go back to the west. He returned to Keesville only to pack his belongings and say good-bye to Evelina, assuring her that he'd send for her once he was "established". He settled in the St Joseph/Pembina area of the Dakota territory, which was close to the Red River Settlement (or Winnipeg, as the settlement was now being called). Many of his friends and family made the trip south to visit him. In the summer of 1879 he relocated to Montana and joined a nomadic, buffalo-hunting band of about 150 Métis families. Riel was planning a "confederacy of Indian and mixed-blood peoples who would fight for a country of their own" (Siggins, p. 293) and he spent a lot of time traveling around, trying to mobilize the Indian chiefs in the area. On April 27, 1881, he married 20 year-old Marguerite Monet Bellehumeur (having apparently forgotten his promise to Evelina Barnabé). He became involved in American politics in a minor way-- he campaigned for a Republican candidate in an 1882 congressional election. (Unlike Indians, the Métis could vote.) On May 9, 1882, Marguerite gave birth to a son, Jean. Riel became an American citizen in March 1883. The following month he was hired as a school-teacher at St Peter's Mission. And a month after that he was arrested and charged with election fraud in relation to his role in the 1882 election. It was believed that he'd "induced Half-breeds who were not U.S. citizens to vote [.... T]he whole thing was patent nonsense". (Ibid, pp. 311, 312.) He was quickly released on bail, and in April 1884 the charges were dismissed. Marguerite gave birth to their second child, Marie-Angelique, in September 1883.

PAGE 117

"By 1886 all of the 1.4 million acres had been granted. Less than 20 per cent of the eligible Metis beneficiaries actually owned the land they were entitled to." (Purich, p. 70.)

PAGES 117, 118

The dispersal of the Métis and native English from Manitoba was gradual but perceptible between 1871 and 1876; it

became remarkable from 1877 to 1880; and the migration increased to a rush of personnel between 1881 and 1884. Overall, more than 4,000 persons participated in the exodus, mainly to Saskatchewan.
[Sprague, p. 139]

In CANADA AND THE MÉTIS, 1869-1885 (which the above quote is from), historian D.N. Sprague contends that the Canadian government consciously worked to deprive the Métis of the land it had promised them by legally rigging things against their interests. (See the Purich quote in the note for panel 77:5 for an example of this type of legal rigging.)

Occasionally historians disagree with one another:

[T]he government's administration of Manitoba lands was creditable. It was slower than people would have liked, but the situation was intrinsically compli-cated [...]. Several thousand Métis left Manitoba in the 1870s and 1880s, but not because the Canadian government deprived them of their river lots or any other lands. They left partly because the arrival of white immigrants changed the character of the Red River settlement, but mainly because the buffalo were withdrawing.
[Flanagan, 2000, p. 33]

Flanagan argues his side of this particular matter (whether or not Canada lived up to its Manitoba Act promises) in his MÉTIS LANDS IN MANITOBA (1991). Anyone interested in getting into this subject in more depth should probably read both authors.

121:3

Father Alexis André (1833-1893) was an Oblate priest.

121:6

I really don't know, but I would guess that an ordinary citizen such as Dumont would have had to make an appointment with George Duck (the Dominion Lands agent in Prince Albert) to see survey maps of the area, and I doubt that Mr Duck would have allowed those maps to leave his presence-- nor would he have allowed those maps to be folded in the way that we fold mass-produced maps today.

122:5

Apparently the square lots lent themselves better to the kind of inten-sive commercial agriculture that the Canadian government was hoping to encourage. But the real reason that so much of the south branch of the Saskatchewan River was divided into "English lots" instead of "French lots" is that surveying long thin rectangles took longer than surveying squares and was therefore more expensive.

123:1

The Dominion Lands office didn't

officially open in Prince Albert until 1881, but George Duck moved to Prince Albert in 1878 and would have been available for consultations with settlers from that point on.

In 1888, the government finally did resurvey the Métis land along the south branch of the Saskatchewan River.

123:2 - 123:6

The Canadian government's homesteading system

involved the following stages:
- making "entry" on a quarter-section [160 acres] through registration at a Dominion Lands agency and paying the $10.00 fee;
- performing "settlement duties," usually uninterrupted residence of three years, construction of a home, and cultivation of thirty acres or raising a certain number of animals;
- obtaining "patent" or title after a Dominion Lands inspector ascertained that settlement duties had been performed;
- "pre-empting" neighbouring land. When a settler made homestead entry, he could also enter a pre-emption on an adjoining quarter-section [...]. Pre-emption was the right to buy those 160 acres at a specified price, once patent had been obtained on the homestead. The price was $2.50 per acre if the land was within a certain distance of a railway, $2.00 per acre otherwise. [Flanagan, 2000, pp. 26, 27.]

If one didn't want to wait three years for title -- if one wanted outright ownership immediately -- one could buy privately-owned land on the open-market (the CPR had lots of land to sell) but the market-price for land was a good deal more than the homesteading price of $10 for 160 acres.

125:2

The land-grants that Father André is referring to here are the lots that made up the 1,400,000 acres mentioned in panels 77:5 and 77:6 and on page 117.

125:2 - 125:4

After the 1885 rebellion, a land-grant was made to the Métis of the North-West in the form of scrip. Scrip was a certificate that could be traded for land or money. Most of the Métis chose to trade their scrip for money. Some argue that the scrip-system was designed to keep the Métis from acquiring more land and that the true beneficiaries were land-speculators who under-paid the Métis for the scrip. (See Purich, pp. 107-127.) On the other side are those who say that the Métis handled the scrip-system to their advantage. (See Flanagan, 2000, pp. 64-84.)

128:1

Charles Nolin had moved to the south branch of the Saskatchewan River and was one of the people who urged that a delegation be sent to Montana to meet with Riel. He was not, however, one of the four men who made the trip. The actual fourth man was named Michel Dumas.

129:3 - 130:4

Concerned that he might be detained at the border, Riel sent his papers up separately to minimize the chance that the police might seize them, so this scene is a fabrication. The book Riel was writing was titled MASSINAHICAN, which was "the Cree word for book or Bible." (Flanagan, 1996, p.125.) I don't know how much of the book Riel managed to write, but it seems that only a few pages still exist. (Riel, pp. 387-399.)

131:1 - 131:3

In late July 1884 Riel "met with twelve chiefs, including Big Bear and Poundmaker". (Siggins, p. 350.)

Treaty No. 6 [signed in 1876] contained the clause whose vague wording would soon make it the most controversial of all the treaty provisions: "That in the event hereafter of the indians comprised within this treaty being overtaken by any pestilence, or by a general famine, the Queen, on being satisfied and certified thereof by her Indian Agent or Agents will grant to the Indians assistance of such character and to such extent as her Chief Superintendent of Indian Affairs shall deem necessary and sufficient to relieve the Indians from the calamity that shall have befallen them." [Beal & Macleod, p. 57.]

The Indians believed the treaty guaranteed them a sufficient supply of food until they were well-established enough as farmers to provide for themselves. [...] But the government took a radically different view of the famine clause. Government officials believed they were under no obligation to supply rations except in the case of a general famine. The Plains Indians had been consistently very hungry since the buffalo suddenly disappeared. Ottawa, however, refused to consider widespread hunger as the famine they interpreted the treaty to mean. [Ibid., p. 72.]

This wasn't the only grievance that the Indians had. "The chiefs complained their reserves were too swampy, [and] that the salty bacon they were usually provided was causing scurvy". (Ibid., p. 88.) They had been promised farming equipment and livestock, but "What equipment and animals the Indians received under the treaty provisions were of such obviously inferior quality that the Indians had understandably refused to take delivery of some of it". (Ibid., p. 63.) Also, the Indian agents and the men hired to teach the Indians how to farm were patronage appointees who had little understanding or sympathy for the Indians and the dramatic changes they faced. Their general unsuitability for the task at hand, often bordering on incompetence, led to a high turnover rate. [Stonechild & Waiser, p. 36.]

131:4

After the Pacific Scandal forced Sir John A. Macdonald from office in 1873, everyone -- including Macdonald -- assumed that he was washed-up politically. He tried to retire but could find no suitable replacement for the leadership of the Conservative party. Meanwhile, the Liberals under Alexander Mackenzie may have been in power, but that doesn't mean that things were going well for them.

The root of the problem was the great world trade depression that began in 1873 [...]. The Mackenzie government could hardly be blamed for the effects of depression on Canada -- but, human nature being what it is, it was blamed. [Careless, p. 268.]

As a result, when the next election came around in 1878, Macdonald found himself to be once again the prime-minister of Canada.

131:5

I mention Riel meeting with the English here. To his surprise, he received a favourable response from the North Saskatchewan's white-anglophone community in 1884. Like the other groups in the Canadian North-West, they were feeling tremendously frustrated with the government, and they hoped that Riel's presence would convince Ottawa to address their concerns along with those of the Métis and the Indians.

Probably the prime concern of the white settlers was the railway.

The rapid construction of the main line ate up money at such a rate that there was none left over to build the branch lines, sidings, platforms, and grain elevators that would make the line usable. The CPR's insatiable appetite for capital and its monopoly position in the West meant that freight rates were set at very high levels, so high that farmers found they needed bumper crops just to get by. The poor crop of 1883 combined with falling prices threatened many with bankruptcy. [Beal & Macleod, p. 32.]

After Riel arrived in [the Batoche area] in early July, there ensued a lengthy period of peaceful political agitation. [...] Riel tried to frame a petition of grievances acceptable to all residents of the area, native as well as white, anglophone as well as francophone. This was no simple task [.] [Flanagan, 2000, p. 14.]

Support from the white community fell away when the Métis and Indians resorted to arms, with one important exception. 23 year-old William Jackson met Riel in July 1884 and became his secretary. The young man was arrested in Batoche on May 12, 1885. He was thought to be crazy and was sent to an asylum.

The logic was simple: Jackson was the only white man among the Métis and Indians who participated directly in their rebellion, and therefore he must be insane." [Siggins, p. 420.]

133:3

In order to get British Columbia to become Canada's western-most province, Macdonald had promised to build a railway that linked it to eastern Canada. There was fear that British Columbia might leave confederation if the railway didn't get built.

132:6 - 137:2

The two disasters -- the revolt on the prairies and the collapse of the railway -- had come together in time. And together they might destroy [Macdonald] and his Canada. [...] They were separate problems. They could even be played off against each other. And in that possibility did not there lie a real hope? He could use the railway to defend the West. He could use the West to justify the railway. [Creighton, p.417.]

Don McLean, in his book 1885: MÉTIS REBELLION OR GOVERNMENT CONSPIRACY?, prints the above quote from historian Donald Creighton -- he then comments:

Creighton saw the success of the CPR and the destruction of the Métis as two separate events that were somehow brought together in time. He recognized that these two "separate" events could be played off against each other by the prime minister in such a way as to save the CPR and the Conservative government. Creighton saw the Métis rebellion as a fortunate coincidence that simply provided Sir John A. Macdonald with the means to politically justify further financial support for the CPR syndicate. They were not, however, separate events. They were intricately interrelated events that came together not through coincidence but by design. [McLean, p. 86.]

D. N. Sprague hints at a similar conspiracy theory in his CANADA AND THE MÉTIS, 1869-1885. The notion that the 1885 rebellion happened by "design" makes a certain amount of sense. If the plan that I have Macdonald outline in panels 136:3 to 136:6 had occurred to him in real life, it's hard to see how he couldn't have been tempted by it. That said, it must be admitted that McLean and Sprague scratch up little in the way of hard evidence.

"The petition [...] had finally, on December 16, been sent off to the governor-general, with copies going to the government." (Siggins, p. 362.)

137:4 - 138:1

Creighton saw Riel's attempt to get money from the government (and apparent willingness to leave Canada if paid) as "cynically, almost brutally, selfish." (Creighton, p. 413.) McLean, on the other hand, reasons that

> By this time he knew that he had done all that he could towards establishing a peaceful and just settlement in the West. Since his presence was now working against further progress, why should he not tend to his own financial affairs and return to his life as a teacher in Montana? [McLean, p. 94.]

138:2 - 139:5

Sprague thinks that this telegram was a deliberate provocation.

> Telegraphed to Dewdney, the news was that Canada would "investigate claims of Half Breeds and with that view [Cabinet] had decided [to make an] enumeration of those who did not participate in Grant under Manitoba Act." The provocation was that only a small minority of the residents of [the area around Batoche] could benefit from awards to non-Manitobans. Moreover, the government already had the figures: 200 of 1,300 potential claimants. Dewdney was so stunned by the news he refused to pass on the information without alteration. Imagining the purpose of the Order in Council was conciliation rather than provocation, he changed the announcement before transmitting the telegram to [the Métis]: "Government has decided to investigate claims of Half Breeds and with that view has already taken preliminary steps." Then Dewdney reminded Macdonald that "the bulk of the French Half Breeds" had "nothing to expect" from the unrevised text. The original news would "start a fresh agitation." No prime ministerial congratulation came back over the wire thanking Dewdney for his editorial intervention[.] [Sprague, p. 170.]

The more conventional view is that Macdonald was not aware that the telegram would be seen as provocative -- that perhaps he was distracted by matters like the CPR crisis and so didn't give the concerns of the Métis the attention that they deserved and/or that perhaps the conflicting reports from the North-West made it difficult to accurately judge how the Métis would react to the telegram. The choice seems to be between believing that Macdonald abused his power or that the government operated inefficiently. People in positions of prominence frequently abuse their power, and governments always operate inefficiently, so both choices seem possible

to me. I've made the McLean/Sprague-theory part of my strip, not because I'm convinced that it's true (I honestly don't have a strong opinion on the matter one way or the other), but because it makes Macdonald seem more villainous -- villains are fun in a story, and I'm trying to tell this tale in an engaging manner.

Incidently, even though I think that Macdonald was capable of abusing his power, I don't think that he actually was a villain. I disagree with much of what he did and stood for, but I recognize that he tried to do what he thought was best for the country. And, quite frankly, I'd rather have lived in a state run by John A. Macdonald than one run by Louis Riel.

140:1 - 140:5

> There is some doubt how far Louis Riel was sincere when he offered to return to the United States. Charles Nolin, a hostile witness, later declared that Riel never really intended to leave the Saskatchewan and that he engineered this demonstration on his own behalf. Schmidt [*] was disposed to take much the same view, writing to Archbishop Taché that it was Riel's personal claque that carried the métis in the demand that Riel stay in the North-West. On the other hand, there is some evidence to suggest that Riel did have notions of leaving the country. Father Vegreville, likewise no warm partisan of Riel, wrote to Taché on February 19, telling him Riel had made arrangements with Louis Marion to drive him to Winnipeg in mid-March -- probably, suggested Vegreville, to see the Archbishop. "The fact is that he is extremely poor and lives by charity," wrote the priest. [Stanley, p. 299.]

140:6 - 141:2

There is no evidence that a conversation like this took place between Clarke and Macdonald or that Clarke saw the prime-minister at all when he was in Ottawa. Whether or not the two men conspired together, it does seem that "Lawrence Clarke was playing a double game." (Sprague, p. 163.) In 1884 Clarke encouraged the Métis to invite Riel back to Canada. When they did, he informed the authorities that the Métis leader was returning and advised them to arrest Riel as he crossed the border. Clarke's advice was ignored -- no effort was made to detain the Montana school-teacher as he re-entered Canada. Clarke then visited Riel, gave him money for his upkeep, and told him to "Bring on your rebellion as soon as you can. It will be the making of this country." (McLean, p. 90.) Then there's the incident described in the next note and also the way that Clarke encouraged the Mounties to fight the Métis. (See panel 153:1.) The Métis believed that they could trust

* Louis Schmidt was a childhood friend of Riel's who opposed taking up arms against the government.

Clarke, but he was reporting their actions to the government. In February 1885, the Métis sent Clarke to Ottawa to "make representations to the government on their behalf." (McLean, p. 96.)

141:4, 141:5

Clarke did not go to Riel to tell him all this.

> On March 18 [...] the French settlements were electrified by a rumour: Clarke had told some freighters whom he met on the trail that five hundred more police were enroute to Saskatchewan and Riel and other leaders soon would be under arrest. [Howard, p. 322.]

"Clarke later denied saying any such thing but the story was quickly and widely circulated." (Beal & MacLeod, p. 139.) According to Beal & MacLeod and Siggins, Clarke met the freighters on the trail on the 17th, not the 18th. (Siggins, p. 371.)

> The truth behind the rumour was that the commander of the police, alarmed by reports of sedition, had ordered a column of 100 men north to reinforce Fort Carlton. [Flanagan, 1996, p. 151.]

141:6 - 142:4

"On March 4, the full details of the government's telegram to Dewdney announcing the Halfbreed Claims Commission were, at last, released." (Siggins, p. 367.) None of the books that I've read mention who released the original telegram to the Métis, or how it was done, but it's rather unlikely that Clarke was responsible, since he went to Ottawa in February and didn't get back to the Saskatchewan area until March 17th. Whoever did it, Dewdney seems to have been right that it would make the Métis angry: on March 5th, Riel, Dumont, and nine other Métis held a secret meeting at which they pledged to "save our country from a wicked government by taking up arms if necessary." (Beal & MacLeod, p. 135.)

142:5, 142:6

Early in the evening of March 18th, Riel, Dumont, and 70 Métis took 3 prisoners -- an Indian agent, his interpreter, and a Batoche magistrate who had been reporting the activities of the Métis to the police. Riel's group then went to the Kerr brothers' store near Batoche and took all the guns and ammunition. From there they headed to the Batoche church (St Antoine de Padoue) where a large crowd was waiting. This is where panel 142:5 takes up the story. The priest who refused to let the crowd into the church was Father Julien Moulin, not Father André. There were several priests in the area, they all disliked Riel, and I'm combining them all into one character.

143:1, 143:2

Refusing the sacrament to any who participated in armed rebellion was threatened on Sunday, March 15th, by Father Vital Fourmond in a sermon delivered at the St Laurent de Grandin church. Riel was in the congregation. He

> rose in his place and denounced the priest. "You have turned the pulpit of truth into one of politics, falsehood and discord. How dare you refuse the sacrament to those who would take up arms in defence of their most sacred rights!" [Siggins, p. 370.]

143:3

It would seem that Riel had others move the priest out of the way. "When Moulin, an elderly, small-boned man, still refused to let them in his church, Louis ordered, 'Take him away! Take him away!'" (Siggins, p. 373.)

146:1

As I mentioned above, three men had already been taken prisoner by the time the Métis got to the Walters & Baker store. By the end of the night they had eight hostages. (Beal & Macleod, pp. 140, 141.) There were more to follow, though (if I've counted correctly), the number of prisoners held at any one time never went over fourteen.

147:5

In December 1884, during a religious ceremony, Nolin's wife had been cured of "a disabling illness" (Siggins, p. 369) that had afflicted her for ten years.

> For the people [in the Batoche area], the recovery of Rosalie Nolin was indeed a miracle. Father André took every advantage of it; he wrested a promise from Charles Nolin that, in thankfulness to the Virgin, he would not engage in any civil disobedience. [Ibid.]

147:1 - 148:1

> Nolin was arrested and brought up for trial along with Louis Marion and William Boyer, two other métis who had refused to take up arms at Riel's request. [...] The trial itself was brief and Nolin, as the ringleader of the opposition, was sentenced to death. According to Philippe Garnot, Riel "made a long speech accusing Ch. Nolin of treason and said that an example was necessary and that it was essential that Nolin should be condemned to death." Riel, however, did not press for an immediate execution of sentence; he knew his man, and he wanted to leave a way open to force the hands of the clergy by granting Nolin his life in return for clerical approval, or at least clerical neutrality during the days to follow. Nolin, badly frightened and encouraged by Lépine, made his submission and agreed to support Riel. So, too, did Louis Marion. Boyer was discharged. [Stanley, p. 308.]

Nolin was arrested on the 19th, not the 25th.

148:2, 148:3

The world-famous Canadian Mounties are finally mentioned in this strip.

> Sir John A. Macdonald envisaged a mounted police force in 1869 to secure Rupert's Land [...] but, true to his nickname "Old Tomorrow," he procrastinated. Consequently, late in 1869 when the first Red River uprising flared, there was no force stationed in the West to deal with it. [Cruise & Griffiths, 1996, p.31.]

> During the early months of 1873, with pressure mounting on Macdonald to produce his police force, the prime minister became mired in a boozy rearguard defence of his office over the [Pacific] scandal. With British Columbia threatening to leave Confederation unless Macdonald kicked some life into the still moribund railway project, the prime minister pulled himself together sufficiently to draw up the legislation needed to make the police force a reality. [Ibid., p.34.]

The force was originally called the North West Mounted Police, but the name was later changed to the Royal Canadian Mounted Police. The Mounties first entered the North-West in 1874.

148:5

Dumont seems to imply here that the Métis were keeping the rebellion a secret, or at least had made no official declaration of hostility.

> On March 19, Riel sent an ultimatum to Major Crozier demanding the surrender of Fort Carlton and threatening a war of extermination if his demand was not obeyed. Major Crozier summarily rejected Riel's demand. [McLean, p.103.]

148:4 - 149:6

These panels simplify the events leading up to the Battle of Duck Lake. Dumont and ten men went over to the Mitchell store on the afternoon of March 25th. Riel and many more armed men joined them and they all went over to a nearby Cree reserve to spend the night. Two police spies were spotted and captured. The next morning, three police scouts were sighted, and Dumont and several of his men chased them to a group of fifteen Mounties and seven militia (local armed citizens -- probably all Anglophones).

150:1 - 151:2

Several of the Mounties were actually in sleighs. The fellow who had the stand-off with Dumont was standing in his sleigh the whole time.

151:2

Dumont's rifle accidentally went off as he struck the Mountie.

151:3

The fellow who's shouting in this panel was also swatted by Dumont's gun. Another one of the Mounties "pushed Edouard Dumont into the snow." (Siggins, p.384.) There was also a good deal more yelling back and forth than I show.

153:2

I imply in the strip that the Fort Carlton fighting force was made up only of North West Mounted Police officers. Of the men, 56 were Mounties, but fighting alongside them at Duck Lake were 43 men from Prince Albert's volunteer-militia.

154:3

Riel's reinforcements actually arrived at around the point when the shooting began.

155:5 - 156:4

The weaponless Assiyiwin is reported to have said to McKay, "If you haven't come to fight, what are you doing with so many guns, grandson?" (Siggins, p.384.) McKay was holding a rifle, and Assiyiwin either grabbed it or reached out to push it in another direction. McKay later claimed that his rifle discharged without killing the Cree. McKay then drew his pistol and shot Assiyiwan and Isidore Dumont. (Charlebois, p.148.)

Assiyiwin, who lived on a nearby Cree reserve, had not considered himself to be affiliated with either side in the conflict. Siggins says that he was at Duck Lake to mediate. But, according to Stonechild & Waiser, he was not there to mediate or to have anything to do with either the Métis or the Mounties -- he had simply been walking his pony home, the path he took happened to lead between the two opposing forces, and he happened to get into an argument with McKay as Isidore Dumont rode up with a white flag. (Stonechild & Waiser, p.66.)

162:5

Only three of the dead were Mounties -- the other nine were militiamen.

162:6, 163:1

If you were to trust my drawings, you'd think that the Mounties fled from Fort Carlton in broad day-light, but that's not what happened. Fearing an attack of the kind that I have Dumont suggesting in panel 163:2, the Mounties decided to leave the fort under cover of darkness in the pre-dawn hours of March 27th. During the rush to leave, a fire started accidentally, and soon the fort was in flames. This drew the attention of the Métis, and the end-result was that the Mounties may as well have left in broad day-light.

The fire caused a great deal of damage to the fort, but there were still supplies and important papers to be found, as I show in panels 164:3 to 164:6.

167:5 - 168:2

The decision to use the CPR imposed serious hardships on the troops and was almost certainly unnecessary. There would have been no difficulty shipping the men through the United States; most of the ammunition and supplies went that way anyway. [Beal & Macleod, p. 172.]

168:4

Saying that Battleford was "attacked" is perhaps overstating what happened, although the inhabitants of Battleford felt like they were being attacked. A large number of Cree ("hundreds" according to Beal & Macleod, p. 181 -- "about 120" according to Stonechild & Waiser, p. 92) advanced on the town and the Battlefordites fled to their fort. Stonechild & Waiser insist that the intentions of the Cree weren't hostile -- nevertheless, finding the town deserted, they decided to loot and destroy much of its property before they returned to Poundmaker's reserve.

168:5

Because he was the chief of the Cree at Frog Lake, Big Bear's name is associated with the Frog Lake massacre, but he himself did not participate in the murders and, in fact, tried to stop them.

To the outside world, it was "Big Bear's band" that had committed unspeakable crimes that early spring day at Frog Lake, and as their leader, he was held personally responsible. [Stonechild & Waiser, p. 118.]

169:5 - 170:2

Amazingly, in just over two weeks since the first shots at Duck Lake, more than three thousand men with all their equipment had been shipped to the West and were ready to be deployed. [Beal & Macleod, p.177.]

Major-General Thomas Bland Strange (I love that name) lived near Calgary, Alberta, and he wouldn't have been in Qu'Appelle -- his orders were sent to him.

In Mid-April, Middleton wasn't in Qu'Appelle either. He started to march toward Batoche on April 6th.

The strip leaves unanswered what happened to Poundmaker and Big Bear, so I'll very briefly deal with that subject here.

Lieutenant-Colonel Otter did find Poundmaker, and on May 2, 1885, the Canadians attacked the Cree camp, but within hours the Indians had the whites on the run. Otter and his men would have all been killed if Poundmaker hadn't intervened and ordered his warriors to let the fleeing soldiers escape. On May 17th Poundmaker and his followers were on their way to Batoche to aid Riel when they heard of the defeat of the Métis. The Cree chief led his people into Battleford and surrendered on May 26, 1885.

Major-General Strange managed to track down Big Bear's group, and on May 28th a battle ensued. The two sides fought for a few hours and then both retreated. On June 2nd Sam Steele of the North West Mounted Police, and 60 mounties and soldiers, attacked the Indians, who managed to get away. The group traveling with Big Bear got smaller and smaller as various factions and individuals went off on their own until the only person left with the chief was his youngest son. On July 4, 1885, the two of them surrendered at Fort Carlton.

Poundmaker and Big Bear were both sentenced to three years, even though Big Bear was clearly innocent of any treasonous or hostile intentions. * He had lost control of his band -- a guy named Wandering Spirit had initiated the Frog Lake massacre. Big Bear had tried to stop the bloodshed. Wandering Spirit and seven other Indians were hanged for the massacre and other murders committed during the Rebellion. If I'm counting right, around 40 Indians who were associated with either Poundmaker or Big Bear were sentenced to various prison terms. (Beal & Macleod, pp. 325-332.)

Poundmaker

sickened rapidly in jail. After less than a year in Stony Mountain Penitentiary he was clearly dying and the authorities released him. Four months later [...] Poundmaker died on July 4, 1886. Big Bear lasted a little longer but he too was seriously ill by early 1887 and was released in March. [...] He spent the last few months of his life on Poundmaker's reserve, where he died on January 17, 1888. [Ibid., p. 339.]

170:6

On the afternoon of April 23rd, Riel and Dumont headed out with

* In their book, LOYAL TILL DEATH, Stonechild & Waiser argue that the same was true of Poundmaker.

200 men (Beal & Macleod, p. 229) or 230 men. (Siggins, p. 397.) They left 20 to 30 men in Batoche to guard it. That evening, "a messenger rode in from Batoche with a report, which later proved false, that the Mounted Police were advancing from Prince Albert." (Beal & Macleod, p. 229.) In case the report was true, Riel took 50 of the men and returned to Batoche.

171:1

A coulee is a ravine.

171:3 - 174:1

[Dumont] tells how one of the [Canadian] scouts came riding towards him. Dumont's combative instinct rose up, and he forgot the need for concealment. "I had no wish to waste my cartridges on such a little matter. He saw us and made off; I chased him and was about to overtake him, when somebody fired at me. My people shouted to me that I was riding into a troop of forty men whom I had not seen, so intent was I on catching my prey. When I saw I had no time to club down the fugitive, I shot him, and at once I plunged into the coulée[.]
[Woodcock, p. 199.]

The way I've drawn the scene implies that, had this incident not occurred, the Métis would have been able to take the Canadians by surprise -- this was not the case. Middleton's scouts had already seen signs of Métis presence in the area, and the soldiers were alert to the possibility of an ambush.

178:5 - 181:3

All day [Dumont] had hoped for help to come from Batoche, but Riel, who prayed for hours on end with his arms held up in the shape of a cross, and exhorted the women and children to do likewise, did not want to send any men, though the attack by Irvine and the Mounted Police did not materialize and the thunder of Middleton's guns could be heard quite distinctly in the village. Finally, Edouard Dumont's patience came to an end. "When my own people are in peril, I cannot remain here," he said, "My brothers are there and I cannot let them be killed without going to their aid." He was supported by an Indian named Yellow Blanket who added: "There is no need to wait until tomorrow to help one's friends." [...T]hey gathered eighty horsemen, and riding hard to Fish Creek, Edouard led his cavalry in a charge into the coulée that forced the Canadians back and made Middleton decide to withdraw[.]
[Woodcock, p. 203.]

According to Morton and Beal & Macleod, Middleton's decision to withdraw had been made before the Métis

reinforcements showed up. (Morton, 1972, p. 68 -- Beal & Macleod, p. 232.)

In panels 179:1 to 180:3, I have a Métis horseman riding from Tourond's Coulee to Batoche and convincing Riel to send reinforcements to the battle. As the above quote by Woodcock makes clear, it was Gabriel's brother, Edouard Dumont, who convinced Riel, and Edouard hadn't yet been at the battle-site. I didn't invent the horseman who rode from the coulee to Batoche -- he's mentioned by Howard. (P. 361.) Perhaps this man was simply deserting the battle with the excuse that he was going for help. A lot of Dumont's men did run away from the fight.

179:4 - 180:3

As mentioned in the above George Woodcock quote, Riel held his arms up in the shape of a cross. "[W]hen his strength had given out, the Métisses had taken turns holding [Riel's arms] up." (Siggins, p. 399.)

181:5

Of the forty-nine, four were mortally wounded.

181:6

One of the two was mortally wounded.

178:3 - 181:6

Snow and rain fell during the day (Siggins, p. 397.), but the precipitation must have been light -- at one point in the battle, the Métis successfully lit the grass on fire, so it couldn't have been very wet or snow-covered.

182:1

While the precipitation was probably light on April 24th, there was a heavy snowfall on the next day, so my depiction of snow on the ground in this panel is accurate.

182:5 - 183:6

The gun-boat (the Northcote) approached from the south. If one was in Batoche, looking toward the South Saskatchewan River, a boat traveling from south to north would float by you from left to right, not from right to left.

Two men on the Northcote were wounded in the exchange of gunfire -- both of them were part of the boat's civilian crew.

183:5, 183:6

The fire that developed on the Northcote would probably not have been as large as I've drawn it in these panels.

"[I]t was quickly smothered."(Siggins, p. 402.)

185:4 - 186:5

I show Father André holding a white flag and walking from the church, past Métis rifle-pits, and toward the Canadian soldiers. Father André was not in Batoche during the battle. Also, the Canadians advanced from the south, and there were no Métis rifle-pits south of the Batoche church. (I'm not sure why -- perhaps because Dumont had expected the attack to come from the east rather than the south. (Siggins, p. 403.) Another reason could have been that the church and the parish-house were located at a bit of a distance from the rest of the village. In addition, the antagonism that had developed between the priests and much of the Batoche community may have influenced Dumont's thinking when planning the rifle-pits.) As they approached the church, the soldiers noticed that a "white handkerchief fluttered from the door of the parish house". (Howard, p. 392.) They walked up to the building and found several priests, nuns, "and the few Métis who had sought refuge with them". (Ibid, p. 393.)

The missionaries in their later accounts of the Battle of Batoche insisted that they remained neutral and that they gave no information to the troops, in obedience to a written pledge the Métis had required of them. But against their words stands not only the testimony of the Métis veterans, inclu- ding Gabriel Dumont, but also the accounts written on the battlefield by Canadian officers, volunteers and newspapermen. [Ibid, p.392.]

The Canadians held the church for the rest of the day (May 9th) but abandoned it when they retreated for their camp in the evening. The next day, the Métis positioned them- selves in front of the church (to the south of it) and it remained behind their line of defence until the Canad- ians' final charge on May 12th.

190:1 - 191:3

Riel had Baptiste Boucher hear his confession on May 8th (the day before the Batoche battle began), not May 10th.

191:5

At some point on May 11th, 150 Mounted Police joined the Canadian force, bringing Middleton's army up to 950 men. (Siggins, p. 405.)

193:3

The Métis believed that General Middleton was waiting for them to run out of bullets. Historian Desmond Morton doesn't think that was the case.

In later years, commenting on his campaign, Middleton sought to leave the world with the impression that he had deliberately conducted a wearing battle at Batoche, seeking to tire out Dumont's men and to train his own. In fact, he does not seem to have known really what to do. [Morton, 1972, p. 87.]

194:2 - 194:6

The decision to charge the Métis was a little less spontaneous than I show in these panels. Lieutenant- Colonel Arthur Williams had gotten fed up with being held back by Middleton. He quietly consulted with his men (the Midland Battalion of Port Hope, Ontario) and they agreed that, if they got an order to advance, they would charge and disregard any attempts to call them back.

[F]rom man to man the word spread [....] Quickly the whispers came back from [other battalions], promising their support. [...] Then the Midland got its orders : a "reconnaissance in force" on the left flank.
The Port Hope Battalion leaped up cheering and started on a run [...] with Williams at their head. The command, "Charge!" rolled along the line [and other battalions] too jumped up and ran, firing as they went.
General Middleton watched aghast as the troops poured over the crest of the hill. "Cease Firing!" he roared. "Why in the name of God don't you cease firing ?"
The bugle sounded the command to retire, again and again, but the troops ignored it. Within ten minutes the whole line was in motion. Middleton, realizing at last that his army was out of control, called up the rear echelons to support the charge. [Howard, p. 403.]

195:5, 195:6, 198:1

Dumont described a conversation that he had with 93 year-old Joseph Ouellette :

What kept me there [on the battle- field], I should say, was the courage of old Ouellette. Several times I said to him : "Come on, Father, we must pull back !" and the good old man always replied : "Just a minute ! I want to kill another Englishman !" Then I said to him, "Very well, let us die here." [Siggins, pp. 406 & 407.]

While they had this exchange "several times" during the battle, there is no reason to think that Dumont and Ouellette repeated it during the Canadians' final charge or that they were side-by-side at that point.

The Métis casualties were

twelve dead and three wounded, but two of these were not soldiers; a young girl had been killed by a burst of shrapnel -- ten-year-old Marcile Graton had been shot dead on the doorstep of Fisher's store, where she had gone looking for her mother -- and a nine-month-old baby had died from machine-gun fire. All the Métis fatalities were suffered on the last day of fighting. The official count for the Canadians was ten dead, thirty-six wounded. [Siggins, p. 407.]

199:1

The two rebels did come across each other in the woods while fleeing the battle, but Riel hadn't yet made up his mind to surrender, or he kept it to himself if he had. Dumont and his wife hid out for several days, and, when he was ready to head for the border on May 15th, he tried to find Riel in order to ask him to come. Dumont was told that Riel had surrendered that day.

203:1 - 232:4

The black backgrounds that I've used here might give the impression of a spacious room. The court-room was actually very tiny and very crowded.

Most of the dialogue in these panels is based on the transcript of Riel's trial, published in book-form as THE QUEEN V LOUIS RIEL (which is listed under Morton, 1974, in the bibliography).

Below are the panel numbers, followed by the relevant page from THE QUEEN V LOUIS RIEL.

203:1, 203:2 -- p. 5
203:3, 203:4 -- p. 44
203:5 - 204:1 -- p. 78
204:2, 204:3 -- p. 83
204:4, 204:5 -- p. 87
204:6, 205:1 -- p. 97
205:2 - 205:5 -- p. 100
205:6 - 206:4 -- p. 108
206:5 - 207:2 -- p. 145
207:3 - 207:6 -- p. 151
208:1 -- p. 153
208:2 - 208:5 -- p. 171
208:6, 209:1 -- p. 194
209:2 -- p. 195
209:3 - 209:6 -- p. 203
210:1, 210:2 -- p. 204
210:3 - 211:4 -- p. 205
211:4, 211:5 -- p. 206
211:6 - 214:4 -- p. 207
214:5 -- p. 209
214:6 - 215:2 -- p. 210
215:3 -- p. 211
215:4 -- p. 214
216:1, 216:2 -- p. 215
216:3 - 218:2 -- p. 229
218:2, 218:3 -- p. 230
218:5 - 219:3 -- p. 244
219:4 - 220:1 -- p. 245
220:2 - 220:5 -- p. 246
220:6 -- p. 256
221:1, 221:2 -- p. 257
222:2 - 223:2 -- p. 262
223:3, 223:4 -- p. 274
223:5 - 224:6 -- p. 275
225:1, 225:2 -- p. 277

225:3 -- pp. 277, 278
225:4 - 226:1 -- p. 278
226:2 - 226:5 -- p. 280
226:6, 227:1 -- p. 281
227:2 - 228:4 -- p. 311
228:5 -- p. 323
228:6 -- pp. 323, 324
229:1 - 229:3 -- p. 324
229:4 - 229:6, 230:6, 231:1 -- p. 349
231:2, 231:5 -- p. 350
232:1 -- p. 371
232:2 -- pp. 371, 372
232:3, 232:4 -- p. 372

203:6

The Crown was represented by five prosecutors : Christopher Robinson, Britton Bath Osler, George Burbridge, David Lynch Scott, and Thomas Casgrain. To simplify things, I've eliminated Osler, Burbridge, Scott, and Casgrain from the story.

204:2

Riel was represented by four lawyers : François-Xavier Lemieux, Charles Fitzpatrick, James Green-shields, and T.C. Johnstone. Only Lemieux makes it into the strip, as if he was Riel's only lawyer.

209:1, 209:4 - 209:6

There is no evidence that such a book ever existed. In order to give Nolin the benefit of the doubt, I invented the scene in panels 129:3 to 130:5 to suggest that he might have gotten the buffalo-blood treaties and Riel's MASSINAHICAN mentally mixed-up in some manner. Still, Nolin was almost certainly lying when he claimed that Riel intended to "give the Province of Quebec to the Prussians [and] Ontario to the Irish" (Morton, 1974, p. 203). Even if Riel had wanted to do so (and there is no indication in his private writings that he did) he could not have gotten away with openly saying so -- the Métis were willing to fight for their homes along the Saskatchewan River, but they would have had no interest in militarily invading Ontario and Quebec.

221:4 - 222:1

Dr Clark testified at the trial, but he did not tell this story there -- it comes from one of his later lectures about Riel. (Flanagan, 1996, pp. 14-15.) Siggins believes that Clark's papers and lectures about Riel "were full of vicious lies". (Siggins, p. 427.) Flanagan admits that "most of Clark's material can be dismissed", but he makes an exception for the doctor's contention that Riel believed he was a Jew named David Morde-chai, because it "is supported by fragmentary evidence." (Flanagan, 1996, p. 16.)

230:1

It took the jury an hour and a half to come to a decision.

232:6

The three doctors "were appointed in secrecy [...]; each doctor was an employee or beneficiary of the federal government; and none was an expert in the field of inquiry." (Flanagan, 2000, p. 162.) Two of the doctors thought that Riel was sane, but the third one, Dr François-Xavier Valade, disagreed and said so in a telegram to Macdonald. When presenting the conclusions of the three doctors in the House of Commons, Macdonald rewrote Valade's telegram to make it look as if Valade had concurred with the other two.

233:2

Macdonald spoke these words to Roderique Masson, the Lieutenant-Governor of Quebec, who "discreetly approached Sir John and pleaded with him to change his mind." (Siggins, p. 442.)

233:3

Riel didn't sleep on the night before his execution. "With the assistance of André and Father McWilliams [...], Louis Riel spent the night in prayer and spiritual exercises." (Stanley, p. 369.) Father Charles McWilliams had been one of Riel's schoolmates in the Collège de Montréal. Flanagan writes that McWilliams didn't join Riel and André until the "early morning hours", by which he seems to mean sometime after 5:00 AM and sometime before Riel was led from his cell. (Flanagan, 1996, p. 194.) On the other hand, Howard thinks that McWilliams joined Riel only on the walk to the scaffold. (Howard, p. 467.)

233:4 - 234:2

> Riel signed a recantation of his heresies on 5 August. Several motives impelled him, including a desire to have the help of the sacraments while facing death, as well as the lingering hope that he might yet bring the Church to support his mission. The abjuration seems to have been only external. Riel subscribed to certain formalities, but in such a way as to leave intact his underlying belief in himself.
> [Flanagan, 1996, p.178.]

> On the morning of November 16th, Riel

> wrote his last retraction and gave it to McWilliams. It was a short declaration of loyalty to the Church. Riel repudiated anything "too presumptuous" in his writings, subordinating himself "to the infallible decisions of the supreme

> Pontiff. I die Catholic and in the only true faith." [Ibid. p. 194.]

233:5, 233:6

Riel described this vision to Dr Augustus Jukes on the evening of November 15th (Flanagan, 1996, p.191), not to Father André on the morning of the 16th. Dr Jukes was a surgeon for the Mounties and had testified at the trial (giving his opinion that Riel was sane). Jukes and Riel became friendly while Riel was imprisoned in Regina.

234:4

"[Riel] embraced me saying: 'How happy and content I am! I feel my heart will overflow with joy.'" (Father André quoted by Flanagan, 1996, p. 194.)

234:5, 234:6

Deputy-Sheriff Gibson arrived at Riel's cell-door at 8:15 A.M. Reluctant to fulfil his task, he stood at the door without knocking or speaking until Riel noticed him.

235:2

I'm pretty sure that I didn't make this up -- that Riel said or wrote something like this about his executioners (i.e. his executioners in general, not the Deputy-Sheriff specifically) but I can't find the reference right now. Anyway, he probably didn't say it to Gibson on the morning of November 16th.

235:4 - 236:5

> Slowly they climbed the staircase towards the exit leading to the scaffold. The two priests recited the office of the dying. At the top, Riel knelt again with McWilliams, while André bestowed upon him a final absolution [....] Riel rose. The hangman approached and bound his hands behind his back. André kissed Riel, and together they walked towards the scaffold.
> [Stanley, pp. 370, 371.]

It seems that Stanley thought that Riel's arms were tied before he stepped onto the scaffold. This is confirmed by Howard, who describes Riel's hands being "pinioned" before he "stooped and passed through the window onto a small ledge above the gallows platform." (Howard, p. 468.) From Siggins' book: "Louis mounted a ladder that led to a window, and climbed outside onto the scaffold without help". (Siggins, p. 445.) Howard writes that, on the scaffold, "The priests and Dr. Jukes shook hands with [Riel.]" (Howard, p. 468.) Flanagan states that Riel "helped put the rope around his own neck." (Flanagan, 1996, p. 194.)

Manoeuvring up a ladder and through a window with one's hands tied behind one's back ("without help"!) would be awkward but probably possible, but I have a hard time seeing how Riel could have shaken anyone's hand or adjusted the noose around his neck. Perhaps Stanley and Howard were wrong about when Riel's hands were tied, or perhaps Howard and Flanagan were wrong about the hand-shaking and noose-assistance.

On a related matter: Of the books before me, only Howard's mentions that Dr Jukes was present on the scaffold. Given his connection to the Mounties, it's possible that he could have been there but, according to Charlebois and Stanley, the doctor's last visit with Riel was on the evening of November 15th. (Charlebois, p. 233 & Stanley, p. 368.)

236:1, 236:2

> He asked God to bless his mother, his wife and children. "My Father bless me according to the views of Thy Providence which are beautiful and without measure." [Siggins, p. 445]

236:3 – 236:5

> The gallows had been erected in a fenced enclosure adjoining the guard-room in which Riel was confined [....] The platform [of the gallows], concealed by the fence, had been placed so that the only access to it was through an upstairs window [...]. At dawn [a crowd] began to assemble in the field before the barracks square. A strong cordon of Mounties had been drawn up around the enclosure and no one without a pass could approach. [Howard, pp. 466, 467.]

236:6 – 237:2

On the evening before the execution, Riel

> asked the sheriff if he would have the opportunity to speak from the scaffold.
> Father André forbade Riel to speak, arguing that he might say something that would disturb his union with God. His mission now was not to prove to the spectators that he was a prophet, but to demonstrate how a Christian should die. Riel submitted, impressed by André's additional argument that he should imitate the silence of Jesus [.] [Flanagan, 1996, p. 193.]

On the scaffold, after the noose had been placed around Riel's neck, Father André

> turned away to conceal his face; he was crying.
> Deputy Gibson spoke. "Louis Riel, have you anything to say before sentence of death is carried out?"
> Riel glanced toward Father André, whose back was now turned to him. "Shall I say something?" he pleaded.
> "No," the priest said. [Howard, p. 468.]

237:4

Riel "asked me not to forget Mr. and Mrs. Forget for their kindness to him". (Father André, quoted by Charlebois, p. 234.)

Amédée-Emmanuel Forget was a clerk of the North-West Council who agitated to have Riel's life spared. (Flanagan, 2000, p. 162, & Howard, p. 466.) Mrs Forget gave Riel a crucifix that he carried to the gallows. (Stanley, p. 370.)

237:6, 238:1

Two versions of the hangman's words:

> "Louis Riel," he said in a hoarse, angry whisper, "do you know me? You cannot escape from me today!" [Howard, p.468.]

> "Louis Riel," he whispered, "you had me once and I got away from you. I have you now and you'll not get away from me." Jack Henderson had been a prisoner in Fort Garry in 1870 and had sworn then to take revenge not only for his humiliation, but for the death of his friend Thomas Scott. [Siggins, p. 445.]

Strangely, Father André claimed that Henderson began weeping after Riel fell through the trap-door. (Charlebois, p. 234.)

238:2 – 238:5

> "Courage, bon courage, mon père," [Riel] called to Father André, who was dissolved in tears. After a few more prayers and farewells, the time had come. Riel and Father McWilliams said the "Our Father" together in English; and on the phrase "deliver us from evil," the trap was dropped. [Flanagan, 1996, pp. 194, 195.]

241:1

My count of 24 men comes from Beal & Macleod (pp. 309-313, 326, 327). (This wasn't the total number of men who were punished for participating in the North-West Rebellion. See the note for panels 169:5 to 170:2 regarding the punishment of the Indians who were associated with Poundmaker and Big Bear.)

241:5

George Stephen, Donald Smith, and James J. Hill

> comprised the triumvirate that formed and controlled the original syndicate of investors in the CPR. [...] At their peak these three associates individually and collectively wielded unmatched financial and political power in North America. A few short years after the last spike [November 7, 1885], they would be among the richest men not just in North America, but in the entire world. [Cruise & Griffiths, 1988, pp. 5,6.]

The above-mentioned Donald Smith is the same Donald Smith who appears in panels 34:3 to 35:3.

BIBLIOGRAPHY

Beal, Bob, and Rod Macleod. PRAIRIE FIRE: THE 1885 NORTH-WEST REBELLION. 1984. Toronto: McClelland & Stewart, 1994.

Bumsted, J.M. THE RED RIVER REBELLION. Watson & Dwyer, 1996.

Careless, J.M.S. CANADA: A STORY OF CHALLENGE. 3rd ed. 1970. Toronto: Stoddart, 1991.

Charlebois, Peter. THE LIFE OF LOUIS RIEL. Toronto: NC Press, 1978.

Creighton, Donald. JOHN A. MACDONALD: THE OLD CHIEFTAIN. 1955. Toronto: Macmillan, 1968.

Cruise, David, and Alison Griffiths. THE GREAT ADVENTURE: HOW THE MOUNTIES CONQUERED THE WEST. 1996. Toronto: Penguin, 1997.

----------. LORDS OF THE LINE: THE MEN WHO BUILT THE CPR. 1988. Toronto: Penguin, 1996.

Ferguson, Will. BASTARDS AND BONEHEADS. Vancouver: Douglas & McIntyre, 1999.

Flanagan, Thomas. LOUIS 'DAVID' RIEL: 'PROPHET OF THE NEW WORLD'. Rev. ed. Toronto: University of Toronto, 1996.

----------. RIEL AND THE REBELLION: 1885 RECONSIDERED. Rev. ed. Toronto: University of Toronto, 2000.

Gentilcore, R. Louis, ed. HISTORICAL ATLAS OF CANADA, VOLUME 2: THE LAND TRANSFORMED, 1800-1891. Toronto: University of Toronto, 1993.

Howard, Joseph Kinsey. STRANGE EMPIRE: THE STORY OF LOUIS RIEL. 1952. Toronto: Swan, 1965.

McLean, Don. 1885: MÉTIS REBELLION OR GOVERNMENT CONSPIRACY? 2nd printing. Winnipeg: Pemmican, 1985.

Morton, Desmond. THE LAST WAR DRUM: THE NORTH WEST CAMPAIGN OF 1885. Toronto:

Hakkert, 1972.

----------, intro. THE QUEEN V LOUIS RIEL. Toronto: University of Toronto, 1974.

Oppen, William A. THE RIEL REBELLIONS: A CARTOGRAPHIC HISTORY. 1979. Toronto: University of Toronto, 1980.

Purich, Donald. THE METIS. Toronto: Lorimer, 1988.

Racette, Calvin. FLAGS OF THE MÉTIS. Regina: Gabriel Dumont Inst. 1987

Riel, Louis. THE COLLECTED WRITINGS OF LOUIS RIEL / LES ECRITS COMPLETS DE LOUIS RIEL. 5 vols. Ed. George F. G. Stanley. Edmonton: University of Alberta Press, 1985. Vol. 2.

Ryerson, Stanley B. THE FOUNDING OF CANADA: BEGINNINGS TO 1815. Toronto: Progress, 1960.

----------. UNEQUAL UNION: CONFEDERATION AND THE ROOTS OF CONFLICT IN THE CANADAS, 1815-1873. Toronto: Progress, 1968

Senior, Hereward. "Orange Order." THE CANADIAN ENCYCLOPEDIA. 1999.

Siggins, Maggie. RIEL: A LIFE OF REVOLUTION. 1994. Toronto: HarperCollins, 1995.

Sprague, Douglas Neil. CANADA AND THE MÉTIS, 1869-1885. Waterloo: Wilfred Laurier UP, 1988.

Spry, Irene M. "The 'Memories' of George William Sanderson, 1846-1936". CANADIAN ETHNIC STUDIES, vol. 17, no. 2, 1985.

Stanley, George F.G. LOUIS RIEL. Toronto: Ryerson, 1963.

Stonechild, Blair, and Bill Waiser. LOYAL TILL DEATH: INDIANS AND THE NORTH-WEST REBELLION. Calgary: Fifth House, 1997.

Woodcock, George. GABRIEL DUMONT: THE MÉTIS CHIEF AND HIS LOST WORLD. 1975. Edmonton: Hurtig, 1976.

INDEX

André, Alexis, 121, 124, 125, 142, 143, **185, 186,** 207, **216, 217, 233-238,** 254, 255, 258, 262, 264, 265
Archibald, Adams G., 251
Assiyiwin, **155, 156,** 162, 259
Astley, John, **205, 206**
Bannatyne, A.G.B., **27-31, 96**
Barnabé, Evelina, 254
Barnabé, Fabien, 254
Begg, Alexander, 247
Bellehumeur, Marguerite, see Riel, Marguerite
Big Bear, 130, **131,** 168-170, 255, 260, 265
Black, John, 249
Black, John, 249
Boucher, Baptiste, **190, 191,** 262
Boulton, Charles, 246, 247
Bourget, Ignace, **99, 100,** 114, 144, 252, 253

Bowell, Mackenzie, 252

Boyer, William, 258
Bruce, John, 244
Burbridge, George, 263
Cartier, George-Étienne, 243, 249-252
Casgrain, Thomas, 263
Clark, Daniel, **220-222,** 263
Clarke, Lawrence, **140-142, 152, 153,** 257, 258
Cowan, William, 19, **20**
Crowfoot, 130
Crozier, Lief, **152-156, 161,** 259
Dennis, John Stoughton, **10-12,** 13, **21-23,** 24, **25, 26, 31,** 245, 246
Dewdney, Edgar, **138, 139,** 141, 142, 257, 258
Duck, George, 254, 255
Dumas, Michel, 255
Dumont, Edouard, 259, 261
Dumont, Gabriel, **78, 79,** 118, **121-130,** 141, **146, 148-152,** 153, **154, 159-**

168, 170-178, 181-184, 188-193, 195, 197-199, 207, 241, 249, 258-263
Dumont, Isidore, 155, 156, 159, 162, 259
Fitzpatrick, Charles, 263
Forget, Amédée-Emmanuel, 237, 265
Forget, Mrs, 237, 265
Fourmond, Vital, 258
Garnot, Philippe, 258
Gibson, Deputy-Sheriff, 234, 264, 265
Goulet, Elzéar, 250
Grant, Ulysses S., 105, 106, 252
Granville, Lord, 73, 74, 248
Graton, Marcile, 263
Greenshields, James, 263
Guernon, Marie-Julie, 245
Guillemette, François, 250
Henderson, Jack, 237, 238, 265
Hill, James J., 265
Howard, Henry, 107, 108, 110-112, 253
Howe, Joseph, 250
Irvine, Acheson, 152, 261
Isbister, James, 127-130
Jackson, Thomas, 208
Jackson, William, 256
Johnstone, T.C., 263
Jukes, Augustus, 264, 265
Kavanaugh, François-Xavier, 250
Laflamme, Rodolphe, 245
Lemieux, François-Xavier, 204-207, 209-212, 214, 216-221, 225, 227, 263
Lépine, Ambroise, 251, 252, 258
Lorne, Marquis of, (John Douglas Campbell) 125
Macdonald, John Alexander, 7, 8, 73, 74, 76, 77, 90, 91, 131, 132-134, 135, 136-138, 139, 140, 141, 162, 167, 168, 232, 233, 241, 243, 245, 248-252, 256, 257, 259, 264
McDougall, William, 8, 12-15, 16, 21, 22, 24, 31, 243-245
Macdowall, David, 137
McKay, Joseph, 155, 156, 161, 259
McKay, Thomas, 204, 205
Mackenzie, Alexander, 102, 104, 105, 256
McLeod, Murdoch, 248
Mactavish, William, 19, 32, 33
McWilliams, Charles, 264, 265
Mair, Charles, 246
Mallet, Edmond, 252
Marion, Edouard, 10, 11, 244
Marion, Louis, 257, 258
Masson, Roderique, 264
Middleton, Frederick, 169, 170, 171, 174, 180-182, 185-187, 194, 206, 226, 227, 260-262
Mitchell, Hillyard, 148
Morton, Oliver P., 252
Moulin, Julien, 258
Nault, André, 9, 10, 244, 250
Ness, George, 206, 207
Nolin, Charles, 34-37, 127-130, 146-

148, 153, 154, 158, 159, 208-210, 246, 255, 257-259, 263
Nolin, Duncan, 38, 39
Nolin, Rosalie, 258
O'Donnel, John, 94, 95
O'Donoghue, William, 248, 250-252
O'Lone, H.F., 250
Osler, Britton Bath, 263
Otter, William, 169, 170, 260
Ouellette, Joseph, 195, 198, 262
Ouellette, Moise, 127-130
Parisien, Norbert, 46, 47, 49-54, 246-248
Poundmaker, 131, 168-170, 255, 260, 265
Provencher, Joseph, 14-16, 244
Richardson, Hugh, 210-213, 215-218, 227, 229, 231, 232
Riel, Jean, 241, 254
Riel, Julie, 90
Riel, Marguerite, 128, 129, 132, 241, 254
Riel, Marie-Angélique, 241, 254
Ritchot, Noel-Joseph, 15, 74-78, 80, 81, 90, 91, 244, 249-251
Robinson, Christopher, 203, 205, 207, 208, 211, 212, 217, 218, 222-226, 265
Roy, François, 218-220
Russel, A.J., 244
Sanderson, William, 247
Schmidt, Louis, 257
Schultz, Anne, 39, 246
Schultz, John Christian, 16, 17, 23-26, 27, 28, 31, 39-43, 46, 47, 48, 52, 53-55, 57, 58, 61, 62, 76, 89, 92, 93-95, 102, 103, 104, 245-247, 250-252
Scott, Alfred, 249
Scott, David Lynch, 263
Scott, Hugh, 249
Scott, Thomas, 54, 55, 59, 61-67, 69-73, 74, 76, 80, 111, 246-251
Sitting Bull, 130
Smith, Donald, 34, 35, 37, 245-248, 251, 265
Spence, Thomas, 250
Steele, Sam, 260
Stephen, George, 132, 133, 135, 136, 137, 241, 265
Stewart, James, 83, 84, 250
Strange, Thomas Bland, 169, 170, 260
Sutherland, Hugh, 48, 51-54, 57, 246, 247
Sutherland, John, 46-48, 246
Sutherland, Mrs, 47, 48, 57, 247
Taché, Alexandre-Antonin, 249-252, 257
Tanner, James, 250
Taylor, James, 248
Tuke, Harold, 253
Valade, François-Xavier, 264
Vegreville, Valentin, 257
Wallace, James, 222, 223
Walters, Henry, 145, 146, 208
Wandering Spirit, 260
Williams, Arthur, 262
Willoughby, John, 203, 204
Wolseley, Garnet, 79, 249
Yellow Blanket, 261
Young, Captain George, 223-226
Young, Reverend George, 69-72, 248

Chester William David Brown was born in 1960 and grew up in Chateauguay, Quebec. He currently lives in Toronto.

TENTH
ANNIVERSARY
SECTION

I drew this portrait in 2003. I liked it and, at the time, suggested to my publisher, Chris, that we use it on the cover of the book. But Chris preferred the drawing of Riel kneeling on a mountaintop (which in this edition is on the inside covers). So the portrait only saw print (miscoloured) <u>on</u> the cover of an "alternative" weekly newspaper. After I sent Chris the extra material for this tenth anniversary edition, he called me up and said, "I really like this portrait of Riel. Why don't we use it on the cover ?"

I based the drawing on a photograph of the man, but I made so many changes that it only vaguely resembles Riel. The nose in particular is all wrong.

279, 280

In early 1998, I began working on the script for LOUIS RIEL. Here are two pages from that script. Compare them to pages 91 to 93.

I didn't yet know how I would depict Riel, and you can see one of my early attempts to draw him on page 279.

281

I was picturing LOUIS RIEL as a book and didn't want to serialize it, but Chris thought that serializing the story in comic-book pamphlets would be a good idea. He wanted the series for "market presence" in the comic-book shops and he pointed out that the pamphlets would give me some sort of income while I created the work. I acceded to Chris's wish.

Chris asked me to draw the cover for the 1999 Drawn & Quarterly catalogue to promote the upcoming first issue of the series. The design (including the image of Montreal at the top of the page) is based on the cover of the April 23, 1870, edition of CANADIAN ILLUSTRATED NEWS. I found reproductions of that newspaper cover on page 209 of Rasky's book and page 144 of Tanner's. (See the bibliography for this notes-section on page 278.) The colours are based on the version in the Rasky book.

282, 283

I wrote the whole script, up to Riel's death, before I began really drawing the project. (I'm not counting the drawings done in the script as "really drawing".) So, when I finished the script near the end of 1998, it was time to start figuring out how Riel would look.

284

I also had to come up with a way to draw Sir John A. Macdonald.

285 - 288

Then, in late 1998, I started "really drawing". These are some of the pages as they were printed in the first issue of LOUIS RIEL. Compare these to pages 7, 11, 19, and 20 in this book. As the series progressed, the way I drew Riel and Macdonald changed. When we reprinted the material in 2003 as a book, I decided to redraw Riel and Macdonald in the early scenes so that they would match how they were drawn later. Almost every depiction of Riel up to page 79 was altered. I redrew other things too. For instance, I got better at drawing guns; look at the rifles in panel 20:6 and in the corresponding panel on page 288.

289

This was the cover of issue number one of the pamphlets. Notice it says it's "the first of approximately ten comic-books". My script indicated that the completed work would be about 200 pages long, but I also knew that, as I drew, scenes would be lengthened, or shortened, or eliminated, or added and that, in 1999, it was impossible to predict the precise final page count. As it turned out, the serialized version ended up being 222 pages, which filled ten issues almost exactly. (Each pamphlet was 24 pages.)

The indicia date for the issue was June 1999.

On page 86 of my 2011 autobiographical book, PAYING FOR IT, I show myself giving a copy of this pamphlet to the prostitute "Anne".

I wasn't happy with how the cover came out and still think it was one of the worst of the LOUIS RIEL covers.

290, 291

I drew this strip for the DRAWN & QUARTERLY 2000 CALENDAR, which was printed in late 1999.

292

The indicia date for the second pamphlet was September 1999.

293

I preferred creating the covers for the pamphlets after the interior artwork was finished. However, the issues had to be solicited months in advance of the publication date, so I began to draw "mock" covers for the distributors' catalogues. While this image is obviously supposed to relate to Thomas Scott's use of an axe in the killing of Norbert Parisien, I decided to stray from an accurate depiction of the event, making it a one-on-one fight in an interior setting. I reasoned that no one was paying attention to the images in the distributors' catalogue.

294

This was the actual cover for the third pamphlet. Its indicia date was December 1999.

295

Compare this with page 79. This was the last scene that I redrew Riel in. I also redrew Dumont.

296

This was the cover for the fourth pamphlet, which had an indicia date of May 2000.

297

Here's another mock cover.

298

And this was the real cover. The indicia date was September 2000.

299, 300

On these pages are examples of my pencils. At the top of page 299 is the pencil drawing that was done for panel 107:4. Usually I pencil various elements for the final drawing on separate sheets of tracing paper. On the bottom of page 299 and on page 300 are the elements for panel 109:6.

301

I must have drawn this for a sequence that got cut. I realized it was unnecessary after I'd done these pencil drawings.

302

Of all the pamphlet covers, the one I did for the sixth issue is the one I dislike most. I had intended to add decorative vegetation but, due to deadline concerns, I had to turn over the cover like this -- plain, unfinished.

The indicia date was May 2001.

303

And the indicia date for this issue was May 2002, a year later. In June 2001, I moved. (See Chapter 23 of my book PAYING FOR IT for details.) That disrupted my schedule a bit. I also spent a few months that year preparing a new edition of I NEVER LIKED YOU.

This image was based on a drawing of the Duck Lake battle (pp. 156-161) that appeared on the front cover of the first issue of a periodical called THE ILLUSTRATED WAR NEWS, which was published in Toronto and had a cover date of April 4, 1885. Perhaps the details of the battle hadn't reached Toronto by April 4th. Or perhaps it was thought that a depiction of the combatants recklessly charging at each other on horseback and fighting at close range might sell better than an image of the Mounties and the Métis cautiously firing from a distance and from behind the relative safety of sleighs and trees. Reproductions of the original drawing can be found in the books by Rasky (p. 220) and Davies. (P. 59.)

304 - 306

Here are the pencil drawings I did for panel 189:3. I put the numbers there to remind myself of the inking order.

307 - 309

This was the series' only wraparound cover. It's based on a Battle Of Batoche print that was marketed in 1885 by the Grip Printing And Publishing Company, which in turn was based on "sketches by the Special Artist of the 'Canadian Pictorial and Illustrated War News,' Sergt. Grundy and others." The image size of the print is 17 inches by 24. At first I wanted to redraw the whole thing, but I quickly realized that would be too daunting a task, so instead I focused on a 10 by 13 detail. I made a few alterations, but I didn't change the sizes of the soldiers, whether those sizes make sense or not.

I managed to find and purchase a copy of the original print, but if you can track down a copy of Tanner's book, there's a large full-colour reproduction on pages 212 and 213.

310

Originally a mock cover for the ninth issue, this artwork was reused as the cover of a Drawn & Quarterly sampler (a giveaway that includes sample pages from upcoming publications).

311

My two favourite covers for the series are this one and the third one. The drawing is a cartoon version of Riel's six-man jury. The photo can be found in Siggins' book and on page 227 of Charlebois' book.

The indicia date for the pamphlet was February 2003.

312

This was another mock cover, but I liked the drawing enough to use it as the real cover.

The indicia date for the final issue was April 2003.

313 - 320

Chris asked if I would do the cover for Drawn & Quarterly's autumn 2003 catalogue. I decided I wanted to create an homage to Harold Gray's Little Orphan Annie. I redrew a sequence from the Sunday, October 5, 1941, installment of the strip, replacing Annie and Daddy Warbucks with Riel and Gabriel Dumont. Let me emphasize that these fifteen panels are fictional. On pages 314 to 320 are the panels reproduced at a larger size.

321

Here's a panel from the October 5, 1941, Little Orphan Annie strip.

322

To promote the publication of the book in the fall of 2003, I drew this poster, which was 17 inches by 22.

323, 324

On page 324 is what the cover looked like on the hardcover edition. I probably drew it in the late spring of 2003.

BIBLIOGRAPHY

Charlebois -- see page 267.

Davies, Colin. LOUIS RIEL AND THE NEW NATION. Agincourt: Book Society Of Canada, 1980.

Rasky, Frank. THE TAMING OF THE CANADIAN WEST. Toronto: McClelland & Stewart, 1967.

Siggins -- see page 267.

Tanner, Ogden. THE CANADIANS. Alexandria, Virginia: Time-Life, 1977.

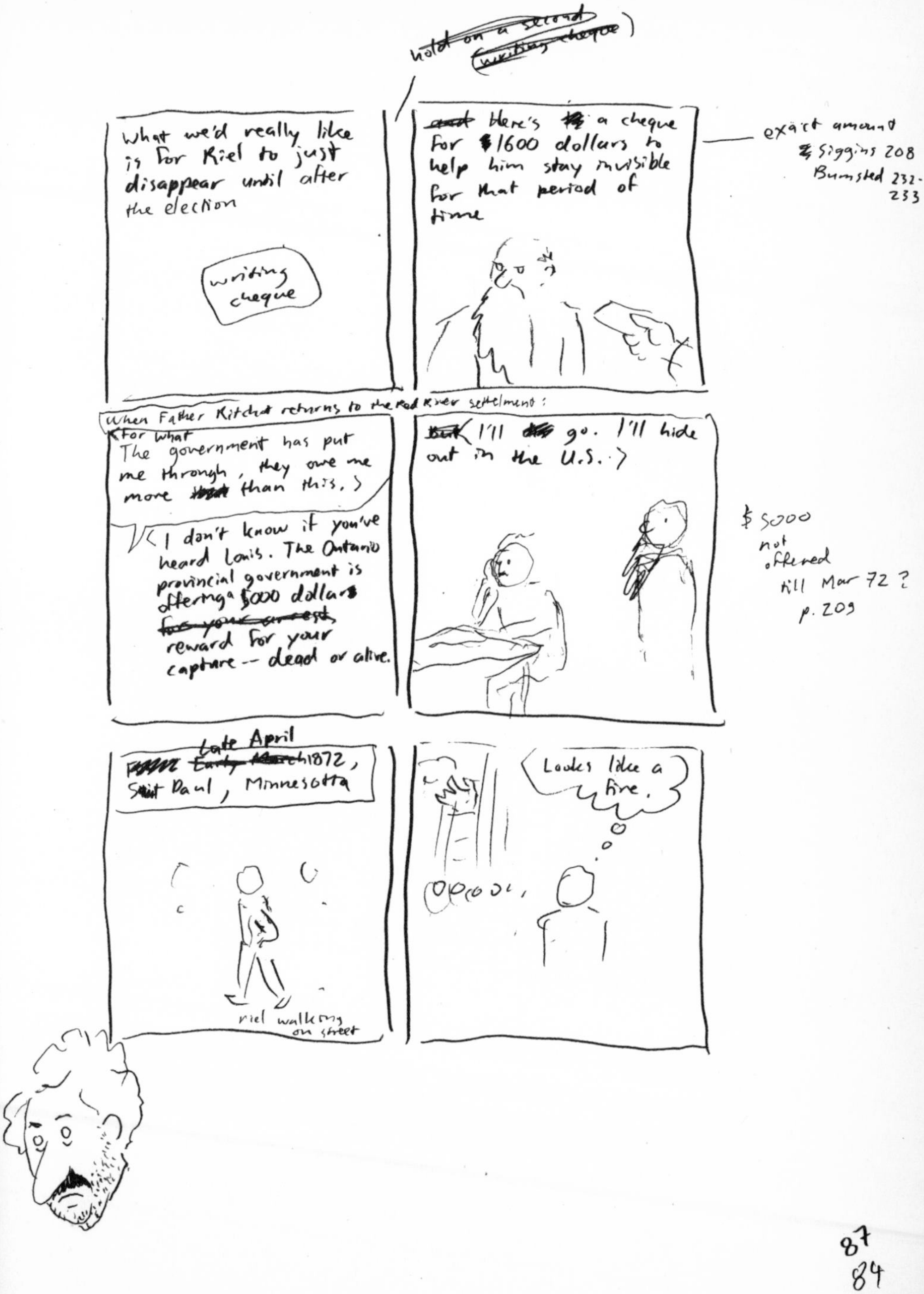

hold on a second (writing cheque)
What we'd really like is for Riel to just disappear until after the election
writing cheque
Here's a cheque for $1600 dollars to help him stay invisible for that period of time
exact amount
Siggins 208
Bumsted 232-233
When Father Ritchot returns to the Red River settlement:
For what the government has put me through, they owe me more than this.
I don't know if you've heard Louis. The Ontario provincial government is offering a $5000 dollar reward for your capture -- dead or alive.
I'll go. I'll hide out in the U.S.
$5000 not offered till Mar 72? p. 209
Late April 1872, Saint Paul, Minnesota
riel walking on street
Looks like a fire.
87
84
78

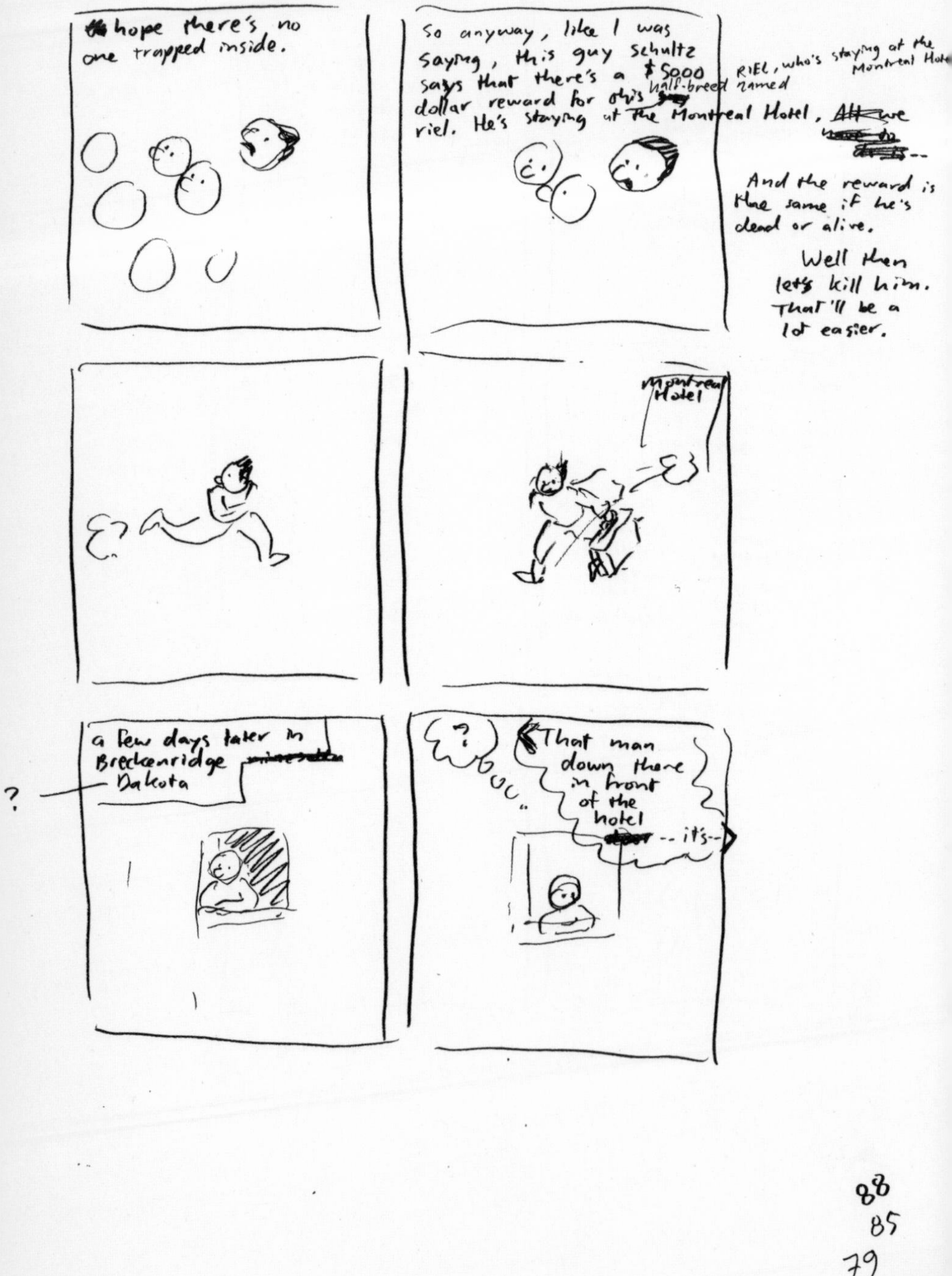
hope there's no one trapped inside.
So anyway, like I was saying, this guy Schultz says that there's a $5000 dollar reward for this half-breed named riel. He's staying at the Montreal Hotel, we --
RIEL, who's staying at the Montreal Hotel
And the reward is the same if he's dead or alive.
Well then let's kill him. That'll be a lot easier.
Montreal Hotel
a few days later in Breckenridge Dakota
?
?
That man down there in front of the hotel -- it's--
88
85
79

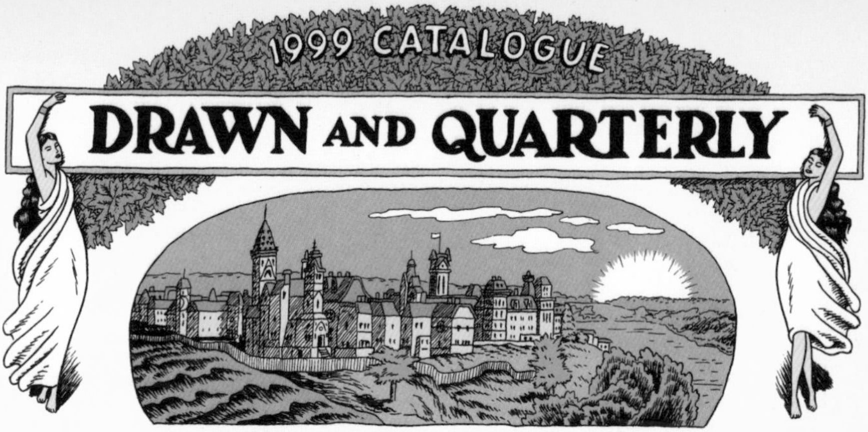
1999 CATALOGUE
DRAWN AND QUARTERLY

MONTREAL -- THE HOME OF DRAWN AND QUARTERLY

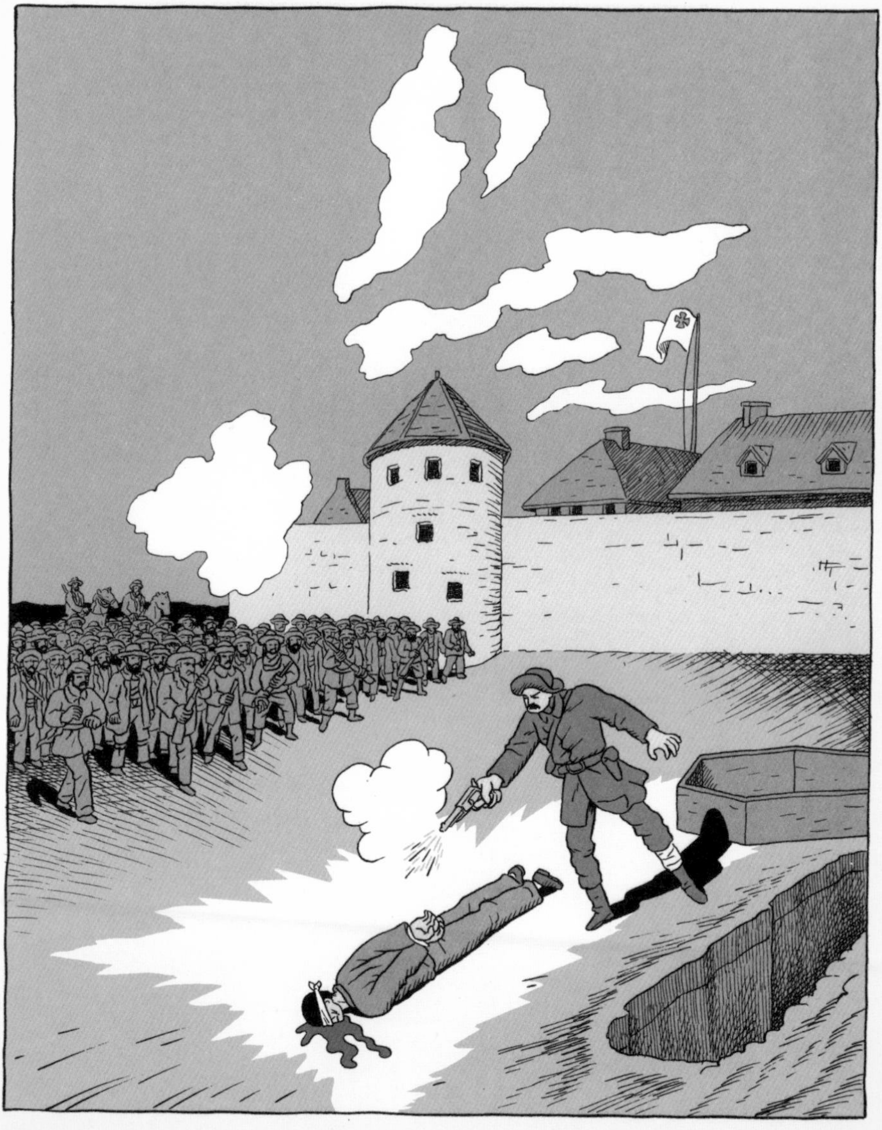

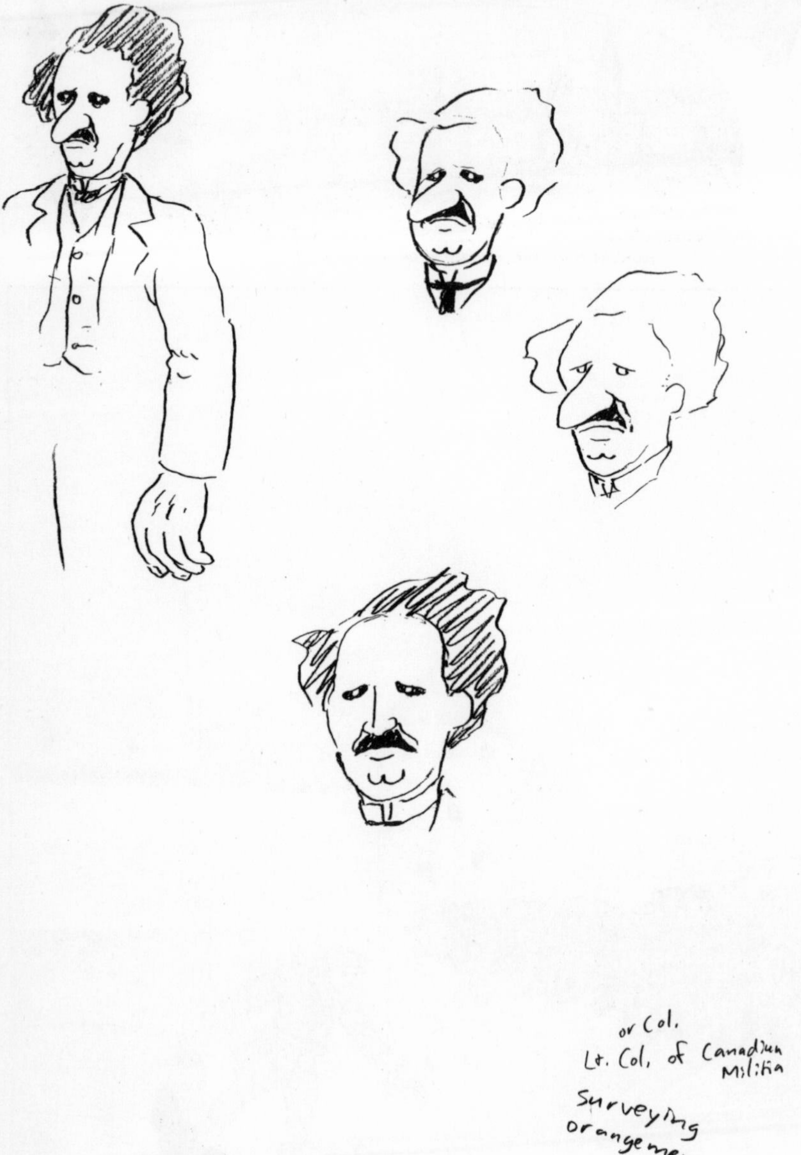
or Col.
Lt. Col. of Canadian Militia
Surveying orangemen

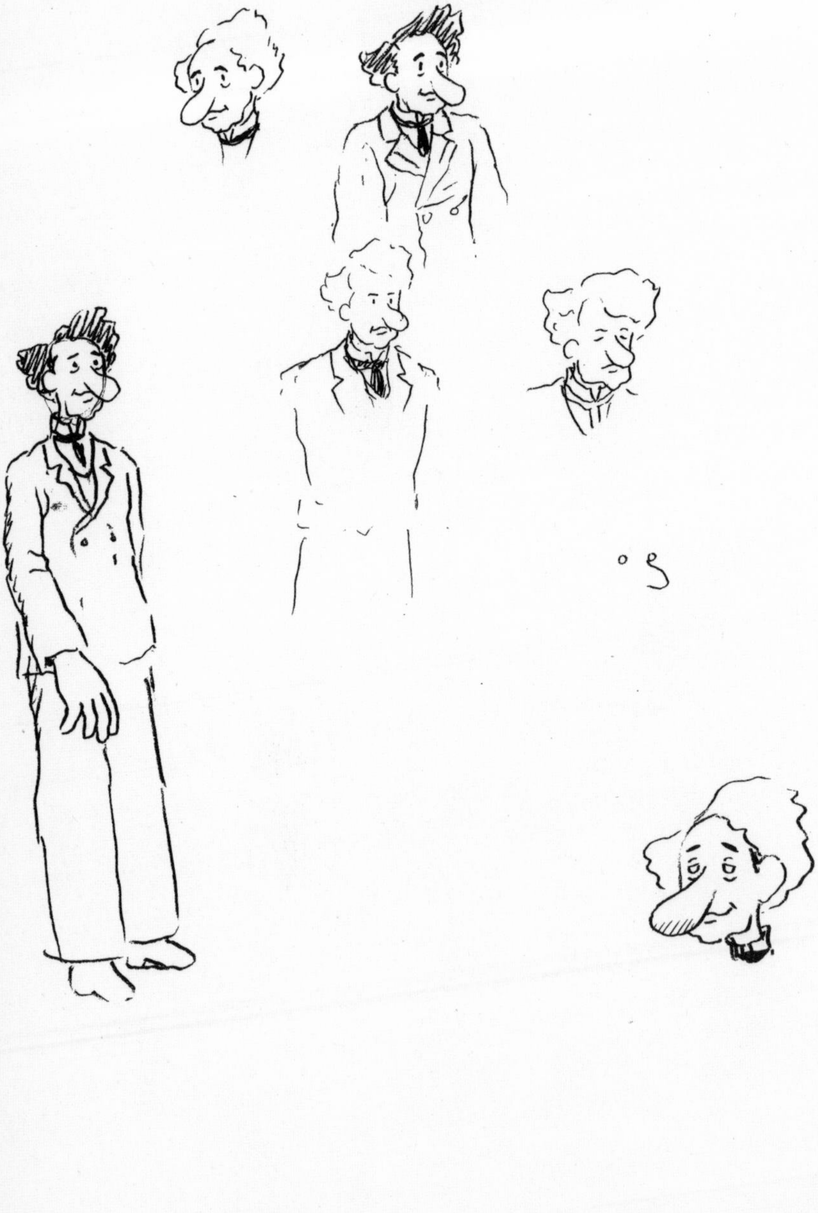

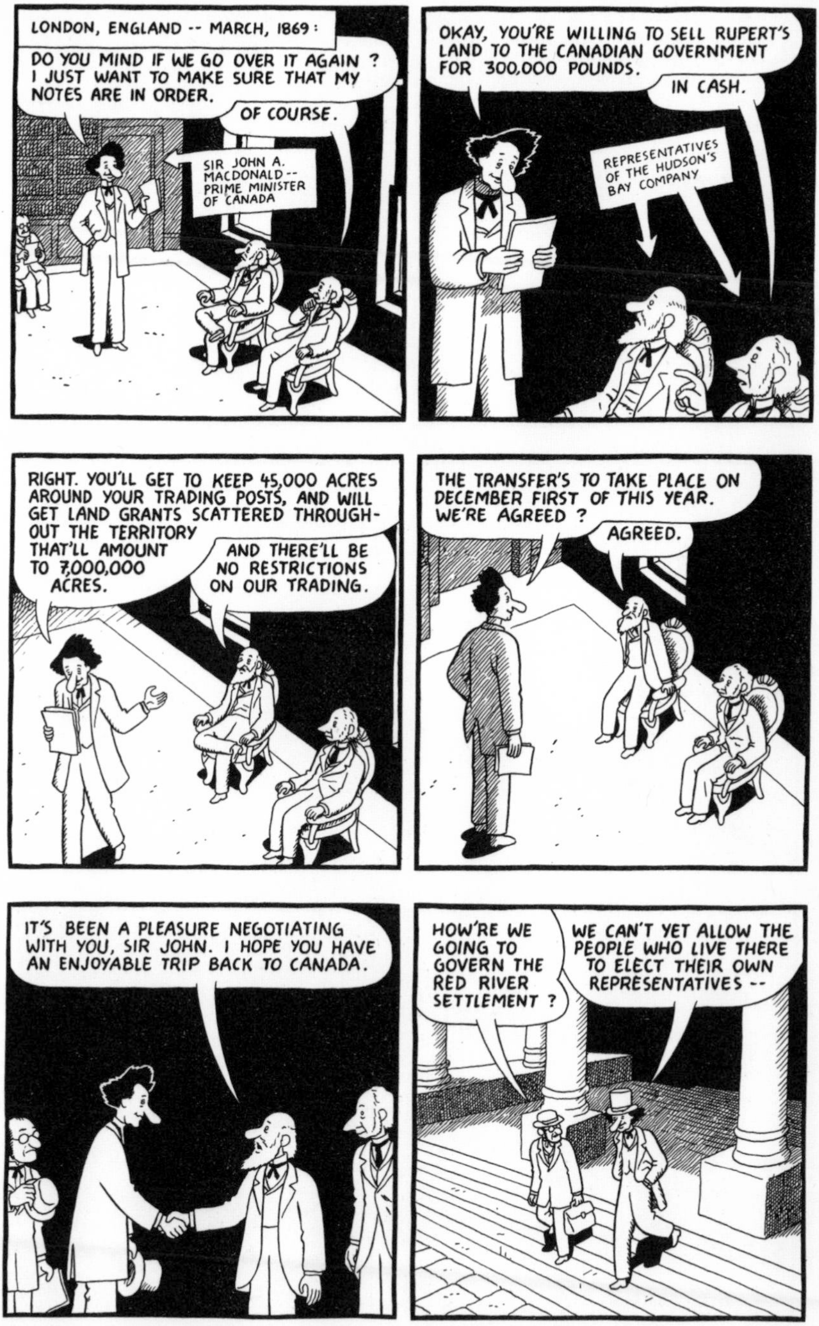
LONDON, ENGLAND -- MARCH, 1869:
DO YOU MIND IF WE GO OVER IT AGAIN ? I JUST WANT TO MAKE SURE THAT MY NOTES ARE IN ORDER.
OF COURSE.
SIR JOHN A. MACDONALD -- PRIME MINISTER OF CANADA
OKAY, YOU'RE WILLING TO SELL RUPERT'S LAND TO THE CANADIAN GOVERNMENT FOR 300,000 POUNDS.
IN CASH.
REPRESENTATIVES OF THE HUDSON'S BAY COMPANY
RIGHT. YOU'LL GET TO KEEP 45,000 ACRES AROUND YOUR TRADING POSTS, AND WILL GET LAND GRANTS SCATTERED THROUGH-OUT THE TERRITORY THAT'LL AMOUNT TO 7,000,000 ACRES.
AND THERE'LL BE NO RESTRICTIONS ON OUR TRADING.
THE TRANSFER'S TO TAKE PLACE ON DECEMBER FIRST OF THIS YEAR. WE'RE AGREED ?
AGREED.
IT'S BEEN A PLEASURE NEGOTIATING WITH YOU, SIR JOHN. I HOPE YOU HAVE AN ENJOYABLE TRIP BACK TO CANADA.
HOW'RE WE GOING TO GOVERN THE RED RIVER SETTLEMENT ?
WE CAN'T YET ALLOW THE PEOPLE WHO LIVE THERE TO ELECT THEIR OWN REPRESENTATIVES --
2

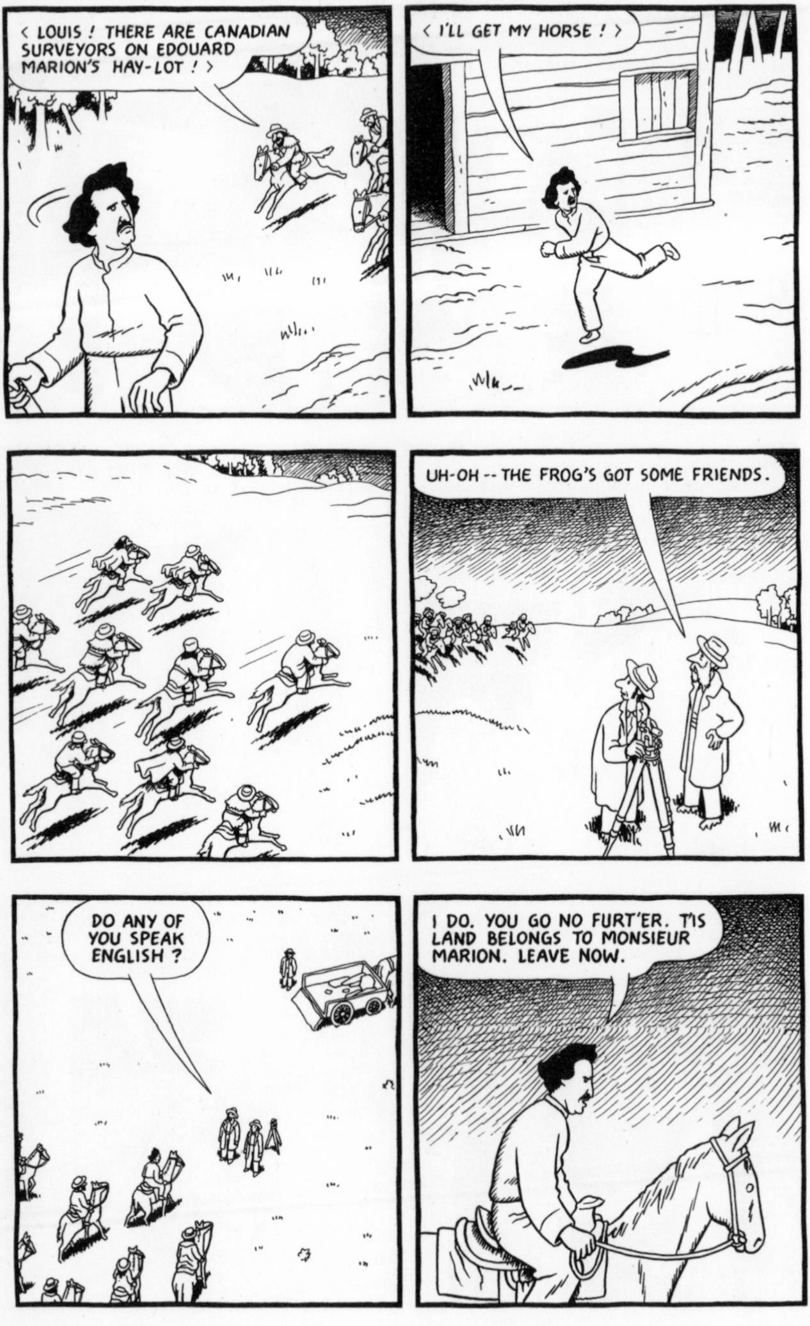
< LOUIS ! THERE ARE CANADIAN SURVEYORS ON EDOUARD MARION'S HAY-LOT ! >
< I'LL GET MY HORSE ! >
UH-OH -- THE FROG'S GOT SOME FRIENDS.
DO ANY OF YOU SPEAK ENGLISH ?
I DO. YOU GO NO FURT'ER. T'IS LAND BELONGS TO MONSIEUR MARION. LEAVE NOW.

6

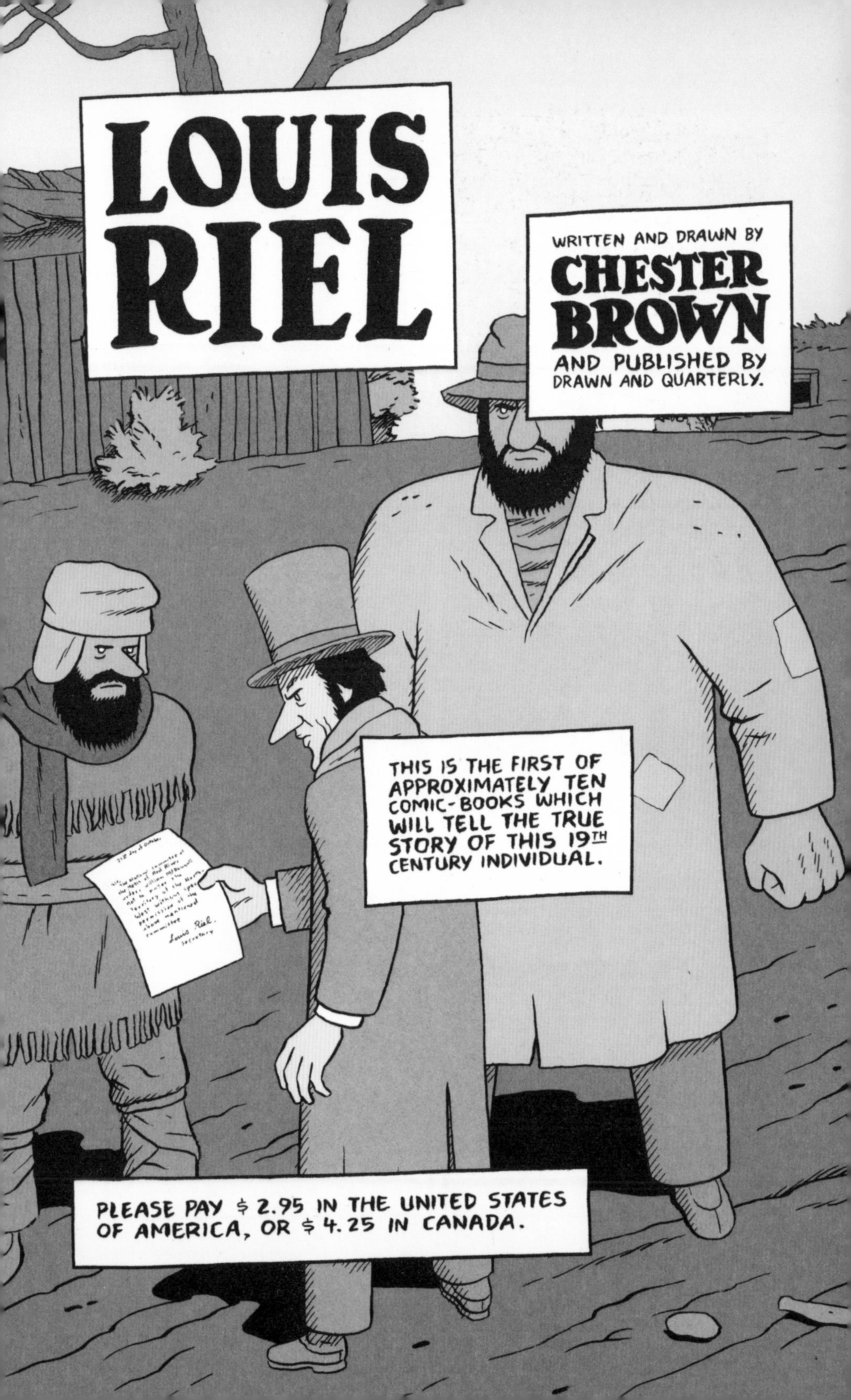
LOUIS RIEL
WRITTEN AND DRAWN BY
CHESTER BROWN
AND PUBLISHED BY DRAWN AND QUARTERLY.
21st day of October.
Sir, The National Committee of the Metis of Red River orders William McDougall not to enter the Territory of the North-West without spec permission of the above mentioned committee
Louis Riel.
Secretary
THIS IS THE FIRST OF APPROXIMATELY TEN COMIC-BOOKS WHICH WILL TELL THE TRUE STORY OF THIS 19TH CENTURY INDIVIDUAL.
PLEASE PAY $ 2.95 IN THE UNITED STATES OF AMERICA, OR $ 4.25 IN CANADA.

WHY LOUIS RIEL'S PARENTS GOT MARRIED

21 YEAR-OLD JULIE LAGIMODIÈRE IS IN CHURCH PRAYING :

THE MILLER WHO LIVES NEXT TO US HAS PROPOSED TO ME.

MY PARENTS WANT ME TO MARRY HIM, AND JEAN-LOUIS *WOULD* MAKE A GOOD HUSBAND -- HE'S EDUCATED AND DEVOUT -- BUT I DON'T WANT TO MARRY.

I WANT ONLY YOUR LOVE, JESUS -- I WANT TO BE IN YOUR ARMS FOREVER. PLEASE HELP ME -- HOW CAN I GET MY PARENTS TO UNDERSTAND ?

AFTER PRAYING, SHE LEAVES THE CHURCH.

FLAMES SUDDENLY SURROUND HER.

AAAA!

SHE LOOKS UP AND SEES AN OLD MAN IN THE CLOUDS.

DISOBEDIENT CHILD! YOU WILL COMPLY WITH YOUR PARENTS' WISHES!

JULIE DOES -- ON JANUARY 21, 1844, SHE MARRIES 26 YEAR-OLD JEAN-LOUIS RIEL. THEIR FIRST CHILD, LOUIS, IS BORN ON OCTOBER 22ND OF THAT YEAR.

Source: Maggie Siggins' RIEL--A LIFE OF REVOLUTION, pp. 29-31.

LOUIS RIEL

PUBLISHED BY DRAWN AND QUARTERLY

WRITTEN AND DRAWN BY
CHESTER BROWN

$ 2.95 IN THE UNITED STATES OF AMERICA -- $ 4.25 IN CANADA

THE SECOND ISSUE

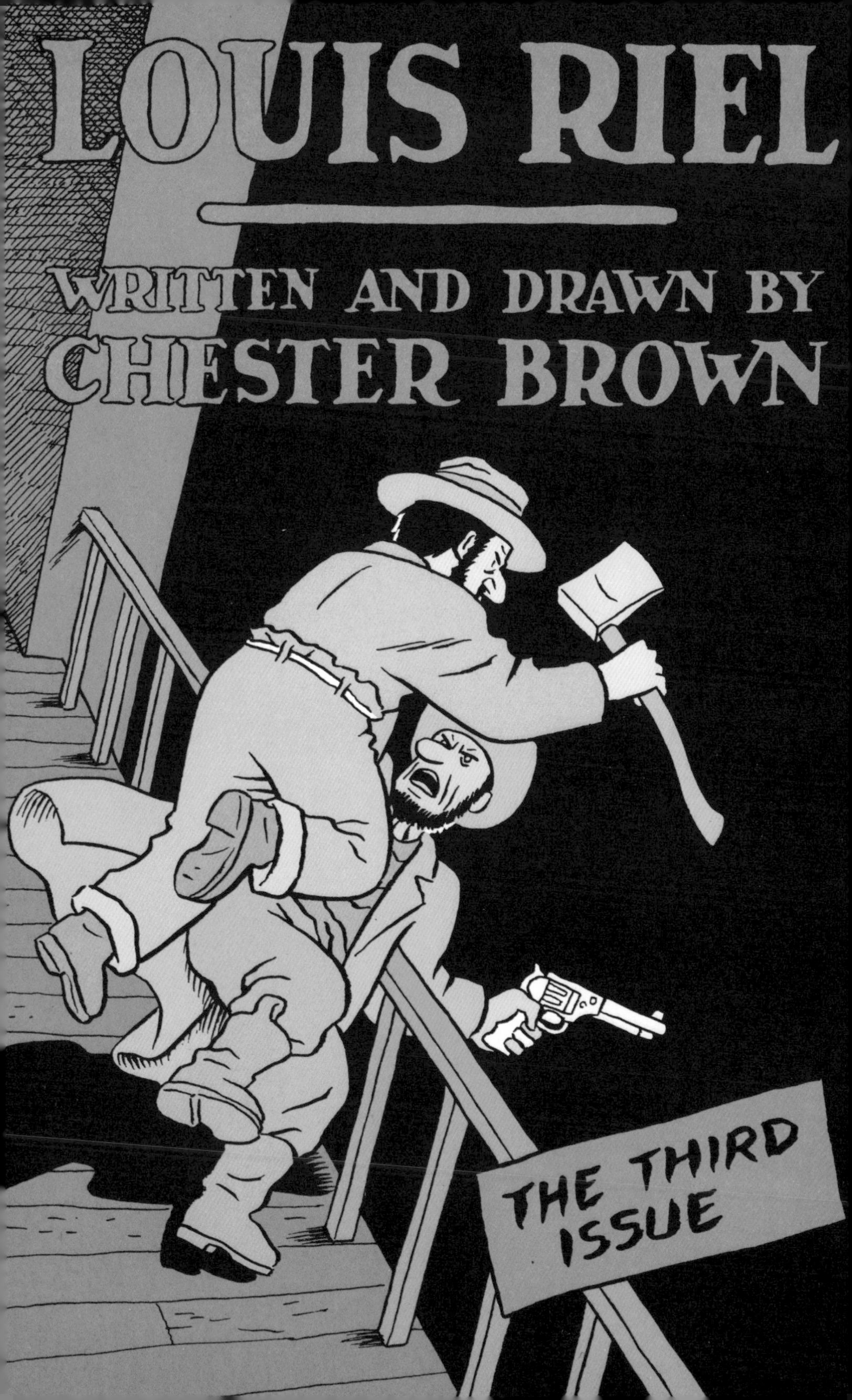
LOUIS RIEL
WRITTEN AND DRAWN BY
CHESTER BROWN
THE THIRD ISSUE

LOUIS RIEL

THE THIRD ISSUE

WRITTEN AND DRAWN BY
CHESTER BROWN

PUBLISHED BY
DRAWN AND QUARTERLY

$2.95 IN THE U.S.A.
$4.25 IN CANADA

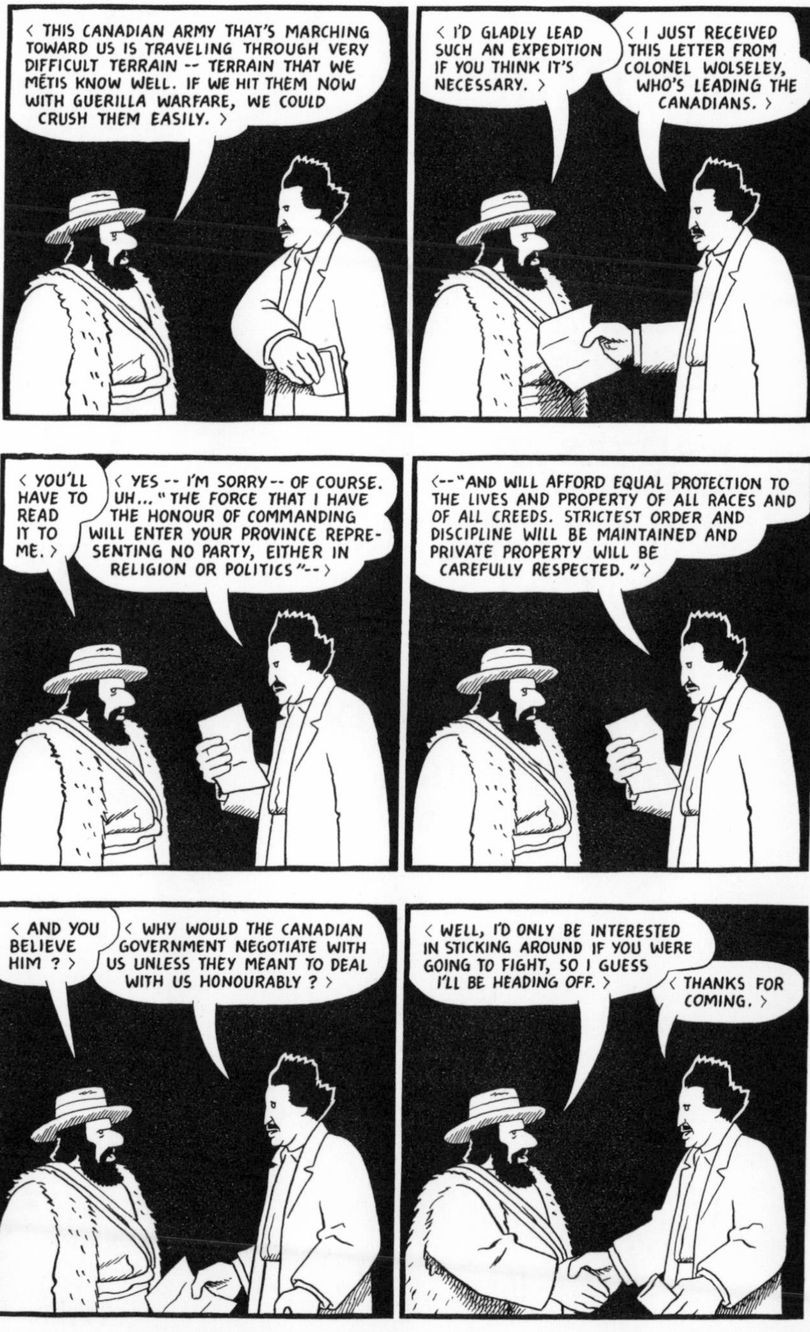

< THIS CANADIAN ARMY THAT'S MARCHING TOWARD US IS TRAVELING THROUGH VERY DIFFICULT TERRAIN -- TERRAIN THAT WE MÉTIS KNOW WELL. IF WE HIT THEM NOW WITH GUERILLA WARFARE, WE COULD CRUSH THEM EASILY. >
< I'D GLADLY LEAD SUCH AN EXPEDITION IF YOU THINK IT'S NECESSARY. >
< I JUST RECEIVED THIS LETTER FROM COLONEL WOLSELEY, WHO'S LEADING THE CANADIANS. >
< YOU'LL HAVE TO READ IT TO ME. >
< YES -- I'M SORRY -- OF COURSE. UH... "THE FORCE THAT I HAVE THE HONOUR OF COMMANDING WILL ENTER YOUR PROVINCE REPRESENTING NO PARTY, EITHER IN RELIGION OR POLITICS"-- >
<--"AND WILL AFFORD EQUAL PROTECTION TO THE LIVES AND PROPERTY OF ALL RACES AND OF ALL CREEDS. STRICTEST ORDER AND DISCIPLINE WILL BE MAINTAINED AND PRIVATE PROPERTY WILL BE CAREFULLY RESPECTED." >
< AND YOU BELIEVE HIM ? >
< WHY WOULD THE CANADIAN GOVERNMENT NEGOTIATE WITH US UNLESS THEY MEANT TO DEAL WITH US HONOURABLY ? >
< WELL, I'D ONLY BE INTERESTED IN STICKING AROUND IF YOU WERE GOING TO FIGHT, SO I GUESS I'LL BE HEADING OFF. >
< THANKS FOR COMING. >

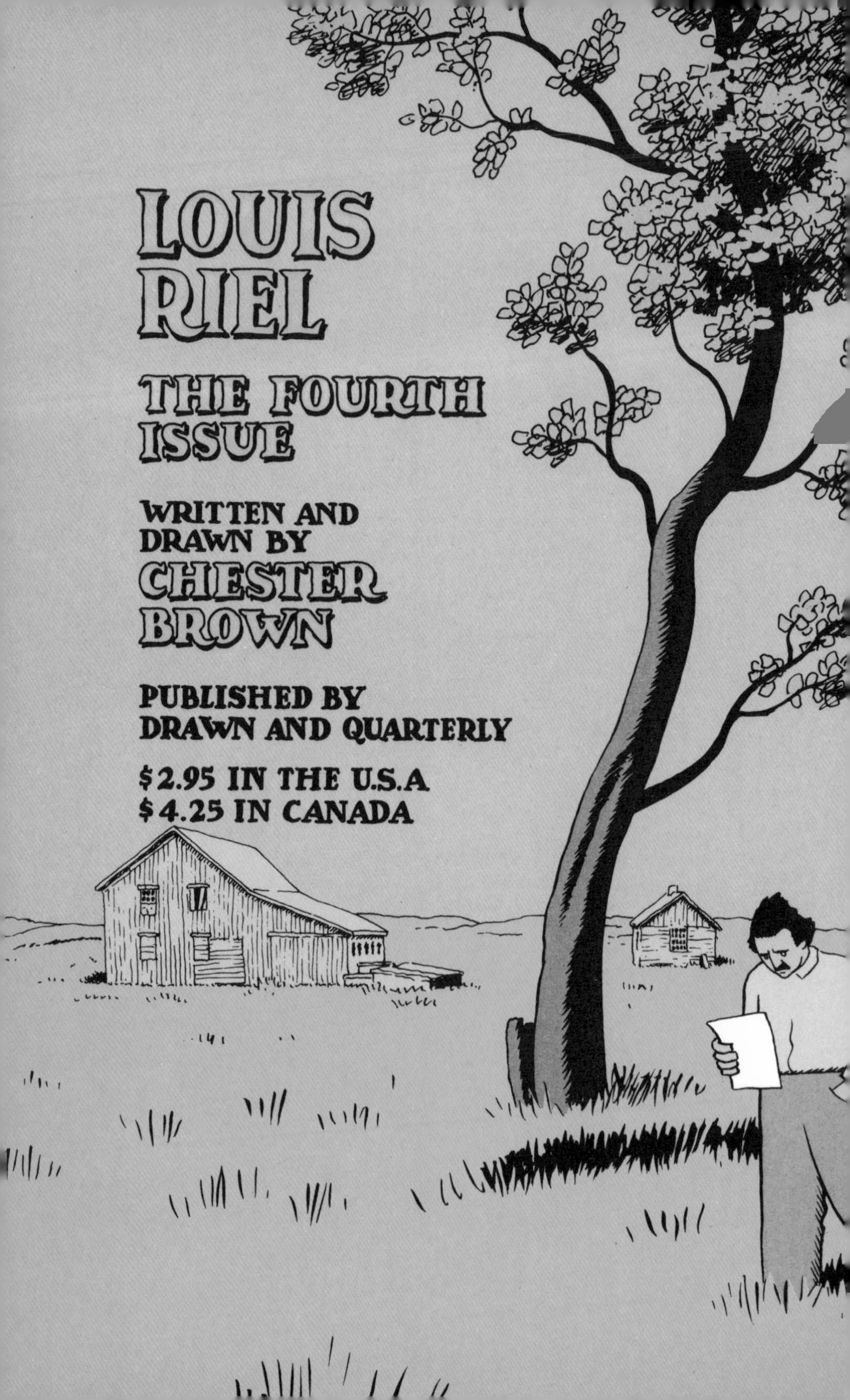
LOUIS RIEL
THE FOURTH ISSUE
WRITTEN AND DRAWN BY
CHESTER BROWN
PUBLISHED BY DRAWN AND QUARTERLY
$2.95 IN THE U.S.A
$4.25 IN CANADA

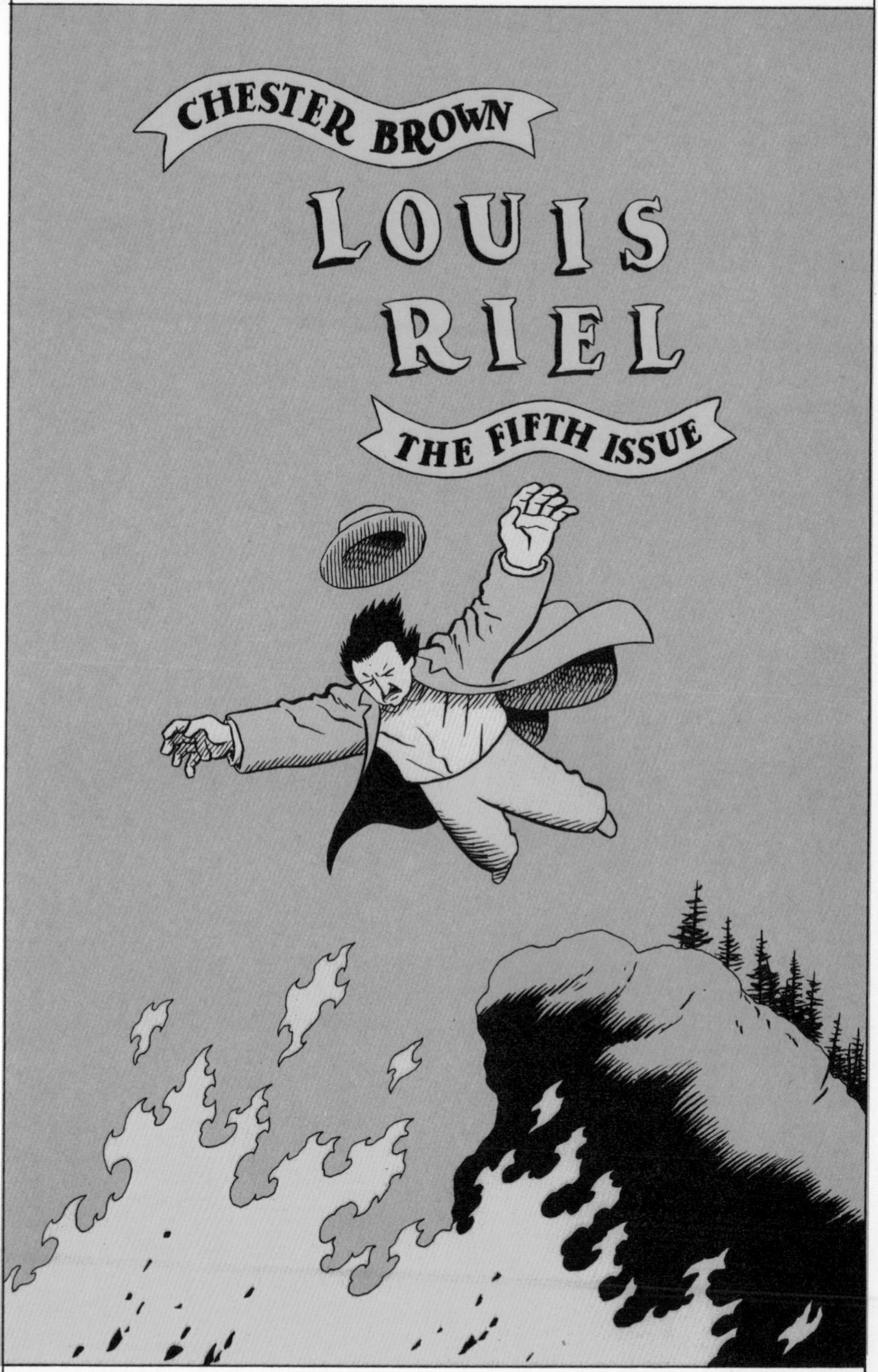
CHESTER BROWN
LOUIS RIEL
THE FIFTH ISSUE

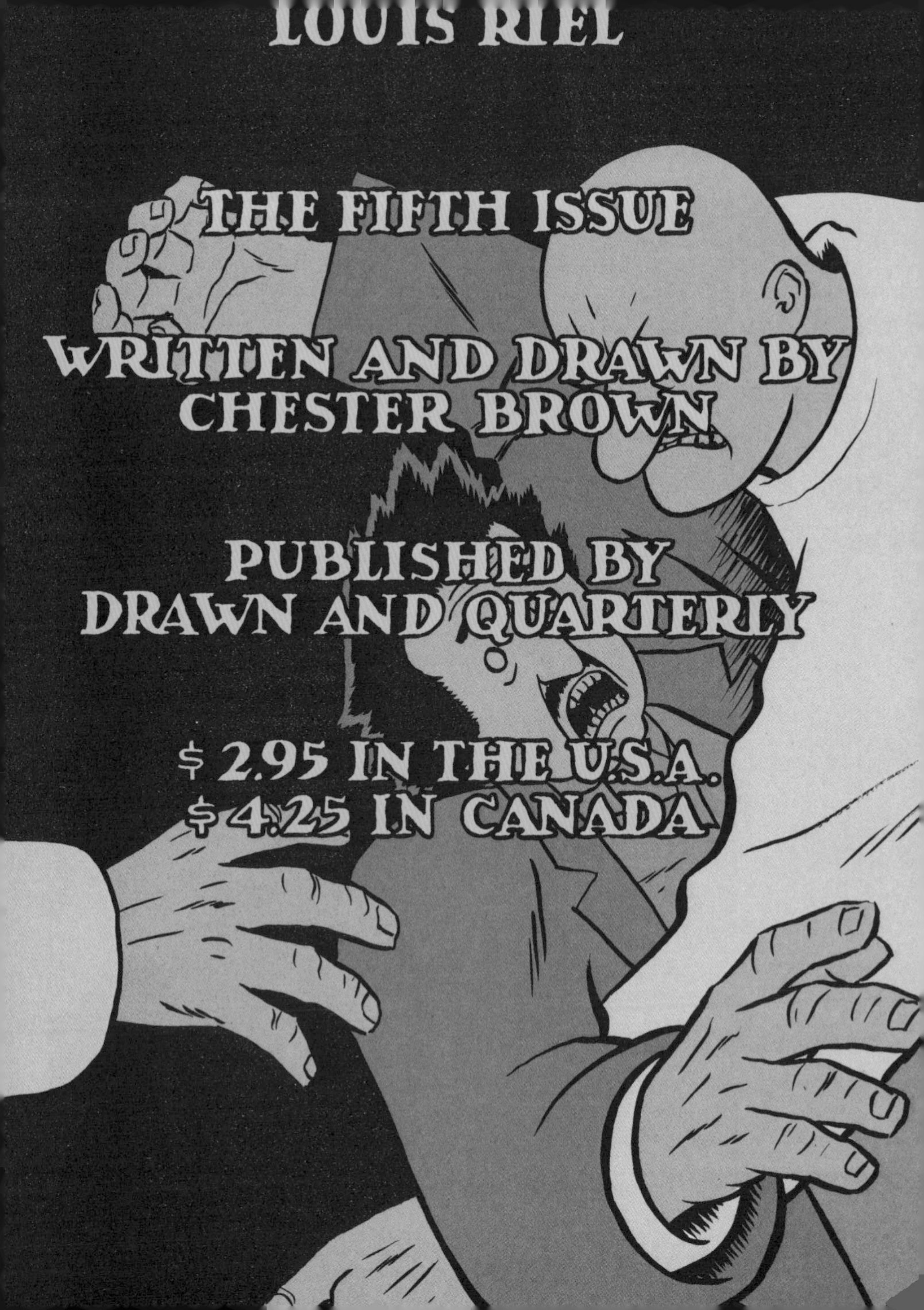

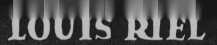

LOUIS RIEL

THE FIFTH ISSUE

WRITTEN AND DRAWN BY
CHESTER BROWN

PUBLISHED BY
DRAWN AND QUARTERLY

$ 2.95 IN THE U.S.A.
$ 4.25 IN CANADA

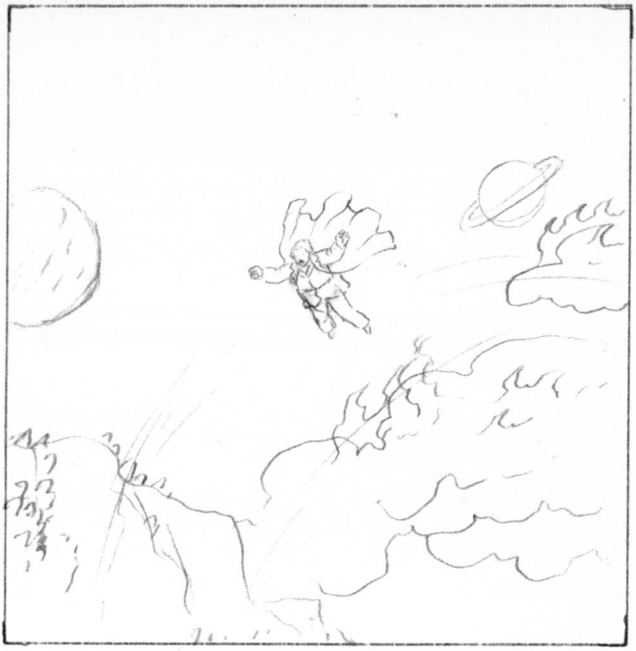

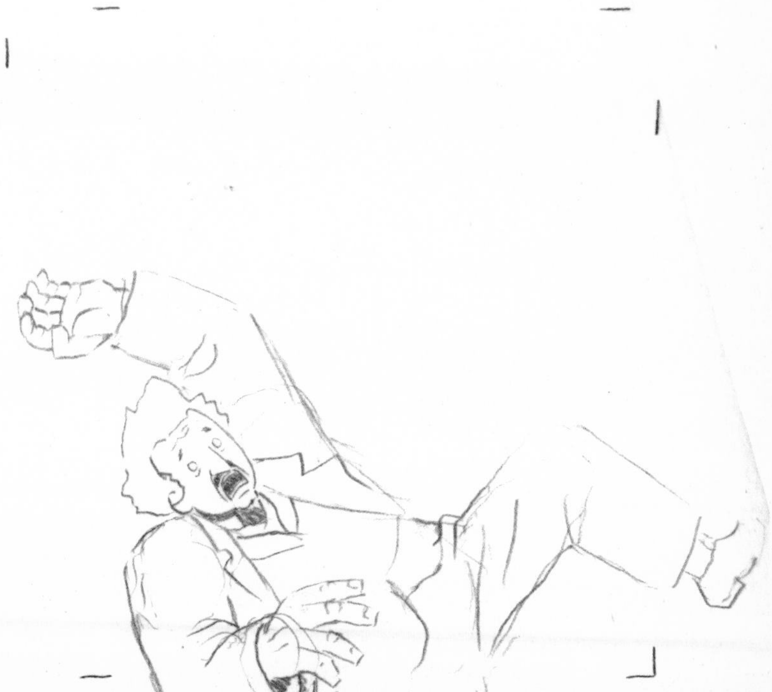

< DON'T RIP IT UP! >
< I'VE GOT THE STRAIGHT-JACKET! >

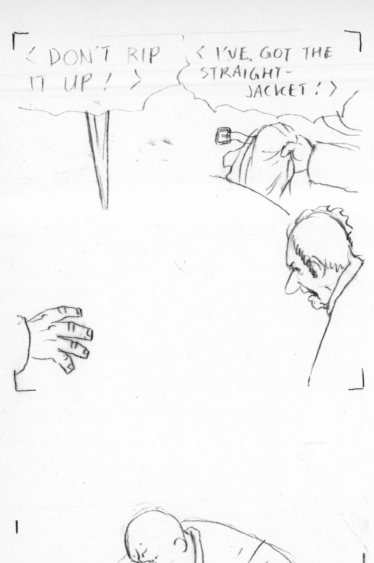

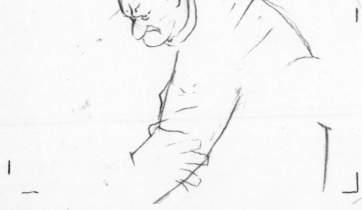

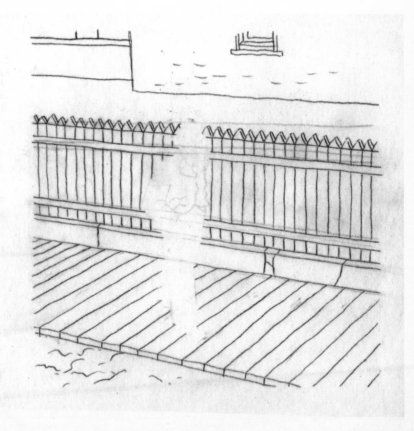

‹ ROME HAS FALLEN ! GET OUT OF MY WAY ! ›

LOUIS RIEL

THE SIXTH ISSUE

WRITTEN AND DRAWN BY CHESTER BROWN

PUBLISHED BY DRAWN AND QUARTERLY

$2.95 IN THE U.S.A. $4.25 IN CANADA

LOUIS RIEL

THE SEVENTH ISSUE $ 2.95 IN THE U.S.A. $ 4.25 IN CANADA

WRITTEN AND DRAWN BY
CHESTER BROWN

DRAWN AND QUARTERLY PUBLICATIONS

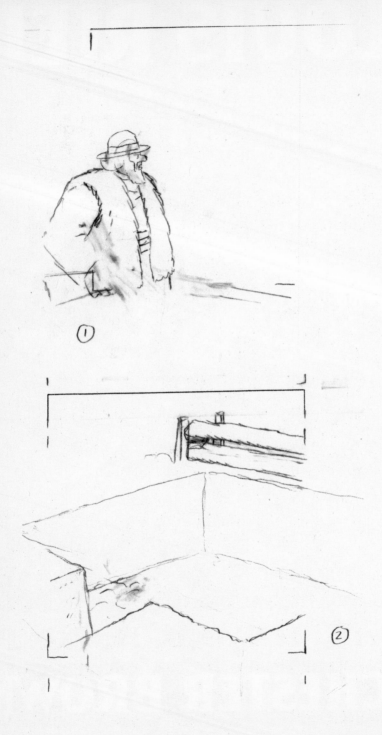

①

②

③

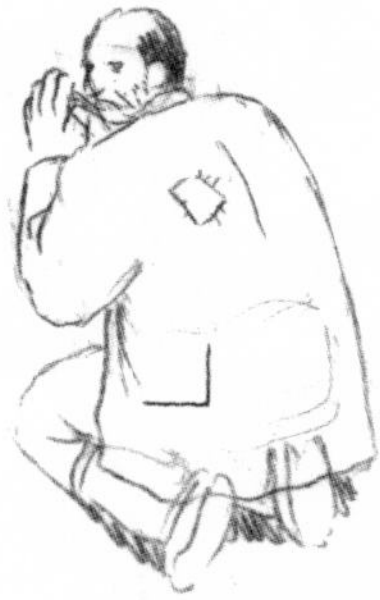

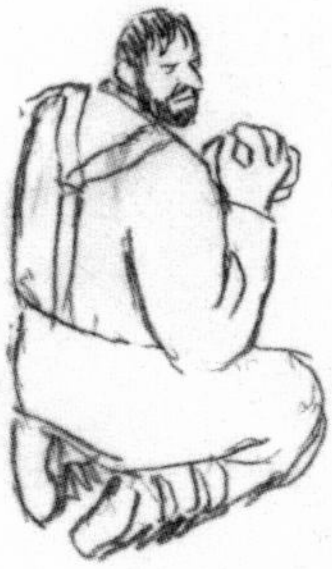

④

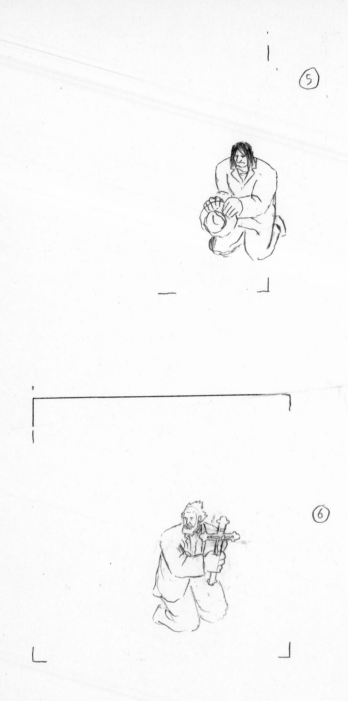

⑤

⑥

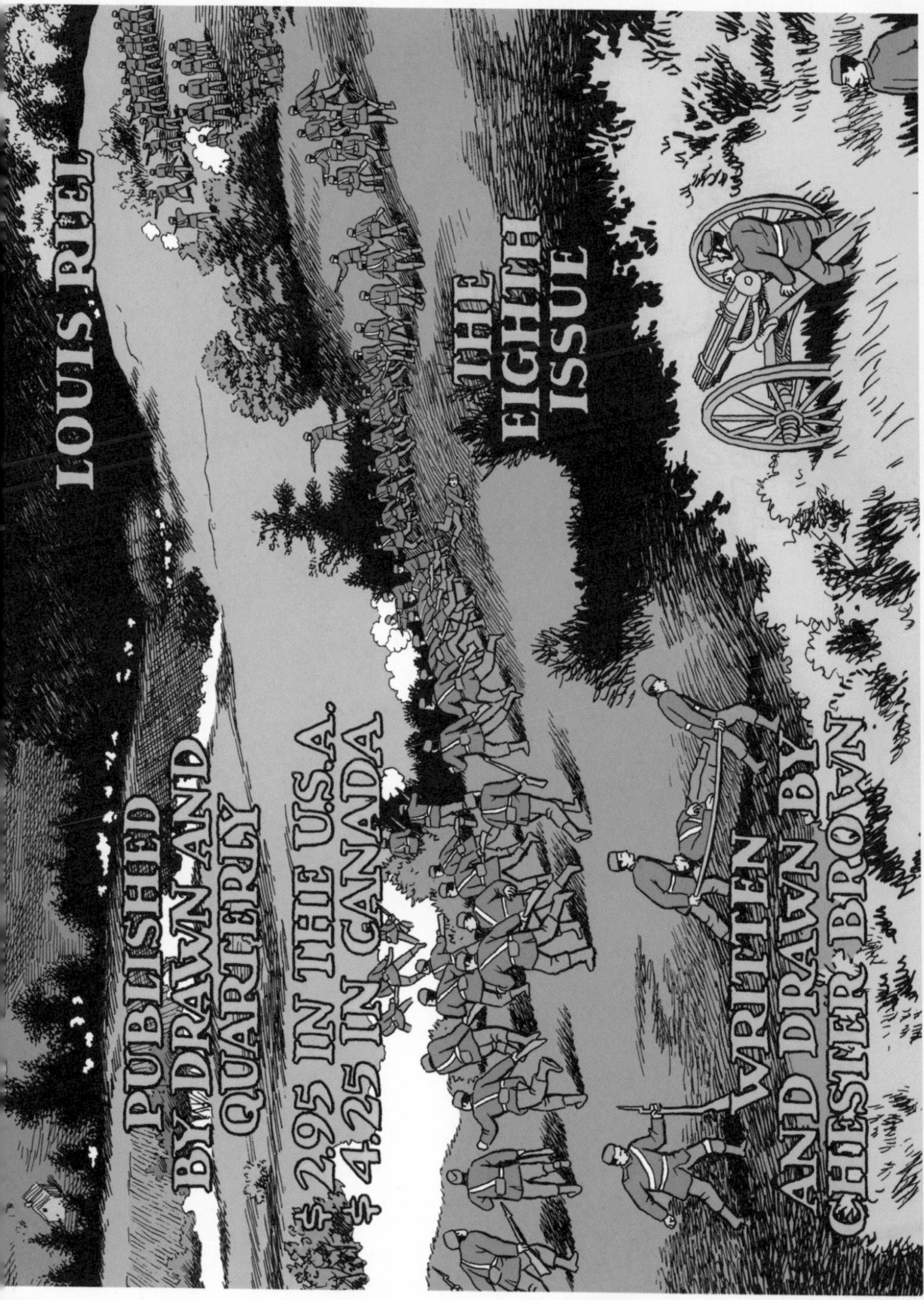
LOUIS RIEL
PUBLISHED BY DRAWN AND QUARTERLY
$2.95 IN THE U.S.A.
$4.25 IN CANADA
THE EIGHTH ISSUE
WRITTEN AND DRAWN BY CHESTER BROWN

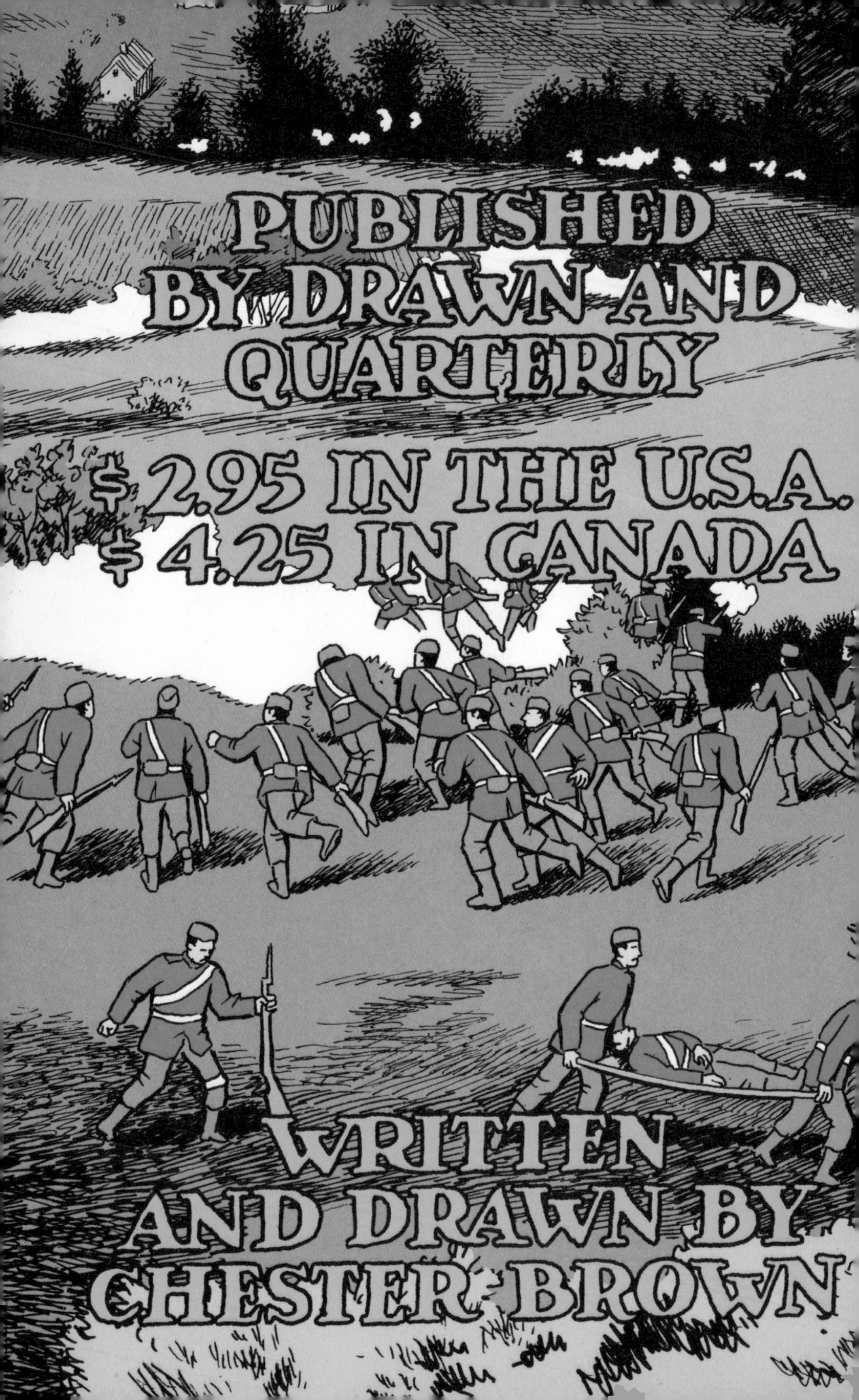
PUBLISHED BY DRAWN AND QUARTERLY
$2.95 IN THE U.S.A.
$4.25 IN CANADA
WRITTEN AND DRAWN BY CHESTER BROWN

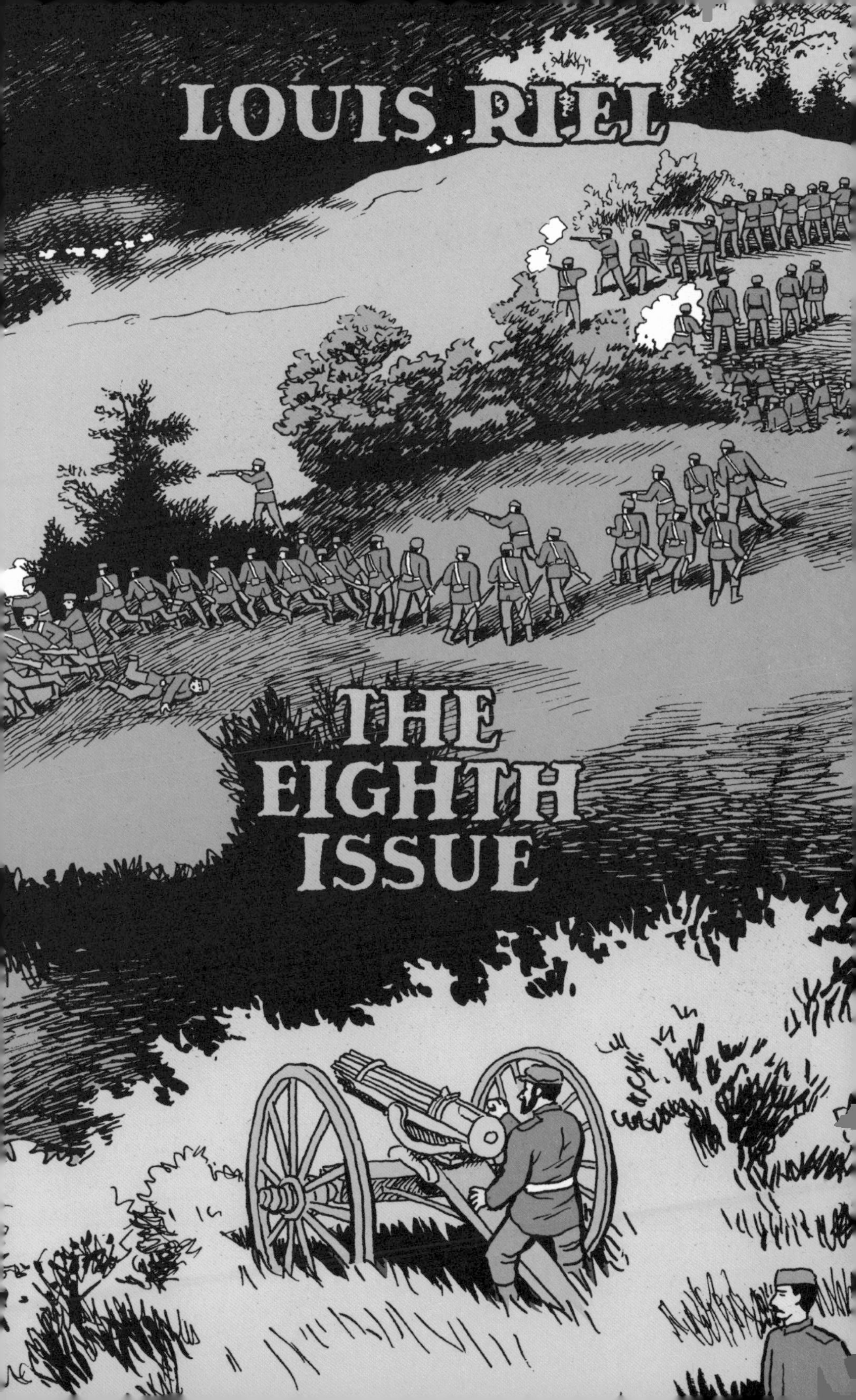
LOUIS RIEL
THE EIGHTH ISSUE

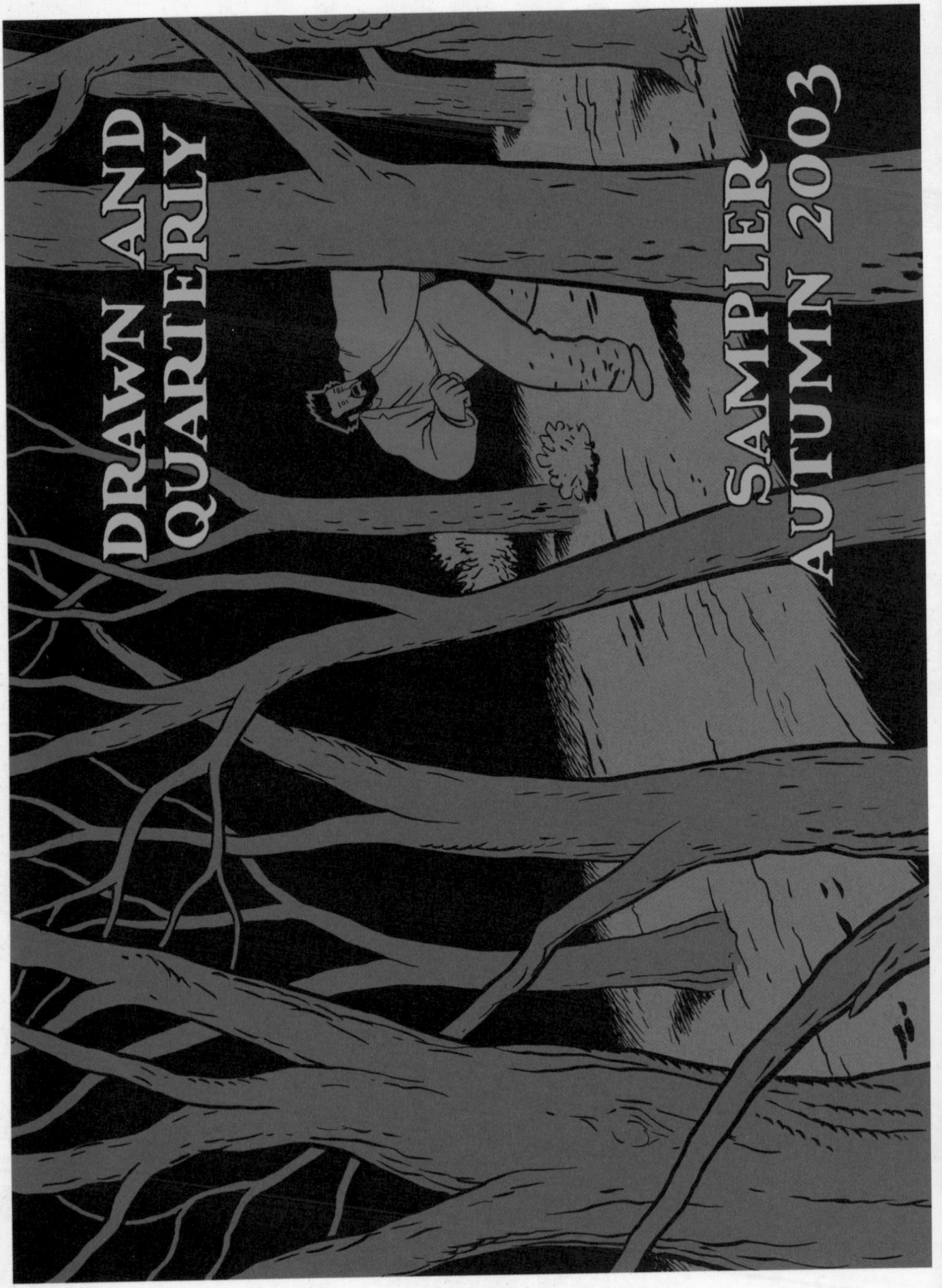
DRAWN AND
QUARTERLY
SAMPLER
AUTUMN 2003

LOUIS RIEL

THE NINTH ISSUE
WRITTEN AND DRAWN BY
CHESTER BROWN
PUBLISHED BY
DRAWN AND QUARTERLY

$2.95 IN THE U.S.A. $4.25 IN CANADA

LOUIS RIEL

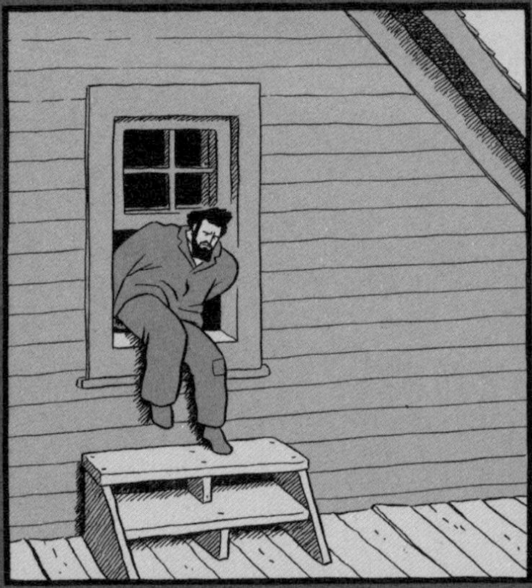

THE TENTH ISSUE

WRITTEN AND DRAWN BY CHESTER BROWN
PUBLISHED BY DRAWN AND QUARTERLY
$2.95 IN THE U.S.A. $4.25 IN CANADA

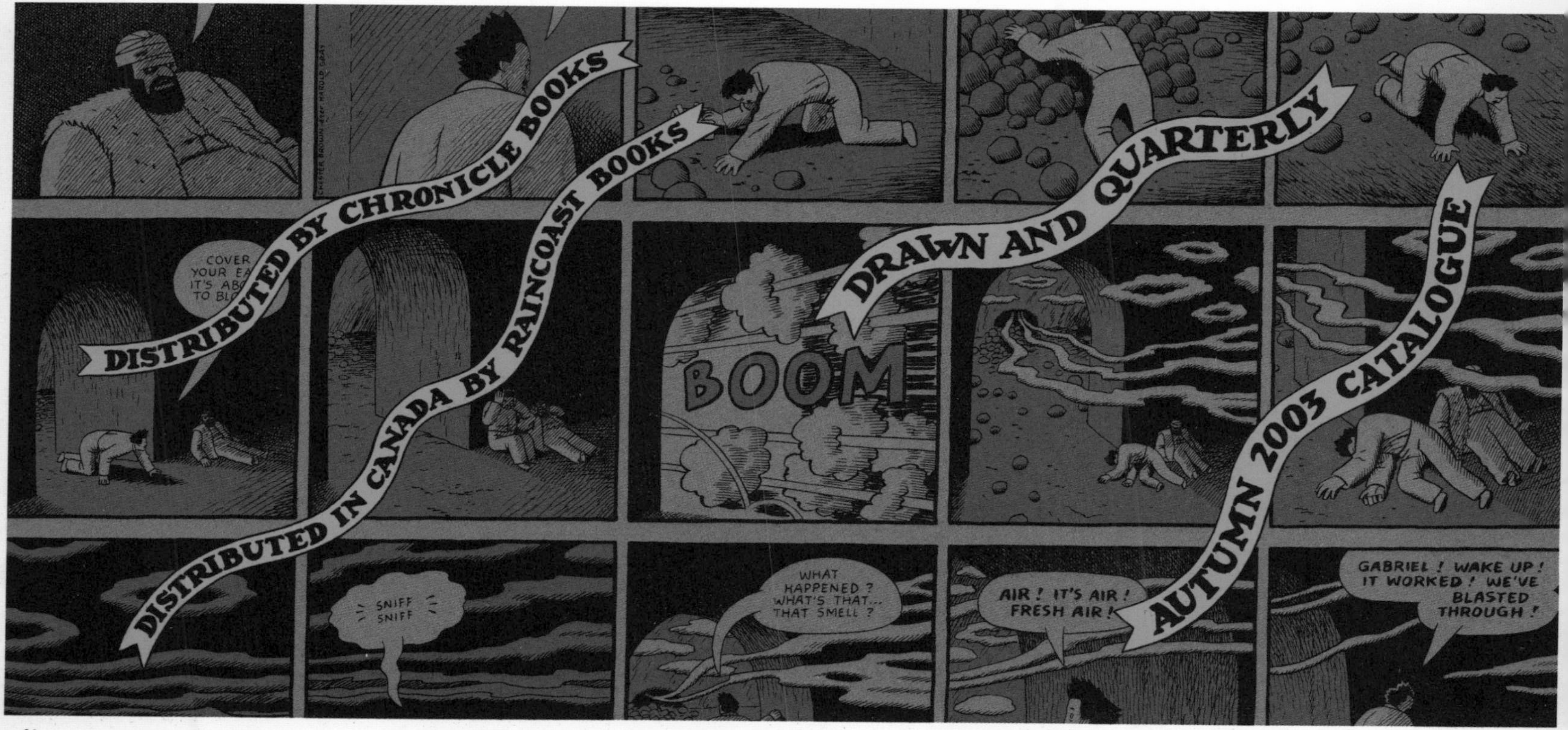
DRAWN AND QUARTERLY
AUTUMN 2003 CATALOGUE
DISTRIBUTED BY CHRONICLE BOOKS
DISTRIBUTED IN CANADA BY RAINCOAST BOOKS
COVER YOUR EA IT'S ABO TO BL
BOOM
SNIFF SNIFF
WHAT HAPPENED? WHAT'S THAT... THAT SMELL?
AIR! IT'S AIR! FRESH AIR!
GABRIEL! WAKE UP! IT WORKED! WE'VE BLASTED THROUGH!

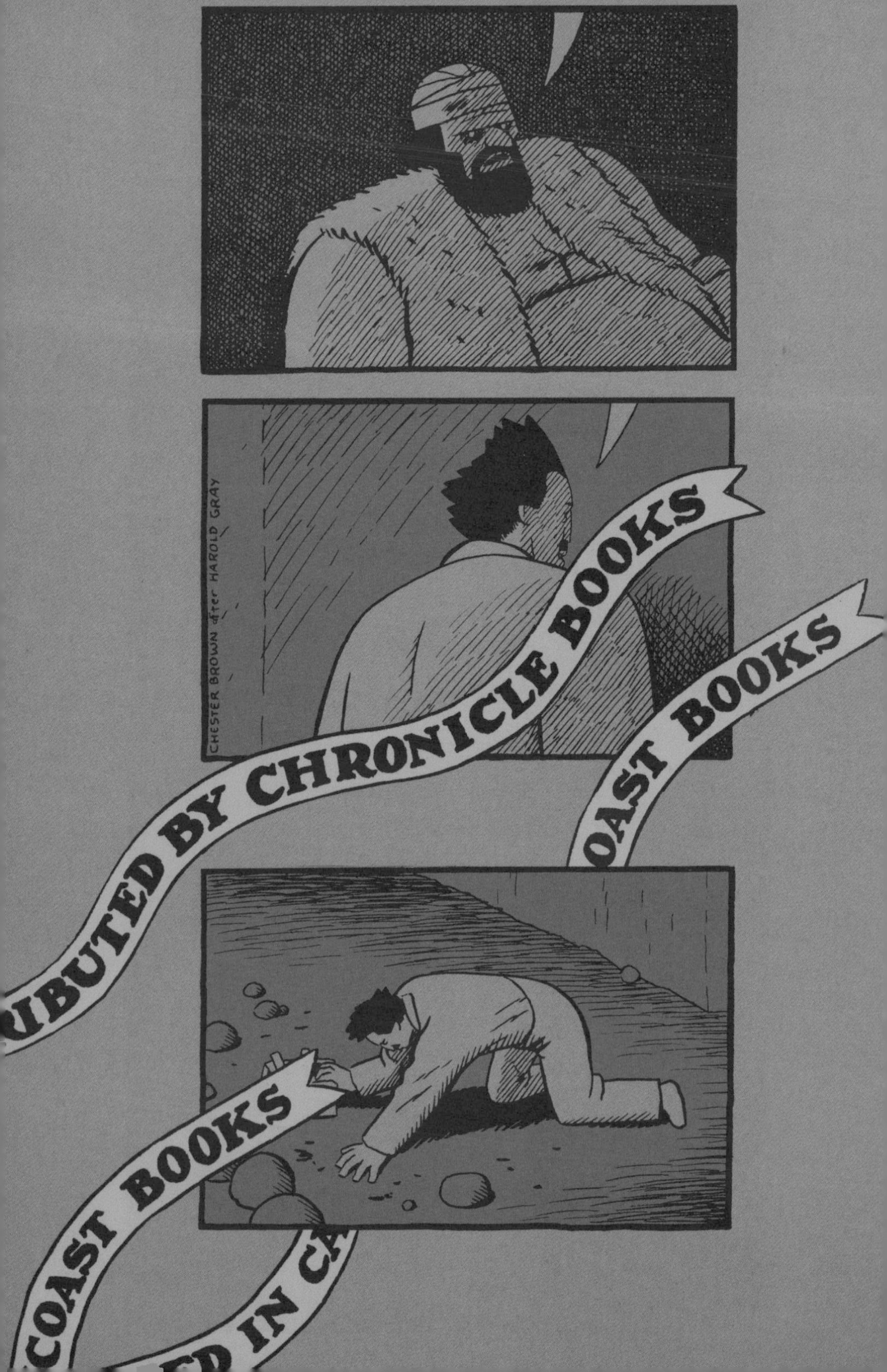
CHESTER BROWN after HAROLD GRAY
RIBUTED BY CHRONICLE BOOKS
OAST BOOKS
COAST BOOKS
COAST
ED IN CA

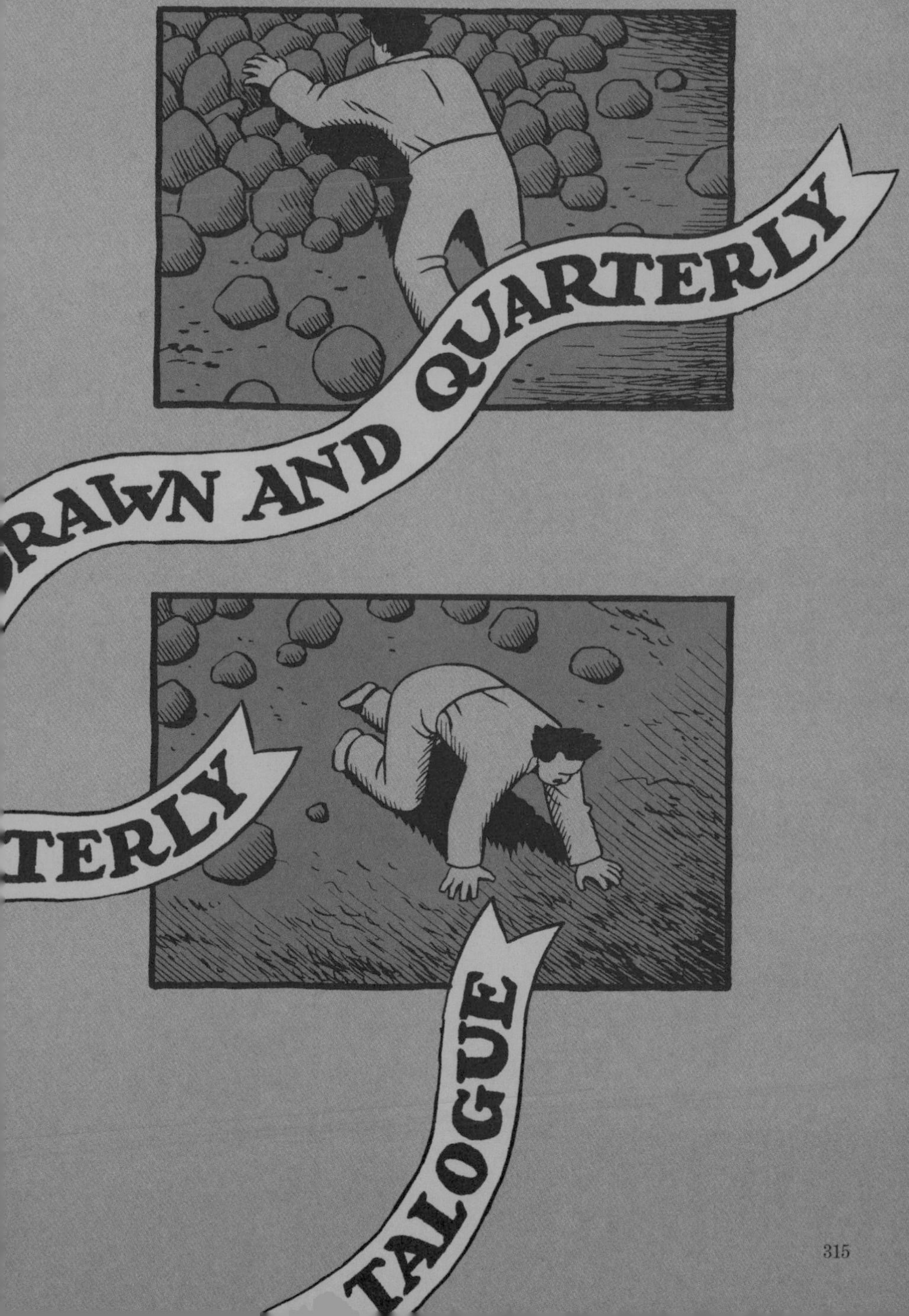
RAWN AND QUARTERLY
TERLY
TALOGUE

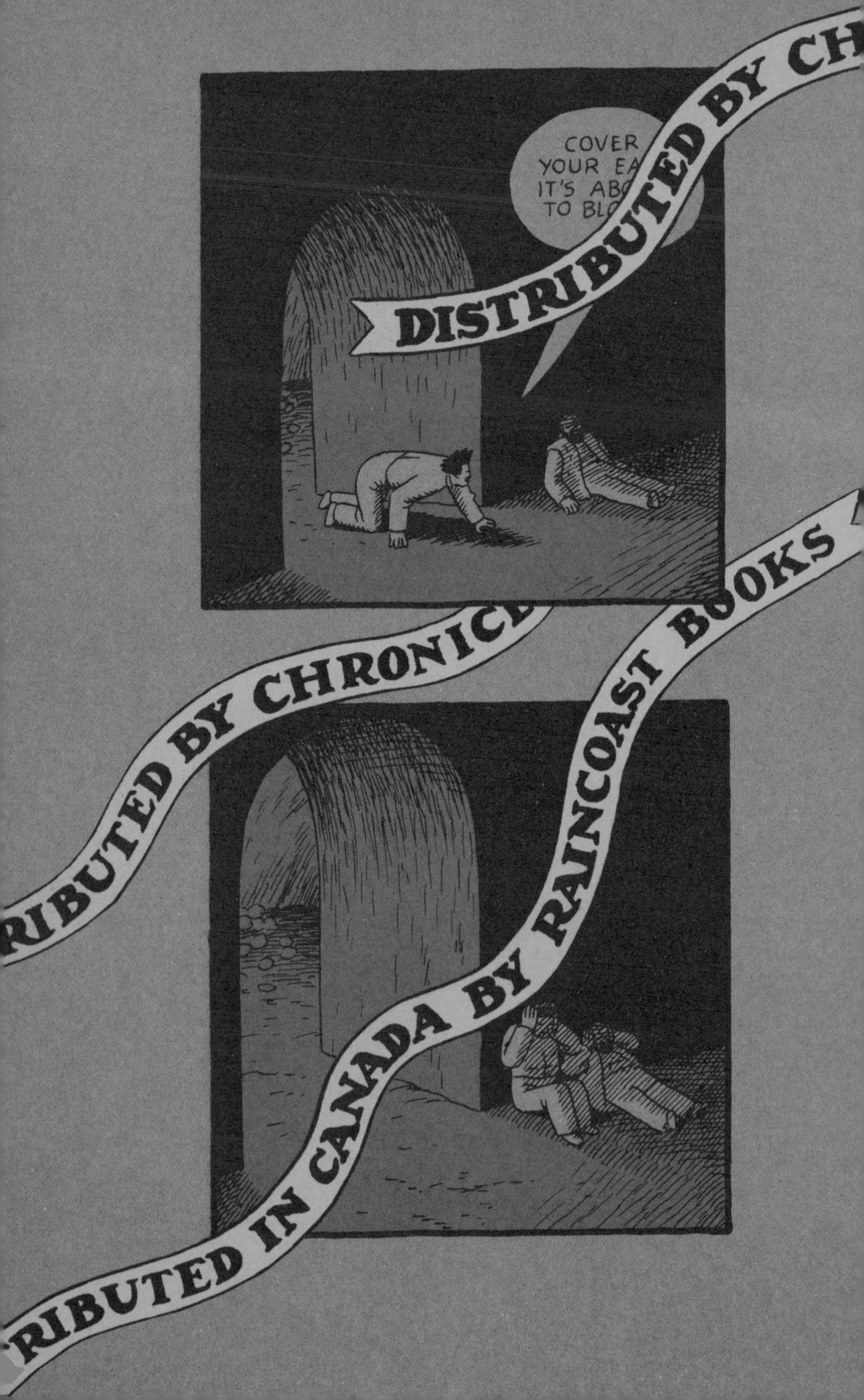
COVER YOUR EA IT'S ABO TO BL
DISTRIBUTED BY CH
RIBUTED BY CHRONIC
RIBUTED IN CANADA BY RAINCOAST BOOKS

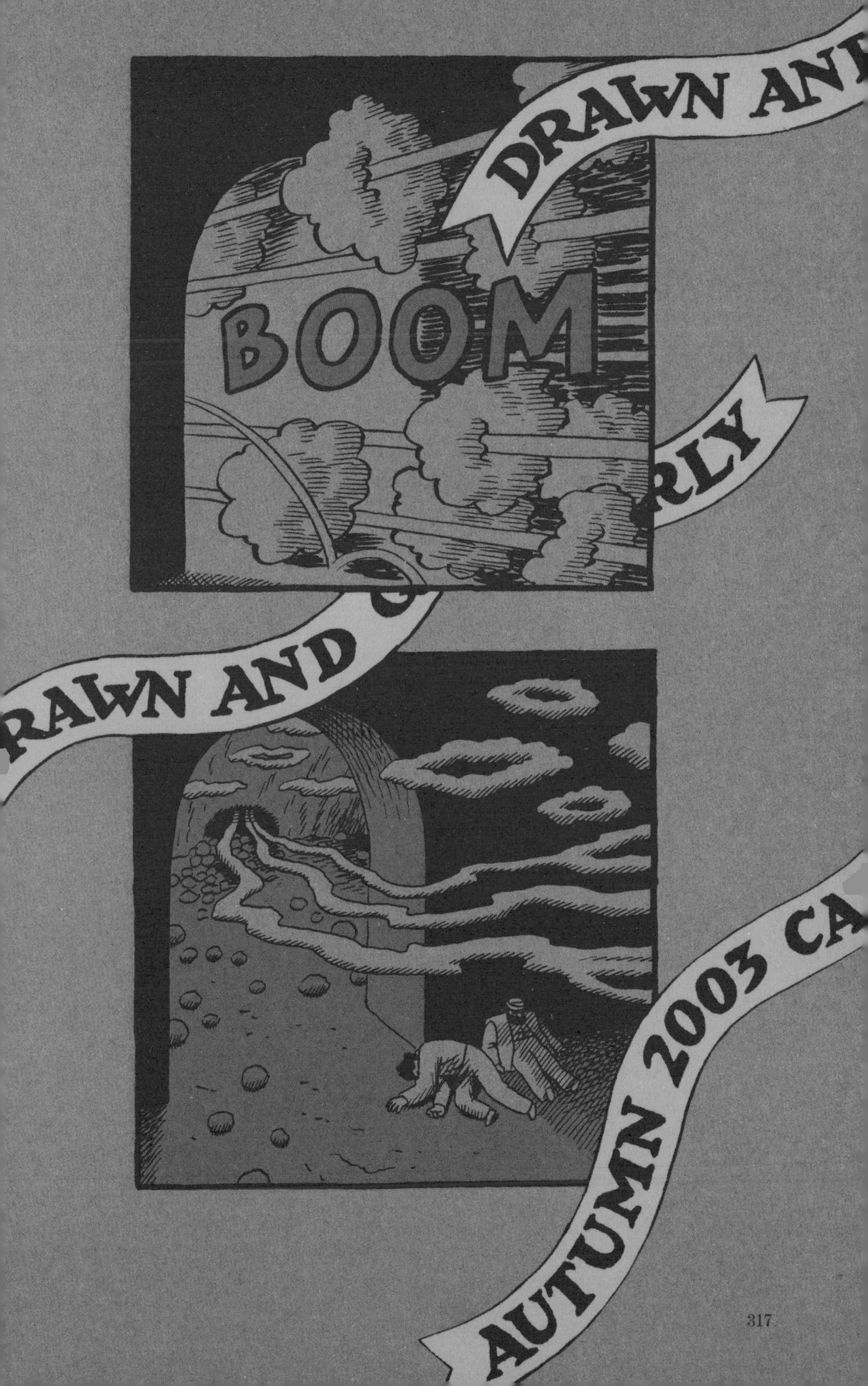
DRAWN AN
BOOM
RLY
RAWN AND
AUTUMN 2003 CA

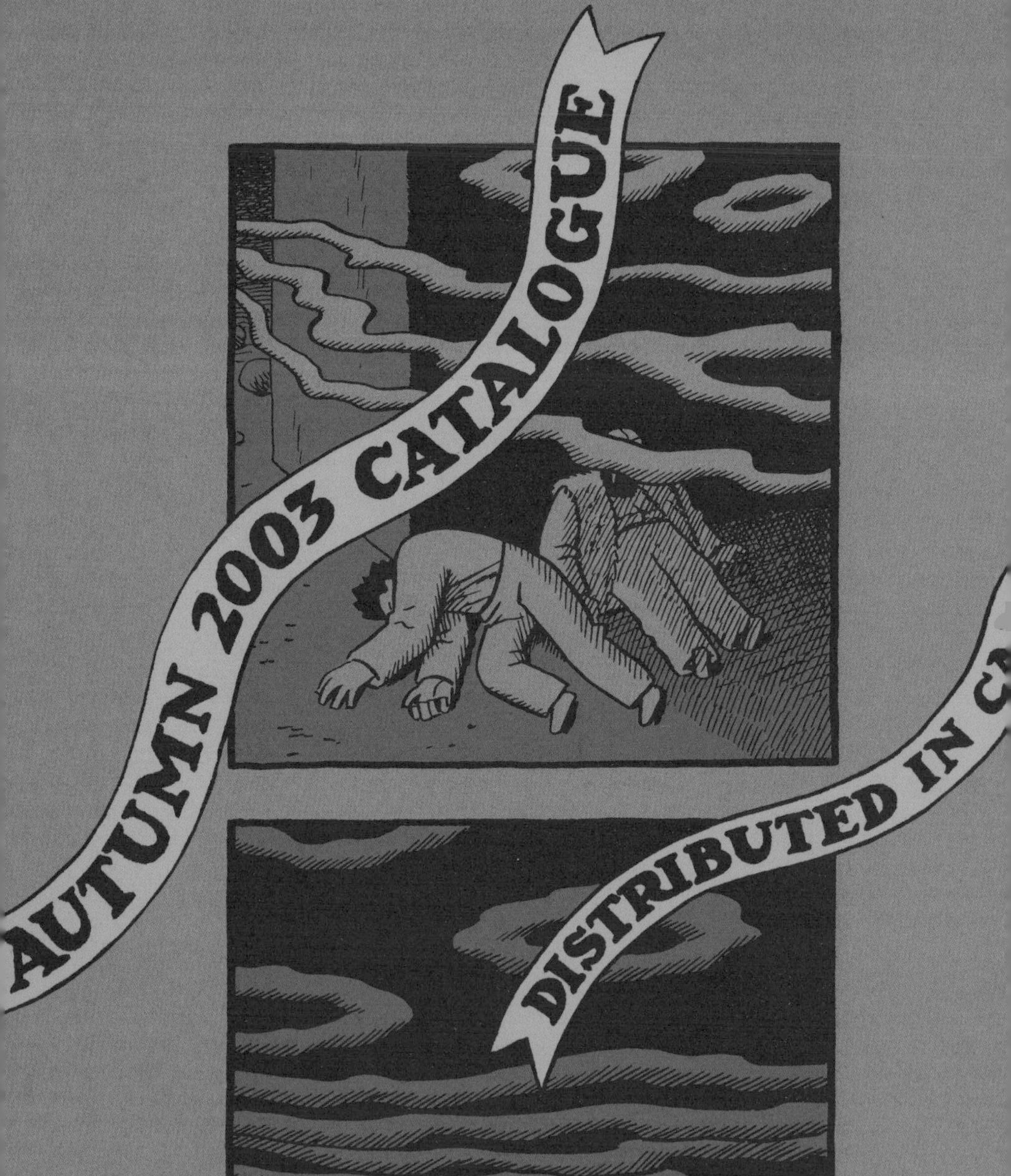
AUTUMN 2003 CATALOGUE
DISTRIBUTED IN CA

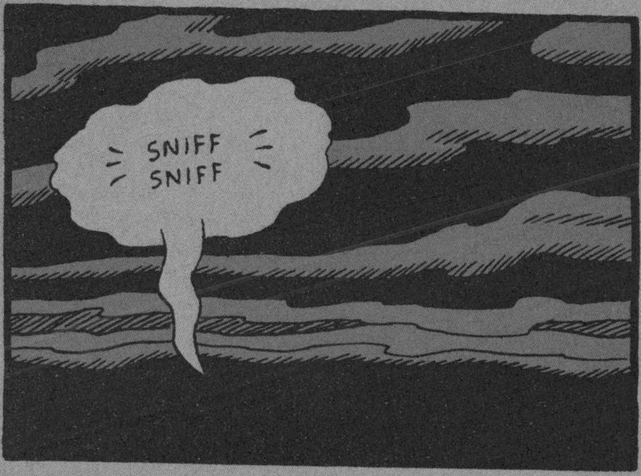
SNIFF
SNIFF

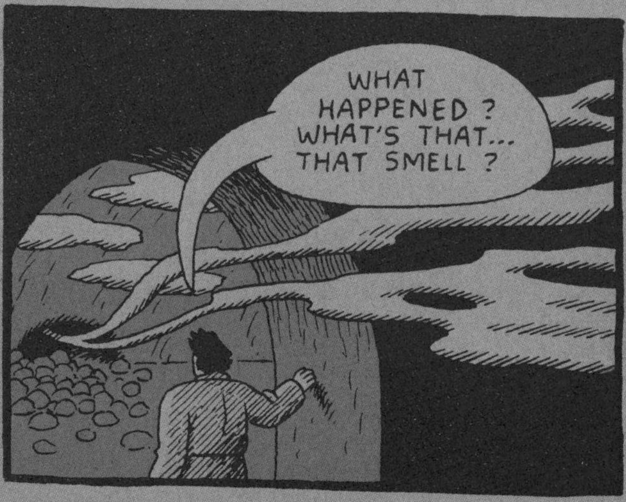
WHAT HAPPENED ? WHAT'S THAT... THAT SMELL ?

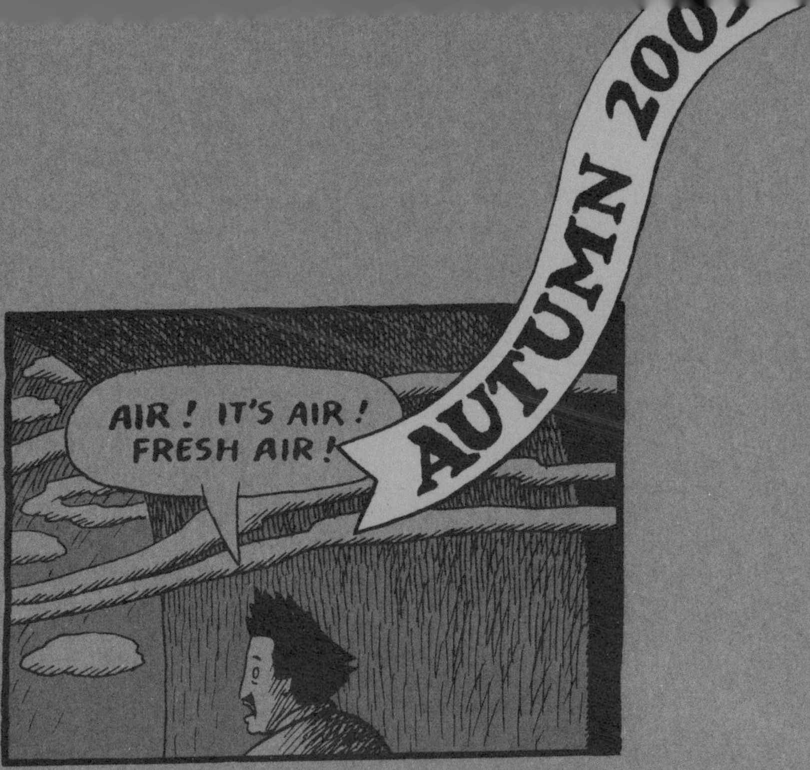
AUTUMN 200
AIR! IT'S AIR! FRESH AIR!

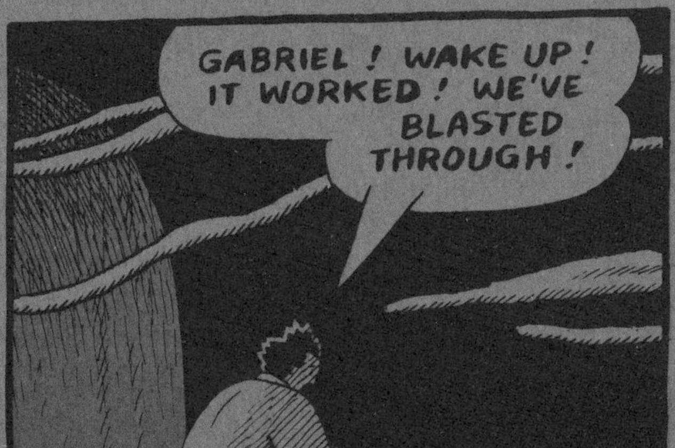
GABRIEL! WAKE UP! IT WORKED! WE'VE BLASTED THROUGH!

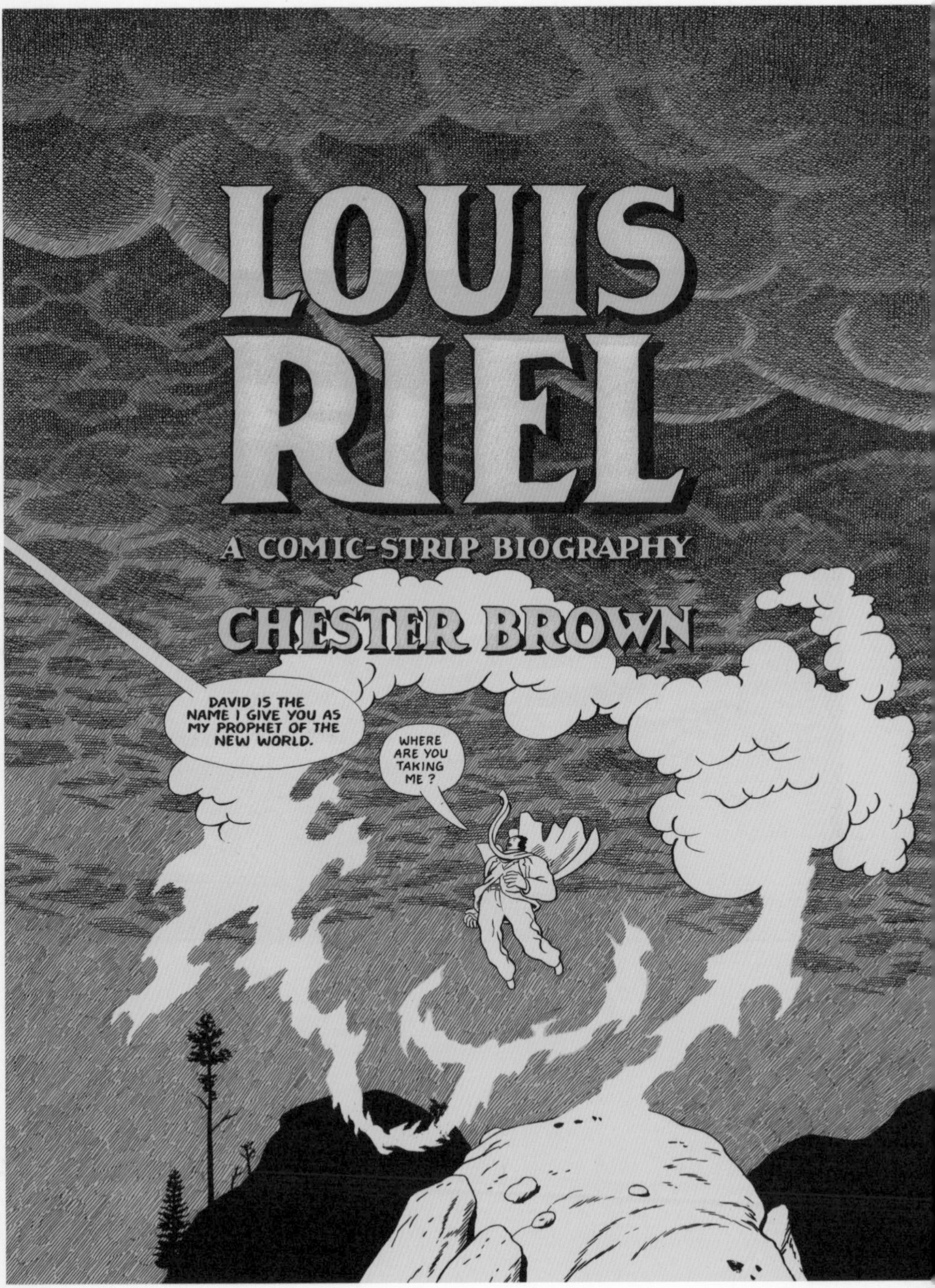
LOUIS RIEL
A COMIC-STRIP BIOGRAPHY
CHESTER BROWN
DAVID IS THE NAME I GIVE YOU AS MY PROPHET OF THE NEW WORLD.
WHERE ARE YOU TAKING ME ?

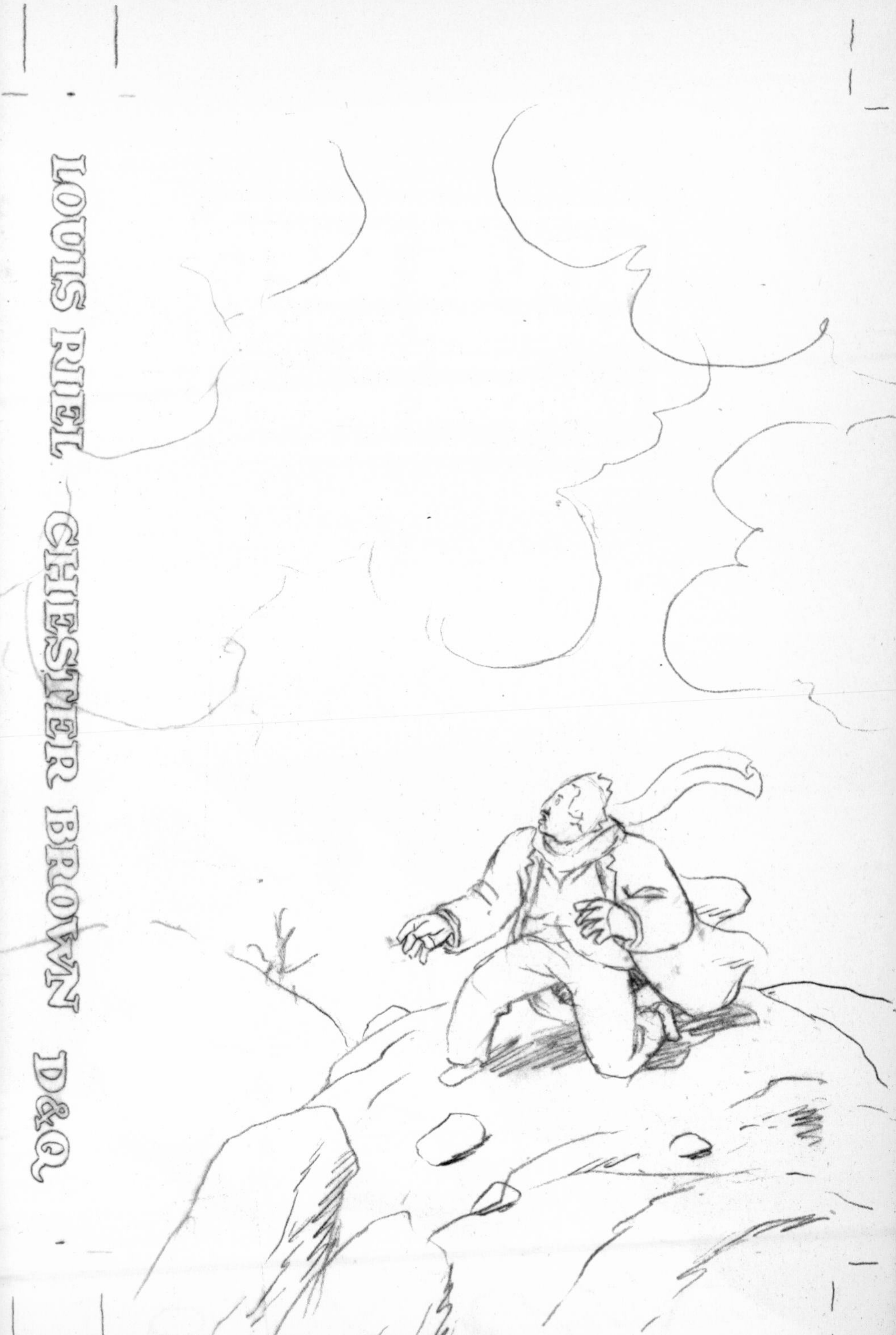
LOUIS RIEL
CHESTER BROWN
D&Q

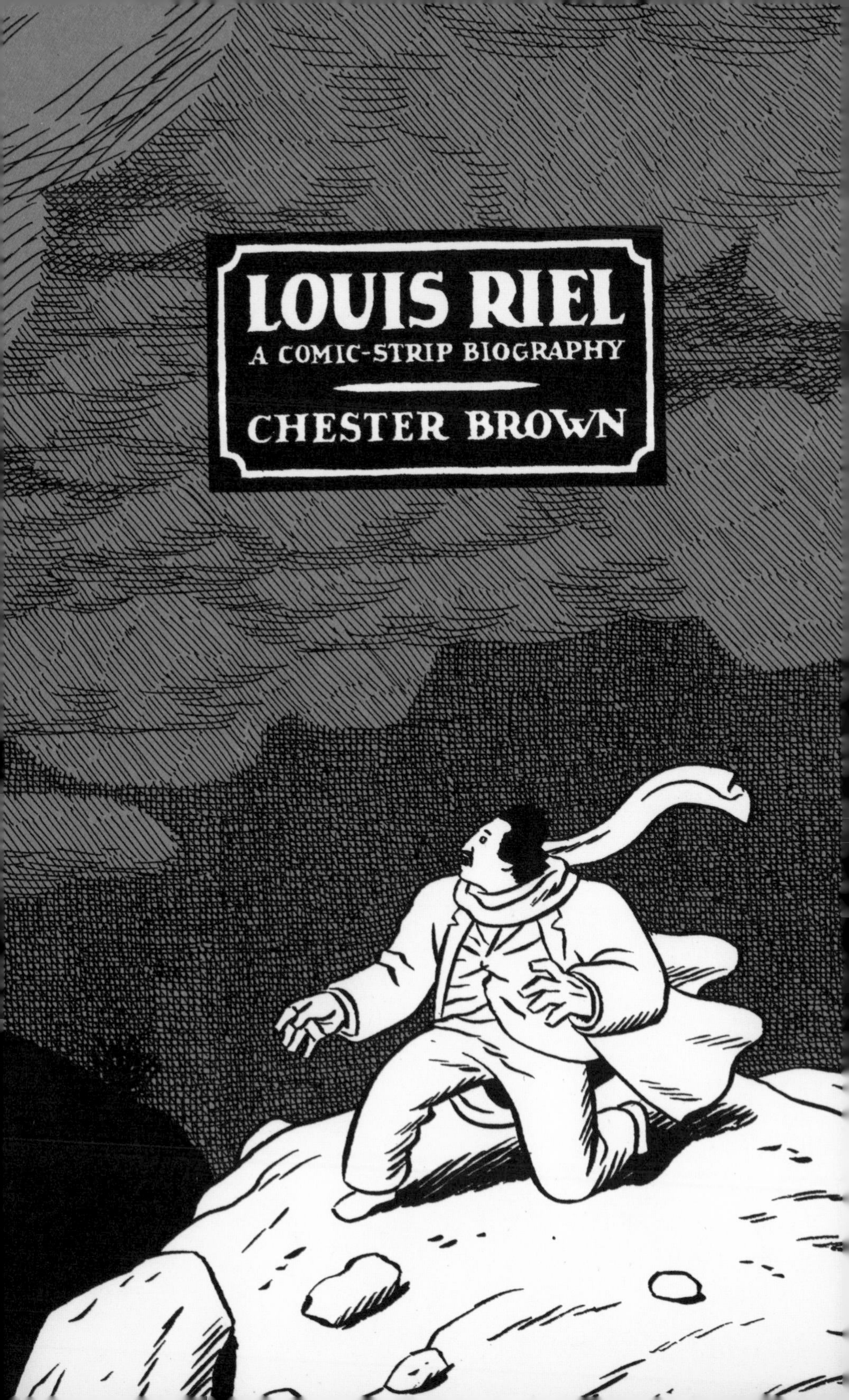
LOUIS RIEL
A COMIC-STRIP BIOGRAPHY
CHESTER BROWN

they killed louis riel & by monday they were feeling guilty
maybe we shouldn't have done it said the mounties as they sat
down to breakfast   louis rolled over in his grave & sighed
it's not enough they take your life away with a gun they
have to take it away with their pens   in the distance he could
hear the writers scratching louder & louder
—bpNichol

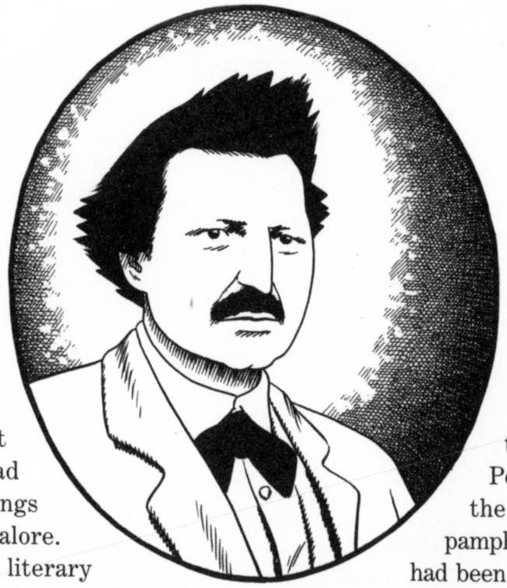

1999. There had been an opera written about Louis Riel. There had been plays and folk songs and children's books galore. One of Canada's great literary modernists had tried to wrestle the man into the pages of a novel. A monument had been erected in Riel's honour in Winnipeg, only to be deemed unsatisfactory somehow, troubling and divisive like the man himself, and replaced with another statue some decades later. The movies had had a go at the myth, too: Riel played the sallow-faced villain in a Technicolor Cecil B. DeMille epic, and in one of the Heritage Minutes, the educational shorts broadcast across Canada, a martyr's pained visage was all we saw of Riel. As the focus of his own made-for-TV biopic Riel would finally be the hero, sure, but he would also be upstaged by Canuck celebrities in walk-on parts—William Shatner, Leslie Nielsen, even *SCTV's* Doug Mackenzie. And then there were the comic books about Riel: French-language treatments of the man and his life, mainly. Respectful, hagiographic, like an issue of *Classics Illustrated*, or one of those old comic books they used to do about the Pope. But until 1999, when the first oddly sized little pamphlet hit the stands, there had been nothing quite like Chester Brown's *Louis Riel.*

Here was a biography in the form of a comic strip, unfolding over ten modest issues and four long years. Here was capital-H history acted out by big-nosed figures with blunk-out eyeballs. Here was desperate, tempestuous action—heated civil war!—but depicted from a cool remove. And here, on these pages, Riel—more myth than man in the Canadian imaginary, and to the rest of the world a mystery, perhaps—lives his life, leads his people, prophesizes, politicks, and dies. Little more than that, since Brown's storytelling is documentary in the truest sense, merely relaying a state of affairs with little in the way of justification, judgment, or commentary. And yet, too, it was so very much more. Over the course of a couple of hundred pages, or one-tenth the length of Riel's own collected writings, Brown conveys the sense of a life, a people, a country, and a cosmology, all while setting a new standard for historical cartooning. That he is able to do so is testament both to his skills, honed to a sharp precision by the time he took on *Riel*, as well as to the fascination inherent in his subject.

"The very essence of Louis Riel is contradiction," writes Maggie Siggins in *Riel: A Life in Revolution*. Brown credits this biography for first interesting him in the story of Louis Riel (loo-EE ree-EL), a man who led his people in two rebellions against the Canadian government in the throes of the nation's birth, and whose hanging for treason remains the only such execution in Canadian history. In all the wringing of hands and raising of voices that accompanied his life and that have followed his death for over a century now,[1] the contradiction that Siggins mentions are everywhere in evidence. The dichotomies of Riel's life live on in the terms in which his legacy is debated: hero or villain, patriot or traitor, madman or prophet? The man means no one thing to any two people—competing versions of his beliefs, his actions, his legacy, all proliferate, like glosses on the Gospels.

This continued fascination with Riel is often chalked up to the almost mythic ways he seems to embody the schisms that constitute Canada as a nation. Being Métis, he could boast of both Native heritage and settlers' blood, and he would have been forced to reconcile the new world's boundless prairies with the old world's "civilizing" order, which was encroaching ever westward. As a francophone versed in English, he could mediate between his people and the institutions and official representatives of anglophone Canada, a francophobic seat of up-with-Britain chauvinism. As a westerner, he was an early agitator against the centralization of power in Canada and the blind administration of western rights and freedoms from afar. Riel's life is so bound up with the founding myths and iconography of Canada— confederation, the railroad, the Mounties, the wilderness—that his own place in the national narrative has become elastic and expansive enough to accommodate any interpretation, from whatever quarter.

How fitting, then, that Chester Brown's version of the man is so often a perfect cipher behind those white eyeballs. His Riel may have great presence on the page, thanks to his hulking proportions, but he is often little more than a placeholder, an agent, a tiny figure who acts and struts and frets, but whose motivations and thoughts remain obscure, withheld, lost to history. This introduction will not attempt to fill in that blank. To do so would be to draw pupils on all Brown's figures, to scrawl cuss words over the astonishing blue streak of X's that Brown has pouring out the mouth of Thomas Scott. "You can't know the truth at this point," Brown has said, and indeed he has worked hard enough to empty his Riel of all preconception and meaning and myth that the man, for once, maintains his ambiguity and mystique. The reader must divine her own truth from the pages that follow, like Riel guessing at his fate on that mountaintop in Washington. What is left, then, is to sketch out the hum and buzz of implication around *Louis Riel's* creation, to hatch and shade the background from which this book emerged.

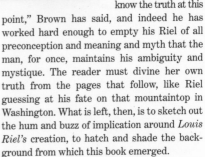

Cartooning the biography of a major Canadian historical figure could hardly have been a predictable course in Chester Brown's career trajectory—except that his work has always been subject to unforeseen swerves. Brown's cartooning first appeared in the pages of *Yummy Fur*, an epochal title in 1980s alternative comics, which he initially self-published.

---

1. Jennifer Reid, in *Louis Riel and the Creation of Modern Canada*, asserts that Riel has been the subject of more "biographical work" than anyone else in Canada.

These early strips featured inventive but aimless surrealism-inflected stories in which toilet paper takes over the world, aliens kidnap a walrus, and a lanky clown suffers sudden, grievous injury. This last character Brown would follow at almost perverse length, once *Yummy Fur* started to take off. The resultant story, collected as *Ed the Happy Clown*, would make a name for Brown as one of comics' great iconoclasts, shocking readers with scenes of scatology, sexuality, and nonsensical political commentary. (Infamously, the head of then-President Ronald Reagan manifests on the tip of Ed's masculine appendage—consider how much more lightly Prime Minister John A. MacDonald gets off in these pages, alkie schnoz and all!) A far cry from the sedate and measured world of *Louis Riel*, perhaps, though at least one critic has noted the anti-authoritarian streak in *Ed* that carries forward into later work like *Riel*.

But while *Yummy Fur* was mostly given over to *Ed's* Dadaist provocations, Brown was also devoting part of every issue to his adaptation of the Gospels. The first stirrings of Riel took place in these back pages, which narrated—straightforwardly and with little pomp—the wanderings and teachings of Christ. Brown renders Christ's behaviour every bit as inscrutable as he would later do Riel's. His Jesus is just as much a wild-haired seer as Riel, and his ability to lead a people is likewise never in doubt. The Gospels would remain the one constant in Brown's oeuvre until he began work on *Riel*, when the Canadian rebel's life story usurped the Nazarene's. In the meantime, however, Brown abruptly ended the *Ed* serial and executed the first of his career volte-faces.

No longer interested, all of a sudden, in *Ed's* fantasies of vampirism and disembodied hands, Brown began to draw inspiration from his own life. His comics were now about the brief but telling conflicts in the rooming house where he lived, or they quietly sketched out

his childhood in a suburb of Montreal, recounting his history with pornography and his reticent relationships with his mother and neighbourhood girls. These autobiographical comics were attentive to the silences in everyday life, the windswept and big-skied suburban landscape, the complex disagreements that simmer and erupt between people—all concerns they share with *Riel*. Most of all, though, they were where Brown first dedicated himself to reconstructing the past, to telling a story about a time that has vanished. In this way, his comics attempt to wring some meaning out of those events, some ethical or moral reflection on how best to live with others. It may be overstating the matter to draw a direct line between Brown's annoying, abusive housemates and blustering jingoists like Doc Schultz or Thomas Scott, but the similarity remains.

Brown would abandon even this mode of comics making, however, as he embarked on a new project called *Underwater*. This would be the most pronounced yet of Brown's sudden departures from reader expectations, as he began telling another life story radically unlike Jesus's, or Riel's, or even his own. This time out, the narrative treats a newborn girl who looks curiously alien, who cannot distinguish between waking life and unconsciousness, and for whom language is little more than an unintelligible pidgin. Brown would grow dissatisfied with this endeavour, too—"I bit off more than I could chew"—but not before publishing a strip that would crucially inform his interest in taking on Riel.

In "My Mom Was a Schizophrenic," Brown consults various sources on psychiatry and weaves together their statements and theories in order to present the case that what we call schizophrenia is not a disease but a construct, a label that society slaps onto unruly individuals in order to reinforce normative ideas of behaviour. The refusal to stigmatize the so-called schizophrenic experience—visions, voices, strange beliefs—and the immersive study of secondary sources would both prove hugely important to *Louis Riel's* sympathetic portrayal of its hero's odd faith, as well as its daunting historical scope. Brown has described the creation of "My Mom..." as "fun": "I wanted to do something like that again—do a lot of research on the subject and cram it all into a story." And he would: a few short years later, leaving both Jesus and the world of *Underwater* behind, Brown would at last begin *Louis Riel*.

The real impact of this innovative "comic-strip biography" would not be felt until several years later. At the time, as Brown noted with equanimity upon his work's completion, "not only were there very few people outside Canada interested in reading a comic book about Louis Riel, but the book didn't do that well *inside* Canada, either." Things have certainly changed: in the ten years since the individual comic books were collected and revised in one single volume, *Louis Riel* has become a certifiable Canadian cultural phenomenon. Upon its release, word of mouth, enthusiastic press coverage, national historical cachet, and the book's undeniable excellence all helped launch *Louis Riel* onto the list of the nation's bestsellers—the first work of Canadian comics to do so. (The analogous American situation would, of course, be the breakthrough of Art Spiegelman's *Maus* some years earlier. The story of how Spiegelman's father survived the Holocaust, *Maus* was, like *Riel*, a biography, but derived from memoir rather than the historical record.)

If we are to judge by those decade-old bestseller lists, *Louis Riel* entered into the national consciousness alongside books by and about war heroes and star athletes, radio raconteurs and Booker Prize–winners. On bookstore shelves, on bestseller lists, on book-of-the-year tallies, Chester Brown's comics rubbed shoulders with Margaret Atwood's science fiction, and *Louis Riel* shared space with Roméo Dallaire. It must have seemed like those other august Canadians were keeping odd company with this curious book of comics—like Riel himself, the rebel, listed on the rolls of Parliament. Before a year was up, Brown's book would require a third printing, having sold through several thousands of copies—more than twice what typically counts as a bestseller in Canada, and unimaginable for a Canadian comic book before *Riel*.

The years to come only brought continued visibility for the book, and continued success. It was praised, debated, and delved into in the pages of the national press—the *National Post* deigned to ask Brown, "Why is a comic strip an ideal format to tell a story like this?" while *Maclean's* praised its ambiguity, as well as its "muted atmospherics and minimalist setting." Abroad, Brown saw his book translated into several languages, acclaimed at Angoulême—the comics world's equivalent of the Cannes film festival—and widely praised as one of the best comics of the decade. Librarians ordered the book in bulk, scholarly papers deconstructed it, and university syllabi made it required reading, pored over by students enrolled in courses as diverse as Comic Book Politics and The Anti-Pioneer: Canadian Settler Writing Then and Now. *Louis Riel*, then—embraced and argued over and deemed a part of legitimate culture—has helped to break the stigma of the comic-book form among booksellers and readers, and along the way has been turned into a kind of institution of its own. And yet the book, like Louis Riel himself, remains elusive, challenging, and never quite what we expect. How has Chester Brown managed to make what's so familiar to every Canadian schoolchild now so strange and new?

Much has been made of *Riel's* debt to Harold Gray, the creator of *Little Orphan Annie*. The stylistic similarities are difficult to

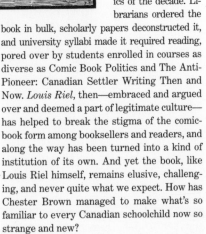

miss—the blank eyes, meticulous hatching, and bulky figures—but Brown has learned from more than just these superficial tics. *Annie* was Gray's Depression-era paean to the gumption, pluck, and stick-to-it-iveness of the American people, even when—especially when—circumstances seemed to loom and lower and conspire against them. Though Riel bears more of a physical resemblance to "Daddy" Warbucks, Gray's avatar of American enterprise, the *character* of Riel hews closer to Annie herself. (Brown has even drawn a Little Orphan Louie, red hair and dress and all, though the look is, let's say, unbecoming.) Louis at times shares Annie's impossible naïveté, a maddening innocence that depends on more able and wised-up compatriots to step in and save the day—in Annie's case, say, her mystical bodyguard Punjab, or the pragmatic Gabriel Dumont in Riel's. Though Riel does not indulge in Annie's brand of nonstop chipper chatter, he does on occasion spout his homespun philosophies in a way similar to the redhead, and Brown is likewise apt to indulge in the same "didactic intensity" that critic Donald Phelps once saw in Gray's work. For *Annie,* like *Riel,* is unabashedly didactic: It wants to tell its readers something about their world, to teach and argue and get political. Gray was an old-school, small-government Republican, and readers can see that same mistrust of intervention and bureaucracy sneaking into Brown's world. Brown's politics would become libertarian by the time he had completed *Riel*—he would even campaign for Parliament himself, as Riel once did—but the true political link binding these strips together is the conviction that the law is no partner to justice, and that what is legislated is not always what is right.

< I'M THE PROPHET OF THE NEW WORLD ! >

The deliberate rhythms and framings of *Riel,* too, may owe something to Gray. His stories, like *Riel,* play out in languorous stretches of real time, only seldom interrupted by flurries of activity which seem all the more troubling after so many consecutive panels of stillness and waiting. But another template for this detached, objective style—in which action is depicted at a sedate pace, from a disinterested angle—is the work of French filmmaker Robert Bresson. Brown has spoken admiringly of Bresson's austere films, which employ non-professional "models" rather than dissembling actors, and whose images are drained of conventional beauty and "postcardism." "It is with something clean and precise," Bresson writes, "that you will force the attention of inattentive eyes and ears." Brown uses precision and simplicity in much the same way: to direct attention, to cast things in an unaccustomed light, cleansed of what we thought we knew.

Brown, like Bresson, takes a kind of monastic vow of aesthetic poverty, in order to attain something truer and more profound—as Bresson puts it, "Production of emotion determined by a resistance to emotion." *Riel's* battle scenes play out like Bresson's *Lancelot of the Lake,* crashingly awkward and disarming in their violence (compare, too, *Riel's* axe murder to the one in *L'Argent*). There's the brute fact of imprisonment in both *A Man Escaped* and *Riel,* represented with true-to-life and stultifying repetition—Louis or Schultz or Brown behind locked doors, desperate for freedom. Finally there's Bresson's *Trial of Joan of Arc,* which rhymes with *Riel's* closing act not only in its strict adherence to transcripts from the trial, but also in how flattened and abstracted is the atmosphere in which the proceedings take place. Joan before the priesthood and Louis before the Crown are crucial historical confrontations, for Bresson and Brown alike. These are the moments when all falsehood and flourish and drama fall away, and simple fact remains, clean and precise. It is no longer the tribunal or the jury who sits in judgment of the plaintiff, but the viewer or reader who sits in judgment over history. What must we make of it all?

There had been historically minded comics before Brown's, to be sure. Harvey Kurtzman, creator of *MAD*, was among the first to turn his cartooning hand to history. In the early 1950s, as the war in Korea was waged, Kurtzman filled the pages of two comic book series—*Two-Fisted Tales* and *Frontline Combat*—with dramatizations of brief episodes from that conflict, and the recently ended Second World War. Kurtzman wrote and blocked out these stories with a mania for detail that demanded exhaustive research into costume, date, terrain, and armaments—a strategy he would pursue, too, for the stories he unearthed from the more distant past of warfare. The cartoonist would take his readers back to Agincourt or Roman times, to the Revolutionary and Civil Wars, and once there he would deliver dispatches from the point of view of the lowly grunt or the civilian at risk, those people whom the history books had so often passed over. Notably, Kurtzman would return to the long wars fought against North America's Native peoples—against the Apache in the desert southwest, against Tecumseh's alliance in 1812 and '13, and against the Sioux and Cheyenne in the Dakota Territory, not far south and west of where Riel and the Métis lived, likewise discontented and likewise rising up.

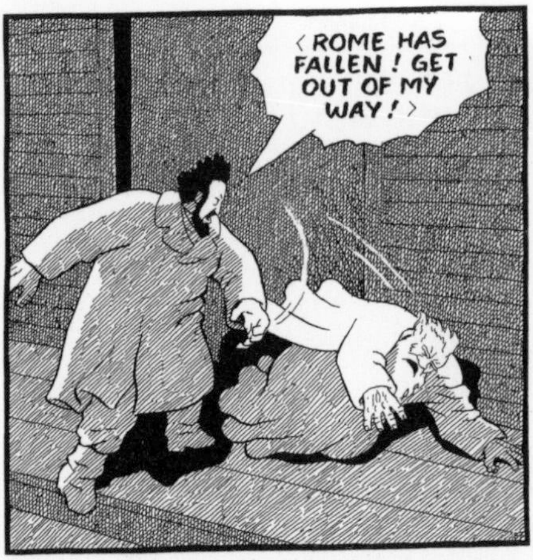

<ROME HAS FALLEN ! GET OUT OF MY WAY !>

History, for Kurtzman, did not exist in order to justify the workings of empire, but rather to condemn the horrors of war. Cartooning allowed him to fictionalize his material ever so slightly, to wrench it into a new way of seeing that was not beholden to prose history's standard narratives of patriotic men and significant events. Brown would learn this lesson, among others, from Kurtzman, though he eschews the older artist's sensationalism ("Custer's hit! He's killed! I'm glad! I'm glad!") and blatantly comic-booky sound effects (the wintry "pk! pk!" of Riel's rifles is no match for Kurtzman's bazooka: "FWOOOSHT! WONK!"). Still, the fatalism and studious pacing of Kurtzman's approach to history, as well as his rankling at injustice, live on in *Louis Riel*.

An even greater kinship exists between Brown's work and that of Jack Jackson, another cartoonist toiling under Kurtzman's influence. Of an earlier generation than Brown, Jackson came up in the American underground comix movement, breaking taboos with as great a frequency as Brown in his *Ed* days. Jackson's early panache for the horrific and grotesque found an unexpected, bracing outlet when his comics began to reconstruct the bloody history of Texas and the American frontier, in comics that the artist calls his "attempts to dispense with the romantic bullshit about the Winning of the West." Jackson's historical work is dense with detail, executed with the steadfast authority of an etching or woodcut, and supplemented by the same apparatus—maps, addenda, and bibliographies—that Brown would later use. It is also righteously angry about the legacy of racism, and concerned with using the popular comic-book form in order to "introduce to the culture at large previously marginalized figures of American history," as Joseph Witek writes in *Comic Books as History*. Jackson's earliest history comics, especially, bear comparison with *Riel*. *Comanche Moon* and *Los Tejanos* are biographical treatments of men like Riel who straddled two or more cultures, and who became leaders of people overcome by the wave of westward expansion, then all too soon dispossessed and maligned.

Comanche Moon is Jackson's version of the life of Quanah Parker, whose white mother lived among the Comanche (her story inspired John Ford's *The Searchers*). Parker grew into a warrior, who at first railed against white America's manifest destiny, before eventually becoming involved in the political life of the Comanche—as Riel had with the Métis—representing his people in trips to Washington, seeking education and peace and rights to the land. Juan Seguin is the subject of Jackson's second book, *Los Tejanos,* named after the people of Mexican heritage who sided with the "Texians" during the Texas Revolution. Seguin plays an instrumental role in the founding of Texas, just as Riel does in Manitoba. Other parallels abound: Seguin is forced to flee his country, is branded a traitor, sees Tejano land and chattels taken by Anglo immigrants. Were it not that Parker and Seguin rebelled and acquiesced, got damned as villains and praised as heroes, on so very different a stretch of frontier than Riel, one could almost imagine Jackson having tackled the Father of Manitoba before Brown got around to it.

There was little worry of that, however—indeed, before Brown's success with *Louis Riel,* few besides Jackson would ever try their hands at history or biography in comic-strip form. (Robert Crumb is, as always, a notable exception—the demons that haunt his Jelly Roll Morton, or the visions that enthrall his Philip K. Dick, make for nice  companions to Riel's dissociative experiences.) After *Riel,* however, the deluge: cartoonists are more eager than ever to give compelling lives the comic-strip treatment. Frank M. Young and David Lasky have taken up the old comic-strip style to tell the history of the Carter Family, the late Spain Rodriguez cartooned the life of another controversial people's hero in *Che,* and the Center for Cartoon Studies has devoted its publishing efforts to comics biographies of crucial American figures like Satchel Paige, Amelia Earhart, or Henry David Thoreau, in an especially thoughtful edition by John Porcellino. Of particular—and Canadian— note, the phenomenal success of Kate Beaton's comics arises at least in part from the irreverent vitality with which she treats even the most inert events of history. One of her earlier strips pits a battle-ready and nonplussed Gabriel Dumont against a credulous Riel, unconcerned with so mundane a thing as strategy. "I have two fists," Riel says; "one is the will of the Lord and the other is miracles. Bam bam!" We have seen this rational Dumont square off with Riel the ingenue before, of course. "Are my likenesses informed by Chester Brown?" Beaton asks, almost needlessly. "Well of course they are!" Ten years on now, how could it be otherwise?

If Brown's example lives on in the world of comics, there can be little doubt Riel's does in the world at large. Books continue to be written about the man; column inches continue to be filled. In 2008, as Manitoba added a February holiday to its calendar year, the call went out to the province's students to select a name befitting the occasion. Louis Riel Day won out over all other comers—including Winnipeg Jets Day, which says much about Riel's significance to that hockey-mad province. And, as the 125th anniversary of his execution approached in 2010, Canada's MPs and news media and ordinary citizens found themselves again divided over the issues Riel raises, even from the grave. Some continue to demand that Riel be granted a posthumous pardon, while others hawk t-shirts showing Riel's neck in the noose.

Chester Brown leaves that noose out of the final panel he draws in Riel's life story, though the hangman's rope still pulls brutally taut. Brown signs and dates the page, in tiny, modest script, in the corner. The space where the next panel should go, however, is another of Brown's blanks—borderless, free, unmarked. Like that final empty space, what *Riel* will mean in the future, and what this book has meant to us, remains emphatically open.

SEAN ROGERS *is a PhD candidate at York University, where he is studying Canadian comics. He has written for* The Walrus, The Globe and Mail, *and* The Comics Journal.

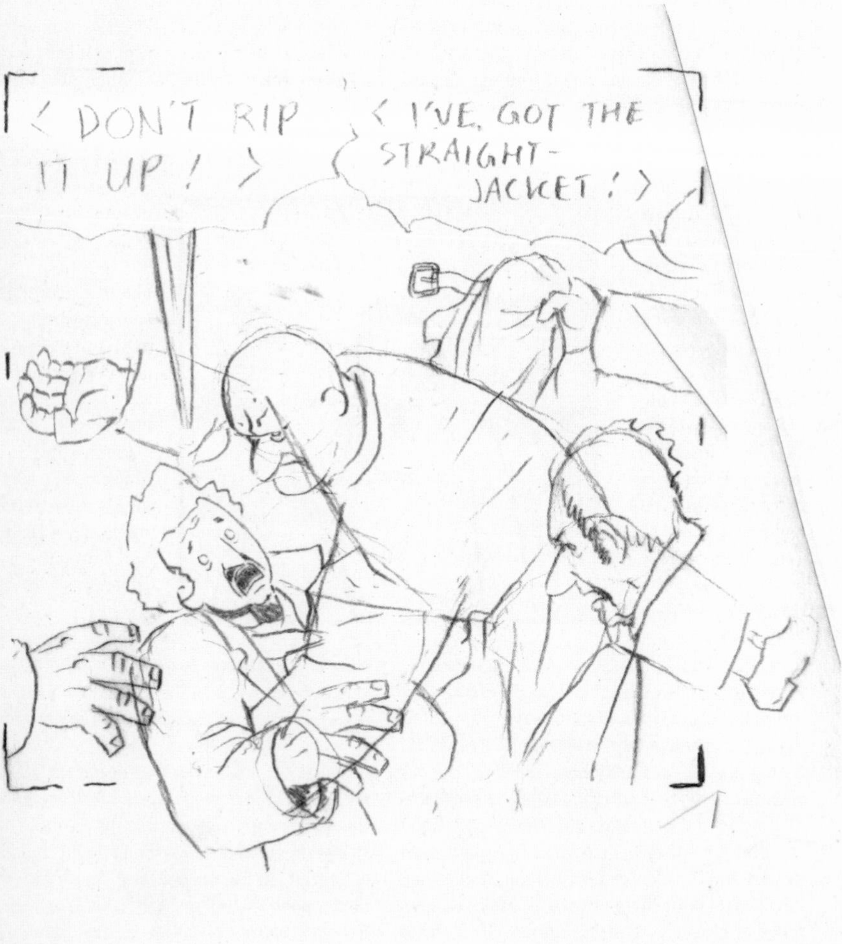
< DON'T RIP IT UP! >
< I'VE GOT THE STRAIGHT-JACKET! >